YOUNG MR. NEWMAN

John Henry Newman

JOHN HENRY NEWMAN, c. 1840
(by Maria Giberne)

Young Mr. Newman

By
MAISIE WARD

"That clever young gentleman of Oriel,
Mr. Newman."—DR. ROUTH

LONDON
SHEED & WARD
1948

FIRST PUBLISHED 1948
BY SHEED AND WARD, LTD.
110/111 FLEET STREET
LONDON, E.C.4

PRINTED IN GREAT BRITAIN
BY PURNELL AND SONS, LTD.
PAULTON (SOMERSET) AND LONDON

75223

To

FATHER HENRY TRISTRAM

WHO KNOWS MORE OF NEWMAN
THAN ANY LIVING MAN
THIS BOOK
IS GRATEFULLY DEDICATED

INTRODUCTION

MUCH OF Newman's story has been told again and again: much has never been told at all. It is partly his own fault. If, in accord with the Cardinal's wishes, his official biographer begins with his forty-fifth year, the host of writers who follow the official biographer will, of course, also begin at that year. And if he does so because he has himself written the history of his religious opinions up till that year, all who write about him are apt to write mainly from the same angle.

I want to write about Newman as a child, a boy and a man: a brilliant and perplexing individual who developed in the midst of an unusual group of brothers and sisters, went to Oxford at a time of great personalities, lived in a period unparalleled in English history and set his mark upon it. Newman is for most people rather a shadowy figure until he becomes an aged Cardinal, but I see him more and more clearly as young Mr. Newman of Oriel.

In gathering the material for this book I have had the most amazing good fortune—for who could have hoped that quantities of unpublished letters and other documents to, from and about a man as famous as Newman, should have remained unpublished over a hundred years?

This is the story.

The development of *this* child into *that* man has for me an intense fascination: so also the gradual unfolding of a mind; as Newman himself says concerning his friend Hurrell Froude, we rarely know much of men in their most interesting years—the years when they were forming—"from eighteen to twenty-eight or thirty." As I re-read my father's biography of Newman, the *Apologia* and the three volumes of collected correspondence, it came over me powerfully that we had never come to know Newman the child or Newman the young man—and that by his own wish. Having in the *Apologia* given his own story of his "religious opinions", having given Anne Mozley his letters for selection, and interwoven with them a brief *Autobiographical Memoir*, the Cardinal seems to have felt that enough had been written of his life as an Anglican. Hence Wilfrid Ward out of two immense volumes gives only seventy-five pages to the first forty-four years of Newman's life.

True we can supplement this by the *Apologia*, and by the Letters, not only the Mozley, but also the Oratorian Collection: *Correspondence with Keble and Others*. But there still seems room for a book that should attempt for the first half of Newman's life the sort of picture that was drawn of the second half in Wilfrid Ward's biography.

The letters are all out of print—and anyhow very few people would read fourteen hundred pages of letters. And if we read both letters and *Apologia* carefully we find ourselves asking questions which Newman cannot answer—for no man knows the whole truth about himself: a painter's self-portrait is a rare artistic gift and its achievement in writing is all but impossible. I would venture the paradox that it is especially impossible for a man with a life-long habit of self-examination. He has been too busy counting trees to get a general view of the wood.

Then, too, there are many gaps in the letters—some omissions naturally made in the lifetime of the writers or recipients, and other omissions dictated by Victorian rules of reticence. Again and again I have found that the most amusing, significant and telling phrases were the very ones omitted. Strangest of all is the fact that no one writing about Newman in recent times has examined the numerous files of unpublished letters to and from his family and friends. "No one except your father," said Father Tristram, when I called at the Oratory, "has asked to see these letters since 1885." That was the year in which Anne Mozley came to Birmingham and Father Tristram painted for me a pleasing picture of three old people in the Oratory parlour—the Cardinal and the old lady (he in his eighties, she in her seventies) in conference over the letters, while Father William Neville hovered over them like a guardian angel. Other letters are still in the possession of the Mozley family—the grandchildren of Newman's sister, Jemima. Besides the letters there are a number of volumes labelled by Newman himself " Autographic Remains." The first and largest of these is a portfolio containing letters, verses, a few drawings, programmes of school prize-days, etc. The rest are exercise books into which he had copied parts of his own journals and such extracts from his family's letters as he thought worth preserving, some with an explanatory note added in square brackets. He then destroyed the originals.

Newman's profound interest in his own past is seen in the care given to arranging and re-arranging letters, copying and re-copying memoranda. The private journal is annotated: "These remembrances of life to 1816, written in 1820, 1821, faithfully transcribed with additions 1823, faithfully transcribed with omissions Lent 1840. Dec. 1872 now to be partially and finally re-transcribed with great omissions and put aside for good. [The superseded copies all burnt.]

"The unpleasant style in which it is written arises from my habit from a boy to *compose* . . . I seldom wrote without an eye to style, and since my taste was bad, my style was bad. I wrote in style as another might write in verse, or sing instead of speaking, or dance instead of walking. Also my Evangelical tone contributed to its bad taste."

Other volumes contain a briefer form of diary, recording day by day events in a few lines. Short bits from all these have been used in the *Autobiographical Memoir* or in linking the published letters together.

The number of Mozleys whose work has helped me or whose personalities pass through these pages is so considerable that I must make an inventory to prevent utter confusion in the reader's mind. First there is Tom Mozley, Newman's pupil, Fellow of Oriel, who married Harriett, Newman's eldest sister, and wrote his *Reminiscences: Chiefly of Oriel College and the Oxford Movement*. This delightful, inaccurate book is full of atmosphere and of good stories.

Harriett Mozley herself wrote "tales" which I have drawn on for the scene of Newman's childhood.

Jemima Newman married another Mozley brother, John, but he made no contribution to literature and she left only a number of excellent letters.

James Mozley, younger brother of Tom and John, was one of Newman's favourite disciples, but attacked him after he left the Church of England. His *Essays Historical and Theological* are useful towards a grasp of the period, but far more his letters which were collected and arranged by his sister Anne. The skill shown by Anne Mozley in making this selection led the Cardinal to ask her to arrange his own correspondence.

Coming to the present generation, we have Jemima's grandson, John Henry Mozley, who has treasured many valuable family letters, and to whom I am immensely indebted both for his help in reading my MS. and for the loan of letters from the boy Newman and from his mother and sisters. Mary Newman's letters are so delightful, I would have liked to use them all. I have also to thank Dr. James Mozley for the loan of other valuable letters.

This book is to some extent a family portrait but also a portrait of university life and friendships—and (I hope) a fairly readable account of the progress of Newman's mind. I have tried too, to sketch in the social and theological background as far as seemed necessary. "Hasn't that been heavily done already?" a friend asked me. I have tried to do it lightly! but the book *can* be read without these parts. An American reviewer of my *Chesterton* assumed that because I told readers they could skip one or two serious chapters I thought those chapters unimportant—and he took me to task severely for so thinking. What I do feel rather strongly is that it is a pity to debar people who are disinclined to read seriously from getting some notion of the *person* whose ideas they feel are beyond them.

In tracing the development of Newman's mind from Evangelicalism to Roman Catholicism, I have tried to be as objective as possible. Like him, I feel that the presenting of Christianity, indeed of God Himself, to save the world in an infidel age is far more vital than argument with one's fellow Christians. Like him, I realise that in his progress he abandoned no positive truth but strengthened, expanded and completed the beginnings of his boyhood. But like him also, I am convinced that the Catholic and Roman Church is the Church directly established by Christ. It is, therefore, impossible that all he says or all I say can please people who do not share this opinion—but I hope I have also shown Newman's love for the Church of England and his admiration and affection for the friends he there left behind him. The saintliness of Pusey and Keble, the affectionate fellowship of Church and Rogers, the graves of Bowden, of Lucy Pusey, of Mary Newman, and of Hurrell Froude must be sacred to Newman's biographer as they were sacred in Newman's heart.

I have not thought it necessary to give in this book all the references that would be needed in the case of a subject less written up. With the letters it would be difficult to give references anyhow. Many of those quoted are unpublished, many of those already printed in the collections contain unpublished fragments used here. Again, Father Tristram is a more accurate copyist than was Miss Mozley and has often made minor corrections in the published letters. To explain all this would lead to a rash of footnotes disagreeable to the eye. In the case of quotations from books other than Newman's letters I have indicated my sources, but have not always given page references, especially when discussing a specific work of Newman's and quoting largely from it. I have used Longman's Standard Edition except for the *Apologia* which was missing in my set and for which I have used the Sheed & Ward edition of 1946.

But this is not a student's book. It is written for people who enjoy reading but have no wish to engage in research, and I have tried to get an all-round picture by reading the works of foes to Tractarianism as well as those of its friends.

Reading for a book is so much more fun than writing it that I have been tempted down a good many by-paths—following the Evangelicals (Wesley, Hannah More, Wilberforce), in one direction, deserting them for Charlotte Yonge and testing her by the country clergy (such as Dean Hook) who were more or less connected with the movement, trying to understand as well as enjoy Sydney Smith, Macaulay, Stanley, Whately, Arnold, and all the other Liberals in their ably-written biographies. The history of Oxford too proved fascinating—I know it was not necessary to read half a dozen volumes about it but I couldn't stop. There was more excuse for dwelling with Newman's contemporaries than with Amherst or Hearne, and it is a period singularly rich in reminiscences and collected correspondence: Tuckwell's *Pre-Tractarian Oxford* and his *Reminiscences*, Bedel Cox, then a little later Hurrell Froude and Blanco White, followed by Rogers (Lord Blachford), Dean Church, both Mozley brothers, Mark Pattison, James Anthony Froude. And then: What Came of It All? brings us to Morley's reflections on Gladstone's Oxford period and Tom Brown, the true disciple of Arnold of Rugby. It is endless: indeed, I have not yet read all I want to read and I fear this is why I write so slowly; and at the end of it all I feel my ignorance when helped by two great scholars: Christopher Dawson and Edward Watkin. To them, to Father Tristram and Sir Walter Moberly I am deeply grateful for reading my proofs and making valuable suggestions. And I must pick out one book from the mass of material—Christopher Dawson's *Spirit of the Oxford Movement*. This short book shows the insight of genius. My debt to Mr. Dawson's guidance in reading rightly and evaluating the various elements in the story is immense.

A WORD ABOUT ILLUSTRATIONS

I DO NOT think buildings are of much value when reduced to the size of a page: but faces are. Then, too, the dress of a period is amusing and illuminating: the Oxford scholar and the fine ladies show us what Newman and his sisters *wore*, which helps a little towards imagining what they *were* as they walked, talked or studied.

As to actual portraits: clearly Maria Giberne had an eye to a likeness and the lovely and touching picture of Mary even taken after death gives some notion of her mature youthfulness.

The family group was, according to Newman, less successful. "Harriett," he wrote to Anne Mozley in 1884, "is represented so unlike the rest that strangers must think that she is a young lady I am sweet upon."

Newman's nose is a great help to the caricaturists, who began early. The picture of "The Spy" is probably not very like him, but it is very much as one boy sees another who has a strongly-marked countenance and who does not please him. The bust is also by a schoolfellow and is a more flattering impression!

On Newman's likenesses in general there is a delightful letter from him to Miss Giberne which belongs here more than anywhere else. Miss Giberne was portrait-painter in chief to the Newman family—whose enjoyment in drawing one another produced much less successful results. When the Movement was at its height caricatures of Newman were appearing on all sides and this letter is concerned with her wish to substitute a true likeness for fancy ones.

April 13, 1842.

Your letter is very kind . . . yet it made me laugh. What a pity it did not come a day sooner. There was Mr. Copeland my curate in Cheltenham till this morning—why should he not represent me. I never have been able to understand, since I could think, what the connection is between a man and his name, or a man and his face —and I really cannot see why every purpose would not be answered if you got another person to sit instead of me, or put out a fancy picture. There would be this advantage in the latter that you could then flatter me. You talk of scarecrows—I have not seen them so

xiii

my imagination is not affected—but tastes differ—how do you know that many persons would not think *me* the scarecrow, and my caricature an improvement. And then again I heard yesterday, truly or not, that a new sketch of Chaucer's Pilgrimage after Stodart has come out, and that a good likeness of me figures as the Priest. . . . My friend Westmacott was flattering enough to take a bust of me, when I did not know the use he meant to put it; and I suspect that that is flattering enough for the most indulgent friend. In truth, were I a person in authority, and did it fairly come to me to have my portrait taken, I would no more object (it would be silly to do so) than to taking my Doctor's degree—but being what I am, . . . it would make me a sort of Demagogue, Popular Preacher, Sectarian Leader and the like—characters which of all others I most abominate . . .

Did I ever do such a thing . . . I should proceed to prefix the said portrait to every one of my books, sermons and all, and would be represented in an elegant dress and attitude, with my hand between the buttons of my waistcoat.

However, he did allow her to draw him after all, and her portrait—far better surely than the well-known Richmond—is the frontispiece of this book.

CONTENTS

CHAPTER   PAGE

INTRODUCTION vii

I. CHILDHOOD I

II. A FAMILY CRISIS 16

III. "MY RELIGIOUS OPINIONS" 23

IV. AT TRINITY 34

V. THE YOUNG EVANGELICAL 54

VI. THE ORIEL FELLOWSHIP 68

VII. WE MUST LOOK BACK A LITTLE . . . 78

VIII. CURATE OF ST. CLEMENT'S 93

IX. TUTOR OF ORIEL 107

X. FAMILY INTERLUDE 117

XI. PREACHER BEFORE THE UNIVERSITY . . 132

XII. A WORLD OF CHANGE 141

XIII. THE PEEL ELECTION 152

XIV. THE THREE BROTHERS 161

XV. FROM THE TUTORSHIP TO THE ARIANS . . 176

XVI. GRAND TOUR 189

XVII. HOW TO ACCOMPLISH IT 204

XVIII. ILLNESS IN SICILY 215

XIX. THE WORLD TO BE MOVED 224

XX. THE MOVEMENT BEGINS 237

XXI. THE *VIA MEDIA* 252

XXII. HUMAN RELATIONSHIPS 268

XXIII. DR. HAMPDEN AND THE DOGMATIC PRINCIPLE . 287

XXIV. CREDO IN NEWMANNUM 298

XXV. FROUDE'S REMAINS 322

XXVI. A PHILOSOPHY OF FAITH 345

XXVII. PEACE AND CONFLICT 1840–1841 . . . 359

xvi / *Contents*

CHAPTER   PAGE

XXVIII.   SUBJECTS OF THE DAY 383

XXIX.   WILLIAM GEORGE WARD 404

XXX.   LAST DAYS AT LITTLEMORE 423

XXXI.   DEVELOPMENT OF DOCTRINE 442

XXXII.   LOSS AND GAIN 449

APPENDICES 460

BIBLIOGRAPHY 468

INDEX 473

LIST OF ILLUSTRATIONS

JOHN HENRY NEWMAN . . . *Frontispiece*
(*From a drawing by Maria Giberne*)

Facing page

THE SPY CLUB 14

THE CLERK OF OXFORD . . . 46

FASHIONABLE DRESSES 126

MARY SOPHIA NEWMAN AFTER DEATH . 150

FAMILY GROUP 174

PORTRAIT 302
(*From the engraving by R. Woodman, after the painting by Sir W. C. Ross*)

MOTHER CHURCH AND HER PUSSEY-ITES . 398

CHAPTER I

Childhood

I

THE CHILDHOOD of a man of genius is much more interesting than his pedigree, yet a word must be said about this, partly because Father Neville was informed by Cardinal Newman, and passed the statement on to Wilfrid Ward, that his family came from Swaffham in Norfolk. This proves to have been a mistake. There are two Swaffhams, one in Norfolk and one in Cambridgeshire—it is from the latter that the Newmans in fact came. J. H. Mozley sent to *Notes and Queries* for November 3rd, 1945, a short pedigree, which he had verified from the local records, tracing them back as farmers at Swaffham Bulbeck in Cambridgeshire, whence Newman's grandfather, John, came to London. He is described in the pedigree as "Citizen and Musician." He was an oil merchant and became a member of the Worshipful Company of Musicians. Newman's father, also John, is described as "son of the above John, of the city of London, Banker." Newman's mother, Jemima Fourdrinier, was descended from a Huguenot family which had settled in England at the time of the revocation of the Edict of Nantes.

John Henry Newman, born February 21st, 1801, in Old Broad Street, was the eldest of six children. Charles Robert was one year younger, Harriett two and Francis four. Then came Jemima, born 1807, and finally Mary, born 1809.

When John was seven months old, his mother writes to her sister-in-law that "the little fellow's scarlet coat is come home— quite dashing—I long to see him in it." (Sending me this, Mr. Mozley adds: "J. H. N. at some time, I believe, fancied himself a soldier, but it was another scarlet to which he was destined!")

Into a portfolio labelled "Autographic Remains No. 1," Newman has pasted other memorials of his childhood. When he was four, a maid writes to his mother: "Marster Jon desires his deuty and wishes me to send you some violets." A year

later comes a letter from his father which confirms Newman's
own memory of being able to read perfectly at five.

MY DEAR JOHN HENRY,
    This is the first letter your Papa ever wrote to his son. I request
you will read it to your Mamma and Charles that, when he sees how
well you can read writing, he will be very desirous of minding his
book that he may also be able to do the same. But you will observe
that you must learn something new every day, or you will no longer
be called a clever boy.
    I, therefore, hope that by next Thursday you will have got your
Multiplication Table by heart and have also begun to learn your
Pence Table. I mean to examine you as to your Multiplication
Table and if I find you improve I intend after a time to buy a nice
Copy Book and teach you to write.

    The promise of a "nice copy book" was probably enticing to one
who was to write incessantly for three-quarters of a century.
A letter to his sister Jemima written in 1861 recalls this
time:

    I have lately been to see our house at Ham, which we had before
you were born—where I was when you were born—and whence I
sent my Mother by my Father the present of a broom-flower on your
birth. I looked at the windows of the room where I lay abed with
candles in the windows in illumination for the victory at Trafalgar.
I had not seen them since I left in 1807. Those famous and beautiful
groves are now in course of perishing—and in not so many years
Dysart House will remain stripped and desolate amid its meadows.

    I went on pilgrimage to see this home of his, and there I found
Newman the child. The house is now fittingly a children's day
nursery: the walls painted with gay frescoes, little blue cots for
the afternoon sleep, a rocking-horse in almost every room (the
Newmans had a rocking-horse to which John later sent his love
from Oxford). It is a large square Georgian house with large
square rooms, none of the nooks and corners common in country
houses. Yet a country house it certainly is: you might be a
hundred miles from London: you expect to meet a cow as you
wander out into the paddock that lies at one side of the large
neglected garden. Here are the shrubberies that we shall meet
again in Newman's dreams. Here he went with Jason on the

quest of the Golden Fleece or was turned to stone by the Gorgon: this garden was the scene for him of all the Greek legends.

There must be acres of it: against a lovely mellow brick wall were growing huge yellow daisies, evening primroses, michaelmas daisies. It was late October, yet a spike of blue lupin was in bloom and clusters of pale blossoms hung from a laburnum. There were roses too in plenty and bushes of pink spiraea, while a border of azaleas showed leaves of deep autumnal red—at their feet brown heather with tiny bunches of purple among the brown. In a beautiful neglected garden is a sand hole where the children play near Newman's favourite plane tree. The plane, a vast chestnut, and other noble trees, must have stood there for centuries.

To the end of Newman's life memories of his childhood recur. Thus on a lonely birthday at Oxford he writes to his mother:

I woke on the morning of February 21, and, without recollecting it was my birthday, my mind involuntarily recurred to the day I was four years old, and said "The Cat and the Cream Bowl" [to a party of little ones in Southampton Street], and the day I was five years old your telling me that now I was a big boy, and must behave myself accordingly; to the day I was six years old, when I spoke Cowper's "Faithful Friend" at Ham.

All through Newman's childhood the addresses are a little confusing. Southampton Street was the family town house. There was a grandmother—his father's mother—at Fulham, with whom he apparently lived, or anyhow stayed for considerable periods. (Perhaps this was when one or other brother or sister was appearing on the scene. How well one knows the pattern: the monthly nurse arriving: the father banished to his dressing-room: any child old enough to "take notice" sent away to relatives.) Jemima and Mary were born in Southampton Street, but after Ham there was a country house at Norwood mentioned in several letters, from which they migrated to Alton in Hampshire.

At seven years Newman was sent from home to a boarding-school at Ealing which we are told was conducted on public school lines, there being in the school at first two hundred, later three hundred boys. We are so accustomed in England to think of a public school as meaning simply a large school for older boys conducted on certain lines and of a private school as a smaller school differently managed, that this description is a puzzling one. Actually the name public school applies to a school run by a governing body of which the profits belong to the school, while a private school is one owned by an individual. The Ealing School under the Reverend George Nicholas of Wadham College, Oxford, was in this sense private, yet run on Eton lines and at this date very popular: the Headmaster was supposed, says a contemporary, to get the boys on. Yet when later Newman told Tom Mozley that he envied him his public school education, it was to elegance in construing that he referred, so it seems probable that the classical studies at Ealing were not up to the highest public school standard.

Newman's father had made a common mistake in urging forward a promising baby, for clearly he began at school as a child among boys. When his parents departed after their first visit, he was found by Dr. Nicholas in tears and urged to cheer up and join his companions.

"O, Sir," said the seven-year-old, "they will say such things! I can't help crying." Obviously he had escaped them to be alone. "O, Sir, but they will; they will say all sorts of things," and taking his master's hand he said, "Come and see for yourself." Only a baby could have done what he then did—led his master into the crowded room where, naturally enough, in his presence there was no teasing. But the story would seem to indicate a wide difference between Ealing and most public schools of that or any period, if a homesick child of seven had nothing worse to put up with than teasing from a crowd of big boys.

No boy, Dr. Nicholas said later, had ever gone from the bottom to the top of the school at such a pace as Newman. An old diary records some of the landmarks of his progress:

1810, May 25	— Got into Ovid and Greek.
1811, February 11	— Began verses.
1812, March 5	— Got into Diatessaron.
May 25	— Began Homer.
1813, May 3	— Herodotus.

At one point the parents thought of sending John to Winchester, but at his own urgent request agreed to leave him at Ealing.

It is good to note that the diary, kept with steadiness astonishing in a child, contains much else besides progress in his lessons. In 1810 the Christmas holidays produce "Had a twelf cake," "Went to see them scate," "Went to the play." Back at school he notes, "Had a whole holiday. Flew kite," "Made glass eyes to kite." Each day has a brief entry, even if it is only "rained" or "hot." "Had chicken pocks," is followed for ten days by the single word "ill." On another page is the rather pathetic entry, "Did no sums—could not get them to answer—ill."

His relations with one of the masters pass through various phases: August 31: "Laurie turned me last. For what? Ask him." But December 11: "I and Mr. Laurie very good friends. He took me up for a reward." December 14: "Very good friends with Mr. Laurie."

Another entry runs:

> Laurie one day
> To his brother did say
> I got a sack
> Of the best tabac.

One wonders whether the little John Henry had seen his father at home in a special velvet coat and cap, practising the strange art of smoking, as Disraeli was presently to describe it, or whether a cigar was a "noxious weed" for the Newman family, as for many English families of that date.

Another attempt at verse is made in the blank pages of the diary:

> Into the palace of the Lord
> Those who do right and keep His word
> Will surely go, but those who don't
> I am quite certain that they won't.

Not yet ten, he makes entries in Latin: "*Sum ire domum in minore tempore quam hebdomada. Huzza. Utinam irem domum cras.*" The next year come the entries "Began music," "Began a tune." By 1812 he is "much better as to bowing," and his father writes: "If the Doctor approves of it, buy the Cremona." He "had paints," "went to see sailing match," "had greengages and pears," "had donkeys and cart"; and there are entries like "Dancing," (mentioned often enough to mean probably a lesson),

"Conjuror came," "My birthday cake sent." June 5, 1812, has the pleasant entry, "Bathed—confirmation."

One summer holiday was spent at Worthing where they "went in a boat and bathed." The entry "Bathed" recurs constantly: at the seaside, at school, later on at Oxford—even in winter. Newman adds, in his Oxford days, the note that the cold bath at Holywell was a "plunging bath" but nowhere does he mention whether he could swim. It is the same in the life of Arnold: he also "bathed" constantly—but whether they just paddled in shallow water or struck out into the deep we are never told. That the Newmans did learn to swim as boys I am inclined to think from a casual allusion Frank made in old age to the difficulty of swimming against currents: "I have known this in the Tigris, in the Nile, and even in the Thames, though the bathing men in several places called me a first-rate swimmer." The amusing point about the early entries in the diary is their destruction of a legend. On the strength of a casual mention by a school-fellow that he had never seen Newman bathe, a theory has been erected that Newman would not undress before his school-fellows, that he is thereby proved morbid and unhealthy. There is certainly no slightest trace of morbidity in the diary or letters of his school days: they are those of a most normal boy: and I have never seen quite so many allusions to bathing in any letters or journals.

Into this volume of Autographic Remains are pasted several letters: among them the formal announcements of the holidays. In his journal he was writing "Huzza all this month at home"; in a very different exquisite copperplate he penned:

June 6th, 1810.
Dear Mama,
I have again the pleasure to announce the approach of our vacation. It begins as usual on the 21st instant when I hope to see you as well as it leaves,

Dear Mama,
Your dutiful son,
John Henry Newman.

(All their lives his letters to his parents are signed "Yours dutifully.")

Twice a year these announcements were sent home: June and December. Every year the writing grows a little smaller, always it is perfect. In December 1813 the letter is written in French, but the heartfelt exclamations of the journal are always in Latin or in English—"*Maximo mihi est gaudio quod domi sum.*" "*Gaudeo loqui quod sum apud me.*"

Although he bathed, went in boats and rode on donkeys, Newman was very far from being an athletic boy. He did not care for games and never played them. His amusements we can partly learn from these early papers. Scott's novels were just coming out and Newman, who had listened at home with delight to his mother's reading of "The Lay of the Last Minstrel," devoured the novels in bed in the early morning. He does not speak of any other books. He must have been *very* young when he wrote out a paper of riddles containing such abstruse questions as:

> Why are there 3 objections to a glass of brandy?
> 3 scruples = 1 dram.
> Which has most legs, a horse or no horse?
> No horse has five legs.
> Which is the greatest Friday in the year?
> Shrove Tuesday.
> When is a man over head and ears in debt?
> Not paid for hat and wig.
> What colour are the winds and storms?
> Storms arose, Winds blew.

As he grew older the chief delight of his life was acting. The school put on a Latin play every year and every year he took a part in it. In 1813 he was Hegio in the *Phormio* of Terence, in 1814 he was Pythias in *Eunuchus*, 1815 Syrus in *Adelphi*, 1816 Davus in *Andria*. He notes in the diary, "Rehearsal in dresses. Supper," "Rehearsal before boys," "Grand night." Besides the playbills for these performances Newman kept a poem composed by himself and a friend, of which his own part gives quite a sense of atmosphere. It is oddly called "Pastoral Scene." He is Tityrus and opens thus:

> Here as we sit and view the boys at play
> Rejoicing in their sunbright holiday,
> While some at fives attack the patient wall
> And others glory in the bat and ball,
> Be our employ in philosophic ease
> Calmly to eat the scanty bread and cheese

Which black-eyed Johnson of the untidy cap
Cuts off for twopence to each hungry chap
And to beguile away the lingering time
To choose some subject gay or grave for rhyme.

They decide to talk about Terence, and Tityrus resumes:

Sweet is the notice that proclaims that all
May lie in bed until a later call;
Sweet is December first or first of June
That shows the holidays are coming soon;
Sweet is the hour that hails the incipient rule
Of the new captain of our numerous school.
But far more dear the glad auspicious day
The doctor tells us we may have a play.

Besides acting, the boys delivered speeches: Newman in 1813 spoke in a reconstruction of a House of Commons debate of 1734, taking the part of Sir William Wyndham: he must have spoken with particular relish the famous speech in which Wyndham, the great Tory, attacked the corruption of the Whig leader, Walpole. In 1816 he "spoke Ajax." All three Newmans took part that year, Charles reciting "The Winter Traveller" of Thomson, and Francis "Queen Mab."

In spite of not playing games Newman attained a position of leadership among a group of boys. He started what was known as The Spy Club. To this belonged the three sons of the American Minister, Mr. Adams, and the eldest of these named their periodical *The Portfolio*. It ran through twenty numbers and the Minister contributed to it. Newman was already writing two periodicals called *Spy* and *Anti-Spy*, written against one another, thirty numbers of one and twenty-seven of the other. "There is not a sentence," he says, "in either worth preserving." But we already see the incredible energy in writing that he never lost.

Frank Newman in an odd little book about his brother's early life gives an account of the affair. We cannot rely on Frank Newman's memory—when able to check up on his statements, I have found them almost always inaccurate: still his description is worth quoting and the book gives the impression that like many old men his memory of childhood is more vivid than of later years.[1]

[1] The book was published after Newman's death, and manifests a strong bias against him. Any statement made in it must be taken with great caution.

In imitation of Addison's *Spectator*, J. H. N. commenced a weekly paper, to circulate among his school-fellows; it filled, in manuscript, four moderate pages. I was too young to care about it, but I saw several numbers, perhaps all that appeared. It had an ugly name —*The Spy*. This word may have been his translation of "spectator": but many of the boys were made sore by the title, and told me that he *quizzed* everybody. Gradually it leaked out that he had initiated a number of the boys into a special Order, with whom he was every week to read *The Spy*. Among these was my second brother, but I, no doubt, was too young. Charles told me that there were degrees in the Order, marked by ribbons of different colours, with J. H. N. as Grand Master. The society met in one of the vacant rooms of this large school—I think afterwards the French master's. But indignation at the rumour of espionage soon culminated and the *profanum vulgus* of the uninitiated forced the door open, swept away the faithful officer on guard, seized the papers, and tore off the badges. Thus came the day of doom to *The Spy*. The victors boasted loudly of their triumph, but neither from Charles nor from any of the initiated did I learn intelligible details.

How did Newmans minor and minimus (if thus they were entitled) hit it off with Newman major? A touching letter from Francis written in 1845 is the only evidence we have. Newman apparently had written to him with great self-reproach about the past. Francis replies:

It is a healthy thing to have a far deeper sense of one's own unworthiness than others have. I do not call it morbid in you . . .

Yet I should not be happy to make any other reply than that I am utterly unaware of any such confessions or apologies being needed. I do not remember any "cruelties at school". It is credible that like other elder brothers you may have expected and enforced more obedience than the younger was always willing to yield; but I am certain that for one act of cruelty there were ten of protection, affection and generosity.

Of letters passing between the boys at school and parents and sisters at home, enough have survived to help the picture of this first stage in Newman's life. To Harriett he writes in April 1815:

Tell Jemima
Once upon a time a
Letter came from her pen
And I did not answer it then:

Therefore tell her I'm her debtor
Of a long agreeable letter.
Of pleasant school and different places
I'll inform her how the case is:
Please do send me then a letter, a
Nice epistle: Yours et cetera
                              JOHN H. NEWMAN.

And to Jemima herself:

Ealing, April 12, 1815.

MY DEAR JEMIMA,

It is always a great pleasure to me to write to you, for the following reason. If I write to Harriett she always requires a laughable letter, which is by no means suited to the dignity of my character, but you Jemima being conspicuously and wonderfully sedate yourself always like a serious, sedate, sensible epistle. One thing in your letter disappointed me very much, and this it was. At the end you say, we all send our love with your affectionate sister, J. C. Newman. I consequently very naturally supposed that you were sent to me, as your letter seems to imply it, and as there was a lumbering *heavy* lump of something or other at the bottom of the parcel, I concluded it must be you, and so I began to unpack this rapidly, to give you (as I thought) some fresh air, of which I did not doubt that you were in want. When to my surprise, having unpacked the said heavy lump, it proved to be a cake! And now I have touched upon the subject I will say two or three things about this said cake. I am very much obliged to Mama that she was so good as to be so punctual, then as to the cake itself I think it is rather too much done, and that Mama must know if she has seen it. I liked Harriett's letter to Charles very much, excepting what related to Trusty, the trusty Trusty.

Believe me ever, my dear Jemima, your
                              affectionate Brother.

To Mary, on her sixth birthday, he writes:

Ealing, November 14, 1815.

DEAR SISTER,

May I not congratulate you though later than I ought. A compliment can never come unseasonably. The 9th of November is no longer winter, the summer sun smiles upon the day. No longer clouds darken the atmosphere and the drizzling rain comes down from above, blue sky appears instead of a uniform gloominess, and the zephyr is heard in the place of the blast of Boreas! What had you on your birthday? Let imagination answer—perhaps you had apples, perhaps cakes, perhaps you had gingerbread, and perhaps you had—

nothing at all. What had we? We had nothing. What shall we have? Difficult to answer. Perhaps we may have our pay sent—perhaps not. Perhaps we may have cake and pay, perhaps—no. . . . I shall conclude and with the most profound respect, am

Your affectionate brother.

There are no letters to help us in picturing the holidays but besides the brief mention of plays, parties and expeditions in his diary the portfolio contains scraps of Newman's own memories of those happy times. He brought home—or more probably he had taken from home to school—a passion for acting, and himself wrote plays for his brothers and sisters. There was a "mock drama" of some sort in 1812 and "a satire on the Prince Regent." For a burlesque opera in 1815 he composed music as well as words. A separate note records that for "our home Christmas play," on January 10, 1815, Mr. Newman contributed a prologue. Probably this play was not the same as the opera. There were many plays and the energies of all the family were thrown into them. Mr. Newman notes:

> The gentlest hearts the costumes have designed
> The nimblest fingers have its folds combined.

The family were all musical and we find Mary later writing to her sisters about songs and scores copied by them, and daring to criticise Handel (the idol at that period of the English public). She found him dull. Newman himself "attained," says Tom Mozley, "such a proficiency on the violin that had he not become a Doctor of the Church, he would have been a Paganini." Quite in his childhood his mother writes to him after a concert: "We were fascinated by the Dutchman [so Newman had christened Beethoven to annoy his music master] and thought of you and your musical party frequently."

II

The family atmosphere is to some extent conveyed in the stories of the eldest sister Harriett, which sold extensively and which show her as a kind of Charlotte Yonge manquée. She cannot draw character or write dialogue with the power that makes Charlotte rise so high above the ordinary moral tale;

what is best in the books suggests memory rather than imagination. In two of her stories are children who talk, their descendants think, as the Newman family might have talked; in both there is an elder brother who, if we do not expect too much of him, will certainly give us something of J. H. N.

In *Family Adventures* the eldest boy is Henry, the second Robert (in actual life John Henry's next brother was Charles Robert). Henry is "a very philosophical young gentleman," he comforts his sister in her troubles, and she him, he is very "considerate" for his elders, especially his parents, he exercises authority over the younger ones not without a touch of priggishness, he has "a peculiar tone of his own."

"I am glad I am not a lady," said Robert, with the grand air young gentlemen assume when they make such speeches. "So much dressing and tidiness, and thought about whether one's fit to be seen or not!"

"And I should say it would be all the better for you, Robert," said his brother, speaking with the superiority which age gives [probably nine or ten], "if you did think a little more about these things. Only look at yourself now. I am sure you don't look fit to go out with a lady!—and no gloves! I cannot bear to see you as you always are—without gloves. It is not respectable, Robert; indeed, it is not respectable."

The family is something of a close corporation, and a little over-confident of their own ways being best. The father, as in all moral tales, is a model of perfection. He is always pointing out what is wrong in attitudes which he had almost certainly produced by his own education.

"You should be willing," he says, "to mix, in a simple, good-humoured manner, with any you may happen to fall in with."

"You mean, papa," said Henry, "that . . . it would be better if we were more social."

"More affable and kind to people in general," added his father.

"It is a great bore," remarked Henry.

"Dreadful," responded Robert. "I had rather be a kitten and cry mew, and live alone all my life."

"I can be civil enough when I like people," said Henry.

In both books we find the elder brother looked to for leadership. His sister "needs" him "to set things right" when they go wrong: his mother and father count on him to look after the younger ones, his father to soothe his mother's fears in an accident. Some part of this is the almost inevitable result of belonging to a large family—if they are to be well brought up. How could the mother and father conduct a brood even of six, unless the elder children helped with the younger? The point is made in these books by the introduction of some intolerable families where only energetic nurses hold utter chaos at bay. Indeed, the above conversation was the result of a visit from just such a family. Henry and Robert felt less than sociable by the time their guests departed. "He is a shallow fellow," remarked Henry. "He likes eating better than reading," observed Robert.

Perhaps because of the identity in the children's names, *Family Adventures* rather than *The Fairy Bower* has been usually thought of as giving a picture of Newman the boy. I at first assumed this to be so and paid little attention to the characters on a first reading of *The Fairy Bower*. Then Mr. Mozley sent me some of Newman's boyhood letters and I suddenly felt that here was the same boy I had met in the story. I re-read *The Fairy Bower*, and while of course there can be no proof, while too there is no family tradition about either character, I have come to believe that George in *The Fairy Bower* is more nearly a picture of John Henry Newman as a boy than is Henry in *Family Adventures*. Curiously enough Newman reading the book on its publication comments on every character in it excepting George.

It is a kind of tract in favour not of the Low Churchism that usually produces tracts but of the moderate Anglicanism of Newman's parents. A family is introduced with an Evangelical governess who is made highly absurd and "quizzed" by George. The book is aimed at inculcating Church principles: we can read in it those of the Newman parents. Attendance at church twice on Sunday, respect for the Prayer Book, daily Bible reading and recitation of the psalms are the ideal.

The children are older than in *Family Adventures*, the heroine, Grace Leslie, is an only child visiting for the first time a large family. George, aged about thirteen, condescends to play with the younger children, likes to "take off the company" when his parents have visitors, "quizzes" his sisters and cousins. He was a young gentleman who "believed he was clever enough to persuade anybody to do anything he chose." He does not like to be defeated either at chess or in an argument, he is constantly described as teasing or quizzing, but good-naturedly. He has a "droll manner" and makes "an odd face." He laughs "provokingly and drolly" at the idea of girls learning Latin—"No Latin was ever learnt except by being *beat* in"—at "satins and pearls and flummery." ("Flummery" was one of Newman's words. He writes to Tom Mozley in the 'thirties of "a letter of the pompous and flummery sort.") He uses the slang of the moment—"What flats you all are," "Here's a pretty go," "How you bamboozled us," "We must have the trial; that's poz! and I'll be the barrister and examine my witnesses." He is a natural leader and is introduced by two lines from Crabbe:

> George was a boy with spirit strong and high
> With handsome face and penetrating eye.

When Grace—a shy child—arrives on the scene, he throws off a string of rhymes (not very good ones) which he describes as a "choriambic." When her health is drunk at a party he replies to the toast:

George was a much better hand at a droll speech than a grave one . . . and this was a tempting opportunity. He told the company that he rose in obedience to his friend Grace Leslie, who had done him the favour to appoint him her champion. He assured them from herself she felt deeply the honour she had just received at their hands; or rather at their glasses; but so amazed was she at their unexpected kindness, that she had not time or power to ascertain her own feelings. She supposed however she was both pleased and gratified. He was quite sure the company would understand his fair friend's sentiments, especially when he added, she would much rather it had never happened; yet at the same time her gratitude was inexpressible, and therefore he would cease attempting to express it.

When his sister Emily and Grace who are sharing a bedroom defy him to guess what they talk about he exclaims: "I know how you spend your time and talk as well as if I was there!"

"Well how?" asked his sister.
"Why first," said he, "you sit over the fire cutting up and quizzing all the people you have been seeing. Emily says 'How I hate Newton Gray and all the Thompsons, and indeed all the rest! I think them

THE SPY CLUB—J. H. N. IN THE CHAIR
by a Schoolfellow

all monstrous disagreeable—don't you, Grace?' 'Yes,' says Grace, 'all but your brother George, and I think him more amusing a great deal than anybody I ever met before!' Then presently up jumps Emily in a great fuss—'Bless me,' says she, 'we shall be *so* late! I must begin to dress! Grace dear, let me *do* my hair first.' Then Grace cries, 'Emily, love, only look! I have got myself into a knot! What shall I do?'—and then Grace falls to crying, though Emily won't tell. 'Never mind,' says Emily, 'there!' and she breaks the string. 'Now, Grace dear, come and *do* my frock!' And so you go on till you are both done enough, or very likely quite overdone, like our goose last Michaelmas day.''

Compare all this with the living boy who recited poetry on his birthday as a child, who led a large group at school and was supposed to be "quizzing" the other boys, who composed comic operas and dramas and led his family in acting them, who would, as Mary tells us later, "make up an odd face" at people and things that amused him, and I think you will see it comes pretty close to a portrait.

B

Chapter II

A Family Crisis

TWO EVENTS that happened when Newman was fifteen were closely linked in his mental history. In March, 1816—in the financial storms and stresses following the end of the long Napoleonic war—his father's bank stopped payment; and he himself experienced a conversion of which to the end of his life he spoke with intense feeling. In his *Memoir* Newman refuses to allow the word failure since the bank paid everyone in full after a brief suspension. He quotes warm praise of his father, whose courage and integrity appear to have impressed all concerned. It would hardly be worth while (even if possible) to track down the details of the affair today, but a vivid picture of the family appears in letters from Mrs. Newman to her sister-in-law during these trying days. The aunt and the grandmother had apparently gone to Norwood to take charge of the three little girls so that Mrs. Newman could be with her husband in Southampton Street during the crisis. Somebody called Boyd (a coachman, I imagine) went constantly between the two houses and letters were sent daily (sometimes even oftener) by him or by the post. Also on occasion, "trowsers, neck-cloths, boot-stockings and pocket hanks."

In these letters we first meet the very feminine, very lovable woman we shall often glimpse later in her relations with her sons. She accepts wholeheartedly her husband's point of view and enlarges on it. Something might have been done to save the situation but for Mr. Newman's colleagues—one "poor man no more fit for business than a baby . . . his apathy and stupidity are past bearing." The senior partner evinced a "*hostile* determination not to lend *voluntarily* a hand to prop up the falling fabric and I must not omit the *art* and *malice* of another individual, *James*."

My great-grandmother used to tell her children that letters must not be written in a colloquial but in an epistolary style: to this canon Jemima Newman adhered faithfully in letters adorned with underlinings and capitals, but deficient in punctuation.

I am looking forward [she writes] with cheerful hope to "a crust of bread and *liberty*" to enjoy the increasing attainments and amiable society of all my dear Children and that with a few additions of friendship in which I flatter myself you will include yourself is the summit of my ambition.

The picture was perhaps a little too black; there was still the house in Southampton Street; there was still the cottage at Norwood with farm attached; there was still her jointure. But certainly nothing could be more honourable than the determination to pay everything possible and let no one suffer whose trust had been put in the bank. Plans were at once on foot to part with the cottage and let the London house:

As soon as I can get away from this house I shall, I tremble at unavoidable *daily* expenses: of course at present we can form no plan, but my idea is if your Brother can possibly manage to come to the Cottage for two months while we collect our poor scattered senses and then it will begin to be in beauty to part with.

Meanwhile:

We shall endeavour to let this house immediately. . . . We shall put up a Bill next week to save taxes, present circumstances emancipate us from certain forms which were highly requisite to submit to before, the peaceful Cot I look to with longing for a little while.

After a few days things began to look more hopeful. There were meetings in Lombard Street of friends: "I cannot but flatter myself they mostly *merit* that name at any rate so far." "I feel so thankful at being so composed and collected I can bear anything."

The same evening she writes that a committee of six has been appointed to investigate, which will be followed by a general meeting: "Your Brother thinks there is no danger of the *Gazette* unless something very adverse should happen . . . the Senior behaved as bad as we expected, he would not come till he had been sent for three times. Our love to our dear Girls and thanks for their letters just received and Harriett's map tell them

I am delighted to find them so industrious and look forward please God to happy day of meeting soon."

The gathering of the bank's friends had been shadowed by "a BRUTAL letter" from the "SISTER" of (apparently) another director "dictated by her Husband . . . it affected *your Brother* and he so much they were scarcely fit to attend the meeting. My hair stands on end while I write about it, but be *mum* as I know it in confidence."

The children, both boys and girls, were naturally much in their mother's thoughts. "We are in a hundred minds about sending for our dear Boys." Mr. Newman had written a "very proper" letter to Dr. Nicholas asking him to send them, but had finally left the decision in the Doctor's hands. One touching letter may be quoted in full since it casts so vivid a light on the married couple, their affectionate relation to the sister Elizabeth Newman and her mother, and the social attitudes of the period:

MY DEAR SISTER,

Your dear Brother and I have enjoyed some rest and feel ourselves rather recruited and I trust shall be able to bear up under all the trials we have to go through if I should be blest with the realising one ardent wish, to make up things quietly, so as no one may be injured, and we retain our name unsullied, all sacrifices will be trifling, nay even delightful, but I fear this is a hope I must not cherish therefore I must keep myself prepared for the worst. Thank God, so far they have been supported wonderfully. They all remained on the spot yesterday to see and be seen by everybody, and received a great many kind visits. Mr. Capel has been at the head of friends, if anything can be done to bring it to a close he is so kind to say he will lend his assistance when the two Johns left here this morning they purposed taking out all the balances with the intention of laying the statement before the principal creditors next Saturday to see if it will induce some to wait and to pay off the smaller. I have just received a very kind letter from Dr. Nicholas, he advises keeping our dear Boys at School and he says every thing considerate and sympathising in our feelings. I am sorry to say he says he is mending *slowly* and he has just lost his Father at 87—it is a great relief for me he has so decided for their presence dear dear Creatures at this moment would I am afraid be more than I could support with firmness— my kind love to your Mother, I hope she will not distress herself about us. Tell her I feel confident the trial although severe will prove for our permanent good and increase our happiness. John and

I already love each other with increased affection. We begin to see the bottom of each other's heart, he begs me to say everything kind and affecte to you both. What shall I say to you in thanks for your kindness and comfort you yield me, in protecting my dear Children and persevering in their education in my absence with my dear John, whom of course I shall not leave while things are any ways unsettled, indeed I assure you it relieved me from a weight that would be too heavy for me to bear, if they were not continued in a proper train and had cause to lament our absence. My Sister Ch. has been sitting with me all the morning and perhaps will call on you tomorrow— I have a hundred commissions to trouble you with which I will inclose. Adieu, ever yours most affectionately

JEMIMA NEWMAN.

Norwood was not, however, many miles away.

We purpose spending tomorrow with our Dears and returning in the evening. I will send something for dinner and bring down Maria and pray *engage* our *three Loves* to dine with us, my head and my heart throb with hope that we shall be protected so as to shield them from all anxiety and mortification.

They decided against a visit to Ealing. It seemed better to bring John, the eldest, already the confidant of his parents, up to town:

March 13.
I have just written to Dr. Nicholas and asked for dear John to come for a day or two. I think it will be a great relief to him and us to talk it over. I am anxious to know how the dear fellow feels, and I trust to be able to soften any keen feelings he may have, Dr. N. having apprised him first, I have said I thought it would [be best not] to tell the other two Dears till John's return, but we are in such good hands with Dr. N. that what he does we shall approve.

John Newman was able to return to school with better news for his brothers than had appeared possible a few short days earlier; and a week or so later he is writing cheerfully to his mother: "I send you the copy of verses that gained the holiday." Within a few weeks all the creditors had been paid in full. But circumstances were changed and the boys remained at Ealing that summer while a family move was being planned and carried out.

I was at first much puzzled by the fact that Mr. Newman should have passed from banking to brewing—or rather, to the management of a brewery. But a little light is cast by one of his wife's letters written on the very day the bank stopped payment: "The Windsor B. of course stopped when ours did, the Distillery goes on. . . . The Brewery is said to go on, but I much fear it will ultimately be so identified with the W. B. it will be impossible to separate them." These close links between two banks, a distillery and a brewery supply a reason for the change which now took the family down to Alton in Hampshire.

For those who enjoy the details of a past age it is lucky that so many of Mrs. Newman's letters are to hand, for, as she truly observes, "Gentlemen do not enter into minutiae so much as we Ladies like." Her own letters are full of them. We learn that Aunt was to bring the girls:

Pray let Joseph order the post chaise in time from the Tiger's Head, Camberwell, First stage Kingston, second Cobham, third Guildford, fourth Farnham, then Alton. Have some brandy for your Mother. I dare say you will not have to change Chaises above twice.

It had been planned for "our wagons to take a load of Ale to town and return with our Goods," but for some reason this idea was abandoned and Miss Newman was to make a bargain with a local man "to bring the things here, fifty miles, his charge you know is £1 10*s*. per day, I suppose he will not charge above four days." The hay should be sold, one stack for £35, the other for £10, potatoes brought to Alton with the "long procession of sheep, ponies, cows, pigs and poultry." Mrs. Newman intended coming to Norwood to clear up "if you can negotiate DECENTLY for a dinner and a bed THURSDAY it would be an IMMENSE accommodation."

There had been one great disappointment: "Harriett and I were" to travel with Mr. Newman "as far as Ealing where we were to dine at the far-famed Mr. Lawes's and to ask the favor of three agreeable Beaus' company to dine with us, which invitation we flattered ourselves would be cheerfully accepted and from which we anticipated much delight. . . . With all these pleasing anticipations in our heads, our Pelisses buttoned, our breakfasts ready," a letter came from Mr. Newman's business friend that *he* was coming to Alton instead of awaiting Mr.

Newman at Windsor. So the expedition was off. One hopes the "three agreeable Beaus" had not been told of the plan. (It is interesting to note that the word Beau, the spelling "favor" are still familiar in America, abandoned in England.) John and Charles and Francis, then, remained unvisited, but they were full of interest in this big-scale move.

John writes to Miss Newman:

Ealing, October 30th, 1816.

DEAR AUNT,

I received your letter this morning, and am very much obliged to you for it, as with the exception of the goose letter, which to be sure was equal to four or five, without detracting from the value of letters, and a short one I received from Mama, written in a hurry, we have not heard from home since the 21st of September. It must be a laborious work, a labour worthy of Hercules, to empty two houses of the accumulations of many years, and what with the distance of their destination from their accustomed home, added to the toil of packing and unpacking it is a most arduous undertaking. Why should Harriett be sorry at leaving Norwood? . . . If Harriett is with the same persons as before (of course I include the chickens) why may she not like Alton as much as Norwood? . . . I hope Grandmama will bear the journey well, it is a formidable one, but a day will suffice, and it will be over. I am rather distressed about Jemima's cough. I hope it may not be her old enemy. The minute I read concerning the horse and chaise it came into my head "How nice would it be to have Trusty back again" and I was agreeably surprised when I came to open Jemima's letter, whom I thank very much for it, that there were hopes. Last night in Mr. Lane's new Assembly Room a Lecturer came and discoursed on Galvanism. I was there—some very curious things. There were some recitations also and imitations of Mrs. Siddons, Jordan, etc. Next Monday there is a ball, I shall not go to it if I can possibly avoid it. I received our pay with thanks to Mama. My trousers have come thanks to Papa. Did you ever read Bishop Newton on the Prophecies? I read them a week or two back, they are extremely ingenious and also *satisfying* (I mean they account and explain well).

I hope you will all get down comfortably to Alton and conclude by signing myself

Your dutiful nephew
JOHN HENRY NEWMAN.

Meanwhile the move to Alton was completed and a budget of family letters followed from all the home folk to the brothers at school. It is one of the huge sheets used at that time on to which four letters are squeezed. Letter 1 is from Jemima to Charles in a large hand, then one from Harriett to John, one from Harriett to Charles or Frank, one from their mother to John. Parts of these letters are lost, but the broken bits can be pieced together to give a fairly vivid view of the new scene. The one letter that is still practically whole is No. 2, from Harriett to John:

. . . Jemima complains that you do not answer her letters. Trusty, the grey horse, the ponies, the cows and the sheep are here and we shall soon have Spot, as Mr. Ramsbottom has got him and will let us have him. Papa is at London and we expect him back today. Tell Charles his description of this house is *almost* right but he must not expect to go through a *little court* to it neither that there is a gate at the back which leads to the Brewery, a few paces before you get into the garden. You remember Grandmama's garden at Fulham? If you do, they say it is like that. At the end there is a seat with trees all round it. You turn to your left and go a little way and there is the gate to the Brewery. The house has two stories. . . . Papa has bought a gig. We have got four cows here, Norwood, Kentish Cherry, Colly and Star. I hope you saw the eclipse as there will not be another like it till 1840 A.D. The new piano cannot be put in the drawing-room till the carpet is . . . and the carpet cannot until stove. They are all new. The two latter I have not seen and what I have seen of the former is very pretty, it is a cabinet piano.

The fragments still remaining of the letter from his mother to John show her already beginning to rely on his judgment and assistance in the education of his sisters, and upon the family situation in general. That reliance was to increase steadily.

CHAPTER III

" My Religious Opinions "

IT IS JUST because for most of us Newman's opinions have been too much abstracted from Newman's self that I have written thus far before alluding to them. To understand the thought we must first know the thinker: underneath the schoolboy exterior the soul was operating—but so it is with everybody. With the ordinary person we are apt to look only at the surface, with the genius, especially if he has a gift of self-expression, we are trying all the time to gaze at the spirit. Yet in the long run the whole man will emerge more clearly if we do not isolate the "history of his religious opinions" but try to see the child, the schoolboy, the youth surrounded by his family and reacting to the circumstances of daily life. I have hoped also to destroy another legend —that the Newman family were Calvinists. Not Calvinists alone but the mildest of Evangelicals would have cast out this family of musicians, of play actors, playgoers and dancers. No, they were, as we have seen, moderate Churchmen. Newman writes:

I was brought up from a child to take a great delight in reading the Bible; but I had no formed religious convictions till I was fifteen. Of course I had a perfect knowledge of my Catechism.

The house at Ham was a place of enchantment: it was the scene of the "angel faces" of "Lead, Kindly Light." "I thought life might be a dream," he says of those days, "or I an angel, and all this world a deception, my fellow angels, by a playful device, concealing themselves from me, and deceiving me with the semblance of a material world." Childlike, the thought of angels was mixed with that of "unknown influence, magical powers and talismans. I used to wish the Arabian tales were true."

It was a beautiful world through which this child could see God Creator of all beauty so clearly that the trees and the flowers became veils for something more lovely than themselves and still more real.

Newman speaks, both in his sermons and in the *Grammar of Assent*, of the attitude towards God of a child brought up in a Christian family. Since Anne Mozley chose several of these passages to illustrate his own childhood it is fair to infer that they did so.

It is my wish to take an ordinary child, but still one who is safe from influences destructive of his religious instincts. Supposing he has offended his parents, he will all alone and without effort, as if it were the most natural of acts, place himself in the presence of God and beg of Him to set him right with them . . .

. . . Though he cannot explain or define the word "God" when told to use it, his acts show that to him it is far more than a word. He listens, indeed, with wonder and interest to fables or tales; he has a dim shadowy sense of what he hears about persons and matters of this world; but he has that within him which actually vibrates, responds, and gives a deep meaning to the lessons of his first teachers about the will and the providence of God.[1]

Exactly how long this sense of God's presence lasted we do not know. Possibly it was destroyed by school life. Anyhow there followed a period during which Newman wished to be virtuous but not religious. "There was something in the latter idea I did not like. Nor did I see the meaning of loving God." This was at the age of fourteen when he argued with a master in favour of Pope's *Essay on Man*, "Virtue alone is happiness below."

Although Bible reading had been inculcated, the Newman boys were left to read unchecked very various literature, for at this same age he found pleasure in thinking of the objections in Tom Paine's Tracts against the Old Testament which he was reading. "Also I read some of Hume's Essays; and perhaps that on Miracles. So at least I gave my Father to understand; but perhaps it was a brag. Also, I recollect copying out some French verses, perhaps Voltaire's in denial of the immortality of the soul, and saying to myself something like, 'How dreadful, but how plausible.' "[2]

Yet too at this time he was superstitious and used always to cross himself when going into the dark. (Before electric light, before gas, the blackness of any moonless night was like the black-out of modern wartime: dinner engagements in the country were

[1] *Grammar of Assent*, p. 112.
[2] *Apologia*, p. 2.

made only at periods of probable moonlight.) Newman's education was quite without Catholic influences and he tells us that years later his breath was taken away on finding that he had adorned his first verse book with a drawing of a cross and (apparently) a rosary. Had he got it from a romance of Mrs. Radcliffe or from a picture? Why had he chosen it? When, in 1864, he thus speculated, had he forgotten the entry in his diary for January 27, 1811, "Went to Westminster Abbey and R. C. Chapel"?

A religious conversion always presents a problem for the biographer. Was the subject of it as different before and after as he appears to himself to have been? Were the sins he laments in the past as grave as they now seem—did Newman's parents, his masters, his brothers and sisters see a great change? All this we do not know. All we have are his own words: "When I was a boy of fifteen," he wrote to Keble in 1844, "and living a life of sin, with a very dark conscience and a very profane spirit, He mercifully touched my heart."

The outward circumstances leading up to the change are of course the one visible part of it and on them we can speculate a little. Suffering often leads the mind to deeper thoughts, and a brilliant sensitive boy, inclined to be responsible beyond his years, probably suffered as much as his parents themselves over the family reverses. "Virtue alone" would bring but cold comfort, and mind and heart would be opened in a new way for the reception of God's light and His grace. Perhaps, brought up on the Bible, Newman would have turned simply to its words and to the church services, perhaps he would have begun his religious life in the same path as his mother, had he been near her at the time. But he was not. The translation of the experimental reality of God's touch on his soul into the language of theology was effected by the influence upon him of the very master with whom he had argued earlier—the Rev. Walter Mayers. A narrow Calvinistic Evangelical, Mayers lent him books "all of the school of Calvin."

These books brought into his mind for the first time distinct impressions of dogma, some part of which he was later to leave behind, and part that remained for life. He wrote in the *Apologia*:

One of the first books I read was a work of Romaine's. I neither recollect the title nor the contents, except one doctrine, which of course I do not include among those which I believe to have come from a divine source, viz. the doctrine of final perseverance. I received it at once, and believed that the inward conversion of which I was conscious (and of which I still am more certain than that I have hands and feet), would last into the next life, and that I was elected to eternal glory. I have no consciousness that this belief had any tendency whatever to lead me to be careless about pleasing God. I retained it till the age of twenty-one, when it gradually faded away; but I believe that it had some influence on my opinions, in the direction of those childish imaginations which I have already mentioned, viz., in isolating me from the objects which surrounded me, in confirming me in my mistrust of the reality of material phenomena, and making me rest in the thought of two and two only absolute and luminously self-evident beings, myself and my Creator.

At the time he wrote, "The reality of conversion as cutting at the root of doubt, providing a chain between God and the soul, that is with every link complete. I know I am right. How do you know it? I know I know." Writing to Anne Mozley in 1885 he commented: "It is difficult to realise or imagine the identity of the boy before and after August 1816 . . . I can look back at the end of seventy years as if on another person."

However great the spiritual change, it was the same eager penetrating mind that had "taken pleasure" in Tom Paine and devoured Hume at fourteen and that now at fifteen set itself upon a very different kind of mental food. Through his books Thomas Scott, who had worked his way through Unitarianism, "planted deep" in Newman's mind the doctrine of the Trinity, in proof of which the boy drew up a series of texts before he was sixteen, to be followed a few months later by a series "in support of each verse of the Athanasian creed." Two thoughts in particular which readers of Newman's sermons will feel to be profoundly characteristic were in his eyes "the scope and issue" of Scott's doctrine: "Holiness rather than peace," and "Truth the only evidence of life." William Law was no Calvinist and his *Serious Call*, read about the same time, may have begun for Newman the "gradual fading out" of the belief in Predestination while fixing firmly in his mind "the doctrine of eternal punishment as delivered by Our Lord Himself."

In the letter to his aunt given in the last chapter Newman had spoken of another book that had on him an extraordinary and a lasting influence: *Dissertations on the Prophecies* by Thomas

Newton, late Bishop of Bristol. The edition I have read was the eighth, published in 1787, and, like Newman's allusions to Tom Paine and to Voltaire, it reminds us that we are still spiritually and intellectually in the eighteenth century: the century of the Deists, the "natural philosophers," the Evangelicals and the Methodists. Newman himself was to be one cause of vast changes in the new century but he grew up in the age of Voltaire and of Wesley, of Fielding and of Johnson, of Hannah More and of William Wilberforce (whose sons in turn were later to be his disciples).

These calf-bound volumes are printed with the old style "s" that so resembled an "f"; each chapter is analysed closely, the footnotes are chiefly in Latin. History and prophecy are treated as interpreting one another with a daylight clarity, and in a dedication to the Archbishop of Canterbury the author urges prophecies as a proof of revelation, both those already fulfilled and those which are "fulfilling even now."

The first volume works steadily through the historical fulfilment of Old Testament prophecies ending with Our Lord's prophecy of the destruction of Jerusalem. All are worked out in immense detail, opposite opinions are refuted in great numbers and at great length, the Fathers and historians introduced in constant confirmation. It is tempting to smile over such headings as "Lord Bolingbroke censured for his indecent reflections on this prophecy," or "'He shall dwell in the tents of Shem' capable of two senses and in both punctually fulfilled." Yet it is easy to see the impression the whole book could have produced on a mystically minded boy of fifteen. We can imagine the young Newman straining his shortsighted eyes over the curious lettering, alternately very black and very pale, and finding the book "extremely ingenious and also *satisfying.*"

The second volume made on his mind the deepest and most lasting impression. The chief part is a consideration of the prophecies of St. Paul and St. John—"copied," says the author, "from Daniel with some improvements. Two most memorable prophecies of St. Paul, the first of the Man of Sin. What the Apostasy. Who the Man of Sin. His exalting himself. His sitting in the Temple of God. . . . The Apostasy charged to the Church of Rome. The Pope the Man of Sin."

With incredible detail and ingenuity the same theme is worked through the Book of Revelation, and here a typical quotation must be made from the text itself if we are to understand the hold it took on the boy's imagination.

Later on we shall see how in his views of Catholic teaching devotions to Our Lady and the Saints would be to Newman an almost insurmountable barrier; in Newton we read:

. . . *The dragon* having failed in his purpose of restoring the old heathen idolatry, delegates his power to the beast, and thereby introduces a new species of idolatry, nominally different, but essentially the same, the worship of angels and saints instead of the gods and demigods of antiquity.

And again:

. . . What first provoked Luther's spirit was the scandalous sale of indulgences; and the doctrine of indulgences having a close connection with the doctrine of purgatory, the refutation of the one naturally led him to the refutation of the other; and his first work of reformation was his ninety-five theses or positions against indulgences, purgatory, and the dependent doctrines. So that he may be said literally to have fulfilled the command from heaven, of *writing*: *Blessed are the dead which die in the Lord, from henceforth:* and from that time to this, this truth hath been so clearly asserted, and so solidly established, that it is likely to prevail for ever.

Remembering his Huguenot ancestry and the one-sided view of history taught at that period, we can see how the historical summaries of the good bishop would seem to Newman to fit and to explain.

Some again may think this prophecy very applicable to the horrid massacre of the protestants at Paris, and in other cities of France, begun on the memorable eve of St. Bartholomew's Day one thousand five hundred and seventy-two. According to the best authors, there were slain thirty or forty thousand Huguenots in a few days; and among them without doubt many true witnesses and faithful martyrs of Jesus Christ. *Their dead bodies lay in the street of the great city,* one of the greatest cities of Europe; for they were not suffered to be buried, being the bodies of heretics; but were dragged through the street, or thrown into the river, or hung upon gibbets, and exposed to public infamy.

And again:

. . . *It was given unto him to make war with the saints and to overcome them:* and who can make any computation, or even frame any conception of the numbers of pious Christians, who have fallen a sacrifice to the bigotry and cruelty of Rome? Sanders himself confesses that an innumerable multitude of Lollards and Sacramentarians were burnt throughout all Europe, who yet he says were not put to death by the Pope and bishops, but by the civil magistrates; which perfectly agrees with this prophecy, for of the *secular beast* it is said, that he should *make war with the saints and overcome them*. No wonder that by these means he should obtain an universal authority *over all kindreds, and tongues*, and nations, and establish his dominion in all the countries of the western Roman empire: and that they should not only submit to his decrees, but even adore his person, except the faithful few, whose names, as citizens of heaven, were inrolled in the registers of life. Let the Romanists boast therefore that theirs is the *catholic church* and *universal empire*; this is so far from being any evidence of the truth, that it is the very brand infixed by the Spirit of prophecy.

The number of the beast is worked out in several ways with incredible skill. ("It agrees to admiration," comments the author.) The scarlet robes of the Cardinals help the picture, the Pope sits above the altar, the Cardinals first create and after worship him:

It is the Roman beast in his last state or under his seventh head: and he hath *a mouth speaking great things and blasphemies*; and what can be *greater things* and *blasphemies*, than the claims of *universal bishop, infallible judge of all controversies, sovran of kings*, and *disposer of kingdoms, viceregent of Christ*, and *God upon earth*!

Newman himself tells us the effect upon him of these volumes whereby he became convinced that the Pope was indeed the Antichrist foretold by Daniel, St. John and St. Paul. It will be seen how as time went on this belief created a stumbling block—almost an impassable barrier on the road he was to walk. "My imagination," he says, "was stained by the effects of this doctrine up to the year 1843; it had been obliterated from my reason and judgment at an earlier date; but the thought remained upon me as a sort of false conscience. Hence came that conflict of mind which so many have felt besides myself; leading some men to make a compromise between two ideas, so inconsistent with each other, driving others to beat out the one idea or the other from their minds, and ending in my own case, after many years of intellectual unrest, in the gradual decay and extinction of one of them."[1]

[1] *Apologia*, p. 5.

The opposite idea sowed in his mind at the same period was
the picture of the early Church as seen in the writings of the
Fathers. Milner's *Church History* which he read this same year
contained long quotations from St. Ambrose, St. Augustine and
others, of which he became "nothing short of enamoured."

But so too did Bishop Newton quote the Fathers. Not until
the originals had been substituted for quotations, not until he
had absorbed them and lived in their atmosphere, did the
Fathers' view of Scripture and of the Church stand out to him in
complete contradiction with the picture given in *Dissertations on the
Prophecies*.

A long prayer written in Latin, asking to be preserved from
anger, pride and impurity, concludes in words of self-condem-
nation similar to those Newman used later. *"Heu miser ego! Pec-
cavi. Aeternam damnationem mereor propter portentosa facinora mea."*

His conversion made him feel a need for some external change
also—some greater strictness in daily life, some restrictions of his
recreations. He feels the need of "presenting my scruples with
humility and a due obedience to my parents"; he jots down the
points of the argument that may follow: "sense of my own
weakness," "the beginnings of sin are small," better "to be too
cautious than too negligent." But he will be "ready to obey in
a matter so dubious," and he concludes: "I think those things
of importance to myself; but I hope I am not so enthusiastic as
to treat it as a concern of high religious importance."

The word "enthusiasm" is one of the very few in the English
language which has grown in stature instead of dwindling; in
the eighteenth century its meaning was uniformly bad—it almost
meant fanaticism. "I do not vindicate enthusiasm," says Hannah
More when defending her work for the poor, "I dread it. But
can the possibility that a few should become enthusiastic be justly
pleaded as an argument for giving them *all* up to actual vice and
barbarism?"

The word still had not a wholly good meaning at this date,
which in part arose from a deep-seated distrust of all that
exceeded the measure of a rather limited measuring rod. Newman
had ventured beyond that measure—he had struck out into the
deep. There was little of what he was now feeling that he could
explain to his parents, loving as they were—least of all the

deepest of the ascetic views that his conversion had opened before him: the "deep imagination" he calls it in the *Apologia*, "that it would be the will of God that I should lead a single life." It was mixed up in his mind with the idea of some full self-devotion —perhaps missionary work among the heathens.

In *Loss and Gain*, written about thirty years later, Newman has shown how through this idea he saw something of the deep incongruity of the ascetic principle with the then Church of England. The discussions with his sister and with his tutor when the hero first speaks of it, the shock, the slight disgust, are illuminating.

"When you afflict yourself on purpose," says the tutor, "then at once you pass from pure Christianity."

"Well," said Charles, "I certainly fancied that fasting, abstinence, labours, celibacy, might be taken as a make-up for sin."

Charles had claimed that an Apostle "unmarried, pure in fast and nakedness and at length a martyr is a higher idea" than a patriarch under his fig-tree and surrounded by his descendants. The tutor objects that he has shifted his ground.

"You began by saying that celibacy was a perfection of nature, now you make it a penance; first it is good and glorious, next it is a medicine and punishment . . ."

. . . "Perhaps our highest perfection here is penance," said Charles; "but I don't know; I don't profess to have clear ideas upon the subject. I have talked more than I like. Let us at length give over."[1]

In the story the tutor's manner after this talk "was not quite his own, as if something had annoyed him." Newman, like Charles, was not yet clear—how was it possible?—on all these deep thoughts that had taken possession of his mind: they must work themselves out. And we must see them working underneath the full life of study, friendship and family affections, of all the novelty and excitement the next few years were to bring.

Meanwhile he began a correspondence with Walter Mayers, and became "very fond" of Beveridge's *Private Thoughts*, both the matter and the style, in which he began to compose sermons that in his old age he would judge severely.

[1] *Loss and Gain*, pp. 200-1.

C

Newman's great love of music makes me choose this passage to illustrate the style of *Private Thoughts* which later gave place in Beveridge's admirer to the utter simplicity of the *Parochial and Plain Sermons*:

When I play . . . the same motion that my hand makes upon the instrument, the instrument makes upon my heart; it calls in my spirits, composes my thoughts, delights my ear, recreates my mind, and so not only fits me for after-business, but fills my heart, at the present, with pure and useful thoughts; so that when the music sounds the sweetliest in my ears, truth commonly flows the clearest into my mind.

Bishop Beveridge can write kindly and humanly:

God, indeed, hath provided a recreation for all sensible creatures; sleep, which is the rest of the spirits in the nerves. When the little animal spirits have been, all the day, running up and down upon the soul's errands, then, to lie down still and quiet, is a great refreshment and revivement to them, provided still that it be moderately used.

But there is Calvinism in the assertion that "by our fall from God the whole soul was desperately corrupted," and a consequent severity towards that poor soul which is "by nature inordinate and irregular in its operations"; and this certainly affected the fifteen-year-old boy. "I am resolved," wrote the Bishop, "by the grace of God, never to speak much, lest I often speak too much; and not speak at all, rather than to no purpose."

Reading Bishop Beveridge suggests one unlucky result of Newman's period of Calvinism: I cannot but feel for many years the exercise of his vigorous if not yet very subtle sense of humour was inhibited by the writers to whom Mr. Mayers introduced him.

When Beveridge is humorous it is certainly most unconsciously —as when considering the possibility of marriage for himself: "If ever it be my lot to enter into that state, I beg of God that he would direct me in the choice of such a wife only, to lie in my bosom here, as may afterwards be admitted to rest in Abraham's bosom to all eternity."

Newman was possibly too young to howl with laughter over this prayer, but one cannot help feeling that the fountain of his mirth was somewhat dried up by the nature of the books he was reading.

For the rest Bishop Beveridge is interesting—especially in the theological sections of his *Thoughts*. He lays down the thesis that we cannot serve God without first knowing Him, and his reflections on the nature of man's soul, his meditations on the Trinity, are valuable enough to explain Newman's fondness for the book. At a first glance we seem far enough from the days when a professor of divinity at Oxford can speak (as did Canon Streeter in this century) of the divine mystery as "mathematically absurd but representatively apt." Actually the best of the Anglican writers were driven by the widespread Socinianism, Arianism and other heresies within their pale to a study of the Patristic theology of the Trinity and Incarnation. Since Catholics had no such problem there was a regrettable concentration on the Protestant Controversy which has left us little that is of value. By good fortune and a profound instinct Newman as a boy chose out, from much that was heretical, material that gave his mind food for deeper and deeper reflection on the central mystery of the faith.

CHAPTER IV

At Trinity

WHAT IF Newman had gone to Cambridge?—and he very nearly did. The post-chaise was at the door and his father still undetermined between the two universities when a friend —Mr. John Mullins, Curate of St. James's, Piccadilly—who came to call turned the scale in favour of Oxford. The scene is a pleasing one: the boy waiting, his luggage ready, the impatient coachman holding in his horses, the two men leisurely discussing a question decided by most parents years ahead. Mr. Mullins, an Oxford man, got into the chaise and accompanied father and son—perhaps to make quite certain they should reach the right university, anyhow hoping to enter John at Exeter, his own college. Since there was no vacancy at Exeter he introduced them to Dr. Lee, President of Trinity and Vice-Chancellor of the University. Newman was entered at Trinity as a commoner, December 14, 1816. On his informing his late schoolmaster, he received plenary approval from Dr. Nicholas. "Trinity, a most gentlemanlike college—I am much pleased to hear it."

Had the post-chaise gone to Cambridge Newman would almost certainly have fallen under the influence of Simeon Vicar of Trinity Church, a leading Evangelical, holding exactly the position he himself was later to hold—a university don in charge of a parish church wielding an immense influence among the undergraduates. It is interesting to speculate on whether this deeply spiritual, powerful but quite unintellectual personality would have held Newman back from the changes that at Oxford made him into Newman.

He was still two months short of sixteen; but his birthday had long passed before he was called into residence—"for want," he tells us, "of the vacancy of a room." It was the very eve of the long vacation of 1817, and Newman came up as most men were on the point of going down. He stayed only a few weeks but the time was long enough for him to fall in love with Oxford. This love which lasted a long lifetime became later the love of a

man. At first it was the love of a boy, and its special quality is
best conveyed in *Loss and Gain,* when Newman, who had just lost
Oxford, remembers the joy with which he first came there. No
one reading the book can help feeling that the hero is young for
his eighteen years—but Newman in fact was only sixteen. As
at Ealing he had been a child among boys, now he was a boy
among men. "When he came to Oxford, he came there with
an enthusiasm so simple and warm as to be almost childish. . . .
As time goes on and we number and sort and measure things—
as we gain views—we advance towards philosophy and truth but
we recede from poetry."

Thus the young Newman found Oxford bathed in poetry:
not the dreaming spires only, but Shotover Wood, the meadows
during haymaking, the may and the laburnum, the trees:

". . . The planes are so touching just now, with their small
multitudinous green hands half-opened; and there are two or
three such fine dark willows stretching over the Cherwell; I
think some dryad inhabits them: and, as you wind along, just
over your right shoulder is the Long Walk, with the Oxford
buildings seen between the elms."

Many years later he wrote:

When the mind is most impressible, when the affections are warmest,
when associations are made for life, when the character is most in-
genuous and the sentiment of reverence is most powerful, [the young
man] comes up to a college in the Universities. There he forms
friendships, there he spends his happiest days . . . when he looks
back on the past he finds himself bound by ties of gratitude and regret
to the memories of his College life . . . he has unconsciously imbibed
to the full the beauty and the music of the *locale.* The routine of
duties and observance, the preachings and the examinations and the
lectures, the dresses and the ceremonies, the officials whom he feared,
the buildings or gardens that he admired, rest upon his mind and
his heart, and their shade becomes a sort of shrine to which he makes
continual offerings of attachment and devotion. It is a second home,
not so tender, but more noble and majestic and authoritative.

Nineteenth-century Commissioners for University Reform noted
that Oxford can hardly be dealt with, as could most of the foreign
universities, simply *as* a university: it is a collection of colleges, each
with its own statutes and customs, each with a very individual
history, each evoking a passionate loyalty from its own under-

graduates and Fellows. "God be with you, Balliol men," cried Belloc, when in bitterest disagreement with his old college; and the love of college with many goes deeper even than the love of Oxford.

With college and university alike hardly a term is in use but has its origin in the Middle Ages, greatly though the meaning may have changed. And the very changes show Oxford, what Andrew Lang has called it, "bitterly historical": the zigzagging course pursued by the Reformation under the Tudors, the triumph of Puritanism and its destructive effects under Cromwell, the glories of the Restoration, the profound modifications of the eighteenth century: all this is written on the stones of Oxford and in her libraries. Many old names of streets still stand, the titles of the colleges, the town and gown riots and the old ceremonial annual fines (a yearly apology for a mediaeval riot was made still in Newman's day by the town to the university). May Day on Magdalen Tower, the very pronunciation "Maudlen," Gaudy, Responsions, Bedel, Act, and hundreds of other terms in daily use call for a glossary for the newcomer to Oxford. All Souls' College reminds him that his ancestors prayed for the dead, All Saints' Church that they invoked them. Our Lady is everywhere, having churches and colleges named in her honour and her name still occurring on solemn occasions. Newman's own college, "dedicated to the Holy and Undivided Trinity," had a history as interesting as that of any in the university. It was the heir of the old Benedictine College of Durham started by the monks of Durham Abbey in 1286, to give hospitality to Benedictines from all parts. At the Reformation, abbey and college were swept away together, and for a short time a hall for students took its place.

Sir Thomas Pope—"an example," says Mallet, "of a successful official in Tudor days"—having acquired some thirty manors from monastic spoils put back a little of his wealth into the foundation of a new college which inherited the site and the buildings of Durham. At Mary's accession the despoilers were allowed to keep their lands, and Pope worked in with Bonner, was for a time guardian to Elizabeth, and died too early in her reign to encounter fresh problems. Mallet thinks he would have had no sympathy for the religious changes that followed: he was, like Henry VIII, a Catholic apart from the Pope, but I fancy he would have managed as well for himself under Elizabeth as under her two predecessors. Anyhow, the college was Catholic enough at its inception: rich altar vessels and vestments had been acquired from the monasteries as well as land, and for the moment these were not wasted. Trinity College was opened with High Mass as well as with a great banquet. The statutes drawn up guarded minutely against heresy, the president was to be a priest, the library windows retained images of Benedictine monks, and one of Thomas à Becket with the murderer's weapon sticking in his head. (After all, the king had not abolished monks as monks, but only as unworthy of their calling.) And the statutes of the college still enjoined prayers for the founder and for the Lady Elizabeth, his wife, "by whose Liberality we are here brought up in Godliness and Learning."

The second president after the founding of the college, Ralph Kettell, was, Aubrey says, a "right Church of England man"; "he sawe how the factions in religions in those days drewe and he kept himself unconcerned." Yet too he "was wont to talk much of the rood-loft and of the wafers: he remembered those times," and, praying for the founder, "he would many times make a wilful mistake and say 'Sir Thomas Pope our Confounder,' but then presently recall himself."

Under the Stuarts the college was mainly loyal, although enough Parliament men were to be found there to produce an attack from a Royalist:

Adire nolui Trinitatem	Old Trinity tho' near I came,
Quam nostis prope stare;	I passed for her impiety;
Haereticam Societatem	Because 'twas dangerous to condemn
Ne videar damnare:	That Heretick Society. [1]

After the Restoration the rebuilding began that made the college we know today, with its lovely low stone buildings, and a wide stretch of green where Newman walked and gazed and dreamed. Two specially memorable elements in this early glimpse of the university were the excitement and novelty of college life and the making of his first close friendship. Mr. Short, his tutor, sent to Newman's rooms another commoner, John William Bowden, to tell him about the college customs and take him in to dinner.

I was much entertained [he wrote to his father] with the novelty of the thing. Fish, flesh and fowl, beautiful salmon, haunches of

[1] *The Clerk of Oxford*, p. 199.

mutton, lamb, etc., fine strong beer; served up in old pewter plates
and misshapen earthenware jugs. Tell Mama there were gooseberry,
raspberry, and apricot pies. And in all this the joint did not go round,
but there was such a profusion that scarcely two ate of the same.

An intellectual man often makes his close friendships at the
university rather than at school—and there too the difference in
age is not such a barrier to intimacy as with schoolboys. Born
the same day as Newman but three years earlier, Bowden was
a congenial companion and the two became known as insepar-
ables, "taking their meals together, reading, walking, boating
together—nay, visiting each other's homes in the vacations."

There is a tantalising quality in the brief mention in biographies
and letters of matters that seem unimportant to the writer, yet
which would greatly help posterity to a vivid picture. We should
like to know more about this boating: did they always row or
sometimes punt? Was Newman skilful in a boat, or may we
picture him with his lank black hair and huge round spectacles
clinging to a punt pole while the boat slid from under his
feet? Or did they punt so long ago?

That they *did* row we know from a map of the river pasted into
the Autographic Remains and endorsed by Newman: "When I
was an undergraduate, perhaps in 1820, I was one of near twenty
Trinity men who skiffed up to Islip together. This is Bowden's
map of the River for me, to prevent mistakes, as I believe I was
to come later than the rest."

At that date cricket was played in a top hat: there seems to
have been no orthodox boating dress. Southey describes the
Isis with pleasure-boats "gliding in all directions and the students
in caps and tassels in curious contrast with their employment at
the oar." Bedel Cox about the same date belonged to a six-oar
crew which took parties down to Nuneham and dressed in green
leather caps with nankeen jackets and trousers. But in the first
recorded eight-oar race in 1815, when Brasenose beat Jesus, top
hats were worn. These two colleges appear to have had the
racing to themselves, but by 1817 Christ Church had a boat on
the river, and in 1819 Christ Church men adopted a sort of
tam-o'-shanter which became popular and drove out the high
hat.

Dr. Jenkyns of Balliol voiced Conservative opinion in declaring
that rowing was no sport for a gentleman, but was won over by

witnessing a crew rowing in perfect unison. "Why," he cried in delight, "it is like the motion of one man."[1]

References in *Loss and Gain* to walks in which a "beaver" was worn are at first sight puzzling—but a beaver was simply a top hat.

> Always wear your Cap and Gown
> Prudent Freshman in the town;
> When a walk you're bent upon,
> You may put your "Beaver" on.

"There were no silk hats," says Tuckwell, "until late in the Thirties. They cost two guineas; only gentlemen wore them." The illustration, which is almost of Newman's date, suggests that gowns (and expressions) were worn with a difference.

Newman had made one friend but that friend had probably gone down with the majority: the next letters home show him very solitary and while disliking the solitude disliking still more the only company that offered. At a wine party he attended, "they sat down," he writes, "with the avowed determination of each making himself drunk. I really think if anyone should ask me what qualifications were necessary for Trinity College I should say there was only one—drink, drink, drink.

"I ought not to envy them [my brothers at home] but I feel very much like it. However, I believe I may come home this day fortnight."

Newman's eyes were weak and all through his life he put on them a tremendous strain. He writes in this same letter:

I was very uncomfortable the first day or two because my eyes were not well, so that I could not see to read, and whenever my eyes are bad I am low-spirited. Besides, I did not know anyone, and after having been used to a number about me, I felt very solitary. But now my eyes are better, and I can read without hurting them, and I have begun to fag pretty well.

Newman's difficulty in getting any directions as to what to "fag" *at* in the Long Vacation is astonishing. He was now a member of a college, he had been assigned to a tutor, yet he went to the strangest expedients to find out. Understanding that he had to ask the president's permission to leave Oxford,

[1] For these details I am indebted to C. E. Mallet's *History of Oxford.* The first Oxford-Cambridge race was in 1829.

he decided to ask him at the same time about his reading! The president, "a courteous gentlemanlike man," naturally answered that he left such matters to the tutors. Seeing a tutor on horseback and thinking it his last chance, Newman dashed into the road and "abruptly accosting him, asked what books he should read during the vacation." This tutor referred him to another and at last he got the information.

A couple more unpublished letters to his father complete the picture of these first few weeks.

June 19th, 1817.
I was in a very good place in the theatre yesterday. Tell Charles he would have liked to have seen the noblemen's dresses, as also the I-do-not-know-what-they-were—very fat men, I suppose DD's in red robes or scarlet, and the Proctors with sheep skins. Mr. Peel was made a Doctor of Laws by the Vice Chancellor.

June 27th, 1817.
Whenever I go out I am stared at; and the other day there was a party of people laughing at my dress. I am the head of the table at dinner, because I am the only one; at least I sometimes nearly finish my dinner before the few remaining drop in. The other day I had a nice dinner set before me of veal cutlets and peas so much to myself that I could hear the noise I made in chewing thro' the empty hall; till at length one came in and sat opposite to me, but I had not been introduced to him, and he could not speak to me. Consequently we preserved an amicable silence, and conversed with our teeth.
I hope the violin is mended . . . I go to bed very early. The candles that you saw are not half burnt out yet.

Christopher Dawson made me notice that an early picture of Newman in his big glasses has a curious resemblance to Mr. Verdant Green as depicted on the cover of that immortal work. At this date he looked young (which he was) and simple (which he was not). "Some of my fellow collegians," he wrote to his mother, "observing perhaps that I did not bluster and make a row, took it into their heads they could make a *butt* of me (take this in more senses than one), but I had not the slightest idea of any such thing."
In his diary this scene is described twice—tersely in Latin, more diffusely in English.

Friday, Nov. 7, 1817.

At about half past six W. came to me and said he had been desired by E. to send me his compliments and he wd. be very happy to see me at his wine party and that I should be so much the more acceptable if I brought my violin . . . The first thing that surprised me on entering the room was a smothered laugh on my conductor announcing "Mr. Newman and his fiddle". I was offered a chair, a glass and a decanter. I took my time in drinking the glass of wine. In the meantime a fresh bottle had been decanted, and my entertainer assured me he was waiting for me to finish the glass before passing the bottle. The bottle waited—those below called out to pass it. I offered to pass it. Oh no—he could not think of my passing it without filling; there was no hurry—he wd. wait. At last I passed it without filling. The bottle came round. I sometimes filled my glass, sometimes passed without filling. Toasts were given—The King—I am sure I wished him well, but I would not fill when the bottle came round with the earth's rapid circuit round the sun.

All this time I was intreated to play. I refused. An hour had passed and I determined to go. I looked at my watch. I finished my third glass, and begged E's leave to depart. E. requested silence and asked me to speak [my wishes]. I did so. "No" assailed me on every side. My voice was drowned but they could not prevent my moving. Then they spoke separately. I ought not to disgrace myself. I was going too soon. I said I had told W. I would go for half an hour. I got up and went.

Clearly the atmosphere had not changed much since the freshmen of the seventeenth century were received "amongst a parcel of honest, merry fellows who think themselves obliged, in honour and common civility, to make you *damnable drunk*, and carry you, as they call it, a CORPSE, to bed."[1]

One more attempt was made in the following week to intimidate the young undergraduate, a visit from two of the party, who proceeded to play the fool noisily while Newman tried to study. One of them (six foot four in height, notes Newman, and broad in proportion), threatened to knock him down. But "the event was," Newman wrote home, "I received a handsome apology." Henceforward he was left in peace to read, to row, and to improve his Latin. "When I got to Oxford," he notes, "Bowden and I made it a rule always to talk together in Latin."

As he has said of himself that he had not in his composition a grain of conviviality, it has usually been assumed that this fact

[1] Quoted from *Terrae Filius*, in Lang's *Oxford*, p. 203.

and his Evangelicalism account for Newman's dislike of wine-parties and objections to the college Gaudy. But in fact Evangelical teetotalism was a later growth than is usually supposed. According to Elie Halévy the sects had no interest in the temperance movement as late as the middle of the nineteenth century. It was confined in the main to the Catholic Father Matthew and the Anglican Evangelicals who themselves had no objection to moderate drinking. At a later date an extreme Evangelical would have refused even one glass of wine: the three glasses Newman had at the party just described seem a fair measure for a boy of sixteen. I cannot but think that the Gaudy must at that date have been a thoroughly drunken scene even if Newman's letter to Mr. Mayers about the Gaudy of 1819 is a little exaggerated. (Writing to an old schoolmaster from whom he had imbibed his Calvinist views he probably to some extent caught his tone.) It took place on Trinity Monday following one of the terminal celebrations of the Eucharist.

. . . It is sickening to see what I might call the apostasies of many. This year it was supposed there would have been no such merry-making. A quarrel existed among us: the college was divided into two sets, and no proposition for the usual subscription for wine was set on foot. Unhappily, a day or two before the time a reconciliation takes place; the wine party is agreed upon, and this wicked union, to be sealed with drunkenness, is profanely joked upon with allusions to one of the expressions in the Athanasian Creed. As it is, I keep quiet, for all have pledged themselves to go—yes, all but one, a poor, despised, awkward man, of unprepossessing appearance and untidy person, who, I really think, has more proper sense of religion than them all together.[1]

To see the secret eagerness with which many wished there would be no Gaudy; to see how they took hope, as time advanced and no mention was made of it; but they are all gone, there has been weakness and fear of ridicule . . .

Oh, that the purpose of some may be changed before the time! I know not how to make myself of use. I am intimate with very few. The Gaudy has done more harm to the College than the whole year can compensate. An habitual negligence of the awfulness of the Holy Communion is introduced. How can we prosper?

In his first full term (October to Christmas, 1817), Newman writes home of the changes that were making Trinity into a

[1] Bowden, he adds in a note, was away—at his sister's death-bed.

reading college. "If anyone wishes to study much, I believe there can be no college that will encourage him more than Trinity. It wishes to rise in the University and it is rising fast. In discipline it has become the strictest of colleges. There are lamentations in every corner of the increasing rigour; it is laughable, but it is delightful to hear the groans of the oppressed."

The diary also notes in this year: "A. C. Dec. Prid. Mane Eucharist. Sacr. accipio." ["This was my first Communion in the Anglican Church."]

Letters home chronicle his progress, both in learning and in his tutor's good graces. It seems pretty clear that Mr. Short began by doubting the scholarship of this sixteen-year-old. But the mathematics do appear to have been surprisingly elementary.

I own I was rather astonished at hearing them begin the Ass's Bridge, nor was my amazement in the least degree abated, when my turn came, to hear him say, with a condescending air, "I believe, sir, you never saw Euclid before?" I answered I had. "How far?" "I had been over five books." Then he looked surprised; but I added I could not say I knew them perfectly by any means. I am sure by his manner he then took it into his head that I was not well grounded, for he proceeded to ask me what a point was, and what a line, and what a plane angle. He concluded, however, by telling me that I might come in with the other gentlemen at 10 o'clock, with the 4th, 5th and 6th books.

The next time I came he was not condescending, but it was "sir" very stiffly indeed.

The next time, after I had demonstrated, I saw him peep at my paper, to see if I had anything written down—a good sign.

And today, after I had demonstrated a tough one out of the fifth book, he told me I had done it very correctly.

As to the classics, Newman tells his parents:

I had a declamation to do last week, a Latin one. I took a great deal of pains with it. As I was going to lecture today, I was stopped by the Fellow who looks over the declamations (the Dean, Mr. Kinsey), and to whom we recite them, and told by him that mine did me much credit.

Although much younger than his fellows and chagrined by finding some of them much more advanced, Newman felt the lectures to be "childishly easy." In a valuable essay on Newman and the Classics, Fr. Tristram has summarised his classical studies during his first year at Oxford. The first term

he offered for Collections, the choice of books being open, Xenophon's *Anabasis* and Tacitus's *Agricola* and *Germania*. Thereupon he felt that he had made "something of a dash," since a single book of the *Anabasis* would have sufficed; and at the same time he regretted that he had chosen a book already studied at school, because it did not extend his range of reading. In the following term for Collections he offered *Herodotus* (5 books) and the *Æneid*. In May 1818, as a candidate for an Exhibition, he was examined in Latin verse and Prose Composition, in Euripides (chorus), Plato, Lucretius, Xenophon and Livy, as well as in Mathematics and an English Essay . . . Before the month was out, he went up for Responsions, offering *Herodotus* (5 books) and Horace's *Odes* and *Epodes*, and he passed without difficulty.[1]

Mr. Short had been urging him to stand for the exhibition just alluded to. To his father Newman writes (April 18, 1818) that he intends to wait another year before trying. "I should stand a good chance of failing and that I cannot say I should relish."

A few weeks later, however, he is writing home for his baptismal certificate and begging them not to ask why, writing also casually of the number of candidates for the exhibition. His tutor had pressed him to stand so strongly that he could not well refuse, but he determined to keep the secret from his family. "How often," he wrote afterwards, "was my pen going to tell the secret, but I determined to surprise you." He felt a deep conviction that the surprise would be a pleasant one, although

I felt the tortures of suspense so much that I wished and wished I had never attempted it . . . I tried to keep myself as cool as possible, but I could not help being sanguine . . . Very few men thought I should get it and my reason thought the same.

The exhibition was for nine years at £60 a year: it was closely contested between Newman and a Worcester man, and Newman's mathematics turned the scale in his favour. In telling the story to his family he exhibits that curious shyness that overcame him all his life. Met by one of the other candidates he was naturally

[1] In *A Tribute to Newman*, Browne and Nolan, p. 253.

asked whether the thing was decided. "What was I to say? 'It was.' 'And who has got it?' 'Oh, an in-college man,' I said; and I hurried away as fast as I could. On returning with my newly-earned gown, I met the whole set going to their respective homes. I did not know what to do; I held my eyes down."

Before they received his letter Newman's family had heard the great news. "My dear Scholar!" his mother writes . . . "By this address you are informed that your mysterious news has flown to us . . . My mind is such a chaos of surprise, pleasure and hope that I can scarcely write to you."

It is interesting to note that Mrs. Newman uses the word "scholar" with pride, for Newman's success came just before the half-way mark in a change noted in Mark Pattison's *Memoirs*. In 1808, he says, scholars were not regarded as gentlemen—they were called "charity boys." But in 1833 "the scholar's gown, far from being the badge of an inferior order had become a coveted distinction."

The relation between Newman and his tutor is puzzling. Mr. Short had come to value his pupil deeply. On one occasion, meeting his father by chance, he went up to him like an old friend and exclaimed, "Oh, Mr. Newman, what have you given us in your son!" Yet he did curiously little to improve the value of the gift by guidance or advice. The story of the next two years is fantastic. Trinity had long failed to attain any first classes: here was a man of first-class material: an ambitious man whose father had just entered him at Lincoln's Inn, who was prepared to work endlessly, and who was so young and inexperienced that he did not realise the limits of his physical powers. He made his eyes the test—as long as they held out he went on reading. Once in chapel he fainted, but after a few hours' rest went back to his books. Reading for a first-class in both classics and mathematics he yet was "much taken up with Hume and Gibbon," he attended Buckland's lectures on geology. (A wit of the time wrote of these lectures:

"Some doubts were once expressed about the Flood,
Buckland arose and all was clear as mud.")

He joined a music club and through the enthusiasm of an old don was kept on at least one occasion "playing quartets on a heavy tenor from seven to twelve! O, my poor arms and eyes and head and back."

Mercifully there was the boating with Bowden, but on the whole both men took their recreation in ways that made it no recreation. Letters home record how they started a magazine. It was to be so deeply anonymous that Newman at first only tells his father: "there is a novel production to be published next Monday, a periodical by name *The Undergraduate*" (February 2, 1819).

But three weeks later he writes to his mother:

. . . Bowden came into my room on Monday morning and spoke these words: "The men of Magdalen universally say that Newman of Trinity is the author of *The Undergraduate*." What imprudence had I committed? I had told no one. I never felt such a dreadful shock. The whole day I was so weak I could hardly walk or speak. One good thing is, no one in Trinity believes it. Why my name should be known and not Bowden's is incomprehensible. I have had a headache ever since I heard of it.

What? Can anyone fag, fag and be an author? Alas! The third day has come a frost and a nipping frost.

The next letter says:

I hope we have completely weathered the storm. You would say we were admirable actors if you saw how we behaved before people, so cool, so collected, so indifferent. The manner of the discovery is to us as great a secret as ever . . .

At length I believe we have decided to give it up. We shall sell it to the bookseller: he will continue it: it will be off our hands and minds. We shall not be distracted in our studies. We shall have gained a great end in gaining experience.

The two friends also composed together a poem on the Massacre of St. Bartholomew. Still in the spirit of Bishop Newton, Newman sketches the false faith that led to terror and persecution.

> Mid the recesses of that pillar'd wall
> Stood reverend Clement's dark confessional.
> Here Rapine's son with superstition pale
> Oft thro' the grated lattice told his tale;
> Here blood-stain'd Murder falter'd, tho' secure
> Of absolution from a faith impure . . .

THE CLERK OF OXFORD, 1817

Mistaken worship! Can the outward tear
Make clean the breast devoid of godly fear?
Shall pomp and splendour holy love supply,
The grateful heart, the meek submissive eye?
Mistaken worship! Where the priestly plan
In servile bondage rules degraded man,
Proclaims on high in proud, imperious tone
Devotion springs from ignorance alone;
And dares prefer to sorrow for the past
The scourge of penance or the groans of fast!
—Where every crime a price appointed brings
To soothe the churchman's pride, the sinner's stings,
Where righteous grief and penitence are made
An holy market and a pious trade!

Like the authors a century later of *1066 and All That*, Newman adds a note to the poem concerning the question of which historical events were truly "memorable" at Oxford. The first canto of *St. Bartholomew's Eve* had already appeared but he had found it was not clear enough.

I take this opportunity of introducing a short sketch of the massacre of St. Bartholomew. It may be thought by many an unnecessary task, and some will not fail to deem it as presuming, to suppose that our learned University is unacquainted with the full particulars. This I thought myself, when I published the First Canto; but an earnest and attentive canvassing of the opinions of those who have done me the honour to peruse my publication has convinced me of my mistake.

These were not the only verses Newman wrote during his time at Trinity. His life must always be pictured against the background of home, and Alton had become home as fully as Ham or Norwood. From a "Prologue to the Masque of Amyntor," written at Alton in 1819, one would gather that the family still continued their acting:

So might the scene yon curtain furled will show
Spellbind each care and charm to sleep each woe.

There are three Eclogues in which Damon and Menalcas, Damon and Thyrsis, Damon and Amaryllis celebrate the summer, the autumn and the spring, not without smiling as the young will always smile at fashions that were passing, not without falling

into the fashions that will provoke the mirth of newer young on
a later day:

> Hail! commonplaces of the pastoral strain!
> Which, once endured, we ne'er endure again;
> Where down the stanza tuneful dullness flows,
> Or ponderous truisms stalk in measured prose.

> . . . . .

> True—blame the folly but the purpose spare;
> Praise we or not, the Spring *is* passing fair.

There are verses to greet brothers and sisters on their birthdays,
verses to commemorate his own. Much later Newman made
some confidences which I should like to call confessions of the
manner in which he turned out verse and expected others to do
the same. He made them when a coach delayed, he made them
to stave off seasickness, he made them when shaving. I confess
to a feeling (in spite of critics far more fitted to judge than myself)
that, except for a very few occasional lines, Newman's verse
cannot be called poetry. That he was a poet no one can doubt—
but surely a poet in prose. What is more, much of the poetry
he admires is not more impressive than the poetry he writes. He
thinks very highly of Southey's "Thalaba"; he told Jemima that
"The Giaour" was definitely his favourite poem. And it is surely
astounding that even at nineteen, he could have written to her
that Pope's translation of Homer "is the finest body of verse,
certainly in this, perhaps in any language; it is so harmonious,
sweet and elegant throughout." In 1828 he wrote an essay on
"Poetry with Reference to Aristotle's Poetics": to illustrate a
point he lists a number of poems which, he holds, no one will
deny to be poetical: among them are Milman's "Funeral Hymn
to the Martyrs of Antioch," Joanna Baillie's "Chough and Crow,"
Campbell's "Battle of the Baltic," Barton's "Dream." It really
seems that the ear so miraculous for prose, so miraculous for
music, was tone-deaf to poetry.

A letter to his mother in 1834 gives a glimpse of the way in
which Alton and Oxford were woven into the pattern of these
earlier university years: particularly interesting is the feeling
many of us know of amazement at finding nature unchanged
when life has changed ourselves:

As I got near the place I many times wished I had not come, I found it so very trying. So many strong feelings, distinct from each other, were awakened. The very length of time since I was here . . . the particular season at which we lived here, when I was just entered at Oxford, so that this place is, as it were, the record, as it was the scene, of my undergraduate studies and opinions. The Oxford reminiscences of that time have been effaced by my constant residence there since, but here I am thrown back upon those years which never can come again . . . There are many little incidents stored in my memory which now waken into life. Especially, I remember that first evening of my return from Oxford in 1818, after gaining the scholarship at Trinity, and my Father saying "What a happy meeting this!" There was something so mysterious too, in seeing old sights, half recollecting them and doubting. It is like seeing the ghosts of friends. Perhaps it is the impression it makes upon one of God's *upholding* power which is so awful—but it seemed to me so very strange that everything was in its place after so long a time. As we came near, and I saw Monk's Wood, the church and the hollow on the other side of the town, it was as fearful as if I was standing on the grave of some one I knew, and saw him gradually recover life, and rise again.

I hope on the whole [his mother replied], you experienced more pleasure than pain from your pilgrimage. Your account revived some very agreeable juvenile recollections in dear J., it was quite a delight to her to follow you through your rambles and at last made her exclaim: "Nothing would give me more gratification than to visit those scenes in the same way!" For myself it was a period of such anxiety and fearful augury of greater trials progressively advancing that I scarcely think I should wish to revisit the place . . . Your recollection of your dear Father's "greeting" cheers me greatly. I have always a nervous dread lest you all can recall him only in pain and sorrow, borne down by injustice and a too sensitive concern for one's disappointed hopes.

At Oxford Newman did not neglect his home correspondence. On December 10th, he writes on the verge of "Collections":

In the interim between studying the beauties of the Rhetoric of Aristotle and enjoying the more substantial sweets of the College cook, allow me to give you a proof of my proficiency in the lessons of the former great man by inditing to you a letter replete with rhetorical graces . . . I promised to give you a description of my rooms and though my feeble pen can ill describe the endless beauties with which it is adorned, yet some slight idea may be obtained and the subject itself may reflect some lustre on my words and sentences.

He continues in the same style, describing every common bit of furniture in grandiose terms, promising to be home on Wednesday week "not without a companion," asking that Frank be admonished that "I shall expect him very much advanced in the science of sounds."

The pressure of work was constantly increasing. Throughout he had never done less than eight hours' study a day. He writes to his father in November 1819: "I am now reading at the rate (I whisper a great secret) of from thirteen to fourteen hours a day." And in the *Memoir* he adds: "I stayed in Oxford during the vacations, got up in winter and summer at five or six, hardly allowed myself time for my meals, and then ate, indeed, the bread of carefulness. During twenty out of the twenty-four weeks immediately preceding my examination, I fagged at an average of more than twelve hours a day. If one day I read only nine, I read the next fifteen." How cold and dark it must have been on winter mornings! He lit his own fire: one hopes it was a good drawing chimney and that the fire blazed quickly.

Looking back forty years later Newman adds that all these hours of study were real study—his mind was all the time concentrated on what he was reading.

Only a very young, a very unguided man could have acted thus. And the amazing thing was that he could still keep a real enthusiasm for the great literature at which he was grinding. To Jemima (aged twelve) he writes:

My attention is at present directed to Æschylus, the great inventor of the Grecian drama; he is the hardest Greek author in the opinion of many, but his obscurity arises from his sublimity; he is a dark, gloomy thundercloud, through which the sheet and forked lightnings glare and dart at intervals, awfully magnificent, sternly beautiful, terribly pathetic. Never, I think, have I read an author with whom I have been so struck; I am much lost in astonishment; I am stupefied, I am out of breath; with much of the style and genius of Shakespeare he has the advantage over him in coming to us in the garb of a foreign language, for everything is novel and strange.

He tells Jemima that he has some thought of setting one or two of Æschylus' choruses to music. In the course of the letter he insists upon Æschylus' superiority to "the dry, stiff, formal, affected, cold, prolix, dignified Sophocles." Jemima naturally charges him with fickleness: to which he replies indignantly: "That I have liked Sophocles I will not deny, that I like him still shall be my firm asseveration, and that I like him better than ever I did shall be a further asseveration." Remembering the group of adjectives with which he had belaboured Sophocles, Jemima must have rubbed her eyes. But her brother continues serenely: "Sophocles may be stiff and yet be majestic; dryness does not preclude strength; nor formality grandeur; affectation admits of beauty, and coldness is generally sharp and biting." This is surely the George of *The Fairy Bower*, who "believed he was clever enough to persuade anybody," and did not like to be defeated in an argument.

The Examination Statute of 1800 declares that all candidates must show "complete proficiency" in the Greek and Latin languages, in Rhetoric and Moral Philosophy as drawn from the Greek and Roman writers, in Logic and in Latin Composition. They must offer at least three books for detailed examination. All this was for a pass degree: a higher standard was demanded for honours. Newman offered a formidable list, comprising Aristotle, Homer, Æschylus, Sophocles, Thucydides, Herodotus, Polybius, Virgil, etc. As time went on he curtailed it. And what precisely was held to constitute "complete proficiency"? No wonder that Newman "read books, made ample analyses and extracts and entered upon collateral questions and original essays which did him no service in the schools."

Surrounded by the conviction that he would take a brilliant degree, he was not buoyed up by it but only made more anxious. Each letter home shows him getting more and more unstrung. There is all the pathos of youth in the letters that chronicle the hopes and fears of this tremendous hour—to no man can the prizes of ambition seem half so important as examination success to a boy. And in Newman's case there was another element. He wanted success, he dreaded failure—and he thought both emotions sinful. To Jemima he writes:

. . . striving to feel that, whether I pass a good or bad examination, God will be bestowing what is best for me, I may rest calm and joyful. I will not therefore ask for success, but for "good". I dare not ask for success, for it might prove fatal to me. Do you therefore, dearest sister, wish for me to obtain that which is best for me, and not for me to gain high honours here; for then, whether I succeed or fail, I shall have the comfort of feeling assured that I have obtained real advantage and not apparent.

And to Frank he speaks of "those emotions which the near prospect of my grand examination and a heart too solicitous about fame and too fearful of failure are continually striving to excite."

How many boys one wonders, with less power of self-expression than Newman, go through this sort of torture. Newman never forgot it: arranging his papers in the early 'seventies he gave an incredible proportion to this story of his youth. Most revealing of all is a letter to Mr. Mayers on the eve of the examination.

. . . in truth I am in no common situation. The very few honours that have been taken by men of our college, the utter absence of first classes for the last ten years, the repeated failures which have occurred, and the late spirit of reading which has shown itself among us, render those who attempt this, objects of wonder, curiosity, speculation, and anxiety. Five of us were going up for first classes this term; one has deferred his examination, one most likely goes up for no honours at all; one is expected to fail; one—whom I think most certain of success —may before the examination remove to another college; one remains. "Unless," I am told, "success at length attends on Trinity this examination, we have determined it is useless to read." . . .

. . . The high expectations, too, that are formed of me; the confidence with which those who know nothing of me put down two first classes to my name; the monstrous notions they form of the closeness of my application, and, on the other hand, my consciousness of my own deficiencies—these things may create a smile, in my future life, to think I feared them, but they are sufficient to dismay me now. I fear much more from failure than I hope from success.

Still may I continue to pray "Give me no honours here if they are to be the slightest cause of sin to my soul."

But, while saying this, I often find that I am acting the part of a very hypocrite; I am buoyed up with the secret idea that, by thus leaving the event in the hands of God, when I pray, He may be induced, as a reward for so proper a spirit, to grant me my desire. Thus my prayer is a mockery.

The tutoring that could lay such a burden on a boy's imagination while giving him so little intellectual help to carry it, explains

Trinity's ten-year absence of Firsts. Newman had both over-read and worried himself into a fever. Called up a day sooner than he expected, he lost his head and broke down completely. In mathematics he failed altogether and in classics took only a second, his name appearing "below the line"—i.e., as low as it could be to be on the Honours List at all, for at that time the names of third-class honours men were not listed. In a very boyish letter he broke the news to his father:

It is all over, and I have not succeeded. The pain it gives me to be obliged to inform you and my mother of it, I cannot express. What I feel on my own account is indeed nothing at all compared with the thought that I have disappointed you. And most willingly would I consent to a hundred times the sadness that now overshadows me, if so doing would save my mother and you from feeling vexation. I will not attempt to describe what I have gone through, but it is past away, and I feel quite lightened of a load. The examining masters were as kind as it was possible to be; but my nerves quite forsook me and I failed. I have done everything I could to attain my object; I have spared no labour, and my reputation in my college is as solid as before, if not so splendid. If a man falls in battle after a display of bravery, he is honoured as a hero; ought not the same glory to attend him who falls in the field of literary conflict?

CHAPTER V

The Young Evangelical

NEWMAN's parents wrote kindly and reassuringly, but the blow was for them almost heavier than for him. The family fortunes were not brilliant and they were getting worse. The unsuccessful banker did not turn into a successful brewer, and Mrs. Newman's income from "the funds" was sinking as the interest fell from five, to four, to three per cent. They had looked to the brilliant eldest to retrieve the family fortunes by an outstanding success at the bar.

His own letters immediately after the examination look back on a bewildering experience. To Mr. Mayers he wrote: "So great a depression came on me that I could do nothing . . . My memory was gone, my mind altogether confused . . . I saw the cataract to which I was hurrying without the possibility of a rescue. It was as if a surgical operation was day after day being carried on upon me, and tearing away something precious."

He did not worry his family with this sort of analysis. To them he dwelt on his gratitude for their kindness and his own resignation to his fate. December 3rd, 1820, he writes: "Much I *have* gone through but the clouds have passed away. . . . Since I have done my part I have gained what is good."

A letter to his aunt ten days later shows the family in London and planning a Christmas reunion: half in jest, half earnest, Newman again shows the strain he had been under.

I write with little to say, for the sake of your receiving from my own hand intelligence of my being well in every respect. I have now got all my cares and anxieties over, and although I have not succeeded I do not feel any vexation and very little disappointment. I expect[ed] a second class in Classics and nothing in the Mathematical list; yet I do not intend to lay my Mathematical books on the shelf for their ungrateful return to my long civilities to them; indeed (excepting Æschylus) my principal amusement is at present in the contemplation of that branch of knowledge which is founded in necessary matter, the Theoria, the greatest good of the philosopher of Stagira. I have no doubt you will think the last sentence obscure enough; the truth is that of late months I have been so exclusively ranging the high paths of philosophy that I find it very difficult to descend into the ways of common conversation. But, without joking, I have really found my memory of common things surprisingly treacherous; I have forgotten things I used to know perfectly and am convinced that the tremendous load of book learning I have been heaping into my mind the last six months has driven out much of what I knew before.

What was now to be done about Newman's career? His exhibition had still some years to run which made it natural enough for him to remain at Oxford. He wanted to see Francis through the University and he could at least hope for a Fellowship later on at some College or other, even if not at one of the first rank.

Meanwhile he had the sense to let his mind lie comparatively fallow. Music and further lectures on geology and mineralogy were pure recreation. He writes home in March:

Thank Harriett for her skill in steaming away the superfluous water of the nitro-sulphate of copper. The mineralogy lectures were finished yesterday . . . I am glad to be able to inform you that Signor Giovanni Enrico Neandrini has finished his first composition. The melody is light and airy, and is well supported by the harmony.

In the long vacation of this year—1821—George IV was crowned and John and Harriett rose at three to view the procession. Harriett wrote to their Aunt, describing the sadly empty seats, the gorgeous dresses, how "old, ugly and ill" the King looked, and the Queen's "extraordinary behaviour". Excluded from the ceremony, Queen Caroline tried to force her way into the Abbey and was kept out on the delightful excuse that she had no ticket! Neither of the royal couple was so admirable as to make a judgment on the rights and wrongs of their quarrel an easy one. Feeling raged. A popular rhyme of the period ran:

> Gracious Queen we thee implore
> Go away and sin no more;
> But if that effort be too great
> Go away at any rate.

But Harriett Newman describes the "great applause" that accompanied cries of "the Queen!" "the Queen!" while Cobbett represented her cause as the popular one. Queen Caroline's trial and acquittal on the charge of adultery, Shane Leslie calls "cruel and comic". After this scene at the Abbey "she was mortally wounded and proceeded to die of the dumps." From Newman's contemporary—another Oxonian—Bedel Cox came the oft-quoted comment "So different, thank God, from the Court Life of our Victoria."

How far were the brother and sister interested in the background of the scene they were witnessing? Newman's part of the joint letter seems only to indicate an interest in the externals of a splendid ceremony; yet it will be remembered that as a schoolboy he had written a satire on the Prince Regent—now being crowned King.

We had all a very good view of the Procession from a booth very near the platform; it was not however till Wednesday evening that we took places, and on the morning of Thursday we still had at 4 o'clock in the morning to obtain a conveyance to go in. At last we overcame all difficulties, set off from home at five o'clock, and got to our places at half past six. The procession commenced at half past eleven, and, as might be expected, was most superb—a gentleman, who sat behind me and knew most of the great personages in it, pointed them out to me as they passed, which made it very interesting. . . . Lord Beresford carried the banner of Ireland, and Lord Harcourt the Standard of England. Prince Leopold was in the robes of a Knight of the Garter—he was much applauded—however grief, diffidence, or ill-nature prevented him from acknowledging the plaudits he received. Of all the nobility the most applauded and the most talked of was Lord Londonderry. He was dressed as a Knight of the Garter—the band of his hat was composed of most brilliant diamonds, to the worth of near £20,000. His person was so graceful and his manner so pleasing, and the way he acknowledged the continued cheers he received so good-natured, that we have not ceased to talk of him. I think him very like his picture in the exhibition. The King looked very pale going, but much better going back. I had a very good view of him. The new crown is very handsome— (I am, however, I believe the only one of us who admires it)—indeed I cannot fancy anything *more* handsome. I can indeed fancy a gew-gaw thing all over colours, which create a vulgar splendour—but I cannot fancy anything more tasteful, more classical, more elegant, more chaste and more brilliant. The green of the emerald, the red of the ruby, the yellow of the topaz, are imitable by coloured glass —and a crown not worth £10 may *look* nearly as well as the most gorgeous that can be made up of these gems—but the sparkling brightness of the diamond and the soft lustre of the pearl are inimitable—and of these is the crown composed.

This is the last letter that shows the family at Southampton Street. Newman writing to Jemima fifty years later, seems to imply that the house had to be given up and an auction of the contents held before 1821 was out. (A note in the diary refers to "the day when our prospects so changed, Nov. 3rd, 1821.") The letter paints a vivid picture and must be given in full:

The Oratory, July 2, 1871.

Mrs. Fox has been kind enough to give me a volume of violin music with "John Henry Newman, 1817" written in it. She got it from an auctioneer—and was naturally curious to know how I lost it. I knew well enough, but was obliged to shuffle. And, as she is soon to see you and will be sure to ask you, you will have to shuffle too. I don't know whether you have the means of recollecting what a point my Father made that I should take all my chattels to Oxford in October 1821, and how I neglected his advice—and how in the following January, when we were at Kentish Town, what a hope there was that we should save the music—and how we bid too low and it went—and how sad my Mother was at dinner, and how my Father said he would try to get it all from the purchaser. I said to Mrs. Fox, "How can I answer for a boy's negligences fifty years ago? Anything may happen in fifty years." It *was* my negligence.

The poor book is like a voice from the grave. It has been worn, and is pieced. It has been thoroughly made use of, pencil marks of fingering for the shifts are put over the more difficult passages. What surprises me is my utter forgetfulness of the greater part of its contents. There is a set of duets by Viotti, which I bought lately—but did not deem I had ever seen before—yet, I recollect, some melodies seemed familiar to me when I tried them. There are pieces by Vaccari and Spagnoletti, whose names I had all but forgotten. At present the book, alas, smells of antiquity, and I must take means for fumigating it.

I wonder what has become of the rest of the music. What a history has gone into the wide world, of names, places and dates, for I suppose these are all inscribed in them. This volume must have been bound at Alton or Oxford—most likely the latter—but I have not written either place in it.

And what a world of history has any single family in it, which perishes like the leaves in Autumn.

At first sight a private diary of Newman's youth appeared the most priceless of discoveries, outweighing all the family letters

and other papers. Actually it proved interesting mainly as a
literary and psychological curiosity, and it surely must have been
as such that he preserved part of it. I have quoted in the Introduction his own criticism of its unpleasant style: "I wrote in
style as another might write in verse, or sing instead of speaking,
or dance instead of walking. Also my Evangelical tone contributed to its bad taste."

Had this been all, the diary might still have been rewarding
as self-revelation, but this is where it most conspicuously fails.
The young Newman of the letters is the joy of parents and
sisters, high-spirited, merry, already self-supporting, shortly to
be the toiling, unselfish supporter of his whole family—inclined
no doubt to overdo his authority, irritable sometimes, but the
centre already not only of his family, but of a circle of affectionate, even admiring friends. The young Newman of the
diary writes: "These are my answers to Doddridge's Questions
in his *Rise and Progress*," and proceeds to an examination in which
he finds himself "very deficient in spirituality, in prayer, in
brotherly love, meekness, humility, forgiveness of injuries, charity,
benevolence, purity, truth and patience.

"I am very bad-tempered, vain, proud, arrogant, prone to
anger and vehement."

In another place he finds himself to be a "mean liar." Yet
again he has "ineffable contempt" for those beneath him and
"mean subservience" towards those above him.

The thing is too wholesale: it is the picture, not of a young
man with virtues and with faults, which Newman was, but of a
young monster, which certainly he was not. Doddridge's
Questions about one's sins all appear to demand an affirmative
answer! Newman, in this matter, reminds one irresistibly of
Jerome's hero who, after reading a medical book, was certain
he had every disease except housemaid's knee.

Nor is it always easy to interpret and evaluate the language
he uses. For example he writes, just after entering Oriel: "I
pray and bless Thee that this temptation, into which I have been
gradually sinking this last half year, is not one of painful and
perplexing doubts and fits of unbelief. I praise and bless Thee
that it is not a fiery attack from my besetting sin. What will
become of me? I am rolling down a precipice . . ." But any
guess we make as we read this of the nature of the temptation
and the desperateness of the danger must surely be shattered

by the resolutions he makes to meet them: "Read prayers with Francis three times a week, repress injurious words, study Bible. I will strive to drive away every wandering thought during my prayers." The editing of the diary by Newman in old age adds to the difficulty. If he had left it untouched, it would be easier at least to get the proportions and to guess which answers are "real" and which are merely "notional" (to use his own famous distinction on Assents). Thus on the matter of sexual temptations, there are occasional comparatively perfunctory references. As the diary now stands, it seems that they bore a very small proportion to the pride, conceit and ill-temper which he records so continually. But we have no means of knowing whether the proportion was greater or less in the original diary.

Then, too, we may see all through Newman's life a peculiarity that has led to many a harsh judgment of him. Most of us have passing feelings of anger, resentment, vanity, to which we either never give utterance, or at most only in the ear of a sympathetic intimate. Newman did not easily speak even to intimates, but he wrote with fatal ease and fluency. A curious text in the Psalms says, "My tongue is the pen of a ready writer that writeth swiftly." I often wondered over this till I studied Newman, for most of us speak more swiftly than we write. Not so Newman. Every passing mood was set down on paper, so that often we come upon puzzling appearances even of self-contradiction. Try to write down your moods for a day—you will be amazed. Thought, fancy, changing sensations are of the essence of the strange being that man is: of the interaction of the soul with a well body or a sick one, of the effect of a harsh or kind word, of sunshine or of clouds. Psycho-analysts try to cure a patient by making him write down the records of past dreams, past fancies. Newman wrote down present dreams, present fancies. Add this habit to the state of mind induced by the Evangelical teaching under which he had placed himself, and you get a document as strange as anything in biography. I shall make some use of this diary both for its record of events and for the light it casts on the phase he was passing through, but I have given up as impossible the effort I at first made to take it seriously as self-revelation.

In another story of Harriett's, *The Lost Brooch*, we get a picture of these years that is very disappointing as regards Newman. The George of the story is only the boy become a young man, with no hint of any spiritual change. But to one of the girl characters she attributes the views that were causing much disturbance and annoyance at this time in the Newman family and we can see a reflection of how the whole thing appeared to father and mother: how exasperating to have two of their sons taking up these ideas, becoming self-righteous (so they thought, knowing naught of Doddridge), lowering the Church of England to a level with the dissenting bodies.

For Frank as well as John had come under the influence of Mr. Mayers, and the two young men diverged widely from their parents' more moderate and reasonable notions of the conduct of daily life.

This is reflected in the diary.

August 13, (1821).
In consequence of my informing my mother of my intention of taking the Sacrament once a fortnight, she seemed to think I began to be righteous overmuch and was verging upon enthusiasm. I was also leading Francis with me.

Actually Francis, though the younger, seems to have been the leader at this stage, John to have had more respect for his father's outlook. Francis would not go to the theatre "for religious motives." John went once or twice and "seemed", he repentantly notes, "so little to feel the impropriety of so doing" that he "mentioned it in the company of religious persons."

Sept. 30, 1821. *Sunday.* After dinner today I was suddenly called downstairs to give an opinion whether I thought it a sin to write a letter on a Sunday. I found dear F[rank] had refused to copy one. A scene ensued more painful than any I have experienced. I have been sadly deficient in meekness, long-suffering, patience, and filial obedience. With God's assistance I will redeem my character.

Monday, October 1, 1821. My Father was reconciled to us today. When I think of the utter persuasion he must entertain of the justice of his views, of our apparent disobedience, the seeming folly of our opinions, and the way in which he is harassed by worldly cares, I think his forgiveness of us an example of very striking candour, forbearance and generosity.

Some very serious advice given by his father to Newman about this time, after he had attended a service at Kentish Town Chapel, is worth quoting:

Take care. It is very proper to quote scripture, but you pour out texts in such quantities. Have a guard. You are encouraging a nervousness and morbid sensibility and irritability of mind, which may be very serious. I know what it is myself perfectly well. I know it is a disease of mind. No one's principles can be established at twenty. Your opinions in two or three years will certainly *certainly* change. I have seen many instances of the same kind. Take care, I repeat. You are on dangerous ground. The temper you are encouraging may lead to something alarming. Weak minds are carried into superstition and strong minds into infidelity; do not commit yourself, do nothing ultra. Many men say and do things, when young, which they would fain retract when older, but for shame they cannot. I know you write for the *Christian Observer*. My opinion of the *Christian Observer* is this, that it is a humbug. You must use exertions—that letter was more like the composition of an old man than of a youth just entering life with energy and aspirations.

The "youth just entering life" after writing down his father's warning and adding a prayer against delusion, pride and uncharitableness, remarks: "How good God is to give me 'the assurance of hope'. If anyone had prophesied to me confidently that I should change my opinions, and I was not convinced of the impossibility, what anguish should I feel."

One is a little sorry for poor Charles between the pair of them. "My father noticed that Charles was not so much with Francis and me as he could wish. We had in the morning been debating how Charles might be more with us. Thank God, Who, without effort, has opened a way to introduce Charles to our readings from Scripture." This was hardly Mr. Newman's idea and I feel the darkest doubts when I read that Charles seemed pleased "when reading [Scripture] with us with Scott's Commentary."

Allied with the decision that John should continue at Oxford was that of his change of profession. Almost all Fellowships were held by clergymen, and his own deepening religious convictions made him desirous of taking Orders. Yet I use the word profession rather than vocation because it is certain that his parents would thus have viewed it. We may recall Edward Ferrars in *Sense and Sensibility*: "I always preferred the Church as I still do. But that was not smart enough for my family. They recommended the army. That was a great deal too smart for me. The law was allowed to be genteel enough." At that period, even for the most serious-minded people, the Church was regarded as one of the professions. In the life of James Robert Hope-Scott, after the Oxford Movement had been on foot some years, we read that he felt the calling of a clergyman to be more powerful for good than any other *except that of a landowner*. To administer large estates offered a yet wider field for beneficence.

Certainly Ordination was always seen by Newman as an opportunity for complete self-dedication—to which one is called by God—but he attached no sacramental value to it. In the diary he wrote:

1822, *Jan.* 11. My father this evening said I ought to make up my mind what I was to be . . . so I chose; and determined on the Church. Thank God, this is what I have prayed for.

Meanwhile parents and son were alike agreed that on leaving Trinity Newman should have Francis with him in lodgings to prepare him for college. Newman writes during the Long Vacation, 1821: "My greatest difficulty is to get good lodgings. I have found one; the place Bowden used to lodge at; being a Coffee House it is handy, as having dinner, etc. all under one roof. There are two sets of rooms. Francis would be £26 a year, candles being found."

The authorities at Trinity approved this plan and Mr. Short got Newman a pupil at £100 a year, so that after returning to Oxford in the autumn, the elder brother very soon offered to take over *all* the expenses of the younger.

Frank Newman spoke in the letter of 1845 of "the collision between us when we were at College," which he said "arose to the very full as much, or far more, from my harsh, blunt, inexperienced and heartless mode of following out dogmas which I received as axioms, than from any fault in you. You have ever had a far more refined and tender heart than I." Tom Mozley speaks of Frank's attitude to his elder brother as "a persistent but amiable antagonism." But after all, the pupil was only between four and five years younger than his master, and on the whole one gets from the correspondence of the time a very pleasant picture both of the relations between the brothers and of the family relations as a whole.

At the very beginning of 1822 there seems to have been some

question of changing the destination of the younger brother from the academic to the business world. John wrote earnestly:

He has improved of late wonderfully. I have been astonished, ever since he has been with me, at the way in which he has dived into things, and the vigour with which he has scrutinized them. In mind he seems to resemble the description I heard of Mr. Wood, who got two First Classes the other day; for he reads *in the way of business*, and, while others stop to admire the beauty of a passage, he has examined it as a critic, not as a poet, observed it in its bearings, and travelled on some way with the author of it. I was astonished for instance, at the way in which he analysed the Greek metres. He made himself master of them, reset a great part of Æschylus, corrected Schutz, and, I really believe, discovered facts no one had known before.

Now, as I said before, I cannot know what my father's "view of things" is, supposing Francis does not come to Oxford, but I must say I think F. very little suited to business. He is in my opinion very quick as to things, and very slow as to persons; he is more expert at mathematical, than moral evidence. To speak from my own judgment, it seems to be taking him from the very thing which is naturally adapted to him. Still, however, all this is only my *opinion*.

The parents might well have been anxious at the burden on the eldest son. Years later, Francis wrote that John had supported him not out of his abundance, but out of his want. Writing to his aunt after getting the Oriel Fellowship, John himself admits, "I was sensible that everything even I ate, I had no idea how it was to be paid for. I knew that every day was adding to what was owing, and I saw no quarter from which relief could come." His diary notes his "precarious situation with regard to money." But to his parents he wrote in a very different strain:

Before I proceed to any other subject, I shall beg leave to satisfy you, which I hope I shall be able fully, with respect to Francis being with me. You have not the *slightest* occasion of the *slightest* uneasiness or anxiety. He is no inconvenience to me. He is incurring no great expense. No bills are owing by him except the tailor's and one for a hat. He now owes nothing for board or lodging: and what he is incurring this term, I expect to be able to pay before he goes down for Christmas. He has been now above a year at Oxford without any inconvenience or trouble to me. And let me, while I say this, thank and bless as I must that most Merciful Providence who has

D

so safely, wisely and mercifully borne us both on, and protected us from all waves and tempests throughout the past year. And doubtless He will preserve us still.

You will therefore distress me very much, if either you or my father have any care about Francis or think he will burden me. He will not do so. Looking at things merely in a human light, if we have got through the last year so well, much more shall we the year to come. *Everything* then as far as relates to Francis and myself is to be cut off from your anxiety.

After varied praise of his brother's abilities, the letter continues:

. . . again, he is a much better mathematician than I am: I mean, he reads more mathematically, as Aristotle would say.

But I am afraid of mentioning Aristotle, for I find you are suspicious lest those sages may have some influence in detaching me from your little chat. You little know my disposition, if you say so; and I smile triumphantly in the consciousness that you have seen nothing in me which should lead to such an uncourteous distrust of me. I am indeed encompassed with blessings for which I can never be properly thankful, but the greatest of them is so dear and united a home. If your fear is, lest my jesting letters to Harriett should unconsciously be written half in earnest, I can only protest, that, however other places may agree with me, I am not in my own proper element when I am away from you and my sisters. Land animals may plunge into the water and swim about in it, but they cannot live in it; and even for the short space they are in it, they must still drink in the air.

As in childhood so too with the young man, a life of intense hidden prayer and thought moulded his visible life and conduct. All through the strain of his approaching examination, Newman had kept up his habits of prayer and meditation. He wrote to Frank, "God sanctifies my studies by breathing into me all the while thoughts of Him." And although the Evangelical phraseology was at moments unfortunate, and Newman was trying to throw himself into a frame of mind alien to his nature, yet on the positive side his grasp of doctrine was deepening with his prayers and thoughts. Meditating on Our Lord's agony and dereliction he writes, "May not this be stated in such a manner as to repel the objection, that His corporal sufferings could not cleanse us from sin which is spiritual?" On the Names of God and of Christ as expressing without exhausting the Divine reality, "If He were in every respect a Lamb, He would not be the Shepherd. If He were in every respect the Husband of the Church, He could not be the Father."

These musings followed him even in his dreams. One night

a spirit came to me and discoursed about the other world . . . Among other things it said that it was absolutely impossible for the reason of man to understand the mystery of the Holy Trinity, and in vain to argue about it; but that everything in another world was so very, very plain that there was not the slightest difficulty about it. I cannot put into any sufficiently strong form of words the ideas that were conveyed to me. I thought I instantly fell on my knees overcome with gratitude to God for so kind a message.

After the examination he notes that he has now more time to give to devotion. And in a most touching group of letters we see at once his concern for his parents' feelings and the ever-deepening humility that resulted from his meditations. After his twenty-first birthday he writes to his mother:

Thank you for your very kind letter. When I turn to look at myself I feel quite ashamed of the praise it contains, so numerous and so great are the deficiencies that even I can see. There is an illusion in the words "being of age" which is apt to convey the idea of some sudden and unknown change. That point, instead of the slow and silent progress of one and twenty years, seems to divide, by some strongly marked line, the past from the to-come . . . Not that I am sorry so great a part of life is gone—would that all were over! —but I seem now more left to myself, and when I reflect upon my own weakness I have cause to shudder.

Newman later records that on this birthday he shed tears "to think I could no longer call myself a boy." The diary runs: "My birthday. Today I am of age. It is an awful crisis."

His mother feeling the expressions in his letter to be morbid, feared that he was ill and wrote an anxious letter:

We fear very much, from the tone of your letter, you are depressed; and if imperious reasons did not forbid us, you would certainly *see* us. We fear you debar yourself a proper quantity of wine . . . Take proper air and exercise; accept all the invitations you receive; and do not be over-anxious about anything.

To this Newman hastened to reply:

I have hardly a moment to write. I am going out to a wine party and to the music room in the evening. I am astonished this morning to find I am very ill! I am very *very* much obliged to you for your anxiety, but never was anxiety so ill founded. I was only the other day congratulating myself on the great improvement of my health to what it was a year ago. I have been to the proctor (Kinsey) and Ogle to send you certificates of my perfect health and spirits . . . To take last week—I dined out once, and was three times out in the evening: to two music parties and one dance. I have walked out an hour and a half every day (except two or at most three rainy days) for the last month. I bathe most regularly. I do not read even an average of four to five hours a day. I am attending a course of lectures on experimental philosophy.

Francis added:

John has been obliged to leave off in a great hurry, and tells me to give my opinion on his health, without looking at his letter. I think he is *extremely* well and in *very* good spirits. We have been out for an hour and a half at least, every day but three I think for five weeks.

At John's request Mr. Kinsey also sent a certificate of his perfect health to Mr. Newman.

But having thus satisfied his family as to his bodily health, Newman pressed on his mother the view that he took of himself in the depths of his soul.

As to my opinions, and the sentiments I expressed in my last letter, they remain fixed in my mind, and are repeated deliberately and confidently. If it were any new set of opinions I had lately adopted, they might be said to arise from nervousness, or over-study, or ill-health; but no, my opinion has been exactly the same for these five years . . . Believe me, those sentiments are neither new nor slightly founded. If they made me melancholy, morose, austere, distant, reserved, sullen, then indeed they might with justice be the subject of anxiety; but if, as I think is the case, I am always cheerful, if at home I am always ready and eager to join in any merriment, if I am not clouded with sadness, if my meditations make me neither absent in mind nor deficient in actions, then my principles may be gazed at and puzzle the gazer, but they cannot be accused of bad practical effects. Take me when I am most foolish at home, and extend mirth into childishness; stop me short and ask me then what I think of myself, whether my opinions are less gloomy; no, I think

I should seriously return the same answer, that "I shuddered at myself."

As years go on we shall, I think, see that while something of this outlook is to be attributed to the views he had imbibed at school, part was the natural outcome of a high ideal of sanctity and the craving for personal purification ever to be found in the Johns, the Pauls, the Augustines, who are called and set apart and sanctified not for themselves alone but for the human race that is so stained with sin and so unworthy to stand before the All Holy God.

CHAPTER VI

The Oriel Fellowship

BY November 1821, Newman had made up his mind to the bold venture of standing in April for the Oriel Fellowship. Superficially he might be said almost to have wasted the last year: he had pursued no settled course of study: he would be the competitor of men with double-firsts: no Oriel Fellowship had ever been given to a man placed in the schools "below the line". Even Mr. Short, who approved his standing, did not for a second expect him to win the Fellowship. He merely hoped that by good work in the Examination he would show his quality and lift from Trinity the stigma of his previous failure—for after all he was one of their chosen scholars. Most of his friends believed him crazy to stand at all; his parents imagined him consumed with the same sort of nervous anxiety that had heralded his last examination. Far from it. Newman was calm and confident with a confidence that increased daily. He knew he was mad to stand, yet he knew he would succeed.

Oriel had already in the previous year given a Fellowship to a second class man against the competition of the holder of a first class, who took his revenge by a bitter article in the *Edinburgh Review*. Once the author's identity leaked out the article became innocuous, but at the time it made a stir, for the accusation was so distinct and unhesitating.

Hardy professions of impartiality are indeed held forth, to attract unwary merit; and selfish mediocrity finds the most exquisite of all its gratifications in the momentary chance of harassing the talent it would tremble to confront . . . Who can be surprised if, under a system like this, genius and knowledge should so seldom strike a lasting root? Or that maturity, which succeeds to a youth so prostituted, should produce, by its most vigorous efforts, nothing better than learned drivelling and marrowless inflation?

It is a little surprising to learn that the author of this tirade, D. K. Sandford, won the English essay prize that year in the

University, but this is not the only surprising element in the story. That a quarterly review should enter with such acerbity into the question of an academic prize seems odd today, although it was not the first time that Oxford and the *Edinburgh* had crossed swords, and the style of attack and reply alike rings oddly in our ears. Rumour had it that the great Sydney Smith himself was the author of one such attack which was answered (also anonymously) by Copleston, the Provost of Oriel. "Hardly a book," he wrote, "is noticed, (for I will not call their ordinary method *reviewing*) which does not furnish an opportunity for this sort of calumny. And latterly the rankling humour has burst out in such exorbitant quantity, and with such malignant aspect, as to call for immediate and strong remedy."

This quotation is from a pamphlet entitled:

A REPLY TO THE CALUMNIES OF THE " EDINBURGH REVIEW "
AGAINST OXFORD
Containing an account of studies
Pursued in that University.

Although published anonymously, the author "will not refuse to account in person, if it should ever be called in question by any respectable name."

The absence of names, respectable or otherwise, resulted in a glorious freedom of expression. Of the charges against the University—"I believe many of them proceed," says Copleston,

from that vile serpent-brood which have been hatched in our own bosom—that hireling tribe of turncoats, who, disappointed of honours or rewards here adequate to their own fancied merits, have carried over to the enemy, as the most acceptable passport, some local information, and have courted the favour of their new employers, by mean detraction and extravagant abuse of their former friends. If any such there be, they will feel the justice of this rebuke without any more particular designation of their persons, and I wish them no severer punishment than that infamy which when their work is done is the common lot of traitors with all parties.

A wit of the moment wrote sending the pamphlet to his country relatives:

Since the cold cutting gibes of that Northern Review
Have tormented and teazed Uncle Toby and you,

I'm exceedingly happy in sending you down
A defence that is making much noise in the town,
Of all our old learning and fame immemorial,
Which is said to be writ by a Fellow of Oriel.[1]

As a whole the pamphlet is not remarkable except in its
attack on the utilitarian school of education. Newman did this
much better half a century later in *The Idea of a University*. Now
he was learning from Copleston, whose *Praelectiones* he made his
text book in studying how to write Latin with ease, and whose
general ideas on education he certainly imbibed whether or no
he read this pamphlet.

The decision once made, Newman had four good months
before him during which to prepare, with a mind freshened and
relieved from excessive pressure.

The diary of these months awakens in a middle-aged reader
a mixture of respect and amusement . . .

Nov. 15. Thou seest how fondly, and I fear idolatrously, my affections are set on succeeding at Oriel. Take all hope away, stop not
an instant, O my God, if so doing will gain me Thy Spirit. . . .
How proud and bitter I am in spirit! How unforgiving—how unclean
—how timid—how lukewarm in prayer.

As the day drew near, confidence in some degree gave way to
apprehension, yet at bottom his conviction of success remained
unimpaired. Writing to his successor as provost some years later,
Copleston says: "Every election to a fellowship which tends to
discourage the narrow and almost technical routine of public
examinations, I consider an important triumph. You remember
Newman himself was an example. He was not even a good
classical scholar, yet in mind and power of composition, and in
taste and knowledge, he was decidedly superior to some competitors who were a class above him in the schools."

Newman could not know the Provost's mind in this matter,
but he did know that importance was attached to Latin composition and general mathematics, and that to have "a metaphysical turn" was a great advantage.

"It was altogether," says Dean Church, who was later holder
of a fellowship and hence an examiner,

[1] Quoted in *The Clerk of Oxford in Fiction*, by S. F. Hulton, pp. 328-9.

a trial not of how much men knew, but of how they knew, and what they could do . . . The Oriel common-room was rather proud of its seemingly easy and commonplace and unpretending tests of a man's skill in languages and habits and power of thinking for himself. They did not care if he had read much, so that he came up to their standard of good Latin, good Greek, good English and good sense . . . It created a prejudice against a man if he should seem to be trying to be flash, or to show off his reading . . . The two papers which were almost invariably the guide to the first decision were the English into Latin and the English Essay, and no man who failed in these had much chance of retrieving himself. Next to these papers the Latin Essay and the translation into English told . . .

A good deal of weight was attached to *viva voce* . . . It was thought to be a good test of the way in which a man met difficulties, and whether he faced them fairly or tried to evade them.

No time limit was set for the various papers and essays, but as artificial light was not allowed in Oriel Hall where the examination took place, the fading daylight set its own limit. In a letter to Bowden, Newman gives details of the examination. It lasted five days, beginning on Easter Eve. There were eleven candidates. Williams of Queen's was the favourite: the rumour ran "he has the last year been working fourteen or fifteen hours per diem and living on pulse and herbs." Besides the Latin and English essays, a passage from *The Spectator* had to be put into Latin; there were twelve philosophical and mathematical questions, ten in Logic and nine books for the *viva voce*.

If I could but have known the success which attended my first day's compositions *at the time*, in how much more correct and superior a manner should I have gone on with the examination. But possessed with the idea that I had all but disgraced myself, and stiff, oh, how stiff! with sitting eight hours on hard benches, I crawled about in the most piteous condition on Easter Sunday and had so bad a night and felt so uncomfortable a heat and as I thought eruption on *my spine*, that I determined the first thing when up to go to Tuckwell. Morning however came and I was better. Before the day was half over, my weakness was such that I was compelled to lay by: consequently through despair, headache and dimness of the twilight I was forced to send in my Latin theme uncorrected.

And in the diary he notes: "April 8: I was so ill I could do nothing and was obliged to walk about" [i.e. up and down

Oriel Hall]. Clearly a very bad examination subject! "It was
the same nervous affliction," he writes on the final copy of the
diary, "which tormented me in 1833 at the commencement of
my fever at Leonforte in Sicily. Then I was obliged to occupy
myself in counting the figures on the pattern of the room paper."

We can stand today in Oriel Hall and imagine the scene:
we can look at the windows and read the motto "*Pie repone te*"
of which Newman wrote towards the end of the examination:
"I have been much comforted today and yesterday by a motto
in Oriel Hall, *Pie repone te*. I am now going to bed and have
been very calm the whole evening."

Meanwhile his first papers had so impressed the examiners
that three of them—Tyler, Dornford and James—hurried over
to Trinity to make enquiries concerning his character and antecedents. This in turn excited Mr. Short so much that he sent
for Newman on the pretext of enquiring of him what the questions
were like and how he was getting on. He was eating an early
dinner at the time and Newman remembered forty-five years later
the lamb cutlets and fried parsley which had almost as great
a share as the cheering words of his tutor in sending him in for
the *viva voce* part of the examination strengthened and invigorated.
Probably he had been forgetting to eat properly during these
anxious days.

All was over on Thursday and the result announced on
Friday. The electors, Newman told Bowden, "were kept up to
one in the morning and then up again at 6 a.m." Newman
awaited the results in the companionship of his violin. The
Provost's butler, on whom curiously enough the task devolved
of making the announcement, entered the room and pronounced
the set form of words that "he had, he feared, disagreeable news
to announce, viz. that Mr. Newman was elected Fellow of Oriel,
and that his immediate presence was required there."

Newman has himself described how he, "thinking that such
language savoured of impertinent familiarity, merely answered,
'Very well,' and went on fiddling."

The puzzled butler wondered if he had come to the right place.
Newman assured him that he had, but let him leave the room
before allowing vent to his own excitement: then flung down his
violin, dashed downstairs and through the streets to Oriel, passing
bowing tradesmen and others with "eloquent faces and eager
bows."

Tuckwell (son of the doctor whom Newman had thought of consulting), in his *Reminiscences of Oxford*, attributes the doubts of the butler not so much to Newman's answer as to Newman's violin: music, like boating, was at that time held to be no occupation for a gentleman. An amusing sidelight is Mark Pattison's account of his father's choice of a college for him a few years later. Balliol and Oriel were the two reading colleges. "We call those," said Lord Conyers, "the two prison houses." But Pattison's father was equally concerned that his son's college should be gentlemanly. "As between Oriel and Balliol," says Mark Pattison, "there could be no doubt that the 'gentility' all belonged to Oriel."

At Trinity the excitement was terrific and shared by all who had friends there. "Men hurried from all directions to Trinity," Newman writes home, "to their acquaintance there, to congratulate them on the success of their college. The bells were set ringing from three towers (I had to pay for them)."

Frank Newman writes that Kinsey, the Dean, "got up from his seat and clapped his hands with ecstasy." A tutor was found "leaping up and down, backwards and forwards," while one undergraduate nearly kicked the door down trying to tell another. A letter from one of the tutors to Newman's parents runs: "In point of emolument it is great; in point of character it is immortality."

It seems curious the extent to which on the one hand a failure in the schools was held a barrier to hopes of a career, and on the other the holding of an Oriel Fellowship to open wide every door to success. A schoolfellow writes to Newman prophesying his career. "Provost, Regius Professor of Divinity, Bishop of ——, Archbishop of Canterbury; or, shall we say thus: Student-at-law, Barrister, Lord Chancellor, or at least Lord Chief Justice of the King's Bench? Which of these ladders is it your intention to climb? You now have it in your power to decide."

In the diary Newman wrote: "I have this morning been elected Fellow of Oriel. Thank God, thank God."

Oriel is one of the smaller colleges although singularly lovely: its area bears no comparison with the gardens of Trinity or the quadrangles of Christ Church. The buildings that face St. Mary's Church did not exist in Newman's day, having been erected with money left to the college by Cecil Rhodes on a site adjoining old St. Mary's Hall, which, long known as "Skimmery", was in Newman's day separate from, but vaguely dependent on, the college. The name derived from a building known as La Oriole. The word itself is, by one theory, old French for a recess or small room more private and better ornamented than the rest of the building. At first Oriel was simply the College of St. Mary the Virgin, just as the University Church was her Church, and as Newman entered the quadrangle from Oriel Lane he was faced by her statue and also by those of Edward II and Charles I.

Oriel's alumni included Bishop Ken, the Non-Juror, and Bishop Butler of the *Analogy*. Tradition also assigned Sir Walter Raleigh to the college—but a tradition not very firmly established. Most of the famous Orielites were still alive when Newman first came there: it was emphatically the college of the nineteenth century. Before that time an old epitaph of one of its Fellows applied to the vast majority of them:

> Of him nothing is memorial
> Save that he was a Fellow of Oriel.

Already in 1822 Newman had won the greatest prize Oxford had to offer a young man. It was something to be a Fellow anywhere, but to be a Fellow of Oriel was to be admitted into the highest intellectual group of Oxford, it was to belong to the reforming college, it was to be a member of the Common Room which already held the greatest collection of talent and to which all aspirers looked. "When a Fellow of the College," writes Tom Mozley, "presented himself in any social gathering he was sure to be reminded of his pretence to intellectual superiority." And perhaps also of the "Oriel tea-pot," for it was the first Common Room where tea was drunk as well as wine, and the remark, "Those fellows drink *tea*," was made not without a sneer.

Had he waited a year, Newman wrote to his family, he could not have hoped for election: Pusey, Churton, Creswell would all be standing.

The Common Room must have been colourful in those days. Dr. Hawkins remembered his first view of Whately (later Archbishop of Dublin) only a few years earlier in pea-green coat, white waistcoat, stone-coloured shorts, flesh-coloured stockings. His hair was powdered. Arnold was wearing a bright blue coat and Heber a parsley and butter one.[1] The Senior Fellow in 1819,

---

[1] *Twelve Good Men*, p. 304.

Edward Miles Rudd, appeared as late as 1847 at the college
Gaudy in black breeches, having travelled from Northamptonshire in a fly, taking two days. A drawing of him as a young man
shows him wearing a wig. The ordinary dress for dinner was
still knee breeches (called shorts in most of the letters of the
period) and silk stockings. Newman describes to his sister the
extreme inconvenience of wading in this attire and thin shoes,
when he had to come from lodgings in bad weather to dine in
hall. Energetic arguments rising to a great height of excitement
were common and sometimes so affected the disputants that they
would avoid one another for a few days after a very hot discussion.

It was a common room, [Dr. Liddon says in his *Life of Pusey*] to
belong to which was in itself an education. Unfriendly critics described this by saying that the Oriel Common Room "stank of logic":
but logic, if liable to misuse, is not without its value. The distinctive
characteristic of the Oriel mind was exactness in thought, as the
basis of exactness of expression. This was exhibited, although in
different ways, by Newman and Keble, not less than by Hawkins
and Whately. Everybody practised more or less the Socratic method
of improving thought by constant cross-questioning; but Whately and
Hawkins especially excelled in this. The result was to discourage fine
words, when homely expressions would suffice; to expose inaccurate
and partial knowledge; to resolve imposing theories into their con-
stituent ingredients; to force men back upon the principles which
really governed their convictions . . . The prose of Cardinal Newman,
unrivalled as it is in this century, owes some of its best elements to
those early years of contact with Whately and Hawkins.[1]

He had stepped into the shoes of Arnold—later known everywhere as Arnold of Rugby. Keble was already a Fellow and when
Newman came into the Common Room for the first time and
received their greetings he wrote to Bowden:

I could bear the congratulations of Copleston, but when Keble
advanced to take my hand I quite shrank, and could have nearly
shrunk into the floor, ashamed at so great an honour—however, I
shall soon be used to this. I am absolutely a member of the Common
Room; am called by them "Newman" and am abashed, and find
I must soon learn to call them "Keble", "Hawkins", "Tyler".

Keble's name recurs in his earlier letters: he is "the first man
in Oxford," he is "perfectly unassuming and unaffected in
manner."

[1] *Life of Edward Bouverie Pusey*, by Henry Parry Liddon, D.D., Vol. I, p. 58.

Yet it was several years before Newman and Keble came to understand each other. Both were, in quite different ways, somewhat isolated from the general trend of the Oriel Common Room which later they were profoundly to affect.

The future lay between two parties which had yet to emerge in clear and definite line and colour from the background of moderate churchmen—the Liberal and the Catholic. And the high interest of Oriel lies in the fact that from that college came the chief leaders of both these parties.

As yet the picture was not clear—it was actually in the making. Oriel was simply the reforming college. Its leaders were known as the Oriel Noetics—"whatever that may mean," says Tom Mozley. Canon Overton derives it from the works of Aristotle and defines a Noetic as "a man who exercised his highest faculties, as opposed to those who let them lie dormant."[1]

At the time the Liberalism of the Noetics was certainly less apparent to Newman than it later became. "In religion," he says, "they were neither High Church nor Low Church, but had become a new school, or, as their enemies would say, a *clique*, which was characterised by its spirit of moderation and comprehension, and of which the principal ornaments were Copleston, Davison, Whately, Hawkins and Arnold."

They were kindly enough to the Evangelicals, their great enemies were "the old unspiritual high-and-dry . . . who were suspicious whither these men would go." A natural enough suspicion in men whose own day, like that of the Evangelicals but less obviously, was fast running out. For Newman as for Oxford the ultimate choice would lie between the Liberal and the Catholic view. And the Catholic view like the Liberal had yet to be uttered.

Meanwhile Newman was a silent figure in the Common Room. We shall find all through his life overwhelming shyness resulting in a chilly silence among people he did not know or like, and expansiveness, a winning and joyous manner that won all hearts when he found himself among friends and intimates. Two comments on him were made, he tells us, by acute observers: one, noting his difficulty in general society, told him that he had had a narrow escape of being a stutterer; the other that he was a man who, when he was silent, would never speak, but if he began to speak would never be silent. He came out of his shell,

[1] *The English Church in the 19th Century*, p. 117.

he says of himself, in 1826 when enjoying his friendships and holding some position in his college and the University and stayed out until 1841. Yet his silence in the Common Room is remarked by Samuel Wilberforce as late as 1835 in a letter, the blanks in which it would be fascinating to fill: "I dined in common room, where the sights and sounds were curious: the cantankerous conceit of ——; ——'s pettishness; the vulgar priggishness of ——'s jokes; the loud ungentlemanliness of ——'s cutlip arguments; the disinterred liveliness of ——, and the silence of Newman, were all surprenant, nay épouvantable."

In these early years his walks were often solitary. The Provost meeting him one day gave him a kindly bow and said, "*Numquam minus solus quam cum solus.*"

Yet beneath the surface shyness and solitariness was a deep spring of joy that made him keep the day of his election, year by year, as one of thanksgiving. "He ever felt this twelfth of April, 1822, to be the turning point of his life, and of all days most memorable." For the moment he did not look forward, even to the bright prospects proposed by his friends. From a full heart he could say he never wished anything better or higher than, in the words of the epitaph, "to live and die a Fellow of Oriel."

Chapter VII

We Must Look Back A Little

IN MOST accounts of the Oxford Movement Evangelicalism is sneered at and the good done by it belittled. Partly this results from the writers being either High Anglican or Catholic, partly from Newman's own revulsion from Evangelical modes of expression, partly from the common reaction against any age that is passing away. Evangelicalism was old and intellectually shabby at the time the Tractarian Movement began (curiously enough William Wilberforce and Hannah More—perhaps the two greatest Evangelicals—both died that very year, 1833) but it had done a great service to religion in England and had far more depth in its best days than could be guessed from such descriptions.

Newman, as we have seen, was still an Evangelical when he came to Oriel: in *Loss and Gain* he later mordantly described one type of that school. The tea party at Freeborn's rooms is an unpleasing and unfriendly picture, and in his note on Liberalism in the second and later editions of the *Apologia*, the tone is hardly more friendly: "The party called Evangelical never has been able to breathe freely in the atmosphere of Oxford, and at no time has been conspicuous, as a party, for talent and learning."

An even more hostile account is given by Tom Mozley, who had, he says, "sat under this sort of preaching for many years":

. . . The doctrine thus everywhere preached was simple enough. Its fortunate discoverers and propagators rejoiced in its simplicity. Simple, I say, it must have been, for it excluded everything else. You were to be quite sure not only that you had received a special revelation that Jesus Christ died for you in particular, but also that your salvation was now such a certainty as to place you above all further anxiety. You might have your faults, but you were saved. Your neighbours might have their virtues, but wanting this personal assurance, they were not saved. They were not even one step on the way to salvation. . . . The impression of the system on my mind, after many years of such sermons, nay thousands of such sermons, with hardly any relief whatever, was that it put the character of

Jesus Christ entirely out of account, and that it reduced the Sermon on the Mount, all the discourses of our Lord, and all the moral arguments and exhortations of St. Paul and other Apostles, to mere carnalities that no real Christian need have anything to do with. All that is tender, all that is touching, all that by which Jesus Christ is the object of unbounded love and adoration even to those who shrink from the attempt to fathom the mystery of His Being, was thrown aside, behind I should rather say, trampled upon, as likely to lead us astray from the real point at issue, namely, whether we ourselves are personally saved to our own certain knowledge.[1]

The High Churchman, Overton, in *The English Church in the Nineteenth Century*, admits that the Evangelical reaction against the worldliness and indifference of the eighteenth century had not been without value, but accuses the Evangelicals of intense narrowness of outlook. Not averse (he says) to the pleasures of a good table, a well appointed house or agreeable society, they declared war with a kind of eclectic asceticism on all sorts of theatrical representations and on all fiction. He quotes an admittedly extreme example from a widely sold book—*Personal Recollections of Charlotte Elizabeth:*

. . . I was permitted to read . . . *The Merchant of Venice*. I drank a cup of intoxication under which my brain reeled for many a year. The character of Shylock burst upon me, even as Shakespeare had conceived it. I revelled in the terrible excitement that it gave rise to, page after page was stereotyped upon a most retentive memory without an effort, and during a sleepless night I feasted on the pernicious sweets thus hoarded in my brain. . . . Oh, how many wasted hours, how much of unprofitable labour, what wrong to my fellow-creatures, what robbery of God, must I refer to this ensnaring book [apparently Shakespeare generally!] . . . But for this I might have early sought the consolations of the gospel. Parents know not what they do when they foster in a young girl what is called a poetical taste. Those things highly esteemed among men, are held in abomination with God; they thrust Him from His creatures' thoughts, and enshrine a host of polluting idols in His place.

Is all this quite fair—or had not the Evangelicals a better case than Mozley, Overton and the rest admit? Surely there was something more than this in the books and ideas that had first converted Newman and long held him, something more in

[1] *Reminiscences*, pp. 186-7.

the movement that had swept England in the eighteenth century, created Wesleyanism and revived a moribund Church. In all fairness a little must be said of the Evangelical revival, and it is helpful, too, as a background for the very different movement now beginning. But I am giving it this chapter to itself, so that those who feel like Mozley, Overton and most heirs of the Tractarians, can omit it and return to Newman at Oriel.

Bishop Porteous said of Tom Paine that he "rendered irreligion easy to the meanest capacity," yet perhaps the most unfortunate effect of the attacks of the Deists and Atheists on revealed religion was the defence put out by its adherents. A deist work entitled *Christianity not Mysterious* published on the threshold of the eighteenth century struck a note which continued to sound until its end and beyond. Blackstone has related how about the middle of the century he went a round of the London churches and did not hear a word in any of them that might not have been spoken by Cicero or any other non-Christian moralist. Richard Watson, Bishop of Llandaff, wrote a long letter on repentance without once mentioning Our Lord, suggested to William Cowper as a cure for melancholy "contemplation of the First Cause," felt he must defend his use of intercessory prayer and did so rather dubiously, saying: "I know perfectly well the philosophical arguments which could be used against the efficacy of all human intercession . . . but the most distant hope of being of use to my expiring friend overcame all my scruples."[1]

Hannah More quotes a clergyman who told the rich and great "that they ought to be extremely liberal in their charities, because they were happily exempted from the severer virtues." She comments: "How do you like such a sentiment from a Christian teacher? What do you think Polycarp or Ignatius would say to it?"

The defenders of Christianity had, in fact, for the most part abandoned their true ground and defended only morality, decency and natural religion. It has been pointed out how miserably poor were most of the deist works, yet the Deists had won one outstanding victory: they had forced the enemy to accept battle on their own ground.

This was the easier because a worldly society was the native home of the clergy of the period. They were country gentlemen, heads of colleges, centres of society in cathedral towns, often spending part of the year in London.

[1] *Some Eighteenth Century Churchmen*, pp. 159-160.

Pluralism, corruption, were not, of course, peculiar to this period, but the complacency with which they were viewed is a little startling. When in the fifteenth century ignorant priests could be found holding several benefices and resident in none, while learned scholars got no preferment, Oxford speaks of it (says Hulton) "with a wealth of allegory and metaphor which increases as the agony grows more intense." Caxton in the Epilogue to his *Æsop* tells the story of "two priestes both Maysters of Art" of whom "the Mayster that was pert and quick, was anon promoted to a benefyce or tweyne, and after to prebendys, and for to be Dene of a grete prince's Chappel."

His simple fellow cleric got only at long last a single parish where he was visited by his pluralist friend:

"I pray yow," said he, "what is this benefyce worth to yow a year?" "Forsooth," said the good simple man, "I wote never; for I make never accomptes thereof, how well I have had it four or five year." "And know ye not," sayd he, "what it is worth? It should seem a good benefyce." "No, for sothe," said he; "but I wote well what it shall be worth to me." "Why," sayd he, "what shall it be worth?" "Forsothe," sayd that other, "if I doo my true dylygence in the cure of my parysshes in prechynge and techinge, and doo my part longynge to my cure, I shall have Hevene therfore; and yf theyre sowles ben lost, or any of them, by my default, I shall be punysshed therfore; and herof am I sure." And with that word the ryche Dene was abasshed, and thought he should do better, and take more heed to his cures and benefyces, than he had done. This was a good answere of a good preest and an honest.

To exult:

> Thus God and Nature planned the general frame
> And bade self-love and social be the same,

was reserved for the Age of Enlightenment.

> Thro' Honour's stages with winged speed he flew,

wrote Samuel Catherall in 1721, in a eulogy on Bishop Crewe of Durham,

> Well poized with Vertue and Nobility,
> He stopped not, till he graced an ample See.

A determination to "grace an ample See" was wholly admirable and pluralism was no cause for shame: indeed, in a work of piety

one Bishop laments the sad case of a friend who could not obtain
"one little sinecure" to give him an opportunity of devoting
himself to writing. Bishop Watson pressing for better emoluments for the parochial clergy gives details of his own £2,000 a
year as "a case full in point." The atmosphere of the period is
probably better conveyed by this contemporary writer than even
by the admirable summary of Lecky[1] or the figures given by
Maximin Piette.[2]

. . . It arises from the tithes of two churches in Shropshire, of
two in Leicestershire, of two in my diocese, of three in Huntingdon-
shire, on all of which I have resident curates; of five more as appro-
priations to the bishopric, and of two more in the Isle of Ely. I
mention this not as a matter of complaint, but as a proof how little
palliations will avail in amending the situation of the stipendiary
curates . . . There may be instances of country clergymen who
occasionally live in towns; but these instances are, comparatively
speaking, not numerous, nor are they in all cases to be blamed. A
man of real talents, and good manners, may, by mingling with the
higher classes of society in great towns, as essentially promote the
belief and practice of Christianity, as if he were constantly con-
versant with a dozen peasants, his parishioners, in a country village.
The want of medical assistance; the desire of giving a suitable education to his own children; the hope of bettering his situation, by
educating the children of others; the being engaged in literary pursuits, where a variety of books is required; these, and such-like causes,
are the main ones which induce some of the clergy to wish for a
town residence; and if their place is supplied in the country by a
resident curate, I cannot think that much mischief will follow from
such an indulgence being granted to a few, and it will never be
desired by many of the body. Nay, if a young man should be accidentally inspired with an ambition to display his talents before a more
respectable audience than his country parish affords him, his ambition
should be rather encouraged than ridiculed and restrained; for a
desire of acquiring professional fame is, next to poverty, the great
source of professional excellence and industry.

Defending Isaac Milner from a charge of meanness, Joshua
Watson wrote: "His Mastership is small; he has no living; his
deanery is not above a third of Canterbury or Lincoln." Milner
combined the Mastership of Queen's College Cambridge with
the Deanery of Carlisle, Van Mildert was at the same time

---

[1] *History of England in the 18th Century.*
[2] *John Wesley in the Evolution of Protestantism.*

Regius Professor of Divinity at Oxford, Bishop of Llandaff and Dean of St. Paul's. Archbishop Manners Sutton of Canterbury presented seven relatives jointly to sixteen benefices: a bishop of Ely, his son and grandson, had together an income of £30,000 from Church properties.

When in 1827 Copleston became Bishop of Llandaff he was utterly horrified at the state of the diocese—but he himself cheerfully combined his Bishopric with the Deanery of St. Paul's. Yet Copleston was among the best, receiving his see at a date when a faint stirring of the churchman's conscience was observable. Most of these quasi-absentee bishops made no attempt to fulfil the duties of any one of their positions. In one diocese, C. P. S. Clarke tells us, no confirmation was held until 1,000 candidates could be collected from various villages and brought into a central town. Bishop Sparks of Chester (1810–12) puts a strain on our imagination by having confirmed in Manchester *eight thousand* children on one day.

Sydney Smith, that most delightful of wits, ardent as he was in the cause of reform was an unashamed pluralist and non-resident. When, at Lady Holland's insistence, he was given the living of Foston ("Don't thank me, Mr. Smith," said Erskine, "if she had desired me to give it to the devil, *he* must have had it") he appointed a curate and in three years paid only one visit to his parish. When forced to reside by a new Bishop who took the Resident Clergy Act seriously, he became very popular with his parishioners; he physicked them and amused them, but he allowed them still to worship in a miserable little hovel with a wooden belfry while spending more than £4,000 on his own house and farm. Later with a stall at Bristol he received another small living —Halberton. He came south and exchanged Foston for a parish nearer Bristol. Not yet content he wrote to Brougham, "I want another living instead of this and as good—about £700 a year clear; and I want a prebend of about £1,000 per annum. . . . These are my objects in the Church."

The measure of zeal in the conduct of services corresponded with "objects" of this nature. Frederick Temple in his youth, wanting to stay for Communion at St. Paul's on a Sunday, was accosted by a verger who said:

"I hope you are not intending to remain for the sacrament, as that will give the Minor Canon the trouble of celebrating which otherwise he will not do."

The squire's pew in many a church was fitted up with cushioned seats, sometimes a table, frequently a fireplace. It simply was a sitting-room if the family chose to use it for other purposes than worship; and in one church, we are told, "when the Commandments are begun, a servant regularly enters at the chancel door with the lunch tray."

"It was a worldly Church," J. A. Froude sums up, "yes, there was no doubt of that." And Jeremy Bentham says: "All her excellencies stand already summed up in the one word *Decency*."

The crop of stories that illustrate what are so often called "the bad old days" can be drawn almost equally from the eighteenth and nineteenth centuries. How far the Oxford Movement exceeded the Wesleyan in its effects on the Church as a whole, how far (as Dr. Brillioth claims[1]) it was the external pressure of Parliament and public opinion rather than an inward self reform it is hard to measure, but certainly widespread changes did take place after Tractarianism had made its mark on the country.

In many respects the parallel between Wesley in the eighteenth and Newman in the nineteenth century is curiously close. Both men started inside the Church of England movements that were to end outside it. Both men were Fellows of Oxford colleges; both appealed to the early Church and sought there for the purest form of Christianity; both were intense students of the Bible; both attempted to revive the daily services and frequent daily prayers of Catholicism; both fasted often, rose early in the morning, held an ascetic view of the Christian life; both had a group of ardent followers at Oxford; each had in that group a friend who died young (Hurrell Froude and Morgan) in part as a result of too much fasting.

And to both movements the attitude of the University was ultimately the same. The *London Chronicle* gave in 1768 some advice to young Gownsmen:

> Ye jovial Souls, drink deep and swear
> And all shall then go well;
> But oh! take heed of Hymns and Prayer,
> These cry aloud—E-X-P-E-L.[2]

[1] *The Anglican Revival*, p. 14.
[2] *The Clerk of Oxford in Fiction*, p. 312.

Dr. Johnson's view was that of the Tory of his age:

Sir, the expulsion of six students from the University of Oxford, who were Methodists and would not desist from publicly praying and exhorting, was extremely just and proper. What have they to do at an University who are not willing to be taught, but will presume to teach? Where is religion to be learnt, but at an University? Sir, they were examined, and found to be mighty ignorant fellows.

Boswell: But was it not hard, Sir, to expel them, for I am told they were good beings?

Johnson: I believe they might be good beings, but they were not fit to be in the University of Oxford. A cow is a very good animal in a field, but we turn her out of a garden.[1]

Ten years before the expulsions of 1768, Wesley had uttered an impassioned Intercession for the University:

> Teacher divine, with melting eye
> Our ruined Seats of Learning see,
> Whose ruling scribes Thy truth deny,
> And persecute Thy saints and Thee,
> As hired by Satan to suppress
> And root up every seed of grace.
>
> Whose knowledge, vain, unsanctified,
> Fills every synagogue and chair,
> Whose guile and unbelief preside,
> And wage with Heaven immortal war:
> The prophet's nursing schools are these,
> And sinks of desperate wickedness.[2]

It was in the matter of knowledge, vain or otherwise, that the great cleavage between the two movements appeared. Wesley was not a man of deep intellectual power, and a first divergence from similar beginnings may be seen in the way the two men set about testing their notions of pure Christianity. Wesley going out to evangelize the American Indians hoped, as his biographer tells us, to learn from them *how* the gospels were really to be understood, hoped that they being simple, natural men—in fact, Rousseau's savage—might reconstruct for him the early ages of the Church. Newman chose the more laborious method of closer and closer study of the Fathers. By the end of Wesley's Oxford period

[1] *The Clerk of Oxford in Fiction*, p. 309.　　　　[2] Ibid, p. 310.

the parallel is at an end: the great thinker long remained at the University, the great evangelist took the road. What he found there is related in his journals; what he took there was an immense revival of belief in Christ as Saviour and Redeemer, a great trust in Him and acknowledgement of man's weakness and sinfulness, and a somewhat heady enthusiasm on the subject of conversion.

Although the Wesleyan movement ended outside the Church of England, its results inside that Church were hardly less significant (here again we have a parallel with Newman).

Most of the writing, most of the labours of Churchmen, down to the first quarter of the nineteenth century, were akin to Methodism, were certainly Evangelical in tone. The resistance to the evangelist himself had come in great part from the more worldly clergy, and among the unworldly his influence was immense. Maximin Piette has pointed out that it also represented a resurgence of the old Puritanism which had alternately conquered and been defeated in English life ever since the Reformation. One is inclined, for instance, to fancy the terrific attack on Sunday travelling to be (as it was so often called) Methodistical, till one remembers that the very unmethodistical Jane Austen instances Sunday travelling as one proof of the depravity of Mr. Elliot's character. "Those destructive engines," writes Hannah More to William Wilberforce in 1820, "Sunday newspapers, stage-coaches and other Sabbath-breaking contrivances." Anyhow, before the end of the eighteenth century religious ardour and severity were almost always called Methodism—and very often were so. Hannah More, an ardent Churchwoman, was currently called "Queen of the Methodists" and she complained to John Newton (in 1794): "My great and *worldly* friends are terribly afraid I shall be too Methodistical (a term now applied to all vital Christianity)."

Evangelicalism really was vital in those days. It inspired William Wilberforce in his attack on the Slave Trade, and it was from its ranks that he gathered most of his adherents. He himself prayed and meditated at least two hours a day during his most overworked period. He tells one significant story of visiting a nobleman hoping for his support: "So you wish, young man," was the reply, "to be a reformer of men's morals. Look, then, and see there what is the end of such reformers,"—and he pointed to a picture of the Crucifixion.

Hannah More compares Wilberforce's ante-room where crowds

were always waiting to "Noah's ark, full of beasts, clean and unclean". Wesley calls him *Athanasius contra Mundum*.

Hero of pious novels in America as well as in England (note Mr. Carleton in *Queechy*), carrying his religion into the House of Commons, boon companion of Pitt in their youth but breaking with him later from principle, an ideal friend and still more ideal parent, William Wilberforce was the apotheosis of Evangelicalism as a worldly force.

He was cultured: he was a man of this world as well as the next: his manual of piety sold its million, yet he could win the admiration of the worldling. He was of small stature, not only insignificant but positively odd in appearance, but his oratory swept all before it. "I saw," says Boswell, after a political meeting, "what seemed a mere shrimp mount upon the table, but, as I listened, he grew and grew until the shrimp became a whale."

The sons of Wilberforce came under Newman's influence. One became a High Church Bishop, two followed Newman to Rome. Zachary Macaulay, friend of Wilberforce and of Hannah More, editor of the leading Evangelical newspaper and chief of the Clapham sect, had as a son the Liberal historian, Lord Macaulay, so little attracted by any form of religion. The tendency in marked characters to react against early home teaching is very strong. While John and Frank Newman had found their father's balance and moderation less inspiring than the Calvinism of their schoolmaster, Macaulay was typical of the children of vehement Evangelicals in reacting violently against the extremes of his youth. Staying with Hannah More as a small child he had been stood on a chair and encouraged to preach to the villagers, while Newman had merely recited verses to an admiring family circle. At school Zachary Macaulay had urged his son to distribute "useful and striking" tracts and to try to convert the neighbourhood. In early manhood when the Newmans were abandoning worldly amusements, Macaulay was taking to them with the zest of a starved man. To a friend who noticed his intense enjoyment of the theatre he said, "According to the most strict sect of our religion I was bred a Pharisee."

One difficulty in getting historical perspective about the periods of Newman and of Wesley lies in the great age to which both men lived: between 1700 and 1900 there were only twenty years in which neither Wesley nor Newman was alive. Thus William

Wilberforce knew both men well. Hannah More, intimate with Wesley and Wilberforce, died only the year the Tractarian Movement began. She, too, did not fall far short of spanning a century (1745–1833), and her biography and voluminous works are about the best thing I have come on as showing the strength and weakness of Evangelicalism inside the English Church.

To Dr. Johnson, Hannah More was "child," "love," "little fool," "dearest"; to Horace Walpole, a close friend and correspondent, although "he took me to task in general terms for having exhibited such monstrously severe doctrine." Burke sat by her at a party for over an hour and recited her own verses to her; she was courted by royalty; Sir William Pepys held that she and Burke "are the only two persons I know who can be safely trusted with a metaphor." Her plays ran neck and neck with those of Sheridan. "Just returned from Percy," wrote one of her sisters, "the theatre overflowed prodigiously, notwithstanding their Majesties and the *School for Scandal* at the other House." The publisher of her poem *Sir Eldred of the Bower*, told her that "if she could hereafter discover what Goldsmith obtained for *The Deserted Village* he would make up the sum, be it what it might." She wrote under her own name, she wrote anonymously —her books sold enormously: *Thoughts on the Manners of the Great; An Estimate of the Religion of the Fashionable World; Strictures on the Modern System of Female Education; Practical Piety; Coelebs in Search of a Wife; Hints Towards the Education of a Young Princess*, etc., etc.

She caught the fancy of the time: probably too she was a brilliant talker. "It requires more wit," one of her friends wrote, "than people are apt to imagine to be foolish; and you are more nearly related to Falstaff than you care to own." An immense reverence for the great men she met doubtless helped to commend her to them: the "sublime and beautiful Edmund Burke; Abyssinian Johnson! Dictionary Johnson! Rambler's, Idler's and Irene's Johnson! Can you picture to yourself the palpitation of our hearts as we approached his mansion?" And of Garrick: "On Monday night he played King Lear, and it is literally true that my spirits have not yet recovered from the shock they sustained. . . . I called today in Leicester Fields, and Sir Joshua declared it was full three days before he got the better of it."

From astonishing success in this world of fashion Hannah More turned aside to the villages that surrounded her native place. Always religious she became far more so in middle life, falling under the influence of that John Newton who was converted in a striking fashion while actually engaged in the Slave Trade and who became a kind of spiritual guide to a number of important people. Hannah discovered with horror the religious state of the English poor. She wrote to William Wilberforce:

The Vicarage of Cheddar is in the gift of the Dean of Wells; the value nearly fifty pounds per annum. The incumbent is a Mr. R——; who has something to do, but I cannot here find out what, in the University of Oxford, where he resides. The curate lives at Wells, twelve miles distant. They have only service once a week, and there is scarcely an instance of a poor person being visited, or prayed with. The living of Axbridge belongs to the Prebendary of Wivelscombe, in the cathedral of Wells. The annual value is about fifty pounds. The incumbent, about sixty years of age. The prebend to which this rectory belongs is in the gift of the Bishop of Bath and Wells. Mr. G. is intoxicated about six times a week, and very frequently is prevented from preaching by two black eyes, honestly earned by fighting . . . No clergyman had resided in it for forty years. One rode over, three miles from Wells, to preach once on a Sunday, but no weekly duty was done, or sick persons visited; and children were often buried without any funeral service.[1]

She started schools in one village after another: in one, out of 108 children "there were not any boys and girls of any age whom I asked, who could tell me who made them . . . these parishes are large and populous; they are as dark as Africa." The poverty was miserable except among "the opulent farmers"—labourers earning a shilling a day, one old woman burning her table, another one of her three chairs, for warmth; not a cup of broth to be had "if it would save a life." Hannah sent in coal as well as starting schools, put her rich friends under contribution, rode horseback in the worst of weather and in the poorest of health from one village to another, was helped by her sisters to conduct the growing number of schools, underwent a real persecution from the infuriated clergy of the neighbourhood and also from some of the rich farmers. She had tried to placate these and writes of one visit: "The next, a farmer of £1,000 a year, let us know that we should not come there to make his ploughman wiser than himself; he did not want saints, but workmen. His wife, who though she cannot read, seems to understand the doctrine of

[1] *Memoirs of Hannah More*, Vol. II, pp. 207-9, 296-7.

philosophical necessity, said, 'the lower class were fated to be poor, and ignorant, and wicked; and that as wise as we were, we could not alter what was decreed'."[1]

In London Hannah was shewn in effigy "at a very great children's ball" with a rod in her hand, the children being told that she would like to prevent all their amusements. "Let the vile abuse vented against you," wrote Horace Walpole, "be balm to your mind; your writings must have done great service when they have so much provoked the enemy."[2]

Hannah's tracts for the poor were no less successful than her plays, novels and verses were among the rich—how much they were read by the poor it is impossible to say, but the clergy bought them by the thousand. Her books went through edition after edition: at that date sales of over a million for a book were sufficiently remarkable, but this was the scale of hers and much of the profit she devoted to her schools, village clubs and other good works. The strength of the evangelical revival may be expressed in one of the titles she chose: *Practical Piety*—earnest prayer and Bible reading flowering into a sincere service of one's neighbour, courage in attacking vice without respect of persons.

The weaknesses of Evangelicalism so much scoffed at in its decay may also, I think, be traced in the letters of this excellent correspondent with bishops, statesmen and people of fashion. She was often accused of Calvinism and as often denied the charge. One of the denials is significant. "It has been repeatedly said that, being a Calvinist myself, I always employed Calvinistic teachers. I never knowingly employed one. As to Calvinism or Arminianism, I should be very sorry if such terms were known in my schools: it never having been my object to teach dogmas and opinions, but to train up good members of society, and plain practical Christians."[3] And again: "I never talk or write of doctrines, as a party matter, thinking it makes our tempers sour and unprofitable. The doctrines peculiar to Calvinism I do not adopt, though I much reverence many good men who maintain them. These differences I conceive to be permitted for the exercise of mutual charity."[4]

She saw as "the distinctive doctrine of Christianity, a deep

---

[1] *Memoirs of Hannah More*, Vol. II, pp. 309-10.
[2] Ibid, p. 379.
[3] Ibid.
[4] Ibid, p. 235.

and abiding sense in the heart, of our fallen nature; of our actual and personal sinfulness; of our lost state, but for the redemption wrought for us by Jesus Christ." But she is "disgusted with much metaphysical nonsense from the pulpit," and clearly sees nowhere the dependence on doctrine of the Practical Piety she inculcates.

We are told of Carlyle that he used to jeer over the Arian disputes and ring the changes on Homoi- and Homo-ousion, talking of the absurdity of expending such fury over a diphthong. Later he came to see that had the Arians won, Christianity itself would have become a legend. So, too, in the English Church of the nineteenth century the terms Hannah More decried meant in plain English the question of *who* God was and of *what* God was. If the Calvinists were right, God was not Love, if the Socinians were right, Christ was not God. The same battle was being fought on the narrower stage of the English Church that had been fought over and over again in the early ages of Christianity, and the later Evangelicals were slipping perilously into Latitudinarianism.

Reading Hannah's letters at the same time that he heard of the lapse into Unitarianism of his intimate friend, Blanco White, Newman wrote to his aunt:

. . . I am sorry to say that the editor of Mrs. More's letters has been ill advised enough to allow letters to appear in which she, in the freedom of private correspondence, speaks slightingly of the Constantinopolitan Fathers (who composed the Nicene Creed as we now use it). Well, what is the consequence? We just now have a most serious and impressive warning if we choose to avail ourselves of it. Poor Blanco White has turned Socinian, and written a book glorying in it. Now in the preface to this book he says: "I have for some time been a *Sabellian*, but the veil is now removed from my eyes, for I find *Sabellianism* is but Unitarianism in disguise." Now what would Mrs. More, or rather her editor, say on hearing this? on seeing that her scoffing at the Creeds of the Church had been a strengthening, so far as it went, of a system of doctrine which ends in Unitarianism? It is most melancholy to think about. What is most painful is that the clergy are so utterly ignorant on the subject. We have no *theological* education, and instead of profiting by the example of past times, we attempt to decide the most intricate questions, whether of doctrine or conduct, by our blind and erring reason.

It was indeed proving impossible to restrain within certain defined limits the right and the duty of private judgment. The

Oxford Movement was to be a last desperate struggle to keep in the Church of England the dogmatic principle. Meanwhile, what perilled it most among the Evangelicals was an excessive concentration on one element, and that a highly subjective one, of the Christian message. Concentration on one's own salvation, one's own acceptance of Christ, produced especially in lesser minds an alarming self-centredness. Many seemed never to get beyond this—their spiritual horizon was a narrow one—and the duty of testifying made them terribly self-conscious. One can see the beginnings of that rather unattractive aspect under which later generations viewed the Evangelicals, yet one cannot read of the eighteenth or early nineteenth centuries without being deeply impressed by what they did for the revival of religion.

CHAPTER VIII

Curate of St. Clement's

IF NEWMAN was at first embarrassed by Oriel Common Room they were no less embarrassed by him. They preferred conversable, "clubbable", to silent, however able, Fellows. It was decided to ask Whately to take him in hand—a task which Whately relished. "He professed", says Newman, "to be pleased to have cubs in hand, whom he might lick into shape, and who, he said, like dogs of King Charles' breed, could be held up by one leg without yelling."

It is possible that he really said "yelping," for he would be better acquainted with canine language than Newman, being possessed of what Tom Mozley calls "a little company of dogs." He would take his daily walk round Christ Church Meadow with them, being always provided "with sticks and big round missiles for their amusement." Whately was one of the many strong individualities of the moment in Oxford and stories about him abounded.

Calling on a bride who had filled her house with spindly-legged chairs Whately sat "swinging, plunging and shifting on his seat while he talked. An ominous crack was heard; a leg of the chair had given away; he tossed it on to the sofa without comment and impounded another chair." At a boring party and unable to reach the door, Whately sat first on the window sill, next half outside and then entirely outside the window, whence he dropped to the ground and made good his escape. Dean Burgon relates that Newman, succeeding later to Whately's rooms in Oriel, found hung outside the window the last of a string of herrings which Whately used to fry for breakfast, adding: "His ways in truth were very peculiar: some of them rather nasty." The rooms were "ill carpeted and indifferently furnished" during both Whately's and Newman's period "as well as encumbered with bookshelves in every part." Dean Burgon regrets that later they were "mercilessly smartened." The devoted daughter who writes Whately's biography says that his influence at Oxford "was lessened by his utter disregard of the customs and regulations of the place." Tuckwell notes his "blatant voice, great stride, rough dress."

But with all this Whately made devoted friends, of whom Newman was among the closest. "There is scarcely anyone," he wrote almost forty years later, "whom in memory I love more than Whately even now." Whately took him out walking and riding, talked to him, was sharp with him and presently told the Oriel Fellows that they had made no mistake in their election and that Newman was the clearest-headed man he knew.

Newman does not mention the dogs, so perhaps they were left at home on these walks. As to the riding, Tom Mozley tells us that Newman if not a brilliant horseman was still a pretty good one. One of the privileges of an Oriel Fellowship was the possession of a horse and he rode a good deal. He long owned a lively animal that, trained in a narrow space, had contracted the habit of making abrupt turns to which Newman accommodated himself successfully. A less good rider, to whom Mozley later lent the horse with a warning, was found lying "sadly contused on the turf" with the horse nowhere in sight.

Whately's influence was the strongest on Newman during his earliest time at Oriel, but he saw a good deal of Dr. Lloyd, Canon of Christ Church and Regius Professor of Divinity, who selected him as one of a small private class. "A very fine class we are," Newman writes gleefully. "Eleven individuals and eight first classes." They went through standard books on the evidences; Lloyd "employed his mind upon the grounds of Christian faith rather than on the faith itself." He disliked Evangelicals, yet he liked Newman and bestowed on him a good deal of attention in which these mingled feelings became apparent. He would walk about the room, taking snuff, asking questions, chaffing his class, and stopping in front of Newman would pretend to box his ears or kick his shins. Perhaps Newman's later impatience of evidences dated from these lectures, friendly though Lloyd became to him. Anyhow Lloyd was not the man to gain the intellectual influence exercised by Whately. The two men were antagonists, representing markedly the rivalry between their colleges, and Newman has drawn out the contrast between them.

Lloyd was a scholar, and Whately was not. Whately had the reputation specially of being an original thinker, of which Lloyd was not at all ambitious. Lloyd was one of the high-and-dry school, though with far larger views than were then common; while Whately looked down on both High and Low Church, calling the two parties respectively Sadducees and Pharisees. Lloyd professed to hold to theology, and laid great stress on a doctrinal standard, on authoritative and traditional teaching, and on ecclesiastical history; Whately called the Fathers "certain old divines", and, after Swift or some other wit, called orthodoxy "one's own doxy", and heterodoxy "another's doxy". Lloyd made much of books and reading . . . Whately's great satisfaction was to find a layman who had made a creed for himself, and he avowed that he was *prima facie* well inclined to a heretic, for his heresy at least showed that he had exercised his mind upon its subject-matter.

As so often happens in friendships, no two men could have been more dissimilar in temperament than Newman and Whately. Newman delicately perceptive of the feelings of others, himself very sensitive, Whately almost coarse-grained. Contrast for instance Tuckwell's stories of the two men. Newman was ready to sink through the floor when Copleston, observing him trying to serve sweetbread, remarked "Mr. Newman, we do not carve sweetbread with a spoon. Manciple, bring a blunt knife." Mark Pattison tells the same story, adding that Copleston "reproved him for not taking wine with the company" and that "Copleston when Provost used to torment Probationers". (For the first year a Fellow was on trial and was called a Probationer: it may well have been Whately's report of him that decided Oriel's confirmation of Newman's Fellowship.) But Whately himself delighted in disregarding all conventions so that Copleston observed of him that he "sadly forgot himself". It was not merely that he had made rings with his tea-cup and scattered the tea leaves at breakfast, or that he had found a hole in his stocking and stuck a bit of plaster on his leg: no, he had gone out walking with the Provost and had thrown a stone at a bird!

In a world where convention prevailed and where a man as shy as Newman had to find his niche, I wonder whether the Evangelical duty of testifying was pressed upon him either by his own conscience or by his brother and his friends. The question is only partly answered by his diary. Before leaving Trinity for Oriel, he had written: "O that I were known to hold those opinions I

E

do hold! how intolerable is the constraint which is now upon me."
About the same time he notes "I commenced a practice of carrying
Tracts about with me for distribution"—but whether he accosted
strangers with them or merely left them about in public places he
does not tell us.

With his intimates it was different. He notes in the diary that
one of his friends "was startled at the idea, when I said that
drunkenness, or rather getting drunk, was, in the sight of God,
nearly as great a crime as murder." To J. Pope, a friend of
Trinity days, he wrote in 1825: "The Play is in my opinion
decidedly improper for a Christian, much more a clergyman."

But talking to chosen friends is not testifying. What of his
colleagues at Oriel? In April 1823, uneasy in conscience at having
dined with the Provost one Sunday and breakfasted with the
Dean another—surely the mildest forms of Sabbath-breaking—
he writes in his diary: "I must explain myself in some way to the
Fellows about my wish to keep Sunday holy."

The impression one gets is that for the most part he took refuge
in silence. The long solitary walks were filled with prayer, intercession chiefly. But one cannot conceive Newman testifying in
public. If we try to imagine him today as a Buchmanite believing
he ought to "share", we shall see the strain of imagination involved
in the idea. It is a type of spirituality that arises periodically and
that might involve positive torture for a sensitive and cultured
mind. In his diary he wrote "I know well what a painful and
ridiculous sense of shame I have on light occasions. It affects me
like bodily pain and makes me cry out. It is like a sword running
through me."

Yet the same man who wrote this also wrote after an early
meeting with Pusey and Churton a prayer that they might be
brought into the True Church, and a few weeks later of Pusey:
"How can I doubt his seriousness? His very eagerness to talk of
the Scriptures seems to prove it. May I lead him forward, at the
same time gaining good from him!" And again: "That Pusey is
Thine, O Lord, how can I doubt? . . . yet I fear he is prejudiced
against Thy children."

It would indeed be a bold man who could doubt Pusey's
seriousness and it is amusing to note that years later Isaac
Williams remarked: "Pusey's presence always checked Newman's
lighter and unrestrained mood; and I was myself silenced by
so awful a person." Pusey was a little older than Newman

but his junior at Oriel. Probably he was not yet "awful" and
the notes about him in the private journal change quickly from a
patronising tone to one of heartfelt admiration. This was part
of a larger change which made these years among the most
important of Newman's life. In his brilliant short biography R.
H. Hutton says:

Newman's was one of the minds which matured slowly, and it was
not until he was twenty-six years of age that it became clear whether
he would be in the main a religious leader or one of the pillars of
the Whately party, that is, the party who threw their influence into
the scale of minimising the spiritual significance of revelation rather
than of maximising it.

This remark is doubly interesting—for Newman had been
a precocious boy and youth. His all-round maturity came late:
the ending of a letter to one of his sisters, "You will not be sought
after by any so facetious a brother
              Asjoh Nhen Rynew Man"
suggests a boy of ten rather than a Fellow of Oriel. But did his
intellect too mature late? I think it did, and that this is often the
result of precocity. There has to be a long pause, a falling-back
to take breath, a fresh start, for young minds which have begun
too early. Surely Hutton is right in this. But on the other question
I am more doubtful. True, Newman spoke later of his own danger
of "drifting into Liberalism", yet in the *Apologia* he also shows the
dogmatic principle so strong in his own mind that he actually
gained from Whately and from Hawkins additions—of which
something will be said in a moment—to his stock of theology, as
well as gaining immeasurably in his powers of expression. Hawkins, he says, first taught him to draw out his thoughts in order,
to weigh, measure and distinguish in a fashion that was later
deemed Jesuitical.

Whately got him to write for the Encyclopædia Metropolitana.
The money must have been a help. For in spite of the income
from his Fellowship the diary for '22 and '23 shows Newman
constantly pressed for ready cash. "By some mistake my pupil
has not paid me yet—so that at present I have hardly more than
a sovereign." "Letter to say that the £50 cannot yet be paid. I
have but a few shillings in my pocket and owe many bills." But
his creditors were forbearing and Tyler, the Dean, lent him £60.

A specimen day in the diary shows six hours devoted to these
pupils so dilatory in their payments, and the chief confessions of
these years are of "petulance and ill-nature" to them and to
Frank. One entry records "A most ungovernable spirit towards
my pupil". In middle life Newman added the remark "a little
wretch aged 17".

Another entry shows a rare degree of honesty in dealing with the
less creditable of one's sins. "I am a great liar, a mean liar—
from pride, lest I should confess myself wrong". This may be
connected with another remark: "I have had much trouble the
last few days with my pupil. . . . It is humbling to find how little
I know in Latin and Greek, and this my pupil forces me to find
out." At seventeen, finding out what the master does not know
is any pupil's principal occupation.

The private pupils, Dr. Lloyd's lectures, the Encyclopædia
articles and the determination to make of himself a classical
scholar worthy to hold the position he had won, caused Newman
to live laborious days. The money difficulty was in part the
problem of help for his family. In 1822 he notes that he "sometimes quite trembled on retiring to rest at [his] own exertions."
For most of the Long Vacation of that year he took only four
hours' sleep. He spent the vacation in Oxford. He was still in
lodgings with Frank who was about to enter Worcester College.
Newman writes to his mother: "Expecting to see Frank, I am
in fact expecting to see you all. I shall require you to fill him
full of all of you, that when he comes I may squeeze and wring
him out as some sponge, affording me refreshment for I am very
thirsty."

The letter continues:

The only way ultimately to succeed is to do things thoroughly. I
lost much time by superficial reading during the whole Long Vacation this time two years. Francis shall not go such bad ways to work.
Liber sum (my pupil having gone), and I have been humming, whistling,
and laughing loud to myself all day.

While educating Frank, Newman was also taking a great
interest in the intellectual development of his sisters. They send
him verses for criticism, he wants to see Harriett's translation of
Tasso, she must "perfect her Andante Minor" before he comes,
if she has leisure time on Sunday she should learn Scripture by

heart. "It is a resource in solitude, on a journey, and in a sleepless night." (He had himself just memorised the Epistle to the Ephesians.) The passage of Gibbon does Harriett "much credit", but what exactly this was does not emerge.

Postscripts in letters to his mother contain "a string of grammatical questions" for Mary, and the remark "Jemima is an ingenious girl and has invented a very correct illustration of the generation of asymptotic curves." A joint letter early in 1824 from John and Francis to Jemima shows the happy family relations.

> . . . give my especial remembrances to Harriett for the very nice and many verses of which her epistle was composed. Tell her that, so far from suspecting them to be extempore, I was much surprised when I found that to be the case. . . . Tell my Mother I have been speaking to my laundress about my shirts, but she is too much for me, and argues most plausibly that a frill which tumbles immediately it is put on is nevertheless very well got up. If Mary were with me, I should get her to put the matter to rights. . . . The other day I rode over to Worton and back again, which was very well for me, being 34 miles. I shall leave Francis to finish and direct this, for you must know, *I* begin things best, and *he* finishes them best.

Frank ends the letter after a good deal of rather unintelligible chaff:

> Love to Grandam and Aunt's rheumatism, and Harriett's hartshorn bottle and Mary's chilblains and your—pretty face. Express to Mrs. *Borum* and Miss Eleanor's *Mr. Pate* (he is her disease) and to all the town when you write or see them, and believe me ever,
> Your very affectionate B with a bad pen.

The background to all this cheerfulness on the part of the eldest brother was appallingly heavy work. A few days before the joint letter to Jemima, Newman had written to his father that Cicero was finished for the Encyclopædia—Dr. Whately had told him that the editor had suddenly been disappointed of an article on Cicero which must be in his hands within two months: John undertook the task (he got £14 for it). So busy was he at the time that one day, after working with his private pupils till the evening, he sat down to his article till four o'clock next morning, then walked over from Oxford to Worton, a distance of eighteen miles, to keep his promise of breakfasting with Walter Mayers.

Ten days later, on June 13, 1824, Newman was ordained Deacon by Dr. Legge, Bishop of Oxford. In the diary he wrote:

It is over. I am Thine, O Lord; I seem quite dizzy and cannot altogether believe and understand it. At first, after the hands were laid on me, my heart shuddered within me; the words "for ever" are so terrible. It was hardly a godly feeling which made me feel melancholy at the idea of giving up all for God. At times indeed my heart burnt within me, particularly during the singing of the Veni Creator. Yet, Lord, I ask not for comfort in comparison of sanctification. . . . I feel as a man thrown suddenly into deep water.

He had not given up the idea of going as a missionary to the heathen. A couple of weeks after his ordination, he called at the Church Missionary House. . . . "They say weakness of voice, shortness of sight, want of eloquence are not sufficient impediments." For the moment, however, he had accepted the curacy of St. Clement's, an Oxford parish lying over Magdalen Bridge. The salary, he anticipates in a letter home, will not be more than forty or fifty pounds a year, but he is "convinced it is necessary to get used to parochial duty early." The suggestion that he take this particular curacy came from Pusey, who "entered into his work and plans with the utmost interest."[1]

His rector, Dr. John Gutch, was an octogenarian invalid. The parish had about two thousand inhabitants and a scheme was on foot for building a new church. Newman had now to take on the work of collecting the necessary five or six thousand pounds, and of winning back the great mass of parishioners who—as a result of the smallness of the existing church and the inactivity of the Rector—had drifted according to their various fancies either into Dissenting Chapels or ale-houses. Newman set about the work energetically. He instituted a Sunday afternoon sermon, which soon became popular (he notes that his voice is getting stronger); and he began a systematic visitation of the whole parish. He wrote to his mother that he had visited "the most respectable third" of the population satisfactorily: "I rather dread the two-thirds of the parish which are to come." But this, too, he managed.

There was a general feeling—shared by his father—that the poor do not like being visited. Newman found that for the most

[1] Liddon, *Life of Pusey*, Vol. I, p. 88.

part they did. They liked his visiting and they liked him: though Pusey records that "the first sick person that Newman visited at St. Clement's refused to see him and shut the door against him, Newman persevered. The man died penitent."[1] He showed a surprising bent for parish work and a sound judgment. He did not try to win over Dissenters—that they were going to Church at all was already something. He speaks kindly of one of their ministers. There was a small Catholic Chapel in the parish. He called upon the priest—a Jesuit named Newsham—not knowing who he was, and asked him why he did not come to Church! Newman went to Communion in the Chapel, years later, as a Catholic.

What Newman had not anticipated was that his parish work would play a part in his personal religious development. The Evangelicalism he had brought with him to Oxford had not lost its fervour but it had lost a good deal of its doctrinal purity: particularly upon the function of the Church. One of the chief links between Methodists outside and Evangelicals inside the Church of England was their disparagement of the Church as a visible organisation. For them the real Church was the invisible society of all who loved Christ, of all who were "saved". Curiously enough it was Whately, from whose Liberalism he was later to recoil, who taught Newman "the existence of the Church as a substantive body or corporation" (at the same time building up in him an awareness of the Church's necessary independence of the State). But it was Hawkins who brought him to see one of the Church's essential functions. As an undergraduate he had heard Hawkins' famous sermon on Tradition which Arnold was later to call the beginning of the Oxford Movement. The only impression he seems to have got from it at the time was that it was very long. But later he read it and was convinced by its main argument—that Scripture was never intended to teach doctrine: for that we must go to the Church, returning to Scripture only to verify what the Church has taught. So thoroughly was Newman won over, that he made the decision (upon which, however, he did not act till later) that he must cease to subscribe to the Bible Society, whose principle was that the Bible alone sufficed. His new vision of the Church was further enriched by the reading (begun in June 1825) of Butler's *Analogy*, with "its inculcation of a visible Church, the oracle of truth and a pattern of sanctity."

[1] Liddon, *Life of Pusey*, Vol. I, p. 88 footnote.

There remained the most distinctive positive element in the Evangelical teaching—the importance attached to the "conversion" of the individual. This conversion was in itself a thing consciously experienced, and carried with it the realised certainty of one's own salvation: it had its prescribed stages, as Newman himself tells us[1]—"conviction of sin, terror, despair, news of the free and full salvation, apprehension of Christ, sense of pardon, assurance of salvation, joy and peace, and so on to final perseverance." It was at this conversion, and not at Baptism, that the soul acquired the Grace without which it could not be saved: and this Grace was not a new life-principle in the soul but an "imputed righteousness"—a kind of legal fiction by which the soul was entitled to point to Christ's merits *as if* they were its own. The world was divided into the saved, who had had the experience of conversion, and the rest who had not: the saved could judge who was converted and who was unconverted. In the Calvinist books which had done so much to form Newman spiritually, the division between converted and unconverted was linked up with Calvin's theory of the elect and the reprobate.

The test of Evangelical orthodoxy upon this central matter was the denial of Baptismal Regeneration. By this test Newman was still, at his ordination, an Evangelical: but with a hint of wavering. According to Frank Newman, his brother shocked both Mayers and himself by a sermon—his first—preached at Mayers' Church at Warton, on the text, "Man goeth forth to his work and to his labour until the evening." It was on behalf of the distressed weavers of Spitalfields, and Newman implied that they were specially worthy of sympathy not merely as men but as baptised men—as our fellow Christians. Newman himself does not tell us that Mayers and Frank were shocked by so much importance attributed to Baptism; but he does tell us that his sermon did not satisfy Dr. Hawkins, who saw in it a denial of Baptismal Regeneration, and held its division of "the Christian world into two classes, the one all darkness, the other all light", to be totally untrue to men as we know them. Hawkins was at this time Vicar of St. Mary's; he and Newman, forced by their parish duties to remain in Oxford during the Long Vacation, had Oriel to themselves and were therefore thrown much in each other's company. Hawkins continued to work upon Newman with the argument from experience against a strict line of demar-

---

[1] *Autobiographical Memoir* (printed in Vol. I. of *Letters and Correspondence*), p. 123.

cation between two sorts of Christian: and he lent him Sumner's *Apostolical Preaching* to reinforce the argument.

A month or so after his first sermon, Newman notes in his diary (August 15, 1824), "The question of regeneration perplexes me very much": and nine days later: "Sumner's book threatens to drive me into either Calvinism or Baptismal Regeneration, and I wish to steer clear of both, at least in preaching. I am always slow in deciding a question; and last night I was so distressed and low about it that the thought even struck me that I must leave the Church". By the following January, he was writing, "I think, I am not certain, I must give up the doctrine of imputed righteousness and that of regeneration as apart from Baptism".

In this same note of January 17, 1825, he shows that he has seen a deeper problem than the connection of regeneration with Baptism; namely the nature of regeneration itself: it must be seen as a real change in the soul (and he adds the comment in his old age that here he had "got hold of the Catholic doctrine that forgiveness of sin is conveyed to us, not simply by imputation, but by the implanting of a habit of grace").

Thus by now his mind is fairly clear about regeneration: it is clearing, but not yet definite, upon the connection of regeneration with Baptism. There is a close connection, as he notes on the day he was "ordained priest" (May 29, 1825), "yet I do not even now actually maintain that the Spirit always or generally accompanies the very act of Baptism, only that that Sacrament brings them into the Kingdom of Grace, where the Spirit will constantly meet them with his influences".

In all this movement of his mind, experience was decisive. He found that the Evangelical doctrine would not work: he had begun to suspect it as theologically wrong, he found it wrong psychologically too. He had already discovered that his own conversion was not according to pattern. In the *Autobiographical Memoir* we read: "He was sensible that he had ever been wanting in those special Evangelical experiences which, like the grip of the hand or other prescribed signs of a secret society, are the sure tokens of a member". He had drawn up, with the support of Scripture texts, a careful account of the Evangelical process of conversion, whose stages we have already seen, and he had to admit that his own conversion had not been like that. It had indeed been accompanied by the assurance of salvation, but as he tells us in the *Apologia* this began to fade a couple of years before his Ordination.

In the parish he found that Calvinism was not a key to the phenomena of human nature in others any more than in himself. That strict line of demarcation between converted Christians and unconverted did not exist. On July 17, 1825, he notes in his diary:

[I am] principally or in great measure led to this change by the fact that in my parochial duties I found many, who in most important points were inconsistent, but who yet I could not say were altogether without grace. Most indeed were in that condition as if they had spiritual feelings, but weak and uncertain.

All this experience he sums up in the *Autobiographical Memoir*: early in his clerical life he had taken the first step towards giving up the Evangelical system: "however for a long while certain shreds and tatters of that doctrine hung about his preaching". Writing to Mr. Edwards close on sixty years later he recalls: "I grew so High Church that Samuel Wilberforce who in 1826 heard me preach at St. Clement's went away wondering". Indeed it was a moment for wonder: all the future hung upon it. With the Evangelical hold broken, he might have been expected either to fall back into an arid not very spiritual churchmanship or to throw himself into Arnold and Whately's new religious Liberalism. He was saved from both by his continuing study of the Fathers of the early Church.

Meanwhile it may have been a result of the wearing through of his Evangelicalism that he was taking a less harsh view of others. On the day he was "ordained priest", May 29, 1825, he writes in his diary:

My feelings as to those ordained with me were somewhat different from those I had this time year. I hope I was not exactly uncharitable then; still I certainly thought that there might be some among them who were coming to the Bishop out of their own head, and without the spirit of God. But when I looked round today I could hope and trust that none were altogether destitute of divine influence; tho' there was difference of spirituality, yet all might be in some degree spiritual.

He was even for the moment taking a less harsh view of himself: in the long self-examination he wrote on the last birthday before his Ordination there is already a break in the fierceness: "[God] has enabled me several times to wrestle with my solitary thought and to drive from me the devilish imaginations of my superiority of intellect . . . I trust my heart is purer than it was . . . I am [selfish] in eating—not that I eat much (tho' this is sometimes the case) but that I am dainty, greedy, indulge my palate. . . ."

On the same day in 1825 he is by comparison almost optimistic: "I seem more pure in heart than I was: I say it with trembling, but this year past God has been most gracious. I do not recollect any grievous attack—one or two momentary temptations I have had, but I have been able to turn my back upon them. Doubtless my incessant engagements is one advantage; besides I am getting older".

1824 was the last year in which the family was whole and complete. The threat of a spiritual rift had shown a few months earlier when Charles had consulted John on the religious doubts which later carried him far away. But for the moment he had gone no further than to talk alone to his elder brother. Father, mother and children were all very close, advising and helping one another. Increasingly the parents' dependence was upon the eldest son. Bearing the weight of the family anxieties he writes to his father saying, "Everything will—I see it will—be very right if only you will let me manage".

His mother wrote of how much the letter had cheered and comforted him. "This is just the text I have preached from whenever your Father and I have discussed the subject. For many months I always begin and end by saying, 'I have no fear, John will manage'".

Financial anxieties seemed light as they looked back a little later. In August 1824 Newman's mother wrote to him of his father's "indisposition". A little later the doctor had asked for a second opinion. She had waited a while hoping to send better news, "but I think it would no longer be kind to keep you in ignorance of his sad illness".

The keenness of Newman's feelings may be read both in his diary at the time and in the heartfelt cry of sympathy with the hero of *Loss and Gain* over "all that long night and that indescribable waking in the morning, and that dreary day of travel which followed it . . . O piercing change! it was but six or seven weeks before that you had passed the same objects the reverse way, with what different feelings, and oh, in what company . . . It was a grief not to be put into words; and to meet mother, sisters—and the Dead".

For the illness had been brief and it was almost over. The diary reads:

That dread event has happened. Is it possible? O my Father! I got to town on Sunday morning. He knew me; tried to put out his hand and said "God bless you!" Towards the evening of Monday he said his last words. He seemed in great peace of mind. He could, however, only articulate "God bless you; thank my God, thank my God"! and lastly, "My dear" . . . On Thursday he looked beautiful. Such calmness, sweetness, composure, and majesty were in his countenance. Can a man be a materialist who sees a dead body?

CHAPTER IX

Tutor of Oriel

RETURNING to Oxford after the Christmas vacation Newman writes to his mother in January, 1825, of his "mortification" at having to wrap his cloak around him on the coach. "I had the satisfaction, however, of observing that the outside passengers in front had close box coats as well as cloaks; and on arriving at Oxford I had the additional gratification of hearing it was the coldest day we have had."

The coach that brought Newman to Oxford was one of seventy-three passenger coaches and mails that left the city every twenty-four hours. "The High Street and the Cornmarket were alive with drags, arriving from London, Birmingham, Southampton, leaving for Cambridge and Bristol, for Hereford and Brighton, North and South and East and West."[1] The coaches a century earlier had taken one day in summer, two in winter, for the trip to London, but G. V. Cox notes in 1828:

In this spring it was recorded, as a remarkable instance of rapid travelling, that a coach went from London, through Oxford, to Cheltenham (100 miles) in nine hours and ten minutes; and that it was expected that the distance from London to Birmingham, through Oxford, would soon be done in thirteen hours and a half![2]

Even with this immense increase of speed Oxford was then as remote from London as Edinburgh is today.

The next morning the chilled passenger plunged into the cold bath at Holywell and found himself in good shape. The hardy method employed of dealing with fatigue and overwork is impressive. Terrific overwork it certainly was. The subscription to the church was proceeding apace, the Sunday school was, says the diary, "in a good train for success. I find I am called a Methodist." There was too a great deal of visiting in the parish. The general harmony disturbed by a dispute with the choir,

---

[1] *A History of the University of Oxford.* C. E. Mallet. Vol. II, p. 191.
[2] G. V. Cox, *Recollections of Oxford*, p. 115.

Newman notes "We now sing en masse". Two sermons weekly were still his rule, yet by Whately's urgent solicitation more work was undertaken for the Encyclopædia—an article on Apollonius with a sequel on Miracles. "I am persuaded, as Whately suggested, that sermon-writing by *itself* has a tendency to produce a loose, rambling kind of composition; nay even of thought."

What he has to say is interesting both as sketching something of Newman's lifelong feeling about miracles and as touching a point on which he was later to change greatly. On the first we find that now as always miracles were not specially valued by him as evidential, in the sense of proving the Christian revelation to the unbeliever, but as manifesting to the believer something of God's character as moral governor of His Universe. Thus he says:

. . . Were a being who had experience only of a chaotic world suddenly introduced into this orderly system of things, he would have an infinitely more powerful argument for the existence of a designing Mind, than a mere interruption of that system can afford. A miracle is no argument to one who is deliberately, and on principle, an atheist.

. . . While writers expatiate so largely on the laws of nature, they altogether forget the existence of a moral system.

. . . Now the Miracles of the Jewish and Christian religions must be considered as immediate effects of Divine Power beyond the action of nature, for an important moral end; and are in consequence accounted for by producing, not a physical, but a final cause.

. . . When the various antecedent objections which ingenious men have urged against miracles are brought together, they will be found nearly all to arise from forgetfulness of the existence of moral laws. In their zeal to perfect the laws of matter they most unphilosophically overlook a more sublime system, which contains disclosures not only of the Being but of the Will of God.

. . . A miracle, then, calls for no distinct species of testimony from that offered for other events, but for a testimony strong in proportion to the improbability of the particular event attested.

. . . As parts of a system, the Miracles recommend and attest each other, evidencing not only general wisdom, but a digested and extended plan.

On the second point it is interesting to note that as yet he confined belief in miracles to those of the Gospels and the *very* early Church: he writes of the miracle "wrought (as it is said) in Hunneric's persecution, long after the real age of miracles was past."

Contrasting these real miracles with the dubious "ecclesiastical" miracles he says:

. . . While the Miracles of Scripture are frugally dispensed as regards their object and seasons, they are carefully varied in their nature; like the work of One who is not wasteful of His riches yet can be munificent when occasion calls for it.

And,

. . . By similar means the pretensions of the Roman hierarchy have been supported.

From the study of Apollonius he had concluded that most Christian treatments of the subject had been unfortunate.

Sceptical writers have been forward to urge the history and character of Apollonius as creating a difficulty in the argument for Christianity derived from Miracles; while their opponents have sometimes attempted to account for a phenomenon of which they had not yet ascertained the existence, and have most gratuitously ascribed his supposed power to the influence of the Evil principle. On examination, we shall find not a shadow of a reason for supposing that Apollonius worked miracles in any proper sense of the word; or that he professed to work them; or that he rested his authority on extraordinary works of any kind; and it is strange indeed that Christians, with victory in their hands, should have so mismanaged their cause as to establish an objection where none existed, and in their haste to extricate themselves from an imaginary difficulty, to overturn one of the main arguments for Revealed Religion.

The Gospels were the work of eyewitnesses, not so Apollonius' biography:

. . . Only an eyewitness is warranted to write thus pictorially; Philostratus was born 86 years after Apollonius' death . . .
. . . Unless, indeed, the history had been perverted to a mischievous purpose, we should esteem it impertinent to direct argument against a mere romance, and to subject a work of imagination to a grave discussion.

The quality of his writing led the editor to ask for more: he suggested an article on the Fathers of the second century which he wanted within a year. Newman offered instead "the Fathers of the second and third centuries" to be completed in two years. The editor refusing this, Newman began to contemplate a serious book on the Fathers—"I am about", he writes to Harriett (May 1, 1826), "to undertake a great work, perhaps."

The great work was to begin with a full reading of the Fathers, and Jemima reminds him that Archbishop Ussher "was eighteen years accomplishing the task", while "Mary desires her love and begs that the next time you write you will be so kind as to enlighten her on the uses of reading the Fathers."

To Pusey, studying in Germany, Newman entrusted the task of procuring for him such works as he could not get in England, and he writes to his mother: "My Fathers are arrived all safe— huge fellows they are, but very cheap—one folio costs a shilling! and all in this extravagantly moderate way".

Newman's sermons were sent regularly to his mother and his sisters who "all agreed a week was much too long to wait", and who "read them repeatedly". And again his mother writes: "I assure you your sermons are a real comfort and delight to me . . . It is, my dear, a great gift to see so clearly the truths of religion; still more to be able to impart the knowledge to others."

Newman's father had cautioned him, now he in turn warns his mother.

I feel pleased you like my sermons. I am sure I need not caution you against taking anything I say on trust. Do not be run away with by any opinion of mine. I have seen cause to change my mind in some respects, and I may change again. I see I know very little about anything, though I often think I know a great deal.

In May 1825, Whately, being made Principal of Alban Hall, chose Newman for Vice-Principal. "I am Dean," he writes to his mother, "Tutor, Bursar and all—in his absence, indeed, Principal."

St. Alban's was one of the five halls that had outlived the reign of Charles I. It was associated with Merton in the same way as St. Mary's Hall was with Oriel, and the two colleges in the later nineteenth century absorbed the two halls. Like all halls and colleges it had its ups and downs and at this time it had fallen, according to Cox, to "a couple or two of members resident at the same time and they generally Gentleman-Commoners, *in statu*

(*sed non aetate*) *pupillari.*"[1]   It had little to offer financially, the
Principal receiving only a salary of £148, curiously contrasting
with St. Edmund Hall's £1,000. Yet Whately returned to Oxford
from a country parish to take it on. And, says Mallet, "one of the
liveliest and most unconventional of teachers had brought new
vigour to St. Alban's Hall, which then sorely needed all the
vigour it could get."[2]

Soon Newman was able to write that the Hall was "rising like a
phoenix from its ashes"; students began to pour in, new buildings
to be needed.

To Harriett Mrs. Newman wrote happily, "I must beg you to
be ready to treat John with the proper respect due to a real
'Don' . . . were it anyone *but* John I should fear it would be too
much for his *head* or his *heart* at so early an age."

Whately having lent his rooms to the Newman family for
the Long Vacation of 1825, Newman writes to his mother of
his hope that Jemima and Mary who had just been confirmed
should receive Communion for the first time at his first celebration.
This took place at St. Clement's on August 7th.

In September he took a short holiday, visiting Bowden in the
Isle of Wight: boating, driving, playing the violin. He wrote on
his return:

I have taken bark according to Dr. Bailey's prescription for three
weeks; and this, added to my excursion, has made me so strong that
parish, hall, college and "Encyclopædia", go on together in perfect
harmony. I have begun the essay on Miracles in earnest, and think
I feel my footing better and grasp my subject more satisfactorily. I
can pursue two separate objects better than at first. It is a great
thing to have pulled out my mind. I am sure I shall derive great
benefit from it in after life.

But in later years Newman admitted that at this time he had
seriously overworked and had got from it a chronic indigestion
that lasted the rest of his life.

The next year brought a great change though no diminution
of work. Tom Mozley tells a story of how the change came about:

One morning, in 1826, Newman received a very short note from
Lloyd: "Dear Newman, step in, please, for a moment." Newman

---

[1] Cox, *Recollections*, p. 177.   [2] *History of Oxford*, Vol. II, p. 223.

thought it might be a reference or a memorandum, something lent or lost, a date or what not, and ran to Christ Church. Upon his opening Lloyd's door the Professor asked, "Newman, how old are you?" "Five-and-twenty." "Get away, you boy;[1] I don't want you," was all the explanation given, and Newman had almost forgotten it when he heard next day that Jelf had, through Lloyd, been selected for the tutorship of Prince George of Cumberland. The only restriction to Lloyd's choice was the limitation of age,—twenty-seven . . . The first consequence of Jelf's leaving Oxford was that Newman became tutor at Oriel in Jelf's place.

Newman himself does not tell this story—still less enter into Mozley's imaginations on the tremendous changes that history would have seen had Newman become "the adviser of the Court of Hanover, and of all the smaller German States" instead of leader of the Oxford Movement. It is probable he would anyhow have refused the post. He had already refused several tutorships including one with Lord Lansdowne. It was the year in which Mozley himself came up to Oxford and his letters record how he became one of Newman's pupils. "My new tutor," he says, "has been very attentive and obliging, and has given me abundance of good advice."

There was much dispute at this time as to whether the duties of a tutor were compatible with the office of a clergyman, some holding that they were derogatory to it, others that they were a matter of indifference—such as whether a clergyman were to be allowed to hunt, shoot or go to the theatre. With both these schools of thought Newman differed profoundly. To him it seemed that the office of a tutor was itself sacred—that it should involve not merely supervision of the studies of his pupils but also a true pastoral office towards them. It was as great a scope for self-devotion as the work of a missionary to which he had such a short time since thought he might be called, connecting it with his "deep imagination" concerning a celibate life.

One of the results of Oxford having been originally clerical was that still at this time there was no provision for married dons other than a few who became Heads of Colleges. A don wishing to marry must resign his Fellowship. This was good in keeping up a flow of young tutors, but it certainly had not the faintest ascetic implication. Newman, however, felt it might be made a fine and a

---

[1] In his own eyes Newman was no longer a boy. He wrote in this year "A reader and thinker must not look for a long life and half mine is gone."

lofty vocation. "To live and die a Fellow of Oriel" meant for him to live and die a missionary to youth.

At his ordination he had said, "I have the responsibility of souls on me to my dying day", and now, taking the tutorship, he was in his own estimation only leaving one kind of work for souls to undertake another. St. Clement's and St. Alban's must both do without him. Whately had offered to make his salary at St. Alban's up to the emoluments of the tutorship—however high they might be. But no, in Newman's view his college called him to duties of first importance. In his diary he wrote: "May I engage in them, remembering that I am a minister of Christ, and have a commission to preach the Gospel, remembering the worth of souls, and that I shall have to answer for the opportunities given me of benefiting those who are under my care."

The youngest of four tutors, Newman entered on his duties with an energy that might well—as indeed it did—disturb the placid surface of the established routine of college life. "The College," he says, "is filled principally with men of family, in many cases of fortune. I fear there exists very considerable profligacy among them." This was in the contemporary diary. In the *Memoir* of years later he records that he

set himself fiercely against the gentlemen commoners, young men of birth, wealth or prospects, whom he considered (of course, with real exceptions) to be the scandal and the ruin of the place. Oriel he considered was losing its high repute through them, and he behaved towards them with a haughtiness which incurred their bitter resentment. He was much annoyed at the favour shown them in high quarters.

"High quarters" meant, in particular, Tyler, the Dean of the College, of whom Newman (according to Tuckwell) said "He was a person inconsiderable in every way". Tyler connived at the keeping by these young men of a pack of beagles at Garsington. The pack became known to undergraduates as Gehazi. Tyler must have had a good sense of humour, for on one occasion he preached a sermon on Naaman in which every mention of Naaman's servant (made very frequently) produced unquenchable giggles in the gallery. He preached the sermon in town, and his vigorous and pleasing manner delighted Lord Liverpool who gave him the rectory of St. Giles in the Fields. Tyler accepted this good promotion, but, says Mozley, did so to his own life-long regret since he lost thereby the chance of the Provostship which shortly became vacant.

Newman writes presently to his mother of "hunting" two men from the college. And he did not scruple to show his feelings to the authorities as well as to the young men themselves.

The evils he was attacking become very vivid both in squibs and pasquinades and in more serious accounts of the period. Gentlemen commoners paid double fees and were allowed to complete their studies in a year less than other undergraduates. Peers, who for long were not obliged to pass any examinations, were distinguished from their fellows at first by a gold hat band, later by a gold tassel on their caps. At all times they wore silk gowns and Tuckwell remembers "the customary attendance of the young noblemen at St. Mary's in their full-dress gowns, at what were called the 'Court-days', their servants robing them at the churchgate, and, after sermon, unrobing their impatient young masters". Earle speaks of a toady as one who "was notorious for an ingle to gold hat bands"; later writers more briefly call him a "tuft hunter". In *The Lounger*, a light eighteenth-century periodical, directions are given for tuft hunting, "this form of sport so little known outside the precincts of the University ". Not expensive, like most sports, indeed often profitable, it may be engaged in all the year round with no interruption from frost. The best places "to find" are detailed and the best methods of hunting: as animals sometimes leave behind a part of their bodies when hotly pursued, so the tuft has been known to drop valuable spoil—commissions in the Army, presentations to a living. May such good luck attend all addicts of the sport!

Arnold's pupils were, like Newman, set against the species Tuft and Gentleman Commoner: T. H. Hughes in *Tom Brown at Oxford* gives a vivid picture of the demoralisation they produced in college life. Exquisite furniture, brilliant clothing, elaborate breakfasts in which figured plovers' eggs, delicately fried fish, "spitchcocked" chicken and cider cup, of which brandy was a principal ingredient, special tobacco of high price, "great wines" at which many got helplessly drunk and others drunk enough to smash their neighbours' furniture or the college windows; dogs, horses and women (the latter reluctantly mentioned by one who was writing late enough to be a Victorian), huge bills run up by obsequious tradesmen, brought many men to the verge of a ruin which money lenders were never lacking to make final. This was the class that Newman set himself against so fiercely and resolved to hunt from Oriel. He was, too, soon at logger-heads not merely with Tyler but with almost all his seniors on the question of compulsory attendance at Communion. One don being told that many of the men became actually drunk at a champagne breakfast immediately after, said, "I don't believe it, and if it is true I don't want to know it."

The changes wrought by time are of extraordinary interest to the delver into old letters. The things that were so important, the people that mattered so very much, the older men that were so revered, the younger ones barely heard of: wait a few years and all the proportions are reversed. In this year Newman's great friend was still Whately, but in a letter home he just mentions the election of Hurrell Froude to be a Fellow of Oriel. This election he saw later as one of the most momentous events in his life. Froude became not only his friend of friends but also a most powerful influence in the growth and change of his opinions. Whately he still loved, but Whately, says Tom Mozley, would not keep a friendship on the terms of an agreement to disagree. Surely this is even more true of Newman. Although, as Christopher Dawson has noted, the Tractarians were more personally charitable to their opponents than were the Liberals they were also so much more deeply concerned with the principles under dispute that they could not simply agree to differ. For the Liberal the only fundamental was personal liberty—for the Tractarian the question at issue was what God had said and what God had meant. Safeguarding this divine Word they grew fierce—and the Liberals realised so little what the fierceness was about that they took it as personal: as the result of pique, annoyance or sheer personal prejudice.

At this date, however, Newman was still Whately's disciple and wrote with profound pleasure when Whately gave generous acknowledgment in the preface to his *Logic* of the help the younger man had given him.

I cannot tell you the surprise I felt on seeing you had thought it worth while to mention my name . . . There are few things which I wish more sincerely than to be known as a friend of yours, and though I may be on the verge of propriety in the earnestness with which I am expressing myself, yet you must let me give way to feelings which never want much excitement to draw them out, and now will not be restrained. Much as I owe to Oriel in the way of mental improvement, to none, as I think, do I owe so much as to you. I know who it was that first gave me heart to look about me after my election, and taught me to think correctly, and (strange office for an instructor) to rely upon myself.

On these last words he looked back later as curiously prophetic for they seemed to indicate his passing (through Whately's help) out of the state of pupillage into what was to be one of profound disagreement with his teacher.

During the vacation he managed to fit in a visit to a friend where sea bathing greatly helped his health. "The truth must be spoken," he writes to his mother, "the air of Oxford does not suit me." But the change of work—however strenuous—did, and he writes of feeling much "the delight of having but one business. No one can tell the unpleasantness of different kinds to get through at once. We talk of its *distracting* the mind: and its effect upon me is, indeed, a *tearing* or *ripping* open of the coats of the brain and the vessels of the heart."

The first term of the tutorship had certainly brought with it considerable problems and called for considerable exertion to meet them. But Newman was not unused to exertion and he returned in October ready for anything.

We who remain are likely to have a great deal of work and responsibility laid upon us; *nescio quo pacto*, my spirits, most happily, rise at the prospect of danger, trial, or any call upon me for unusual exertion; and as I came outside the Southampton coach to Oxford, I felt as if I could have rooted up St. Mary's spire, and kicked down the Radcliffe.

CHAPTER X

Family Interlude

I THINK with constant anxiety [Newman's mother wrote to him], that you suffer from over-exertion, that I and we may enjoy comforts. Pray always bear in mind that good air and rustic entertainment will ever be perfect happiness to me, when you are all well; and that I can enjoy your society as circumstances permit. I cannot help smiling at the idea of your *selfishness*. You know, like yourself I am no flatterer; but I know though imperfectly to value the many many blessings I have always possessed, dear loved ones departed, and *dears* now possessed, who are ever desirous of sacrificing too much to me. For yourself, you were the *silent* pride of my early life, and I now look to you as the comfort and guide of my age.

She was not very old, but we can fancy her in widow's cap and gown feeling that life was over except as she might live again in her children, especially the brilliant eldest, whom she calls in one letter her guardian angel. The other two brothers were rather self-centred and opinionated: she adored them but was worried by them. Her dependence was on John in a double sense, for he had now assumed almost the full financial support of the family. For some time they had had no settled home and John clearly had hard work to persuade his mother that he was able to carry this burden. In August 1826, he wrote:

While on the subject of houses, let me say a word on a subject which I fear harasses you. Do not think about *me* and what I undertake. I think Francis and I *ought* to have a home. Again, I look upon it as a *duty* to you. Can I be wrong in doing a duty? Is it for us to look forward to the future, and *fancy* distant evils, when a duty stands before us? It is a duty to you and my sisters. I am sure it is a measure so proper and so desirable that there can be no hesitation about it. Why should I be eager to save money? may not I trust that I shall, ten years hence, and twenty, have fair health and mental powers, and (with the connections I have) can I ever be distressed while I have them? Why should my sisters be immured to the injury of their health? Nay, after all, I *shall* save. I shall have at least three

hundred *over*. Is this beggaring myself? Shouldn't I be a miser if
I laid by more?

The whole Newman family wrote incessantly to one another.
One would be staying with a grandmother, another with an aunt,
while the rest were in lodgings. Some bundles of letters (mostly
unpublished) paint a vivid family picture.

The summer vacation of 1826 found the brothers leaving
Oxford in high spirits, secure of Frank's success. Frank was to go
home first. John writes to his mother:

I hereby send to you a young person from Oxford, to whom I hope
you will be kind for my sake; his stay will be short, so I trust the favour
I ask will not be too great. You must indulge him in some things—
poor young gentleman—he has got some odd ideas in his head of
his having been lately examined, of his having been thanked for the
manner in which he acquitted himself, particularly in the mathematical school, and of a general belief in Oxford that his name will
appear in both first classes. You must not thwart him in these fancies,
but appear to take no notice of them and gently divert his attention
to other subjects . . . He is very docile, while kindly treated, and
quite harmless. Do not frighten him.

On Frank's getting a brilliant double first Mrs. Newman writes
to the elder brother: "I think I must congratulate you equally
with Frank on his success, as I suspect your anxiety on the
occasion has been much greater than even his."

Again: "It is very delightful about Frank. I am more thankful
on your account than on his. He is a piece of adamant. You are
such a sensitive being."

So sensitive that the harsh doctrine he had made his own
tormented him in his tenderest feelings. A little earlier than this
letter, a note in his diary, about his mother and sisters, runs:

O how I love them. So much I love them, that I cannot help
thinking Thou wilt either take them hence, or take me from them,
because I am so set on them. It is a shocking thought.

It was indeed and so was the feeling that long persisted with
him that God directly sent bereavements and heavy sorrows for
his correction. Yet mixed up with this was a thought not

shocking but of deep consolation which has been curiously misinterpreted by Newman's less sympathetic biographers. Again and again Newman shows his belief in a special Providence—a special fatherly care from God in the details of daily life. This idea has been treated as a proof of overwhelming pride and self-importance—that Newman should believe God was interested in the details of *his* life. But in fact he believed that God was interested in the details of every man's life: in giving good gifts to *all* his children, or in drawing out of life's evils material for yet richer good here or hereafter. The theory is not rightly to be treated as throwing a shadow on Newman's character but rather a light on the character of God.

A vivid light on the pleasantness of the relations of mother and children is cast by a phrase of Mary to Mrs. Newman: "How sorry I should be to have a mother I was afraid of. I can write *almost* as much nonsense and as easily to you as I can to Jemima."

Everything Mary writes is vivid. She was a most lively correspondent and the adored of the entire family. A few of her letters were printed by Anne Mozley but there are many more. "The receipt of your letters has perfectly ecstaticised me," she writes to Jemima. "I was very right to begin on a sheet of foolscap, for the ideas in the thermometer of my brain are rising rapidly, and I expect that if they have not room to expand they will overflow and make terrible havoc; besides the name of the paper has something congenial with their nature."

"O, I wish I could write as fast as I think," she begins one letter and it is her constant complaint that she cannot. And again:

. . . I sit down, dear Harriett, in a frenzy of delight, sorrow, impatience, affection and admiration; delight at your happiness, sorrow at your letter [Harriett had complained of headache] disappointment, impatience to see you, admiration at you all!

How much I should like to know Mr. and Mrs. Rickards! And yet, I don't know, perhaps I should be afraid; but no, I should not be afraid. O Harriett! I want to say such an immense number of things, and I cannot say one. I will try to be a little quiet; but how is it possible while Mamma is reading to Aunt your charming description of John's "ordeal"? Poor girl with a headache, poor girl —"outrageous"; sweet girl; nice girl! dear girl! Oh, what shall I begin with? Mamma's arrival on Friday quite revived me just as I was sinking in a torpid despondency.

Harriett and John were at this time at Ulcombe. Samuel Rickards, the vicar, must with his wife have been among the most delightful of Newman's friends. Young Oxford clergy often took country duty during the vacation, and Newman, with Harriett to keep house for him, had been doing so at Ulcombe. The Rickards and their children having returned, the Newman brother and sister were invited to stay on as guests. Newman writes to Jemima:

Harriett is very stingy, and dribbles out her morsels of information from your letters occasionally and graciously, and I have told her I mean to complain to you of it. I, on the contrary, am most liberal to her of my letters. And in her acts of grace she generally tells me what you and Mary etc. say in *her* words. Now it is not so much for the *matter* of letters that I like to read them as for their being written by those I love. It is nothing then to tell me that so and so "tells no news", "says nothing", etc.; for if he or she says *nothing*, still he or she *says*, and the saying is the thing. Am not I very sensible? You have received from H. such full information of our, I cannot say *movements*, but sittings, here, that it will be unnecessary for me to add anything.

Oh, [writes Mary to Jemima] I shall have to wait until this day week before I see Harriett! that seems a long time, but however I am glad that she *is* coming at all, there really seemed great danger in the case, lest she should forget which was her home . . . I suppose you mean to do the same, Miss; upon my word it is very pretty of my two sisters to leave all the fag of finding a house to Mamma and me, while they are enjoying themselves and then to return just in time to place themselves comfortably in the house which we have had the trouble of procuring! but though I say this you must not believe me, for I assure you that I like this *trouble* very much and now am watching the weather very anxiously lest it should prevent our projected expedition to Bayswater where are two promising houses, though I hardly wish them to suit because we saw one on Saturday at North End, Hammersmith, which has quite won all my "suffrages" so clean, neat, genteel and pretty.

A few days later Newman is house hunting in Brighton while Mary and his mother are doing the same around London. He writes of having "heard of a house in Regency Square" but adds "I have no sort of objection to Bayswater". Their next letters crossed . . . John wrote from Worthing where he had been "enquiring about houses" before "Bowden and I set off for the Isle of Wight which we propose circumnavigating or circumequitating."

"At Portsmouth ", he tells Harriett a little later, "we had a private room, dined on venison and cod and a bottle of port—had tea, bed, breakfast, fire in bedroom—they charged us only £1 6s."

Mary writes:

Just before we set out a letter from John came, saying that he had almost decided to engage a house at Worthing for six months—this rendered our expedition *useless*, therefore it was declined. A letter from Harriett likewise arrived—poor girl! I think her *brain is rather turned* from the style and matter—saying that she would go to St. M[ary] C[ray] on Friday and bring you home with her the next day, *lest your visit should linger on too long!* Bag! how long has *her* visit lingered?

However they go to Bayswater in case John should "alter his mind". "On Sat. (I tell you as a *secret* lest it should *frighten* less *able walkers* than ourselves) we (M and I) walked at least 10 miles! Hammersmith, Kensington, Fulham was our circuit, in and out etc. 3 houses viewed, which is very fatiguing." (A later letter tells us that it took Mrs. Newman some weeks to recover from the effects of this walk.)

On the next sheet Harriett writes a letter to Jemima, Mary puts in a piece and Mrs. Newman writes in a corner; on another Mary writes to Jemima and John adds "I have generously let her write on 3 sides and the turn down of my letter, so am pent up in this corner."

A house was found in Brighton and we may see the family from outside through the eyes of Maria Giberne who was to become a close friend. She it was who went thirty years or so later to Italy to collect Newman's witnesses for the famous Achilli trial. Her friendship began not with the eldest but with the third Newman brother. Her sister Sarah was married to Walter Mayers and Frank Newman had been helping Mayers with his pupils while Maria Giberne was visiting her sister. They were all of the body of the elect, all "saved" people who interchanged experiences and became very intimate. Frank (who incidentally had fallen over head and ears in love with her) confided in Maria his anxiety over the spiritual state of his sisters. One assumes that he feared they were *not* saved, but it is possible that other motives increased his eagerness that the young ladies should know one another. Anyhow the account written by Maria is both amusing and illuminating.

An important era in my life was now about to commence . . . November (dear month) the 6th 1826 after repeated solicitations the Newmans first set their foot in this house, and thus began a friendship which is dearer to me than life and which on my part shall last for ever I trust. When at Worton I had sent a message to Harriett about coming, and she said she would and they came altogether at dusk . . . I shall never forget the day. I did not like the looks of any but sweet Mary who so resembled my favourite Frank that I was very sorry when I found that she was not going to stay; however I resolved to like the other two since they were his sisters. I could not bear their style of dress nor their manner of talking but was determined to like them. I thought they looked so worldly, but recollected what Frank had said that he so much wished they should know us, as they had never been accustomed to religious society and he hoped we should have patience with them for they never talked much on the subject. So I resolved not to force the subject but talk on any other for I had heard they were very clever, so I think poetry amongst other things formed the topic of our conversation the first evening of their arrival. The first thing Harriett said which startled me was about beasts being annihilated when they die. I said it was so because the Scriptures said so. She said you assume it but it need not follow, or something to that purpose. This struck me as strange because it differed from the usual way in which religious people expressed themselves, but I did not like what she said, was almost vexed . . . After a few days I began to discover fresh beauties in the uncommon character of these two sisters. Their truth, their love for each other, and sympathy with each other such as existed among us concerning trifles which I had never seen before in any but ourselves, greatly endeared them to me, but on the other hand I thought them terribly reserved as I began to discover how I had been opening my mind to them and they in return never told of anything concerning themselves . . . They stayed one fortnight with us, none of the family liked them, but I saw there was something that was quite inestimable about them and though I still thought them very cool to me my affection for them increased daily . . . I felt my very great ignorance and stupidity when with them as I did when with Frank but that only inflamed my desire to form with them an everlasting friendship, the more so as in all my other friends I had always felt unknown to myself till this time a decided superiority in mental attainments. I had never contemplated it before, but here I found myself so low that I hoped through their means to improve, which I trust I have done. I called Harriett "Mother Church", because she was so strict a Churchwoman, but it never influenced me at all . . . I was greatly puzzled from not finding . . . fervour and readiness to talk on religious subjects. Any other subject they entered into readily, but this they always paused and seemed averse to engage.

Maria and Mary struck up a close and rather philosophical friendship:

I must tell you, [Mary writes to Jemima] my dream of the other night—I thought I was with you at Wanstead and the Miss Gibernes were drawing up very neatly on *ruled paper* the *tests* of *friendship*; by which we were determining to regulate our ideas. I approved entirely of their judgment in the execution, my only objection was that I feared a strict adherance to these rules might make us somewhat *mechanical* and *formal*!!! what is your opinion? Mamma expects you fully this week, but I do not know what to think. Aunt's love.

Mary was always inclined to philosophise. She quotes a letter from a cousin who "thinks me a very droll girl for asking her if she likes thinking." She speaks of a thousand "indescribable, subtle, pleasant ideas which I cannot enumerate, insinuating themselves into the bottom of my mind and making me feel as light as a balloon." She asks Jemima her opinion of

the difference between "impatient patience" and "patient impatience" I think the latter means a sort of *impotent* impatience—as to the former, I doubt; what led me to think of this was the manner in wch I waited for the different letters I expected . . . dear Jem, how clever you are! how nice you are! I do not wonder one particle of a degree at the love and admiration wch you must always attract. I only wonder at my astonishing (comparatively) insensibility—no, not that, but—I can't tell what—to it—the only reason must be because I am so used to it and in all my brothers and sisters.

In one letter she confesses to John "Whatever I write to you I am always ashamed of. I think it must be vanity; and yet I do not feel so to most others." The learning and authority of the brother of twenty-five probably seemed vast to the girl of sixteen, but after a gay letter in which she first calls him absurd and then begs his pardon for doing so Mary ends: "Well I really think I have found out the secret of my difficulty in writing to you. It is because I never told you that difficulty."

Maria Giberne's idea that the clergyman brother and his clerical friends did not constitute "religious society" is quite typical of the brotherhood of the saved. It indicates too that at least in Frank's eyes John was no longer of their company. To his mother and sisters, however, the young cleric seemed the perfect guide and I have been entertained by one letter which would seem to show that he still took life along his own lines quite as seriously as did Frank and his methodistical friends. To Harriett he writes:

As to your question about steering a middle course in mixing in general society, it is difficult to advise. I meant in my last to hint a caution concerning *parties*, mixed parties, invitations to places where there will be *many* people, a most irrational mode of spending time. If I had my will, no lady should go where she could not take her work. Do not think me silly enough to lay down any *strict* rule. I cannot bear legislating for particular cases. I am sure you will do right. I think it highly desirable that all of you should see as many persons as you can—though *not all at once*. People get contracted notions and narrow ideas by being always at the bottom of a sugar canister or sewed up in a pincushion.

Probably the last sentences of this letter would have appeared terribly worldly to the Gibernes, Mayers and Frank Newman. And what would they have felt of a letter to his mother concerning her table silver?

I write to prevent, if possible, the engraving of the additional forks you have bought, by the person who has spoilt mine. Spoilt they truly are—they came Friday; and on opening the parcel I found a huge crest, looking like a great scar upon the handles. I am quite in earnest when I say I fear I must get others. The spoons are still worse than the forks. As vulgar as you can well imagine. Like a great coachman's button.

Evidently the family opened one another's letters pretty freely, for Mary writes a warning to Jemima that Aunt's letter to their mother is *not* to be read while she assumes that in Jemima's absence Mrs. Newman will read Mary's letter to her. A letter from Mary to Jemima runs:

I have broken the seal to tell you about John: he is very well. Bowden is gazetted. John hopes to tempt Blanco White who is very musical to Brighton, besides Wilberforce and Froude! and to get an introduction to Mr. Anderson of Balliol, curate of Brighton. Mrs. A. is a very superior woman! Whately's Logic published, John mentioned in preface. Bishop of Oxford in a very precarious state. Lloyd supposed to succeed him. Do not forget Mamma's cap. If the weather will admit Mamma intends being in town on Wednesday or Thursday, but she supposes there is no chance of *inveigling you away so soon.* Cop. by desire of bish. of Ches. publish. a sermon preached Nov. 5. John to preach at St. Clements tomorrow, is in very good spirits.

The year 1827 started with severe pain from toothache. Newman underwent, he writes to his mother, "many operations", "more severe than I ever experienced ". It must be remembered that this was before the days of gas, ether, or any other anaesthetic. The letter continues:

I am sure many surgical operations would have been less painful. Two teeth were stopped up—two cut about . . . I have been nearly in constant pain since, and my face is swollen up. But the vinegar has made my nerves so much stronger that the toothache is not now the prostrating overwhelming, downthrowing, flattening pain it was to me. The pain, however, of the operation was very considerable— more especially as two of the teeth were eye-teeth—and the decayed part of a third lay close up to the nerve. In the midst of my agony the wretch had the face to murmur out, "A very ungrateful sensation this ".

All through his Oxford life toothache was to be Newman's constant companion. We learn of it chiefly through letters to Bowden at whose house in London he usually stayed for engagements at the dentist. In one letter he says, "I must come up to London for a day or two about my teeth (which I almost think will not be quiet while they exist) ".

Mary's prophecy that Lloyd would be Bishop of Oxford proved true. Newman writes to his mother when Lloyd has been installed:

The new Bishop presented himself in his wig in church last Sunday. He is much disfigured by it, and not known. People say he had it on hind part before . . . Blanco preached a very beautiful sermon at St. Peter's last Sunday. What is the matter with Jemima, so mum is she? But she is industrious. Ah, I believe I owe her a letter, so the fault is mine. Young Oakeley was elected Fellow of Balliol the other day.

A few days later:

Tell Jemima Miss M. [Miss Mitford?] is clever, but her natural-ness degenerates into affectation and her simplicity into prettiness. She is rather the ape of nature—a mimic—*ars est celare artem.* But some of her pieces are very good, e.g. the old bachelor. Tell her she has no business to say *we* are getting old. Let her speak for herself. Tell her I am quite vigorous.

And again: "We are having rows as thick as blackberries. What a thing it is to be vigorous, J., and to be dignified, H. I am so dignified it is quite overpowering. Yours ever most dutifully."

Harriett writes: "John, your quiet, sober, innocent sister Jemima amuses herself with making griffin faces in the glass like *you*." Jemima adds "I cannot deny it, but, if you like, I will make the same before your face. Will that do?"

"I have nothing to send you, dear Johnnie," she writes in another postscript, "but my love."

Mary writes to him, "How I long to see you, nice creature! I can fancy your face. There it is looking at me."

Maria Giberne's first view of John Newman accorded more with that of his college—where he appeared rather a formidable personage—than with the attitude of the home circle. Her narrative continues:

The summer of 1827 Rebecca Charlotte and Emily went to lodge at Brighton. I went down for ten days and the Newmans lived at Eastern Terrace. I of course trotted up there almost every day gener-ally with Emily and here I saw a good deal of dear Mary, the other two leaving shortly after for Ulcombe, and was first introduced to J. H. N. against whom I had taken a violent prejudice chiefly I believe from having heard that he was a stiff Churchman . . . I drank tea there with Emily the night before H. and J. left and was introduced to him which at first increased my dislike and yet I felt an excessive curiosity about him for I observed he paid not the slightest attention to me, did not seem to hear when I spoke (not to him of course) and this was so unlike what I had been accustomed to from other gentlemen that I could not make it out. However he was particularly attentive to his mother and sisters and this uncommon

Fashionable Dresses.

FASHIONABLE DRESSES

From Mary Newman's copy of The Ladies' Polite Remembrancer, 1826

circumstance first awakened a much greater interest for him than if
he had been like most other men. I conceived a great respect for
him mingled with fear before the evening was over and was half
sorry half amused that he said he would walk home with us. He did
it so simply without any fine speeches I felt exceedingly awkward
particularly at the long silences which seemed unending. He never,
I always broke them and awkwardly enough I dare say, then came
that very honest speech that quite delighted me being so uncommon.
I said near home "Do not trouble yourself to come any further for
we do not mind this short distance at all."—"Now I have come so
far I may as well go on." Not the smallest remark as most men
would have made as to the pleasure of escorting me . . . I wished
to see more of him now from curiosity but I scarcely ever spoke to
him after this . . . The November of 1827 Mama kindly asked
them again and this time sweet Mary came with H. E. N. The
former I thought particularly attractive though others to my great
annoyance would have it that she and H. were affected . . . They
talked of their brother John but I felt no interest in him for I fancied
him cold hearted reserved and dry and that I could never derive
any good from so stiff a Churchman.

It is the theory of practical people that intellect and above all
genius make men incapable of dealing with the affairs of daily
life. This is sometimes so, only because no mind can do everything
at one time and therefore profound thought produces temporary
abstraction. Absence of mind as Chesterton truly said means
presence of mind on something else. But a good mind when it is
turned on practical matters is likely to be able to handle them
better than an inferior mind. Newman was already well practised
in moving his mind from subject to subject, and we are not really
surprised to find him giving excellent practical counsel to his
mother about the second house to which they moved at Brighton.
Has she considered whether its newness may mean dampness;
if there is no back drawing-room may they not be cramped;
but if there is a back drawing-room will they be short of a bedroom; will the house be easy to let; if they are going to buy
furniture will it not be wiser to sign a three years' lease, etc.

It is not always possible to tell from what house or lodging
Mary is writing. We know that in 1827 they were established in
Brighton, but Newman took duty for Mr. Marsh at Hampstead
for several weeks and lived in the Vicarage, while the Brighton
house was let for the season. Names occur that meant much in
his life. His pupils and younger friends come to stay, and the

F

scrambling manner of living (by the standards especially of that day) produces mishaps to which the family sense of humour proves quite equal. Hampstead was not like Ulcombe—the Vicarage even proved to be dirty, and Mr. Golightly, a pupil of John's, was staying there. Mary writes to Jemima:

Poor Golightly! how we have laughed at his amusingness's, his manner is indescribable, but you know it. When John gave him a hint the evening he came of the dirt, etc. "Dear me, sir, I hope you do not mean . . . for I am such a *complete prey* to them!" then—"Dear me, Ma'am, what an extraordinary man Mr. Marsh must be!" "Dear me, how shocking!" Mama has just come up to say she must write to Harriett so I must close. John is writing to Mr. Marsh. Adieu dear Jem, I am in consternation about this house.

Poor G., [she says in the next letter], he makes us laugh as usual, [and then] Did you ever know anything like the people? Here came a letter to John yesterday from Henry Wilberforce to beg, to entreat of him to allow him to read with John! "he is very anxious to read, but he wants incitement"—"he throws himself on his benevolence" and all that; and he is very jealous of Golightly, I believe; John seemed much inclined at first, though unwillingly, to consent; but I hope and I think he will not; I am sure it would be too much for him. Bag and a half! we were going to use the lamp which is here, but I hear that *a piece has come out*, and it has *all come* to pieces! everything seems of a piece! You delight me with what you say about those Rics. pray tell me more . . . Charles is quite well, and he never scarcely comes home of an evening but we have a tremendous laugh at something that has happened absurd in the day. If you had heard them laugh the night the *malodour* was perceived in the house you never would have forgotten it. We were just going to bed, Golightly and I had both retired, when I heard such overwhelming laughter from Mama, John and Chas., as led me out of my room to inquire the cause—I had no sooner opened the door than the malaria rushing into the room answered my question. We have never told G. of this for as he was in his room at the time and left the next day, he did not discover it; I think, poor fellow, it would have completely *done* for him—such a passive sufferer I never saw, too polite to complain and yet horrified beyond measure at being such a *prey* to those animals.

Although they laughed at him Golightly clearly became intimate with the family for we find his hostess helping him to look for lodgings:

After having looked over twenty lodgings with Mamma all equally dirty and expensive, he exclaimed, "Really, Ma'am, I'm quite in despair, indeed Ma'am it's quite *awful* what they ask for them" (quite seriously).

Miss Giberne said that the Newman family impressed her by their care to say nothing unkind about anybody. In their intimate letters there is a certain amount of "quizzing", a good deal of discernment of character, but very little that could be called unkind. John laughs and makes faces, but more over those he dearly loves than over acquaintances.

Pray do not let Mrs. Ric. send those sketches to Padcombe, you will get the credit of being quizzes. Why did you scratch out "cunning Lucy is?" I'm just come from dinner. I wish you could see the faces John and I make at each other at dinner. John desires me to ask you to tell us in your next letter *every*thing you have heard about this house; . . . Does Mr. Ric. really mean to learn the piano? I read that to John, and he laughed in that impertinent, malicious way that he always does about *him*. J. was extremely amused with the sketches, he says the one of "Rickards" is like, but the head too large—Mama says the one of Cobi is "a shame"—John does nothing but laugh queerly as if he was thinking of the *originals*.

Herself at Ulcombe in 1827 Mary writes to John "What nice creatures these are. Mr. Rickards skipt into the room looking as if he were sure of being welcome and saying 'Well little girls, well ladies' and all the time seeming so self-satisfied. It is enough to make me feel glad only to look at him."
The Wilberforces—sons of the great William—are always coming in. "I am just wishing to be able to write as fast as H. Wilberforce speaks; in two minutes I should cover this sheet I am sure."

That nice little Henry W. what a nice fellow he is! has Mamma told you of his absurd impudence last Friday? I like them all better and better; and R. W. with all his quietness and gentleness, he is as bad as H. W. and worse, because he is not so honest. H. W. says, "I am impudent, I am a torment"—and he is so. R. W. says, "I am gentlemanly and timid" and he *is*—impudent and tormenting.

One would dearly like to know why

Harry has just looked up with her Ulcombe curly face and said, "Really, Robert W. has made no apology—he has used me very ill" bag! what a face of displeasure! I wish he could see it! he would not feel very much ashamed of himself; how beautiful she looks when she makes that pretty face!

And again:

Harry certainly did encourage H. W's absurdity altho' she denies it and says she scolded and told him he was impudent, but what is this but encouraging him?

We have seen that *The Lost Brooch* does not shed much light on young Mr. Newman. But it sheds a good deal on this group of girls with their work boxes and verses and duets, their fun and their gravity, their attitude to their brothers and friends and their views of life in general. Newman said that Harriett could depict a girl but not a boy. The best part of the book is the outline of the family group. But there is certainly a suggestion in Grace of the delicate high spirits, the depth yet gaiety that mark these letters, and there are flashes in "Emily" of the Mary who never fully developed her powers of wit and irony, who was growing into a character unusually blended from elements very various, even opposite.

It was a full, rich, happy life. Several of the letters are written in French, surprisingly good French for an English girl of fifteen to seventeen. Mary learnt Keble by heart ("Very diligently in dressing of a morning and other spare times"); she made her own dresses ("our claret coloured frocks have no side pieces"—she had just put the finishing touches to hers); she read widely: *Charles XII* three times, *Sketches of Russia*, Napoleon "in a multitude of volumes," *The Edinburgh Review*, *The Conscript's Bride*, *Evelina* which she thought a copy of Sir Charles Grandison—"Evelina herself is exorbitantly silly." She sang a lot; to Jemima she writes:

Oh, by the bye, I have such an excellent plan! Let me see, what time of the day shall I say—if you will sing "My pretty page" taking the *second* part and waiting for me to and fancying you hear me singing the *first*, you understand? on Friday morning at 10½ o'clock I will be doing exactly the same and singing the first part—and then, when we come to the part where we sing together! ha! ha! ha! how absurd! but mind you do so if you possibly can, for I shall most undoubtedly, and fancy you doing the same.

The one curiosity about these letters is that though Mary was so young there is no mention anywhere of schoolroom, governess or even visiting masters. Nor do we in the earlier letters find any reference to the formal education of Jemima or Harriett. Mother and Aunt saw to their "going on in a good train" when they were little children, as older girls one has the impression that they picked up culture—and quite a lot of it— as birds might pick up crumbs from their brothers' richly furnished table, from their friends and from much reading. Frank later asked a pupil he was visiting if she and her mother would like him to read aloud as he did to his own mother and sisters over their needlework.

All the sisters taught in the infant school: later Jemima and Harriett had "to train nearly 100 wild children" and Mrs. Newman writes to John of this occupation being "unfitted for delicate girls". Mary draws and "engraves"; she writes verses; she has an immense correspondence, carried on under the difficulties of quill pens, made or mended by herself— "remember it that I may hear (Oh the pen!) it when we (Oh the ink) meet (Oh my knife)."

There is a touch of Jane Austen in some of these letters, especially when the question arises of an unwelcome correspondent:

I have had a letter from Fanny this morning; she has furieusement embarrassed me, or rather, I should say, Margaret has, by announcing the intention of the latter to write to me! and hoping that I will allow her to become one of my correspondents! Would you believe it? is it not horrid? and astonishing! I should have had the pleasure of a letter from her this morning, but she is not yet well enough. If she writes what *shall* I do? I can't imagine how she can be so entirely *denuée* of *shame*. . . . Dearest, sweetest, how delightful writing to *you* is! how could I possibly write to M. Y.? what could I say? would it not be hypocrisy? undoubtedly.

Thus might Marianne Dashwood have written to Elinor, but Mary has more character than Marianne and is less prone to dream of ideal love. Her age had only brought her to ideal friendship and the light on her life was shed chiefly by the happiness of her home. "I am so happy," she writes, "and so much engaged in the past and present, that I can but find time to steal one glance of hesitating pleasure at the future."

CHAPTER XI

Preacher Before The University

WHEN FIRST publishing the *University Sermons*, Newman spoke of the book as his best though not his most perfect. On the title-page are the words: *Mane semina semen tuum, et vespere ne cesset manus tua. Quia nescis, quid magis oriatur, hoc aut illud; et si utrumque simul, melius erit.*

Unlike the *Parochial and Plain Sermons* the volume is chronological in arrangement, the first half consisting of sermons preached before the journey to the Mediterranean. Then follows a gap of over six years—the years in which the Movement was launched and developed. In those six years Newman's intellectual growth was surely gigantic.

The earlier sermons are far less developed than the later—they recall Chesterton's Note Book in which were contained the seed thoughts later so richly developed. In the Introduction of 1871 and in the footnotes, it is especially one of these early sermons that Newman himself corrects and criticises. Nor are the earlier so rich as the later which take us to the verge of his full Catholic development. The earlier sermons belong to the young Newman, still partly an Evangelical, still influenced by Whately but passing gradually under the influence of Keble and Hurrell Froude. Perhaps a passage in the sermon "Personal Influence as the means of propagating the Truth" has reference to Keble, so unassuming, so gentle, believed by Froude to be a saint.

These, perhaps, by chance fell in with their destined father in the Truth, not at once discerning his real greatness. At first, perhaps, they thought his teaching fanciful, and parts of his conduct extravagant or weak. Years might pass away before such prejudices were entirely removed from their minds; but by degrees they would discern more and more the traces of unearthly majesty about him; they would witness, from time to time, his trial under the various events of life, and would still find, whether they looked above or below, that he rose higher, and was based deeper, than they could ascertain by measurement. Then, at length with astonishment and fear, they would become aware that Christ's presence was before them; and, in the words of Scripture, would glorify God in His servant. . . .

The first of the University Sermons was the second sermon preached by Newman in St. Mary's, which was not only a parish church but also the religious centre of the University. The group of buildings forms an epitome of the religious and scholastic history of Oxford. The Congregation House, to the north-east of the Church and appearing part of it, was the earliest meeting place of the University and the home of its first library. The Church occupies the site of a Saxon Church, succeeded by an early English one. The present building is fifteenth century.

Wyclif preached before the University from the pulpit of St. Mary's. Cranmer, Ridley and Latimer were cited there for a disputation with the doctors of Oxford and Cambridge on the "presence, substance and sacrifice of the Sacrament"; here they were brought to trial, and here (on a platform the marks of which may still be seen on one of the pillars) Cranmer, discovering that all his recantations of Protestant doctrine were not going to save his life, made his final recantation of "Papistical doctrine."

Over the west door, with its Italian porch and lovely spiral columns, stands a statue of Our Lady and her Child erected by Archbishop Laud's chaplain. This occasioned so much offence to the Puritans that it formed one of the articles of the Archbishop's impeachment. It is lucky that the statue was left in place when he was beheaded.

In the pulpit of St. Mary's are delivered both University Sermons and Bampton Lectures, so that, as the "Guide to Oxford" informs the visitor, "men of the most diverse schools of thought have occupied the pulpit." Ten times every year there is a sermon by a preacher specially chosen. A solemn procession of Vice-Chancellor and Heads of Houses in their robes threading their way through the narrow streets adds solemnity to the occasion. In the "bidding prayer" before the sermon, fifty public benefactors of the University are introduced on Act Sunday and on other solemn occasions.

It was probably at Whately's suggestion that the Vice-Chancellor invited Newman, at the early age of twenty-three and still only a deacon, to preach before the University. He had at that

time refused the honour, and the first sermon in this volume was
preached on Act Sunday, July 2nd. 1826. (After this sermon, he
notes in the diary "I lay on my sofa writhing, at the thought what
a fool I had made of myself.") The Act is now known as Commemoration, and the expression "Act Sunday" has become
unfamiliar. Newman, quoting from Huber on the English
Universities, explains in a footnote the meaning of the term:

The candidate, emancipated from his teacher, makes himself known
to the other teachers by taking part in the disputations in the schools.
These services afterwards became formal public acts, *disputationes,
responsiones, lecturae cursoriae.* A more especially solemn Act formed the
close of the whole course of study. The licence was then conferred on
him by the Chancellor. A custom arose that all the final and solemn
exercises should fall in the second term of the year (hence called the
Act Term), and be closed on the last Saturday in term by a solemn
general Act, the Vesperiae, by keeping which the candidates of all
degrees in their different Faculties were considered qualified and
entitled to begin the exercises connected with their new degree upon
the following Monday. This fresh beginning (*inceptio*) took place with
the greatest solemnity, and formed the point of richest brilliancy in
the scholastic year. In Oxford it was called emphatically "the Act",
in Cambridge "the Commencement".

Commemoration had long been a time for visitors to Oxford,
especially a time for the women to rejoice in their menfolk's
triumphs, and I had liked to fancy Newman's mother and sisters
watching the procession in an ecstasy of joy over the young
preacher, marred only by anxiety about the set of his gown or
the fear that he might be nervous. Mary's delight especially
would have passed all bounds: we can imagine her trying to catch
John's eye and squeezing Jemima's hand in a frenzy of excitement.
But alas Mary's diary shows she was elsewhere in 1826, so she
never had the opportunity to hear and see her brother as Preacher
before the University. An undated letter a few years later shows
Mrs. Newman and Harriett both rather overcome by the scene
when John had them conveyed to Oxford from Iffley.

Thanks for sending the Fly [wrote his mother]. I should have lost a
great pleasure if I had been absent, such an Assembly must be to the
mere spectator an interesting and imposing spectacle, but it made
my heart beat high with many combined feelings, too deep to express.

And Harriett:

I was absurdly nervous this morning for you—and let myself be so—since I fancied there would be less for you in case you were inclined to feel so—but it is a good thing men are stouter than women for if I lived to 100 I should be frightened to preach before such a congregation—I had no idea it was so imposing a sight—but you are all used to these things which are new and affecting to others.

It is easy to picture Newman in Oxford: still easier perhaps to see the University peopled by the monks and friars and wandering scholars of a time far more remote. There is in the buildings a power to make time serve as we would have it: not as though it simply stood still, but as though in a kind of fulness it gathered experience and treasured it without loss. If time is the *nunc fluens* of man, and eternity the *tota simul* of God, Oxford surely is a little like man's life in Heaven: there is an aeviternity about it. Newman loved it, we know. What we do not know is how far his mental history was affected by those buildings, that living reality of its past held collectedly in its present. Froude and Keble were beginning the process of turning a Liberal Evangelical into a Catholic: the Fathers of the Church were benevolently assisting, but was not Oxford bearing its part in the work of development of doctrine in John Henry Newman?

Going into the Church today, trying to picture Newman in that pulpit where he was to stand so often, feeling the great waves of history that have there advanced and receded, I thought I would try something like the *Sortes Vergilianae*—as it were to sense the story that was just beginning when Newman first mounted the steps of the University pulpit. I opened first the Hymn Book and my eyes fell on a verse from Luther's "Ein' feste Burg":

> And though they take our life,
> Goods, honour, children, wife,
> Yet is their profit small;
> These things shall vanish all,
> The city of God remaineth.

It seemed to fit the man for whom the city of God was indeed the one transcending reality, but as I turned to the Psalter the page at which I opened seemed even more fully to fit the story that was about to unfold, and in which the young man now entering the pulpit was to be the chief actor:

My heart was hot within me and while I was thus musing the fire
was kindled:
And at the last I spake with my tongue.

. . . . .

For man walketh in a vain shadow and disquieteth himself in vain
He heapeth up riches and cannot tell who shall gather them
And now Lord what is my hope?
Truly my hope is even in thee.

The title of this first sermon is "The Philosophical Temper
first enjoined by the Gospel". Reference is made to the motto
of the University, *Dominus Illuminatio Mea*, and both title and tone
are more nearly akin to Whately than those of any other sermon
in the volume.

It is a striking treatment of the philosophical (what would in
some aspects have been called a little later the scientific) temper
as taught by Christianity. For Christianity first taught men to
work patiently for the common good and first inculcated a spirit
of serious enquiry into truth.

. . . It is obvious that to be in earnest in seeking the truth is an
indispensable requisite for finding it. Indeed, it would not be necessary
to notice so evident a proposition, had it not been for the strange
conduct of the ancient philosophers in their theories concerning nature
and man. It seems as though only one or two of them were serious
and sincere in their inquiries and teaching. Most of them considered
speculations on philosophical subjects rather in the light of an amusement than of a grave employment,—as an exercise for ingenuity, or
an indulgence of fancy,—to display their powers, to collect followers,
or for the sake of gain.

Christianity too first brought home to men the truth of the
operation of nature's laws. For these laws are given by nature's
Creator: heathenism supposed arbitrary interference with them
by various forces but Christianity in its teaching on miracles
assures us of a uniformity never broken save by the will of the
Law Giver—rarely exercised and always in accord with His own
higher moral governance of the universe.

Abbott has made much of the changing influences on Newman
—Mayers, Whately, Froude, Keble—and both he and Bremond
have inferred a lack of stability, a mind at the mercy of surrounding currents. Bremond has made it a point of *The Mystery*

of Newman[1] whether there was in fact a real Newman independent of these currents: he can hardly have read the *Apologia* very attentively.

The advantage of a strong mind holding a dogmatic principle is exactly that he can learn without losing. A weak mind or a mind unfortified by a principle changes opinion readily—Newman did not change, he developed. His own simile for the Church —sitting in the midst of the doctors, hearing them and asking them questions—is true in its degree of himself. He tells us in the *Apologia* of much learnt from Whately, from Hawkins, from Froude—of no positive truth unlearnt. It was a steady process of growth, and we can trace much of it both in the *Arians* and in the *Sermons before the University*.

Both books mark the period of Newman's first deep plunge into patristic reading. If the sermon on the philosophical temper is akin to Whately, that on God's Justice is far more akin to St. Augustine. There are always two currents in Newman's thought about God: overwhelming realisation of His love and His individual providence, and the equally overwhelming realisation of God's justice and man's carelessness. In an age when, for most of his listeners, a comfortable view of religion was super-added to a life of luxury, he felt keenly the need to stress this last aspect.

Thus he defended even superstition as preferable to carelessness:

. . . If our race *be* in a fallen and depraved state, what ought our religion to be but anxiety and remorse, till God comforts us? Surely, to be in gloom,—to view ourselves with horror,—to look about to the right hand and to the left for means of safety,—to catch at everything, yet trust in nothing,—to do all we can, and try to do more than all,— and after all, to wait in miserable suspense, naked and shivering, among the trees of the garden, for the hour of His coming, and meanwhile to fancy sounds of woe in every wind stirring the leaves about us,—in a word, to be superstitious,—is nature's best offering, her most acceptable service, her most mature and enlarged wisdom, in the presence of a holy and offended God. They who are not superstitious without the Gospel, will not be religious with it: and I would that even in us, who have the Gospel, there were more of superstition than there is; for much is it to be feared that our security about ourselves arises from defect in self-knowledge rather than in fulness of faith,

---

[1] This is the title of the English translation of Bremond's *Essai de biographie psychologique*.

and that we appropriate to ourselves promises which we cannot read.

With many of these sermons we have to recall the period and its dangers, so different from today. Newman dwelt on these dangers especially in this sermon on Justice, in "Contest between Faith and Sight" and in "Human Responsibility as Independent of Circumstances."

The triumph of the world is the triumph of sight over faith, it is the triumph of imagination, "of trusting the world because it speaks boldly". "The world overcomes us, not merely by appealing to our reason, or by exciting our passions, but by imposing on our imagination".

. . . This in fact is the fault incident to times of political peace and safety, when the world keeps well together, no motions stirring beneath it to disturb the continuity of its surface, which for the time presents to us a consistent and finished picture. When the laws of a country are upheld and obeyed, and property secure, the world appears to realise that vision of constancy and permanence which it presented to our youthful imagination. Human nature appears more amiable than it really is, because it is not tried with disappointments; more just, because it is then its interest to respect the rights of others; more benevolent, because it can be so without self-denial. . . . But, fairly as this superficial view of human nature answers in peaceful times; speciously as it may argue, innocently as it may experimentalize, in the rare and short-lived intervals of a nation's tranquillity; yet, let persecution or tribulation arise, and forthwith its imbecility is discovered. It is but a theory; it cannot cope with difficulties; it imparts no strength or loftiness of mind; it gains no influence over others. It is at once shattered and crushed in the stern conflict of good and evil; disowned, or rather overlooked, by the combatants on either side, and vanishing, no one knows how or whither.

To Newman the conflict between good and evil raging in the world was ever present and while it is hard to forget it in a time of stress, it is hard to remember it in a time of tranquillity and prosperity. Newman was the prophet of danger and even of doom to an over confident generation. Like Savonarola he would willingly have staged a burning of the vanities. It was only much later that he saw a better way when he wrote, after a dramatic description of Savonarola's brief triumph:

His history brings to mind that passage in sacred history, where the Almighty displayed His presence to Elias on Mount Horeb. "The Lord was not in the wind", nor "in the earthquake", nor "in the fire"; but after the fire came "the whisper of a gentle air".

So was it with the Lord of grace Himself, when He came upon earth; so it is with His chosen servants after Him. . . .

. . . When He began to preach, He did not "contend nor cry out, nor break the bruised reed, nor quench the smoking flax"; and thus "He sent forth judgment unto victory". So was it in the beginning, so has it been ever since. After the earthquake and the fire, the calm, soothing whisper of the fragrant air. After Savonarola, Philip.[1]

Bremond's *Mystery of Newman* is an exasperating book, because in it a lesser man is patronising a greater one, and also because it is based chiefly on the findings of the anti-Catholic Abbott. Reading the *Mystery of Newman* gives one a sort of shuddering fear of theorising about his self-revelations. Bremond sees Newman as identified with almost anyone he ever happened to describe or discuss: with Charles in *Loss and Gain*: with Agellius in *Callista*:

He has himself in view whenever he represents to us the heroes of his choice—the Patriarch Jacob, St. Paul, St. John Chrysostom, St. Athanasius, Theodoret, St. Philip Neri. . . . It is also well to pause in the Parochial Sermons at every mention of the Patriarch Job.[2]

This gives us rather too wide a choice—and of types so various as not to be very helpful. Yet there is surely one very definite pointer by which again and again Newman indicates his own view of his own temptations—which is found both in sermons and in letters, which agrees too with the verdict of his intimates.

The sermon on "Wilfulness the Sin of Saul" is of quite extraordinary interest in this respect. Not in the gentle weak Agellius did Newman see himself mirrored, but rather in the two Sauls—in him who became Paul and in the other who, endowed with kingly gifts and called by God to a great destiny, fell miserably at last:

. . . Those minds, which naturally most resemble the aboriginal chaos, contain within them the elements of a marvellous creation of light and beauty, if they but open their hearts to the effectual power of the Holy Spirit. Pride and sullenness, obstinacy and impetuosity

[1] *Occasional Sermons*, pp. 218-219.   [2] *Mystery of Newman*, p. 9.

then become transformed into the zeal, firmness, and highmindedness of religious Faith. It depended on Saul himself whether or not he became the rival of that exalted saint, who, being once a fierce avenger of his brethren, at length became "the meekest of men", yet not losing thereby, but gaining, moral strength and resoluteness. . . . A comparison of him in this respect with the Apostle who originally bore his name, is not perhaps so fanciful as it may appear at first sight. St. Paul was distinguished by a furiousness and vindictiveness equally as incongruous as Saul's pride, with the obedience of Faith. In the first persecution against the Christians, he is described by the sacred writer as ravening like a beast of prey. And he was exposed to the temptation of a wilfulness similar to that of Saul—the wilfulness of running counter to God's purposes, and interfering in the course of Dispensations which he should have humbly received. He indeed was called miraculously, but scarcely more so than Saul, who, when he least expected it, was called by Samuel, and was, at his express prediction, suddenly filled by the Spirit of God, and made to prophesy. But, while Saul profited not by the privilege thus vouchsafed to him, St. Paul was "not disobedient to the heavenly vision," and matured in his after-life in those exalted qualities of mind which Saul forfeited. Every attentive reader of his Epistles must be struck with the frequency and force of the Apostle's declarations concerning unreserved submission to the Divine will, or rather of his exulting confidence in it. But the wretched King of Israel, what is his ultimate state, but the most forlorn of which human nature is capable? "How are the mighty fallen!" was the lament over him of the loyal though injured friend who succeeded to his power. He, who might have been canonized in the catalogue of the eleventh of Hebrews, is but the prototype of that vision of obduracy and self-inflicted destitution, which none but unbelieving poets of these latter ages have ever thought worthy of aught but the condemnation and abhorrence of mankind.

The temptations of young men often seem in Newman's thoughts not to have the same reference as in those of the generality: not so much sensual temptations as pride, self-sufficiency, wilfulness, worldliness. One feels, studying his sermons, that for him sins of the flesh were not the main problem: his temptations were primarily of the spirit. With this agrees his saying in old age—that as a boy before his conversion he had been a devil: devils commit no sins of the flesh because they have no flesh: they are spirits and their sins are of the spirit.

CHAPTER XII

A World of Change

THE YEAR 1826 brought two men to the Oriel Common Room whose advent was to be of primary importance in the development of the schools of thought from the contest between which the Oxford Movement was born.

By the bye [Newman writes to his mother], I have not told you the name of the other successful candidate—Froude of Oriel [Robert Wilberforce was the first]. We were in grave deliberation till near two this morning, and then went to bed. Froude is one of the acutest and the clearest and deepest men in the memory of man. I hope our election will be *in honorem Dei et Sponsae suae Ecclesiae salutem,* as Edward II has it in our statute.

And again, "We have just given a diploma degree to Blanco."

Joseph Blanco White was a Spaniard of Irish descent, an ex-Catholic, a priest. In his *Life of Pusey,* Dr. Liddon declares, "Of Blanco White's positive influence it is not too much to say that he is the real founder of the modern Latitudinarian school in the English Church. Whately and Hampden were in different senses his pupils; Arnold and even Hawkins felt his positive influence, though less directly . . . It is within the truth to say that but for Blanco White's visit to Oxford, Hampden's Bampton Lectures could never have been written".

These lectures will be discussed in a later chapter. Hampden himself—also a fellow of Oriel—stood with Arnold in the public mind as the chief champion of Liberalism. In character no two men could have been more dissimilar: Hampden a shy recluse rendered miserable by the attacks he unwillingly provoked, Arnold joyous and sociable, rushing into battle on every possible occasion. Arnold was perhaps a great man, Hampden (although with greater intellectual ability) certainly a small one. A story told in Arnold's life by his great-grandson illustrates their temperaments:

It was once remarked of the family of his friend Bishop Hampden, that they were always dejected and ready to burst into tears "because Papa had so many enemies". Arnold's children on the other hand were always full of good spirits, and would often come bursting into his study with the triumphant cry, "We have another story against you, Papa!"[1]

Liddon's estimate of Blanco White's influence may be an exaggeration, but it is the exaggeration of a truth. The vague Liberalism of the Noetics became something much more definite after his walks and talks with Whately and Hampden—and with the latter he certainly discussed the lectures that were in preparation. Newman has written in his Memoir: "Fifty or sixty years ago the intellectual antagonist and alternative of the Evangelical creed was Arminianism:[2] The Catholic faith, Anglo-Catholicism, Irvingism, Infidelity were as yet unknown to the religious enquirer." "Romanism", wrote Pusey, "in our early days was scarcely heard of among us."[3] The infusion of Blanco White's scholasticism tended to clarify what many would have preferred to leave vague: Liberalism began to reveal its two chief principles, hatred of dogma and hatred of mystery.

Reading the biographies of the Liberals we see whither their minds were tending: they might differ from one another in degree or detail, but there was one underlying desire which might be phrased in the title of the book already mentioned—to render *Christianity Not Mysterious*. While Newman was pondering with increasing earnestness on the deep mysteries of the Incarnation, Arnold came to feel that the title of Christian "should be given or withheld," not on doctrinal grounds, but purely on those of "the spirit and temper of the parties alluded to." He deplored "metaphysical questions as those between Homoousians and Homoiousians."[4] Whately desired to be as much as possible rid of theological subtleties: but he was, said Blanco White, an unconscious Sabellian.

Of Blanco's own books the most important are the *Letters from Spain* and the posthumous collection of letters and diaries made by him and completed by his Unitarian friend, Mr. Thom.

---

[1] Arnold Whitridge, *Dr. Arnold of Rugby*, p. 4.
[2] A seventeenth century Dutch revolt against the ultra-Calvinist doctrines on Predestination and Election. In England the early Methodists were divided—Wesley's followers being Arminian, Whitfield's strictly Calvinist.
[3] Liddon, *Life of Pusey*, Vol. II, p. 2.
[4] Stanley, *Life of Arnold*.

From these we learn much that he wanted to tell and much also of unconscious revelation. There is charm and colour in the glimpses of a deeply Catholic people, given by Blanco almost in spite of himself. Those rosary processions at daybreak when the tinkling bell brought crowds of men hurrying to greet Our Lady before the day's work, those Mystery Plays which had since the Middle Ages brightened the daily life of town and village: innumerable popular shrines; life impregnated by a vital and colourful religion—all this is the background of a fierce attack on the Church, her superstitions, her creed, her discipline.

Blanco White loved books, and to be a student instead of a merchant he chose to become a priest. Admitted to Minor Orders at the early age of fourteen he writes disgustedly of secret revolts, of the terrible burden of the Divine Office, daily meditation, endless Sunday services. Yet he writes too: "In vain did I exert myself to check exuberance of feelings at my first Mass. My tears bedewed the corporal in which with the eyes of faith I beheld the disguised lover of mankind whom I had drawn from heaven to my hands."[1]

The Inquisition still ruled over the Spanish intellect, and side by side with profound beauty of devotion we see in these books the disastrous results of substituting suppression of false ideas for their open examination and defeat. None of the infidel literature of France or England could penetrate openly into Spain: after the French invasion Blanco discovered some worm-eaten volumes interred in the halls of the Inquisition. But meanwhile he and his friends had been reading smuggled books, and by his account atheists were to be found among the Spanish clergy.

For Newman this was a confirmation of his anti-Catholic prejudices. "There is a general impression," he writes to Harriett, "which Blanco White's book confirms, that infidelity and Romanism are compatible, or rather connected with each other."

But I doubt if the intercourse between the two men had much relation to theology. Having left Spain a declared atheist, Blanco shortly afterwards gathered together sufficient divinity to become a clergyman of the Church of England. It was as such that he was admitted to Oriel, but surely James Mozley is right in holding that he was only a theologian, as it were, by accident. He was happier far thinking of other matters, of *belles lettres*

[1] *Letters from Spain*, pp. 124-5.

especially, and it was of these that he liked to have Newman think
also. For some time they lodged in the same house and several
of his letters are included in the collection of Newman's correspondence. Starting a magazine he writes:

It gives me great pleasure to find that you consider the intended
Review almost as an Oriel cause. But you must contribute to its
success with your pen. I know how difficult it is to persuade a mind
like yours to write without preparation; but I should certainly advise
you to venture upon the strength of your *household stuff*—on the reading
and reflection of many years. Write without much concern; you are
sure to write well. Take up any book you like; imagine yourself in
our Common-Room, myself in the corner, Dornford passing the wine
etc., and tell us your mind on paper. Should you prefer a subject
connected with your daily occupations, tell us how the leading classical
writers should be read.

They played the violin together: "Listeners," says Tuckwell,
"noted the contrast between his excited bowing and Newman's
sphinx-like immobility." He had, Newman says, an exquisite
ear. One can feel this in the astonishing ease with which he could
turn the English language, which, although learnt in boyhood,
was not his native tongue.

For ink you must use the first tints of the Spring;
Your pen you should take from a Butterfly's wing;
Of Gossamer words all your Lines should be wrought,
Then beware lest you crush the whole work—with a Thought.

It is a thousand pities that he did not take his own words to
heart—for thought was not what Blanco White was best at. He
was excellently equipped with scholastic phraseology—he had
studied all those books *Ad Mentem divi Thomae* which were then
in use, doubtless he had memorized them for he was held in his
Spanish seminary to be a brilliant student. And he had the
illusion that he had grasped this majestic structure of Catholic
thought. When Newman's *Arians* was published, he wrote to
Dr. Hawkins: "The whole of what Newman has worked out for
his last publication has been quite familiar to me since my youth."
Yet read what account he gives of the doctrines he was again, but
more slowly, abandoning. Either he is deliberately distorting the
Christian doctrines of the Trinity, of the union of two natures in

Christ, of the Atonement—or he had never understood them. Much of Christianity he abandoned merely because of its supernatural character: thus he who had seen superstition in devotion to Mary came to see it in belief in the Incarnation: he who had blamed the exuberance of Spanish devotion came to have an intense dislike of the very idea of an ardent love of God. More and more he aimed at a religion that should be a mere exercise of the intellect. But in all this, though aridly, he states fairly enough the position he rejects. When it comes to deeper theology, he has, it would seem, no realisation that he is caricaturing the doctrines he attacks.

In the Oriel Common Room Newman and Whately were Blanco White's intimates. He walks with Whately one day, with Whately and Newman another, he takes tea with Newman, he plays duets, quartets, quintets with him. Yet he was ill at ease at Oxford, never able to believe he was accepted as an equal, seeing insult (says Tom Mozley) in the kindness of a Magdalen don who sent a loaf of bread daily to his lodgings because he had praised the Magdalen baker. "He knew not how to refuse it dexterously, or to accept it good-humouredly, and lived in terror of its daily advent." It must surely have been he who uttered the phrase which became a family joke with the Newmans: "What, send me jam? am I come to that, Newman?" (Whately, being richer—and also being Whately—was less touchy. Newman suggests to his mother to send him "some remembrance, a cheese or a dogfish or a barrel of oysters.") Blanco voted at Peel's election largely to prove his rights as a naturalised Englishman, was horrified to learn—accidentally—that he ranked below Probationer Fellows in the Common Room. It was all too much for him, and when his friend Whately left for Dublin, Blanco packed up and followed him.

Blanco White passed from the Oxford scene, but he had acted as a precipitate on elements already present that needed only this touch to separate and to declare themselves. Whately and Arnold avoided Unitarianism only by refusing to look at the doctrine of the Trinity. Hampden, using a form of scholastic words with much reference to Aquinas, abandoned in his Bampton lectures all but the gospel announcement of the mystery, and declared the creeds to be not only inadequate but misleading. For Newman, at this date, while Whately's was the dominant influence, Blanco too aided the dangerous drift towards Liberalism made so inviting by the Oriel Common Room. And did he not see in Blanco that very thing from which he later thanked God for shielding him—the dangers of a sceptical mind?

With the choice of Hurrell Froude as a Fellow, the College of the Noetics had gathered in the last of the four men who were to lead the Movement against Liberalism for the restoration of full Catholic dogma and worship to the Church of England: Newman, Keble, Froude and Pusey. Which of the first three did the greatest part of the work Christopher Dawson holds open to doubt. To James Anthony Froude it later appeared that " the rest were but ciphers, Newman the indicating number", but his brother Hurrell was as yet far ahead of Newman in his grasp of Catholic ideas. Perhaps because his time was to be short his development spiritual and intellectual was unusually swift. Perhaps too since Newman supremely was to wield "the iron club of dogma" against Liberalism, he needed to understand Liberals profoundly, to understand them always because for a while he had sympathised with them. He did not yet know Froude and Keble; his friends were Whately, Hawkins, Blanco White and Pusey, who in early years was half Protestant, half Liberal.

Pusey's own deep piety was drawing him towards the more Catholic-minded group, but his German friends were amazed at his later Catholic developments. He had been, they said, "stark evangelisch, ganz protestantisch."

Richard Hurrell Froude was the eldest son of Archdeacon Froude of Dartington, Devonshire. Born in 1803, educated at Eton, he was two years younger .than Newman and not, like Newman, two years ahead of his contemporaries. His father belonged to the traditional High Church Tory party; James Anthony has given us an idea of a happy home life in country surroundings, Sunday a delight, the " intensest reverence" for religion. "We had our father, our mother, brothers, sisters; and the old faces of the old servants, and the sheep and the cows in the meadow, and the birds upon the trees, and the poultry in the bushes, and the sky, and God who lived in it; and that was all. And what a beautiful all!"

Hurrell too was a devotee of nature and outdoor life. He loved to sail his own boat, he was a brilliant horseman and would as a young don take his pupils with him boating, riding, skating. Though a tutor, he was not, says Rogers who knew him well, "squeamish" in helping the young out of a scrape. "I remember climbing Merton gate with him in my undergraduate days, when we had been out too late boating or skating."

So utterly unlike an ordinary don was he that Rogers also remembered his confessing ignorance of a Greek passage and asking his best pupil to construe it. Yet too he was merciless with them against sham knowledge or any conceit and unreality. His own views were marked and unconcealed. He loved argument and would take it "as he took his fences in riding."

"He was," says Tom Mozley, "a High Churchman of the uncompromising school, very early taking part with Anselm, Becket, Laud and the Non-Jurors. Woe to anyone who dropped in his hearing such phrases as the Dark Ages, superstition, bigotry, right of private judgment, enlightenment, march of mind or progress. When a stray man of science fell back on a 'law' or a 'subtle medium' or any other device for making matter its own lord and master, it was as if a fox had broken cover; there ensued a chase and no mercy."[1]

He liked to startle and would put his thoughts in paradoxical form, but brightness, playfulness are the words most constantly used of Froude by all who came in contact with him. "That bright and beautiful Froude", says Harriett Newman. "That air of sunny cheerfulness," writes Oakeley, "which is best expressed by the French word *riant*, never forsook him." Yet "I thought", wrote Isaac Williams, "that knowing him I better understood Hamlet, a person most natural, but so original as to be unlike anyone else, hiding depths of delicate thought in apparent extravagances. *Hamlet* and the *Georgics* of Virgil, he used to say, he should have bound together."

Hamlet was not wholly a cheerful character and Samuel Wilberforce remarked in his early days, "They talk of Froude's fun but . . . I was overwhelmed with the deep sense which possessed him of yearning which nothing could satisfy and of the unsatisfying nature of all things." This was the side known before his death only by the slightest of hints, only to his most intimate friends. A man of intense reserve, he had been deeply moved by two influences—the posthumous reading of his adored mother's journal and the friendship that grew up with Keble at a reading party under his direction. In his mother's journal Froude found both prayers for himself and the record of difficulties experienced by her that were similar to his own. He would read the journal

[1] Mozley's *Reminiscences*, Vol. I, p. 227.

for hours at a time, it "sends me back", he notes, "to her in my childhood; it gets such a hold of me that I can hardly think of anything else."

Of the time spent with Keble much is said by Isaac Williams in his Autobiography and much may be read in Froude's own letters to Keble. Williams has related how Keble's sanctity became to both men a source of deep reverence. Neither cared much for *The Christian Year* which was then in the making, and Froude told Keble so with complete frankness. "There is something I should call Sternhold and Hopkinsy in the diction." One must believe in the saintliness of a man who accepted such criticism from a pupil! And in fact Keble became for Froude far more than a tutor—a spiritual father and an inspiration, although his dislike for "sawniness" (his word for sentimentality) forbade Froude to speak in the glowing terms used by Isaac Williams.

Keble was not resident in Oxford when Froude became a Fellow, and Froude was slow in his advances towards Newman. Immediately after his election he wrote prophetically, "He is to my mind by far the greatest genius of the party, and I cannot help thinking that some time or other I may get to be well acquainted with him."[1] But in a later letter: "He is a fellow that I like the more, the more I think of him; only I would give a few odd pence if he were not a heretic."

From Newman himself we shall learn later how much of his Catholic development he owed to Froude, while Froude on his side claimed to be like the murderer who had done one good deed in his life—he had made Newman and Keble understand one another.

As we have seen, Newman spent part of the Long Vacation of 1827 at Ulcombe. Mrs. Rickards wrote of trying to make John

idle enough to rest himself; for we think his looks bespeak that he has been reading too hard. If he improves in looks at Ulcombe, how delightful it will be! . . . And now here is John come to keep me company, or rather to be plagued by the children. I wish you only could see him with both on his lap in the great armchair, pulling off and then putting on his glasses. They are quite overjoyed to see him.

But the time at Ulcombe was not long enough, and he returned to Oxford unrestored. "We have not neglected," he writes to

[1] Hurrell Froude: *Remains*, Vol. I, p. 199.

Mary, "to take prodigious walks", but he complains in the same letter of being "lazy" and "rather stupid".

It was of course the usual story with him of over-work, and a month later comes a note in his diary, "Taken ill in the schools while examining, was leeched on the temples". As an undergraduate Newman had fainted from overwork, this attack was similar but more severe.

In his diary he describes his state as

a confusion, an inability to think or recollect. Once or twice indeed, when my head was on my pillow, I felt a throbbing so distressing, though it was not violent, to make me sensible I had never experienced a real headache. It was not pain, but a twisting of the brain, of the eyes. I felt my head inside was made up of parts. I could write verses pretty well but I could not *count*. I once or twice tried to count my pulse, but found it quite impossible; before I had got to 30 my eyes turned round and round and inside out, all of a sudden.

This was the illness which in the *Apologia* he classes with bereavement in its effect upon his life.

I was beginning to prefer intellectual excellence to moral: I was drifting in the direction of Liberalism. I was rudely awakened from my dream at the end of 1827 by two great blows—illness and bereavement.

Maria Giberne tells the story of the bereavement which followed so soon after. She went in January 1828 to stay with the Newmans at Brighton.

. . . Dear Mary ran down stairs to meet us and was most affectionate and kind as were the others but not so warm in their manner. As she hung over me that evening she was telling me she hoped I would assist her in drawing etc., expressing the pleasure she felt at my coming to stay there. The next day, Friday, she complained of a pain in her chest. . . . At dinner she felt so ill as to leave the table and that was the last time I saw her alive. . . . Mr. Woodgate and Mr. Williams were dining there, and I was beginning to admire Mr. Newman with astonishment; that very day he said some things at dinner showing a great mind but not of a religious character. Jemima soon followed Mary and after dinner the mother left and returned with a countenance full of alarm and anxiety—saying, "John, I think we must send for Dr. Price. Mary is very ill."

Miss Giberne herself had had toothache and in the morning, hearing that Mary, though weak, was now free from pain, she went to have the tooth extracted. The instrument broke and she returned with the tooth still there and in great discomfort.

When no one appeared but J. H. N. and he as pale as ashes ushering us into an empty parlour saying, "Will you come in here," my heart sank within me and I felt like a stone. . . . J. H. N. offered us chairs and leant himself against the table facing the fire, I see him now, his serious face, eyes fixed on the fire, his cheek deathly pale, his lips firmly closed except when speaking to prepare us for the sad truth, they quivered, his hands crossed and closed, his whole deportment showing a frame under perfect control of a high toned manly mind and yet my eyes were not opened. After telling us a good deal about her he said the Doctor said she could not live beyond the morning.

Slow to understand Maria asked Newman to pray with her, hoping, as she rather quaintly says, that he would thus show signs of a religious character.

He then with an effort over himself said, "I must tell the truth . . . she is gone already." . . . He kindly fearing the tidings would be too much for me begged me to sit down, kept his own feelings in, told us a little detail of this sad event and then thinking only of our comfort wished us good night.

The Gibernes went to stay with other friends but Maria returned daily to make a last sketch of Mary.

One day John came up to look at my drawing and while standing by the coffin I cannot forget the tone of these few words, "It's very like." All this time I grew fonder and fonder of them all even John and this seeing him such a noble character first made me think other than Evangelical people might be bearable.

At the funeral she notes: "I thought as I looked at John who seemed like a walking corpse, 'You will be the next'."

In a letter long years after to Newman himself she says: "You told us a little about her, with gasping sobs in your voice, and then you left us."

In the letters that follow we hear sometimes those gasping sobs, but more often there is a sense of Mary's being now one

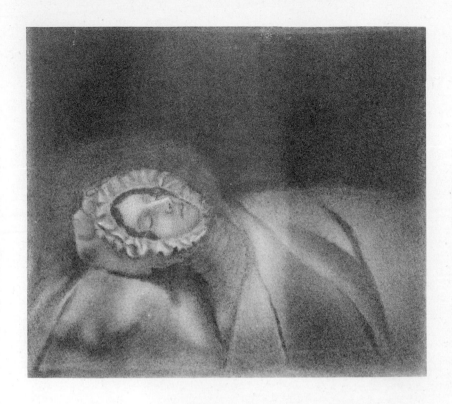

MARY SOPHIA NEWMAN AFTER DEATH
(by Maria Giberne)

of those angelic presences of which he was always so keenly aware. He sees her form hidden behind the beauties of Nature, coming to his side in dreams. "Dear Mary seems embodied," he writes to Jemima in May, "in every tree and hid behind every hill. What a veil and curtain this world of sense is! beautiful but still a veil." And months later, "Her form is almost nightly before me, when I have put out the light and lain down. Is not this a blessing?"

One of the best known of Newman's poems, "Consolations in Bereavement," was written three months after Mary's death:

> Death was full urgent with thee, sister dear,
>   And startling in his speed;
> Brief pain, then languor till thy end came near:
>   Such was the path decreed,
>   The hurried road
> To lead thy soul from earth to thine own God's abode.
>
> Death wrought with thee, sweet maid, impatiently;
>   Yet merciful the haste
> That baffles sickness;—dearest, thou didst die,
>   Thou wast not made to taste
>   Death's bitterness,
> Decline's slow-wasting charm, or fever's fierce distress.
>
>   *   *   *   *   *
>
> Death came and went: that so thy image might
>   Our yearning hearts possess,
> Associate with all pleasant thoughts, and bright
>   With youth and loveliness.
>   Sorrow can claim
> Mary, nor lot nor part in thy soft soothing name.
>
> Joy of sad hearts and light of downcast eyes!
>   Dearest thou art enshrined
> In all thy fragrance in our memories;
>   For we must ever find
>   Bare thought of thee
> Freshen our weary life, while weary life shall be.

Chapter XIII

The Peel Election

THROUGH illness and through sorrow the business of life has to go on. Pusey had returned to England in a bad state of health and was staying at Brighton near the Newmans. In a letter suggesting that his mother should "send her card and he will call" Newman speaks of Copleston's bishopric and adds "Shall we have a new head or not? Which will be best, Keble or Hawkins?"

Acknowledging Mrs. Newman's "obliging present" (was it a dogfish or a barrel of oysters?) Pusey says "Should there be a difference of opinion as to the successor, it is a satisfaction to agree with J.N."

Newman wanted Hawkins. He thought he knew his mind and that they would be of one opinion as to the government of the college. When Froude urged on him that Keble if elected "would bring in with him quite a new world, that donnishness and humbug would be no more in the college, nor the pride of talent, nor an ignoble secular ambition", Newman "answered with a laugh that, if an angel's place was vacant, he should look towards Keble, but that they were only electing a Provost".

A delightful interchange of letters followed between Newman and Keble. Newman explained his own admiration for Keble but his belief in Hawkins for this special job. "It is ungracious to go on", for "you could easily be made to believe anyone alive was more fit for the Provostship than yourself". Keble replied that Newman's knowledge of Hawkins was "enough to prevent anyone with a spark of commonsense in his head from being hurt at your preference of him."

Keble withdrew his candidature and it was many months before Newman began to doubt whether Hawkins and himself were so entirely of one mind as he had believed. Not merely in the beginning but for a long time Provost and tutors worked in complete harmony. This seems surprising if we compare Newman's attitude—to social rank for example—with that of Hawkins, described by Tuckwell from the memories of "old Orielites". Hawkins, they declared, made a custom of giving "one finger to a Commoner, the whole hand to a 'Tuft'" so that he was greatly embarrassed when Mr. —— went down one term to come back as Lord —— of ——. Another story is pleasant: that an Oriel undergraduate took to preaching in St. Ebbe's slums and was angrily inhibited by the Provost. "But Sir," he said, "if the Lord Who commanded me to preach came suddenly to judgment what should I do?" "I," said Hawkins, "will take the whole responsibility of that upon myself."

He would grant an exeat during term time only in very special cases. A man begged leave to absent himself in order to bury his uncle. "You may go," was the reluctant permission: "but I wish it had been a nearer relation." His high and dry churchmanship made him impartially intolerant. Of the Newmania he always spoke as "the late unhappy movement", nor was he less severe upon *Essays and Reviews*, not perceiving that their teaching sprang lineally from that of his own Noetic brethren. . . . When Jowett was bitten by a Balliol dog, and the culprit was expelled from the College, the joke went round that Hawkins had received the animal and tenderly entertained it.[1]

Hawkins had been Vicar of St. Mary's which included in its parish the village of Littlemore, about three miles from Oxford. To this position Newman succeeded. Several important dates are briefly noted by him:

March 9 [1828]—Did duty at St. Mary's in the afternoon and preached.
March 23—I read in—i.e., read the Thirty-Nine Articles.
March 27—Disputed with Arnold for B.D. degree, Provost presiding.
March 28—Dined with Provost to meet Arnold.

How far are we from the Movement in atmosphere although only five years in time. Newman undertook the disputation "merely to keep Arnold company, since one man cannot dispute with himself."

Newman's health had forced comparative quiet upon him but it was never more than comparative. Work in the parish; work with his pupils; much reading and writing; a series of catechetical

---

[1] *In Praise of Oxford*, Vol. II, p. 469.

evening lectures at Littlemore; the weekly preaching at St. Mary's and a Sermon as Whitehall preacher; the arranging of his letters (348 since August 1826); the start of a fortnightly dining club of which the "fundamental rule is to have very plain dinners", and the aim of which was to draw together men from different colleges; the College Bursarship—all these matters are mentioned casually in 1828. Dr. Copleston, now Bishop of Llandaff, writes that year "It is well that Oriel has so good a treasurer as yourself." And a year later Dr. James says "Two hundred pounds and possibilities is good gifts . . . If you were to treat us so every year I shall vote that you be made perpetual treasurer".

But Newman, obliged to refuse a visit to Bowden—"a pleasure which I would put second to no other that could be mentioned"— emphasises the trials of this "most odious Bursarship." Oxford tradesmen, Anne Mozley tells us, were amazed at the despatch with which he cast up accounts and paid their bills, but efficiency is seldom painless. The office, Newman continues, "besides teasing me by an inconceivable number of little businesses in Term-time, has hitherto tied me especially to this place in Vacation as the only leisure time for its greater duties. It is very well to have such business, when it is one's main business, but as a business by the way it is insupportable. It has, I believe, been more than anything else the cause of my continued indisposition."

The quiet months from Mary's death to the beginning of the following year were followed by perhaps the most surprising incident in Newman's life, his one whole-hearted (indeed hot-headed) intervention in a political election.

Through all that first quarter of the century, the question of Catholic Emancipation filled the horizon, especially as it affected the right of a Catholic to a seat in Parliament; Catholics were kept out by the necessity of taking a Protestant Oath. The Liberals were for Emancipation, the Tories under the Duke of Wellington and his Home Secretary Robert Peel (since 1817 member for Oxford University) were against. When, in 1828, the Catholic Daniel O'Connell was sent to Westminster as member for Clare the moment had come. Hating Catholic Emancipation as much as ever, Peel concluded that the alterna-tive was civil war in Ireland: he persuaded Wellington, and with endless trouble they persuaded George IV. The Bill was brought into Parliament. Peel felt bound, after so complete a reversal of the policy on which he had been elected, to resign and offer himself anew. The University found itself faced with a by-election.

The result of his action was a sudden outburst of electioneering, in the course of which some curious shifts of position were seen. Hawkins led the fight for Peel's re-election: the whole Liberal Group to which Newman had so far belonged were for him. Pusey was for him. Newman took the other side. His letters home must be quoted to convey the atmosphere of those days.

February 17, 1829.
Peel resigned; Ch. Ch. [Christ Church] *gave him up.* This was a great thing, and among others I exerted myself to gain it. Unluckily our meddling Provost [Hawkins] just then returned from London, where Oxford men, being chiefly Liberal lawyers, were for Peel. He joined the Merton men—Whately,[1] Shuttleworth, Macbride, etc.— in nominating Peel. He suddenly formed a committee in London, and—vigorously employing the Ch. Ch. interest, which Ch. Ch. had precluded itself from using—began an active canvass. The party opposed to Peel's re-election consisted of all the College Tutors and *known* resident Fellows in Oxford; but they agreed in one point, only differing in their view of the Catholic question, but all thinking Mr. Peel unworthy to represent a religious, straightforward, unpolitical body, whose interest he had in some form or other more or less betrayed. Besides, they thought it an infamous thing if Oxford was to be blown round by the breath of a Minister, signing a petition one day and approving of the contrary the next. . . . The great Captain, wise as he is, has thought the Church and Oxford his tool—and that we should turn round at the word of command. When Oxford is spoken of, the *residents* are always meant. Oxford, by seventy residents, has rejected Mr. Peel, and, if it elects him, elects him by non-resident lawyers.[2] It is said we shall all be in great disgrace, and that certain persons have ruined their chances of promotion. Well done . . . the modest Keble has come forward with a paper of questions against Mr. Peel, signed with his own fair name . . . Pusey is against us, thinking Peel an injured man, and us hot-headed fellows.

His mother and sisters, knowing Hawkins and Whately as Newman's best friends, were naturally startled. A few days later he writes: "I will tell you why the Provost is 'meddling'— because when Ch. Ch. had *resigned* Peel, he chose to turn the

[1] Alban Hall was an appendage of Merton College.
[2] Every holder of an M.A. degree if he leaves his name on the books of his college has a right to vote whether resident or not.

opposition to him, without inquiring, into a *cabal*; and suddenly got up an opposite party without speaking to any of us (i.e. the Oriel Common-Room) on the subject, and brought clamour and faction in."

Newman's next letter to his mother is a song of triumph:

March 1, 1829.

We have achieved a glorious victory. It is the first public event I have been concerned in, and I thank God from my heart both for my cause and its success. We have proved the independence of the Church and of Oxford. . . . The "rank and talent" of London came down superciliously. . . . They would make use of their suffrage, as members of the University, to degrade the University. No wonder that such as I, who have not, and others who have, definite opinions in favour of Catholic Emancipation, should feel wé have a much nearer and holier interest than the pacification of Ireland, and should, with all our might, resist the attempt to put us under the feet of the Duke and Mr. Brougham.

Their insolence has been intolerable; not that we have done more than laugh at it. They have everywhere styled themselves the "talent" of the University; that they have rank and station on their side I know; and that we have the inferior colleges and the humbler style of men. But as to talent, Whately, with perhaps Hawkins, is the only man of talent among them; as to the rest, any one of us in the Oriel Common-Room will fight a dozen of them apiece—and Keble is a host; Balliol too gives us a tough set, and we have all the practical talent, for they have shown they are mere sucking pigs in their canvass and their calculations. Several days since, their London chairman wrote to Mr. Peel assuring him of complete and certain success. They strutted about (peacocks!) telling our men who passed through London that they should beat us by eight to one, and they wondered we should bring the matter to a poll. . . . Well, the poor defenceless Church has borne the brunt of it, and I see in it the strength and unity of Churchmen. An hostile account in one of the papers says, "High and Low Church have joined, being set on rejecting Mr. Peel."

I am glad to say I have seen no ill-humour anywhere. We have been merry all through it.

The defeat made no difference to Peel's parliamentary career. A few days later he was elected for the close borough of Westbury. Two days after that he proposed Catholic Emancipation in a four-hour speech in the House of Commons. The bill was, in due course, passed.

With all Newman's powers of expression, he does not manage to tell us why he felt such a frenzy of excitement about the need to defeat Peel. It was not because Peel stood for Emancipation. Newman's own attitude on the subject was exactly like Peel's. In the first place he thoroughly disliked the Catholics. In 1827, while refusing to pronounce against Emancipation, he wrote: "At the same time I must express my belief that *nothing* will satisfy the Roman Catholics. If this be granted, unquestionably they will ask more", and in 1829 he expresses the fear that Emancipation would endanger the Irish Protestant Church. But he thought it inexpedient, perhaps impossible, to oppose it. A year or so before the election he had been against a Petition calling upon Parliament to reject it—this, as he tells us in the *Apologia*, on two grounds: first, he had been reading a work (attributed to Whately) on the necessary separation of Church and State: second, he "shrank from the bigoted 'two-bottle Orthodox' who formed the main opposition to the Catholic claims".

But if Emancipation was not the point at issue, what was? Peel had acted with the strictest correctness in resigning (which he was under no legal obligation to do) and re-offering himself to his constituents. By returning him to Parliament the University would be reversing the stand it had recently taken against Catholic Emancipation—but it seems strong language to describe this as "an infamous thing if Oxford is to be blown around by the breath of a Minister, signing a petition one day and approving of the contrary the next".

His family were still puzzled, still pressing him to explain. In a not very coherent letter to Harriett he tried to make his reasons clearer: "It is rather too much that Mr. Peel's change is to be sheltered by our change, and that we are to whitewash him by our own disgrace"—this because "Oxford has never turned with the turn of fortune." Further "I am anti-Catholic in principle—i.e. I think there is a grand attack on the Church in progress from the Utilitarians and schismatics—and the first step in a long train of events is *accidentally* the granting these claims." But at the end of the letter he feels that he has not done his position justice.

Writing about it in the *Apologia* thirty-five years later, Newman says that he "took part against Mr. Peel on a simply academical, not at all on an ecclesiastical or political ground: a great University ought not to be bullied even by a great Duke of Wellington".

Looking back upon all this, it is curious that he did not see, or at least did not say, that youth was a very operative factor in the whole matter. He was twenty-eight, Hurrell Froude twenty-six, Wilberforce about the same age. Have not we all seen in a young group some practical issue handled in this excited over-wrought fashion? The other side have brought in outsiders, have failed to consult their friends, are electioneering, are getting at people, the skies will fall if they are not defeated.

When the smoke of battle cleared away changes might be seen at Oriel. Whately's "humorous revenge" on Newman is described in the *Apologia*. He invited to dinner all the dullest men of the University, those fondest of port, the "two-bottle orthodox" and placing Newman between Provost This and Principal That asked him if he was proud of his friends. He saw more clearly than Newman that it was the parting of the ways between them.

Newman says in the *Apologia* that he was at this time under the influence of Keble and Froude. Naturally enough he does not trace this in detail, but we can imagine how the visit (recorded in a letter) to Keble's country home, how the endless talks with Froude, had been working on him during the past three years. To my mind we see it especially in the curious identification between Conservatism and Churchmanship so much more natural to men of their antecedents than of his. Thus, though Emancipation may be expedient, it is "carried by indifference and by hostility to the Church", is "an alteration in our constitution" and "will endanger the Irish Protestant Church", perhaps lead to disestablishment in England.

Far more original, far more characteristic, are the thoughts on tradition (in which Newman comes near to de Bonald) and on the workings of the fallen human intellect on which he dwells in a letter to his mother, when the heat of the conflict is two months behind him and the young politician has once more given place to the philosopher:

. . . What a scribbler am I become! But the fact is my mind is so full of ideas in consequence of this important event, and my views have so much enlarged and expanded, that in justice to myself I ought to write a volume.

. . . We live in a novel era—one in which there is an advance towards universal education. Men have hitherto depended on others, and especially on the clergy, for religious truth; now each man attempts to judge for himself. Now, without meaning of course that Christianity is in itself opposed to free inquiry, still I think it *in fact* at the present time opposed to the particular form which that liberty of thought has now assumed. Christianity is of faith, modesty, lowliness, subordination; but the spirit at work against it is one of latitudinarianism, indifferentism, and schism, a spirit which tends to overthrow doctrine, as if the fruit of bigotry, and discipline—as if the instrument of priest-craft. All parties seem to acknowledge that the stream of opinion is setting against the Church. . . .

. . . It is no reply to say that the majesty of truth will triumph, for man's nature is corrupt; also, even should it triumph, still this will only be ultimately, and the meanwhile may last for centuries. Yet I do still think there is a promise of preservation to the Church; and in its Sacraments, preceding and attending religious education, there are such means of Heavenly grace, that I do not doubt it will live on in the most irreligious and atheistical times.

The enemies of the Church, he considers, are

. . . the uneducated or partially educated mass in towns . . . who are almost professedly deistical or worse, the Utilitarians, political economists, useful knowledge people . . . the Schismatics in and out of the Church . . . the Baptists, whose system is consistent Calvinism . . . the high circles in London.   I might add the political indifferentists, but I do not know enough to speak, like men who join Roman Catholics on one hand and Socinians on the other. . . . And now I come to another phenomenon: the talent of the day is against the Church. The Church party (visibly at least, for there may be latent talent, and great times give birth to great men), is poor in mental endowments. It has not activity, shrewdness, dexterity, eloquence, practical power. On what, then, does it depend? On prejudice and bigotry.

. . . This is hardly an exaggeration; yet I have good meaning and one honourable to the Church. Listen to my theory. As each individual has certain instincts of right and wrong antecedently to reasoning, on which he acts—and rightly so—which perverse reasoning may supplant, which then can hardly be regained, but, if regained, will be regained from a different source—from reasoning, not from nature—so, I think, has the world of men collectively. God gave them truths in His miraculous revelations, and other truths in the unsophisticated infancy of nations, scarcely less necessary and divine. These are transmitted as "the wisdom of our ancestors" through men—many of whom cannot enter into them, or receive them themselves—still on,

G

on, from age to age, not the less truths because many of the generations through which they are transmitted are unable to prove them, but hold them, either from pious and honest feeling (it may be), or from bigotry or from prejudice. That they are truths it is most difficult to prove, for great men alone can prove great ideas or grasp them. Such a mind was Hooker's, such Butler's; and, as moral evil triumphs over good on a small field of action, so in the argument of an hour or the compass of a volume would men like Brougham, or, again, Wesley, show to far greater advantage than Hooker or Butler. Moral truth is gained by patient study, by calm reflection, silently as the dew falls —unless miraculously given—and when gained it is transmitted by faith and by "prejudice".

CHAPTER XIV

The Three Brothers

THE WORD Littlemore has venerable associations; we think of Newman's long period of waiting: of the *Essay on Development*: of Father Dominic. But Littlemore was associated with Newman long before Newman was associated with those things— and not with him alone but with his family. As we have seen, it was part of the parish of St. Mary's of which Newman became Vicar early in 1828. His mother and sisters came to live at Iffley close by for lack of a suitable house in Littlemore itself. Iffley is even then talked of as Oxford in some of their letters, and they went into the University for Newman's lectures and sermons. To see the family relations as a whole at this period we must, I think, retrace our steps and glance at the budget of letters from Mary's death (1828) to Newman's departure for Sicily in 1832. Of some of these letters Newman copied extracts and destroyed the originals. This is a pity both because we lose "munitiae" that might today be interesting, and we lose vividness—by the omission especially of Mrs. Newman's capitals and italics.

A death often seems to draw the survivors more closely together, and the family letters after the loss of Mary are even more intimate and tender than before. Especially to Harriett, John writes with deep affection combined with that religious note which (Maria Giberne nothwithstanding) always permeated their intercourse.

November 23rd, 1828.

It is Sunday evening—the duties of the day are over, and I am by myself. Can I raise my mind more entirely upwards than by writing to you? For I hope we are each associated with each by ties not of this world. Home has the memory of too many trying events to inspire a merely earthly pleasure. What confidence can I have, or you, or any of us, that we shall continue blest in each other's love, except as we are members of Him whose life and rule belong to another world?

Harriett, he says, being nearest his own age, and most like him in character, can best enter into his thoughts and feelings.

Even more than Mary and Jemima are they united. "No
calamity, I think, could occur to me here so great as to lose your
love and confidence".

He visited them again at Brighton, more than once going on
horseback, having a minor accident on one journey through
"musing" too much while riding, walking as much as fifteen
miles in the day to spare his horse Klepper. Between the visits
a lively correspondence is maintained. Harriett writes him fiery
letters about the Brighton clergy: "Do you know that owl
(O for shame) talked in his sermon on Sunday of 'the softer
sex'?"

In the next letter she asks, "Pray, who is 'Miss Minx'? Who
is 'Miss Spitfire'? I cannot but shrewdly suspect you mean me,
you old wretch . . . you do not know how cautious I am, Mr.
Worldly Wiseman—though I do not pretend to rival you, and
at best can only be Miss W. W."

And after another visit:

It was very good of you to write such a nice (nice for you), long
(long for you) letter immediately on your return. . . . I am ashamed
of your letter, which was certainly penned with the quill of a wild
goose. I long to expose you, and to read it to some of the sober folk
here who are so deluded still with the belief of your wisdom.

To Jemima, John writes much about the music for his church.
There is one indignant letter:

Mr. Gould, who is perhaps somewhat conceited . . . not only
disapproves of the Chant we fixed on, but attempted to convict me of
making discords and mistaking keys in certain alterations I suggested,
and lastly suggested a dull melody which I cannot approve of.

Brighton did not suit Mrs. Newman very well, and the girls
also were tried by the harshness of the winters. (One rather
shudders at reading of the remedies applied for the mother's
inflammation of the chest—besides being leeched, she was twice
bled with the lancet.) Then too, they wanted to be together,
and John needed help in the parish at Littlemore.

My mother [he writes retrospectively of the cause of their move]
complains in one of her letters that there were no steam carriages,

little thinking there were soon to be. And another [reason for moving] was a wish not to ask of me so great a contribution to their income, now that I had lost the Tutorship, as the Brighton house required. So they came to me nearer and nearer, first stationing themselves at Horspath, then at Nuneham, then at Iffley.

At first they still kept their house at Brighton though on the move towards Oxford. During the long vacation of 1829, Newman rode every day to Horspath for dinner, returning to Oxford next morning. Henry Wilberforce had lodgings close at hand. Blanco White came over for music, "Woodgate's piano" having been sent to Horspath. Quintets in which Blanco White and Newman both performed are often mentioned. The weather though uncertain was "excellently well adapted for enjoyment". Just occasionally he got wet through, but on the whole enjoyed the daily rides and spent four to six hours of his day at Oriel "discovering arrears". Probably this means arrears of work, but possibly of money, since he was working on the college accounts. He wrote to Froude about pupils, saw friends passing through Oxford, arranged his papers and read some history—finding the times of James I and Charles I rather like the present, but adding "all times may be like all times for what I know". He wanted a Curate for Littlemore where he was trying to have a chapel, and proposed it first to Wilberforce, next to Froude. It was ultimately accepted by Isaac Williams.

A pleasant glimpse of their relationship is given in the letters Williams writes after Newman had thanked him for staying at his post when cholera was in Oxford:

. . . But you know, my dear Newman, you have yet to learn how to be a vicar, or you would see the impropriety of saying to a curate, "I am obliged to you for staying," for it is my business to be here always.

(His relations with his curates seem to have been of the easiest. According to Ffoulkes, who was one of them, Newman would say to a man quite casually "You be my curate" and the man would last a year or two—till the work proved too much. He often paid his curates more than the parish paid him).

Newman finds the Fathers go too slowly amid all his occupations. He doubts if the beauties of Froude's home are greater

than "the inland Shotover. . . . I never saw tints half so enchanting". "It was," says Anne Mozley, "a harmonious period that
might well live in the memory of all concerned in it, and perhaps
raise gloomy contrasts as time went on".

The harmony between the brothers grew steadily less. Francis
Newman was branching off into rather curious religious views
of his own. "I have had a delightful letter from Frank", writes
Miss Newman shortly after Mary's death, "half full of our
beloved Mary, and the other half on the Millennium."

This letter probably came from Ireland where Francis was
for eighteen months tutor in a Dublin family and where his
religious views became even more pronounced through the
influence of an interesting personality—John Nelson Darby,
founder of a sect known at first as Darbyites and later as Plymouth
Brethren (Darby later lived at Plymouth). In Ireland Frank
Newman met this man at the house where he was tutoring.
Darby had been living in a primitive hut, evangelising "the
Romanists", half-starved and self-neglected he had become "a
cripple on crutches, with fallen cheeks, a bloodshot eye, seldom
shaven beard and a shabby suit". He looked "like a monk of
La Trappe" and powerfully affected Frank, both in his "strivings
after a more primitive form of Christianity" and in the desire
for Church disestablishment in Ireland. The association of the
Protestant Church with the State was in Darby's eyes a chief
bar to spreading the gospel among the natives! Frank Newman
liked Romanists no better than did his brother, but he became
convinced that justice demanded their admission on equal terms
to Parliament, found arguments for this in St. Paul's epistles,
and "looked with amazement and sorrow at spiritual Christians
who desired to exclude the Romanists from full equality."[1]

Thus while John Newman was at once becoming more Catholic
and fighting against Emancipation, Frank was becoming more
Evangelical and contending for it! He returned to England having
planned to go on a Missionary Expedition to Persia with one of his
Irish friends and a small group who perhaps were not yet a sect
but certainly very near becoming so. Frank says himself that
anticipating that he would be ordained for the Church of England,
his brother made use of him at Littlemore in 1826. This is, of
course, impossible: it could have been in 1829, but one feels that

[1] See John Henning, "Cardinal Newman's Brother in Ireland" in *The Irish Monthly*,
May 1947.

if so the elder brother must have felt very anxious as to what sort of teaching Frank would give when he was allowed "to call on and look after the poor people at Littlemore." I think myself that Frank, writing as an old man, confused two things—that it *was* in 1826 but at St. Clement's not at Littlemore that he had helped his brother.

Frank Newman never took his M.A.—religious difficulties made him unable to sign the Thirty-Nine Articles. The parallels and divergences in these two brothers' lives are interesting. Mayers had given Doddridge to both, and tried to mould them both in the same shape, but both broke the mould. Their portraits show a strong resemblance: their handwriting in later life appears to me identical.

Frank started for Persia in 1830. His family were grieved at losing him and still more at the irregular ideas he was taking with him. John describes the parting as having "had its sufficient share in knocking me up" but adds, consoling both himself and his mother, "Frank so completely put himself into His hands that we can have no fear for him, whatever becomes of his projects."

It was the strangest, wildest expedition. Francis Newman's biographer notes how little trace can be found of the party doing any evangelising. They had many prayer-meetings among themselves, they learned to smoke (and Frank sent home long, half-apologetic disquisitions on the various forms the art may assume); they travelled under terrible conditions, they could not handle the language, three of the women missionaries died, once they were stoned. Frank himself was twice very ill: the second time he almost died. He was away two years. New ideas were pressing upon him during this time. As with his eldest brother the acid test of real life dissolved the Calvinism he had embraced in his boyhood. John Newman issued from this test a Catholic: Frank's biographer thinks that on this journey he "crossed the Rubicon" dividing the Christian faith of his youth from the Unitarianism of his later life. The change was not immediately apparent with either brother when they met in England, each having nearly died, each having deeply altered, arriving home on the same day in 1833, one from Bagdad the other from Sicily.

In refusing to sign the Articles, Frank was sacrificing—as John was later to sacrifice—a brilliant career at Oxford. For a while his future seemed quite uncertain, but there were new colleges coming into existence designed to receive men who were not

members of the Church of England or who could not con-
scientiously sign her tests; Frank went first to Bristol, later to
London where he became Professor of Latin.

Many of his students told stories of Francis Newman from
which we can form a picture of him, especially as he grew older.
A brilliant teacher with attentive students, he "did not always"
his biographer says, "discover the pranks and designs for diverting
the course of true knowledge in which the average young Englishman loves to indulge". (A pleasant description of legpulls.) He
had absolutely no sense of humour and said of himself that he
could speak clearly and forcibly but without wit. In winter he
would wear three coats, the top one green with age; and over the
coats a rug with a hole for his head. Beneath these appeared
trousers edged with several inches of leather and above all an
immense dirty white hat. Yet he had, one pupil says, "courtly
genial manners". "A very brilliant scholar," said another,
"with a tendency toward eccentricity". His eldest brother
remarked, "Much as we love each other, neither would like to
be mistaken for the other".

Religiously they went steadily in opposite directions—had
their father been alive he would have thought Frank's the
reaction of a strong, John's of a weak mind, from the creed of
their youth. Frank remained for some time a Protestant of one
type or another, getting himself immersed as a member of the
Baptist sect at Bristol in 1836. But by 1850 he had written *Phases
of Faith: Passages in the History of My Creed*, while the titles of others
of his many books indicate something of what these phases were:
*The Defective Morality of the New Testament, The Historical Deprava-
tion of Christianity*, etc. etc. Augustine Birrell used to relate how
after lectures at Frank Newman's house, his wife would apologise
to the young listeners for her husband's strictures on our
Lord's character: "Frank doesn't mean any harm. He is the
very best of men."

To some extent he seems to have filled the place of faith with
a large number of fads. He was anti-vaccination, anti-vivisection,
anti-tobacco, anti-alcohol, anti-flesh-food. He called these last
the triple abstinence, and once described himself as anti-every-
thing.

But he talked amazingly good sense about what he calls the
problem of "Un-Employ" and at moments almost rivalled
Cobbett in his attacks on Enclosure and his claims for the labourer

to have some stake in the land. He seemed more aware than John of the horrors of modern poverty. Writing later than Cobbett he is brilliant over the damage wrought by drainage to the soil's fertility and, although anxious to avoid the name of Socialist, he became vice-president of the Land Nationalisation Society.

But first and foremost Frank Newman was a scholar—not of Greek and Latin only but of Berber, Numidian, Scythian,[1] Modern Arabic, Kabail, Libyan and other strange tongues, for many of which he gathered dictionaries or wrote essays in aid of students. A sentence in a letter to another professor conveys a picture of a man living in a world as remote from his fellows as the Patristic world inhabited by his brother:

I feel on perfectly solid ground in Medo-Persian or Scythian. Difficulties in them are like difficulties in Greek or Sanscrit: that is all. In the Assyrian, I do not yet know whether to believe at least half of the characters, and many fundamental alleged principles. . . .

Of his relations with John, Francis Newman once said, "You know how very strongly my brother and myself differ in opinion: yet this has never created *the slightest personal discord*". They did not meet often. Soon after Newman's conversion he remarked on Frank's wanting to visit him, "Why should he come? I believe he has some obscure idea about thumbscrews"; while Frank visiting the Oratory in old age wrote that he could not sleep for two nights after from excitement. The clashes of opinion and temperament are reflected in the little book referred to earlier which Francis lived to write after his brother's death. It was emphatically a case of having the last word.

The brother between these two—Charles—early became a problem and remained so all his life. To begin with he seems hardly ever to have been out of debt: most letters to his mother contain mention of some pressing bill, requests for money or thanks for money sent. "I have sent John an account of money affairs," he writes to Mrs. Newman early in 1827, "and shall in future consider him the proper person for these topics, for it is obvious that the money comes out of his pocket and to plague

---

[1] A friend, to whom I showed this, comments: "Nothing is known of the Scythian language—not even to what speech group it belonged. Some, it seems, think it was an Iranian language; if so, it was allied to, perhaps identical with, the Medo-Persian alluded to below."

you on the subject is roundabout and troublesome." Clerk for
a while at a bank, he sent an abusive round robin to the Directors;
they were, says Mrs. Newman, very forbearing—surely "a tribute
of respect to a dear departed". But I sometimes wonder whether
filial piety and wifely devotion have not cast a cloak over Mr.
Newman's own financial incompetence—anyhow after his death
his sister as well as his children became John's burden. Perhaps
John was apt to assume more in the Aunt's case than the strictly
necessary: one of Charles' letters contains an intimation that
John had paid Aunt Newman's debts, while to his mother John
writes of her money troubles: "Why cannot I bear to be told
as well as Harriett, who reads me little driblets of her letters as
if I were some infant or puny schoolboy?" No, but much too
responsible a young man! One of the notes added later to his
diary tells us that John and Frank between them paid £700 of
debts contracted by their Aunt.

To return to Charles, religiously he ran quickly into negation.
"My head, hands and heart are all knocked up", Newman
wrote to his mother, "with the long composition I have sent
Charles . . . he revived the controversy we had five years ago.
I have sent him what is equal to nine sermons". Charles became
a Socialist—for the sake of the company. "Conventional or very
religious society is no society for me. I would as soon live among
Caribs, as among persons who do not aim at justice." Justice
meant partly his own right to be supported by society, and society
in this case meant John and Frank. They both rather nobly
fulfilled the obligation—receiving scant thanks from Charles.
One or other of them would get him a post which he would
abandon or lose, to turn up again starving on their hands. Most
of the energy used by John and Frank in their work was put by
Charles into quarrelling with them and with all around him.

Because, (he writes to his mother), I did not feel the same as them
on dear Mary's death, because I made light of it, it was "painful".
Squeamishness!
You view things in so melancholy a light. Ours is a great loss but
why it should cloud you so, I by no means see. . . . Did not Mr.
Williams of York St. lose an only daughter? When I mentioned it to
Mr. Hayes he made light of it. "Well, these things will happen."
And very properly he felt. Do not men of sense drink their wine on
the field of battle with friends dead and dying around them. It is
always my method in correspondence to put down what comes to

the end of my pen, and if it is not allowed me to do so . . . I must decline all correspondence.

It might have been well if he had. Newman writes to Jemima:

I had a letter from Mr. Mullins [was this the man who had caused Newman to go to Oxford not Cambridge?] complaining of Charles having sent him a newspaper with a direction he enclosed me. The direction was to "Parson Mullins, Pharisee Cottage, etc.," and the paper contains an account of a pauper of the name of Mullins who was brought up to Bow St. Office.

Charles himself delights in describing the rows he is having and his own dignified bearing. "I want no womanish advice," he writes to Mrs. Newman, "what method I am to pursue to shake off insult."

Just as a paragraph reveals the character of Francis, profoundly learned in useless languages, so one letter may be given which amusingly depicts the quarrelsome, self-centred, half crazy yet immensely intelligent third brother. It is written to his doctor:

SIR,

As I shall be often going to London it is better that you should put an end to your visits. Either I greatly overrate the efficacy of the materia medica or else you have declined duly putting forth its resources in your attendance on me. You have prescribed me nothing but pills, together with some black draughts and at length an alternative medicine which operated very coarsely and like the continued use of the pills in a manner quite contrary to that regularity of the functions which you professed it to be your special aim to produce. I cannot attribute this to want of skill on your part, or to your not having medical remedies at your command unless both yourself and your establishment are greatly degenerated from what I know them to have been many years ago. Formerly you spared no expense, now you have given me nothing but the cheapest of all medicines, pills. And when I complained of fever etc., you have said you must send me stronger pills, but have not done so, and have prescribed me no remedy whatever, and yet (strange to say) have continued calling on me. Until my opinion of the resources of the materia medica and of your ability to use them becomes greatly changed from what it is at present I shall continue to think your conduct very extraordinary. What your motives have been I know not: it is not worth enquiry.

I am, sir,

Yr obdt servt,

C. R. NEWMAN.

Meanwhile Charles was deeply concerned that John and Frank did not get on with one another, sympathising alternately with each and to some extent with both.

"I do not say that Frank is positively low-minded," he writes to John, "but he is decidedly not high-minded, and I believe he does not nor ever will do you justice, and perhaps you not him."

For a short while the eldest brother, in the strange fashion of the period, would not (as he has told us in the *Apologia*) consort with Frank because Frank had left the Church of England and made a religious party of his own. Presently, although not holding Frank orthodox, he saw that he was no longer a member of a definite schism and the breach was healed. But all the time both aided Charles. At one time they thought him odd enough to be certifiable as a lunatic, but decided finally that this was not so. He writes himself:

The state of society in England either makes people mad naturally or gives them artificial madness from their efforts to escape from that natural madness. The family of the Newmans is as mad a family as perhaps can be found in that mad country. Frank, the moment he gets out of his line, is the maddest person I am acquainted with. Next to him I rate either you or I . . . as for Frank I never felt in his company as if I was in the company of a man. Half a man is the utmost I can concede him. Of you my criticism would be different. I should say you were a whole man prevented by privilege from proper operation.

Many years later, a friend of Frank's, commenting on the home influences that had shaped himself and John, received in return a murderous sketch of Charles.

You evidently do not know (he wrote), that I have *two* brothers. The eldest, Dr. J. H. N.; the second, Charles Robert N., three years older than myself, of whom we do not speak, because he is as unfit for society as if insane. He is a Cynic Philosopher in modern dress, having many virtues, but one ruinous vice, that of perpetual censoriousness, by which he alienates every friend as soon as made, or in the making, by which he ejected himself from all posts of usefulness. . . . He has lived now more than thirty years in retirement and idleness. His moral ruin was from Robert Owen's *Socialism and Atheistic Philosophy*; but he presently began his rebukes on Robert Owen himself. His sole pleasure in company seems to be in noting down material for ingenious,

impertinent, and insolent fault-finding; hence no one can safely admit
him. He formally renounced his mother, brothers, and sisters about
forty years ago, and wrote to other persons requesting them not to
count him a Newman . . . because we were religious and he was an
Atheist. He had *all the same dear sweet influences of home* as all of us; yet
how unamiable and useless has he become! still loving to snarl most
at the hands that feed him. Is not this an admonition not to attribute
too much to the single cause of home influences, however precious?

Perhaps a better last word is in a letter from John Henry
Newman to Anne Mozley:

I write a line to tell you that my poor brother Charles died yesterday.
He must have had some curious natural gifts, for eccentric, violent
and self-willed as he was, he attracted to him the mother and daughter
with whom he lodged, and, the mother having died, the daughter has
refused a nurse and has nurst him day and night through his last
illness.

Before he went to Persia in 1830, Frank proposed to Maria
Giberne. He proposed again on his return but met with a steady
refusal. The drawing of the family group was done by her. Mary
is not in it but Frank looks so young that it must have been made
before his departure for Persia. Maria, engaged to a man in
India, was more interested in Mary than she was in Frank, and
was now beginning to be more interested in the elder brother's
ideas than in the younger brother's adoration. She was one of
the women for whom the Oxford movement opened a deeper
view of religion issuing in a vocation to the religious life.

August and September 1830, Newman was busy preparing to
receive his mother and sisters at Iffley. He notes:

August 6—walked with Pusey and his wife to see the cottage at
Rose Hill. . . .
September 30—walked with Froude to Rose Hill to inspect the
furniture. . . .
October 22—my mother and sisters came to Rose Hill. . . .

One would imagine Newman must have met Mrs. Pusey
during the long engagement, but the first mention in his letters
is of an early call after the marriage when he "had a long gossip
with Mrs. Pusey" and wrote to Jemima, "She is a *very* pleasing
person."
The friendship grew steadily and Newman writes to Jemima:

"Pusey and 'Maria' request me to express an earnest hope that whenever you come, you will (while your abode is preparing) take up your quarters in Ch.Ch."

A bundle of Mrs. Newman's letters of this year shows her deeply concerned with two subjects—this move to Iffley, and the lives of her two difficult children Charles and Frank.

"How nice that *long* visit was," she writes to John after seeing him, "it has made me quite gay and young, and this mood will last till I see Frank on Sunday morning."

Frank was preparing for the Persian expedition—"such a fearful wild plan". She wants John to convince him that "he is following his own enthusiastic inclinations and usurping duties to which he is not called or fitted". Yet both she and Harriett were clearly half afraid of a clash between the brothers: "I need not say," writes Mrs. Newman, "how anxiously I hope you will hear and receive all he has to inform you with the cordiality of old and brotherly affection forgive me the anxiety I feel on this point it is a subject so near my heart". Harriett on the turn-down of the letter adds her own plea to the same effect.

It was an anxious problem for the poor woman. Charles, his mother is sure, "would not listen to a Female, that weak sex he would pity" while "our other Anxiety is equally self-sufficient though he means to be and thinks he is the most *humble* Christian". Was it wiser to appeal herself or to let John speak? Would he say just what she wanted: would the brothers quarrel? At least she could relieve her own mind to John! She hopes that poor Charles's "gross deviations may increase our own watchfulness, warn us against self-dependence and make us anxious to obtain an increase of faith to be if possible the means of bringing him into the right mind".

One feels that if John was not always patient with his brothers he was almost infinitely so with that weak sex that Charles despised. The details are endless on which his opinion was wanted after the move had been decided. Mrs. Newman shows at once a lot of commonsense and the need to have every decision confirmed and a good deal of the work done by her one amenable son. "I had no idea," says Newman to Jemima, concerning one maternal letter, "she required an answer, being fully persuaded her judgment was right."

He is to enquire into the cost of hiring "cottage furniture" if the landlord will not leave his, also "moderate apparatus, glass

and crockery, carpets and floor cloth . . . and I should like
to know what would be the reduction if we found carpeting,
glass and crockery". Perhaps man-like he felt her over-careful,
for she writes, "put all the disgrace of bargaining on me".

Things not hired were to be "bought for ready money" either in
a London shop or by Newman or his clerk at a sale. On October
1st she writes: "You are a most superlatively excellent Manager,
and your Clerk a most able Assistant. . . . I hope you will be
able to make *me* as well as your sisters useful at Littlemore. . . .
There can be but one obstacle to our coming on the 12th the
D^{vds} will not be paid and to speak in a round term taking in six
weeks' rent and travelling we shall require £45."

An immense list follows of things needed for the cottage,
including tent bedsteads, feather beds, "stump" bedsteads,
"sopha", crockery, etc. etc. Newman might "meet with some
of the expensive things at a sale the bedsteads are the only thing
to be feared. . . . Do not perplex yourself about bed-hangings
we shall bring something to put up."

A second letter on the same day runs, "I have not mentioned
Drawers . . . perhaps by the assistance of the Carpenter I may
plan for a few shillings what may be as useful . . . another
requisite for our embellishment I have omitted Looking-Glasses,
I hope you will give us some credit for this omission, it is not so
with all Ladies . . . I suppose you have ordered an Honest
Woman into the House who will arrange things decently till we
come . . ."

"Do not," writes Newman on the 4th, "buy any furniture for
a week to come—as I send my agent to sales on Wednesday and
Thursday. . . . I have already my eye on a carpenter who will
do wonders".

On October 15th, she has bought beds, bedding, etc., at the
cost of £33; "I should thank you to order the Respble 'Body' to
air all the Bedding and Blankets carefully . . . I sometimes think
you must wonder what I do with the money, but I endeavour
annually to account for it and you see it goes on *uncontrollable*
items which I am *longing* to reduce. . . . I am very glad to hear
the House is *small* and do not fear but we will use our skill to make
it *neat*".

Mother and sisters delighted in their efforts to "repair and
beautify by stages", largely with John in mind. Harriett writes
to her Aunt the next year:

The long vac. has begun and John has taken possession of his new
apartments—consisting of a hall, staircase, study and bedroom—
quite grand, is he not?—His study is very pretty and comfortable
for summer—we have made a new large window in it, allowing him a
view of our garden and a very pleasant lookout towards Oxford. He
is very much charmed with all his arrangements, which we did not
allow him to see till everything was completed.

Of the family's work in the village Tom Mozley writes:
". . . They attended to the schools, the charities, and the sick
people of Littlemore, which though without a Church, and at
that time with scarcely a genteel residence, had more care
bestowed on it than many a village furnished with all the outward
symbols of parochial completeness".[1]

The family letters do not cease with the move: now they are
largely notes carried by any messenger that can be found, sometimes Rogers, Copeland or other friends, sometimes less reliable
messengers. Harriett writes on one "*J'ai peur que les yeux de l'homme
de lait ne soit peutêtre que trop perçants*". Evidently sharp eyes could
read the turn-down of a letter, for Mrs. Newman writes of having
much to tell her son, "but not on the turnings". Newman sends
this quaint note to his friend Johnson (a friend of Bowden)
who was enquiring about a maid who had been with Mrs. Newman: "*Non est praecellentis ingenii in coquina. Credo tibi eam non
fere idoneam* . . . She has many good qualities *sed tu post litteras meas*
have explained to me more fully what you wanted. *Mater ejus*
so pressed on me to name her to you, *ut non potuissem non loqui.*"

The family are constantly in and out of Oxford: they take
"Flys"; they call on Mrs. Hawkins, Mrs. Whately, Mrs. Pusey.
They walk with Newman or some other "Escourt" or even alone.
Mrs. Newman writes: "We all agree it is not at all disagreeable
to walk at Oxford, London is hateful for young ladies, but O.
is a quiet and well-ordered place, we were in hopes of being
Proctorised by *you* or your Colleagues but although we returned
partly down the High Street we did not succeed".

The year after the move to Iffley the cholera came to England
and Mrs. Newman writes to her son:

. . . Should it increase, I wish you could have that Cottage at
Littlemore for Head-quarters for Nurses to be on the spot, without
mixing with uncontaminated families, and for a Depot of Medicines,

[1] Mozley: *Reminiscences*, p. 137.

FAMILY GROUP

Left to Right: FRANCIS, MRS. NEWMAN, HARRIETT, JOHN HENRY, JEMIMA

(by Maria Giberne)

etc. And I should think it a privilege while health permits, for you
to consider me *Head Nurse*. I have the whole in my head, should it be
ordained that our vicinity is to suffer under the visitation. Pray take
care of your own health. *Your* usefulness is before you, I trust for the
comfort of many, for many years.

In this year no case occurred at Littlemore, although there
was one the year following—outside Newman's parish, though
he says it kept him busy. Mozley has an amusing story in this
connection. Various Evangelicals had been in the habit of
cross-questioning him about Newman:

In the summer of 1831, I was urged, besought, and invoked a dozen
times over in one evening, to say truly and outright, with no faltering,
or speciality of tone, but in the orthodox accents of unflinching
certainty, whether Newman was a "good man". . . .
An Oxford clergyman of the same school gave a remarkable . . .
testimony to this oft-challenged "goodness". There was cholera in
Oxford, and he had to take his usual holiday. There might be some
visiting necessary, and funerals involving danger. Clergymen under
no obligation to incur the risk might hold it their duty to avoid it.
So he carefully drew up a long list of clergymen to be applied to in
the order stated, and gave it to his clerk in case of need. One of the
clergy applied to took the list out of the clerk's hand, and found it
headed with Newman's name, followed by those of his known friends
in the order of their reputed devotion to him. After this came the
clergymen of this gentleman's own school. It was never known whether
he made this arrangement as thinking the clergymen first in his list
more likely to attend the summons, or as deeming their lives less
precious than those of his own friends.[1]

[1] Mozley: *Reminiscences*, Vol. I., p. 240.

CHAPTER XV

From the Tutorship to the Arians

NEWMAN himself later saw the germ of the Oxford Movement in the grouping of Keble, Froude, himself and Robert Wilberforce and in the ideas with which they combated Peel's election. Clearly by the autumn of 1829 his views on the Church were finding more pronounced expression. In November he preached three times on the "Unity of the Church," November 8, 15, and 22, and followed on November 29th by a sermon on "Submission to Church authority." The final form of the first sermons is No. 17 of Vol. VII of the *Parochial and Plain Sermons*. It distinctly teaches the doctrine of the Mystical Body and the gift of Grace *through* the Church. Speaking of the common cry against party spirit (one of Arnold's bugbears), Newman makes the statement "that the Christian Church is simply and literally a party or society instituted by Christ."

In the sermon on "Submission to Church Authority" he teaches Apostolical Succession, and also the value of outward forms. "Faith," he says, "sees things not to be forms, if commanded, it realises consequences."

In what sense is adherence to the Church a form in which prayer is not also? The benefit of the one is not seen, nor of the other; the one will not profit the ungodly and careless, nor will the other; the one is commanded in Scriptures, so is the other. Therefore, to say that Church-union is a form, is no disparagement of it; forms are the very food of faith.

On a smaller stage Newman's changing views were again manifested by his quarrel with the Church Missionary Society of which he had been made secretary in March 1829. In December we find him writing to his fellow secretary to protest against the society being held responsible for doctrinal views expressed in some sermons preached on behalf of their funds, but the other secretary replied:

I would not, on any account, allow myself to become a party to any measure which might appear like a disclaimer against either of the individuals in question. I should, on the contrary, deem such a proceeding totally inconsistent with Christian candour and love. Both the men are devoted servants of Christ, and actuated in an eminent degree by love of God and man—as their whole conduct and spirit testify. Both are, as to the general character of their preaching, faithfully announcing the gospel of Jesus Christ.

With regard to the point of difference between them, I conceive (so far as I can judge from the reports I have received of their sermons, and from my previous knowledge of their sentiments), that Mr. Bulteel is most correct, because more clearly adhering to the spirit and language of Scripture; yet I entertain at the same time a very high regard for the piety and usefulness of Mr. Sibthorpe; nor can I believe that the difference between them on the particular subject in question is so great as some casual expressions may have led some to suppose.

Tuckwell's *Reminiscences* throw an amusing side-light on this letter.

At the opening of the thirties [he recalls], Evangelicalism was dominant, trumpeted by a tremendous Boanerges named Bulteel, whose powerful but sulphurous sermons filled St. Ebbe's Church. He made a name for himself outside his squalid parish, attacked the Heads of Houses for sloth and unfaithfulness in a violent University sermon, whose impeachments they but feebly answered, practised faith healing successfully in cases where physicians were in vain, ministered in conventicles, found his license revoked by Bishop Lloyd, whom he thereupon denounced publicly as "an officer of Antichrist", built a chapel of his own, and founded a not long-lived sect of Bulteelites.

Newman tried next to get the rules of the Society changed. Dissenters had been admitted to membership, but he urged that the Society should be made an integral part of the Church of England. He writes to Jemima of a circular letter he is preparing:

. . . I am printing 500 copies, and if it takes (which I do not expect but take the chance of), I shall send it campaigning all over the country. I shall make Woodgate, perhaps our friend Mr. Rickards, distribute it in Kent. . . . I shall send it to Davison at Worcester and Benson in town, and to the Bishops of London, Lincoln, and Llandaff —perhaps Exeter. Perhaps the Bishop of Ferns! Ha ha! Are you not laughing? I am. There is a fine fricassee of fowl before the eggs are laid. . . . Now, if it be a silly thing, why, I am exposing myself and doing what is unsafe; but one must run risks to do good, and fortune favours the bold; so I must hug myself if no one else will hug me.

Woodgate, (a fellow of St. John's and friend of Newman) writes chaffing him on his recent change of front but agreeing with his line of argument:

. . . I have withheld the author's name as you requested me, but told them there was no cause for alarm, as he was one who, however he might once have betrayed symptoms of sectarianism, or be called Evangelical, was now as staunch a Churchman as Addison's landlord, who, when he could not find time to go to Church, headed mobs to pull down meeting-houses; that you drank Church and King every day in a bumper after dinner, voted for Sir R. Inglis, stood neutral on petitions, and sang, "God Save the King", and "A Health to Old England, the King, and the Church", every night after supper.

On March 8th, 1830, Newman notes, "Turned out of the Church Missionary Society because of my pamphlet."

Tom Mozley in a letter to his sister explains that Newman's proposal, which would have resulted in the exclusion of Dissenters, was carried in a Committee chiefly of clergy; but at a general meeting to elect officers, "when they generally re-elect the old ones and just fill up vacancies, he was ousted by an immense majority, Bulteel and his satellites, and half Edmund Hall being in attendance. He has, to be sure, given the Low Church Party great provocation."

We must turn back a little in time in order to get a clear view of what was happening in the College before, during and after these agitations. Newman has given in his *Memoir* an account of the difficulties that arose between the younger tutors—himself, Robert Wilberforce and Froude—and the Provost, but his account is vague as to date; the letters make the order of things clearer. From the *Memoir* we get the impression that differences began very shortly after his election, but Hawkins had in fact been Provost more than a year when Newman wrote to Samuel Rickards:

We have gone through the year famously; packed off our lumber, parted with spoilt goods, washed and darned where we could, and imported several new articles of approved quality. Indeed, the college is so altered that you would scarcely know it again. The tangible improvements of system have been, first, the diminishing the Gentlemen Commoners from twenty to eight or nine; then the dismissal of the Incurables; then the rejecting unprepared candidates for admission —the number is awful, some twice; then the giving chance vacancies to well-recommended and picked men; then the introduction of paper work into the Collections Examinations; then the refusing testimonials to unworthy applicants; then the revival of a Chapel sermon at the Sacrament; then the announcement of a prize for Greek composition. The most important and far-reaching improvement has been commenced this term—a radical alteration (not apparent on the published list), of the lecture system; the bad men are thrown into large classes, and thus time saved for the better sort, who are put into very small lectures, and principally with their own tutors quite familiarly and chattingly. And, besides, a regular system for *the year* has been devised. But we do not wish this to be talked about. We hope soon to give some Exhibitions or Scholarships. All these alterations are, you observe, additional to that grand act at the election, of throwing open two fellowships. Pretty well, we hope, for a year.

Hawkins's spirits are not what they used to be, and persons who have known him long say he is ageing. I have sometimes been made quite sad at the sight of him. But this, of course, *entre nous*. He has not (nor should a Head), taken the initiative in these innovations, but has always approved—sometimes kept abreast with us—and at Collections has slain the bad men manfully. It is said in college by the undergraduates that, "Now, alas! the Provost was as bad as a Tutor." Whereas, at Collections they used to hope the Provost would retaliate on the Tutors the blows they received from the latter.

This letter was written on February 6th, 1829, but on February 17th Newman is writing about "our meddling Provost", and is in the very thick of the Peel election troubles. "We have been merry all through", he says of those troubles—but then he had been on the winning side and the winning side is often the merry one. The Provost had met with ignominious defeat in an open field at the hands of his own tutors; was it likely that he would be "merry" or that his attitude to them would remain unchanged?

The occasion of the tutorship dispute was a question of the arrangement of time-tables; the principle was the question of whether a special pastoral relationship existed between a tutor and his own pupils, and further, whether it was lawful for tutors to concentrate on the ablest men—the material for first classes, which were, says Newman, "once more looming". The Provost's view, he adds, "was disciplinarian, that of the tutors pastoral". Dr. Hawkins claimed that they neglected the mass of the students for the sake of the élite, they that this was a part of their very office as tutors. Froude wrote:

In order to comply with such a system I should be obliged to abandon all hope of knowing my pupils in the way in which I know them at present, and, consequently of retaining that influence over them which I know I now possess.

That very influence was probably in the Provost's view one of the chief arguments against the system. Whately had seen in Newman a tendency to become the leader of a party. One feels rather sorry for him and Hawkins, as they watched the promising young Liberal whom they had rescued from the jaws of Evangelicalism turning into a red hot zealot of an equally dangerous kind. Anything red hot would have annoyed them—a High but not Dry Churchman, a furious Church-and-King bigot, was gathering a formidable influence through the rising talent of the College. It must be stopped.

The correspondence between Provost and tutors dragged on through 1829 down to June 1830 and ended with the Provost's decision to give no more pupils to the three men if they would not comply with his views. By an interesting irony, almost all Newman's pupils came out with first classes, while, in order to keep the college going at all, Hawkins had to import Hampden as a lecturer and to abandon to all intents and purposes the tutorial system that had been, with his own backing, working so fruitfully.

Many years later Newman said to Mark Pattison that "it did not answer for Heads to turn out their tutors in a body; they put themselves entirely in the power of the succeeding tutors, it being a measure they could never repeat." Pattison is interesting about all this, for he came into residence shortly after it had occurred, and in his opinion Oriel, which had possessed "the true revolutionary spirit", had already begun its decline, and no college precisely took its place, especially for great talk in the Common Room. Eveleigh and Copleston had both set aside the old custom of choosing clubbable rather than able men for fellows; both had sought out talent, and Oriel was the first college to make this the criterion.

Pattison saw "thinness and superficiality" in the character of

Hawkins contrasted with "the sterling force and richness of that of his predecessors". When he came up in 1832, "There was a goodly array of silk gowns—gentlemen commoners they were invidiously called at the High Table". But with all this Pattison thinks that in the hands of the three young tutors Oriel would have soon become a seminary!

It is very hard to see in the action of Hawkins simply what Newman saw—a question of opposing principles. There was that, of course, also. Some letters a couple of years later when Newman might have been Dean, show the nature of the gulf more and more plainly apparent between the older and the younger Oriel. Newman writes to Dr. Jenkyns, who had apparently asked him about his willingness to accept the office.

> . . . Let me come to the practical point of the Sacrament: for if the question is to turn on this, we are both of us losing time.
> . . . I have at present no formed opinion about administering it to the mass of undergraduates; but if I have to make up my mind (which I cannot do all at once on an important subject), I think it very likely I shall make it a point of conscience to act upon it. Then the question will be whether the Provost will make it a point of conscience, on the other hand, to bid me administer it when I object. If so, dropping abstract views, it is frank to say, I should not consider myself bound to obey him in a matter so solemn. I will further say, that, at this very time (I may change my opinion next week), I am disinclined toward the present rule of (practically) obliging the undergraduates to communicate.

The point was part of a larger question Newman was putting—the delimitation of disciplinary authority between Provost and Dean. But this letter, with its announcement of a conscientious objection which may be removed by a change of opinion, does, I think, show that the Provost had a case for being on his side aggravated by his high-minded young colleagues!

He did not take away their existing pupils: but as each departed, the vacant place was not filled, so that by 1832 none remained to them. Newman writes to his mother on June 18th, 1830:

> It is at length settled that the Provost gives us no more pupils—us three (R. Wilberforce, Froude and me)—and we die gradually with our existing pupils. This to me personally is a delightful arrangement;

it will naturally lessen my labours and at length reduce them without at once depriving me of resources which I could not but reckon upon while they lasted. But for the college I think it a miserable determination.

"The Fathers arise again full before me", was Newman's immediate reaction to the fading out of the tuition, but he adds, a little bewilderingly, "This Vacation I should not wonder if I took up the study of the Modern French Mathematics". And again he writes to Froude, ". . . When I was at home, I wrote out all that correspondence, which I mean to be a document to my heirs; and I made a bold inroad into Trigonometry, and have this morning got through about a quarter of Hamilton's Conics".[1]

In his *Anglican Career of Cardinal Newman*, Abbott makes much of these and similar letters which he takes to imply that Newman's interests were far too scattered for serious work on his "great project" of reading the Fathers. A couple of years ago he had been learning Hebrew, still earlier he had procured a Persian-Arabic grammar, he was full of business for his college and his family: what chance of his being a serious student of any one thing? Of course some of these schemes were merely thrown out in letters, not acted upon. And Newman's capacity for work was certainly extraordinary. He could drive at top speed through a day of sixteen to twenty hours, taking in and analysing his reading, and with almost no recreation.

Nor did he care to make a show of scholarship such as often carries a little learning a very long way. In reply to a suggestion that he should write one volume in an Ecclesiastical History, he says:

I hardly know what answer to make to your inquiry without knowing more of particulars. For instance, what I feel most clear about is this: I never would undertake to write lightly on any subject which admits of being treated thoroughly. I think it is the fault of the day. Now this probably will be a great objection to my engaging in a professionally popular work. Not that it is necessary to compose a long treatise, but more time (I feel) ought to be given to the subject than is consistent with the dispatch of booksellers, who must sacrifice everything to regularity of publication and trimness of appearance. An Ecclesiastical History for example, whether long or short, ought to be derived from original sources, and not be compiled from the standard authorities.

---

[1] Always a good mathematician, Newman took up the study again about 1860.

He undertook the work, and it became *The Arians of the Fourth Century*. To Froude he writes in August 1831:

My work opens a grand and most interesting field to me; but how I shall ever be able to make one assertion, much less to write one page, I cannot tell. Any one, pure categorical would need an age of reading and research. I shall confine myself to hypotheticals; your "if" is a great philosopher as well as peacemaker.

Still determined to devote himself to Oxford, it is curious how little Newman seems to have realised how deep the Peel affair had gone with his colleagues; with Hawkins, and even more with Whately. We find him writing to Harriett after Whately had been made Archbishop of Dublin in September 1831, fully expecting to be asked to join him there, and afraid it would seem selfish and ungrateful and cowardly not to do so.[1]

. . . However, by this time I think my mind is quite made up that it is my duty to remain where I am, so remain I shall. (Is it not good to answer before I am asked?) My reasons for remaining are these: first, I am actually engaged to Mr. Rose for a succession of works, the composition of which is quite incompatible with the duties of a post about an Archbishop; next, this engagement will be in itself a channel of exclusive usefulness, which I should be abandoning just as I had begun it; thirdly, the study of theology is very much neglected in Oxford, and I may be doing peculiar service to the place (by "peculiar" I mean what others will *not* do) by cultivating it; fourthly, if times are troublous Oxford will want hot-headed men, and such I mean to be, and I am in my place; fifthly, I have some doubts whether my health would stand an Irish engagement.

Whately, naturally, did not ask him. Indeed, Newman was to see the Archbishop only twice more, casually and for a moment, in 1834 and 1838. Letters interchanged between the two men in 1834 are printed in Newman's Correspondence and in Whately's biography. They are melancholy enough, for a broken friendship is always melancholy, and these two men had loved each other too well and come to misunderstand each other too profoundly for superficial courtesies. Whately by then had voted for the Irish Bishoprics Bill and we shall see presently what that meant

[1] Actually Whately in this month offered Newman the Vice-Principalship of Alban Hall!

for Newman. The Liberal anger at intolerance, the Tractarian fierceness at betrayal, are manifest in the letters.

Newman had started the last year of his tutorship, "weak and deaf" from overwork, and suffering from want of sleep. But all through that year and the next, work proceeded on *The Arians of the Fourth Century*.

In his diary he occasionally notes progress:

October 21 (1831)—Resumed my task at the Councils, though with many interruptions, for a while.

October 24—On my return from my walk, found a present from my pupils, consisting of the *Fathers*.

And in December:

Resumed opusculum after many weeks' interruption.

Froude tells him to "stop fiddling" with his introduction. Newman answers in January 1832:

Your advice about my work is not only sage, but good; yet not quite applicable, though I shall bear it in mind.

Recollect, my good sir, that every thought I think is thought, and every word I write is writing, and that thought tells, and that words take room, and that, though I make the introduction the *whole* book, yet a book it is; and, though this will not steer clear of the egg blunder, to have an introduction leading to nothing, yet it is not losing time. Already I have made forty-one pages out of eighteen.

Anne Mozley records:

All through June Mr. Newman had been engaged upon his *Arians*, or, to give it its original title, *First Volume of Councils*. . . .

Mr. Froude had warned his friend not to go fiddling on with his preface. Mr. Newman's solicitude over this first work showed itself throughout. He grudged no pains; wrote and re-wrote; read passages to his home circle; sought the criticism of his friends. Mr. Henry Wilberforce made free to tell him that the style was not, in his judgement, equal to that of his sermons; finally, he notes in his diary, "The last days of my working upon the *Arians* I was tired wonderfully, continually on the point of fainting away, quite worn out."

Work on the *Arians* was one of the elements gradually converging towards the Oxford Movement. And curiously enough one of the prime movers at this moment was a Cambridge man—the editor of the series, Hugh Rose. Dean Burgon in his study of Rose is disposed biographer-like to exaggerate his position, but there is no doubt he bore a significant part in the early phases and the letters from Newman published in *Twelve Good Men* make this clear.

The first mention of Rose in Newman's own correspondence is in a letter from Samuel Rickards: "I wish somebody would be so good as to convince me that he is a very first-rate man, because I find it mighty inconvenient to stir among Cambridge men and not think him so."

On this letter Newman notes: "Here Rickards wrote hastily. I am a bad hand at criticising men, but the admiration and love I had for Rose was inspired, I think, by his elevation of mind, his unflagging zeal, his keen appreciation of what was noble and saintly, his insight into character, and his vigorous eloquence."

Whatever his qualities, Rose was a cautious man. Newman on finishing the *Arians* noted his suspicion that Rose thought it "scarcely safe," but he later tells Robert Wilberforce: "Rose objects to my history, not my doctrine. He says I begin it too soon. I have grounds, whether good or bad, and do not mean to knock under." Rose and his advisers did, unfortunately, decide against including *The Arians* in their proposed historical series. But meanwhile he had visited Oxford and wrote enthusiastically of having derived "the very highest gratification" from meeting "such a body of learned, powerful and high-minded men ". Newman returned the visit in July, 1832, and "was taken by surprise and overcome by delight,"—not so much, apparently, by the men as by the buildings: "in spite of my regrets at her present defects and past history, and all that is wrong about her. I seemed about to cry 'Floreat aeternum' . . . I do really think the place finer than Oxford."

Rose was editing the *British Magazine* and Newman threw himself wholeheartedly into the scheme of making it a means of the revival of Catholic thought. He wrote for it and solicited contributions right and left. We find him asking Froude to "send Mr. Rose one or two more architectural articles," suggesting to Henry Wilberforce to write an article on Loyola or St. Francis. "I am much set on understanding the *mode* in which the Monastic Orders rose, in order to see whether one could not found such a society if times got bad."

To Rose he proposes to run a poetry department for the Magazine:

to bring out certain truths and facts, moral, ecclesiastical, and religious simply and forcibly,—and with greater freedom and clearness than in *The Christian Year*! I will not go on to say with greater poetry. If it answered on trial we should be content to carry it on *ad infinitum*. It might be called *Lyra Apostolica*.

And to Rogers he writes, wanting him to contribute:

As to my notice about verses, do not be so surprised—I had a reason. If you do not already write them, I can only say the sooner you do the better, for while your eyes are bad, it would be an amusement . . . Do not stirring times bring out poets? Do they not give opportunity for the rhetoric of poetry, and the persuasion? And may we not at least produce shadows of high things if not the high things themselves?

Newman did not want his friends to write for Rose solely for the sake of the *British Magazine*. There was probably much more at the bottom of his mind than he yet realised, but quite consciously he wanted all his pupils to be reaching out to "high things", quite consciously he wanted them to aim at work for the Church and for God. He and Froude had from the first spent themselves in the service of the young men committed to them, asking these in turn to spend themselves in a higher service. (Little details are interesting, such as Newman's refusal of payment from one pupil in difficult circumstances, his returning part of another's cheque.) Nor did either of them think that the relationship ended when the pupil ceased to be a pupil. A bunch of letters, all belonging to this year (1832) are most illuminating. Tom Mozley had long taken his degree, he was an ordained clergyman, but Newman still felt towards him, and Mozley still accepted, the attitude of mentor. Writing a long epistle of college news, passing on the offer of a curacy, Newman continues:

I am truly rejoiced to find your desire for parochial employment has not diminished, and your opinion of your own health not such as to deter you. For myself, since I heard your symptoms, I have not been alarmed, but some persons have been very anxious about you. I trust you are to be preserved for many good services in the best of causes. I am sure you have that in you which will come to good if you

cherish and improve it . . . I cannot but sorrowfully confess to myself
(how much soever I wish to hide the fact from my own mind) that
you have lost much time in the last four or five years. I say I wish to
hide it from myself, because, in simple truth, in it I perceive a humiliation to myself. I have expected a good deal from you, and have said
I expected it. Hitherto I have been disappointed, and it is a mortification to me. I do expect it still, but in the meanwhile time is lost,
as well as hope delayed. Now you must not think it unkind in me
noticing this now, of all times of the year. I notice it, not as if you
needed the remark most now, rather less, but because you have more
time to think about it now. It is one especial use of times of illness to
reflect about ourselves.

You have various gifts and you have good principles. For the credit
of these principles, for the sake of the Church, and for the sake of your
friends, who expect it of you, see that they bring forth fruit. I have
often had—nay have—continually anxious thoughts about you, but
it is unpleasant to obtrude them, and now I have hesitated much
before I got myself to say what I have said, lest I should only be making
a fuss; yet believe me to speak with very much affection towards you.

This is not Polonius writing to Laertes, or Lord Chesterfield to
his son, but a man of thirty-one writing to a man of twenty-six.

To Henry Wilberforce, about to take a curacy, he writes
(October 1832):

Perhaps on the whole I am sorry you are going to be Mr. Sargent's
curate. You must have more work, responsibility and anxiety, if you
are to be worth anything. I fear the ladies of the house will make you
idle. You will be lounging and idling with them all day. There is this
mischief attends all familiar society between us and the fair sex. We
cannot talk without being idle, but ladies are employing their fingers
in a thousand ways while they encourage idleness in us.

To another pupil, Rogers, Newman writes (November 1832):

. . . I have been thinking you may be at present exposed to danger
from the state of your eyes; thus—Are you not naturally idle? and
are you not now *reduced* to a state of idleness? Beware of getting into
a way of muddling away your time; shuffling through the day doing
nothing, etc. I know that when you get to the Bar you must work;
yet there are degrees of exertion, and it is possible to be absent with
your books before you. I throw out this merely because it strikes me,
as a raw material which you may convert as far as possible into something real and practicable.

And again:

When I spoke of muddling, it was merely that I thought your eyes at present kept you from doing *anything*, and that you were literally idling. I did not mean that you must be reading or thinking. You may hunt in Hampshire three days in the week, and I shall never call it muddling; that is, *it will not incapacitate you* from working in its season. But to be doing absolutely nothing is injurious.

Comparatively few of these letters remain—how many were there? Small wonder if the work of the Tutorship, while new men were coming on each year, new correspondences starting with the men going down, a mass of teaching and college affairs, had stood in the way of greater matters. Twelve years later he wrote to his former pupil William Froude:

I should have gone on with Mathematics (which I was bent on doing and did, till Jenkyns, *on the ground of* my leaving the Tutorship, introduced me to *Rose* and so to the History of Arianism) I should have gone on with Niebuhr and Aristotle.

Later still he wrote of himself in the third person:

In the year after his relinquishing the Tutorship, on his return from abroad, the Tract Movement began. Humanly speaking, that movement never would have been, had he not been deprived of his Tutorship; or had Keble, not Hawkins, been Provost.

Chapter XVI

Grand Tour

A FORETASTE of Newman's only prolonged journey (in a
life of almost ninety years!) was his first visit to Devonshire
with Hurrell Froude in 1832. His fear of being captured by
earth's glory always comes out most strongly in relation to
Devonshire and a long letter to his mother on this first visit shows
him almost overpowered by beauty. He writes of the

extreme deliciousness of the air and the fragrance of everything
. . . I think I should dissolve into essence of roses, or be attenuated
into an echo if I lived here . . . The rocks blush into every variety of
colour, the trees and fields are emeralds, and the cottages are rubies.
A beetle I picked up at Torquay was as green and gold as the stone
it lay upon, and a squirrel which ran up a tree here just now was not
the pale reddish-brown to which I am accustomed, but a bright brown-
red. Nay, my very hands and fingers look rosy, like Homer's Aurora,
and I have been gazing on them with astonishment . . . The scents
are extremely fine, so very delicate yet so powerful, and the colours
of the flowers as if they were all shot with white. The sweet peas
especially have the complexion of a beautiful face. They trail up the
wall mixed with myrtles as creepers. As to the sunset, the Dartmoor
heights look purple, and the sky close upon them a clear orange. When
I turn back and think of Southampton Water and the Isle of Wight,
they seem by contrast to be drawn in Indian Ink or pencil. . . . I
have heard of the brilliancy of Cintra, and still more of the East, and
I suppose that this region would pale beside them; yet I am content
to marvel at what I see, and think of Virgil's description of the purple
meads of Elysium.

No wonder that, exhausted by the *Arians*, released from pupils,
Newman felt Froude's suggestion a few months later of a winter
in the Mediterranean "very tempting. It quite unsettled me, and
I have had a distracted night with the thought of it". He is sad
to think "how little real stability of mind I have yet attained".
Afraid of intruding on Hurrell's father, anxious about the expense,
about the length of time away, he yet cannot bear to refuse.

"What a name the Mediterranean is! . . . And I feel the need of [travel]. I am suspicious of becoming narrow-minded . . . I wish to experience the feeling and trial of expansiveness of views . . . to say I had and to know how to meet it in the case of others . . ."

They set out in December, Newman "despatching" verses for the *Lyra* on his way to Southampton and writing to his mother of casual encounters on the journey—"I have been talkative and agreeable without end . . . now that I have set up for a man of the world it is my vocation . . . at times it seems to be miserable going away for so long . . ."

Oddly enough he made trouble for himself with a man (obviously drunk) on the coach.

The first act ended by his calling me a d... fool. The second by his insisting on two most hearty shakes of the hand with the protest that he certainly did think me very injudicious and ill-timed. I had opened by telling him he was talking great nonsense to a silly goose of a maid-servant stuck atop of the coach; so I had no reason to complain of his choosing to give me the retort uncourteous . . . He assured me he reverenced my cloth. It is so odd, he thought I had attacked him under personal feeling.

The vessel was a steam-packet and as such Newman tells his mother "under the Navy". He likes the officers but they "have made very few inductions and are not in the habit of investigating causes—the very reverse of philosophers". How amazed these unphilosophic officers would have been at the philosopher's description of his own seasickness that follows.

It is an uncomfortable feeling certainly; but in saying that, I have said the worst of it. Never certainly had I ailment more easy to bear; and, so far from having my spirits depressed, I could do nothing but laugh at the oddity of my plight. It began on going down to dinner on Saturday. The motion is felt much more below, and the cabin is close. A strange feeling came over me; the heaving to and fro of everything seemed to puzzle me from head to foot, but in such a vague, mysterious way, that I could not get hold of it, or say what was the matter with me, or where. On I ate; I was determined, for it is one of the best alleviations. On I drank, but in so absurdly solemn a way, with such a perplexity of mind, not to say of body, that, as I have said, I laughed at myself. How I wished dinner over! Yet, on I sat, heaving

up and down, to and fro, in an endless, meaningless motion, a trouble
without a crisis; the discomfort of an uneasy dream. I went upstairs
and got better. Then I lay down and was well. Got up at eleven at
night, walked about and was better again—went to bed and slept
soundly.

The selected letters of this tour fill 150 pages of Anne Mozley's
collection. They show Newman's relief from overwork "like
steam expanding itself", the classical and historical associations
that made each new place a sort of homecoming, the intimate
understanding of his family. Every passing thought and feeling
is of interest. Only the merest hint of all this can be given by
occasional quotation. And the verses pour out: on Athanasius,
on the Church of Rome, on the Nature of Man; he enjoys the
fireflies and the Great Bear "close to the water's edge" which
however "quite squints, like a word ill spelt". Passing the
Portuguese coast he sees "visions such as I can hardly believe to
be real . . . the first foreign soil I have come near", sights Cape
St. Vincent and the Rock of Gibraltar, and writes a curious
letter home on the effects on himself of all this excitement.

I no longer wonder at younger persons being carried away with
travelling and corrupted; for certainly the illusions of the world's
magic can hardly be fancied while one remains at home. I never
felt any pleasure or danger from the common routine of pleasures
which most persons desire and suffer from—balls, or pleasure parties,
or sights—but I think it does require strength of mind to keep the
thoughts where they should be while the variety of strange sights—
political, moral, and physical—are passed before the eyes, as in a tour
like this.

"Off the Lizard" he dwelt on this thought in the poem
"Wanderings"; also "Off Cape Trafalgar" on his home "now a
thousand miles away"; he saw

> The vision of my past innumerous deeds,
> My deep heart-courses, and their motive-seeds.

He looked with dread on his country's earthly power and
wealth, so very manifest to a traveller. Unlike Hannah More,
who while lamenting the sins of a worldly society glanced joyfully at the increase of trade as hopeful for a prosperity that

H

should later extend to the poorest, Newman saw this prosperity itself as terrifying. Leaving Gibraltar he wrote:

> Tyre of the West, and glorying in the name
>   More than in Faith's pure fame!
> O trust not crafty fort nor rock renown'd
>   Earn'd upon hostile ground;
> Wielding Trade's master-keys, at thy proud will
>   To lock or loose its waters, England! trust not still.
> Dread thine own power! Since haughty Babel's prime,
>   High towers have been men's crime.
>
>   . . . .
>
> He who scann'd Sodom for His righteous men
>   Still spares thee for thy ten;
> But, should vain tongues the Bride of Heaven defy,
>   He will not pass thee by;
>
>   . . . .

The landing at Gibraltar had been entirely delightful. He sends home a case of oranges, a packet of letters—and more verses. On December 19th he writes again from the ship . . .

What has inspired me with all sorts of strange reflections these two days is the thought that I am in the Mediterranean. Consider how the coasts of the Mediterranean have been the seat and scene of the most celebrated empires and events which are in history. Think of the variety of men, famous in every way, who have had to do with it. Here the Romans and Carthaginians fought; here the Phoenicians traded; here Jonah was in the storm; here St. Paul was shipwrecked; here the great Athanasius voyaged to Rome.

And again:

Mount Atlas soon showed itself again, and went with us the greater part of the day. A sublime range, indeed, with its head every now and then in the clouds, and three or four tiers of heights under it, till the eye came down to the cliffs overhanging the sea—*vide* the first fifty lines of the "Odyssey". . . . This morning (the 23rd), we neared Cape Bon, and saw the track to Carthage. An island lies to the west, and the course is between the two. Nothing I had seen so touched me as this. I thought of the Phoenicians, Tyre, of the Punic Wars, of Cyprian, and the glorious Churches now annihilated; the two headlands looked the same then as now; and I recollected I was now looking at Africa for the last time in my life.

Christmas Day near Malta brought a bitter disappointment. Not allowed to land, the Captain taking in coal all the morning, the three clerical travellers could not achieve any kind of service.

But what provokes me is that the coal will be got in by the afternoon, and they are making preparations for a Christmas dinner, which seems incongruous. This morning we saw a poor fellow in the Lazaret close to us, cut off from the ordinances of his Church, saying his prayers with his face to the house of God in his sight over the water; and it is a confusion of face to me that the humblest Romanist testifies to his Saviour, as I, a minister, do not.

He adds:

Yet I do what I can, and shall try to do more, for I am very spiteful . . . One of the first sights we came to in Malta was St. Paul's Bay, where tradition goes that the Apostle was wrecked. Above St. Paul's Bay is Citta Vecchia, where probably was the Roman garrison spoken of, Acts xxviii . . . The bells are beautiful here, as at Gibraltar and Cadiz, deep and sonorous, and they have been going all the morning, to me very painfully (for reasons given above).

Between Zante and Patras he writes again:

It is so strange in a vessel: you go on at your employment downstairs; you are called on deck, and find everything new. A scene is spread before you as if by magic, and you cannot believe it is real. I am now in the Greek sea, the scene of old Homer's song and of the histories of Thucydides. Yesterday was the most delightful day I have had.

Of Zante he says:

Virgil calls the island "nemorosa"—it still deserves the title. The whole face of a beautiful and varied rock was covered with olive-trees in an exquisite way. . . . The mountains are multiplied without end, one piled on the other, and of such fine shapes and colours; some very high and steep like giants, and black at top, or bleached with snow; and to think that here were Brasidas, Phormio, Demosthenes, Cimon, and the rest!

And again:

When I was for hours within half a mile of Ithaca, as I was this morning, what did I not feel! Not from classical associations, but the thought that what I saw before me was the reality of what had been the earliest vision of my childhood. Ulysses and Argus, which I had known by heart, occupied the very isle I saw . . . Homer calls the island "dear and little". I gazed on it by the quarter of an hour together, being quite satisfied with the sight of the rock. I thought of Ham, and of all the various glimpses which memory barely retains, and which fly from me when I pursue them, of that earliest time of life when one seems almost to realise the remnants of a pre-existing state. Oh, how I longed to touch the land, and to satisfy myself that it was not a mere vision that I saw before me!

At Corfu:

It is an overpowering thought to recollect that the place looked precisely the same in the times of Homer and Thucydides, as being stamped with the indelible features of the "everlasting hills".

. . . Here that famous faction fight began which eventually ran through Greece; and what a strange contrast was the scene last night at the Palace—the ball on the anniversary of Constitution Day—at the magnificent palace of a nation in the time of Thucydides not merely barbarous, but unknown. Dresses, novel to them, and unbecoming, but rendered fashionable as being the garb of their masters, soldiers in a like costume, and Greek names and faces in the midst of them all; all mixed up and dancing together, as if it were the most natural thing in the world. Let me set it down in my books, a proposition settled and indisputable, that no change is so great as to be improbable . . . January 4 . . . I have a great deal to say, but fear I shall forget it. No description can give you any idea of what I have seen, but I will not weary you with my delight; yet does it not seem a strange paradox to say that, though I am so much pleased, I am not interested? That is I don't think I should care—rather I should be very glad— to find myself suddenly transported to my rooms at Oriel, with my oak sported, and I lying at full length on my sofa. After all, every kind of exertion is to me an effort: whether or not my mind has been strained and wearied with the necessity of constant activity, I know not: or whether, having had many disappointments, and suffered much from the rudeness and slights of persons I have been cast with, I shrink involuntarily from the contact of the world, and, whether or not natural disposition assists this feeling, and a perception almost morbid of my deficiencies and absurdities—anyhow, neither the kindest attentions nor the most sublime sights have over me influence enough to draw me out of the way, and, deliberately as I have set about my present wanderings, yet I heartily wish they were over, and I only endure the sights, and had much rather *have* seen them than *see* them, though the while I am extremely astonished and almost enchanted at them.

Here they land and begin to travel by road. Mrs. Newman was an enthusiastic gardener and her son sends her the seeds of rare flowers, giving too descriptions of the growth of myrtle, olive, cypress, vine, and arbutus. He writes:

Our rides across country have given me some definite notion of the state of travelling in Greece in the times of Thucydides, etc. (also I have some drawings). It is astonishing I should have so long read about a country without realising it, and I am amazed how it ever *became* one country; how its inhabitants ever had intercourse with each other, how they ever could go to war, etc., etc.; for it is one heap of mountains thrown together in the wildest way conceivable.

They meet for the first time the Greek Church.

The churches are Venetian; but why it was that the Venetians extended the Greek communion I have not made out . . . The Greek clergy of these islands, as of the Morea, are of a lower rank, as our Methodists. They are said to be very ignorant, but moral in their lives. They interfere little, or not at all, with their flocks, who pay them their offering and receive the rites of religion as a *quid pro quo*. There seem to be no endowments, but the clergy are dependent on their people . . . The Greeks are very rigid in their fasts; besides the forty days in Lent, they have forty before Christmas, and some others. At these times they eat no meat; the pirates are as rigid in keeping them as others. I turned over the leaves of one or two books in the country church; one was a collection of prayers by John of Damascus. There was little objectionable that I saw in either of the books; much that was very good. There was a prayer to the Virgin, a prayer to the Guardian Angel; but the doctrine of the Trinity was the prominent subject in all of them. The pictures I spoke of abounded in representations of the Deity; in one I saw the Trinity. St. Michael seems a principal saint here; his figure is prominent in the pictures of the Last Judgment. At St. Spiridion's people were ever coming in, weeping and bowing and kissing the pictures.

At Corfu for the first time for five weeks the travellers attended a service at an English Church "and it was quite a comfort to get there. I had hoped there might have been the Sacrament." This was on the Epiphany, "the Greek Christmas Day".

All this time he had had no news from home. He writes:

> I do so long to hear from you; there is just a chance of my hearing at Malta by the packet that left London about the 19th. I dream about you all, and that letters are brought me; but, when I begin to read, they are illegible, or I wake up, as if there were men trying to tell me and others preventing it. And the ship bells are so provokingly like the Oriel clock, that I fancy myself there.

Back at Malta on January 10th the travellers have to submit to quarantine. In the Lazaretto Newman is still full of all he has seen. To Bowden he writes:

> Only imagine my pleasure at being in these places! I was in silent wonder; and everything so grand and beautiful, and the mode of conveyance such that I could look on without stop and without fatigue. I had Homer's *Odyssey*, Virgil and Thucydides with me, and seemed transported back to their times, for everything looks now just as it did then. Mountains cannot change . . . well did Homer in the beginning of the *Odyssey* speak of [Mount Atlas] as supporting the heaven. It has just that effect if you take the Mediterranean as the great centre of the earth, and the sky stretched over it as a curtain.

The time in the Lazaretto begins prosperously. He admits to a fatigue in the hand from much writing:

> My dear Mother will say I am doing too much; but to one who has been employing his mind actively for years, nothing is so wearisome as idleness, nothing so irksome as dissipation. I assure you, I feel much more comfortable now than when I was on that restless element which is the type of human life—and much less wearied in prison than in seeing sights . . . The *Hermes* left this place on Saturday last—the 12th—and I saw it go off with strange feelings. I had been securely conveyed in it for five weeks, during which time I had never once slept ashore. It was a kind of home; it has taken me up from England, and it was going back there. I shall never take a voyage again. As it went off, I seemed more cast upon the world than I ever had been, and to be alone—no tie remaining between England and myself; nor any assignable path by which I can get back . . .
> I believe in the whole Lazaret there is but one fireplace beside our own. We burn olive wood. I assure you we make ourselves very comfortable. We feed well from an hotel across the water. The Froudes draw and paint. I have hired a violin, and, bad as it is, it

sounds grand in such spacious halls. I write verses, and get up some Italian, and walk up and down the rooms about an hour and a half daily; and we have a boat, and are allowed to go about the harbour.

Apparently the Lazaretto was haunted or had that repute. Newman and the Froudes all heard strange sounds and Newman does not repudiate this explanation as impossible.

You may say the noises came from some strange transmission of sound; or you may say that the quarantine island is hardly Christian ground. Anyhow, we cannot doubt that evil spirits in some way or other are always about us; and I had comfort in the feeling that, whatever was the need, ordinary or extraordinary, I should have protection equal to it.

Even before he reaches Rome, Newman's strange mixed feeling about the Catholic Church becomes apparent.

I have hitherto seen little of the Greek and Latin Churches, but what I have seen fires me "with great admiration". I do not perceive that my opinion has in any respect changed about them; but it is fearful to have before one's eyes the perversion of all the best, the holiest, the most exalted feelings of human nature. Everything in St. John's Church is admirable, if it did not go too far; it is a beautiful flower run to seed. I am impressed with a sad presentiment, as if the gift of truth when once lost was lost for ever. And so the Christian world is gradually becoming barren and effete, as land which has been worked out and has become sand. We have lasted longer than the South, but we too are going, as it would seem.

. . . As to the number of sects which have split off from the Church, many of them have already ended in Socinianism and heresy worse than any in Rome or Constantinople. . . . Rome is the city of the Apostles, and a place to rest one's foot in, whatever be the after-corruption. We shall go almost by the track of St. Paul from Malta to Rome.

Before, however, the party leaves Malta one letter must be quoted—the typical utterance of a sick man. Newman had caught a cold sitting up in bed the better to hear the ghost in the Lazaretto. He writes:

I am properly taken at my word. I have been sighing for rest and quiet. This is the sixth day since I left the "Lazaret"; and I have hardly seen or spoken to anyone. The Froudes dine out every day, and are out all the morning of course. The two last days they have been on a visit to a friend [I wished and insisted on their doing all this]. Last night I put a blister on my chest, and, never having had one on before, you may fancy my awkwardness in taking it off and dressing the place of it this morning. I ought to have had four hands. . . . Well, I am set upon a solitary life, and therefore ought to have experience what it is; nor do I repent. But even St. Paul had his ministers. I have sent to the library and got *Marriage* to read! Don't smile—this juxtaposition is quite accidental. You are continually in my thoughts, of course. I know what kindness I should have at home; and it is no new feeling with me, only now for the first time brought out, that I do not feel this so much as I ought. Thank God, my spirits have not failed me once. They used, when I was solitary, but I am callous now. Last night, as I put on my blister, I reflected it was just a week since I caught my cold at the Lazaret by speaking to a ghost. I wonder how long I shall last without any friend about me. Scripture so clearly seems to mark out that we should not be literally solitary. The Apostles were sent two and two, and had their attendants, so I suppose I should soon fail. I am glad Frank [in Persia] has the comfort of friends about him.

The words in brackets were added by Newman himself later. Meanwhile his family were evidently much upset. "As to Froude, whom Jemima blames," Newman writes, "I cannot have fully stated how it was, I was left alone at Malta. . . . You know I can be very earnest in entreating to be left alone. If I said anything else in my letter, it was the inconsistency of the moment."

Naples none of the party liked, but to Sicily Newman lost his heart and determined to return for a more prolonged stay.

I am drawn to it as by a lode stone. . . . It has been a day in my life to have seen Egesta . . . its ruins with its temple. O wonderful sight! full of the most strange pleasure.

The history of Sicily

beginning with the highest antiquity—unites in due time both with the Greek history and the Roman. It was the theme of almost every poet and every historian and the remains in it of the past are of an earlier antiquity and more perfect than those of other countries. And now it lies in desolation.

One longer description must be quoted.

The hill on which we stood was covered with ruins, especially of a theatre. Opposite to it, a precipitous rock started out of the ravine below. On the hill beyond it there were, as on our hill, ruins; and we conjectured they might mark the site of the Greek town, but on the circular hill there was nothing but a single Temple. Such was the genius of ancient Greek worship—grand in the midst of error, simple and unadorned in its architecture; it chose some elevated spot, and fixed there its solitary witness, where it could not be hid. I believe it is the most perfect building remaining anywhere—Doric—six gigantic pillars before and behind, twelve in length, no roof. Its history is unknown. The temples of later and classical times have vanished—the whole place is one ruin, except this in the waste of solitude. A shepherd's hut is near, and a sort of farmyard—a number of eager dogs—a few rude intrusive men, who would have robbed us, I fancy, had they dared. On the hill on which the theatre stood was a savage-looking bull, prowling amid the ruins. Mountains around and Eryx in the distance. The past and the present! Once these hills were full of life! I began to understand what Scripture means when speaking of lofty cities vaunting in the security of their strongholds. What a great but ungodly sight was this place in its glory! and then its history; to say nothing of Virgil's fictions. Here it was that Nicias came; this was the ally of Athens; what a strange place! How did people take it into their heads to plant themselves here.

To Tom Mozley Newman writes of the Church news:

On reading the papers of the beginning and middle of February I hate the Whigs (of course, as Rowena says, in a Christian way) more bitterly than ever. We do so wish to know what the Church in general, then Oxford, and then certain of our friends in particular think of the atrocious Irish sacrilege Bill.[1] What Magister Præpositus, *e.g.*, says about it, and what poor Whately (*entre nous*).

To another friend he writes in sarcastic fashion:

Froude heard from Keble the day before yesterday, and so received news of Arnold's plan of Church Reform, which seems very comprehensive. If I understand it right, all sects (the Church inclusive), are to hold their meetings in the parish churches, though not at the same hour of course. He excludes Quakers and Roman Catholics, yet even with this exclusion, surely there will be too many sects in some places for one day. This strikes me as a radical defect in his plan.

[1] See infra page 232–3.

If I propose an amendment, I should say pass an Act to oblige some persuasions to *change* the Sunday. If you have two Sundays in the week, you could accommodate any probable number of sects, and in this way you would get over Whately's objection against the Evangelical party and others; make *them* keep Sunday on Saturday. This would not interfere with the Jews (who would of course worship in the parish church), for they are too few to take up a whole day. Luckily the Mahommedan holiday is already on a Friday, so there will be no difficulty in that quarter.

In the *Apologia* he says:

At this time I was specially annoyed with Dr. Arnold, though it did not last into later years. Some one, I think, asked, in conversation at Rome, whether a certain interpretation of Scripture was Christian? It was answered that Dr. Arnold took it; I interposed, "But is *he* a Christian?" The subject went out of my head at once; when afterwards I was taxed with it, I could say no more in explanation, than (what I believe was the fact) that I must have had in mind some free views of Dr. Arnold about the Old Testament;—I thought I must have meant, "Arnold answers for the interpretation, but who is to answer for Arnold?"[1]

To Jemima a few days later he writes:

We have encouraging accounts about Prussia from M. Bunsen, who has received us very kindly. There is every reason for expecting that the Prussian Communion will be applying to us for ordination in no long time. We hear, also, much about Germany, in the way of painters! which leads us to hope that a high reverential spirit is stirring among them. And the Wilberforces tell us that the recently ejected ministers of Geneva are applying to England for Episcopal ordination. Further, our friend the Yankee, whom we fell in with again here, gave us so promising an account of the state of things in America, that we mean, when turned out of St. Mary's, to go preaching through the churches of the United States.

Meanwhile the first sight of Rome itself had been overwhelming and the feeling persisted. He writes to Harriett:

And now what can I say of Rome, but that it is the first of cities, and that all I ever saw are but as dust (even dear Oxford inclusive)

[1] *Apologia*, pp. 33-4.

compared with its majesty and glory? Is it possible that so serene and lofty a place is the cage of unclean creatures? I will not believe it till I have evidence of it.

From Rome a burst of correspondence with all his friends conveys much of Newman's strange state of mind: passionate admiration fights with lifelong suspicion. To Rogers he writes:

We arrived at this wonderful place only Saturday last (March 2) from Naples. It is the first city which I have been able to admire, and it has swallowed up, like Aaron's rod, all the admiration which, in the case of others, is often distributed among Naples, Valletta, and other places. It is scarcely with patience I hear people talking of Naples in comparison—nor will I degrade Rome by dwelling on the notion. Of course, I have seen very little of it; but the effect of every part is so vast and overpowering—there is such an air of greatness and repose cast over the whole, and, independent of what one knows from history, there are such traces of long sorrow and humiliation, suffering, punishment and decay, that one has a mixture of feelings, partly such as those with which one would approach a corpse, and partly those which would be excited by the sight of the spirit which had left it. It brings to my mind Jeremiah's words in the Lamentations, when Jerusalem or (sometimes) the prophet, speaks as the smitten of God. Oxford, of course, must ever be a sacred city to an Oxonian, and is to me. It would be a strange want of right pride to think of disloyalty to it, even if our creed were not purer than the Roman; yet the lines of Virgil keenly and affectionately describe what I feel about this wonderful city. Repeat them in your memory every word, and dwell on each. "*Urbem, quam dicunt Romam, Meliboee, putavi stultus ego!*" etc. And if you had seen the cypresses of Corfu, and the graceful, modest way in which they shoot straight up with a composed shape, yet boldly in their way, being landmarks almost for miles round, you would see the beauty of the comparison of the *inter viburna cupressi*. Since I have been abroad I have been taking in stores of pleasure for many years to come. It is impossible to enter into the full power of what one sees at once—the sights of celebrated places are like seeds sown in the mind. I have often felt the retrospect more delightful than the first enjoyment, great as that was. It is strange, too, the different kind of pleasure one has in different places. Only think, I have seen Ithaca—seen it for hours—coasting, in fact, all round it; and then again Rhium and Antirrhium and Corcyra—and again Sicily—and the landmarks leading to Carthage. All these places had their own pleasure, and as different as Homer is from Thucydides. I have so often wished for you and others to share my gratification, but the plague is, one feels it *never* can be. In other cases one says, "Well, some other day, perhaps"; but, though you may see, I shall not—it is a thing past with me, not to return. . . .

No words can describe [the churches]. They could not have been in any place but Rome, which has turned the materials and the buildings of the Empire to the purposes of religion. Some of them are literally ancient buildings—as the Pantheon, and the portion of the Baths of Diocletian which is turned into a church. And all—St. Peter's, St. John Lateran, etc.—are enriched with marbles, etc., which old Roman power alone could have collected. The first effect produced on the mind by these noble piles (and I can as yet speak of no other), arises from their gigantic dimensions—everything is proportioned to the size of the building. The statues of the Apostles (*e.g.*) —all that the Germans would call *insanae molis*—produce quite a moral effect of humiliation on the *homunciones* who gaze on them. Thus we have all the riches of the latter ages of the arts added to the magnitude which is the peculiarity of the early Egyptian, Cyclopean, etc. It is a realisation of the skill and power of Daedalus, who was beautiful while he was stupendous (*posuitque immania templa*, etc.).

While most of the letters dwell on the glory of the city and condemn the existing Church, one to Samuel Rickards, written a few days later from Naples, works out in some detail a curious theory. Rome is Babylon, is accursed, but this means the city of Rome, not necessarily its Church. St. Gregory had recognised this when he ordered the destruction of the monuments of pagan Rome. A Roman tradition emphasised that no human power could destroy the city. St. Gregory had believed it "reserved for future superhuman judgments." The temporal power of the Papacy had in some way involved the great Apostasy. By an old Irish prophecy the line of Popes was now within nine or ten of its close—at the end of the list we read, "Then shall she that sitteth upon the seven hills be destroyed when the Lord shall come to judge the earth."

Rome has had one character for 2,500 years; of late centuries the Christian Church has been the instrument by which it has acted—it is its slave. The day will come when the captive will be set free; but how a distinction is to be drawn between two powers, spiritual and devilish, which are so strangely united, is as much beyond our imagination as it was beyond the power of the servants in the parable to pull up the tares from the wheat; but that it is incomprehensible is no objection to the notion of God's doing it.

And to Christie:

. . . Well then, again, after this, you have to view Rome as a place of religion; and here what mingled feelings come upon one—you are in the place of martyrdom and burial of apostles and saints; you have about you the buildings and the sights they saw, and you are in the city to which England owes the blessing of the Gospel. But then, on the other hand, the superstitions, or rather, what is far worse, the solemn reception of them as an essential part of Christianity. But then, again, the extreme beauty and costliness of the churches; and then, on the contrary, the knowledge that the most famous was built (in part) by the sale of indulgences. Really this is a cruel place. There is more to be seen and thought of daily. It is a mine of all sorts of excellences.

The Froudes went on their way to the South of France but Newman stuck to his determination to return to Sicily. On April 11 he writes to Jemima:

How shall I describe the sadness with which I left the tombs of the Apostles? Rome, not as a city, but as the scene of sacred history, has a part of my heart, and in going away from it I am as if tearing it in twain. I wandered about the place after the Froudes had gone with a blank face. I went to the Church of S. Maria in Cosmedin, which Dionysius founded A.D. 260, and where Austin is said to have studied rhetoric. I mounted the height where St. Peter was martyred, and for the last time went through the vast spaces of his wonderful basilica, and looked at his place of burial, and then prepared for my departure. Also I have lost my companions, and I was going among strangers into a wild country to live a wild life, to travel in solitudes, and to sleep in dens of the earth—and all for what? For the gratification of an imagination, for the idea of a warm fancy which might be a deceit, drawn by a strange love of Sicily to gaze upon its cities and mountains.
. . . I ought to tell you about the Miserere at Rome, my going up St. Peter's, and the Easter illumination, our conversation with Dr. Wiseman and with M. Bunsen, our search for the church of St. Thomas of Canterbury, my pilgrimage to the place of St. Paul's martyrdom, the Catacombs, and all the other sights which have stolen away half my heart, but I forbear till we meet. Oh, that Rome were not Rome! but I seem to see as clear as day that a union with her is *impossible*. She is the cruel Church asking of us impossibilities, excommunicating us for disobedience, and now watching and exulting over our approaching overthrow.

CHAPTER XVII

How To Accomplish It

HURRELL FROUDE too was writing letters, some of which were later published in his *Remains*. To Keble he wrote on his way home:

> The only thing I can put my hand on as an acquisition is having formed an acquaintance with a man of some influence at Rome, Monsignor Wiseman, the head of the English college, who has enlightened Newman and me on the subject of our relations to the Church of Rome. We got introduced to him to find out whether they would take us in on any terms to which we could twist our consciences, and we found to our dismay that not one step could be gained without swallowing the Council of Trent as a whole. We made our approach to the subject as delicately as we could. Our first notion was that the terms of communion were within certain limits under the control of the Pope, or that in case he could not dispense solely yet at any rate the acts of one Council might be rescinded by another; indeed, that in Charles the First's time it had been intended to negotiate a reconciliation on the terms on which things stood before the Council of Trent. But we found to our horror that the doctrine of the infallibility of the Church made the acts of each successive Council obligatory for ever. . . .
>
> . . . So much for the Council of Trent, for which Christendom has to thank Luther and the Reformers. Newman declares that ever since I heard this I have become a staunch Protestant, which is a most base calumny on his part, though I own it has altogether changed my notions of the Roman Catholics, and made me wish for the total overthrow of their system. I think that the only τόπος now is "the ancient Church of England", and as an explanation of what one means, "Charles the First and the Nonjurors." When I come home I mean to read and write all sorts of things, for now that one is a Radical there is no use in being nice.[1]

Newman in the *Apologia* gives briefly his own account of their Catholic contacts:

[1] Hurrell Froude. *Remains*, Vol. I, p. 306.

We kept clear of Catholics throughout our tour. I had a conversation with the Dean of Malta, a most pleasant man, lately dead; but it was about the Fathers, and the library of the great Church. I knew the Abbate Santini, at Rome, who did no more than copy for me the Gregorian tones. Froude and I made two calls upon Monsignore (now Cardinal) Wiseman at the Collegio Inglese, shortly before we left Rome. Once we heard him preach at a church in the Corso. I do not recollect being in a room with any other ecclesiastics, except a Priest at Castro-Giovanni in Sicily, who called on me when I was ill, and with whom I wished to hold a controversy. As to Church Services, we attended the Tenebrae, at the Sestine, for the sake of the Miserere; and that was all. My general feeling was, "All, save the spirit of man, is divine. . . ." When we took leave of Monsignore Wiseman, he had courteously expressed a wish that we might make a second visit to Rome; I said with great gravity, "We have a work to do in England."[1]

Of the three men Wiseman seems to have been most deeply affected by the meeting. He wrote twenty years later:

It remains marked with gratitude in my mind as an epoch in my life. From that hour I watched with interest and love the Movement of which I then caught the first glimpse. My studies changed their course, the bent of my mind was altered, in the strong desire to co-operate in the new mercies of Providence.[2]

To realise the annoyance caused by Froude's letter when it came to be published we must remember that to call oneself a Radical in those days was more extreme than to declare oneself a Bolshevist today. Then, too, the idea of re-union with Rome had long died, would not soon rise again and was felt to be utterly disloyal to the Church of England. Abbott makes great play of this letter as disproving Newman's own account of the same visit given in the *Apologia*. Even if Newman had been Froude it is hard to see how anyone could miss the ironic note, but Newman was not Froude and on this question of Rome there was a marked difference in their views. Froude, it is true, was *more* shocked than Newman by such things as the Catholicism of Naples: (". . . I have seen priests laughing when at the Confessional; and indeed it is plain, that unless they habitually made light of very gross immorality, three-fourths of the population would be excommunicated.")[3]—

[1] *Apologia*, pp. 32-3-4.
[2] Dawson: *Spirit of the Oxford Movement*, p. 54.
[3] Hurrell Froude: *Remains*, Vol. I, p. 294.

but his view of Rome's position as a Church was far more definite, his criticism of the Church of England more pronounced.

In the main however, both men were thinking along the same lines. While furious with the Liberal attack, they felt deeply that the alternative to an external parliamentary 'reform' of the Church must be a true inward self-reform. They desired for the Church of England a Counter-reformation that should restore all that belonged to her Catholic past. They believed her a living branch of the one Church founded by Christ.

Their minds at this time were giving birth to all the elements later to be drawn out as the doctrine of the *Via Media*.

The Oxford Movement in embryo may be seen in Newman's "Home Thoughts Abroad", published three years later in the *British Magazine*, and republished in *Discussions and Arguments*, under the title "How to Accomplish It".[1]

The two Englishmen, "looking out from the Capitol" over "a city which the Christian can never survey without the bitterest, the most loving, and the most melancholy thoughts," get into talk:

My friend began by alluding to a former conversation in which I had expressed my anticipation, that Rome, as a city, was still destined to bear the manifestation of divine judgments. He said, "Have you really the heart to say that all this is to be visited and overthrown?" His eye glanced at St. Peter's. I was taken by surprise, and for a moment overcome, as well as he; but the parallel of the Apostle's question in the Gospel soon came to my aid, and I said, by way of answer, "Master see what manner of stones and what buildings are here!" He smiled; and we relapsed into our meditative mood. . . .
. . . He replied by one of his occasional flights—"If Rome itself, as you say, is not to last, why should the daughter who has severed herself from Rome? The amputated limb dies sooner than the wounded and enfeebled trunk which loses it."

"To cut off a limb", Ambrose goes on, "is anyhow a strange mode of saving it from the influence of some constitutional ailment".

I answered, "I will grant you thus much,—that the present is an unsatisfactory, miserable state of things; that there is a defect, an evil

---

[1] I am glad that Christopher Dawson in his *Spirit of the Oxford Movement* (see p. 51, *seq.*) attaches the same importance as I do to this paper and I entirely agree with his identification of "Ambrose" with Froude.

in existing circumstances, which we should pray and labour to remove; yet I can grant no more. The Church is founded on a doctrine—the gospel of Truth; it is a means to an end. Perish the Church Catholic itself (though, blessed be the promise, this cannot be), yet let it perish *rather* than the Truth should fail. Purity of faith is more precious to the Christian than unity itself. If Rome has erred grievously in doctrine (and in so thinking we are both of one mind), then is it a duty to separate even from Rome." . . ."You allow much more," he replied, "than most of us; yet even you, as it seems to me, have not a deep sense enough of the seriousness of our position. Recollect, at the Reformation we did that which is a sin, *unless* we prove it to be a duty."

Ambrose continuing to urge the duty of unity next makes use of those very quotations from St. Augustine, that very argument from the story of the Donatists, which were in the event to bring Newman into the Catholic Church. At this date he could set them down and remain unmoved—or perhaps not unmoved but quite unconvinced—by them. He answers:

". . . after all, they [i.e. Roman Catholics] are but a part of the Christian world. Is the Greek communion to go for nothing, extending from St. Petersburg to Corinth and Antioch? or the Armenian churches? and the English communion which has branched off to India, Australia, the West Indies, the United States, Canada, and Nova Scotia? The true state of the case is this: the condition of the early Church, as Augustine and Cyril describe it, exists no more; it is found nowhere. You may apply, indeed, the terms which they used of it to the present time, and call the Romanists Catholics, as they claim to be; but this is a fiction and a theory not the expression of a visible fact. Is it not a mere theory by which the Latin Church can affect to spread itself into Russia? I suspect, in spite of St. Cyril, you might ask in vain for their churches under the name of Catholic throughout the autocrat's dominions, or in Greece, as well as in England or Scotland. Where is the Catholic Bishop of Winchester or Lincoln? where the Catholic Church in England as a visible institution? No more is it such in Scotland; not to go on to speak of parts of Germany or the New World. All that can be said by way of reply is, that it is a very considerable communion and venerable from its consistency and antiquity."

Newman's view in fact is that the state of the Christian world is so far altered that the Fathers cannot be held to be "representatives of things now existing." Not only are there divisions in the

Church Catholic, but there exist also bodies of Christians separated from it retaining something of tradition and of truth. And he draws a parallel which he was to use and develop for many years to come:

" . . . In the latter ages of Judaism, the ten tribes, and afterwards the Samaritans, and then the proselytes of the gate, present a parallel, as having a position beyond the literal scope of the Mosaic law. I shall scruple, therefore, to apply the strong language which Cyprian uses against schismatics to the Scottish Presbyterians or to the Lutherans. At least, they have the Scriptures. You understand why I mention this—to show, by an additional illustration, that not every word that the Fathers utter concerning the Church Catholic applies at once to the Church of this day. The early Christians had not the complete canon, nor were books then common, nor could most of them read."

On the other hand they had then the tradition of the early Church—historical yet so close at hand that the Fathers "did not in their writings curiously separate the Church's intrinsic and permanent authority as divine, from her temporary office of bearing witness to the Apostolic doctrine as to an historical fact."

Ambrose says he must take time to think of this; and the writer, who calls himself Cyril, adds, "To tell the truth I did not see my way clearly how far my own view ought to carry me."

They continue to discuss how far expediency is justified in existing conditions, how far primitive rules can be followed even if not absolutely binding, what can be looked for and arrived at:

My companion went on in his ardent way: "After all, there is no reason why the ancient unity of Christendom should not be revived among us, and Rome be again ecclesiastical head of the whole Church." . . .
. . . "You will," said I, "be much better employed, surely, in speculating upon the means of building up our existing English Church, the Church of Andrewes and Laud, Ken and Butler, than attempting what, even in your own judgment, is an inconsistency. Tell me, can you tolerate the practical idolatry, the virtual worship of the Virgin and the Saints, which is the offence of the Latin Church, and the degradation of moral truth and duty which follows from these?"

Cyril's claim to build upon the ground of Laud and Stilling-fleet is disallowed by Ambrose on two grounds:

"The actual English Church has never adopted it: in spite of the learning of her divines, she has ranked herself among the Protestants, and the doctrine of the Via Media has slept in libraries. Nay, not only is Anglicanism a theory; it represents, after all, but an imperfect system; it implies a return to that inchoate state, in which the Church existed before the era of Constantine. It is a substitution of infancy for manhood."

As good High Churchmen both men are agreed on the desirableness of the union of Church and State as "a wonderful and most gracious phenomenon in Christian history. . . . It is a realization of the Gospel in its highest perfection, when both Caesar and St. Peter know and fulfil their office. I do not expect anything so blessed again. Charles is the King, Laud the prelate, Oxford the sacred city, of this principle; just as Rome is the city of Catholicism, and modern Paris of infidelity".

By this time they have left the Hill of the Capitol and walked as far as the Pincio where they are joined by a third friend designated as Basil, whose views are those of Cyril a little more emphasized. Before the conversation ends all three are agreed upon a practical line of action. "To do anything effectually", says Basil, "we must start upon *recognized* principles and customs, 'developments' not 'innovations', like St. Paul who developed Judaism into Christianity, we must 'take and use what is ready to our hands'. This means first Scripture which all Anglicans accept, next 'existing constitutional and ecclesiastical precedents among ourselves'."

Cyril reminds him that "Providence always says, '*Stand still* and see the salvation of God' and that we 'who are in captivity, must *bide our time*'." This thought of waiting upon a sign from God is intensely characteristic of Newman. The others agreeing that they should build upon what they have, Basil proceeds to summarize: Ordination, which implies both Apostolical Succession, the power of the Bishop, and the Priest's power of remitting and retaining sin.

Next the necessity of sacraments for salvation, the recognition of Confirmation and Matrimony "as spiritual ordinances", forms of absolution and blessing.

"Further, we have the injunction of daily service, and the solemnization of fast and festival days.

. . . "Lastly, we have a yearly confession of the desirableness of a restoration of the primitive discipline.

. . . "On these foundations, properly understood, we may do anything."

. . . "Still you have not touched upon the real difficulty," interrupted Ambrose. "Hildebrand governed an existing body, and was only employed in vindicating for it certain powers and privileges; you, on the other hand, have to make the body, before you proceed to strengthen it. The Church in England is not a body now, it has little or no substantiveness; it has dwindled down to its ministers, who are as much secular functionaries as they are rulers of a Christian people. What reason have you to suppose that the principles you have enumerated will interest an uninstructed, as well as edify an already disciplined, multitude? Still the problem is, How to do it?"

Cyril retorts that Hildebrand himself, that all great reformers, have had to create, that Hildebrand found a Church practically incorporated into the world:

"In planting his lever, which was to break all these irreligious ties, he made the *received* forms and rules of the Church his fulcrum. If master minds are ever granted to us, to build us up in faith and unity, they must do the same; they must take their stand upon that existing basis which Basil has just now described. . . . So far well; but you will say, how is all this to be made interesting to the people? I answer, that the topics themselves which they are to preach are of that striking and attractive nature which carries with it its own influence. The very notion, that representatives of the Apostles are now on earth, from whose Communion we may obtain grace as the first Christians did from the Apostles, is surely, when admitted, of a most transporting and persuasive character. . . . He who is told that the Church is the treasure-house of spiritual gifts, comes for a definite privilege; he who has been taught that it is merely a duty to keep united to the Church, gains nothing, and is tempted to leave it for the meeting-house."

He goes on to show how from lack of use of "the provisions of the old Catholic System" there have grown up clumsy substitutes —calendars of texts for the Scripture lessons, prayer-meetings for the daily service, "individual and self-authorised preachers" for the legitimate priesthood, charitable societies "instead of the strict and enthusiastic Religious Institutions", popular hymns for Psalmody.

Supremely Cyril feels and states the need of some form of monachism.

". . . indeed, I conceive you necessarily must have dissent or monachism in a Christian country;—so make your choice. The more religious minds demand some stricter religion than that of the generality of men; if you do not gratify this desire religiously and soberly, they will gratify it themselves at the expense of unity. . . . We can but desire in our day to keep alive the lamp of truth in the sepulchre of this world till a brighter era; and surely the ancient system I speak of is the providentially designed instrument of this work . . . great towns will never be evangelized merely by the parochial system. They are beyond the sphere of the parish priest, burdened as he is with the endearments and anxieties of a family, and the secular restraints and engagements of the Establishment. The unstable multitude cannot be influenced and ruled except by uncommon means, by the evident sight of disinterested and self-denying love, and elevated firmness. The show of domestic comfort, the decencies of furniture and apparel, the bright hearth and the comfortable table, (good and innocent as they are in their place,) are as ill-suited to the missionary of a town population as to an Apostle. . . ."

. . . "I have been watching with some interest," said Ambrose, who had been silent all this while, "how near, with all your protestations against Popery, you would advance towards it in the course of your speculations. I am now happy to see you will go the full length of what you yourselves seem to admit is considered one of its most remarkable characteristics—monachism." . . .

. . . "I know," answered I, "that is at present the popular notion; but our generation has not yet learned the distinction between Popery and Catholicism. But be of good heart; it will learn many things in time." . . .

. . . The other laughed; and, the day being now someway advanced into the afternoon, we left the garden, and separated.

"Charles is the King, Laud the prelate, Oxford the sacred city . . ." The idealisation of Laud is curious—they must have been rather insensitive not to be haunted by the ears of Prynne and of others severed in the pillory by his orders. But Oxford could be idealised. And so could the Royal Martyr. The doctrine of the divine right of Kings, and the duty of passive obedience or non-resistance to the rightful sovereign, both Newman and Froude realised as distinctively High Church. Newman upholding the union of Church and State was thinking of it as did Hooker, to whom it seemed a "very wicked and brutish opinion" that the royal authority should be limited to merely temporal matters.[1] The relation between Church and State was in the High Anglican tradition (as Christopher Dawson has pointed out) "an almost sacramental bond which moulded the inner life and spiritual ethos of the community". Newman certainly realised this bond and accepted this double loyalty.

The Non-Jurors, who are increasingly in Newman's mind, hold an honourable place in relation to this tradition, despite Johnson's detestation and the contempt of Macaulay and Arnold. For they were the men—Ken and several other bishops, some hundreds of clergy and a small number of the laity—who caused a schism in the Church of England because they would not forswear themselves or abandon their hereditary monarch for a foreign succession when James II was dethroned in 1688—this, though James II was a Papist and the new King was the Protestant William of Orange. When Lake, Bishop of Chichester, was told that if he refused the oath his suspension would take place August 1, and his deprivation the following February 1, he answered that "He considered that the day of *death* and of *judgment* are as certain as the 1st of *August* and the 1st of *February*, and acted accordingly."

But there was something else about the Non-Jurors besides their uncompromising courage and loyalty that made them to a startling degree the forerunners of Newman, Froude and Keble. There are pages, especially in the story of the group called "Usagers" that find a perfect context in the efforts of the nineteenth century Oxford men "to accomplish it". They demanded the restoration of the Prayer Book of Edward VI, especially stressing four points of "usages":

1. The mixed chalice.
2. Prayers for the faithful departed.
3. Prayer for the descent of the Holy Ghost on the consecrated elements.

[1] In the Prayer Book, for instance, Newman would still find the collect (May 29): "Almighty God, our heavenly Father, who of Thine infinite and unspeakable goodness towards us didst in a most extraordinary and wonderful manner disappoint and overthrow the wicked designs of those traiterous, heady and highminded men, who under the pretence of Religion and Thy most holy name, had contrived and wellnigh effected the utter destruction of this Church and Kingdom. . . . Strengthen the hands of our gracious Sovereign King N., and all that are put in authority under him, with judgment and justice, to cut off all such workers of iniquity, as turn Religion into Rebellion, and Faith into Faction; that they may never again prevail amongst us, nor triumph in the ruin of the Monarchy and Thy Church among us."

4. The Oblatory Prayer, offering the elements to the Father as symbols of His Son's Body and Blood.

And they demanded these usages because they were "Primitive and Catholic".

They attacked the more extreme Reformers—especially Calvin and Knox—as Froude was soon to attack them:

> These were the men that laid aside the Mixture; that declared against Prayer for the Dead; that allowed no Eucharistick Sacrifice, nor any Oblatory Prayer which might carry to that sense. . . . I should rather suggest a preference for Justin Martyr and Irenaeus, etc., those primitive non-resisting Fathers, than resign to the novelties of the 16th century and be governed by the tenets of those men who in several countries turned the World upside down, and pressed their Reformation with Fire and Sword.

The Non-Jurors restored daily service morning and evening, claiming justly the authority of a neglected Rubric of the Prayer Book; one even went so far as to administer the Eucharist daily, morning and evening, to his family.

The Non-Jurors failed. The world was against them, and by their splits and divisions they became in some sort against themselves. The schism lasted for about a hundred years, growing weaker with time and at last vanishing wholly away. But it remained as a memory and became for Newman and his friends a high point of that Catholic tradition in the Anglican Church which, though attenuated, had never been wholly lost. Whatever their feelings, they knew that the atmosphere of sanctity attaching to the royal supremacy was gone forever.[1] They might sigh over it, they would waste no time over it. But the Non-Jurors had asserted a profounder principle still, of the rightful independence of the Church. In his most interesting history of the movement, Canon Overton writes:

> The ejection of bishops, simply by an Act of Parliament, without any synodical action, without anything that bore the faintest resemblance to an ecclesiastical judgment; and the putting into their sees— that is, into sees not canonically vacant—new bishops by the civil

---

[1] "I have doubt," Newman had written to Froude in 1830, "whether we *can* consider our King as a proprietor of land on the old Tory theory. The rightful heir was lost in the Revolution; then the nation took the property of the island and gave it to William, and then to George, *on certain conditions*—that of being chief magistrate. Has not the constitution since that time been essentially a republic?"

power, was about as glaring a violation of this principle as can well be conceived; and it is hard to see how those who held the principle could help feeling, not only justified, but in duty bound to continue to exercise the functions which the Church had given them, and which the Church had not taken away from them.

The London Library copy of this book belonged to Leslie Stephen: his autograph is on the title page. The words "simply by an Act of Parliament" are underlined (apparently by him), and in the margin is written the sardonic note, "cf. 1559". This comparison did not apparently suggest itself to Newman for many years to come.

CHAPTER XVIII

Illness in Sicily

RETURNING to Naples en route for Sicily, Newman writes to Jemima of his grief at parting with the Froudes. He had travelled as far as Naples in the company of an English acquaintance met in Rome, but would rather have been in solitude "at a time when my heart was full and when I would fain have enjoyed the only remedy of grief, the opportunity of grieving."

The letter continues:

We had passed Terracina with its white rocks by moonlight; at dawn we had before us a circle of beautiful blue hills, inclosing a rich plain, covered with bright green corn, olives, and figs just bursting into leaf, in which Fondi lies. Then came Mola, where Cicero was murdered, and the country I saw was still more beautiful; and so at length we got to Naples in twenty-nine hours from Rome, including two hours stopping, the distance being about 148 miles. . . . You will ask how I like Naples in a better season; I shall return substantially the same answer . . . the town is essentially a watering place, and more like Brighton than any place I know; the same glare, the same keen brightness of the hills, the same disposition of houses opening upon the sea, the same boisterous wind, the same stimulating air, the same sparkling water, the same bustle, or rather tenfold, and the same apparent idleness of the people. Oh, what a change from the majestic pensiveness of the place I have left, where the Church sits in sackcloth calling on those who pass by to say if anyone's sorrow is like to her sorrow! . . .

. . . I am interrupted by the thought that the decision of the Oriel election is at this very time taking place. The Provost is in the Common-Room, and the Fellows are sitting round. Would that I knew how it was to be! . . .

Delayed in Naples they decided to go up Vesuvius and they started about eleven in the morning, "just," interjects Newman, "as the names of the new Fellows are being given out." A long description concludes: "This is the most wonderful sight I have seen abroad."

It did not tempt him to linger in Naples, but warned of the difficulty of getting provisions in Sicily, he laid in a store of food there—most of which turned out to be bad—"curry powder, spice, pepper, salt, sugar, tea and ham; cold cream, a straw hat, and a map of Sicily. I shall want nothing from the island but macaroni, honey and eggs." He had engaged an Italian servant who had been in various English families, and had taken passage on a sailing vessel. While he was still worrying about whether Rogers had won the Fellowship, some cheese eaten at Naples produced a nightmare which he describes to his mother:

First a weight and horror fell on me, after which I found myself in the tower at Oriel. It was an audit and the Fellows sat round. Jenkyns and the Provost had been quarrelling [what a shame! I suppose they never did in their lives],[1] and the latter had left the room, and Jenkyns to expedite matters had skipt on in the accounts and entered some items without the Provost's sanction (the extreme vividness of all this was its merit; after waking I could hardly believe it was not true). I shook hands first with one Fellow then with another. At last I got a moment to shake hands with the gallant Dornford, who was on my right, with Denison, who stood next, and then Copleston [these were the new tutors in our place],[1] who said: "Newman, let me introduce you to our two new Fellows," pointing to two men who stood on his right round the table. I saw two of the most clumsy, awkward-looking chaps I ever set eyes on, and they had awkward unintelligible names. With great grief of heart, but a most unembarrassed smiling manner, I shook hands with them and wished them joy, and then talked and chatted with the rest as if nothing had happened, yet onging to get away . . . to the shrubberies, which were those of Ham. "There," thought I to myself, "on this seat or that arbour, which I recollect from a boy, I shall recover myself"; but it was not allowed me. I was in my rooms, or some rooms, and had continual interruptions. A father and son, the latter coming into residence, and intending to stand for some Sicilian scholarship. Then came in a brace of gentlemen commoners with hideous faces . . . lastly, my companion with whom I travelled down here from Rome, with a lady under his arm (do what I will I cannot recollect who I thought it was—I saw him with a lady at St. Peter's on Good Friday). This was part of the dream, but only part, and all, I say, so vivid. What shall we say to a bit of cheese awaking the poetical faculty? I hope simply poetical, and not historical. Indeed I have grown calm out of spite, and am now so confident that Rogers has succeeded that I do not think about it.

[1] Added by Newman when editing his letters.

In Sicily at last, horrible beds, abounding in fleas, general dirt and discomfort could not spoil the glory of the country.

> . . . I never knew that Nature could be so beautiful; and to see that view was the nearest approach to seeing Eden. Oh happy I! It was worth coming all the way, to endure sadness, loneliness, weariness, to see it. I felt for the first time in my life, that I should be a better and more religious man if I lived there . . . Etna was magnificent. The scene was sombre with clouds, when suddenly, as the sun descended upon the cone, its rays shot out between the clouds and the snow, turning the clouds into royal curtains, while on one side there was a sort of Jacob's ladder. I understood why the poets made the abode of the gods on Mount Olympus.

Probably Newman's illness was already upon him but the next letters tell of circumstances that certainly aggravated it. The transitions of the climate between heat and cold were extraordinarily severe, and twice he had to spend the night in an open boat; he had several sleepless nights from the fleas, several famished days owing to the bad provisions; there were rough roads and sirocco and at last a doctor who had no English, very little Latin and perhaps not much medical skill.

The whole matter of this return to Sicily and his almost mortal illness is absorbingly interesting from the tremendous importance it held in Newman's own eyes. First his extreme determination to come back to Sicily despite the opposition of his friends and his own deep pain in leaving them, and secondly his care to write out afterwards so minute an account of every detail—written partly in 1834, completed in 1840—the *abridged* account fills seventeen large pages. Anyone who has experienced a severe illness knows how, looking back, it may become fully apparent as a physical medium whereby God was working on the soul. Hence the fascination of every detail—for oneself. "The thought", he says in 1840,

> keeps pressing on me, while I write this, what am I writing it for. Whom have I, whom can I have, who would take interest in it? I was going to say I only have found one who ever took that sort of affectionate interest in me as to be pleased with such details—and this is H(enry) W(ilberforce) and what shall I ever see of him? This is the sort of interest a wife takes and none but she—it is a woman's interest—and that interest, so be it, shall never be taken in me. Never, so be it, shall I be other than God has found me. All my habits for

years, my tendencies, are towards celibacy. I could not take that
interest in this world which marriage requires—I am too disgusted
with this world—and, above all, call it what one will, I have a repugnance to a clergyman's marrying. I do not say it is not lawful—I
cannot deny the right—but, whether a prejudice or not, it shocks me.
And therefore I willingly give up the possession of that sympathy,
which I feel is not, cannot be, granted to me—yet, not the less do I
feel the need of it.

This is omitted by Miss Mozley, and so is another important
element. "The devil" writes Newman, "thinks his time is come,
I was given over into his hands." He had a terrific sense of
struggle. "What I wanted first to speak of was the Providence and
strange meaning of it. I could almost think the devil saw I am
to be a means of usefulness and tried to destroy me."

In his sermons always, later in *Gerontius*, in *Callista*, Newman
showed keen awareness of the devil as our personal relentless
enemy. Yet God's power and providence was over all and he was
confident he would not die. The phrase recurs, "I thought God
had some work for me."

The last sermon he had preached in England had been "Wilfulness the Sin of Saul", and the danger of self-will was ever a note
of his sermons. Whether solely in the delirium of fever, or partly
because these sermons were in some degree preached against his
own temptation, Newman felt now—as he lay three days miserably ill at Leonforte, having ridden and walked forty-two miles
the day before with the fever on him—that he had been self-
willed in leaving the Froudes, in insisting on taking this journey:
"yet I felt and kept saying to myself, 'I have not sinned against
light' and at one time I had a most consoling, overpowering
thought of God's electing love, and seemed to feel that I was His."

Looking back he saw that his thoughts were "heightened" by
delirium, yet he makes these thoughts the occasion for that severity
and self-searching always so startling yet so usual in men of
profound spirituality. In the lives both of Pusey and Keble we find
the same comparison of themselves with one another, the same self-
condemnation. Newman writes:

I seemed to see more and more my utter hollowness. I began to
think of all my professed principles, and felt they were mere intellectual
deductions from one or two admitted truths. I compared myself with
Keble, and felt that I was merely developing his, not my, convictions.

I know I had *very* clear thoughts about this then, and I believe in the main true ones. Indeed, this is how I look on myself; very much (as the illustration goes) as a pane of glass, which transmits heat, being cold itself. I have a vivid perception of the consequences of certain admitted principles, have a considerable intellectual capacity of drawing them out, have the refinement to admire them, and a rhetorical or histrionic power to represent them; and having no great (i.e. no vivid) love of this world, whether riches, honours, or anything else, and some firmness and natural dignity of character, take the profession of them upon me, as I might sing a tune which I liked— loving the Truth, but not possessing it, for I believe myself at heart to be nearly hollow, i.e. with little love, little self-denial. I believe I have some faith, that is all; and, as to my sins, they need my possessing no little amount of faith to set against them and gain their remission.

He goes on to say "I thought I had been very self-willed about the tutorship affair, and now I viewed my whole course as one of presumption".

He was haunted especially by a feeling that later "faded"—that the illness was a judgment for "profaning the Lord's Supper, in having cherished some resentment against the Provost for putting me out of the Tutorship." This feeling reached such a pitch that in imagination "I dictated to myself (as it were) a letter to the Provost stating in very strong terms my self-reproach; and I was not to preach at St. Mary's or anywhere for a length of time as a penitent unworthy to show himself . . .".

How truly amazed would Hawkins have been if the letter had ever been sent.

His servant Gennaro wanted Newman to leave some kind of will bequeathing his baggage to him. Newman gave him Hurrell Froude's address in case he should die, but said "I do not think I shall. 'I have not sinned against the light', or, 'God has still work for me to do'—I think the latter."

The delirium continuing he insisted on travelling on, sucked some magnificent oranges by the roadside, began to eat leaves of the trees and finally had to be taken from his mule and laid on his travelling cloak in a rough hut by the roadside. Late in the day he went on to Castro Giovanni. The doctor was called in and they had to correspond in Latin: "I have the papers still with me. He, I suppose, was no deep Latin scholar, and pretended my Latin was nonsense; but it is very good, particularly considering I was so ill."

The scent of some camomile flowers by the bed was delicious to him and camomile tea refreshing. Slowly he began to get better, would look for the daylight and greet it with "O sweet light: God's best gift", but still very weak, tormented by any noise and especially by the daily Mass bell:

I used quite to writhe about, and put my head under the bed-clothes, and asked Gennaro if it could be stopped. He answered with a laugh of surprise that it should not annoy me, and of encouragement, as if making light of it. I have since thought they might suppose it was a heretic's misery under a holy bell. . . . It seemed like a dream or absurdity how I should ever get to England again. As to the Oriel election, I first saw the news of it in a "Galignani" at Palermo, and on seeing that Rogers was elected, I kissed the paper rapturously.

This tiny incident gives an interesting clue to some unusual elements in Newman's make-up. He had been pursued by the question of Rogers and the Fellowship, he had dreamed a nightmare about it: it had wound in and out of his delirium. Very few men would feel thus passionately about one friend's success or failure: but Newman felt intensely over the fortunes of half a hundred. At times we see him concentrated on his own troubles, at others poured out on those of his mother, his sisters, the men he knew. There was in him a combination—quite unique I should say—of interest in self and in others. It was not merely the commoner mixture of unselfishness in action and self-centredness in thought. Newman's whole mind would focus itself—on someone else's troubles, on his own. And because he was a man of unusually powerful personality the effect on the reader of his letters is rather extraordinary. It is hard to find a simile: can one imagine a sensitive tornado or a brooding earthquake—anyhow the elements seem moved and the earth shaken by the force of his concentration.

The joy of recovery made food delicious: "life from the dead" he called a cup of tea. "I had never had such feelings". It was three weeks before he was fit to go on to Palermo. The country had always seemed exquisite but now: "My joy was too great for me at first. I never saw such a country—the spring in its greatest luxuriance. All sorts of strange trees—very steep and high hills over which the road went; mountains in the distance—a profusion of aloes along the road. Such bright colouring—all in tune with my reviving life."

Yet looking forward in his state of weakness "I sat sometime by the bedside crying bitterly, and all I could say was that I was sure God had some work for me to do in England."

"What a dream is life," Newman concludes. "Time is nothing except as the seed of eternity."

"I have a work to do in England." This was the thought that made him wild with impatience. In the *Apologia* he writes, "I was aching to get home; yet for want of a vessel I was kept at Palermo for three weeks. I began to visit the Churches, and they calmed my impatience, though I did not attend any services. I knew nothing of the Blessed Sacrament there."

Here at Palermo he wrote:

> Oh that thy creed were sound!
> For thou dost soothe the heart, thou Church of Rome,
> By thy unwearied watch and varied round
> Of service, in thy Saviour's holy home.
> I cannot walk the city's sultry streets
> But the wide porch invites to still retreats,
> Where passion's thirst is calm'd, and care's unthankful gloom.
>
> There, on a foreign shore,
> The homesick solitary finds a friend:
> Thoughts, prison'd long for lack of speech, outpour
> Their tears; and doubts in resignation end.
> I almost fainted from the long delay
> That tangles me within this languid bay,
> When comes a foe, my wounds with oil and wine to tend.

With returning health the verse-making had begun again and now the solitude was profound, external as well as spiritual. At Corfu he had written:

> Thrice blest are they who feel their loneliness

and at Tre Fontane he had seen himself

> A pilgrim pale with Paul's sad girdle bound

But in Palermo he saw that his solitude could not be that of the hermit or the solitary student. Had Paul chosen such a life

> Men had not gnash'd their teeth, nor risen to slay
> But thou hadst been a heathen in thy day.

Overflowing with zeal he now had above all to preach patience to himself:

> Lord! who Thy thousand years dost wait
> To work the thousandth part
> Of Thy vast plan, for us create
> With zeal a patient heart.

Christ alone could say of His work: "It is finished"; all we are but day-labourers:

> List, Christian warrior! thou, whose soul is fain
> To rid thy Mother of her present chain;
> Christ will avenge His Bride; yea, even now
> Begins the work, and thou
> Shalt spend it in thy strength, but, ere He save,
> Thy lot shall be the grave.

At last he got off in an orange-boat, bound for Marseilles. Becalmed a whole week in the Straits of Bonifacio he wrote his best known poem:

> Lead, kindly Light, amid the encircling gloom,
> Lead Thou me on!
> The night is dark, and I am far from home
> Lead Thou me on!
> Keep Thou my feet; I do not ask to see
> The distant scene,—one step enough for me.
>
> I was not ever thus, nor prayed that Thou
> Shouldst lead me on.
> I loved to choose and see my path; but now
> Lead Thou me on!
> I loved the garish day, and, spite of fears,
> Pride ruled my will; remember not past years.
>
> So long Thy power hath blest me, sure it still
> Will lead me on
> O'er moor and fen, o'er crag and torrent, till
> The night is gone;
> And with the morn those angel faces smile
> Which I have loved long since, and lost awhile.

Newman was homesick. To his mother he writes from Lyons:

I trust when you receive this I shall not be far from you. Really it seems as if some unseen power, good or bad, was resisting my return.

The thought of home has brought tears in my eyes for the last two months. God is giving me a severe lesson of patience, and I trust I am not altogether wasting the opportunity of discipline. It is His will. I strive to think that, wherever I am, God is God and I am I.

From Lyons he rushed home, sleeping only one night out of the seven that the journey took. "It was", he says in the *Apologia*, "the success of the Liberal cause which fretted me inwardly. I became fierce against its instruments and its manifestations. A French vessel was at Algiers; I would not even look at the tricolour. On my return, though forced to stop twenty-four hours at Paris, I kept indoors the whole time, and all that I saw of that beautiful city was what I saw from the Diligence."

Deciding in Rome on a motto for the Lyra, Froude had paraphrased the words of Achilles returning to the battle: "You shall know the difference, now that I am back again."

CHAPTER XIX

The World To Be Moved

EARLY writers on the Oxford Movement see a special strength in the narrowness of its scene. Oxford, says Dean Church, was like a Greek republic, or an Italian city state of the Middle Ages. But this is only partly true. Oxford had indeed an intense life of its own, and men there were who hardly looked beyond its walls and towers. But it was also the intellectual centre of England: in a sense the spiritual centre. The movement gained from Oxford its historical basis, but Oxford was not isolated. Clergymen came and went between their parishes and their colleges, legislators returned to vote in Convocation; even before railways "a scheme to London" was a term-time event, while Oxford residents spent at least part of every year away from Oxford. For a young don success at the University was but a preparation for success on the wider stage of law or politics or the Church.

Later writers have seen in one respect more truly that the weakness of the movement lay in its appealing only to one section of the community—but this had little to do with its connection with Oxford: it was rather the unfortunate result of the fact that England was becoming, as Disraeli put it, two nations.

The intention of the leaders was far otherwise. Hurrell Froude says: "We will have a *vocabularium apostolicum* and I will start it with four words: 'pampered aristocrat', 'resident gentleman', 'smug parsons', 'pauperes Christi'. I shall use the first on all occasions: it seems to me just to hit the thing."[1]

Newman writing from Rome to a former pupil says:

If we look into history, whether in the age of the Apostles, St. Ambrose's or St. Beckett's, still the people were the fulcrum of the Church's power. So they may be again. Therefore, expect on your return to England to see us all cautious, long-headed, unfeeling, unflinching Radicals.

[1] *Remains*, I. 329.

To Rogers he enlarges further on the same topic:

I confess, Tory as I still am, theoretically and historically, I begin
to be a Radical practically. Do not let me misrepresent myself. I,
of course, think that the most natural and becoming state of things
is for the aristocratical power to be the upholder of the Church; yet
I cannot deny the plain fact that in most ages the latter has been
based on a popular power. It was so in its rise, in the days of Ambrose
and in the days of Beckett, and it will be so again. I am preparing
myself for such a state of things, and for this simple reason, *because*
the State has deserted us and we cannot help ourselves. You must not
think, however, that I myself mean to hasten the downfall of the
Monarchy by word or deed. I trust the Whigs and Radicals will reap
their proper glory, and we but enjoy their fruit without committing
ourselves. On this ground, I am against all measures on our part
tending to the separation of Church and State, such as putting the
Bishops out of Parliament, etc., though, I confess, if the destructives
go much further in their persecution of us—e.g., if they made Arnold
a Bishop—I might consider it wrong to maintain that position longer,
much as I should wish to do so.

All the confusion which makes it hard to write about the
Movement in the larger setting of the period is visible in this
letter. The people must be called upon to support the Church
because the aristocracy have deserted it. But had not the Church
first deserted the people?

How can one characterize this age in which were sown the
seed of the dragons that are today devouring us? It is hard
because we see now what has happened: our ancestors did not
see. By one of the greatest revolutions in human history England
was being changed from an agricultural property-owning community into an industrial society which substituted a large urban
middle class for the ancient peasantry. Elie Halévy considers
that this middle class assured a more widespread distribution of
wealth than most peasant lands could show. But on each side
of this comfortable class were social groups of great extremes of
wealth on the one hand and on the other of a poverty so abject
that today we are ashamed to contemplate it. Yet a man who
saw this as clearly as Chesterton could speak of that "mood of
liberty and liberality that we call the nineteenth century." As
in all ages good and evil worked together: today we are inclined
to see only the evil—perhaps because the age itself saw nothing
but the good. All—or almost all—who were writing, were praising

the times: the growth of trade, the improvement of agriculture, the increase of liberal ideas.

They could see the network of canals that had begun to cover the country and along which barges carried coal and timber and iron. They could see the roads, on which a multitude of wheeled vehicles were replacing the tedious packhorse. Soon they could see "steam carriages" proceeding at a delirious rate. Blanco White after travelling more than thirty miles in two hours calls the railway "a giant of romance at our service. I was intoxicated with pleasure during the rapid journey". They could see the increased weight of cattle sold at Smithfield, the improved methods of sowing and drilling, the immensely greater fertility of the enclosed fields. For the first time in human history, says Trevelyan, cattle were no longer slaughtered before the winter, scurvy was disappearing. Small uneconomic farms were thrown into "great" ones, the great farmers were also paying great rents—and contentedly, for their profits were great. England led the world in agriculture.

Keble complained of "high farming" when it destroyed the hedgerows. He never seems to have asked whether it was destroying the peasant. Arnold, who wanted the clergy "to come forward as one man denouncing the high rents and the game laws and the carelessness which keeps the poor ignorant", speaks of Enclosure as if it were only one method of agriculture. Arthur Young at first thought the benefits of common land taken from the people by the enclosures "perfectly contemptible". The Board of Agriculture, which reckoned the increased harvest, took no count of the small losses of the dispossessed commoners— of their rushes for thatching and wood for firing, of their geese and pigs and cows fed on the common pasture. Enclosure of common lands was universally alluded to as though a common meant simply a waste—as of course it sometimes did.

We have begun [Elie Halévy quotes Lord Sinclair as saying in 1803], another campaign against the foreign enemies of the country. . . . Why should we not attempt a campaign also against our great domestic foe, I mean the hitherto unconquered sterility of so large a proportion of the surface of the kingdom? . . . let us not be satisfied with the liberation of Egypt, or the subjugation of Malta, but let us subdue Finchley Common; let us conquer Hounslow Heath; let us compel Epping Forest to submit to the yoke of improvement.

A perfect example of that strange ignorance which was almost innocence is given by Tom Mozley in relation to lands owned by Oriel College:

The Provost, however, had received applications from a number of labouring men at Littleworth, a hamlet on the property, asking for cottage gardens, or pieces of land to cultivate as they pleased. As luck would have it, under the instigation of some local agitator they had used language which indicated *a theoretical right rather than an appeal to benevolence.* . . .[1] The Provost and Senior Fellows had their case ready. A labourer's best chance is his wages. His time and strength are due to his employer. Land above the scale of a garden is an encumbrance. Who is to pay rates and taxes upon it? What is to be done when the holders increase and multiply? . . . The labourers could only repeat that they would like some land to do what they pleased with, and that they had been told manors were for the poor as well as for the rich. Oriel College was a very great body. It had taken Wadley House from the builder. It could do anything.

Men imprisoned for poaching to feed their hungry children or for taking a little wood from a hedge to warm them felt, Mrs. Fry tells us, that not they but the laws were wicked; so these labourers were conscious of their right to a bit of land. They could not put it clearly or set out evidence from the past, but they knew that manors were for the poor as well as for the rich—and Mozley apparently, the Provost, and the other dons did not, though they were living in the midst of a social revolution in the course of which about 40 per cent of Oxfordshire had been enclosed.

Cobbett, throughout, was crying in the wilderness: was described as a revolutionary because he was trying to prevent a revolution—what Chesterton has called the revolution of the rich against the poor. And in this revolution the clergy profiting solidly by the enclosures were for the most part simply a section of the rich.

Chesterton has said that if you want to understand a period you must look carefully for the things that go unmentioned. Suffering caused by Enclosure was to that age what the slaughter and maiming of millions by motorists is to this—the dark side of a benefit so unquestionable that it is never questioned. The Tractarians never sound the inhuman note of Whately suggesting

[1] Italics mine.

that the hair of "any female receiving relief" should be cut off and sold—to contribute towards their keep and discourage pauperism: "the number who would exert themselves to save their hair is beyond belief". Pusey bought an estate, to give away the income from it in charity. Newman, while keeping his family and paying his curates more than the college paid him as rector, writes to his sister to bear in mind his wish to give away one sixth of his £600 earnings in direct charity.

But it may be, it has been, asked—could not Newman have seen what Cobbett saw, had he not at least as good a mind as the great democrat? He had as good a mind, but it was a mind exclusively occupied with the work that was uniquely his vocation. On the social scene he cast only a tired man's cursory glance—disliking most of what he saw: disliking trade, disliking wealth, disliking disorder. "I am confirmed", he once wrote to Bowden, "as a staid dull old Tory unfit for these smart times".

No man can concentrate, can gather all his powers, on everything. The artist, the poet, the creative thinker has the load of genius to carry, its life to live, its message to express. The contemplative has the spiritual vocation to draw the world nearer to God by prayer. Newman's genius found its scope in a unique vocation—at once spiritual and intellectual—of drawing the world nearer to God not by prayer but by thought. His was perhaps the greatest theological vocation since St. Thomas: he lived and moved more among the early Fathers than among his living friends close as these were to him.

And it may be that Newman's work was a vital preliminary because first things must come first. It may be that Cobbett's words fell on deaf ears because Newman must be heard first—because the rebuilding of Christian thought can alone prepare men to build a Christian social order. It might be worth trying.

Meanwhile, most of the country clergy were not, I am sure, the callous beings they are often represented. They shared sincerely if naïvely in the fashionable optimism of political economists who were explaining lucidly that the whole country would soon be sharing in the benefits of an era of unexampled prosperity. For it was not only in agriculture, but in inventions, manufacture, trade, that England was ahead of all her competitors—so far ahead that it was many years before her supremacy could even be challenged in any field. The figures of her exports rose astoundingly after the French wars. Every day new machines were being invented, cotton was booming, iron and steel were booming, the aggregate wealth of the country was rising year by year. The word "trade", dear to Defoe, had become a fetish a hundred years later. And England had almost a monopoly of all the most lucrative trades. Seeing this, few looked at the destruction that went with it, at the small insanitary houses run up back to back to shelter the "hands" that were working sixteen hours a day in the factories, at the actual starvation that followed each feverish crisis of over-production.

Here, however, some of the clergy were more alert than they were about the countryside. It was obvious that these vast new cities were almost without spiritual ministrations: the dissenting chapel was often the only church, except perhaps some Popish rendezvous for the immigrant Irish labourer. An establishment is slow to move, a state slow to spend money on things spiritual. The best of the clergy were agitating both for churches and for justice for the workers. Among these was Arnold, who stated nobly the horror of the new estrangement between masters and man and the obligation of every Christian man to become alive to it.

A man sets up a factory and wants "hands"; I beseech you, sir, to observe the very expressions that are used, for they are all significant. What he wants of his fellow-creatures is the loan of their hands—of their heads and hearts he thinks nothing. These hands are attached to certain mouths and bodies which must be fed and lodged; but this must be done as cheaply as possible; and, accordingly, up starts a miserable row of houses, built where ground is cheapest, that is, where it is least generally desirable to get it; built as close as possible, to have the more of them on a given space, and for the same reason without any sort of garden or outlet attached to them, because the comfort and enjoyment of the human being is quite independent of the serviceableness of his hands. But further, sir, these hands are not only attached to mouths and bodies, but to reasonable minds and immortal souls. The mouths and bodies must be provided for, however miserably, because without them the hands cannot work: but the minds and souls go utterly unregarded. And is this any other but a national crime, a crime in the civil government, a crime in the Church, a crime in all the wealthy and intelligent part of the English people, that while hands have been multiplying so enormously in the last forty years in every corner of the kingdom, no greater efforts have been made to provide for the welfare of the human beings who have multiplied with them; beings born not for time only, but for eternity.

It was Arnold, by the way, who exclaimed, "Woe to that generation that is living in England when the coal mines are exhausted and the National Debt not paid off."

Few of the clergy followed even Arnold, whom they condemned as a radical, while Arnold himself condemned the radicalism of Cobbett. Religion was always mixed up with these apparently political judgments. Had Arnold not been a religious Liberal he might have carried the orthodox clergy with him; had Cobbett not exalted the Catholic Church of the Middle Ages in his much abused *History of the Protestant Reformation*, he might not have antagonized Arnold. With all its faults of haste and temper the book had pointed to a happier England in the past identified with the Catholic faith. The "old religion" as it was still so often called had been driven into obscurity: it still did its primary task of caring for the souls of its children but, like the dissenting bodies, it was powerless in the social field. Yet in all fairness it must be admitted that the Church and the social scene in nineteenth-century France were not unlike England and her establishment. In his brilliant study of Proudhon (only nine years younger than Newman) Père de Lubac has made this abundantly clear. The great ages of Christianity as a social power lay in the past— and in the future. The privilege which had identified the French clergy with the aristocrats in the eyes of the Revolution did the same for the English clergy in the days of Reform.

The main complaint of the Liberals in England was that the House of Commons was in no sense representative of the people of England: the constituencies had been set up before the Industrial Revolution had drawn large masses of the population into the coal-bearing midlands and north; and in any event a great number of the constituencies were actually owned by private individuals who decided at their pleasure (and profit) who should be member. The Liberals under Earl Grey and Lord John Russell fought for reform in this matter. The nation clearly wanted it: the success of the Revolution which drove out the French Monarchy in 1830 added impetus to the demand: in 1832 the Reform Bill became law. It redistributed constituencies with some reference to the balance of population, abolished the private ownership of constituencies altogether, and widened the franchise (not very much—five-sixths of the adult males of England, including the whole of the working class, still could not vote).

What would come of the Reform Bill? Nobody knew, but everybody was agitated with strong feelings of enthusiasm or despair. The one thing no one doubted was the value of a vote. Cobbett was certain he could no longer be kept out of a reformed Parliament and equally certain that once there he could undo the evils of the past—including apparently the Enclosure Acts. The masses in the cities believed that the bill would ameliorate their lot, neither realizing that for them it would not even mean the possession of a vote, nor how little that vote could do to set them free from economic slavery.

When the House of Lords threw out the bill, the bishops who had voted against it, and who were everywhere identified with the anti-reform party, were alarmed by the degree of popular fury that followed. The Archbishop of Canterbury was mobbed in his Cathedral city, the walls of the Bishop of Bath and Wells were scaled in the night, every pane in his glasshouse broken and a deer killed in his Park! The Bishop of London cancelled an engagement for fear of violence, while the more courageous Doctor Jenkyns of Balliol going out to remonstrate with a mob of townsmen was felled by a heavy stone. Tom Mozley has given a vivid description of the riots in the Midlands. Dr. Arnold noted "a great wish for church destruction and church robbery", and mobs who "cry for no bishops, no tithes, and no rates".

In the House of Commons itself the reform party was energetically opposed to Church privilege. One speaker expressed a wish, even, that "these foolish ordinations would cease" and spoke of the coming disendowment of the Church "now that it is condemned by the country, when its charter is on the eve of being cancelled by the authority which gave it, when it is admitted on all hands to be not useless only but absolutely detrimental". It was not the Church alone that was threatened. The word "freedom" was in the air: reform was to break all bonds and fetters, to make the gains of trade available to all, to destroy privilege. "The institution of the Peerage," said Macaulay, "is evidently dying a natural death." And "the national situation", says Douglas Macleane, "may be gauged by Earl Grey's words in the Upper House of May 7th, 1832: 'I do not like in this free country to use the word "monarchy"'."[1]

The Reform Bill was supposed to do for England what the Revolution had done for France. The first reformed Parliament

[1] *Famous Sermons*, p. 205.

met in 1833 and Macaulay declared that this aim had been accomplished. He said in an address to his Committee:

They boast and justly of those three days of July; but I will boast of our ten days of May. We, too, fought a battle, but it was with moral arms. We, too, placed an impassable barrier between ourselves and military tyranny; but we fenced ourselves in with moral barricades. Not one crime committed, not one acre confiscated, not one life lost, not one instance of outrage or attack on the authorities or the laws. Our victory has not left a single family in mourning. Not a tear, not a drop of blood, has sullied the pacific and blameless triumph of a great people.

Reform of the Church was to be one of the first concerns of the new Parliament. A Commission to examine into ecclesiastical matters was threatened now, appointed three years later. The Church Temporalities Act, known also as the Bishoprics Bill, and the erection of the Privy Council into the supreme court of appeal in spiritual causes, were both passed. Lord Grey adjured the Bishops to "set their house in order". And it was widely believed that this legislation was only a beginning; that the Church was to be first despoiled and then disestablished, above all to have her formularies, perhaps her doctrines, altered by Act of Parliament. Palmer in his *Narrative of Events* writes:

Pamphlets were in wide circulation, recommending the abolition of the Creeds (at least in public worship), and especially urging the expulsion of the Athanasian Creed: the removal of all mention of the Blessed Trinity; of the doctrine of Baptismal Regeneration; of the practice of absolution. In fact, there was not a single stone of the sacred edifice of the Church, which was not examined, shaken, undermined, by a meddling and ignorant curiosity.

It is hardly necessary to say that Newman hated all this: Liberalism was the enemy, in religion primarily, but one spirit ran through it all, and this external activity was only a preliminary to its total triumph: it must be resisted at every point. Of the Revolution in France in 1830 he wrote to Jemima (August 10) "The French seem to me the most wicked nation on earth . . . and King Charles and his ministers are a set of poltroons for not staying to be shot or guillotined." Following the success of the Reform Bill and Lord Grey's warnings to the bishops, he wrote to Bowden (August 20, 1833): "The gift of excommunication will not for ever remain unused. If I were a Bishop, the first thing I should do would be to excommunicate Lord Grey and half a dozen more, whose names it is almost a shame and a pollution for a Christian to mention."

All this formed the background of Keble's famous sermon on National Apostasy, which was preached in July 1833—a few days before the Bishoprics Bill became law. It is hard to avoid a strong sense of unreality as one considers the occasion of this sermon—the abolition[1] of ten bishoprics in the state Church of Ireland. For we have in all this the strange confusion of Catholic-minded men prepared to oppress a Catholic people and of anti-Catholics defending them. Demanding not only freedom for Irish Catholics but also endowment of their priests, Sydney Smith remarked: "The Scotch were suffered to worship God after their own tiresome manner, without pain, penalty or privation." And in all the biting irony of *Peter Plymley's Letters* he does not attempt to conceal his intellectual contempt for the cause he is espousing.

I am astonished at the madness of the Catholic clergy, in not perceiving that Catholic emancipation is Catholic infidelity; that to entangle their people in the intrigues of a Protestant Parliament, and a Protestant Court, is to ensure the loss of every man of fashion and consequence in their community. The true receipt for preserving their religion, is Mr. Perceval's receipt for destroying it: it is to deprive every rich Catholic of all the objects of secular ambition, to separate him from the Protestant, and to shut him up in his castle with his priests and relics.

Keble, Pusey, Newman, would have had far more respect for the relics and the religion, yet they were prepared to continue an oppression of Ireland which it is hard to characterize in terms sufficiently strong. The Protestant Church was imposed upon that country by an external foreign power; was maintained by a forced levy from a starving people; by its side was the Catholic Church which was in unbroken continuity with her past and to which belonged almost the entire population. It would surely seem that the government in freeing Irish Catholics from the necessity of supporting ten alien bishoprics had only made a first step towards a greatly needed reform.

[1] So it was usually called. In fact they were merged in other sees.

But Oxford knew little enough of Ireland, while the theories
of High Churchmen claimed a sacredness for the episcopacy
which attached to the individual see and made the suppression
of a diocese in their eyes an act of sacrilege, a destruction of one
of the seven candlesticks of the Book of Revelations. In one
respect High Churchmen and Protestants were agreed in a view
that separated them both from the Liberals. If the Church had,
in the sixteenth century, rightly protestantized herself, her endowments belonged to the reformers whether or no they possessed
Apostolic Succession. If, as the High Churchmen held, the Church
of England or of Ireland was still one with the pre-reformation
Church this was equally so. Newman wrote "The Church thus
deprived was founded by St. Patrick. It has been continued by
regular succession of clergy ever since, the Romish priests being
mere intruders, and a creation from Rome of these last centuries.
Thus it is one of the oldest ecclesiastical bodies in the world." Sydney
Smith and Macaulay read history very differently. Macaulay said,
a few years later: "Of all the institutions of the civilized world,
the Established Church of Ireland seems to me the most absurd".

And demanding as a measure of justice the improvement and
endowment of Maynooth College—he uttered one of his most
famous bursts of oratory:

When I think of the spacious and stately mansions of the heads of
houses, of the commodious chambers of the fellows and scholars, of
the refectories, the combination rooms, the bowling greens, the stabling,
of the state and luxury of the great feast days, of the piles of old plate
on the tables, of the savoury steam of the kitchens, of the multitude of
geese and capons which turn at once on the spits, of the oceans of
excellent ale in the butteries; and when I remember from whom all
this splendour and plenty is derived; when I remember what was the
faith of Edward the Third, and of Henry the Sixth, of Margaret of
Anjou and Margaret of Richmond, of William of Wykeham and
William of Waynefleet, of Archbishop Chichele and Cardinal Wolsey;
when I remember what we have taken from the Roman Catholics—
King's College, New College, Christ Church, my own Trinity; and
when I look at the miserable Dotheboys Hall which we have given
them in exchange, I feel, I must own, less proud than I could wish of
being a Protestant and a Cambridge man.

But none of this Keble saw, nor Newman, nor Froude. Theirs
was, they believed, the faith of William of Wykeham and of

Waynefleet, they lived by right in their colleges. That "reform" should come from without and by Act of Parliament was by no means to be endured. The Church should indeed reform herself and Newman often used the phrase "There was need for a second Reformation."

It is difficult to paint a picture with statistics: we must try to see what a particular village looked like, what it meant to live in a factory town, by scanning closely the letters, the memoirs and the fiction of the time. And the difficulty is that before Dickens little enough was written that got inside the lives of the poor. Still there are glimpses—some of them from unexpected quarters. The author of *Cranford* paints with lurid accuracy conditions in mills and factories a little later than Dr. Arnold. Charlotte Yonge gives in *The Carbonels* a village scene of the late twenties and early thirties. In most of the Yonge novels there is a vague background of some neglected area which a clergyman (always a portrait of Keble) will presently transform. But in *The Carbonels* we find ourselves actually inside such a village. The rector is the principal of an Oxford college coming down only in the summer to preach sermons more suitable for a university than for rustics. Celebrations of the Eucharist are few and far between, and attended by old men for the sake of an almsgiving which follows. There are two public houses but no school. When the Carbonel family inherit a farm and small estate they are told by the local gentry that the villagers are worthless and irreclaimable. The story is written from the point of view of the family, telling their sacrifices —the new carriage-drive for example that is never built, so that the Duchess paying them a call drives through a farmyard over a road full of holes—sacrifices made to help the villagers and requited by the destruction of the Carbonels' threshing machine and the burning of their house.

But as we move through the story the picture of the village grows clearer and more horrifying. Women work long hours in the fields, often in broken boots. The weeding woman in the garden begins to change and look almost fat from the bounties carried to her by the young Carbonels from their own table. Prizes bestowed when the school starts largely take the form of warm garments (and the mothers grumble—because the Duchess in the next parish had none of this nonsense about rewards but gave every child in the village a warm red cloak). Captain Carbonel starts a coal club and persuades the gentry to back him in order to save the thefts of wood from their forests. He lets out a field in cheap allotments and the villagers are persuaded that he makes a good thing out of it. Hunger and cold form a permanent background. Buns are given to the children with their prizes, blankets to their mothers. Skim milk is denied to the pigs in favour of the children. The dependence of the village on the family who are loved by a few, hated by most, emerges more clearly than I think the author realizes, and nothing seems more improbable than the winning of their affections with which the story ends.

And yet it may have happened, for good people can create good relations in the worst of systems. This perhaps was not the worst, but it was very bad. It was precisely in Belloc's sense— the Servile State. Often today we meet with the remark that Belloc's prophecy has been fulfilled and that we are living in his servile state. But we are not. We are living in *a* servile state but quite a different one. In his vision part of the population was going to be enslaved to work for the other part. But today we are all enslaved to the state. Belloc was in fact looking back rather than forward. His servile state existed: it was Disraeli's two nations. The factory hands were slaves of the owners, the villagers were slaves of the squires. And by this slavery they were being conditioned to be happy slaves of the state.

Obviously today, thanks chiefly to trades unions, one of those nations, created by Enclosures, Industrialism, the old Poor Law, the new Poor Law and the rest, is better off, more secure and no more enslaved than of old. And we of the other nation look on and wonder when the electorate will strike a blow for liberty. *We* are conscious of slavery because we are unused to it. But would that our ancestors had seen what they were creating and had saved England as a property-owning democracy and a Christian land.

CHAPTER XX

The Movement Begins

Tracts for the Times, published at Oxford. "If the trumpet give an uncertain sound, who shall prepare himself for the Battle?"[1]

NEWMAN preaching on "The Mysteriousness of our Present Being", on "The Greatness and Littleness of Human Life," is supremely the Newman who was now opening the scene of the Oxford Movement. The groaning and travailing of the creature awaiting the revelation of the sons of God was ever in his ears, and a part of this groaning arises from the narrowness and the confusion of this human stage of action. How deep is the mystery of our nature, how impossible it is for this world to witness its full realization and manifestation. So seldom do men say what they really mean, or rightly choose the moment for saying it: "the best in this kind are but shadows" of a more profound reality.

When Keble preached on National Apostasy he chose as we have seen the wrong occasion and hence gathered around him many of the wrong men, men who later fell away dismayed by the principles of the movement. Froude, Keble, Pusey, Newman, were all concerned not with tithes or benefices or the outward glory of the Church except insofar as they viewed these as the outworks and protections of its inner character. Newman especially was appalled by his own vision of an onrushing flood of infidelity. God and the soul were his chief, his haunting thoughts. Like the mediaevals who built a stage in three levels—heaven above, hell below and this world between—so Newman saw human life. Dr. Brillioth finds a contradiction between the deep spiritual aims of the Movement and its insistence on such matters as Apostolic Succession, but there was no contradiction in Newman's thought. Only a religion of authority could ever be for the mass of men a religion of the spirit, could save men's souls from the world and the devil and make them

---

[1] Advertisement written by Newman for the Tracts.

ready to stand before God. Such a religion—Christianity—God Himself had made. Half a century later a visitor to the Oratory noted that Newman hated having to spend on the Anglican controversy time that he desired to consecrate to the deepest issues of faith and unfaith. And at this earlier date he was not a mere controversialist for the Establishment. The Church was "the concrete representative of things invisible", the heir of the Apostles, Christ's Mystical Body through which as through the name of Jesus "all men must be saved." If the Church had the gifts of divine truth and divine life to impart to mankind no scandals could prevent that power from functioning.

Thus thinking, he and Keble alike found it horrifying that men of no definite Christianity could legislate for the Church. Such in their eyes were the Liberals, and in his sermon on National Apostasy Keble compared the England of his day to the Jews when they demanded a king to rule over them. Thus in England a legislature, "*the members of which are not even bound to profess belief in the Atonement*", was usurping the position of the Apostles. The Jews had asked for Saul the ruler instead of Samuel the prophet, a king like the nations around them instead of God. For the Jewish state had been a theocracy: "The Lord God was your King."

Newman returned from Sicily with health restored and in a more buoyant state of spirits than he had known since childhood. The illness and the voyage had meant a ceasing from his habitual overwork; the high fever in Sicily had taken away most of his hair and on his return many of his friends did not recognize him, but this was less from the loss of the hair than from the change in his walk and general aspect. He says of himself that he undertook the work of the Movement in a spirit that was "fierce yet sportive". James Mozley describes him as "perfectly ferocious in the cause, and proportionately sanguine of success—'We'll do them,' he says at least twenty times a day—meaning, by 'them', the present race of aristocrats, and the Liberal oppressors of the Church in general."

Soon after Newman's return, a meeting took place at Hadleigh rectory, the home of Hugh Rose. Rose was a man of considerable learning and high character: a true historian: a cautious churchman, although strongly imbued with a desire for reform: it is doubtful whether he would appreciate the apocalyptic outlook

of Newman, Keble and Froude. His health was bad: he died
before the Movement had reached its height, but although at
the beginning he was whole-heartedly with them, Newman wrote
of him later to Keble: "I never have reckoned him as in his
opinion one of ourselves, so to say . . . Our view, whether
right or wrong, he has not seemed to grasp, or to be likely to
grasp."

William Palmer, who was at the meeting, later wrote *A
Narrative of Events Connected with the Publication of the Tracts for
the Times, with Reflections on Existing Tendencies to Romanism, and
on the Present Duties and Prospects of Members of the Church.* Like
Rose, Palmer was a man of learning. His *Origines Liturgicae,*
published the previous year, was a book that had given him
authority with divines and scholars. He was of a scholastic turn
of mind and many years later the Roman theologian, Perrone,
approved his logical periods, with the note: *optime Palmer.* This
was, by Father Ignatius Ryder, combined into one sentence
with another remark made by Perrone on another occasion—
Newman miscet et confundit omnia—an admirable summary of the
effect of genius on the tidy and uninspired. While Rose may not
have fully understood the other three, he was bold along his own
lines. Palmer was desperately cautious and Newman had to overcome his scruples and difficulties at every step.

Those present at Hadleigh were Rose, Froude, Palmer and
Perceval. Newman writes to Keble, 5th August 1833:

I fear they did not get on very well at Hadleigh. Froude wants
you to give your friend Arthur Perceval a bit of advice, which I
think Froude himself partly requires. We shall lose all our influence
when times are worse, if we are prematurely violent. I heartily wish
things may keep quiet for a year or two, that we may ascertain our
position, get up precedents, and know our duty. Palmer thinks both
Froude and Perceval very deficient in learning, and therefore rash.

Keble replies:

As concerning Mater Ecclesia, think, if the Hadleighans could not
agree, where *inter quattuor muros* will you find six men to agree together?
But I quite agree with you that Rose's *Magazine* must be supported—
unless he actually rats, which I never will believe till I see it. As for
Hurrell, he is so annoyed just now at his project not being accepted
that I count his dissatisfaction for very little.

The main practical question which divided the group was whether the work of the Movement should be done through an association or through the issue of tracts. At first the compromise agreed upon was that there should be an association through which tracts should be issued. Newman writes to Rogers on August 31st:

. . . Entre nous, we have set up Societies over the kingdom in defence of the Church. Certainly this is, you will say, a singular confidential communication, being shared by so many; but the *entre nous* relates to *we*. We do not like our names known. You may say as much as you will to any one about the fact of the Societies and their object. They are already started (in germ) in Oxfordshire, Devonshire, Gloucestershire, Berks, Suffolk and Kent—the object being "to make the clergy alive to their situation, to enforce the Apostolical Succession, and to defend the liturgy". We mean to publish and circulate tracts. I have started with four. We think of a quarterly magazine. I wish I had more money (a respectable wish), but I have squandered mine in Sicily. All this plan of publication will not interfere with Rose's *Magazine*. Everything as yet promises well—but we are merely talking about it as yet, and have got no rules even.

And on October 2nd:

. . . We are getting on famously with our Society, and are so prudent and temperate that Froude writes up to me we have made a hash of it, which I account to be praise. As to Gladstone, perhaps it would be wrong to ask a young man so to commit himself, but make a fuss he will sooner or later . . .

This—the first I think—mention of Gladstone in connection with the Movement recalls the aspiration a few years later. In "Oxford 1840", the poet longed for the hour when

England at one shall stand at the Church gate
    And vesper bells o'er all the land be borne
And Newman mould the Church and Gladstone stamp the State.

In an Introduction to the first volume of Tracts, Newman showed his faith in the "English branch" of that Church of Christ which "was intended to cope with human nature in all its forms, and surely the gifts vouchsafed it are adequate for that gracious purpose." Why were so many lost to the Church of

England? Simply because "the more gracious and consoling truths" were being omitted from the teaching of the day. Whately had once bitterly said of most preachers: "They aim at nothing and they hit it." This absence of positive teaching drove men "to prayer and bible meetings", "to the solemn and captivating services by which Popery gains its proselytes."

The awakened mind knows its wants, but cannot provide for them; and in its hunger will feed upon ashes, if it cannot obtain the pure milk of the word. Methodism and Popery are in different ways the refuge of those whom the Church stints of the gifts of grace; they are the foster-mothers of abandoned children.[1]

The Tracts were at first designed to be a product of the Society but this would not do. It called for endless revision to make a Tract such as would be acceptable to the whole committee, and by much revision all individuality, all personality, was lost. "I doubt," Newman wrote to Keble, "whether the Society ought to pledge itself to more than a *general* approval of the principles of *any* tracts. One thing strikes one reader, one another. If you correct them according to the wishes of a board, you will have nothing but tame, dull compositions, which will take no one; there will be no rhetoric in them."

This difficulty presently reappeared in a measure to which all had agreed—an address to the Archbishop of Canterbury. Newman wrote to Bowden on October 18th:

We talk of getting up at once a Declaration or address from the clergy to the Archbishop against material alterations in doctrine and discipline, and against extra-ecclesiastical interference; at the same time granting improvements, if such, and the completion of our system. We have also instituted a bureau for newspaper influence. We have about twelve country newspapers already in our eye, which are open to our friends, and we hope to introduce tracts into them by their means. If you can do anything for us in the North in this way, it will be a service. Our papers are to appear in the *British Magazine*, with a notice that all who please may reprint them cheaply, or have them from us.

The sense that the Church was in peril had—whatever their individual views of what the Church meant—momentarily

[1] *Tracts*, Vol. I, p. iv.

drawn together representatives of all sections of the Establishment (except the Liberals). Froude and Newman designated their supporters as "Apostolicals" who were wholly to be relied upon, "Z's" or "Establishment men", who were roughly speaking the old High-and-Dry-Churchmen, and "Peculiars" or Evangelicals of whom there were at first a fair sprinkling in the Associations—but only at first.

Newman managed to get five letters into the *Record* before the editor decided no longer to admit "the apple of discord which had rolled into their columns from Oxford". "So these people," wrote Newman to Froude, "have just managed to give us a most flaming advertisement." And "I have lately heard that the *Christian Observer* has a furious attack on us, nay, upon Oriel, in this last month. Can we have more favourable signs? Men do not cry out till they are frightened".

"Go on and prosper," wrote Keble to Newman, "and let the *Record* dry in its own ink."

The attempt to make the Movement nation-wide involved a committee in London supposed to work with the group at Oxford. The address went to and fro. To Froude Newman writes:

November 8. (1833)—The address is done today. Such a composition I never saw; we have re-written each other's (London and Oxford) three times; but now we have made a few alterations *nostro periculo* and have printed it off. The word "Bishops" at the close has been put in here and taken out there five times *sub silentio*.

Meanwhile Palmer wanted the Tracts stopped altogether. Newman writes to Froude:

Palmer musters the Z's in great force against the tracts, and some Evangelicals. He presses, and I am quite ready to admit, a disclaimer (in the shape of a circular) of the tracts. But he goes further, and wishes us to stop them . . . What will be done I know not; but I want advice sadly. I have no confidence in anyone. If I could be sure of five or six vigorous co-operators in various parts, I would laugh at opposition; but I fear being beaten from the field. Keble says we *must* be read, unless we grow stupid; but I am not oversure of our fertility even . . . One proposition is that we should cease the issue of the tracts till the address is happily got over; but I say, "Palmer, you delayed us five weeks with your scruples, which you yourself got over at last; and now you are playing the same game again". Yet I should shrink from spoiling the address, and I do not know what to do. . . . My dear Froude, I do so fear I may be self-willed in this matter of the tracts. Pray do advise me according to your light.

Froude attacks the address and insists on the Tracts: " . . . have you not been a spoon? . . . to leave out your key-words. . . . My father is annoyed at its being such milk and water; do make a row about it."

"As to giving up the tracts, the notion is odious . . . We must throw the Z's overboard; they are a small, and, as my father says, daily diminishing party . . . Do keep writing to Keble and stirring his rage; he is my fire, but I may be his poker."

Froude was indeed the poker of the whole business—had Newman needed a poker. He did not, but at times he sorely needed encouragement. While Froude was for throwing over "the Z's" and Palmer for dropping the enthusiasts, Newman alone could hold both groups and win fresh adherents. This involved an immense and difficult correspondence in which he explains over and over again the aims and objects of the Move-ment. Then too as Tom Mozley has pointed out, he was the only one of the group who could really write a tract: something short and pithy with a sharp point to it.

"A tract," he wrote to Perceval, "would be long enough if it filled four octavo pages." And again "We hope to publish tracts for hawkers' baskets in time. Are you disposed to draw up a series of translations from Eusebius's *Ecclesiastical History*? Or what do you think of such a measure? I mean for instance the account of St. John and the robber, whom he had baptised in youth, the martyrs of Lyons, the account of the persecution at Alexandria given by Dionysius, etc. These are *popular* in their nature and to the people we must come."

In the event very few of the Tracts were of a popular character: and if in one aspect this was a weakness, in another it was a strength. The whole idea of tracts written by the educated for the educated was a novel one. Tracts had hitherto meant at the best Hannah More's *Village Politics*, for the most part something much weaker, distributed by maiden ladies with time on their hands or by reforming Mrs. Jellybys and Pardiggles to drunken labourers.

Now the flower of Oxford were both writing and distributing them. An interesting paper is preserved in the *Letters and Correspondence* which Newman gave to the men sent out by him:

Objects of your Journey

To form local associations.

To instruct the corresponding member.

To sound men on certain questions.

Our object is to get together immediately as large a body as we can, in defence of the *substance* of our spiritual rights, privileges, our Creeds, &c.; but we wish to avoid technicalities and minutenesses as much as possible.

The posture of affairs will not allow of delay.

We wish to unite the clergy and create channels of correspondence between them.

We have it in view to get up petitions on a sudden, through the country, should any bold measure of the country against the Church be contemplated, or other event require it.

We are of no party nor interfere with party questions.

We have no concern with politics.

We have nothing to do with maintaining the temporalities of the Church, much as we deprecate any undue interference with them by external authority.

Queries in Prospect

1. Petitions against lax men about to be appointed bishops, &c.
2. Alterations in Burial Service and in Baptismal.
3. On the competent authority to alter Liturgy.
4. On protests.

Beware of any intemperance of language.

You may mention *facts* illustrative of the present tyranny exercised over the Church as much as you please, according to your discretion.

If men are afraid of Apostolical ground, then be cautious of saying much about it. If desirous, then recommend prudence and silence upon it at present.

Everything depends on calmness and temperance. Recollect that we are *supporting* the Bishops; enlarge on the unfairness of leaving them to bear the brunt of the battle.

Newman himself—though feeling rather awkward, for, as he says, that sort of thing was hardly in his line—went on horseback to country rectories carrying tracts. At one the rector met him with obvious suspicion. "He paused awhile, and then, eyeing me with significance, asked, 'Whether Whately was at the bottom of them'."[1]

Samuel Rickards wrote to Newman from Ulcombe (November 28, 1833):

In the whole circuit of a very large neighbourhood which I have been searching with no little care and labour, I have not been able to find a single person, lay or clergyman, X, Y, or Z, who believes that the Church or its liturgy or anything belonging to it is in danger. The tracts they either utterly abhor or else they consider them the work of men whose brains are cracked by their own melancholy and fanciful temper working in very partial and cloudy views of the subject.

(Seven years later Henry Wilberforce told Newman of a parson in Warwickshire or Worcestershire who explained the whole Movement by the fact that Newman, having failed in the Schools because he could not answer a simple question on the Bible, had vowed that he would turn the Bible out of the Church of England and substitute the Fathers of the Church—"And, sir, that was the cause of all this noise.")

Rickards went on to express his own agreement with Newman, but he added the warning (borne out by the event):

I am sorry that there should be any danger of your ever seeming to be a Papist, because so far as you do, I shall be really your antagonist.

The suspicion that the Movement meant Papistry was natural enough, though it cannot often have been more oddly expressed than by an anonymous writer in the following year:

If with Protestant pay you save the *Apostate Church* how can you shun the doom of Judas if you do so? Be wise therefore and consider in time and see your delusion—Can the Pope preserve your soul when the Universe is floating about your ears in dissolving flames?

But these discouraging reactions were rare. Tom and James Mozley were among those enlisted for the distribution and the former relates the puzzled friendliness with which he was usually received. James sent packages to his family with suggestions for their distribution. Bowden disseminated them in London. "We

[1] *Apologia*, p. 41.

are very strong (I hope)," Newman writes, "in Leicestershire, Cheshire, Oxford and Northamptonshire."

Says Tom Mozley:

> The tracts had to be circulated by post, by hand, or anyhow, and many a young clergyman spent days in riding about with a pocketful, surprising his neighbours at breakfast, lunch, dinner, and tea. The correspondence that ensued was immense. Nobody was too humble in intellect or in clerical position not to be invited, and enrolled as an ally. Men survive, or have but lately passed away, who can never have known what it was to share a glory and a greatness except at that happy time. . . .[1]

> High and Low Church stood by amazed, and very doubtful what it would come to; but meanwhile equally pleased to see life in the Church, which the House of Commons seemed to think incapable of thought, will, or action. The correspondence grew. Oxford resumed its historic place as the centre of religious activity. This was the golden age of the movement, and men talked rather gayly. Some readily accepted the charge of conspiracy, and were far from prompt to disavow that there was more in the background.[2]

For most of the younger men this glory and greatness emanated from the person of their leader—John Henry Newman. They recked little of meetings at Hadleigh or addresses to Archbishops: Newman's ideal of the Church, Newman's personality were their motive force. The inner circle of his younger disciples showed towards him an interesting mixture of awe, frankness and affection. At first awe would predominate—the power to inspire it being an essential element in the make-up of a leader. He was, says Rogers, "Master of a formidable and speaking silence calculated to quell any ordinary impertinence"; and Lockhart records that a man had up before Newman for some serious matter and asked what he had said replied, "I don't know, but he looked at me."

Lockhart was also told by a "muscular Christian", the stroke of his college boat, of their both meeting a "furiously drunken butcher", foul mouthed and blasphemous. Newman stood straight in the man's path: the oarsman expecting violence got ready to fell him "when he saw the man stop short. Newman was speaking to him. Very quietly he said, 'My friend, if you thought of the meaning of your words you would not say them.'

---

[1] *Reminiscences*, Vol. I, p. 313.　　　　[2] Ibid, p. 341.

The savage was tamed on the spot, he touched his hat, turned round, and went back."

Part of Newman's strength lay in the sense of great forces kept in leash: and nothing was more strongly curbed than his sarcasm and severity. An illuminating sentence in a letter to Pope deprecates an attack on Milman: "To raise an outcry against him is just the way to confirm him in his error—and *being useless becomes uncharitable.*" [1] Only a few times in his life did Newman feel justified in taking the sword—and then how effectively. But he could certainly utter judgments which, if just, were less than kind. Of Whately: "Of course to know him now is quite impossible— yet he has so many good qualities it is impossible also not to feel for him. I fear his love of applause, popularity etc., has been his snare." Of Sam Wilberforce (known later as Soapy Sam): "whom Froude and I have stigmatised as a humbug for many years." And again, "Samuel Wilberforce is so far from anything higher than a dish of skimmed milk that we can hope nothing from him." A letter to Jemima has a tantalising postscript: "Do you know what makes H. such a little fool?" There are few of these things but one feels there might have been many.

"I fear John will scare them," wrote Pusey later when hoping to gather undergraduates for discussions. But those who had been Newman's pupils, Rogers, the Mozleys, the Wilberforces; those who, never his pupils, yet looked upon him as their master, all discussed his moods with some freedom and felt towards him more affection than fear. They speak of him as Neander, to him as Carissime and sometimes Antiquissime.

We have seen in an earlier chapter how readily his pupils sought and he offered advice; now he had no more pupils, but there always appeared towards his younger followers an immense sense of responsibility—leading him to shield them when he could from the severity of authority, but also to show privately a severity of his own.

James Mozley, with inconceivable carelessness, arriving two days late for his deacon's examination, writes to his sister that Newman "took it into his head to feel hurt about it, not to say considerably enraged". Newman however, quickly relenting, offered James the surplice used at his own Ordination, "with every kind thought", in a letter beginning "Carissime" and

[1] Italics mine.

ending "ever yours affectionately". "But," says James, "he looked amazingly black at first, I can assure you."

Frederick Rogers tries more than any of the group to analyse the character of their leader: he speaks of

his strong and tenacious, if somewhat fastidious, affection (not, it must be confessed, without a certain tenacity of aversion also). . . . As the Movement gathered power in his hands he became somewhat more disinclined to men who affected an independent position, and was quick in detecting a growing divergence, though sometimes curiously over-confident in his power of counteracting an adverse pre-possession.

There follows an annoying line of dots which one would like to replace by the rest of the sentence. Rogers speaks of "his genius, depth of purpose, his hatred of pomp and affectation; his piercing insight into the workings of the human mind."

With those who understood him, the intercourse was perfect.

Newman seemed to have an intuitive perception of all that you thought and felt, so that he caught at once all that you meant or were driving at in a sentiment, a philosophical reflection or a joke—within a certain circle, no doubt, but within a circle which comprehended all your common sympathies. And so there was in talking with him that combination of liveliness and repose which constitutes ease; you seemed to be speaking with a better kind of self, which was drawing you upwards.[1]

On his side, Newman was all through his life deeply dependent on the affection of his friends. He was soon to lose Froude who went that winter (1833) to Barbados in a vain search for health, and whose letters were all that remained of him to Newman during almost the whole remainder of his short life. The group of younger men, especially Rogers and Church, now supplied both devoted affection and the element of hope which had been especially Froude's contribution and of which, says Church, Newman's own store was never very abundant. Enthusiastic he was, but not optimistic. Richard Church, later Dean of St. Paul's, wrote an admirable *History of the Oxford Movement* in which he reconciled to a degree that might well have been deemed impossible devotion to Newman and loyalty to the Church

[1] *Letters of Lord Blachford*, p. 14.

of England. One can feel in his pages the opposing currents that run so strong in Froude's letters and in Palmer's Narrative.

Turning to the Tracts one hardly wonders that Palmer so hesitated about them as an advertisement for the Society. Newman's personality might for a while keep together men of different shades of opinion, but the very first Tract was eminently calculated to blow the Society to pieces. Its subject was the Apostolic Succession, and Dean Church tells the story that one of the Bishops after reading it sat in much perplexity wondering whether or not he believed in the doctrine. And if he did believe, what of it? Dean Church sees in the Establishment the blot of "a quiet worldliness", and indeed a state Church is seldom free from it. How would such a prospect as "the spoiling of their goods and martyrdom" appeal to those Bishops who had opposed Reform from fear of loss of benefices and diminished revenues. . . . Nothing could show more clearly the cross purposes already at work. Of this first Tract a few paragraphs must be quoted:

I am but one of yourselves,—a Presbyter; and therefore I conceal my name, lest I should take too much on myself by speaking in my own person. Yet speak I must; for the times are very evil, yet no one speaks against them.

Is not this so? Do not we "look upon one another" yet perform nothing? Do we not all confess the peril into which the Church is come, yet sit still each in his own retirement, as if mountains and seas cut off brother from brother? Therefore suffer me, while I try to draw you forth from those pleasant retreats, which it has been our blessedness hitherto to enjoy, to contemplate the condition and prospects of our Holy Mother in a practical way; so that one and all may unlearn that idle habit, which has grown upon us, of owning the state of things to be bad, yet doing nothing to remedy it.

Consider a moment. Is it fair, is it dutiful, to suffer our Bishops to stand the brunt of the battle without doing our part to support them? Upon them comes the care of all the Churches. This cannot be helped; indeed it is their glory. Not one of us would wish in the least to deprive them of the duties, the toils, the responsibilities of their high office. And, black event as it would be for the country, yet, (as far as they are concerned), we could not wish them a more blessed termination of their course, than the spoiling of their goods, and martyrdom.

To them then we willingly and affectionately relinquish their high privileges and honours; we encroach not upon the rights of the

SUCCESSORS OF THE APOSTLES; we touch not their sword and crozier. Yet surely we may be their shield-bearers in the battle without offence; and by our voice and deeds be to them what Luke and Timothy were to St. Paul. . . .

The Tract concludes:

. . . But, if you will not adopt my view of the subject, which I offer to you, not doubtingly, yet (I hope) respectfully, at all events, CHOOSE YOUR SIDE. To remain neuter much longer will be itself to take a part. *Choose* your side; since side you shortly must, with one or other party, even though you do nothing. Fear to be of those, whose line is decided for them by chance circumstances, and who may perchance find themselves with the enemies of CHRIST, while they think but to remove themselves from worldly politics. Such abstinence is impossible in troublous times, HE THAT IS NOT WITH ME, IS AGAINST ME, AND HE THAT GATHERETH NOT WITH ME SCATTERETH ABROAD.

And the country clergy we know best, Jane Austen's clergy, how did they receive this Tract? Did Henry Tilney, middle-aged now, read it out to Catherine in "the prettiest room in the world," looking out at the cottage that the General spared only because Catherine approved it as an object? Did Edmund Bertram talk it over with Fanny before walking across the park to see Sir Thomas? And what on earth did Mr. Elton make of it? Was Lady Catherine de Burgh still alive and did Mr. Collins call at Hunsford to get her opinion?

I feel sure the word enthusiasm was uttered in its worse sense if Tom Mozley called at any of these rectories.

I may be told that it was the Charlotte Yonge clergy who were beginning to spring up to whom the Tracts were directed, but would you not in fact be as much surprised to meet a Charlotte Yonge rector as to meet Black Giles the poacher or one of the rich farmers or the good shepherd of Salisbury Plain out of Hannah More's tales? Charlotte had grown up in Keble's parish and all her good clergy were sketches of Keble. They were figures that belonged in an old style tract rather than readers of this new style. Did not Jane Austen's clergy pass by a natural development into Trollope's and what would be felt about the Tracts in the Cathedral Close and in the country parsonages of Barsetshire: would even Mr. Harding have approved—or Mr.

Arabin? I shudder to think of Mrs. Proudie's feelings or the Charge she would write for the Bishop, and I almost fancy that for once in their lives she and Archdeacon Grantly would be of one mind.

What, on the other hand, would Cobbett have made of the suggestion that bishops should be ready to endure despoiling of their goods and martyrdom? We can fancy a sardonic smile on his lips as he read, riding the while past rich glebes and parsonages supported by an almost starving populace, changed with the assistance of these bishops from a peasantry into a proletariat.

As we try to recall in imagination the actual England in which Newman and his friends were working we feel the truth of Richard Holt Hutton's comment—that they lived "more like a colony of immigrants amongst a people of different languages and customs than like a band of patriots who were reviving the old glories of their native country."[1] He noted in their efforts "an air of anxious venturesomeness, of hesitating audacity, of careworn courage": but it took an outsider to notice it: for them the courage had lifted their hearts high and they were living in an unreal world in which they were carrying all England with them on a tide of returning Catholicism.

[1] *Life of Newman*, p. 55.

CHAPTER XXI

The Via Media

IN OXFORD itself, that "home of lost causes", the atmosphere would be very different from that of the countryside. It was right to utter with respect the name of Laud, to celebrate the virtues of Bishop Ken whose life Keble wrote and in whose honour Newman composed an office after the style of the Breviary. The appeal to the Fathers, the constant reference to the great Anglican divines, were here wholly in place. Then too a liking for "characters" made Newman acceptable in the same fashion as Whately or Arnold or Lloyd. And as long as extreme views were aired chiefly in Common Rooms even the most conservative were highly tolerant.

Newman certainly had no intention of keeping his views in Common Rooms. He had said in *Home Thoughts Abroad*, that a great reformer' must usually begin by creating his own instruments. The instruments of the Oxford Movement were measures and they were men—both for the most part of Newman's creation. In the first year appeared twenty Tracts of which nine were of his writing; late in 1834 he took over from his friend Benjamin Harrison a controversy-by-correspondence with the French Abbé Jager: the correspondence lapsed after Newman had written a couple of long letters but he incorporated much of what he had written in the lectures entitled *Prophetical Office of the Church*, later republished as Volume I of the *Via Media*. In the *British Magazine* the *Lyra Apostolica* made the principles of the Movement attractive in the verse of the period, while Newman emphasized and illustrated them in a series of articles on the Church of the Fathers.

These principles he has told us were in his mind, chiefly three: the dogmatic, the sacramental, the anti-Roman.

My battle was with liberalism; by liberalism I mean the anti-dogmatic principle and its developments. . . . From the age of fifteen, dogma has been the fundamental principle of my religion: I know no other religion; I cannot enter into the idea of any other sort of religion; religion, as a mere sentiment, is to me a dream and a mockery. As well can there be filial love without the fact of a father, as devotion without the fact of a Supreme Being. What I held in 1816, I held in 1833, and I hold in 1864. Please God, I shall hold it to the end.[1]

On this foundation of dogma was erected the teaching of the Church to be found in her creeds, her great divines and above all the Fathers of the early undivided Church.

Some portions of their teaching, magnificent in themselves, came like music to my inward ear, as if the response to ideas, which, with little external to encourage them, I had cherished so long. These were based on the mystical or sacramental principle, and spoke of the various Economies or Dispensations of the Eternal. I understood these passages to mean that the exterior world, physical and historical, was but the manifestation to our senses of realities greater than itself. Nature was a parable: Scripture was an allegory: pagan literature, philosophy, and mythology, properly understood, were but a preparation for the Gospel.[2]

The Anglican divines whose works Newman read deeply at this period were themselves imbued with Patristic doctrine. Accepting from them this Catholic tradition Newman accepted along with it their attitude towards Rome. Some years later, as he relates in the *Apologia*, he wanted to "bite off their ears", for what he could not but feel the dishonesty of their polemic. But at this moment his inclinations increased his docility towards these teachers of his own Church. Probably too, the adherence of Dr. Pusey to the movement confirmed his attitude—for Pusey had learning on which Newman tended to rely as far deeper than his own.

Isaac Williams tells in his Autobiography how Pusey at first hesitated, not wishing to be identified with the Tracts. He agreed to contribute on condition that his own Tract—on fasting—should be initialled. The others were anonymous. But the result was, naturally enough, the opposite of his intentions. So far from his initials separating him from the rest they succeeded in identifying the Movement with his name—it began to be called "Puseyite", (this was not common before 1840)[3] although still "Tractarian" and oftenest of all "Newmanite". Pusey was the

[1] *Apologia*, p. 32.   [2] *Apologia*, p. 18.   [3] Liddon, *Life of Pusey*, II, 139.

first man of real standing—a professor, a man of social position and of almost legendary learning—to join the Movement. "Froude and I were nobodies", Newman says.

Fortunate the man who finds a skilful and sympathetic biographer. While Coleridge's dry treatment of Keble leaves one cold, Liddon's life of Pusey kindles an enthusiastic affection for his subject. I had absolved myself in advance from reading more than the first half of this four-volumed work, but found I could not put the book down. He really was a heavenly man, and "Maria" and the delicate children and the whole home atmosphere of love and sorrow shining out under the terrifying severity of his outlook, make a unique picture with which Newman is closely identified. A stray visitor to Oxford describes seeing Newman with Pusey's children.

Presently, after dinner, Dr. Pusey's children ran into the room. One climbed Newman's knee and hugged him. Newman put his spectacles on him, and next on his sister, and great was the merriment of the Puseyan progeny. Newman, it is said, hates ecclesiastical conversation. He writes so much that when in society he seems always inclined to talk on light, amusing subjects. He told them a story of an old woman who had a broomstick which would go to the well, draw water, and do many things for her, how the old woman got tired of the broomstick, and wishing to destroy it broke it in twain, and how, to the old woman's great chagrin and disappointment *two* live broomsticks grew from the broken parts of the old one![1]

Newman, the visitor adds, "is a dark middle-aged, middle sized man, with lanky black hair and large spectacles, thin, gentlemanly and very insinuating."

Constantly with the family, Newman is presently described by Mrs. Pusey to her husband as "Mr. Newman (I beg pardon 'John', I might almost say St. John)" She writes to him of the comfort of his sermons in sickness, later he was to help both husband and wife to bear the separation as her life drew to a close.

Pusey's adherence to the Movement altered the nature of the Tracts and brought in some new features. Least of all the writers could Pusey express himself briefly; in his hands a tract became a treatise. He started establishing doctrines by means of unwieldy "catenae" of texts from the Anglican divines. With

[1] Liddon, *Life of Pusey*, II. 406-7.

Newman and Keble he started the *Library of the Fathers*, and a letter from Newman entreats him to admit the principle of idiomatic English instead of literal verbal translation! Pusey's sense of effect was never equal to his learning and as time goes on we find several of the younger men in despair at his determination to put the Movement in the worst possible light in the eyes of its opponents.

Newman had said that he and Froude were nobodies, but he was fast becoming a somebody. *The Arians* had caused a stir among the learned of the University, and James Mozley describes Newman as "closeted the other day two hours with Routh of Magdalen" receiving complimentary opinions of the book. The first volume of his Parochial Sermons too had an immense success. The second was in the Press, and Newman decided to stand for the Professorship of Moral Philosophy. "There is no situation", he wrote jestingly to Bowden, "which combines respectability with lightness of responsibility so happily as the office of a Professor." Up to the eve of the election he was the only candidate. But James Mozley writes:

Hampden offered himself the very day before the election, and being a Bampton Lecturer and an Aristotelian, and a Head of a House, and a Liberal, and moreover, a stupid man in his way, he was of course the successful candidate. It is a pity, if only for the title-page of Newman's volume of sermons, which has just come out.

Meanwhile all was going well with the Movement. The years 1834 and 1835 brought much work but no great problems. Both as an Apostolical and an Oxford man, Newman objected to other English Universities, not barred to Dissenters by Oxford's tests, being allowed to grant degrees. He writes to Bowden, (March 14, 1834): "The Duke has begun his campaign by advising us strenuously to resist London University's granting degrees in Arts and Divinity—Indeed it does seem a little too bad that the Dissenters are to take our Titles—why should they call themselves M.A. except to seem like us?" (In the same year his mother writes to tell him that "Francis has engaged himself as Classical Tutor! at the Bristol College.")

The parish ran smoothly, apart from some excitement over Newman's refusal to perform the marriage service for an unbaptised woman: "As to refusing marriage to unbaptised persons," he writes to Bowden (July 1834), "we must make a stand somewhere. . . . I am determined, please God, that, as far as I am concerned the Church shall not crumble away without my doing in my place what I can to resist it."

There was one development in the Movement itself. "Next," he writes to Bowden (September 1835), "we have determined to commence a series *against* Popery, i.e. to devote next year at length to the subject." In the same month he writes to Henry Edward Manning on the same subject, with a minuteness of detail which verges on the eccentric. He wants Manning to find a bookseller to handle the Tracts:

> . . . giving him a percentage on all he sells and providing him with a bit of wood painted black with an inscription in paint (of another colour) to the following effect: "Tracts of the Times sold here"— the said board to be suspended by two strings meeting in an angle and connected with a nail in the wooden frame of the window-pane in his shop.

The reasons for Newman's decision to attack Rome in the Tracts are, as he suggests in the *Apologia*, mixed. One certainly was his desire to refute the charge that he was himself popishly inclined. It was a charge he could answer with complete sincerity. A couple of months after the directions to Manning just noted, he wrote a most interesting letter to Henry Wilberforce's wife, who had told him of her own attraction to Rome and her resistance to it. He confesses that he has felt the same attraction as she, but "the more I examine into the R.C. system, the less sound it appears to me to be." He lists four main objections—the belief that Christ's body is carnally present on the Altar, the polytheism involved in saint-worship, praying to images ("is there not a still small voice telling us not to do so?") and purgatory. (The letter is given in full in Appendix A.) He had one further objection: he wrote to Bowden (August 1835): "Dr. Wiseman . . . is to be here . . . in a few days. He sent before him a Roman Catholic priest named Maguire a few days since, who dined with me and had some talk. It is quite painful to see how they are hand in glove with O'Connell and Co." The willingness of Catholics to consort with "such vile persons" as O'Connell, who was willing to consort with Liberals, was for long a major stumbling block in Newman's path.

But his desire to clear himself was not a major motive. In fact

Rome *had* to be attacked—it was a necessity of principle because the Anglican Church as he conceived it was essentially anti-Roman; and it was a strategical necessity because the *via media* could not be justified unless Rome were shown to be wrong. The development of the *via media* was the vast work upon which he was now embarking.

In the assertion of a dogmatic principle and in the attack upon Romanism, Newman could take with him the Evangelicals, Conservative Churchmen, even many dissenters. How far did they go with him in his view of a Church that was primitive but not Roman, the minister to man of God's truth and grace through her teaching and her sacraments, a *via media* between Protestantism and Romanism? So confident was he in the strength of his position that at one moment he had felt half afraid of unsettling the Abbé Jager (with whom, as we have just seen, he was in controversy) and making it difficult for him to go on in his own "branch" of the Church. A devout Anglican himself, he chose from another devout Anglican the perfect words with which to introduce his thesis.

The printed edition of the *Via Media* he prefaced with the words of Bramhall:

No man can justly blame me for honouring my spiritual Mother, the Church of England, in whose womb I was conceived, at whose breasts I was nourished, and in whose bosom I hope to die. Bees, by the instinct of nature, do love their hives, and birds their nests. But, God is my witness, that, according to my uttermost talent and poor understanding, I have endeavoured to set down the naked truth impartially. . . .

Howsoever it be, I submit myself and my poor endeavours, first to the Judgment of the Catholic Œcumenical essential church, which if some of late days have endeavoured to hiss out of the schools as a fancy, I cannot help it. From the beginning it was not so.[1]

And in choosing the man to whom to dedicate the Lectures as a volume Newman rightly selected one who more than any other in Oxford represented the scholarly, patristic and anglo-Catholic tradition of the English Church, Martin Routh of Magdalen, known as "the old President", who was to live to his hundredth year and had been a don when Dr. Johnson visited the University. Born in the reign of George II, he lived

[1] *Via Media*, Vol. 1 (Advertisement), XII-XIII.

to within two years of the birth of Bernard Shaw. His learning was legendary, his *Reliquiae Sacrae*—a collection of little-known Patristic literature—had brought him fame not in England alone but on the Continent. Tom Mozley absurdly suggests that Newman's dedication was a political move, that he really thought little of Routh, but we are hardly to suppose that Mozley had read the *Reliquiae* with any care.

Routh always fasted on the anniversary of Charles I's death. He did not like the non-jurors but had a great reverence for royalty and a considerable contempt for the House of Commons. He had been of the party that opposed Peel on Emancipation but he was one of the very few who remained on the friendliest of terms with those who went over to Rome—a rare thing indeed at that period.

Oxford abounded in stories about the President of which perhaps the best became traditional and was told of later Heads of other Colleges. Some men asking leave to stay in College after the Michaelmas term, they said to read, but meant to hunt, were confronted by a notice from the President that they would have to attend Chapel twice daily, and that the kitchen would be closed till further notice. Watching next morning the departure of crowded coaches the President observed, "This kind goeth not out except by prayer and fasting".[1]

We can see him watching them in the heavy wig he wore all his life, knee breeches, huge buckles to his shoes, and over all his robes ("and cassock" adds one visitor)—"as different" says one of the Mozley sisters "from anything one is used to as maybe".

Writing to Routh to ask his acceptance of the dedication Newman says, "I have tried as far as may be to follow the line of doctrine marked out by our great divines, of whom perhaps I have chiefly followed Bramhall, then Laud, Hammond, Field, Stillingfleet, Beveridge . . ."

And on the title page he described Routh as one "Who has been reserved to report to a forgetful generation what was the theology of their fathers". Thus Routh has been called a Tractarian before the Tracts, for he embodied the High Church tradition which the apathy of the early eighteenth century and the later Evangelical revival had combined in obscuring.

Routh for his part had been observing Newman—"that clever

[1] There are various versions of the story. This one was told my father by Jowett —on whom it had been fathered, coaches being altered to trains.

young gentleman of Oriel"—ever since the publication of the *Arians*. Later he used to call him "the great Newman". And in the final volume of his *Reliquiae*—published three years after Newman's reception into the Catholic Church, Routh (then ninety-two), called him "Vir valde perspicax et eruditus".

A Professorship would have given Newman a lecture platform. Without it, if he wanted to lecture he must create a platform. "He anticipated," says Dean Church "a freedom—familiar now, but unknown then—of public lecturing." The question of locality was a minor difficulty to be overcome. He decided to make use of a neglected part of his parish Church—Adam de Brome's Chapel, the Lady Chapel of St. Mary's, inconveniently crowded by the large tomb of Oriel's founder. To-day the Chapel is again simply part of the Church, but at that date it is called by Dean Church "a dark dreary appendage to St. Mary's." The Dean goes on:

At the end is a high seat and desk for the person presiding, and an enclosure and a table for officials below him; and round the rest of the dingy walls run benches fixed to the wall, dingy as the walls themselves. . . . On occasion of a university sermon, a few minutes before it began, the Heads of Houses assembled, as they still assemble, in the chapel, ranging themselves on the benches round the walls. The Vice-Chancellor has his seat on one side, the preacher, with the two Proctors below him, sits opposite; and there all sit in their robes, more or less grand, according to the day, till the beadle comes to announce that it is time to form the procession into church. This desolate place Mr. Newman turned into his lecture-room: in it he delivered the lectures which afterwards became the volume on the Prophetical Character of the Church, or Romanism and Popular Protestantism (this is Vol. I of the *Via Media*); the lectures which formed the volume on Justification; those on Antichrist, and on Rationalism and the Canon of Scripture, which afterwards became Nos. 83 and 85 of the Tracts for the Times.[1]

Through these lectures which began in 1834 came many of the younger adherents to the Movement, among them Stanley, who later gravitated into extreme Liberalism, and William George Ward. Both Stanley and Ward were at this time followers

[1] Dean Church. *The Oxford Movement*, p. 165. A footnote adds: Romanism and Popular Protestantism, from 1834 to 1836, published March 1837; Justification, after Easter, 1837, published March 1838; Canon of Scripture, published May 1838, Antichrist, published June 1838.

of Arnold, and Stanley in many of his letters laments the gulf between Arnold and Newman who "seem to be almost antagonist powers, whereas really they are of the same essence so to speak." Coming straight from Rugby he was immediately impressed with the force of Tractarianism as "a magnificent and consistent system . . . all that I see here against it is weak and grovelling". Ward, who had a powerful and logical mind but none of Stanley's power of imaginative sympathy, merely refused at first to hear Newman. "Why should I go and listen to such myths?"

Dean Goulburn writing to Wilfrid Ward has described the scene in Adam de Brome's Chapel when Ward, persuaded by Stanley, became a member of Newman's audience.

Your good father was the most demonstrative of men—wholly incapable of suppressing any strong emotion which for the time got possession of him; and as these lectures awakened in him the strongest emotions both of admiration for their power, and (at that time) indignant repudiation of their conclusions, he put the preacher somewhat out of countenance by his steadfast gaze, his play of feature as some particular passage stirred him, his nudges of Stanley, and whispered "asides" to him, ("What would Arnold say to that," etc., etc.) Your father's manner and gestures were so pronounced that no one in the congregation could help noticing them; . . . at the lecture immediately succeeding one at which Ward had been specially demonstrative, we found the benches of the congregation turned sideways (as in college chapels), so that he and Stanley could not, without turning their heads askew, look the preacher in the face.[1]

At times it seemed as though in Newman's eyes the *via media* already existed in the Church of England and he would appeal with confidence to her Prayer Book, her formularies, and the writings of her great divines. Yet again he would seem to feel that he was all but the "onlie begettor" of a disembodied dream. To his sister Jemima he wrote when the lectures were in progress (October 2, 1834):

. . . Somehow my own confidence in my views seems to grow. I am aware I have not yet fully developed them to myself. There are opinions as yet unknown to me which must be brought out and received; inconsistencies, too, perhaps to be set right; but, on the whole, I seem to have a grasp of a system, very comprehensive. I could go on a great way with Rome, and a great way with the Evan-

---

[1] *William George Ward and the Oxford Movement.* Wilfrid Ward, p. 83.

gelicals; nay, I should not despair of religious Dissenters. I think our system will be very taking from its novelty, its sublimity, and its argumentative basis. . . . I am conscious to myself I easily bring a person to a stand, and to say: "Really I have not considered it in that point of view." (Whether a permanent effect would be produced is another matter.) I attribute this, not to any powers of argument which I have (for, if I had my will, I never would argue, and I suppose, on the other hand, one *likes* to do what one can do well), but simply to my having got hold, somehow or other, of an imposing *view*, call it right or wrong. I should not be surprised (though sorry) if an Apostolical School started up at Cambridge, as the Shelleian, Utilitarian, etc.

Novelty seems a curious claim from a man whose "stronghold was antiquity", yet as an Anglican expounding Anglicanism the novelty he saw was in the arrangement of ideas already present: it was his Church's mission to bear witness to a Catholicism primitive yet not Roman:

Primitive doctrine has been explored for us in every direction, and the original principles of the gospel and the Church patiently and successfully brought to light. But one thing is still wanting: our champions and teachers have lived in stormy times: political and other influences have acted upon them variously in their day, and have since obstructed a careful consolidation of their judgments. We have more than we know how to use; stores of learning, but little that is precise and serviceable; Catholic truth and individual opinion, first principles and the guesses of genius, all mingled in the same works, and requiring to be discriminated.

This quotation comes from the Introduction to the Lectures when first collected into a volume, and in it Newman faced with complete frankness the threefold attack that his system had to repel. (1) The *via media* was unreal, its supporters "mere antiquarians or pedants, amusing ourselves with illusions or learned subtleties, and unable to grapple with things as they are". (2) The true Church of England even if accidentally episcopal was "set", and the form in which it was set was essentially Protestant. (3) The Church—and this was, he held, the most plausible attack—"as established by law, and existing in fact, has never represented a doctrine at all or been the development of a principle, has never had an intellectual basis; it has been but a name, or a department of the state, or a political party, in which religious opinion was an accident, and therefore has been various.

In consequence, it has been but the theatre of contending religionists."

The question at issue was then whether "what is called Anglo-Catholicism, the religion of Andrewes, Laud, Hammond, Butler, and Wilson, is capable of being professed, acted on, and maintained on a large sphere of action and through a sufficient period, or whether it be a mere modification or transition-state either of Romanism or of popular Protestantism, according as we view it."

The actuality of Anglo-Catholicism Newman firmly believed he could prove: All parties in the Church of England rejected Rome, all held by antiquity and by the Bible. Popular Protestantism had indeed erred in one direction as Rome in another, yet there might be found in the Church of England "the nearest approximation to that primitive truth which Ignatius and Polycarp enjoyed, and which the nineteenth century has virtually lost".

This is not the only Introduction which we can read today if we pick up this volume of lectures. Forty years later Newman the Catholic commented on the lectures given by Newman the Anglican. Ruskin and others have adorned with footnotes later editions of their early books, but there remains an unique quality about this late edition of the collected works of Newman which although belonging in the main to his Catholic life has a certain significance here.

The footnotes must have been written with a smile, especially on p. 312. "This is incorrect, and I cannot guess where the author got such a statement." But the Introduction shows us that apart from the bias against Rome—the "false conscience" created in boyhood and strengthened by the Anglican divines—we have the same Newman talking without realising it about the same Church. The *via media* is in fact what has been later called "the Catholic Centre". In dealing only with the Church as Prophetical the lectures inevitably missed that centre, for the Church is the Mystical Christ working in the world with a three-fold anointing—that of prophet indeed, but also that of priest and that of king. The introduction of 1877 is needed to complete the lectures by giving the harmony and balance only to be found by considering all these aspects, but this completion is not (except in some details) any contradiction. The Catholic Church holds in truth the middle way of Newman's dreams by holding the fulness and the balance of the whole Christian revelation.

Viewing generally the "errors" he was attacking, Newman in the first lecture drew the distinction: "Rome retains the principle of true Catholicism perverted; popular Protestantism is wanting in the principle." The Reformation he desiderates for Rome will be of her popular devotions not of her main teachings. "Romanism may be considered as an unnatural and misshapen development of the Truth; not the less dangerous because it contains traces of its genuine features." He considers in this lecture the nature and ground of both Roman and Protestant errors, and in the next three discusses Rome as neglectful of antiquity and Infallibility under its moral and political aspects. "How hopeless then is it to contend with Romanists, as if they practically agreed with us as to the foundation of faith, however much they pretend to it! Ours is Antiquity, theirs the existing Church. Its infallibility is their first principle; belief in it is a deep prejudice quite beyond the reach of anything external."

Seeing Infallibility as too systematic and complete—"the Church of Rome is in fact led on to profess to know not only infallibly but completely"—he confuses (as the Catholic Newman notes), the vast field of theological opinion with the rare pronouncements of authority.

It [Roman Theology] arranges, adjusts, explains, exhausts every part of the Divine Economy. It may be said to leave no region unexplored, no heights unattempted, rounding off its doctrines with a neatness and finish which are destructive of many of the most noble and most salutary exercises of mind in the individual Christian. That feeling of awe which the mysteriousness of the Gospel should excite, fades away under this fictitious illumination which is poured over the entire Dispensation . . . This technical religion destroys the delicacy and reverence of the Christian mind . . . Christian holiness, in consequence, loses its freshness, vigour, and comeliness, being frozen (as it were) into certain attitudes, which are not graceful except when they are unstudied.

And in a footnote the Catholic Newman comments: "This is plausible, theoretical, and untrue."

Yet the wish to be fair drew from the writer of these passages a picture of Catholic tradition that no writer inside the Church could have surpassed.

It is latent, but it lives. It is silent like the rapids of a river, before the rocks intercept it. It is the Church's unconscious habit of opinion and sentiment; which she reflects upon, masters, and expresses, according to the emergency. We see then the mistake of asking for a complete collection of the Roman Traditions; as well might we ask for a full catalogue of a man's tastes and thoughts on a given subject. Tradition in its fulness is necessarily unwritten; it is the mode in which a society has felt or acted during a certain period, and it cannot be circumscribed any more than a man's countenance and manner can be conveyed to strangers in any set of propositions.

The lectures on Private Judgment are so Catholic in tone that hardly a corrective note was needed forty years later. The chaos into which the Bible Christian must necessarily come has never been shown more powerfully. The Bible alone is simply not sufficient. Men must at last "either cease to think orthodoxy necessary, or allow it to be taught to them".

But who was the teacher to be? Not the existing Church. In its sinfulness and in its divisions it too obviously fails to correspond with the promises of Christ. "Infallibility, were it ever intended, might require the presence of a superhuman charity and peace"; and these were no longer to be found in the Church. We must therefore find our guide in the Church of Antiquity. Commenting so long after as a Catholic, Newman is ironical about this assumption that the Church of the first four centuries had that degree of holiness the absence of which invalidated the teaching of the Church of today. At the time the difficulty hardly seems to have occurred to him. The important point was "The creed of Rome is ever subject to increase; ours is fixed once for all." Antiquity did not in his eyes actually teach a creed, but it is the witness of the teaching of the undivided church, and he was ever listening to its voice: "If the voluminous remains of that period, including the works of Ambrose, Austin, Jerome, Chrysostom, Basil, Gregory Nyssen, Gregory Nazianzen, Athanasius, and Cyril of Jerusalem, will not afford a standard of Catholic doctrine, there seems little profit to be gained from Antiquity at all."

"Voluminous" is surely the operative word. Strange that he did not see that this was a somewhat impracticable guide for men who wanted the truth of Christian doctrine here and now. One sympathizes with Whately's summary of the appeal to Antiquity: "this depends on their being governed on the Apostolical models, of which the Apostles have left us in their writings no precise description, but which we are to collect by a comparison of what St. A. saith in such a book, with what is reported by St. B. to have been reported by St. C. as the practice of the Church in D."

Actually Newman did see the problem of sorting out what was essential in the great mass of patristic teaching. But he sees the answer in the Creed, or rather in the Creeds, for the Nicene Creed must be admitted too. But is not the Nicene Creed an addition to the Apostles' Creed? No, it is merely an explanation. (The Catholic Newman sees the weakness: "New questions, new opinions are ever rising in the Church. . . . If she cannot say Yes or No, how can she teach the Truth?") Nor are the Thirty-Nine Articles an addition. They are valuable as a test against Romanism, as "portions of Catholic teaching, as expressing and representing that Ancient Religion, which of old time found voice and attained consistency in Athanasius, Basil, Augustine, Chrysostom and other primitive doctors."

If Antiquity is the one sure test, is there any way in which the living voice of the Church may be heard? Yes, the Anglican believes:

She speaks in her formularies and services. The Daily Prayer, the Occasional Offices, the Order of the Sacraments, the Ordination Services, present one and the same strong, plain edifying language to rich and poor, learned and unlearned . . . The very titles of the Prayers and Creeds show this; such as, "the Apostles" and "the Nicene Creed", "the Creed of St. Athanasius", "the Catholic Faith", the "Catholic Religion" a "Prayer of St. Chrysostom" and the like . . . a stranger taking up the Prayer Book would feel it to be no modern production. . . . It claims to be Catholic; nor is there any one of any party to deny, that on the whole it is. There is no mistaking then in this day in England, where the Church Catholic is, and what her teaching. To follow her is to follow the Prayer Book.

Here is the main foundation and justification of the *via media*.

R. H. Hutton has noted that his anxiety to admit difficulties and his sensitiveness to them made Newman appear often less convinced than he was of the position he held. This comes out strongly in the last lecture of the Course:

. . . And now that our discussions on what may fitly be called the Prophetical Office of the Church draw to a close, the thought . . .

is not unlikely to recur, when the excitement of the inquiry has sub-
sided, and weariness has succeeded, that what has been said is but
a dream, the wanton exercise, rather than the practical conclusion of
the intellect. Such is the feeling of minds unversed in the disappointments of the world, incredulous how much it has of promise, how little
of substance; what intricacy and confusion beset the most certain
truths; . . . Without some portion of that Divine Philosophy which
bids us consider "the kingdom of God" to be "within us" and which,
by prayer and meditation, by acting on what is told us, and by anticipating sight, develops outwardly its own views and principles, and thus
assimilates to itself all that is around us—not only the Church in this
age and country, but the Church Catholic anywhere, or at any time,
Primitive, Roman, or Reformed, is but a name. After all, the Church
is ever invisible in its day, and faith only apprehends it . . .

Yet surely we may expect:

that the true Faith, the one way to heaven, the one message from the
Saviour of sinners, the Revelation of the Gospel, will be plain and
unequivocal, as the sun in the heavens. In the English Church, however, we shall hardly find ten or twenty neighbouring clergymen who
agree together. . . . The laity wander about like sheep without a
shepherd . . . they walk in darkness and disquiet, far removed from
that "peace" which the Prophet describes as resulting from the
"teaching" which the children of the True Church receive.

Having stated the case as strongly as possible he answers it
along two lines—the weakness, anomalies, defects in the Jewish
Church and those in the history of the Church Catholic: the
Council of Ephesus, Pope Vigilius, simony in the appointment
of Bishops, scandals in the Papacy, the great schism, the testimony against Catholic Authorities of St. Basil, against the Roman
See of St. Thomas à Beckett.

In a famous passage he concludes:

. . . But in truth the whole course of Christianity from the first,
when we come to examine it, is but one series of troubles and disorders. Every century is like every other, and to those who live in it
seems worse than all times before it. The Church is ever ailing, and
lingers on in weakness, "always bearing about in her body the dying
of the Lord Jesus, that the life also of Jesus might be made manifest
in her body." Religion seems ever expiring, schisms dominant, the
light of Truth dim, its adherents scattered. The cause of Christ is ever
in its last agony, as though it were but a question of time whether it

fails finally this day or another. The Saints are ever all but failing from the earth, and Christ all but coming: and thus the Day of Judgment is literally ever at hand. . . . Well may prophets cry out, "How long will it be, O Lord, to the end of these wonders?" how long will this mystery proceed? how long will this perishing world be sustained by the feeble lights which struggle for existence in its unhealthy atmosphere. God alone knows the day and the hour when that will at length be, which He is ever threatening: meanwhile, thus much of comfort do we gain from what has been hitherto,—not to despond, not to be dismayed, not to be anxious, at the troubles which encompass us. They have ever been; they ever shall be; they are our portion. "The floods are risen, the floods have lifted up their voice, the floods lift up their waves. The waves of the sea are mighty, and rage horribly; but yet the Lord, who dwelleth on high, is mightier."

CHAPTER XXII

Human Relationships

IN THIS first period of the Movement, a long letter from John to Frank gives something of the atmosphere of home and parish. It is wonderfully characteristic of the period that Frank had felt it his duty to protest against his brother's waste of money on the house at Iffley. Mrs. Newman was only too apt to worry over being an expense: "I have long been anxious to release you from some of our expenditure; and your sisters and I have often talked it over to find the best means, with Respectability, to effect it."

But what she saw as Respectability Frank saw as pride of life. The line he took is clear from John's answer (September 7, 1834):

> I agree with you that you are not bound to support any collateral relative who can without you provide for himself,—or *herself* . . . but it seems to me a very poor ground to take, to debate about strict obligation, when affection may lawfully come in—and again it is totally out of place to speak of me, as if I *maintained* my sisters. This is surely quite a mistaken view of the case: so I give you my thoughts upon it.
>
> You speak of our keeping up "the lust of the eye and the pride of life". Now really the only point I can make out in which we succumb (even in your view) to these bad principles, is in my mother's having a servant in livery. She does with as few servants as possible—and perhaps your own experience abroad will show you that to dispense with servants altogether and keep one's own house in order oneself is not the way to improve one's talents or to do most good. Everyone has his place in society—there is a difference of duties and of persons fitted to them. "High" and "low" are mere names, and invidious ones. I would rather speak, if I could, of right hand and left hand ranks, all being on a level. When I engage servants, it is a mutual engagement, for the good of all. They do what they are fitted to do, and which I for want of training cannot do—and I in turn do good, first to them, then to others, or at least ought to do. Whatever I may give my Mother and Sisters is indeed in the first way of viewing it a free

gift—but, if I must be utilitarian enough to trace its operation, I will affirm that one very great portion of it passes from them in direct charity, another portion in *indirect*, and the whole of it places them in a position to benefit a number of persons variously whom otherwise they could not benefit. My mother cannot do good to herself without benefitting others. If she told Charles she wanted more, depend upon it, nine-tenths of that more would not have found its way to her. The other day I heard her lamenting she could not take another servant: *you* would have said this was "the pride of life"; but I happen to know that it was solely with the view of keeping a girl from bad example, and teaching her a servant's work. Here she would have given away in board (say) twenty pounds a year, and got nothing for it. This will explain to you Charles's report.

Now I must think she is thus making herself more useful than if she threw herself out of her place in society. Depend upon it, this does not answer; a person is then worth nothing at all. He has been trained for a certain place—he does not know his business in another. You yourself confess it in your letter. You say that, having been trained in Latin and Greek, you cannot make money, now that you have left the church. Had my mother religious reasons for leaving her post, as you have had, that would be another matter. But as things are, I say that she and my sisters are doing their duty "in that state of life in which it has pleased God to call them", are spreading God's glory far more than if they lived simply on their own means, and gave away what they had beyond those means in the lump in charity. They are the instruments of temporal good to two hundred people at Little-more—they teach the children, set an example to the parents, and even when they cannot do all they wish, they make people better who otherwise would become worse: and moreover they have friends, whom they otherwise would not have, through whom they do good to my people in various ways, as to finding the young women places, etc., etc.

True, they might give up housekeeping and live in lodgings as some-what cheaper, but then where would be the kitchen for Littlemore, with broth and messes? Where the rice and tapioca from a house-keeper's closet?—in a word, they enable me to spend a large sum upon the poor which I could not spend satisfactorily myself. (How can I manage a parish without women?) They take all my trouble upon themselves. What could I do better with the money? Give it to some Religious Society, to be spent by strangers in whom I had not reason to feel confidence? I suppose my money goes further than yours in journeying to Persia.

I have spoken merely on the ground of *utility*. As to myself person-ally, I shall say nothing. You know little or nothing of my principles or practice, if you should think I go by the mere fashion of society.

"Broth and messes" seem at first sight suggestive if not of Lady Catherine de Burgh (who was fonder of scolding than of feeding her villagers into prosperity and plenty), at least of Emma Woodhouse or Mr. Elton. But even the distribution of broth is only a part of a personal relationship, and whether its social setting was right or wrong, the personal relationship between the Newman family and Littlemore was deeply right.

Visitors to Newman's own catechism classes noticed the eager alertness of the children: every family in the village petitioned for the building of the church: the children brought stories that the builders themselves vied with one another to be bellringer calling all to work each morning. The church completed, the people to Newman's great pleasure decorated it with "bunches of bright flowers" for the consecration. Forty years later, Anne Mozley found the memory of both the rector and his family alive in the parish. To one woman he was "the old gentleman", while his sisters were "the young ladies"—but this may well have been because of his own later visit to the place. He had grown old: their memory was young, and another parishioner, writes Anne Mozley to Jemima (1875), "still sees you and Harriett in green silk cloaks, in which you looked so nice. You were her ideals of goodness and taste." It had been an honour for her to help in the kitchen at Rose Bank (to which the family had moved from Rose Hill). "Dr. Newman examined her for Confirmation, and she and another were the head candidates. Also she was of your mother's class, has most devoted recollections of her kindness to people, knows still her taste in needlework, and how particular she was."

"We will be your Deacons," Mrs. Newman writes, wanting John to rest a little; and her letters report faithfully: "Your Church was well attended as usual and the service done as you would wish. Jemima will tell you of our Saturday's Fête which will not be soon forgotten." He asks them where he shall put the school and Jemima draws a plan. Mrs. Newman, glad there are so many candidates for Confirmation, rejoices in "seeds of promise sown by yourself . . . but I am not so sanguine as those who think permanent good quickly effected nor so desponding as those who relinquish their efforts if not speedily successful". Summing up she writes, "everyone is very grateful and I do hope the people are something better and happier than they were some time ago."

An amusing touch which may relate to their happiness occurs in a letter from Newman to Bloxam, who succeeded Williams as curate in June 1837: "Whitman has come to me with a strange request from some young ladies—to be allowed to have a ball in the school room next week. It does not look well—but they say you have hitherto allowed it. Enlighten me." One hopes it was still allowed, especially as Bloxam tells the story that W. G. Ward coming over for "the Littlemore Festival . . . said to me loud enough for Dr. Pusey to hear him, 'I understand that you are going to give a ball tonight, and that Dr. Pusey has consented to come and dance at it'."

The rustic congregation described in *The Carbonels* included labourers in white smocks, many of them beautifully stitched, farmers in drab coats with large pearl buttons and long gaiters, boys in green smocks and girls in cotton dresses with coarse white straw hats and bright ribbons. James Mozley later described the Littlemore girls as dressed up in pink bonnets and white tippets for some great occasion; and when he resigned St. Mary's Newman gave frocks and bonnets to them all as a parting gift. Probably they wore some such uniform for the laying of the first stone of the church, on July 21, 1835. In her diary Mrs. Newman wrote: "A gratifying day. I laid the first stone of the church at Littlemore. The whole village there . . . J.H. a nice address." She calls the occasion "that day of triumph".

The touching memory of one woman was that, in burying her baby, Newman had *added* some additional words to the service to express his conviction of the child's blessedness. *Cor ad cor loquitur*, and this sense of a personal contact was vivid with all who met Newman. "We don't seem so comfortable now as we used to, I thinks " was the repeated remark of one old woman soon after his departure.

In all this he knew well how great was the debt to his women-folk. How, he asked Frank, could he manage a parish without them? How was a man to have women in his parish who had determined on celibacy? Pusey, although himself married, held strongly that the answer lay in the revival of sisterhoods in the Church of England, but to most of Newman's friends a married clergy seemed the obvious, the time-honoured solution. Newman never wavered in his own determination. His sisters jokingly call him a monk, and he writes to Maria Giberne of her being "lionised" in Oxford in his own absence, "by one who was under no monastic vow to love it and be true to it for life ". The word vow was not literal. Froude had evidently suggested vows of celibacy, but Newman replied to this, "I have thought vows are evidences of *want of Faith.* Why should we look to the morrow?" To Mr. Rickards he wrote of his determination to love and be faithful to Oxford alone. Life in a country rectory had, he admitted, an unspeakable charm for him, "but this is the only great temptation I fear. I feel as if I would rather tear out my heart than lose it ".

Newman himself was, I think, by nature a bachelor, by grace a celibate. It seems clear that his attitude upon clerical celibacy in general was misunderstood by some even of his most intimate friends. Thus (late in 1833) Henry Wilberforce came to tell Newman of his own engagement and went away without doing so. "I did not tell Neander (as who would)," Wilberforce writes to Rogers, "yet I did tell his sister and give her leave to tell him . . . whether Neander will cut me I don't know." And Rogers to Newman, "How can you possibly suppose that after your way of treating that *perditum ovem,* H. Wilberforce, you would be his first confidant? The fact obviously is that he came to Oxford with the intention of breaking the matter to you; but when he came near and saw how fierce you looked, his heart failed him and he retreated."

Rogers clearly thought that Newman objected to clerical marriages: later staying with the Wilberforces he writes "I . . . like my friends' wives although presbyterae "—lady presbyters![1] (But by that time Newman had already stood godfather to Henry's first baby!) Although once or twice Newman speaks strongly of his *feeling* against married clergy, I am sure he did not object to them in principle. He told Rogers to "bear to be candid towards" their wives, until at least a substitute for them could be established in parish work. I find no trace of his disliking Pusey's marriage, although he admits to feeling "sick" over Keble's. No, Newman believed a married clergy to be perfectly legitimate: but he also believed that alongside of it there should be scope for more absolute self-devotion in the religious life.

First for the sake of the Church. "Alas," he wrote of Rose to his mother, asking her to pass the information on to Froude,

---

[1] The word is only a joke here. But according to Duchesne the title presbytera was conferred in the early Church on wives who, when their husbands received priestly orders, continued to live with them as sister and brother.

"he *is* married. This has quite troubled and grieved me—still, if he manages to give his whole soul to the Church it matters not—*though it seems impossible.*"[1]

In a letter to Henry Wilberforce himself, Newman had pressed the need of asceticism if the clergy are in fact to be more than a "'working body', which is now the fashion, like farmers or excise-men". Actually he wants an interfering clergy—interfering even in politics—if he can but have a live one.

I only wish our spiritual governors were more like men and less like cows . . . I do believe we are corrupt in grain far more than we know it,—lovers of ease with not even the self-mastery which a worldly ambition inspires. Surely the veriest heretic, who, as Arius, has learnt to bear asceticism, or an infidel like Julian, who can bear to neglect himself, claims more respect from us than a professed Christian, much more minister, who sets out with purposing to be comfortable, and allows himself in dreams of "tellus, et domus et placens uxor" as the τελος of his life (an unintentional pun).

But the single life was valuable not only for the sake of the Church but of the spiritual development of the individual. If the dogmatic was a leading principle of Tractarianism certainly the ascetic was no less so: for almost everyone who adhered to it seriously, this found expression in their long fasts. An inner circle found it also in celibacy—but they did not exclude "presbyterae" in the case of their weaker colleagues. None could have merited the title more than Mrs. Henry Wilberforce and her sisters. They may be said as a family to have married into the Oxford Movement. John Sargent, Rector of Lavington, had four daughters known as "the beautiful Miss Sargents". The eldest, Emily, had married Samuel Wilberforce in 1828, Caroline had married Henry Edward Manning in 1833. It was the society of these girls which Newman had feared would lead Henry Wilberforce—their father's curate—into "lounging and idling". Actually it led in 1834 to his marriage with Mary. In the same year George Ryder married the remaining sister Sophia Lucy. (I knew their daughter who at ninety was still so lovely an old lady that I can well believe in the legendary beauty of the famous sisters.)

To Ryder, contemplating marriage two years earlier, Newman had written:

[1] Italics mine.

It is quite absurd to suppose that you are not *at liberty* both to marry and to go into the Church—indeed I think that country parsons ought, as a general rule, to be married—and I am sure the generality of men ought, whether parsons or not. The celibate is a high state of life, to which the multitude of men cannot aspire. I do not say that they who adopt it are necessarily better than others, though the noblest ethos is situated in that state.

He thought Ryder too young to marry, did not know "who it is your heart is set on". But:

What can you know of others at your age? How likely are you to be captivated by an outward show, though not show in the common vulgar meaning of the word! Depend upon it, many a man would repent of his marriage, if he did not think it right (as it is) to repress the rising sigh . . .

This letter belongs to the high moment of Newman's tutorial zeal: when he was exhorting Rogers, Mozley, Wilberforce against idleness and urging upon them an ardent zeal which he certainly hoped would flower with some into the self devotion of the religious life. Froude was self-dedicated, so was Newman himself, perhaps he thought Keble was. Almost certainly Tom Mozley—for he writes to Bowden later when Tom and Harriett Newman were engaged: "I never can approve of a fellow like Mozley marrying—but if it must be, it is a great happiness to find him brought nearer to me by his offence against monastic rule."

My feeling is that Henry Wilberforce (perhaps Robert too), thrown into intimacy with Newman and Froude, had talked big in the same direction. The ideal is outlined in *How to Accomplish It*—and we can well imagine how much further the young men went as they talked in their studies or walking together through the meadows. There was ever an atmosphere of crisis about Newman and Froude—accentuated in Froude probably by an obscure sense of how short his time was to be. They saw visions and dreamed dreams of a vast work to accomplish in the saving and restoration of the Church, of the world. They asked of one another what Froude gave: life unto death. Into such an atmosphere Wilberforce had, nervously, to introduce his surprising news. I think his letter to Rogers shows that he was conscious of retreat from his past and needed reassuring. Part of the letter has been omitted by the editor but after expressing the fear Newman will cut him Wilberforce continues "Nor, again, am I without a feeling of the danger, as you know, of married priests in these days of trouble and rebuke, but I have taken my line."[1]

He really was a very silly young man: he came to Oxford; he stayed several days; Newman wrote, "Though we often talked on the subject, he said nothing about it, which I am sure he would have done were it a fact . . . I am spreading my incredulity, and contradicting it in every direction, and will not believe it, though I saw the event announced in the papers till he tells me." To Froude he presently summarises what had occurred: "H. Wilberforce engaged to marry Miss S. last December—was afraid to tell me, and left Oxford without; spread abroad I had cut R. for marrying. Yet he has not ratted and will not (so be it). Marriage, when a crime, is a crime which it is criminal to repent of."

Naturally too the personal element was not absent. It would have hardly been human had Newman not been annoyed when one of his most intimate friends spread abroad the news of his own engagement and then left it to be communicated to Newman by Newman's sister after his own departure! Poor Newman, contradicting it right and left—looking foolish enough to be annoyed had he been the most insensitive of men. Actually he was clearly in a raging temper with the *perditum ovem*—not improved by Henry's later assumption that their friendship could remain equally open on the side of one who had a wife to share his secrets and one who had not.

This in itself constituted a difficulty in the sort of "ideal" group of friends drawn together in the early Movement days. Robert Wilberforce several years later wrote of a confidence Newman had made him: "in justice to you I cannot communicate what occupies my thoughts even to the natural partner of all my feelings." Many an old bachelor has gone through moods of annoyance and despondency when his friends are all married and the old open-hearted sharing of confidences, the old open-hearted friendship, seems closed. This feeling often leads in the healthiest way to further marriages—but unhappily the celibate may also be an old bachelor on his human side. If he must not have his pleasing wife and hearth and children he badly needs the com-

---

[1] I have not seen the original. It is quoted in Newman's *Letters and Correspondence*, II, 21.

panionship in his monastery. Among the letters that Newman wrote while enraged—none of them sent—one escaped destruction. Perhaps it is hardly fair to quote it since it was not sent, yet it represents a mood that is visible also in Newman's relations with his mother and sisters, and which, tiresome as Henry had been, does sometimes make one want to shake Newman himself. It becomes necessary to remember his utter unselfishness in action, his perpetual overwork, and his hatred of being made to look a fool, if we are to understand a note of querulousness in a letter that after all was never posted.

Henry Wilberf. *NOT SENT.* Jan. 8, 34

My poor dear foolish Henry,

Dear, for auld lang syne—foolish, for being suspicious of me—poor, because I suppose you have been pained at your own suspicions; why have you left it first to a casual word of yours, next to a letter of Christie's, to acquaint me that the time is fixed for your changing your state and commencing to be a citizen of the world that now is? . . . When have I ever questioned the propriety of your marrying . . .? But you surely are inconsiderate—you ask me to give you my heart, when you give yours to another—and because I will not promise to do so, then you augur all sorts of ill-treatment towards you from me. Now I do not like to speak of myself, but in self-defence I must say, it is a little hard for a friend to separate himself from familiarity with me (wh. he has a perfect right, and perhaps lies under a duty, to do) and then to say "Love me as closely, give me your familiar heart as you did, though I have parted with mine". Be quite sure that I shall be free to love you, far more than you will me—but I cannot, as a prudent man, so forget what is due to my own comfort and independence as not to look to my own resources, make my own mind my wife and anticipate and provide against that loss of friends which the fashion of the age makes inevitable. That is all I have done and said with regard to you. I have done it towards all my friends as expecting they will part from me, except to one, who is at Barbados. I dare not even towards my sisters indulge affection without restraint . . . You know very little of me, if you think that I do not feel at times much the despondence of solitariness . . . and why may I not arm myself against what is inevitable?

. . . My dear H. You really have hurt me—you have *made* a difficulty in the very beginning of our separation. You should have reflected that to remove it, you wd. not only have to justify it to yourself but to explain it to me.

Ever yours affectionately,

In contrast—and most entertaining contrast—with this letter is one written later in the same year to Newman's early Trinity friend, Pope, who was a celibate not from choice or dedication but merely by chance—who was neither a pupil of Newman's nor one of the chosen band who were to move the world.

. . . When did I ever hint you were petulant and unreasonable? Not I! Certainly you have a good deal to harass you—your being alone is especially against you. But do not suppose that you alone have cares in this world. I suppose everyone has in his way. Were you married, at the head of a fine and flourishing family, I may say an increasing family, with nine altogether, four boys and five girls and another expected, would you not have troubles? Or were they all girls would you not say "girls are such an expense, and my girls are not particularly showy or well favoured", or if they were boys, one would be sent away from school for striking a praepositor, another would dabble in wet and dirt till he got the scarlet fever, and the eldest would run off to Gretna Green with some milliner's apprentice. Or Mrs. P. would be for ever on the look-out for balls and sights, in spite of your grave admonitions that a Parson's wife should keep at home. Or she would have a tongue and a temper, and make your home twice as doleful as it is now. And then bad times would come, and you would say "Why really I cannot afford to keep a conscience; give me a large fat rectory and I can suffer a little taxing and fining, but what with my four sons (now going on to college) and my five daughters (the youngest turned nine) I cannot stand on punctilios. True it is this new Bishop [that] Ministers have put in, has avowed himself a Unitarian, and I hate his principles, but my family has claims on me etc. etc. etc." Now I think with all your grumbling, you are a happier man now than you would be under such circumstances.

The whole question of a celibate life, the struggles, temptations, difficulties that it must bring, were certainly intensified by the fact of belonging to a Church which took no account of it. Newman had from boyhood held to the belief that he himself had this vocation (excepting, he tells us in the *Apologia*, for very brief periods up to the year 1829, but never after). On his father's death he had written in his journal, "When I die, shall I be followed to the grave by my children? My mother said the other day she hoped to live to see me married, but *I* think I shall either die within college walls, or a Missionary in a foreign land." Was his mother still hoping and longing for his marriage?

Probably no one except Froude took Newman's resolve as absolute.

Those who are not called to the celibate life are sometimes apt to fancy that those who are receive an inclination with the call that makes it painless to follow. They do in fact receive strength, they receive (I suppose) a profound sense of its rightness that may be termed inclination, but seldom or never is it painless. And it is noteworthy that the priest son is in most families the most tenderly attached to his mother, the most homeloving.

Certainly this was so with Newman. There must anyhow have been pain as life went on with its natural partings and the natural breaking-up of an unusually prolonged family life. But for him the breaking-up was not simply that which the order of nature brings, for him it was more painful, more prolonged.

He had met with an unusual degree of understanding at home. His early friends had been also his mother's and his sisters' friends. "The great Dr. Whately himself," Harriet writes, had visited them at Brighton and "talked in his way", he had "seemed as content as I was at our listening"; Mr. Rickards and his wife had almost adopted the sisters of their friend, his pupils had grown into the family life. The letters written to him in Sicily evidence this intimacy, for half of every packet is filled by the family, half by friends, while Newman's own letters teem with messages and assume a closeness of contact throughout the whole group. Then too some of Newman's most striking ideas were adumbrated in letters to his sisters, while on their side they studied to bring their attainments to the level he would wish. Their mother writes of "H. engrossed with German, J. with Greek." Their French was probably better than either and Harriett writes in 1834: "We send you all the French. I hope somebody has a French Prayer Book for the Articles . . . the last part has been very troublesome and you must look sharply over it please." (Whether this sharp look over would have been of much use one doubts, if Newman's French is represented by a sentence in a letter to Jemima: "*Prenez garde que vous n'avez aucun d'embarrassement avec les amis tres obligeants chez les quels vous vous demeurez le Vendredi*".)

"The Miss Newmans," wrote James Mozley about to be introduced to them, "are very learned persons, deeply read in ecclesiastical history, and in all the old divines both High Church and Puritanical. But, notwithstanding this they are, I believe, very agreeable and unaffected. In fact, to have such a brother as Newman is a sufficient pledge of their carrying off their learning well."[1]

Yet the intellectual was the least of the bonds that made "such a brother as Newman" all in all to his sisters. In *Loss and Gain* he has touchingly shown something of the faint shadow first falling in anticipation. An old friend has just been visiting, and the brother (confusingly called Charles!) and sister agree that he is no longer what he was to them in their childhood.

"Indeed it isn't he that is changed," said Charles, "but we; we are in the time of life to change; we have changed already, and shall change still."

"What a mercy it is," said his sister, "that we are so happy among ourselves as a family! If we change, we shall change together, as apples of one stock; if one fails, the other does. Thus we are always the same to each other."

"It is a mercy indeed," said Charles, "we are so blest that I am sometimes quite frightened."

The sister is startled, and he explains his meaning:

". . . we can rely on nothing here, and are fools if we build on the future."

"We can rely on each other," she repeated.

"Ah, dear Mary, don't say so; it frightens me."

She looked round at him surprised, and almost frightened herself.

"Dearest," he continued, "I mean nothing; only everything is so uncertain here below."

"We are sure of each other, Charles."

"Yes, Mary," and he kissed her affectionately, "it is true, most true"; then he added, "all I meant was, that it seems presumptuous to say so. David and Jonathan were parted; St. Paul and St. Barnabas."

Tears stood in Mary's eyes.

"Oh, what an ass I am," he said, "for thus teasing you about nothing; no, I only mean that there is One *only* who cannot die, who never changes, only one."[2]

As early as 1832 a slight beginning of strain may be seen in Newman's relations with his mother and sisters. He writes to his mother on January 29th:

[1] *Letters of Rev. J. M. Mozley.* p. 27.   [2] *Loss and Gain*, pp. 102-4.

I wish I could convey to you any notion of the pain such accidents as that the other night give me. I say so, because possibly you have no idea that it is so. Without going into the cause of disagreement, and how far I am or am not in fault, I only mean to assure you that the very notion of having vexed you pains me in the very keenest way— and sometimes I have been brought to profuse tears and that for a long while, on the recollection that possibly I might not have been as kind to you as I ought to be.

Mrs. Newman answered by return of post:

Jan 30, 1832

When I err, it is often from over-anxiety or delicacy, and, if you will at any time, without letting it dwell on your mind show me where you think me wrong, I will be quite willing to explain and have done with it. And I hope you will allow me, with the most anxious affection, to caution you against over-sensibility. If not guarded against in high wrought minds, it becomes a real trouble. I wish I could do anything that would at all express my sense of your anxious kindness on all occasions, and how sincerely I am your truly affectionate Mother.

These letters might only be the expression of a momentary disagreement such as all families know—most of all perhaps the most devoted families. The only way to avoid jars and disagreements is to avoid too great an interest in one another. But letters from Harriett later in the same year show that the trouble was fairly serious. She explains the problems she finds in their intercourse:

First is your own manner, which I am sure you must know is sometimes very trying to me, and which I cannot always understand. You cannot I think yourself be aware of the discouragement it is to me, when I have been most desirous of speaking openly to you . . . Another difficulty is the great difference I see in our opinions . . .

"Then think," she continues, "how few opportunities there have been for our talking together at ease, for *years* past, I may almost say." Clearly in reply to a complaint of Newman's, she confesses to not liking three of his friends, but

I think you are apt to forget that when your friends become our acquaintances, we must regard them in a different light.

I think we are both inclined to exaggerate our causes of complaint and I hope I shall not do so in future, but I shall be glad to feel you as kind and affectionate as I know you are. I daresay you will think this a great weakness.

I feel sure he did not. Brother and sister as he had noted were so much alike—too much for their comfort, when causes of disagreement arose. And if Harriett was over-sensitive to John's manner in one mood he was in another over-sensitive to it himself, and she became the comforter. In one of his letters from the Mediterranean, he had spoken of a consciousness of his own deficiencies and absurdities. Harriett had answered:

I wish I could say anything to persuade you not to think of your "deficiencies" and "absurdities" which I well know exist only in your own mind, and the idea of which I daresay often deprives yourself and perhaps others of great pleasure . . . I do not know a manner or bearing I more admire in society when it pleases the owner to be himself; or to add that my opinion is far from singular.—I never will believe that anyone with a gentleman's heart and common sense to help him can ever find himself in any position to which he may not get accustomed in a day.

But later Harriett is again wishing John would show the tenderness he feels: "You are not aware you are often apparently wanting in manner to us. I hardly know what to call it, but I feel it . . . my dear, and only left Brother."

I imagine it was only in some moods that the sisters felt Frank entirely lost to them. Of Charles everyone except his mother had despaired by the early thirties: and it is wonderful, reading his rude letters to her, to find that she—although saddened by "hostile letters" and "bitter feelings to us all"—still clung precariously to hope. John's one idea seems to have been to save her and his sisters. She writes in 1832 grieved that John "should have to attempt an interview", in 1834 wanting to "authorise Aunt to make some proposition to C." If he will "relinquish that Person" (called elsewhere "his Destroyer" and "this miserable deceptive object") his "Cloaths [shall be] redeemed" and an unspecified sum per week allowed "for Board, Lodging and Washing". But the mother could not rest content with helping vicariously. One touching letter must be given.

June 12, 1834

My dear J.H. (Most of her letters so begin)

The style of Charles' letter pains me greatly, and I fear that if
he is left quite desolate his nervous symptoms may increase so as to
render him incapable of helping himself—I do not ask you to *approve*
what I have determined to do, I only ask you not to *condemn me*, and
allow for my decision, as I feel if any melancholy results should ensue,
I should condemn myself for having omitted my Duty as a Mother
and a Christian if I had omitted such a marked opportunity of trying
to be useful to him—I think you will anticipate that I intend to ask
him down here for a short time that is I mean to devote a fortnight
to him, instead of going to Barford, by that time his Aunt N. will be
able to have him, with, or near her, and he will be more capable of
looking after an engagement—As you purposed living at Oxford
during my absence I hope the plan will not be inconvenient to you,
I feel every day I shall lose from enjoying your company *alone* a sacrifice
as I had anticipated much delight and profit in enjoying your undivided
attention, but the *hope* of giving consolation to such a poor desolate
Being, makes me yield it, and should my humble but sincere efforts
be blessed with some permanent good effects we shall all have reason
to rejoice. I do not pretend to influence your conduct, I am sure you
will act up to your Character and privileged Profession, and if the poor
Wanderer seems desirous of being brought to a right judgment, you
will not withhold your assistance—I think I shall name next Wednesday the 18th for him to come, the day that H. goes and every one
will be gone,—I shall enforce certain conditions of Conduct while
under my roof, and I shall *trust*, to the [rest of letter missing].

Charles came and she writes (June 22, 1834) that the "poor
fellow" proved "very desirous to perform every Sunday duty and
much I think with good and great feeling". They read

with great attention by his wish two very impressive sermons of
yours. . . . Indeed my Dear though I will not allow myself to be too
sanguine, I hope we may all be blessed by this being a profitable week.

June 25: Pray think kindly and hopefully of him.

June 30: Poor C. is evidently comforted by having been here, he
was very grateful for yr. attention to his wants, and wished me to
offer you anything you wd. feel acceptable from him.

John's early sermons had been the joy of his family, but
presently Harriett was saying "They are very High Church. I
do not think I am near so high, and do not quite understand

them yet." And in 1835 his mother wrote of a volume he had given to her:

Thank you for the sermons which I shall read with attention. I see there are several that I have not heard: . . . I have felt many of your sermons as blessings to correct, strengthen and console me—and I lament that this volume should be presented to me with the sad reproach that "I do not feel any particular interest or sympathy in your opinions". My dear John, I would ask you, who of your friends anywhere, who have equal means of judging with yourself, agree with you in everything? Is it then wonderful that I, unschooled in your learning, should not always be able to follow you close? . . . I know I am a very weak arguer, and on most occasions feel much more than I venture to express.

Poor mother, poor son. She had perhaps allowed herself too fully to accept him for her guide if she could not really abrogate her own judgment. Mother and sisters had for years thought it so natural to be guided intellectually and spiritually by him that the cleavage was much harder than it would have been in an age when a brilliant woman had a career of her own, or in a family in which the other men had borne their part.

Yet I think that Newman copying these letters as an old man gave too large a proportion to the sense of strain, too small to the immense pride and joy his mother still took in him and to the affectionate enjoyment that marked the greater part of their intercourse. Letters pass inviting Newman to bring friends to Littlemore "to eat a Woodbury pheasant", he is asked to order more sherry, he will find cold beef for dinner should he care to come unexpectedly. In an undated letter probably of summer 1835 his mother writes: "If Mr. Keble is disengaged and you will make an unceremonious invitation acceptable to him we shall have much pleasure in seeing him . . . Poor C. is as strange as usual, he treats me much as you do 'Prince', boxes my ears and coaxes me." And on a round of visits, in Aug. 1835, she writes:

If it should prove your lot to superintend a "Parish" I am sure you would do it most efficiently, and it would be (I think) most for your personal comfort but your many gifts fitted to the exigencies of these perilous times make me anticipate that you are likely to be called to more active and energetic Duties—You ought not to have any cares about temporal concerns, and this makes us anxious, to make some alterations in our plans, etc.

A few days' later, staying with some relatives, Mrs. Newman misses the Oxford atmosphere: "I confess I feel rather a craving for more mind than we are likely to find here."

And from Derby a month later: "Horses and field sports engross the leisure time and conversation of the vicinage . . . It is a melancholy thing that the large population of the Potteries have not judicious clergymen."

Meditating deeply on the past Newman wrote in 1875 a touching "*Apology for Myself*":

It was a great mistake in all of us, though a very natural one, to fancy that, if my Mother and sisters came nearer to me, they would see more of me. Their coming near me did not lessen the work of various kinds which engrossed my time: it did but involve them in a necessary disappointment, and made it seem as if I did not avail myself of opportunities of our meeting which they had done their part in securing.

When they were at a distance, I went to see them from time to time for weeks together, for a whole Long Vacation; and then I was at a distance from all such work as at once fell upon me when at Oxford; but, when they came near to me, they came to the seat and scene of my occupations, and, when they still found me at a distance from them practically, as it was not a distance of the body, it seemed to be one of the mind. And, when they, in their kindness, tried, however delicately and considerately, to overcome what was to them an invisible obstacle, then I got worried; I got worried by their affectionateness.

Moreover, there was always the chance of their not liking those whom I liked; and, in matter of fact, they did not like some of my greatest friends.

And again, from the first, they did not like the distinctive principles of the Oxford Movement; and the more it developed, the wider did their difference from me in respect to it grow.

And then again, there was the different position in which they stood from mine, and the different judgment they formed, as regards each of my brothers.

These differences, though they tried to hide them and to make the best of them, made me very sore. They had a full right to their own views; but I did not imitate them in bearing patiently what could not be helped.

Yet their residence near me bore ultimately this good fruit. It ended in the happy marriage of my two sisters to the two Mozleys.

To Jemima, about to become engaged to John Mozley, Newman writes:

November 19, 1835

Brother never had a greater loss nor another a greater gain. I have been thinking, praying, dreaming of you ever since. You must be a blessing wherever you are—not the least, when you are the bond of union between those who already, as friends, love each other, without tie of relationship.

Joy and sorrow lay close together in those years. To talk of heartstrings has become terribly hackneyed yet one cannot avoid with Newman the thought of his own favourite instrument. No violin could vibrate more sensitively to life's touch than he, and none express better life's changing melodies.

The wedding took place on April 28, 1836, and on May 17, almost suddenly, Mrs. Newman died.

Isaac Williams describes Newman "clinging to my arm in great distress". "Dreadfully dejected," says James Mozley, "his countenance perfectly clouded with grief." Anne Mozley saw him at the funeral, "kneeling in prayer at the altar when all was over, lost in prayer and memory."

Memory was indeed misery. We all know its habits when we have lost one we loved. Pictures of the past bring with them overpowering loneliness. We forget all we have done to show our love, we remember nothing but omissions, unkindness and misunderstandings dreadfully magnified by grief.

Poor Charles had small need of a magnifying glass: he wrote a letter of genuine love and contrition to John:

You tell me very heavy news indeed. I feel deeply indebted to my brothers and sisters for having so amply filled the office in which either from my fault or misfortune I have failed, of good children towards my mother . . . it was just as if I were her only son so kind has she been to me. But it is a great satisfaction to me that so many points of her character are so exactly reflected in my brothers and sisters, that I shall scarcely seem to have lost herself if they remain alive . . . I thought it probable that she would have lived many years yet, but when I consider how she has grieved on many accounts I do not wonder, but during her last years she has been greatly blessed in the affection of you and my sisters and that must be a great consolation to you all.

The sense of solitude was strong on Newman now. There had been deep differences between this loving son and mother, and writing to Jemima he cannot but dwell on them: at their very last meeting "she mistook something I said", and "was very hurt at it". But mistakes might have been cleared up—the thing went far deeper. "My mother has much misunderstood my religious views, and considered that she differed from me." Unfortunately she really did. Mother and son had gone along so long in perfect harmony that he was slow to believe the disagreement real. "I never thought anything more precious," he wrote, "than her sympathy and praise." But he could have it only on conditions—conditions that he could not fulfil. He could not hold back; she could no longer follow. All that remained to him was to look forward. Returning from the funeral, as if he "thought grief had reigned long enough he seemed," says Isaac Williams, "in a sort of resolute effort to throw it from him". And to Jemima he wrote: "God I trust will support me in following whither He leads . . . in heaven there will be no misunderstandings."

CHAPTER XXIII

Dr. Hampden and the Dogmatic Principle

THE EARLY months of 1836 were marked by a grand flare-up in the troubled relations of Dr. Hampden with the University.

The steps in the Hampden story are worth recapitulating. He had delivered the Bampton Lectures of 1832 in St. Mary's—presumably to a sleepy audience for we are told that his voice was dull. Anyhow no notice whatever was taken of them. They were just that year's Bampton Lectures. They were printed. They were forgotten. But the fame of having delivered them was enough, as we have seen, to get for Hampden the Moral Philosophy Professorship in March 1834. The electors were the Vice-Chancellor, the Proctors, and the Heads of Christ Church, Magdalen, and St. John's. They gave Hampden a majority of two over Newman. The same year he caused the first clash of principle between Tractarians and Liberals, and the principle involved was the dogmatic. In view of what happened later, it is odd enough that the occasion should have been a proposal for the abolition of the signing of the Thirty-Nine Articles so that Dissenters might be allowed to enter Oxford. This was advocated by Dr. Hampden in a pamphlet—*Observations on Religious Dissent.* In November 1834 he sent the second edition to Newman who thus describes it:

In this Pamphlet it was maintained, that Religion is distinct from Theological Opinion, pp. 1, 28, 30, etc., that it is but a common prejudice to identify theological propositions methodically deduced and stated, with the simple religion of Christ, p. 1; that under Theological Opinion were to be placed the Trinitarian doctrine, p. 27, and the Unitarian, p. 19; that a dogma was a theological opinion formally insisted on, pp. 20, 21; that speculation always left an opening for improvement, p. 22; that the Church of England was not dogmatic in its spirit, though the wording of its formularies might often carry the sound of dogmatism, p. 23.[1]

[1] *Apologia*, p. 38.

Newman, acknowledging the pamphlet, expressed to Hampden his "very sincere and deep regret" that it had been published. Arnold, Whately and Hawkins all supported Hampden's proposal: Arnold and Whately for the same reason: that the Articles were obscure and led to differences of interpretation. "That exposition of the Articles," writes Arnold, "which bishops and divinity professors now recommend was censured (at the time of Burnet) by the Lower House of Convocation as Latitudinarian."

Whately said:

The *mode* of a man declaring himself a member of the Established Church, by subscribing to the Articles, I always thought highly objectionable. It may be done with a safe conscience when the meaning is duly explained. But the best way in all cases is to say in plain English exactly what you do mean. There is always danger in teaching men to form habits of explaining away words. It has always appeared to me a breach of the Third Commandment to trifle with the language of solemn obligation.

Rogers describes the scene in Convocation at which the motion to abolish the signing was defeated by 459 to 57. On one of the anti-reformers crying out *Non placet* and walking to one side of the theatre——

It seemed from the gallery, where I was, as if the whole crowd were following him. You just saw a few spots here and there stationary, in the midst of the great current, and rather struggling not to be carried away in it, as little bits of dirt do when you are pouring water out of a basin: and after a short settling we saw about forty gentlemen left "alone with their glory" in the middle of the room, looking very foolish, and hardly knowing whether to stand boldly forth or not, to bear as best they might the shoutings of the opposite party, and the undergraduates.

The oddest part, notes Rogers, was that "these very young gentlemen whom people are so anxious to liberate from the yoke of subscription are the most vehement and noisy opponents of any 'relief bill'" . . . Crowding the galleries they not only applauded the decision but also hissed "our respectable Provost who is the great patron of change".

Deprecating Hampden's pamphlet Newman had prophesied that it would prove the first step "towards interrupting that peace and mutual good understanding that has prevailed so long in this place," and that there would result "dissensions the more intractable, because justified in the minds of those who resist innovation by a feeling of imperative duty". It was very true—and even truer than he realised, for while in Tractarian eyes the abolition of tests was an innovation, in Liberal eyes the Tracts were equally so. On their first appearance in book form Newman writes to Bowden (July 7, 1835) in some amusement at a letter from Hampden "in which he said I was guilty of 'duplicity' (or dissimulation) falsehood, and dark malignity, the latter quality arising from a 'fanatical persecuting spirit'—and he affirms that I should have been afraid so to have acted except under shelter of my 'sacred profession' which means, as Froude says, that he, *to prove himself a Christian*, would have fought a duel with me, but for my being in orders."

To Pope, Newman writes, "I, myself, even I, have received a letter from a Head of a House accusing me of 'falsehood and dark malignity' . . . I really do believe, were it not for the restraint of society etc. he would take up a knife and stick me in the fifth rib. Now I trust I have excited your curiosity which I will not gratify a bit more except by word of mouth".

In 1836 Lord Melbourne, who has been described as "an amateur theologian", had to appoint a Regius Professor of Divinity. He seems to have thought a Bampton Lecturer and a Professor of Moral Philosophy would be acceptable enough to the University. Of course he was glad to have a man of his own party (and Liberals were scarce in Oxford). The appointment aroused bitter opposition. Arnold attributes this to Hampden's efforts to repeal the Tests. This is probably true, but indirectly. For Hampden's pamphlet (against Tests) was crammed with unorthodox views, concisely and readably stated: and by its mere existence it drew attention to the Bampton Lectures, in which the same views were set out so lengthily, diffusely and boringly, that no one had noticed that they were there. Indignation mounted that a man holding such views should be Professor of Moral Philosophy. And now he was appointed Regius Professor of Divinity. The effect was what might have been described at that date as perfectly electrical.

A considerable body in the University vainly petitioned the King to rescind the appointment. Protestants and Tractarians alike seemed to forget how recently Hampden had been the choice of the University itself, and raised the cry of Erastianism. "The more the matter is thought of, the more I hope people will see the absurdity of allowing all the King's Church Patronage to be distributed by a premier, who may be himself a heretic, or anything else."[1]

The *Watchman* declared that "Protestantism was stabbed to the very vitals". The Principal of St. Alban's Hall was "going about for two or three days quite furiously with a passage from Hampden's moral philosophy lectures in his pocket, and declaring that he ought to be turned out of the Professorship and hall, house and home, and everything". But as Rose wrote to Newman, the great argument with Lord Melbourne and the Ministers— and undeniably it had a "deplorable strength"—was that Oxford itself had chosen Hampden *after* the Bampton Lectures as Professor of Moral Philosophy: Copleston also had assured Lord Melbourne of Hampden's soundness, and James Mozley declared that the Ministers were "exceedingly angry" with him "for having taken them in". An Orielite of his acquaintance wrote to Mozley that Melbourne had said to him:

Pray, Wood, how is it that in the bosom of your sluggish University, and out of a College by no means the largest in it, so many heresiarchs have lately sprung up? First there is Whately, Arnold, and Hampden, then there is Mr. Keble and Mr. Newman, who, I hear, are quite as great theologians as the others, only in another way.

For the moment the orthodox party were united and were in the ascendant. Postponed in March by the proctors' veto a decree was carried in May 1836, by a huge majority of Convocation—474 to 94—depriving Hampden—the Regius Professor of Divinity—of the right of participation in choosing university preachers because "the University had no confidence in him in theological matters".

Although the size of the majority shows that the resolution was not the work of any one party but that the University had acted as a whole, Newman was especially identified with what became known in Liberal circles as the "persecution" of Dr. Hampden, both because he and Pusey had been to the fore, and also because Newman by request of "the leaders of Orthodoxy" undertook an "elucidation" of the Lectures directly his appointment was

---

[1] *Letters of Frederic Lord Blachford*, p. 29.

rumoured. Another man was supposed to have undertaken the task, but this proved a false rumour. So Newman set about it. He proceeded, says James Mozley, "in a most miraculous way—day and night I might almost say, for he sat up reading and writing the whole of Wednesday night".[1] He certainly wasted no time. The news of Hampden's appointment came on February 8: the pamphlet was out on February 13. Hampden's friends declared that Newman's *Elucidations* misrepresented Hampden's meaning. Even a hundred years later, a critic could write: "He made an unmerciful use of the well-known controversial method of giving as unfavourable a combination as possible of passages taken out of their context in his opponent's writings."[2] I suppose it is hard ever to believe in the absolute fairness of an opponent's statement of your case; but it seems to me, as it did to Dean Church, that the meaning of the Bampton Lectures is so obvious that Newman had no need to exaggerate it, and so closely woven into every page that there was no need to choose out careful combinations of passages: almost any passage would do, from almost any page.

I tackled Hampden first, then the *Elucidations*, and I hope that I shall not be suspected of what Stanley called "garblements" if I subjoin a few quotations and summaries.

For Hampden, *the* enemy is logical Theology. Revealed truth is to be found in Scripture and only there: any interpretation men make of the text of Scripture, however obvious it may be, is only a human opinion: it is theory: it is not part of divine revelation:

> The Scripture intimates to us certain facts concerning the Divine Being: but conveying them to us by the medium of language, it only brings them before us darkly, under the signs appropriate to the thought of the human mind. . . . There must be in fact a repeated revelation, to authorize us to assert that this or that conclusion represents to us some truth concerning God.

The Roman Church had proceeded through the centuries to build up a mass of such interpretation, following the principles of the Scholastic Philosophy. That is how dogmas came to be enunciated: that is how creeds came to be drawn up. It is a weakness of the human mind to want to do this sort of embroidering: over and above that the attack of the heresies forced the

---

[1] J. B. Mozley's *Letters*, p. 51.   [2] Brillioth, *The Anglican Revival*, p. 143.

orthodox to it: "It was the necessity of the case that compelled the orthodox as themselves freely admit, to employ a phraseology by which, as experience proves, the naked truth of God has been overborne"—overborne because human philosophy, relied on for the defence of revealed truth, is of no more than provisional and temporary value. The Trinity is a perfect example, but he applies his view to other dogmas as destructively. This is his view

not only of our Articles at large, but in particular, of the Nicene and Athanasian Creeds, as they stand in Ritual, or are adopted into our Articles. If it be admitted that the notions on which their several expressions are founded, are both unphilosophical and unscriptural; it must be admitted that they do not impress these notions on the Faith of the Christian as matters of affirmative belief. They only use the terms of ancient theories of Philosophy . . . to exclude others *more obviously injurious*[1] to the simplicity of the Faith. The speculative language of these Creeds, it should be observed, was admitted into the Church of England as established by the Reformers, before the period when the genius of Bacon exposed the emptiness of the system, which the schools had palmed upon the world. . . .

Surely nothing could be more scrupulously just than Newman's balancing of all this with Hampden's professions of faith:

Dr. Hampden's views then seem at length to issue in the following theory: that there is one and one only truth, that the truth is the record of facts, historical and moral, contained in the text of Scripture, that whatever is beyond that text, even to the classifying of its sentences, is human opinion and unrevealed; that, though a thoughtful person cannot help forming opinions and theories upon the Scripture record, and is bound to act upon and confess those opinions which he considers to be true, yet he has no right to identify his own opinion on any point, however sacred in itself, with the facts of the revealed history, or to assume that a belief in it is necessary for the salvation of another, or to impose it as a condition of union with another; that, though he considers he cannot be more sure of being right than another, and does not hold his own opinions to be more pious than another's, and will not pronounce heretical opinions (so called) to be dangerous to any being in the world, except to those who do *not* hold them, yet he himself firmly believes the Church's dogmatic statements concerning the Trinity, etc., and at a proper season could contend as zealously against Arian or Socinian doctrines, as those who think that in the

[1] Italics mine.

case of others belief in them is of importance to eternal salvation; and this, though he considers those statements, as such, and so far forth as they are distinct from those Scripture facts, which Arians and Socinians hold as religiously as himself, to be "a system of technical theology by which we are guarded" only "in some measure from the exorbitance of theoretic enthusiasm", a system of phrases borrowed from those who differ from us, and useful only in excluding *their* use of them.

The copy kept at the Oratory of Newman's *Elucidations* had clearly been the possession of an enemy of its author. "Newman", he scrawls on the title page, "you should have put your name. The Provost will watch you". And again "The Oxford logic is studied for bad purposes. . . . It has been asked whether Mr. N. is a Roman". He is called "the calumnious Elucidator", and advised to "Consult the Head of your College and he will direct you in the right way, for he is humble-minded and pure in heart". These are not the adjectives his best friends would have picked for poor old Hawkins! Indeed one can almost see him squirm at such a description of his dignified scholarly self. Whoever scrawled these comments was expressing an honest indignation—which Hampden himself seems to have felt—at the accusation of heterodoxy. After all had he not affirmed his belief in the Trinity? He had indeed:

"The truth itself of the Trinitarian doctrine emerges from these mists of human speculation, like the bold, naked land, on which an atmosphere of fog has for awhile rested, and then been dispersed". But this is not a great deal: he accepts the Trinity, but will not attach a meaning to what he accepts, because meanings are only human opinion.

The only ancient, only catholic, truth is the scriptural fact. Let us hold that fast in its depth and breadth—in nothing extenuating, in nothing abridging it—in simplicity and sincerity; and we can neither be Sabellians, or Tritheists, or Socinians. *Attempt to explain*,[1] to satisfy scruples, to reconcile difficulties; and the chance is, that however we may disclaim the heterodoxy which lurks in every step of our path, we incur, at least, the scandal at the hands of others. . . .

James Mozley had said that "the length, stupidity and obscurity" of the lectures "had deterred most people from looking

[1] Italics mine.

into them; so that he might have maintained the Mahommedan system in them for anything the majority of people knew". Long they are: but they are not very obscure, and they are not stupid at all. Hampden had completely failed to grasp St. Thomas's statement of the doctrine of the Trinity, but one hardly imagines that Mozley was holding that against him. His position has one fatal weakness—the repeated assertion that he accepts Scripture as revealed truth combined with his view that any meaning attached to Scripture is only human opinion—but this is only because he is a man born out of due time. A few years more and he could have thrown the authority of Scripture overboard, and taken his stand foursquare upon the inadequacy of human language to express the infinite—which after all is a real problem. In the Modernist movement of this century he would have ranked high—not with the very ablest like Tyrrell, but well above Bishop Barnes. What he did for his own moment was to place his finger upon the fundamental weakness in Anglicanism. Remember how he said that, if theology is to go on reasoning from Scripture, reasoning from its own reasonings, "there must be in fact a repeated revelation to authorize us to assert that this or that conclusion represents to us some truth concerning God". In principle he was right: dogmatic formulas *do* require a guarantee higher than human reason can give: in the Catholic Church, her God-guaranteed actually operative power of infallible definition provides it: but what provides it in the Church of England? Not yet did Newman conceive the doubt whether there was any middle ground between the Roman Catholic Church and total scepticism. But the germ of it was here in Hampden.

Scrupulously fair as Newman was it was foolish of him, had he been considering consequences, not to leave to some other man—preferably some Evangelical—the invidious task of elucidating Hampden. For after all Hampden had succeeded him in the tutorship at Oriel, Hampden had defeated him for the Moral Philosophy Professorship, while they had crossed swords pretty fiercely about tests and Tracts. Added to all this he did most heartily disapprove of Hampden. "In his Moral Philosophy," he wrote to Pope, "he adopts the lowest and most grovelling Utilitarianism as the basis of Morals—he considers it a sacred duty to live in this world, and that religion by itself injuriously absorbs the mind. Whately, whatever his errors, is open-hearted, generous and careless of money. Blanco White is the same, though he has turned Socinian. Arnold is amiable and winning—but this man *judged by his writings*, is the most lucre-loving, earthly-minded, unlovely person one ever set eyes upon".

It was the natural reaction of the generous against a philosophy later described by Chesterton as a belief that God will give us the good if we are greedy enough about the goods. And probably few of the men who abused Newman ever compared the Bampton Lectures and the *Elucidations* or even read the other lectures on Moral Philosophy.

The word persecution was a favourite with all parties. The Liberals, enraged by the action of Convocation in withdrawing Hampden's right to a say in the nominating of University preachers, made particularly free use of it.

Whately considered there had never been—taking times and manners into consideration—a more unjust and cruel persecution, "for impudence I never knew the like", its perpetrators displayed "combined folly, cruelty and baseness". Had he been still at Alban Hall it would never have been allowed to happen.

For months Blanco White was haunted by the part Newman was playing. He wrote to Professor Norton (Feb. 25, 1836): "The grossest spirit of Mysticism and Popery has revived at Oxford, not without persecution against those who, though feebly, venture to oppose it."

To Lord Holland he wrote a whole series of letters:

March 3, 1836.

What do you think of the impudence of the *Intolerants* at Oxford? I only hope Hampden and his supporters will run stout.

March 6.

I am incessantly haunted by the Oxford persecution against Hampden. A more impudent display of bigotry, and thorough priestly spirit, it is impossible to conceive. There are, as usual, sincere bigots and hypocrites concerned in the case. The most melancholy instances of the former, are two men whom I love for their talents and good nature; Pusey, the Professor of Hebrew, and Newman, a Fellow of Oriel. The latter, in particular, was one of the most liberal, well-informed, and kind-hearted men I knew. He is now one of the most forward leaders of persecution. He is a man of great influence with the most reading young men at Oriel, all of whom he has for the last four or five years gained over to bigotry and Toryism.

April 27.
Newman who has raised himself into a Protestant Pope.

April 30.
Among these persecutors I pity no one but Newman. . . . Pusey is a vain man: Newman's deceiving pride is more deeply seated, and more difficult to be suspected by himself than the sources of the other's practical error.

To John Stuart Mill he writes next year: "Newman is a real enthusiast; I do not believe that Pusey deserves that name, though I should be sorry to believe him a hypocrite."[1]

The most serious attack on the University and on the Tractarians came from Dr. Arnold who wrote in the *Edinburgh Review* an article entitled "Oxford Malignants". He said later that this title had been the editor's but it was no stronger than the contents of the article. He began by cataloguing Hampden's University honours: doubtless Oxford would rejoice when one of her own most favoured sons was selected by the Ministry as Regius Professor. But no, for since receiving these honours he had tried to abolish the tests and let Dissenters into the University: this was in fact the reason why Oxford had so lately discovered his unorthodoxy.

Totally ignoring the numerically powerful Evangelical opposition (a minor sign of how unimportant they had become), Arnold concentrates on the Tractarians. Other persecutions had been conducted at least to support something great and majestic—the Romanist system, the ideal of freedom, a passion of devotion towards God. But

the fanaticism of the English High Churchman has been the fanaticism of mere foolery, a dress, a ritual, a name, a ceremony, a technical phraseology—the superstition of a priesthood without its power—the form of Episcopal government without its substance—a system imperfect and paralysed, not independent, not sovereign—afraid to cast off the subjection against which it was perpetually murmuring—objects so pitiful that, if gained ever so completely, they would make no man the wiser or the better; they would lead to no good, intellectual, moral, or spiritual.[2]

The pages of the article devoted to the defence of Hampden's orthodoxy show the same curious obliquity of vision as Hampden's

---

[1] These letters are printed in Blanco White's *Life and Autobiography*.
[2] *Edinburgh Review*, vol. lxiii, p. 235.

own defence of himself. To the end neither of them seemed to understand that you cannot both affirm a creed and attack it as absurd and unmeaning. To those who showed that he had done the latter, Hampden and Arnold triumphantly proved that he had also done the former. I have never seen an argument so perfectly designed to get nobody anywhere.

Philosophy was never Arnold's strong point; he viewed everything historically and he was now and henceforth obsessed by a peculiar historical view of the Oxford Movement. He saw in it a repetition "of the Non-Jurors reviling Burnet, of the Council of Constance condemning Huss—of the Judaizers banded together against St. Paul".

The article leads up to a terrific climax of attack on the Tractarians:

> The attack on Dr. Hampden bears upon it the character, not of error, but of *moral wickedness* . . . for such persecution, the plea of conscience is not admissable; it can only be a conscience so blinded by wilful neglect of the highest truth, or so corrupted by the habitual indulgence of evil passions, that it rather aggravates than excuses the guilt of those whom it misleads.

But perhaps the best word was Whately's (in a letter to Mrs. Arnold).

> I think the "holy men" who garbled and distorted Hampden's Bampton Lectures with the deliberate design of holding him up to the hatred and persecution of unthinking bigots, are the genuine descendants of those Roman emperors who dressed up the early Christians in the skins of beasts, and then set dogs to worry them to death.[1]

[1] *Life of Whately*. Vol. ii, p. 120.

CHAPTER XXIV

Credo in Newmannum

ATTACHED to a bundle of Newman's letters is the note:

March 1836 is a cardinal point of time. It gathers about it, more or less closely, the following events:

1. Froude's death.
2. My mother's death and my sister's marriage.
3. My knowing and using the Breviary.
4. First connexion with the "British Critic".
5. The Tracts becoming treatises.
6. Start of the "Library of the Fathers".
7. Theological Society.
8. My writing against the Church of Rome.
9. Littlemore Chapel.

} A new scene gradually opened.

For ten years Hurrell Froude had been Newman's most intimate friend, at first sharing his college life, later kept close by a constant correspondence. For each of his friends, it has been noted, Newman had a separate tone of intimacy, but only with his mother and with Froude perfect unreserve. Froude died two months before Mrs. Newman. "I shall be truly widowed," he writes to Jemima, "but I hope to bear it lightly." To Bowden he wrote of how Froude had succeeded at Oriel to their own youthful intimacy: "I was from time to time confusing him with you, and only calling him by his right name by an act of memory. . . . [His loss is] a very heavy visitation to all who were intimate with him. Yet everything was so bright and beautiful about him, that to think of him must always be a comfort."

Henry Wilberforce saw Newman weep ("not a common thing for him") because he could not see Froude again to tell him all he owed him, and to Keble he wrote, "I would fain be his heir".

"My sister's marriage", following "my mother's death", clearly refers not to Jemima but to Harriett. Writing to her in June Newman expresses the fear that she stayed on so long at

Iffley for his sake and reassures her as to his future solitude. It is but a return to what he had experienced before the intimacy with Froude and he does not dread it. "I am learning more than hitherto to live in the presence of the dead."

In July there follows a flurry of letters concerning Harriett's engagement to Tom Mozley. Very quaint some of them are. Looking back over the earlier correspondence one rather wonders that the engagement came as such a complete surprise. For in 1834 Mrs. Newman had described Harriett as "safely and agreeably lodged at Derby. . . . The House full of company as well as a numerous party domiciled. . . . The family are *eleven*. . . . Thomas the only unoccupied person, she had been to Church and was much pleased with the chaunting and general mode of service."

Reading these letters one sees always the two month or longer stays made by Elizabeth Bennett at Hunsford Vicarage or Mary Crawford at Mansfield. The young gentlemen are in attendance, the pianoforte and the harp, the strolls in the shrubbery, the rides on horseback, the reading aloud all form a perfect setting for romance. But this particular romance was in Newman's eyes of dubious quality. To Jemima he writes:

How strangely and unexpectedly providence works—I introduced another person to you all some years since, with the hope that an attachment might follow between him and H.—and I cannot but believe that my desire so far was justified, that my Mother wished it also. But God's ways are so different from ours—I doubt not it is H's. *duty* to do as she is doing and that is what I *mean*—we must act by duty, and form our likings according to God's will. Still, it is most marvellous. . . . I hope H. will consider £30 at her service from me for her necessary preparatory expenses. I heartily wish it was more—and heartily that I had been able to offer anything to *you* some months ago—but you none of you know how I have been hampered (I do not mean distressed) by want of money. Also I am much relieved at having found a use for the furniture, if T. M. will accept it—for it has been much on my mind—and for the plate. It will be the greatest comfort to be free from the charge of both, without any breach of duty—which it wd not be in this case. I am sure it is far happiest for H. that things should be as they are to be—her happiness is bound up in being settled—though God certainly does work strangely. . . . Take care to make H. easy with herself—she talks of her "fate" being to do what she is doing.

Apparently Mrs. Newman had not been very fond of Tom. John writes to Jemima a few days later:

I am quite aware of H's. main difficulty and did not impute her hesitation to anything else. At the same time I am happy to be able to say, as you do, that my dear Mother's feelings towards T. M. changed very much the last month or two. . . . I have no doubt at all, could she now say what she would like, she would wish H. to do what she is doing. . . . The only disadvantage which strikes one at first hearing of it, is the question of ages—but then that is much more to us, or rather to me, who have known T. M. from a schoolboy, than to others.

She was in fact about two years younger than Newman and three years older than Tom. The voice of the elder brother and the ex-tutor is audible in all these letters. "Tell H. if she manages to make T.M. read, she will do what *I* have not been able to do."

But after all he was very fond of Tom Mozley and that most likeable young man returned the fondness with a passion of humble adoration for his future bride and his bride's brother who was already his leader and his hero. He writes on July 12th:

MY DEAR NEWMAN,

I have scarcely time to say anything, but if I had a day I could not express the delight your few lines offered me. I confess I marvel to see the confidence with which you commit your sister to one so weak and dependant as I am. . . . You might well be surprised at the event, as the attachment which for years I have felt for your sister was always so mixed with a kind of awe and veneration that it was not likely ever to disclose itself by ordinary signs, even if I had ever so present intentions or sanguine hopes. If you needed any new proof of her lofty qualities, I am sure you would find it in every step of her conduct to me since I first ventured to address her. I only wonder more and more at my boldness, and still more at my success. My father and mother and all my brothers and sisters cannot contain their joy at acquiring such a sister.

Yours most affectionately,
TH. MOZLEY.

All was now, one would suppose, happily concluded. The Rectory of Cholderton was at Tom's disposal. Newman had called on the Provost and arranged for him to give up his rooms at Oriel, had provided furniture and plate. But the young couple were too precipitate: Mrs. Newman had not been dead for the statutory mourning period.

Newman writes to Jemima:

H. tells me she has *settled* to be married in October. If so, there is no help for it—so I do not write to her direct, lest, if so, I shd only needlessly annoy her. And I do not speak to Tom, wishing, if any thing comes, that it should come to him from her. But it strikes me six months ought to be suffered to pass first, the 17th or 19th of November should be the earliest day. I do not know the reasons, but it seems, before I hear, as if no good one could be given—and surely it is soon enough even at the end of six months. For instance it would be most painful, I should think, to leave off mourning—I think I could not do so anyhow. I write to you this, as I feel it, without circumlocution—were I writing to H. herself, I should study my words.

Nothing is more curious in studying Newman's character than the boundless defiance of convention where he saw defiance as a duty and the dutiful acceptance of it in daily life. And now lack of respect seemed implied to his Mother's memory and the thing went deep with him. On August 18th he writes again:

I am much pained the marriage is so soon. I cannot help saying so—and think I ought to say so. I do not think my Mother would have been pleased from what I have heard her say; and I do not think it will be a pleasant thing to look back on 20 years hence. Perhaps it would not have happened, had I been consulted. Perhaps I am superstitious about these things, but I do not like it.

Before September was out the marriage took place at Derby, Samuel Rickards officiating. Derby was the home of the Mozleys, and the Newman home had ceased to be with the Mother's death. One is happy to learn how successful was the much debated marriage. The stately Miss Newman became "Birdie", could hardly bear the briefest separations from her husband, and abounded in anecdote concerning their one child—a little girl.

"A new scene gradually opened" writes Newman after he had "given away" the last of his sisters—and this new scene was laid almost wholly in Oxford. A resident curate at Littlemore, his Mother's grave, an empty house at Iffley—for the first time he was entirely Newman of Oxford.

A frequent visitor has described the room at Oriel where Newman lived and worked:

You entered from the staircase by a door in the corner of the room. On your left were the two windows looking into the Quadrangle. Opposite to them two windows looking into Merton Lane. Between the latter were engravings of St. Christopher, and the three different portraits of Charles the First. On the side of the door were bookcases filled with folio volumes of the Fathers. Opposite to these was the fireplace, over which was a small portrait of his Mother, and a crucifix from which, however, the figure had been removed. [Newman was always careful in these things to do only what he believed his own Church clearly permitted. To Faber he wrote later (1844), of direct prayer to Our Lady "I have a great repugnance at mixing religions . . . a system is a whole. . . . I do not like decanting Rome into England; the bottles may break."] In the centre of the room was a table covered with books and papers. Newman's own chair was on one side of the fireplace near the table with its back to the Merton Lane windows.[1]

Home life was at an end. Nor could the gathering of younger disciples take the place that had been Froude's or the intercourse of the University break the inner silence into which he was increasingly gathered. That silence was peopled chiefly by the Fathers of the early Church with whom he dwelt constantly in study and imagination. And it was surely no mere coincidence that he should have read them to the accompaniment of the Breviary. Asked to choose a book of Hurrell's for a memorial, he selected Butler's *Analogy* but found it had already been chosen. "An intimate friend at my elbow said 'take that'. It was the Breviary which Hurrell had had with him at Barbados."

So from the hand of his dead friend Newman received the book which became his constant companion, and in which the New Testament interprets the old, the Fathers illuminate the Gospel meaning—all in a unity of incomparable beauty that grows as the Church grows. Antiphon answers to psalm, old feasts take us to the catacombs and new ones into the cities of the modern world; the early Church, the mediaeval, the modern, all are laid under tribute, each bearing its special witness yet each a part of the whole.

[1] Quoted in *John Henry Newman Centenary Essays*, p. 129, from a MS. at Magdalen College.

JOHN HENRY NEWMAN
From the Engraving by R. Woodman, after the
Painting by Sir W. C. Ross
(*By kind permission of Picture Post Library*)

To Henry Wilberforce Newman wrote:

If we are to give hours to prayer during the day it is quite impossible without forms. . . . The Breviary devotions take up from three to four hours a day, a time which may be easily redeemed from the world. I like them uncommonly. Latin devotions are majestic and austere; Greek are much more pathetic and animated, they are better fitted for praise and earnest expostulation. The great advantage of a dead language is that it keeps one sober.

The Psalms should be the basis of all devotion: the more one knows of them the more surprising they are: of course being inspired.

The reaction from his Evangelical period is often visible in Newman's thoughts about prayer:

. . . the bulk and stress of the [Breviary] service is in the morning, that is, when our time is most our own, and our mind most fresh. To leave the body of our prayers for night is like putting off religion to a death bed. Here is a curious contrast between "peculiarism" and the Catholic way. Evening services are peculiar and they are exciting in order that they may answer.

Another excellence is "its precise method . . . it does seem a good thing to have a definite *number* of prayers and psalms. This led the Romanists to the rosaries, etc. I feel the principle to be important, though it may be abused into formalism".

Hurrell's Breviary lay on Newman's desk as his constant companion when he was writing the *Apologia*. It is there still. It became for Newman not only the interpreter of the Fathers, but the source of a Tract and the accompaniment of a tremendous volume of work of all sorts: Tracts, translations, editing, lecturing, preaching, as the Movement swept on in a flood that seemed irresistible. To those inside it, the first five years appeared its greatest and most triumphant period. To Oxford, I think, the peak seemed reached a few years later—probably on the eve of the publication of Tract 90; but Newman has placed it in 1838.

Littlemore Church was consecrated on September 22nd, 1836, and both that day and the anniversary next year gave Newman deep joy. Friends had sent beautiful Church vessels, the people had (on both occasions) brought "out of their own heads" "a profusion of bright flowers". After the consecration two children were baptised. On the anniversary Newman was "asked to have Afternoon Service when Morning Service was over, and complied". Many letters contain requests for the plans of the Church: one clergyman told another of its perfections. Rickards thought it the nicest small church he knew and Newman asks Tom Mozley to send him a sketch of it.

An interesting contrast between the attitude of the Littlemore parishioners and those of St. Mary's, Oxford, emerges in the letters. These last were chiefly tradesmen and their families and servants in the Colleges. A letter kept by Newman shows that his ministrations were not without difficulty:

High St.

SIR,

I am desired by my Aunt (Mrs. W. Wyatt) to present her respects to you and say that a severe cold has prevented her from writing to acknowledge the favour of your call. She feels much indebted for your kind offer to visit her servant which she is obliged to decline having consulted her in the matter. She (her maid) prefers for the present the attentions of her mistress in the way of reading, etc.

I am, Sir,
Your obdt. scrvt.
ANNE WYATT.

And to Miss Giberne he wrote:

I have had a second anonymous present of plate for St. Mary's altar. The parishioners received it in the vestry in silence, and then began disputing about the expense of repairing a pinacle of the Church.

Very different was it at Littlemore, where the fact of a curate by no means lessened the vicar's interest. All his friends regarded the little Church as a Movement cause: numbers came from Oxford on all great occasions. Pusey ministered on the anniversary. All were ready to help if Newman or his curate was away. . . . A letter from James Mozley apologises for being unable to secure a tried friend to take the duty. He had fallen back on Tait (later one of the tutors who protested against Tract 90, later still Archbishop of Canterbury). Mozley writes:

It is rather a floor perhaps having recourse to this quarter: for persons ought not to officiate at Littlemore except they chime in in some way with the disposition of things there. However Tait is a respectable man, and has not committed himself one way or another; though I believe he is a bit of a Presbyterian. . . . However I hope it does not much signify. Tait is a person to comply with the customs of the Church he officiates in; and he attends prayers sometimes in the mornings at St. Mary's which is to his credit.

Parochial work taken seriously eats into the day, especially if to preaching be added lecturing and a correspondence as vast as Newman's. "My hand", he writes to a friend, "is too tired to write letters, unless I am forced—literally my hand is in a continual ache." And to Jemima: "My hand is so tired I can but scrawl." To make it worse, in 1837 and into 1838 he was having special trouble with his old enemy, toothache.

A man in Newman's position today would doubtless have one or more secretaries to whom he could dictate letters, a typist would copy his lecture and sermon notes, and he would only have the work of revising and polishing. What drive and energy must it have taken to work as he did at turning lectures into a book. This was done first with the *Prophetical Office* and he writes to Jemima in January, 1837—a month in which he had continual trouble with his teeth—that the book is almost finished. It will be

a systematising, consolidating, supplying premises, &c. I say nothing, I believe, without the highest authority among our writers; yet it is so strong that everything I have yet said is milk and water to it, and this makes me anxious. It is all the difference between drifting snow and a hard snowball. It seems to me like hitting the Peculiars &c. a most uncommon blow in the face. Pusey however compared it to a blow that takes the breath out of one. He says they will be so out of breath as not to be able to answer—and that before they recover one or other of us must give them another.

In *The Difficulties of Anglicans* published in 1850 Newman underlines what his lectures of this period make apparent—his greater zeal in attacking Protestantism than in attacking Romanism. "Their great and deadly foe," he says of the Tractarians in general, "their scorn and their laughing stock was that imbecile, inconsistent thing called Protestantism." And of himself: "The author's feeling then seems to have been—I should have a perfect case against this Protestantism but for these inconvenient 'Romanists', whose claims I do not admit indeed, but who, controversially, stand in my way."

Actually at this time all he knew of Romanism was his external view of it in Italy, and the idea of its tenets which he had gathered from the Anglican divines. He had not yet thought of it as a

conceivable alternative to the Church of Antiquity—or that of
the seventeenth century—hardly even as a serious enemy. The
men of the Movement

> were accustomed to regard theology generally, much more upon its
> anti-Protestant side than upon its anti-Roman; and from the circum-
> stances in which they found themselves, were far more solicitous to
> refute Luther and Calvin than Suarez or Bellarmine. Protestantism
> was a present foe; Catholicism, or Romanism as they called it, was
> but a possible adversary; "it was not likely", they said, "that Roman-
> ism should ever again become formidable in England"; and they
> engaged with it accordingly, not from any desire to do so, but because
> they could not form an ecclesiastical theory without its coming in their
> way, and challenging their notice. It was "necessary for their position"
> to dispose of Catholicism, but it was not a task of which they acquitted
> themselves with the zeal or interest which was so evident in their
> assaults upon their Protestant brethren.[1]

We have already seen that this was the spirit in which the
anti-Roman Tracts were written. It becomes evident again in
the succeeding series of lectures, begun after Easter 1837, in
which as a Catholic Newman found little enough to correct,
from which Father Przywara has chosen such magnificent passages in his *Newman Synthesis*. The *Lectures on Justification* are in
fact a marvellous treatment of the doctrine of divine grace.
They are more interesting to read today than the *Via Media*
because—like all great theology—they are intensely actual. "I
hear the Peculiars say," Rogers wrote, "'Well now Mr. Newman
is coming out with a work on Justification you will see he is a
Roman Catholic' so they bide their time." Clearly Newman
did find it hard to keep in these lectures any kind of *via media*
—controverting a "Romanist" view in one place he makes use
of the curious phrase "as Roman writers *seem*[2] to speak".
Of what Protestant writers say, however, he has no doubt; and
against it he builds up, largely in scriptural words, the Catholic
doctrine concerning Faith, Grace and good works—and supremely,
with a power shown by no contemporary Catholic writer, the doctrine of the Mystical Body.

With this book also, a letter to Jemima shows how hard he worked.

> My book on Justification has taken an incredible time. I am quite
> worn out with correcting. . . .

---

[1] *Difficulties of Anglicans*, p. 126.   [2] Italics mine.

I write, I write again: I write a third time in the course of six months. Then I take the third: I literally fill the paper with corrections, so that another person could not read it. I then write it out fair for the printer. I put it by; I take it up; I begin to correct again: it will not do. Alterations multiply, pages are re-written, little lines sneak in and crawl about. The whole page is disfigured; I write again; I cannot count how many times this process is repeated.

I shall make no attempt to convey by quotation any idea of these lectures. Even were I competent to do so, I think it could not be done. Quotations need either their context in Newman's writing, or their context in his thought. Read then the entire book or read Father Przywara's selections in *A Newman Synthesis* to get some notion of these grand lectures—which, curiously enough, R. H. Hutton found the only dull thing Newman ever wrote. That is just the trouble: sheer theology is held to be dull by the average Englishman: it is a matter, they think, of words, meaning little but producing endless arguments and quarrels. Hence, Newman's attitude to Hampden was held by so many to be unreasonable as well as uncharitable—for, as he saw with anguish, Protestants were fast becoming Liberals by the abandonment of the dogmatic principle.

He had never, he told Rogers while this was in progress, had so much important work on hand at one time—the Library of the Fathers, the book on Justification, the Tracts, Froude's papers. (Of these something must be written in a separate chapter.) To all this, running parallel with ministering, preaching, studying, Newman added constant help to other men, working under his direction or on similar lines. "Have you not", a friend asks, "work enough of your own on hand that you father so many bantlings of other folks?"

But that of course was one of Newman's chief concerns: never was creator more anxious that a movement should not be regarded as *his* movement, never leader more concerned to bring forward his followers and make their importance equal with his own. Dr. Routh said of him that he did not want to get on in life—and Newman was gratified at this comment. Not personal aggrandisement but the spread of ideas, the winning of men to views that "elevate the Church but sink the individual".[1]

Pusey had tried to start a theological society and Newman had

thrown his energies into its support, but at the beginning of
1837 he himself initiated something in a lighter vein. He called
it simply having men to tea but it became known as "Newman's
soirées". James Mozley writes (February 21, 1837):

Newman gives a tea-party now every Monday evening, in term.
He has just started the thing. Last night went off very well—about
eight or nine men. Conversation flowing continuously, and every one
at his ease. Newman can manage a thing of this kind better than
Pusey. . . . We talked on a variety of subjects.

That Newman should speak of "the young ladies of the
congregation" as an "interesting class" who should "employ
themselves in working altar cloths and ornamenting service
books" seems irresistibly comic today. He even designed to start
"a set of quarterly little volumes or semi-volumes—verse or
prose as it may happen, for the edification of young persons and
the fair sex". He writes this to Harriett in 1837, and asks both her
and Maria Giberne for contributions. Miss Giberne, now no
longer a Peculiar, is described by Harriett Mozley as behaving
extremely well and exercising self-denial with her former friends,
by not calling clergymen priests or nonconformist meetings "false
teaching houses".

The affection between Newman's sisters and Maria was now of
long standing, but the friendship with Newman himself grew
slowly: the first letter is of 1833 and appears to have been
dragged out of him. It begins "My dear Madam", answers
some questions and is signed "Yours faithfully". But she was
a very intelligent woman, her questions were, it seems, intelligent
questions and her gratitude for information was unbounded.
Newman is soon writing: "To have contributed at all to the
satisfaction of a mind like yours, must be a gratification to any
clergyman and a cause of thankfulness." And again: "What is
to be done? Say some way _in which_ you can be convinced that
we are right and we will try to satisfy your test."

I suppose they met fairly often in the family circle but there are
few letters until 1835 when Jemima, writing four pages to Maria,
gives her brother the turn-down of her sheet. This short letter
is signed "Yours very sincerely with very real esteem". Both
Maria Giberne and Anne Mozley became more and more
associated in the close relationship between Newman and his
sisters—but with one great difference. The sisters and the

Mozleys went with him only a certain distance, Miss Giberne followed every move of his mind so that she remained his confidant to the end of their long lives. She had done a drawing of Froude and was one of the few to whom Newman wrote on Froude's death. "I love to think and muse upon one who had the most angelic mind of any person I ever fell in with—the most unearthly, the most gifted. . . . You will do me a most exceeding kindness in giving me your sketch of him." And a little later: "I hope I need not say, I am sure I need not, how very acceptable the portrait of my dear Mother was—I value it most highly." By 1837 Miss Giberne is permitted to be concerned about Newman's health. "As to fasting," he writes, "this week I confess to being emaciated, but the influenza is the cause." Now, when planning his "little volumes", he writes: "I am sure we shall do nothing till we get some ladies to set to work to poison the rising generation".

A correspondence follows on what she is most fitted to do— in which one may note that Newman never lets the editor weaken into the friend. Her first attempt is "done with spirit . . . still I think you must not write more tales for children. . . . What say you to biography? . . . An English Calendar, arranging all our worthies on their death-days. Or it would be a great thing if we had lives of saintly women."

Maria, however, persisted with her children and produced a "story of little Mary which is quite beautiful", writes Newman. "If I am to decide I should make the aunt and cousins Peculiars . . . do not go to the Acta Sanctorum—you are very well employed." A little later he is writing: "I am too little acquainted with children to say how far it is to the life. . . . I suppose even little children *do* give themselves religious airs . . . the effect of the narrative admits of heightening."

The next letter (July 24, 1837) shows both how important the right attitude towards children is felt to be by the correspondents and how completely serious Newman was in this plan of his. It is another example of his belief that the Movement was not for what today would be called highbrows but rather for those who in his own period were often classed together—women, children and the uneducated (meaning roughly all who knew no Greek). "I have not a clear view how far in a book written for children a *mother* (though a Peculiar specimen) may allowably be made absurd and faulty—that is I literally do not see my way."

The "little books" were changing in idea. "We have thoughts of starting a quarterly publication . . . strictly a Miscellany, taking in whatever comes to hand during the Quarter—verses—prose—story or history—dialogue or sermon."

From this he passes straight on to the Library of the Fathers. "It seems to me the great use of our Library will be to make the clergy read the originals—and its giving a general *impulse* in a *certain* direction".

He had been corresponding with the *Christian Observer* and had succeeded in frightening the Peculiars. "I wish them to be regularly frightened and perplexed. They have been sailing along with all things their own way and I wish to take them in flank. It is remarkable how plans to alter the Liturgy have died away ever since our movement began. We have given them other things to think of."

At the end of this year the *British Critic* changed hands and Rogers wrote, glad that it had not gone to a nominee of Newman's: "it seems almost as if one ought to wait until F.'s Remains come out before accepting anything from the Z.s lest they should think afterwards we had got it under false colours." Maitland, the new editor, wanted, however, "a promise of our assistance", and the liberal giving of this would "come in the way", said Newman, of the new light periodical.

Practically, as the correspondence shows, he was already Editor and he became so formally by the middle of 1838. Newman was an excellent editor and the *British Critic*, although not as light as the projected periodical (which was now finally abandoned), makes excellent reading. "I wish you joy of the B.C.," wrote Rogers. "What shall you make of it?"

The Record, The Christian Observer and the rest of the opposition papers flash in and out of these letters and usually Newman's note is a high-spirited one. "I am getting into controversy", he writes to Rogers, January 7, 1837, "with the 'Christian Observer' *in its own pages*. I fervently hope I may be able to tease them *usque ad necem, insaniam,* or something else equally bad." And in the same year to Bowden, "I heard the other day of a young man in an office being led to Apostolical views by the 'Record'. He . . . has become a propagandist".

An unpublished anonymous letter may be briefly quoted (the letters themselves are seldom brief) as typical of the attacks fathered by these newspapers and their reports of Tractarian activities.

DEAR SIR,

What a thing to bow to a piece of bread and a little wine! To bow to them and then to eat one and drink the other! Popery glares thro' these forms—yet *I* will not call them "tricks". . . . I think you will be kind enough to inform me whether scarfs were worn in Edward 6th's time with crosses. . . . Is it also true that you have ordered a celebrated architect to have ready for you "tabernacle work" as it is called or something of that kind [at Littlemore].

Newman annotates this letter:

N.B. *I* had no crosses on my scarf. I wore *no* scarf. Nor did I bow to the elements. Tabernacle work!

The externals that were later to mark the High Church party had in fact no existence in Newman's day. The wearing of vestments was not introduced until several years after he had left the Church of England. To the end of his life Pusey never wore them in his private chapel. In any case such details would have seemed to either man supremely unimportant.

Newman wrote to Rogers: "To be recognised as a fact is everything. If you form a knot in London and set about puzzling the Peculiars, etc., I shall not regret one bit being left alone." And to Maria Giberne: "We seem to be making way very remarkably here in Apostolical views: so much so that our success quite frightens me, as being unnatural—may it be supernatural." The correspondence of the next few years shows many "knots" forming, much puzzling and enraging of the Peculiars, and an increasing recognition of the "fact" of Tractarianism.

Rogers reported to Newman that he had heard a "coxcombical diner-out", talking of religious enthusiasm and insanity, remark that "those Oxford men" were "just on those confines where it is so puzzling to pronounce". And again

one cannot go anywhere without hearing of the "Oxford Tract Party" etc. I could scarcely write a letter in the club-room the other day, so much was my attention distracted by two men who were discussing you—and you appear by degrees to be taking possession even of the public streets; at least the last time I crossed St. Paul's Churchyard I heard the words "Newmanite" and "Puseyite" (a new and sonorous compound) from two passers-by.

Stanley cherished as a kind of natural curiosity a solitary undergraduate of his acquaintance who never heard the name

Newman from one end of term to the other: "of his existence however he had a dreamy notion." The profane spoke of New-mania and Neomaniacs. And, of course, as Newman himself admitted at the time and brilliantly sketched later in *Loss and Gain*, the camp-followers of the Movement were not all sensible men. There was a danger, he says in a letter to Rogers, "of getting *peculiar* in externals, i.e., formal, manneristic, etc.". Actually his own unconscious mannerisms were closely imitated by some of his young and ardent followers, and this was sardonic-ally noted by Frederick Temple (later Archbishop of Canter-bury), who wrote to his mother soon after coming up as an under-graduate: "It is, however, very absurd to see them all hold their heads slightly on one side, all speak in very soft voices, all speak quick and make very long pauses between their sentences, and all on reaching their seats fall on their knees exactly as if their legs were knocked from under them."

The letters abound in brief notes such as "Stanley attends Sacrament in St. Mary's now", "Hook has converted three Wesleyan preachers", "The only real news is the accession, I trust, of Ward of Balliol to good principles. He is a very important accession". And there is no doubt that while on the one hand Tractarian principles were very early a bar to advancement in many quarters (James Mozley was rejected in 1837 for a fellow-ship at Lincoln, another man in the same year for a school at York) the Tractarians whenever possible gave as good as they got. Not in the case of Hampden alone but whenever a Professorship was vacant letters pass urging the election of men of "good principles", the defeat of men suspected of Latitudinarianism. That they had a case in the very statutes of the University was true but the age was against them. "What I fear", wrote Newman prophetically to Bowden, "is the *now* rising generation at Oxford, Arnold's youths. Much depends on how they turn out."

But at present Tractarianism was in the ascendant and had even won to itself temporarily many of Arnold's young men. William George Ward, converted, not temporarily, to Newman, went to Rugby to discuss matters with Arnold, who, Stanley sorrowfully notes, used the most savage phrases about Newmanism that he could invent . . . "The evil spirit is evidently upon him for a season, and everyone who will be bold enough to act the part of David is likely to be run through with a javelin."

Principal Shairp, a Presbyterian from Scotland, Stanley and
Lake, Liberals from Rugby, Church and Rogers in the heart of it,
casual visitors to Oxford, all bear the same testimony—that the
Movement was profound and widespread in its influence and was
the one absorbing topic of the hour. "It was allowed", said one
visitor, "that Newman and the doctor (i.e. Pusey) governed the
University." But actually the attitude of the University was
divided by a very simple barrier—that of age. All the adherents
of the Movement were young men and most young men adhered
to it. Heads of houses were suspicious—perhaps jealous—of its
influence. Newman in *Loss and Gain*, Oakeley in his *Tractarian
Movement*, have described how its enemies fought it. Just as a
hundred years previously practice of Methodism had "cried
aloud Expel", so now with Newmanism. Undergraduates were
watched, were warned, were rusticated; young dons who joined
the movement could expect no promotion. To be called a party
man brought with it a definite stigma, and by the appointments
they were making now, the Heads were preparing the reaction
which followed—and which was equally hated by so many of
them.

J. C. Shairp, not at first wholly in sympathy with a view that
"unchurched" a Presbyterian like himself, has described the
impression made on him by "the purity of life and elevation
of aim, generosity of purpose and depth of devotion" that he saw
among the young fellows and scholars:

> Could the movement which produced these qualities, or even
> attracted them to itself, be wholly false and bad? This movement,
> moreover, when at its height, extended its influence far beyond the
> circle of those who directly adopted its views. There was not a reading
> man, at least in Oxford, who was not more or less indirectly influenced
> by it. Only the very idle or the very frivolous were wholly proof
> against it. On all others it impressed a sobriety of conduct and a
> seriousness not usually found among large bodies of young men. It
> raised the tone of average morality in Oxford to a level which perhaps
> it had never before reached. You may call it overwrought and too
> highly strung. Perhaps it was. It was better, however, for young
> men to be so, than to be doubters or cynics.[1]

The *via media* was, a critic assures us, "crowded with young
enthusiasts". Newman writes joyfully to his sisters of the numbers

[1] J. C. Shairp, *John Keble*, p. 8.

at the weekly celebration at St. Mary's, showing "a steady growth of seriousness among the clergy of the place . . . the change whatever it is is not from *undergraduates*".

Newman continued, after he had become Vicar, to administer Communion not at the altar but in the chancel. This had been the custom since the Reformation. Napkins were laid out and the clergy came round and administered Communion to the congregation in their places. Golightly alludes to the custom in a letter of 1836 and there is no later reference to Newman's having discontinued it. We can stand in St. Mary's today and vividly picture the gowned figures kneeling before their pastor. Forty one day, forty-three another, coming early through the dark winter mornings as well as in the summer.

Shairp saw the whole movement as a mighty power emanating from one man, "perhaps the most remarkable whom the English Church has produced in any century—John Henry Newman" . . .

"Newman and Froude to breakfast," notes one of the Mozley sisters a little before Hurrell's death, "striking entrance. The whole not to be described." Newman's very stillness had in it a dramatic quality, and now he stood alone on the centre of the stage for the climax and the closing acts of the drama. "A certain wonder and awe", says Dean Church, "gathered about him." Hurrell Froude was dead, Keble at his country rectory, taking little part in events, Pusey in Oxford indeed, but a recluse and in his occasional appearances anything but dramatic. Dean Church says of the theological gatherings at his house that they were "irresistibly sleepy". And in the fullness of his powers there was no intellectual comparison possible between Newman and these others. In his youth he had learnt from Hurrell, Keble, Pusey, but now James Anthony's dictum stands: "The rest were but ciphers, Newman the indicating number."

Admirers or opponents, the whole University was alive to the presence of "one of those persons of indisputable genius who was likely to make a mark upon his time. The literary critics of the day were puzzled. They saw he was not an ordinary man; what sort of an extraordinary man he was they could not tell. 'The eye of Melpomene had been cast upon him', said the omniscient Athenaeum; but the glance was not fixed or steady".[1]

Some contemporary descriptions of Newman may help us to picture him. Of his appearance, they are very various. Dean

[1] Froude: *Short Studies*, Vol. IV, 192-3.

Lake thought him "rather like the picture of Louis XI in the red *Quentin Durward*". James Anthony Froude thought he resembled Julius Caesar: "His appearance was striking. He was above the middle height, slight and spare. His head was large, his face remarkably like that of Julius Caesar. The forehead, the shape of the ears and nose, were almost the same. The lines of the mouth were very peculiar, and I should say exactly the same."

Aubrey de Vere describes a first impression:

Early in the evening a singularly graceful figure in cap and gown glided into the room. The slight form and gracious address might have belonged either to a youthful ascetic of the middle ages or to a graceful high-bred lady of our own days. He was pale and thin, almost to emaciation, swift of pace, but when not walking intensely still, with a voice sweet and pathetic, and so distinct that you could count each vowel and consonant in every word. When touching on subjects which interested him much, he used gestures rapid and decisive, though not vehement.[1]

Newman refused the name of a party for himself and his ardent band of followers: yet a party, says Dean Church, they certainly were. And when, speaking of his break with Whately, Newman disclaims all wish to lead a party of his own, I think we should rather interpret this as meaning that he did not set out to create one. "Blessings of friends that to my door, unasked, unhoped have come." But he must have enjoyed using his powers of leadership.

"The influence of his singular combination of genius and devotion," says Dean Lake, "has had no parallel (at Oxford) before or since." "In Oriel Lane," says Principal Shairp, "light-hearted undergraduates would drop their voices and whisper, 'There's Newman!' when, head thrust forward, and gaze fixed as though on some vision seen only by himself, with swift, noiseless step he went by. Awe fell on them for a moment, almost as if it had been some apparition that had passed."

Half inside, half outside, the intimate circle of Tom and James Mozley, Rogers, Church, Henry and Robert Wilberforce, James Hope, were many such as J. A. Froude, Stanley, Clough, Ward, Oakeley, Mark Pattison, Gladstone, Faber, Manning and others who went to "Newman's soirées", saw him from

[1] Ward: *Newman*, Vol. I, p. 66.

time to time, and were in varying degrees for varying periods under his influence.

Stanley writes home that the thought of Newman is "the point that most occupies my mind." He sees in him, "a thorough Christian . . . a man of the purest charity . . . of the most self-denying goodness that can well be conceived."

Fresh from Rugby, both he and Clough were amazed to find that here in the mixed world of Oxford, Newman had a greater and stronger grip on the consciences of his followers than had Arnold who had seemed to them so tremendous in the smaller world of school.

Samuel Wilberforce, still a young man but never completely a Newmanite, wrote of a talk with him:

> It was really most sublime, as an exhibition of the human intellect, when in parts of our discussion Newman kindled and poured forth a sort of magisterial announcement in which Scripture, Christian antiquity, deeply studied and thoroughly imbibed, humility, veneration, love of truth, and the highest glow of poetical feeling, all impressed their own pictures on his conversation.[1]

Sister of two of Newman's greatest admirers and herself one of the family circle, Anne Mozley had written:

> If Mr. Newman expected great things from his friends . . . he always thought them capable of performing them. The "heroic" was a sort of natural element with him—his presence inspired a sense of greatness in his friends, a sense of his greatness and the greatness of companionship with him.

This sense breathes still from dusty letters that have lain over a hundred years in their boxes.

James Anthony Froude, like Stanley an undergraduate, saw Newman as supremely a leader, felt his genius more powerfully than his spiritual influence. The resemblance to Caesar, that he had noted, was not facial only but extended to the temperament.

> In both there was an original force of character which refused to be moulded by circumstances, which was to make its own way, and become a power in the world; a clearness of intellectual perception, a disdain for conventionalities, a temper imperious and wilful, but along with it a most attracting gentleness, sweetness, singleness of

---

[1] *Life of Bishop Wilberforce*, Vol. I, p. 95.

heart and purpose. Both were formed by nature to command others, both had the faculty of attracting to themselves the passionate devotion of their friends and followers, and in both cases, too, perhaps the devotion was rather due to the personal ascendancy of the leader than to the cause which he represented. It was Caesar, not the principle of Empire which overthrew Pompey and the constitution. *Credo in Newmannum* was a common phrase in Oxford, and is still unconsciously the faith of nine-tenths of the English converts to Rome.

. . . We, who had never seen such another man, and to whom he appeared, perhaps, at special advantage in contrast with the normal college don, came to regard Newman with the affection of pupils (though pupils strictly speaking he had none) for an idolised master. The simplest word which dropped from him was treasured as if it had been an intellectual diamond. For hundreds of young men *Credo in Newmannum* was the genuine symbol of faith.[1]

Many years later, indignant at Kingsley's allegations, Principal Shairp wrote:

Those who witnessed these things and knew that, if a large following had been his object, he might, by leaving the Church of England three years earlier, in the plenitude of his power, have taken almost all the flower of young Oxford with him, needed no *Apologia* to convince them of his honesty of purpose.[2]

Newman did not, James Anthony says, enter on the great topics of faith and unfaith with undergraduates or at social meetings: there he talked on any common topic, "literature, public persons and incidents. Never didactic or authoritative," he was in conversation, "lightness itself—the lightness of elastic strength."

But in the pulpit of St. Mary's the brilliant talker was transformed into the inspired prophet.

These weekly sermons were by common consent the motive force of the Oxford Movement. Some few had attended the lectures, many had read the Tracts, but everyone listened to the sermons. The congregation every Sunday numbered more than the population of the parish. Every man of note in the University attended, and many visitors.

When the sermons came to be thought a serious menace, Heads of Houses tried to prevent undergraduate attendance by

[1] Froude: *Short Studies*, Vol. IV, pp. 192-3, 199.
[2] Shairp: *John Keble*, p. 26.

such devices as changing the dinner hour so that a hot dinner and a sermon became incompatible. (One dean who had done this came regularly himself.)

It is hard, Dean Church says, for anyone of a later date fully to realise the uniqueness of these sermons, because of the degree to which they transformed preaching in the Church of England. James Mozley admits that he imitates Newman just as an Evangelical preaches in an Evangelical style—he was perhaps the first of the long line of Newmanite preachers.

Urging Keble to publish his own sermons Newman had said "it seems to me a great object, as Sir Walter Scott beat bad novels out of the field, in like manner to beat out bad sermons by supplying a more *real* style of sermon".

Tastes differ of course as to what is real—and even as to whether calm reality is suited to a pulpit rather than "oratory of the Boanerges sort". Newman took the trouble of copying a comment made on his own sermons by the Rev. J. Clark of Philadelphia (in *Glimpses of the Old World*), "He is a thin sallow-looking man and appears as cold in the pulpit as an icicle. . . . Mr. Newman did not in his sermon exhibit any of his particular views. The discourse upon the whole was exceedingly dull and uninteresting". Upon which Newman's comment is "The impression produced on an intelligent foreigner, perfectly impartial". Impartial Mr. Clark probably was—but his opinion which is interesting chiefly because entirely unique seems to represent a rather *un*intelligent reaction to novelty.

For pre-Newman preaching had been either the clear cold intellectual type of which Whately was a good example, or else gush of the Evangelical school—a sermon aimed at both heart and head was almost unheard of. And both types were quite removed from the realities of daily life—there was a special pulpit school of eloquence that took little account of its hearers. W. G. Ward used to recall listening in a village church to a clergyman reading to a rustic congregation a sermon which abounded in such phrases as "Hark ye gilded voluptuaries", or "Pause ere it be too late, ye butterflies of fashion"—and this was scarcely more remote from reality than the average preacher of the day from the lives and thoughts of his hearers.

There was an interesting irony in Newman's situation when he stood in the pulpit of St. Mary's Parish Church. The University had the right to appoint preachers on many Sunday mornings:

men came to Oxford from London or from some cathedral city, men came from colleges as University Preachers; and standing in that pulpit attacked ever more vigorously the Movement he was leading. They came and they went and Newman remained. They were preachers before the University, Newman the Vicar. They each preached once and Newman preached every week. But those who listened to him were amazed at not hearing from him what they at first deemed the doctrines he had most at heart. Nothing about Apostolical Succession, or the authority of Bishops: no peculiarities in the service, only a careful carrying out of the liturgy of the Prayer Book. Nor did Newman answer the attacks on his position, he was concerned with greater matters, the matters for which in his mind the Movement really stood.

What was the Church but the "concrete representative of things invisible", what was her office but to save souls through the truth and grace God had given her to dispense. Listeners of every kind were struck most of all by the reality of Newman's sermons. It was to real men he was speaking, living in a real world and suffering from real temptations. James Mozley notes his extraordinary power of entering into those temptations even when most remote from his own. He could picture the mind of a successful tradesman eager for gain, of a man of the world afraid of ridicule, of a waverer afraid of truth. "He spoke," says James Anthony Froude, "with such piercing insight that you thought the secrets of your own heart had been revealed to him." But you were not afraid, for a sympathy no less profound went with the insight.

Forty years later a listener described the scene as though it were yesterday, the intense stillness, the "hands literally not seen. The sermon began in a calm musical voice, the key slightly rising as it went on", then as the preacher warmed to his subject "it seemed as if his very soul and body glowed with suppressed emotion".[1]

It was the sense of great forces held in, that made in part the drama of a scene which many have described and in which each seized and made his own a different passage.

The very tones of his voice [says this listener] seemed as if they were something more than his own. . . . The great Church, the congregation all breathless with expectant attention. The gaslight,

---

[1] Quoted in *Letters and Correspondence of J. H. Newman*, Vol. II, p. 219.

M

just at the left hand of the pulpit, lowered that the preacher might
not be dazzled; themselves perhaps standing in the half-darkness under
the gallery, and then the pause before those words in the "ventures
of Faith" thrilled through them—"They say unto Him, we are able."

To a natural power of reading character, Newman had added
a life-long study both of men as he had known them and of the
immense portrait gallery of Scripture. He knew the men both
of the Old and New Testaments. Jacob and Joseph, Saul and
David and Jonathan, Peter and Paul, appear in his sermons as
friends with whose strength and weakness he is familiar and
who all carry lessons for the Christians of today. All with varying temperaments, under different circumstances had one task—
the salvation of their souls. And the treatment of these characters,
like his touch on the souls of his listeners, was, to use Newman's
own phrase, "real" not "notional".

Browning speaks in one of his poems of "the truth of things . . .
their very superficial truth", and to Newman all this external
world only represented the "superficial truth". His sermons
were real where others were not, just because he came, as his
hearers noted, from another world, remote to them but to him
far more real than the one in which they lived. It is fancifully
thought by men of this world that belief in another diminishes
the reality of this. The truth is the exact opposite. We can see
the reality of this world, only in the measure in which we grasp
a greater reality. Those who listened to Newman experienced
this even if they could not explain it. He revealed them to themselves, they said. He showed them the truth of this world in the
light of its Creator. And he could do this because his own conversation was in Heaven. Different ambassadors of God to men
show forth different virtues, and if one were set to choose Newman's one would answer unhesitatingly—he was supremely, in
an unbelieving age, a man of Faith.

Another thing on which all agreed who went to St. Mary's
was that the sermon was only a part, although a great part, of
what touched and moved them. Newman's voice, like a silver
bell, was heard first in the Lessons. "He was," says Oakeley,
"reader, preacher and celebrant": the music and ceremonial
were his also, for if others ever filled these departments "they
have faded from the memory which has settled down on him
alone."

"Why is it," asks another, "that, while many things at the time even more impressive have faded from the memory, one scene, or perhaps one cadence, remains fixed in it for life? Thus it is that one who more than forty years ago stood just before him almost a boy in the College Chapel, has at this moment in his ears the sound of the words, 'Oh, magnify the Lord our God, and worship Him upon His holy hill—*for the Lord our God is Holy.*' "[1]

As year followed year his listeners would look forward to certain lessons as special examples of Newman's power: the sacrifice of Isaac, the story of Joseph, the passage of the Red Sea, the history of Balaam. "He stood before the sacred Volume," says Oakeley, "as if penetrating its contents to their very centre." And looking back thirty years later, he saw in these afternoons at St. Mary's "that sublime idea which the Church has embodied in the quasi-dramatic recital of the Passion in Holy Week".

If there was a dramatic quality in Newman's very stillness, how much more when he was speaking to men in God's presence and to God Himself? The word actor has come to sound unreal, but think of its true meaning: a great actor forgets self, he is intent upon the action of the drama. So Newman was intent upon the action of worship—in his eyes the greatest action man can perform. The boy had thrown himself into his part in Latin plays, but for the man, only what was real was truly dramatic.

As David danced before the Ark, as Callista in the story of her dream went forward in a rhythmic dance towards her sacrifice, as the celebrant lifts his hands and moves solemnly in the greatest of all sacrifices, so in his movements, in his cadences, the swift speech, the long pauses, was Newman offering before God the drama of his worship and the worship of those around, one with him in the action of praise and adoration. If the young men gathered around him had come with *Credo in Newmannum* on their lips, it was for him to change it in that hour to the confession: *Credo in unum Deum, in Filium ejus unigenitum, in Spiritum Sanctum, in unam sanctam et Apostolicam Ecclesiam, ad vitam aeternam.*

[1] Quoted from *The Dublin Review*, April 1869.

CHAPTER XXV

Froude's Remains

HURRELL FROUDE had left behind him a quantity of papers: and these were sent by Archdeacon Froude to Newman and Keble. Newman's first impression, written to Henry Wilberforce (July 16, 1836), is startling in the light not only of what happened but of the documents themselves: "I am engaged on Froude's papers, which are so keen and well-tempered, that I feel they will fulfil the story of the man beheaded by the Damascus blade, who did not know his head had been taken off, till he shook himself and it fell. So expect the world to see nothing in them."

Of course it was Newman, in the midst of all his other activities, who set to work transcribing for Keble's "imprimatur" the first instalment that came from Devonshire. He was "deeply impressed" with the "attractive character" of the *Private Thoughts*. "If you say 'yes' and send them to me, I propose to go to press almost immediately." This was in June, 1837. In July he sent to Rogers a number of extracts from Froude's letters to himself. At Isaac Williams' suggestion he proposed to print these to follow the thoughts.

Read them attentively. If you think there is a chance of their doing, I must apply for yours, Keble's, Williams' and his home letters. . . .

Vaughan was observing the other day that we never have the history of men in the most interesting period of their life, from eighteen to twenty-eight or thirty, when they are *forming*: now this gives Froude's . . . his change from Tory to Apostolical is curious . . . the interesting *growth* of his mind, how indolence was overcome . . . his remarkable struggle against the lassitude of disease, his working to the *last* . . . the intrinsic merit of his remarks.

Six weeks later the Archdeacon sent more papers. Newman commented:

Hurrell's private journal (1826–1827) giving an account of his fastings, etc., . . . more interesting than anything I have seen except perhaps his letters to Keble, which are also come. Does it not seem as if Providence was putting things into our hands for something especial? There is so gradual and unexpected an accumulation. . . . These new papers have quite made my head whirl.

A whirling head was not perhaps the ideal instrument with which to take a delicate decision. On the earlier elements for the book Newman had taken a good deal of advice. He realised, as he wrote to Rogers, the need of a critic "more impartial than ourselves, in order to ascertain his *impression* . . . I thought of Acland, except that he is a fastidious man. What say you to Hope?"

James Hope (he took the name of Hope-Scott on his marriage to Sir Walter's grand-daughter) became later one of Newman's most intimate friends and correspondents. This wish to have his judgment on a practical problem was typical. People were, all through his life, asking and acting on his advice—often with the worst results. My mother, who was his daughter, used to say that with all her father's qualities of head and heart she thought his practical judgment peculiarly weak and could not imagine why people continued to rely on it! (She herself was only seven when he died but she judged from letters and other remains). It was probably the result of his unusual powers of advocacy—he was a very successful parliamentary barrister—combined with good looks much out of the ordinary, and a genius for friendship that held him in closest relationship to the end of his life with his Oxford friends: Newman, Manning, and Gladstone.

"Things seem," wrote R. F. Wilson, ". . . at a turning point. A trifle will give the inclination on one side or the other. . . . We cannot afford by any shock to throw back . . . some who are now leaning our way."

The first shock was given and its impression communicated to the editors by a curious accident before publication. Agitated letters from the publishers to Newman seem to be answers to some expostulation. Then comes a letter from W. H. Hale to Newman explaining that no blame attached to the Rivingtons at whose works he had been calling. "My eye caught the word 'humbug' printed upon a rough proof which was lying near. So unusual a word naturally excited my curiosity, and I took

up the sheet, which the foreman told me was already in the
press, and cast an eye over two or three paragraphs, the nature
of which very much surprised me, since they evidently were the
secret confessions of the author's most secret thoughts." He
only read a few passages: "they were indeed of so striking a
character, that I felt as if I ought never to have had the power
to read even those." He had written first to Keble whom he
knew best and had hoped this intervention "would not only
have been looked upon as one of pure friendship, but would also
have caused the question of publication of such a journal to be
again considered".

Whether considered again or not, publication was not abandoned, but it dragged slowly and by January, 1838, Newman
appears less excited and more despondent about the event.

Anxious I have been, and am, about several things. Froude's
volumes will open upon me a flood of criticisms, and from all quarters.
It is just a case when no two persons have the same judgment *about
particulars*, and I am fully conscious that even those who know one
will say, "What *could* he mean by putting this in? What is the use of
that? How silly this! How trifling that! What is it to the world if
so and so? How injudicious! He is cutting his own throat!" But *on
the whole* I trust it will present, as far as it goes, a picture of a mind;
and that being gained as the *scope* the details may be left to take their
chance.

He was throwing himself open to attack upon a wide field, for
besides the personal revelations, Froude's historical and ecclesiastical views were unusual and vehemently expressed. This
first publication consisted of two volumes containing letters,
thoughts, private journal, sermons and a few recorded sayings,
with an introduction by Newman. In the second series—two
further volumes, with a preface by Keble—was included a study
of St. Thomas à Beckett with material towards a biography
of him.

Froude had thrown himself into the resurrection of the Church
of England, the Church of the Non-Jurors, nay more, the Church
of the Middle Ages. While Newman was studying the Fathers,
Froude was living with Thomas à Beckett (contrast his sketch
with James Anthony's later treatment of the same subject, for a
perfect example of the attitudes of the two brothers). While
Newman was discovering St. Athanasius, Froude was less

pleasantly discovering Luther. "Some of the Oxford men," Arnold wrote, "revile Luther as a bold bad man; how surely would they have reviled Paul; how zealously would they have joined in stoning Stephen."[1]

Froude's language about the Reformers did not go further, as Dean Church notes, than most Anglicans would have gone by the eighties; but in the thirties it came as a shock and—thrown out in most startling form without (says the Dean) the winning smile, the qualifying phrase of the living man—Froude's words startled and estranged many. But however vivid his smile, however graceful his manner, Froude would have been perfectly willing to let the naked word stand unsupported and unmitigated. He would surely have hated the publication of his asceticisms, but of the gauntlet thrown down to Protestantism, he would be without repentance.

How beautifully [he had written to Newman] the *Edinburgh Review* has shown up Luther, Melancthon and Co.! What good genius has possessed them to do our dirty work. . . . *Pour moi*, I never mean, if I can help it, to use any phrases even, which can connect me with such a set. I shall never call the Holy Eucharist "the Lord's Supper", nor God's priests "Ministers of the Word", nor the Altar "the Lord's Table", etc.: innocent as such phrases are in themselves, they have been dirtied: a fact of which you seem oblivious on many occasions.

Not the character of the Reformers only but a whole view of the Church was unfolded in Froude's pages—the "Apostolical" view as the Tractarians called it—set out abruptly, in startling language and without the preparation of the reader's mind, without the careful balance of language that came naturally to Newman, who also would not at that date have condemned the Reformers so vigorously. On the nature of the Church, its sacraments, its membership, they both stood in sharp contrast to the Protestants and Liberals who were alike enraged by the *Remains*. "Its predominant character," wrote Arnold to Hawkins, "is extraordinary impudence."[2] And "these men would exclude John Bunyan and Mrs. Fry and John Howard from Christ's Church, while they exalt the Non-Jurors into Confessors and Laud into a martyr."[3]

Newman writes to Jemima: "Old Faussett has been firing off at us. He is like an old piece of ordnance which can do

---

[1] Stanley, *Life of Arnold*, p. 388.   [2] Stanley, *Life of Arnold*, p. 324.   [3] Ibid.

nothing but fire, or like a macaw with one speech. He fired off at Milman and against Hampden—and now at us. He can do nothing but fire, fire." Faussett was Lady Margaret Professor of Divinity. "I have just published a letter," Newman wrote a few weeks later, "to that goose Faussett who literally knowing nothing at all on the subject has thought fit to publish his sermon." The reply was written so quickly it was printed ahead of the attack—and sold more copies. "Who would have thought," Newman commented, "persons would buy an *answer* without a *question?*"

One drawback of the haste in which he first wrote was stated by J. F. Christie, "Your mode of expressing yourself is hard and inconsiderate to the feelings of those who differ from you. . . . You say 'if I may so speak'—but *may* you so speak?"

Conscious of overboldness towards his leader, he remembers "you once floored Rogers and Henry Wilberforce for not telling you of something they did not quite like in what you had published . . . I will allow you to call me micropsyche—and Boy—on condition you modify in your second edition."

In a debate in the House of Lords on the grant for educating the Irish Catholic clergy, Lord Morpeth said: "If they were to be always talking of the objectionable doctrines taught at Maynooth, they must not be surprised if they sometimes heard of the not very satisfactory doctrines which had recently become fashionable at Oxford"—and he quoted some of Froude's remarks about the Reformers. Gladstone, I think characteristically, looks bold but is really cautious in his reply. He "had never heard a speech more cruelly unjust . . . he had no hesitation in characterising the assertion as a mere vulgar calumny." But ignoring the general agreement between the editors and their subject, he goes on to stress those passages in the preface in which Newman and Keble state that they do not in publishing commit themselves to agreement with all the ideas of a deeply original mind.

The book and the debate were a glorious opportunity for the Protestant press, and Newman sends James Mozley an extract from a ragged paper sent to him by post.

The Debate was rendered remarkable for bringing before the notice of the country, through Lord Morpeth, a sect of damnable and detestable heretics of late sprung up in Oxford: a sect which evidently affects Popery, and merits the heartiest condemnation of all true Christians. We have paid a good deal of attention to these gentry, and by the grace of God we shall show them up, and demonstrate that they are a people to be abhorred of all faithful men. We do not hesitate to say that they are criminally heterodox.

Nor were the Protestant the only newspapers interested. The *Oxford Herald* called Froude and his editors "amiable and fanciful men". But Newman adds: "*Fraser's Magazine*, I am told has opened on us. We must expect a volley from the whole Conservative Press. I can fancy the Old Duke sending down to ask the Heads of Houses whether we cannot be silenced."

By October he is writing to Jemima of the first suggestions for that excrescence on Oxford (since put to many curious uses) the Martyrs' Memorial. "They are getting up a sort of Cranmer and Latimer testimonial here. . . . They told the President of Magdalen (so it is said) that it was for the Primitive Martyrs and so got his name—they also told the Vice Ch. it was done against me, and he withdrew his; so they say."

The Martyrs' Memorial certainly was intended as a move against the Tractarians, and there seemed a beginning of confusion in their views if not in their ranks when Pusey appeared willing to subscribe. But very soon he was writing to the Bishop of Oxford that the memorial was "a counter movement against Froude's Remains". One of its supporters had said "It will be a good cut against Newman." Pusey goes on to give the Bishop his considered view: "I fear lest this plan should tend to increase the vulgar impression that we were a new Church at the Reformation, instead of being the old one purified."[1]

This was written in November 1838. The following year Newman's files are full of letters on the subject. Many of his followers write hoping he *will* subscribe to prevent talk of his popery, saying the absence of his friends' names is widely noted, that it is rumoured that no one concerned in the Library of the Fathers will subscribe to the Memorial. "P.S." adds one friend. "My wife wishes to hear from your own lips that you do not want us to pray to the saints or the Blessed Virgin."

In April Newman is able to tell Jemima "the unfortunate Memorial is acknowledged to be a failure. What then has

[1] Liddon: *Life of Pusey*, Vol. II, p. 68.

Goose Golightly and Co. done but raised an enquiry upon Cranmer whom it is truest charity to say nothing about?"

Golightly had been ardent in gathering subscriptions and he thus comes again upon the scene in a very different character from his earlier appearance as the amiable, not very bright, friend of the family. Readers of the published correspondence and of Tom Mozley's *Reminiscences* may feel he had been harshly treated when in 1836 Newman asked him to be Curate at Littlemore and then objected so strongly to a sermon he had preached as to make him feel obliged to resign before he had even begun upon his duties. But he himself took it quite amiably and the unpublished letters[1] bring out fully both how correctly Newman acted and how perfectly it was understood by all that Newman's attitude was invariably governed by impersonal considerations of orthodoxy. Though the unhappy episode ended the old warm friendship between the two men, Golightly continued for some time to sign his letters "Yours affectionately", offered to take, if Newman desired, any part of the duty "which you will trust me to undertake" and refused to have back his subscription to Littlemore. "I look upon it as no longer my own but consecrated."

As time went on he would take part more and more violently against Newman—Tom Mozley says he had promised to hide them in his house when persecution came but was in the event one of the worst persecutors. But I think it is pretty clear that *odium theologicum* and not personal feeling was his driving force.

---

[1] The published accounts had given me the impression that Newman had treated Golightly rather shabbily. The private correspondence removed the impression. In May, 1835, Newman invited Golightly to be his curate at Littlemore. Golightly, in a long letter, urged Newman to examine his doctrinal views carefully before sending him to Littlemore. He feared that, if Newman came to discover later that his views differed too widely, he would turn him out, "which I should not like." Newman was satisfied with the letter and Golightly undertook the work. A year later Pusey heard him preach and complained to Newman. Golightly sent the sermon and Newman found it "most objectionable; quite irreconcilable with the avowal of baptismal regeneration, you made in your considerate and satisfactory letter of last year." He informed Golightly that he could not "take an irrevocable step about Littlemore." Golightly decided that in the teeth of so strong an expression of want of confidence—"accompanied as it is by a refusal to licence me, I should not be justified as a prudent man in undertaking the charge." He was clearly puzzled. He felt confident that the unsatisfactory sermon gave the same teaching on Baptismal Regeneration as the satisfactory letter of a year earlier. But it did not. The letter questioned whether baptised sinners "have the spirit of God or not"—which is orthodox; the Sermon questioned whether they had really "been born again"— which is heterodox. Had the letter used this second phrase, Newman would have dropped the matter instantly. Golightly saw so little difference that, as Newman pointed out, he actually quoted the letter as containing the second phrase, whereas it had contained the first.

The attacks of enemies were expected: Golightly he never took seriously, to neutrals he was indifferent; but the real blow for Newman was that the publication of Froude's *Remains* alienated some friends and annoyed many more. At the end of March, when the book had just appeared, he warned Keble to expect "a somewhat excited letter from Edward Churton". Several months later Churton was still unhappy. He wrote to Newman:

> I could wish you had used a little of the reserve which Isaac Williams recommends. . . . I ever shall regret that the pruning knife was not more extensively used in the preparation of those extraordinary papers . . . they have sadly encumbered a plain good cause . . . your opponents will never find ground to stand upon, *unless you are so kind as to give it to them.* . . .
> You must perceive that since the publication of Froude's *Remains*, your friends are perplexed, and some who were neuters have declared against you. . . . I have not found one who defends that publication except Dr. Pusey. . . . Pray, think of the perils of new divisions, and on points confessedly unnecessary.

In answer to Newman's answer he writes again. "You say 'the pain persons feel is no proof we were not right. Operations which save life are often painful.' If the pain which has been felt were confined to persons opposed to your principles, I would allow the force of such an argument," but the pain is felt "by those who want to approve of everything you do." Not only the unfortunate criticisms of the Reformers but the publication of the diary seems to him a grave mistake. He had surely heard Newman express opinions on such publications "with which these selections cannot be held to harmonise".

Churton's feeling about the diary was widely shared, although not as universally as he supposed. Ward of Balliol liked the book better than anything of the kind he ever read: it completed his conversion from Arnold's to Newman's party. But the general feeling was that of an admirer who wrote, "I must say I felt I was committing an impertinence in reading his private journal— perhaps the most private journal that ever was written. For conceive his horror while writing some of the confessions to think that all that would be read." One wonders certainly that his friends did not shudder at the thought of publication. And this for the reason Chesterton gives why the Browning love letters ought not to have been published—not because it reveals Hurrell Froude to the world but precisely because it does not. The "bright and beautiful Froude" of their memories is unrecognisable in the tortuous analyses of his own motives, the morbid note of the journal.

Holding the clue through their knowledge of his personality, Newman and Keble failed to see that they had not given it to others in such fashion that most readers could seize it. Some could and did, but most not—so that a view commonly held of Froude became that of a man concerned with "tithing mint and cummin", reducing Christianity to a system of fasting and negations, making himself miserable over the daily trifles of conduct that are hardly worth noticing. His fasts were serious— no food all day except a piece of bread in the evening: no food till the evening and then self reproach for a meal of buttered toast. From sleeping on the floor he would rise for early service and a day almost without food. Nor was this a rare exception: fast days occur often in the diary.

He seizes on his own weaknesses to magnify them, sees poor and even bad motives in all he does.

I have kept a tolerable fast today; have read my journal, though I can hardly identify myself with the person it describes: it seems like having some one under one's guardianship who was an intolerable fool, and exposed himself to my contempt every moment for the most ridiculous and trifling motives.[1]

There is a kind of savagery against self which reads like a very young man—which does not read unlike an early chapter in some life of a saint. He had no guidance, he calls himself "disgustingly enthusiastic", but he saw the elements of daily life as the elements of sanctification or of selfish deterioration and he made war on himself with a laugh of self-contempt. He was, complains Abbott, "bordering on abjectness towards God."

Dean Church compares Froude with Pascal and he was indeed willing to wager all for all. What, asked Newman in one of his sermons, have most of us ventured for faith, how would we be worse off if it proved an illusion? Froude had ventured. James Mozley compares not only the contrasting intellectual outlook but the character of Arnold with that which made Hurrell Froude the witness to another ideal.

[1] *Remains*, Vol. I, p. 18.

Arnold, gushing with the richness of domestic life, the representative of high, joyous Lutheranism, is describable—Mr. Froude hardly. His intercourse with earth and nature seemed to cut through them, like uncongenial steel, rather than mix and mingle with them. Yet the polished blade smiled as it went through. The grace and spirit with which he adorned this outward world . . . the severe sweetness of the life divine, not so much rejected as disarmed those potent glows and attractions of the life natural: a high good temper civilly evaded and disowned them. The monk by nature, the born aristocrat of the Christian sphere, passed them clean by with inimitable ease; marked his line and shot clear beyond them.[1]

But Mozley had known Froude in what little flesh there was of him, the whole Newman group shared the memory of a vivid and gracious person. Outside the charmed circle it was otherwise. James Stephen in the *Edinburgh* spoke contemptuously of Froude's fasts, contrasting him with Whitefield who "when he would mortify his body set about it like a man. The paroxysm was short indeed but terrible." Stephen could not see the wasted figure, the brilliant smile, the good companion who secretly, with continued effort (so much harder than a brief paroxysm) brought an almost dying body under the spirit's control. The Reformers' prophecy that *they* would light up a flame in England will not, says Stephen, "be defeated by the successors of the Oxonian divines who listened to it, so long as they shall be vacant to record, and to publish, contrite reminiscences of a desire for roasted goose, and of an undue indulgence in buttered toast."

Men often admire austerity or penitence described in general terms who shrink from its embodiment in concrete details. Yet there is a right element surely in this shrinking. Froude's confessions of the temptation brought by the smell of food after a long day's fast might touch and help a fellow-struggler, but on the whole they would be better left as private (and, by the way, as incidental) as he intended them. To Stephen it seemed that Newman had consigned his friend "to lasting ridicule". "Mr. Froude," he says, "left behind him a great collection of papers, which affection would have committed to the fire, though party spirit gave them to the press."

Most serious of all was a Charge from the Bishop of Oxford, Dr. Bagot. While praising the zeal of the Tractarians, he warned

[1] J. Mozley's *Essays Historical and Theological*, Vol. II, pp. 50-51.

them of the need of caution, saying that some words and expressions in the Tracts might lead people into error—he feared more for the disciples than the masters. To Newman this caution, slight as it was, was agitating in the extreme. From St. Ignatius of Antioch, from Antiquity, he had imbibed a profound sense of the sanctity of episcopal authority. It was in the person of the Bishop that the visible Church of Christ commanded and must be obeyed. "What he said," Newman wrote to Bowden, "was very slight indeed, but a Bishop's lightest word *ex Cathedra* is heavy." "My Bishop," he added later, "was my Pope." He at once offered to suppress any Tract that was in his power, to suppress them all.

The Bishop appeared surprised, and Newman told Keble:

> He had, he said, been forced to give judgment on account of anonymous letters and of other bishops having spoken . . . had approved of much . . . censured nothing only warned. . . . Nothing could be kinder or more sympathetic than his letter. . . . I think he has not considered that a Bishop's word is an act, that I am under his jurisdiction, that he cannot criticise but commands only.

Both to Bowden and Keble, Newman expresses the thought that the Bishop was in fact helping on their ideas while giving them "a slap" "just as men revile Popery in order to say strong Catholic things." But to Keble he slips in a revealing sentence "I am not sure if he was not rather annoyed with me when he delivered his Charge whether on account of the 'Remains' or for other reason." We may feel pretty sure he was, for he was a cautious man and no lover of extremes.

I think Newman, although looking back later he saw the tide beginning to turn against the Tractarians, was unwilling then or ever to admit how great a share the *Remains* had in the change. He is eager to assure Keble that most people think they were wise to publish and to minimise any attacks other than the Protestant. But a strong note of alarm had been sounded in the camp and continued to echo for many months. John Keble's brother, Tom, voicing Conservative opinion—chiefly that of the country clergy—felt that things were being done too hastily at Oxford. He wanted Newman to go away, to be "a little while out of the way of your Faussetts, Shuttleworths, etc." And in one letter he sends Newman a message from a Mr. Burke—the kind of "message" in which one feels the transmitter has allowed his own feelings very free scope: "You never give yourself time to cool. You cannot survey from its proper point of sight the work you have finished before you decree its final execution. You never go into the country soberly and dispassionately to observe the effect of your measures on their objects . . ."

Meanwhile two of the younger men, Wood and Williams, were translating the Breviary. Newman tells Keble he had proposed its being corrected "by some standard"—the Articles or the Prayer Book or both. Williams wanted total publication, perhaps accompanied by an introduction on the errors of Popery. Tom Keble and Sir John Prevost wanted the whole thing dropped. The correspondence dragged on for months, the parties interested not writing to one another but to Newman, who continued to be the recipient also of letters against the *Remains*. "I am sorry to find," writes John Marriott, "on meeting strangers how many of them are violently set against Froude's *Remains* . . . many are quite outrageous." Archdeacon Froude began to doubt the wisdom of publishing the proposed second series—but this is the only thing that Newman did not suggest abandoning, in some letters that followed of wholesale submission to John Keble's judgment.

If you will tell me what not to do, I will not do it. I wish parties would seriously ask themselves what they desire of me. Is it to stop writing? I will stop anything you advise. Is it to show what I write to others before publishing? It is my rule already. Pusey saw my letter to Faussett. Williams and others heard and recommended the publishing of my lectures. Is it to stop my weekly parties, or anything else? I will gladly do so.

. . . If I ought to stop I am ready to stop, but do not in the same breath chide me (for instance) for thinking of stopping the Tracts, and then be severe on the Tracts which are actually published. If I am to proceed, I must be taken for what I am.

There is a fascinating contrast between the impression given to the younger men of Newman's attitude to criticism and the tone of the letters to Keble. Rogers was on the whole against the Breviary publication, and Newman, he says, took his attitude "as very unkind, and showed it in a certain flinty way which he had at command on great emergencies . . . the pain of keeping up this severe outside was at times to him visibly overpowering."

He is sometimes reproached, says Rogers, with hardness, but "you occasionally saw what this flintiness cost him. And when you came to frank explanation there came from the rock a gush of overpowering tenderness."

With Keble there was no show of flintiness nor even of firmness but a frank confession of underlying doubts. Newman could face a thousand foes but when friends attacked, he distrusted his own judgment. He speaks of "that sense of disgust which the steady contemplation of his own doings is sure to create in any serious man". And again "When a man like your brother *does* object, he has my own latent witness on his side, and he goes just the way, whether he wishes it or not, to reduce me to silence." This silence, however, would not mean inaction but "reading and preparing for future writing on the Fathers" and giving up "off-hand works"—the *British Critic*, the Tracts, even St. Mary's.

But the Tracts were selling "faster than we can print them"— sixty thousand in a year. Newman's fourth volume of sermons which "I meant to be my best" came to a second edition in half a year—"nothing of mine has ever been so quick before"—the *British Critic* was being read increasingly. A stranger writes early in 1839 proposing a Tractarian newspaper; but "the hope of the Church," replies Newman, "does not lie with newspaper readers. It lies with thoughtful men and young men—whether lay or clerical . . . And they will in their sphere and place spread the truth against the newspapers."

Yet, too, there were newspapers on the side of the Movement and this Newman brings out in an unsigned article written in April for the *British Critic* called "State of Religious Parties"[1] in which he quotes a commentator: "The *Morning Post* sustains the character of their apologist in London, and the *Liverpool Mail*, the *Coventry Herald* and other journals identify themselves with them in the country."

This article has a triumphant ring which seems the stronger after the mood of depression of the previous year. Planning it, he seems to have been in high spirits: he wrote to Miss Giberne "N.B. I should be obliged if you could send me at once any *good* absurd lies about us which are current in your parts." One such good absurd lie he had mentioned earlier in the year to Henry Wilberforce. "I heard yesterday that the master of University

[1] Re-published in *Essays Critical and Historical* under the title "Prospects of the Anglican Church".

had been assured by a lady at Cheltenham that we offered sacrifice every morning . . . she knew for certain we killed something, she did not know what. Qy. little children? or each other? or frogs? spiders? what?" Another, he told Bowden, was "that I carried my austerity to such an extent that I would not let my wife wear anything but sad-coloured ribbons in her hat". Indeed lies about himself always amused him. He wrote to Ryder (in November 1838): "There is a great fat lie, a lie to the backbone, and in all its component parts, in its soul and body, inside and out, in all sides of it, and in its very origin, in the Record of yesterday evening. It has no ultimate element of truth in it, it is born of a lie, its father and mother are lies, and all its ancestry—and to complete it, it is about me."

In this article Newman shows the great variety of origin and outlook in the men of the Movement, some representing the "High Church dignitaries of the last generation", others "the Tory Aristocracy", Keble "is of the country clergy", Pusey moulded by German universities and Arabic studies, Newman himself indebted to the friendship of Whately. These men have come together by no mere external influence but moved by deep moral causes that are not seen. Among their followers some are unwise, extravagant or over-enthusiastic. "It must be so in the nature of things; it cannot be helped; a mixed multitude went out of Egypt with the Israelites." The leaders "are not answerable for the dust and din which attends any great moral movement. The truer doctrines are, the more liable they are to be perverted."

The Liberalism and the "motley Protestantism" that disfigure the Church of England will not always obscure her essential Catholicity. "It is very certain that neither Puritanism nor Liberalism has any permanent inheritance within her." The confusion of the moment contains within it the seeds of ruin "it does but occupy the space between contending powers, Catholic truth and Rationalism . . . Then, indeed, will be the stern encounter, when two real and living principles, simple, entire and consistent, one in the Church, the other out of it, at length rush upon one another, contending not for names and words or half views, but for elementary notions and distinctive moral characters."

In one sense the Movement, he claims, is part of something larger than itself, something world wide. Catholicism is stirring in other countries and waking from a long slumber, and the current of opinion, no longer Protestant, points either to Popery or to Pantheism. "The spirit of Luther is dead; but Hildebrand and Loyola are alive . . . Would you rather have your sons and daughters members of the Church of England, or of the Church of Rome?"

It is rare to find a man so deeply absorbed in ideas and so entirely immersed in friendships as was Newman. His friends' grief became his own. Very soon after this article came for one of the chief of these friends, Pusey, the greatest of all possible human sorrows. All through his wife's last illness, Newman kept very close to him in prayer and affection.

"I am afraid of intruding on you," he writes, "and yet I do not like day to pass after day without your hearing from me. You know, should you *like* me to walk with you in the morning, there is no reason why I should not come to you at six as well as any other time. You have but to send me a note overnight . . . I am continually thinking of her, and pray (what I doubt not) that you may have grace so to part from each other that you may meet again in peace."

It has been said that great love marriages are a creation of Christianity. Pusey and his wife had been married for ten years (and in love eleven years before that). Their marriage had been a deeply happy one. Human intercourse seemed unbearable after the loss, but Pusey's mother insisted on his seeing Newman.

". . . Your first visit, 'in the embittered spirit's strife,' was to me like that of an angel sent from God; I shrank from it beforehand, or from seeing any human face, and so I trust that I may the more hope that it was God's doing . . . I pray that he may make you what, as you say, there are so few of, 'a great saint' . . ."[1]

Pusey's prayer for Newman had long been Newman's conviction about Pusey. Several years earlier he had written to Miss Giberne: "I am sure that never was there a man in this world on whom one should feel more tempted to bestow a name which belongs only to God's servants departed—the name of a saint—never a man who happened [more] unconsciously to show . . . entire and absolute surrender of himself in thought word and deed to God's will."

[1] Henry Parry Liddon, D.D., *Life of Pusey*, Vol. II, p. 102.

That Froude, Keble, Pusey, he himself were Catholics, Newman did not doubt. And the Protestant attack on the *Remains* had been a furious attack upon its Catholicism. Many years later, analysing the elements that made up the Movement, Oakeley dissented from this view, especially in the case of Froude—both the journal and the man whom he had known in person.

He observed in Froude, towards the end of his short life, "something of Old Testament religion", a growing severity, a loss of his earlier "bright and sunny cheerfulness" not chargeable solely to ill-health. He found in the journal "an extraordinary suppression of the sentiments of love and joy."

"I think the journal is melancholy," says one reader, "but then every sincere thing of the kind must be so."[1]

Surely the fact was rather that the religion of the *via media* was a melancholy religion with those who took it seriously. Not with Mr. Vincent of *Loss and Gain*, who, because it was a fast day, ordered a plain beef steak and a saddle of mutton ("no Portugal onions, Watkins—or currant jelly"), and a simple pudding ("Charlotte pudding, Watkins—that will do"); not with the young curates whose rector bitterly complained that they praised celibacy and immediately married, and praised fasting but neglected to fast;[2] not for all those on the fringe of the Movement, excited over the eastward posture, or Gregorian music, or Gothic architecture, or candles on the altar, or the length of a surplice. But for those men to whom the Movement was a reality changing and remodelling their lives, it was melancholy, and in so being was exceedingly unlike the Catholicism with which its friends and enemies alike identified it.

The gradations were many in the seriousness with which the way was followed and they are all reflected in Newman's correspondence. Dean Hook writes of Lady Eastnor's daughter who "is one of the Maids of Honour to the Queen and to her I am Confessor. I may state one thing which will shew her excellent training. She and another young Maid of Honour she has brought over to Catholicism *fast* every Friday at the Queen's table by abstaining from pleasant food and by stating their reasons for so doing to the few whose minds are prepared to attend to sacred things."

It seems a world away to turn from this letter to one from Rogers about his sister's death from consumption. She had read

---

[1] Footnote to J. B. Mozley's *Letters*, p. 75. Probably one of the Mozley sisters.
[2] Dean Hook to Newman.

Pusey's Tract on fasting and had long eaten and drunk too little. In winter she had stayed much in a north room without a fire. Rogers writes of her profound unselfishness and of how she had given up her drawing and other pursuits in an unconscious preparation for death. She was not the only but one of the most lovely feminine counterparts of Hurrell himself, and Pusey even more than Newman was their inspiration to asceticism.

But the preachers of the *via media* were reviving Catholicism incompletely: with almost every doctrine the part revived was the less human part: and this because they were always prevented by the rules of their "Branch" of the Church from following out any doctrine to its logical consequences.

Thus, Newman preaching on the Communion of Saints finds a deep consolation in the thought that we are encompassed by a cloud of witnesses, that the invisible Church of the Saints is by far more numerous than the part visible on earth. But he warns his hearers against invoking the Saints. He bids us remember our dead who "beneath the altar wait"—but may we pray for them? Pusey, after his brother's death, wrote to Newman: "They are not separated who are not visibly with us. Dare one pray for them? Will you answer me when I see you? Nothing, I am sure, can be found in Scripture against praying for the dead."[1]

(Incidentally the hesitation on this point was not felt by all Anglicans. For the "Usagers" had introduced a prayer for the dead into the Communion Service, Dr. Johnson prayed for his dead wife, Dr. Routh composed an epitaph showing he believed in it. Moreover the draft of an Article condemning the practice had been altered and the condemnation dropped.)

More and more Newman grew to realise the meaning of Our Lady's office as the Mother of God. Yet he hesitated to say too much of this glorious doctrine, lest his hearers should be led into Roman errors and exaggerations. Pusey asks in another letter whether it is permissible, with caution, to let a dying man look at a crucifix. James Mozley feared the Bishop would comment unfavourably on the crosses in the stonework of Newman's Littlemore church, while a cross and flowers on the altar were very extreme and usually forbidden. Oakeley was accused of justifying candles on the altar by London fogs, and incense by bad smells. There were no statues of saints, no rosaries, no votive candles, or sanctuary lamps, no crib or Stations of the Cross.

---

[1] Liddon, *Life of Pusey*, Vol. II, p. 112.

Newman and Froude believed in celibacy, but they were forbidden the consolations of a religious home in a community of like-minded men. They fasted rigorously but can we imagine them feasting heartily? They were hedged with cautions lest they slip at any time from the *via media*. Even talking of Holy Communion they must be careful—they believed in the Real Presence, but they must not fall into the Roman error of Transubstantiation. Might they recognise *some* sacrificial aspect in the Communion Service—or would that be admitting "sacrifices of Masses?" Despite its real beauties, the *via media* was a bleak road and hard to walk.

Newman's sermons with all their glory are often in the same minor key as the *Remains* and have been, therefore, called Calvinist. (Dean Church speaks of "that severe and solemn minor which reigns throughout.") There is, it is true, a tinge of his old Calvinism in a few of the sermons, but Newman was far too good a theologian for this to be frequent. Calvinist is not the right word: it would be more exact to say of Newman that he had the Bible without having the Church to explain it.

He got far more than most men out of the Bible—far more than most Catholics: yet he, like all of us, needed the Church even to get from the Bible all that genius could find there. One interesting example is a sermon on Christ's Eucharistic Presence. There is a marvellous treatment of the analogy between the miracle of the loaves and the Blessed Sacrament, between Christ's treatment of the doubting Jews over His Divinity and over His Sacramental Presence—and then he uses against "Roman" developments the exact argument that Hampden had used about the Trinity. We must leave, he says, this sacred mystery simply as given to us by Scripture, "Our Lord's own words contain marvel enough, even without adding anything to them by way of explanation."

Newman is to the full a Bible Christian. Whenever he is arguing with Protestants, it is easy for him to show how far more Biblical he is than they. They were highly eclectic, he knew every line of the inspired volume and there was no part he did not use. Like medieval sermons his are often for pages on end a mosaic of Bible texts. He preaches constantly from Biblical topics—and many of the sermons cannot but frighten us: on Balaam, on the Indignation of the Lord, on the Unprofitable Servant, on Christ's Fasts, on Apostolic Abstinence, on the Cross of Christ, on the Weapons of the Saints, on Warfare the Condition of Victory.

His discussion of the forgiveness of post-baptismal sin is especially interesting. Revolted by the Evangelical assurance that faith alone is needed for the sinner's acceptance by God, Newman stresses the gospel emphasis on repentance—St. Peter, St. Mary Magdalen, the Prodigal Son. But without the Catholic teaching on the Sacrament of Penance, he dares not pronounce that repentance is followed by full forgiveness in this life.

I have listened to sermons almost infinitely inferior in power to Newman's on Mary Magdalen or St. Peter, but they have ever had this advantage: they have bidden us look less at the weeping penitent than at the loving Master saying: "Thy sins are forgiven thee"—nay even "Lovest thou me more than these"—"Feed my lambs, feed my sheep." We miss in the Tractarians the thought that even sin may "serve"—that

> ......only Heaven
> Means crown'd not vanquished when it says forgiven.

The absence of the Church gives us, I think, a key to the absence of joy in many of the sermons. Chesterton has pointed out the falsity of the common idea that the Church has obscured the Gospel picture of a loving gentle Saviour and has substituted a God of wrath. The truth is almost opposite. We can, indeed, find in the Gospels a God of love, but at first view, it is the God of justice that we see there. The Christ who scourged the money-changers out of the Temple, called the Pharisees whited sepulchres, said to the first of His Apostles: "Get thee behind me, Satan," and in the Sermon on the Mount spoke six times of the eternal punishments of Hell, needed not that the Church should emphasise the fear of His anger.

The Church has ever turned to us the merciful and loving face of God. She has shown us His Sacred Heart pierced for man. She has taken us back to His Childhood and bidden us gaze at the Baby with His arms around His mother's neck. She has told us that that mother is also our mother and has pity on all poor sinners.

Never explaining away the hard sayings of the Gospel, the Church in her history, her liturgy, her living daily commerce with men's souls, has cast a light upon the Gospels that at once clarifies and humanises them. Where they tell us of men making themselves eunuchs for the Kingdom of Heaven, she does not deny the inmost meaning of this fearful image; but she shows us the virgin saints shining in their glory and beside them the saints of home and married life. Every virgin has had a mother, and we all have for our own Christ's virgin mother.

The hidden life of Nazareth has only one verse given to it in the Gospels, but by the Church is drawn out into meditations that make us realise its significance: the carpenter helping in Joseph's shop, sawing and planing, joining and hammering, eating and sleeping, talking to His neighbours, obeying His parents—for thirty years.

The Church gathers up the fragments of the Gospels lest any be lost: she changes the proportions just so much as life must change the proportion of the written word. The teaching of three years, the sufferings of three days, take longer to tell than the labours of thirty years—but they did not take longer to live. The Church gives Christ's life by living it, for she is His Mystical Body upon earth.

In all their refinements on the Church, how could the Tractarians experience this? Theologically, Newman almost knew it; but although in solitude he read his Breviary, he could not so join with the Church's joy as fully to rejoice with all her children.

To one who felt strongly drawn towards Rome he wrote, "You are framing in idea a religion all of joy. No, a sinner's religion must have gloom and sorrow. Even in speaking of Rome you dwell upon the more beautiful and glorious views it sets before you; you forget what a true Church must have . . . its abasing, its chill, its severe doctrines."

Wearied out with his Lenten fast, he preached one Easter on the subdued rejoicing, the sober joy with which we should keep the feast. But the Catholic Church is not sober: she is ringing bells, she is unveiling statues, she is crowding flowers on to the altar, she is lighting lamps and candles, exclaiming *Lumen Christi*, she is crying *Exultet*. Let the choirs of Heaven rejoice over the victory of their King, let the faithful on earth rejoice, for they share in His triumph: *Alleluia! Alleluia! Alleluia!*—Did Newman, I wonder, ever quote St. Paul's amazing words: "Be ye not drunk with wine . . . but be ye filled with the Holy Spirit?"

Often, indeed, the sermons are saying with perhaps more perfect poetry than the hymn itself: "Lead kindly light, amid the encircling gloom, Lead Thou me on."

Four Advent sermons in Volume V are preached on the text:
"Thine eyes shall see the King in His beauty: they shall behold
the land that is very far off." Their note of yearning for something distant contrasts curiously with the Liturgy. Christ is
not far off in Advent. He is very near to us. The skies are called
on to rain down, the earth to open and bring forth, our Saviour.
Day by day expectation grows intenser: there is something almost
breathless in the excitement of the last weeks. *Regem venturum
Dominum, venite adoremus* turns into *Prope est jam Dominus*—the
Lord is nigh. *Veniet et non tardabit,* Alleluia. He is coming in
splendour, let all the world adore, be ready and go forth to meet
Him, fear not, He will come to thee, for all things are accomplished
that the Angel spoke to Mary.

The subjects of some of Newman's Advent sermons are curious:
"Unreal Words", "Shrinking from Christ's Coming"—and at
Christmas: "Equanimity", "The State of Innocence". In
reaction from Evangelical excitement his key expressions seem
to be: reverence, peace, tranquillity, holy fear, rejoicing with
trembling. But who can tremble at Christmastide? Nor is the
Liturgy tranquil, peaceful, or fearful. At moments it seems
hardly reverent: the excitement is too great. In the Parochial
Sermons we are looking back at Bethlehem or forward to the
Judgment and the end of the world. But in the Church's Liturgy,
something is happening here and now. God is coming again as a
man to men, as a child to children: He will come tomorrow:
mane videbitis: wait a little, a very little and it is today. The child
wakes up and seizes his Christmas stocking, he hears the rustle
of the Christmas tree in the next room, the Baby Jesus is lying
in the straw where yesterday Our Lady and St. Joseph were
waiting for Him. Something is *happening*: today Christ is born:
today angels are singing on earth: archangels are rejoicing:
today the just exult as they cry out: "Glory be to God on
high."

O no, don't let us be sober: above all, don't let us be tranquil
over the most exciting thing that ever happened.

In January, 1839, Newman gathered together the strong things
that he and others had said against Rome and used them in the
Advertisements at the end of the Movement publications. No
shadow of a doubt had yet crossed his own mind, and this was
only "to meet the public clamour against myself and others and

to satisfy the Bishop . . . Conscious as I was that my opinions in religion were not gained, as the world said, from Roman sources, but were, on the contrary, the birth of my own mind. . . . I had a scorn of the imputations which were heaped upon me."[1]

One way in which Newman later described that organic growth of doctrine which he traced in his *Development* was by saying that the Catholic Church had magnified all the great truths revealed to her. But at this time he was looking back over the centuries through the diminishing glass of time: what had been living reality became through that glass an unsubstantial wraith. Yet too it was through that glass that his first glimpse came of a vision that at first dizzied and appalled him.

The letters of 1839 show him earnestly working on the Fathers, especially the period of the Monophysite heresy. At first he saw in the historical scene material for each side in the Anglo-Roman controversy "the great power of the Pope (as great as he claims now almost) and the marvellous interference of the civil power, as great almost as our Kings." But a little later to the same correspondent (Rogers) he writes, "Since I wrote to you I have had the first real hit from Romanism which has happened to me . . . Dr. Wiseman's article in the new 'Dublin'. I must confess it has given me a stomach ache."

Two things had come upon him together—the position of St. Leo in the Monophysite heresy and that of St. Augustine against the Donatists. "The drama of religion," he wrote later "and the combat of truth and error were ever one and the same . . . The shadow of the fifth century was on the sixteenth. It was like a spirit rising from the troubled waters of the old world with the shape and lineaments of the new."

Jean Guitton sees Newman bending over the mirror of the past that he might discern in it the Anglican Church—but now that vision was clouded by another, "I saw my face in that mirror and I was a Monophysite. The Church of the *via media* was in the position of the Oriental Communion, Rome was where she now is and the Protestants were the Eutychians."[2]

Rome was where she now is: this was the stab, the haunting doubt that might leave him but would return again. He had, he tells us, seen a ghost.

[1] *Apologia*, pp. 62–63.
[2] He sets all this out fully in a letter to Mrs. William Froude, given in Appendix B.

The Wiseman article was another trouble. Wiseman had shown how St. Augustine had applied to the Donatist controversy not Antiquity but a simpler test—the judgment of the living and universal Church: *securus judicat orbis terrarum*. Here then was Antiquity deciding against itself.

Walking in the New Forest with Henry Wilberforce, Newman confided to him the blow he had received, adding that he felt confident that on further reading and consideration he would see his way out of the difficulty. Much agitated, Wilberforce expressed the hope that Newman would die rather than join the Church of Rome. "He replied with deep seriousness, that he had thought, if ever the time should come when he was in serious danger, of asking his friends to pray that if it was not indeed the will of God, he might be taken away before he did it." [1]

In the *Apologia* he writes, "I had seen the shadow of a hand upon the wall . . . The heavens had opened and closed again. The thought for the moment had been 'The Church of Rome will be found right after all'; and then it had vanished. My old convictions remained as before."

[1] *Letters and Correspondence*, Vol. II, p. 257.

CHAPTER XXVI

A Philosophy of Faith

NEWMAN occasionally preached at St. Mary's not as parish priest but as the selected University Preacher. Further, every M.A. of the University had his "turn" in the University Pulpit and he might delegate this turn to another. So Newman had his own and his friends' turns. The attacks on Tractarianism were met not by contrary polemic but by the deep philosophy of faith that can be read today in the *Oxford University Sermons*.

Six years, as we have noted, separates the first from the second half of the book, but a profound continuity of thought bridges those six years and the later sermons are a deep and ripe fulfilment of youth's promise. The book is, Newman said, the least theological he had ever published. But it was the most philosophical and perhaps the most penetratingly psychological: from its lines of thought grew the *Grammar of Assent* and *The Development of Christian Doctrine*.

In the *University Sermons* Jean Guitton sees a philosophical commentary on the *History of the Arians* (finished just before the Mediterranean journey in 1832). Newman's chief masters were the Fathers of the Alexandrian School. *The Arians* was undertaken in the spirit of Traditional Anglicanism—the defence of the Council of Nicaea, the return to early Christianity. Newman believed, like Bishop Bull, that in defending the faith of Nicaea he could oppose the Socinians and the Deists on the one hand and the Roman innovators on the other. "He had too", writes Guitton in a passage already referred to, "a special predilection for the Church of Alexandria: learned, well-read, mystical, ascetic, liberal, self-contained, alert in its faith it was in his eyes the prototype of the Church of England. The religious philosophy of the Alexandrian Fathers recalled the Platonism of the Oxonians. . . . The Sophists were the Noetics. Paul of Samosata was not unlike Whately. The Arians might be compared to the Protestants. Bending over this far-away past Newman saw in a mirror an idealised picture of his surroundings and reassured himself with the reflection."[1]

Although in 1839 Newman had received the first blow from Rome on his own chosen ground of the Fathers, there is little trace of this in the *University Sermons*, preached in that year and the two or three years that followed. Their commentary on Church History lies rather in their discussion of *how* men believe in Christianity and on the relations between faith and reason. To the first Christians Revelation had come as a fact offered for their acceptance, and Newman held strongly that the modern insistence on evidences tended to obscure its unique and startling quality.

In these sermons he treats of faith, "as the chosen instrument connecting heaven and earth, as a novel principle of action most powerful in the influence which it exerts both on the heart and on the Divine view of us." The common idea of faith, in part a heritage of the eighteenth century *Christianity not Mysterious*, reduced it to almost nothing beyond an acceptance of evidences:

but investigation and proof belong to man prior to the Gospel: therefore Faith is something higher than Reason . . . The word of God is offered to a man; and, on its being offered, he has Faith in it . . . Faith is the reasoning of a religious mind, or of what Scripture calls a right or renewed heart.

If children, if the poor, if the busy, can have true Faith, yet cannot weigh evidence, evidence is not the simple foundation on which Faith is built. If the great bulk of serious men believe, not because they have examined evidence, but because they are disposed in a certain way,—because they are " ordained to eternal life", this must be God's order of things.

This is not to deny the intellectual quality of faith. "Faith is an intellectual act; right Faith is an intellectual act done in a certain moral disposition." Faith is "an exercise of the Reason, so spontaneous, unconscious and unargumentative as to seem at first sight even to be a moral act." "Almighty God influences and works in us, through our minds, not without them or in spite of them." Religion is "the system of relations existing between us and a supreme Power." "The philosopher aspires towards a divine *principle*; the Christian towards a divine Agent." God is "the object of the mind's contemplation."

[1] Guitton, *La Philosophie de Newman*, p. 3.

The idea of the mind's *contemplation* is vital in Newman's thought. Too much had the age in which he grew up thought of reason only as analytical, discursive, argumentative. "It is as absurd", said Newman, "to argue men as to torture them into believing."

Many professed Christians believe on habit from heredity and surroundings,

but today as in the first ages of Revelation there are men who accept the divine fact with personal realization . . . They go out of themselves to meet Him Who is unseen, and they discern Him in such symbols of Him as they find ready provided for them . . . they feel that the external religion offered them elicits into shape, and supplies the spontaneous desires and presentiments of their minds . . . The safeguard of Faith is a right state of heart. This it is that gives it birth; it also disciplines it . . . It is love which forms it out of the rude chaos into an image of Christ . . . It was from lack of love towards Christ that the Jews discerned not in Him the shepherd of their souls. "Ye believe not because ye are not of My sheep. My sheep hear my voice and follow Me." . . . It is the new life and not the natural reason, which leads the soul to Christ . . . The divinely enlightened mind sees in Christ the very Object whom it desires to love and worship—the Object correlative of its own affections; and it trusts Him or believes from loving Him.

"True faith admits, but does not require, the exercise of what is commonly understood by reason." And "Reason may put its sanction upon the acts of Faith, without in consequence being the source from which Faith springs." We must not "mistake a critical for a creative power." "Reason may be the judge without being the origin of Faith . . . Faith may be justified by reason without making use of it."

Paley's *Evidences of Christianity* was in much use as an examination book and Newman did not agree with Paley's view which "would imply the necessity of a conscious investigation and verification of [Revelation's] claims." He added that it would be "as paradoxical to prohibit religious enquiry and inference as to make it imperative". He did not deny the usefulness of the usual type of evidence—for some minds. He pointed out that Hume in rejecting the mass of evidence for miracles was doing so purely on a presumption, "the antecedent improbability is a sufficient refutation of the evidence".

The danger was that excessive stress on one *type* of reasoning smothered the deeper and less producible lines of thought—that the reasons put forward were not the most real but the easiest to express. ". . . only such reasons are in point as can be exhibited in simple propositions; the multiform and intricate assemblage of considerations, which really lead to judgment and action, must be attenuated or mutilated into a major and a minor premise."

While Hume had rejected the evidence for miracles simply because of their antecedent improbability, "for a believing mind" it is antecedent probability that gives meaning to those arguments from facts which are commonly called the Evidences of Revelation; "whereas mere probability proves nothing, mere facts persuade no one . . . probability is to fact as the soul to the body; . . . mere presumptions may have no force, but mere facts have no warmth. A mutilated and defective evidence suffices for persuasion where the heart is alive; but dead evidences, however perfect, can but create a dead faith."

Newman has said of himself that he had an exceedingly sceptical intellect and he thanked God for saving him morally from what might have come upon him intellectually—general scepticism. To this may be added the remark in his 1871 Introduction that while preaching these sermons he got no help from Anglican, and knew no Catholic, theologians. Lines of thought that he was to draw more completely in *The Grammar of Assent* are brilliantly indicated here but certain expressions he later changed. For instance he said as a Catholic: "Ten thousand difficulties do not make one doubt", but here he seems to suggest that we can at once believe and doubt. Likewise he guards in a later footnote the very startling remark, "It is indeed a great question whether Atheism is not as philosophically consistent with the phenomena of the physical world *taken by themselves*, as the doctrine of a creative and governing power." He italicised "taken by themselves", in the footnote and added St. Paul's judgment that atheists are "inexcusable"; but whether in reaction from Paley or because the moral element was to him always the overwhelming one he does appear in this sermon, "Faith and Reason contrasted as Habits of Mind", to undervalue—indeed to despise—external evidences. No man can be strong at all points: nothing would have been easier for Newman than to repeat the traditional arguments as efficiently as any other clergyman would have repeated them. But this he would never do. His thought was his own and was real creative thought. "Reasoning", he said, "or the exercise of Reason, is a living spontaneous energy within us, not an art." Any treatment of evidences that did not admit "the legitimate influence and logical import of the moral feelings"—would have been unconvincing to himself and he would not use it. He writes:

For is not this the error, the common and fatal error of the world, to think itself a judge of religious Truth without preparation of heart . . . "The pure in heart shall see God": "To the meek mysteries are revealed . . . the darkness comprehendeth it not." Gross eyes see not; heavy ears hear not. But in the schools of the world the ways towards Truth are considered high roads, open to all men, however disposed, at all times. Truth is to be approached without homage . . . Men . . . will enter upon the most sacred points of Faith at the moment, at their pleasure,—if it so happen, in a careless frame of mind, in their hours of recreation, over the wine-cup. Is it wonderful that they so frequently end in becoming indifferentists, and conclude that Religious Truth is but a name, that all men are right and all wrong, from witnessing externally the multitude of sects and parties, and from the clear consciousness they possess within, that their own enquiries end in darkness?

Many years later James Anthony Froude wrote a novel entitled *The Nemesis of Faith* in which he says, "We thought we were Catholics but we were only Newmanites." It is rather a feeble story and one wonders today that in its time it was held highly dangerous to men's faith. Perhaps it was, being a vigorous expression of the irreligious mood of the moment. Adoring the memory of Newman to his life's end, indignantly repudiating Kingsley's attack on his honesty ("he was on the contrary the most transparent of men"), Froude yet assigns to him a chief share in the destruction of his own faith. He had been quite content with the arguments of Paley, and had accepted Paley's account of such writers as Hume so that it came as a shock to hear Newman's admissions of the force of their arguments. "It was injudicious in Newman", he says, "to throw out before us thus abruptly an opinion so extremely agitating." Not philosophical himself, he had been helped not at all by Newman's line on faith and reason: he gained from it only the idea that the best to be said for Christianity was that it was "probable."

Are we to take literally Froude's assertion that Newman began the destruction of his faith? Jean Guitton accepts it. He speaks of a terrible remedy that poisoned those it did not cure and lists with Froude, Matthew Arnold, Stanley and Mark Pattison. But surely (except for Pattison, who gives quite different reasons for his own loss of faith) these were rather the pupils of Arnold than of Newman, under whose influence they came only briefly and superficially. Newman speaks in letters and diaries of the rising tide of infidelity and of his fears concerning Arnold's pupils. Wilfrid Ward says that Arnold injected his followers with a little rationalism just as Newman injected his with a little Popery, to immunise them. But in neither case was the injection successful: the diseases assumed in these very men their most virulent form!

Guitton thinks that Newman offered to his followers only the alternatives seen by himself—unbelief or Catholicism. This was later Huxley's view: there are in fact, he said, only two alternatives: Newman chooses one, I the other. But Newman denied that in being thus logical for himself he had insisted on the same logic for others.

My father is probably more nearly right than Guitton in saying that Newman did not sow scepticism in Froude's mind. He recognised that it was already sown and tried to supply an antidote—unsuccessfully in Froude's case, very successfully in that of others. But while the *University Sermons* are marvellous in their positive philosophy, I think we must recognise a certain wilfulness in Newman's repeated attacks on evidences. He really knew better than to say that atheism is philosophically consistent even with material creation alone. Because it isn't. The traditional arguments for a First Cause have often been laughed at, never answered. The fact that there are intelligent men who cannot grasp them in no way invalidates them.

Newman was building a new and magnificent psychological and spiritual form of apologetic—the apologetic of an understanding of revealed doctrine and of the mind that is to receive it. But surely he might—as he sometimes did—leave the old arguments to do their work in their own way, however irritating Paley's book was to a mind like his own.

It is almost certain that Froude would anyhow have become an agnostic: his mind was acute but shallow, he could never have kept his childhood's faith as he seems in *Short Studies* to fancy he might have done in face of the nineteenth-century world. He was one of those men described by Newman, "who are commonly Latitudinarians in religion . . . who regard the pursuit of truth only as a syllogistic process."

To W. G. Ward, also a sceptical intellect, these sermons brought a renewal of Faith: forty years later he gave them to his son to save him from doubt: for multitudes of young men in that dawning of an era of scepticism they did the same thing: offering the object of faith as a reality that the mind could seize, not merely as the conclusion of a logical process. In this as in so much else Newman lived in the early Church where Revelation was a fact which Christians apprehended with that whole soul which is our whole mind.

These sermons should be read with the Introduction in which Newman later distinguished the various meanings in which he used the word "reason". Haunted by the Scriptural teaching that the Gospel was for the poor, the little ones, yet certain too of its intellectual power, he was led into the consideration that thought is deeper than argument can manifest, deeper, indeed, than its own expression or its own realisation in the mind. Men in general, he said, reason well though they may argue badly: "their professed grounds are no sufficient measure of their real ones." "All men have a reason but not all men can give a reason." "The mind ranges to and fro, and spreads out and advances forward with a quickness which has become a proverb and a subtlety and versatility which baffle investigation."

In this famous passage he compares the genius in any field of thought to a climber "who by quick eye, prompt hand and firm foot, ascends how he knows not himself, by personal endowments and practice, rather than by rule." But he will not allow that this is only true of the genius: "Such mainly is the way in which all men, gifted or not gifted, commonly reason—not by rule but by an inward faculty."

"The act of mind," he says in another place, "by which an unlearned person savingly believes the Gospel, on the word of his teacher, may be analogous to the exercise of sagacity in a great statesman or general, supernatural grace doing for the uncultivated reason what genius does for them."

In nothing do we more see the influence of his work on the *Arians* than in the two last sermons, "Wisdom as contrasted with

N

Faith and with Bigotry", and "The Theory of Developments in Religious Doctrine." There is no better way of tracing the progress of Newman's own mind than by reading these sermons preached respectively in 1841 and 1843 after reading the early ones. In a sermon of 1831 on "The Usurpations of Reason", he had said, "The forward Reason stepped in upon the yet unenclosed ground of doctrine, and attempted to describe there, from its own resources, an image of the Invisible. Henceforth the Church was obliged, in self-defence, to employ the gifts of the intellect in the cause of God, to trace out (as near as might be) the faithful shadow of those truths, which unlearned piety admits and acts upon, without the medium of clear intellectual representation."

But in the later sermons he sees definitions no longer as a regrettable result of heresy but as the fruit of the Church's contemplation of the Divine Idea revealed to her.

Faith, he tells us, is the beginning, and wisdom the crown, of our life as Christians. "Faith is the elementary grace which is required of all." But it is "a principle of mental growth also in an especial way." Both Faith and Wisdom are intellectual habits, Faith being elementary and Wisdom "that orderly and mature development of thought, which in earthly language goes by the name of science and philosophy."

Comparing the natural order with the supernatural, he touches on the sources of mental enlargement: splendid scenery, the heavens thrown open by the telescope, the sight of foreign animals, "their strangeness and startling novelty, the originality (if I may use the term) and mysteriousness of their forms and gestures": again, seeing the world by entering into various societies of men: nay, sin itself which "brings with it its own enlargement of mind", so that its victims "look upon their state of innocence with a sort of pity and contempt, as if it were below the dignity of men."

Religion on the other hand "has its own enlargement", so that the uneducated on "looking into themselves . . . and studying the inspired Word seem to become, in point of intellect, different beings from what they were before." And men (here he glances at his own history) who have known nothing better than the nonconformist or Latitudinarian schools, "introduced to the theology of the early Church, will often have a vivid sense of enlargement."

In this sermon Newman's enthusiasm for philosophy is given full scope. "No arguments in favour of Religion", he tells us, "are of much account but such as rest on a philosophical basis," and we feel there is another side-kick at the unlucky Paley in the allusion to "the rhetorical or forensic Evidences" which "whatever their merits, which I have no wish to disparage, are not philosophical."

"Philosophy is reason exercised upon knowledge": it "implies a connected view of the old with the new; an insight into the bearing and influence of each part upon every other; without which there is no whole and could be no centre. It is the knowledge not only of things, but of their mutual relations. It is organised and therefore living knowledge."

Returning again to the possibility that uneducated men can be Christian "philosophers", he also returns to his thoughts on implicit or unconscious reasoning. "Since Faith is the characteristic of all Christians, a peasant may take the same view of human affairs in detail as a philosopher; and we are often perplexed whether to say that such persons are intellectually gifted or not . . . they cannot defend themselves; they are easily perplexed and silenced; and if they set themselves to reason, they use arguments which appear to be faulty, as being but types and shadows of those which they really feel, and attempts to analyse that vast system of thought which is their life, but not their instrument."

In the final sermon Newman brands as Protestant that fear of definition which he himself had felt ten years earlier, which he had combated in Dr. Hampden, which he had come to see as "the badge of heresy; its dogmas are unfruitful; it has no theology. . . . Deduct its remnant of Catholic theology and what remains? Polemics . . . protests . . . Biblical Criticism . . . Evidences of Religion . . . Heresy denies to the Church what is wanting in itself." It had come to suspect all theology as "words without meaning, and deductions which come to nothing . . . private opinions, which if individuals will hold for themselves, at least they have no right to impose upon others."

Against all this he set the vision gradually dawning upon him, choosing Our Lady for its exemplar and preaching from the text, "Mary kept all these things and pondered them in her heart."

"She does not think it enough to accept; she dwells upon it; not enough to possess, she uses it; not enough to assent, she develops it; not enough to submit the Reason, she reasons upon it. . . . And thus she symbolises to us, not only the faith of the unlearned, but of the Doctors of the Church also." She will be our example in "the use of Reason in investigating the doctrines of Faith."

Faith is assent to divine truth: it is acceptance of fact—and "realising" this divine truth "is the very life of true developments." Fresh definitions do not add to the original truth. They "are used to express portions of the great idea vouchsafed to us, can never really be confused with the idea itself, which all such propositions taken together can but reach and cannot exceed."

This sermon is a first step towards the book on Development— and in it Newman remarks that he would need a volume to draw out all he has to say on the subject. But two special characteristics of his thought may be touched on here that are much in evidence in his earlier as well as his later works: his love of analogy and his views on economy.

Following Butler he delights in drawing comparisons between the order of human life and the divine revelation built upon it: he is always saying with St. Thomas that grace builds upon the order of nature—but I think that in some of these sermons and in the *Development* itself the very original quality of his thought makes the transition occasionally confusing. Very close attention is necessary to follow his meaning with any exactness.

The word "Economy", Newman tells us, got into the language in an especial sense through Froude's *Remains*. Divine Reality is so far beyond human languages that God teaches us as we might teach children by an economy that is an accommodation to our intelligence: much must be held back, much taught only analogically. We in our turn can only teach the unbeliever or the child by expedients which adapt our teaching to their state. Rogers is quoted in Newman's correspondence as reproaching him with "economising" too much. For Rogers never fully understood Newman's meaning.

"We must dispense and 'divide'," wrote Newman, "the word of truth, if we would not have it changed as far as they are concerned into a word of falsehood; for what is short of truth in the letter may be to them the most perfect truth, that is the nearest approach to truth, compatible with their condition." Obviously, as Newman himself says, this theory is open to abuse; and a tract by Isaac Williams, called "Reserve in communicating

Religious Knowledge", got very rough handling from the Bishops of the Establishment in a number of Charges to their clergy. But while they laid stress on the word "reserve", Newman's stress was on the word "communicate". Simply to say something may not be to communicate it. If our senses were different equally different would be our perception of the world around us. Thus the sound of a trumpet typified for a blind man the colour scarlet—typified it but did not fully convey it. Our ideas even of the external world are not adequate: "the senses do not convey to us any true idea of matter, but only an idea commensurate with sensible impressions."

Thus with the definitions of theology, "there may be a certain correspondence between the idea, though earthly, and its heavenly archetype, such, that that idea belongs to the archetype, in a sense in which no other earthly idea belongs to it, as being the nearest approach to it which our present state allows." Our minds cannot "fathom the depth" or measure the course of the deep mysteries of God, yet we should use them if it be but to reach "a shadow of the unseen", "the nearest approximation to truth which our condition admits."

For an example of the difficulty he is analysing, Newman chooses the scriptural statement "that the sun moves and the earth is stationary" and that of contemporary science "that the earth moves and the sun is comparatively at rest". He comments:

How can we determine which of these opposite statements is the very truth, till we know what motion is? If our idea of motion be but an accidental result of our present senses, neither proposition is true, and both are true; neither true philosophically, both true for certain practical purposes in the system in which they are respectively found; and physical science will have no better meaning when it says that the earth moves, than plane astronomy when it says that the earth is still.

Against this passage Edward Watkin told me Leslie Stephen had pencilled a comment giving vent to the honest anger of the scientific rationalist at the "priestly sophistry" that made such a statement possible. "Little did he anticipate," writes Mr. Watkin, "that, rightly or wrongly—for one cannot build on scientific fashions of thought—twentieth century science would accept as its new truth the sophistry of this clerical reactionary. Newman in an age of scientific dogmatism anticipated Einstein's relativity view of the astronomical statement of the motions of the heavenly bodies. Whitehead has stated it and applied it precisely to this point. . . . Neither Galileo nor his opponents stood for the absolute truth," though Galileo's seems to have been rather "the better economy". Scientists of the last century did not certainly see Einstein in a vision. It is a mark of Newman's genius that with no scientific training he almost did so.

I hastened to the London Library to read Stephen's words for myself. But, alas, the volume could not be traced and I was told that a bomb had fallen on the very middle of the Sermon section. There remained a set of the *Parochial Sermons* annotated by Stephen showing the same curious contempt for the "narrowness" and duplicity of Newman's mind. Carlyle said Newman had "the brains of a moderate sized rabbit" and Kingsley asked "What then does Dr. Newman mean?" So too with Stephen. The greatest talent can come to terms with its own age, genius hardly ever.

Newman's *Parochial Sermons* on the existence and the power of angels, the need of repentance for sin, the littleness of man, the almighty power, the sternness yet the love of God, man's free will and God's foreknowledge, Heaven and Hell, Leslie Stephen does not so much attack as dismiss with the scorn of the grown person for the toys of a child. "A very queer statement," "eternal torments—the genuine article", "If God loves me why does he hit me?" "Oh J.H.N. a bit of bluster!", "*Oh* J.H.N.!"

It is surely the commentator rather than the writer of these sermons who looks childish—but of all those old rationalists one feels that they were also childlike. They accepted their teachers with simplicity, they were humble before the facts of nature— which they did not recognise as economies of God's devising. Surely they have entered the Kingdom of God as children—and been considerably surprised by what they found there!

Explicit theology was not for Newman the only instrument through whose notes God sounds His harmonies. In his youth he had suggested that poetry was the mysticism of the age, and music had always been for him supreme in that "whole series of impressions made on us by the senses" in which he saw "a Divine economy suited to our need and the token of realities distinct from themselves." So now perhaps as he pondered he took his violin and tried through it to learn the unknowable and to utter the unutterable.

Let us take another instance, of an outward and earthly form, or economy, under which great wonders unknown seem to be typified; I mean musical sounds, as they are exhibited most perfectly in instrumental harmony. There are seven notes in the scale; make them fourteen; yet what a slender outfit for so vast an enterprise! What science brings so much out of so little? Out of what poor elements does some great master in it create his new world! Shall we say that all this exuberant inventiveness is a mere ingenuity or trick of art, like some game or fashion of the day, without reality, without meaning? We may do so; and then, perhaps, we shall also account the science of theology to be a matter of words; yet, as there is a divinity in the theology of the Church, which those who feel cannot communicate, so is there also in the wonderful creation of sublimity and beauty of which I am speaking. To many men the very names which the science employs are utterly incomprehensible. To speak of an idea or a subject seems to be fanciful or trifling, to speak of the views which it opens upon us to be childish extravagance; yet is it possible that that inexhaustible evolution and disposition of notes, so rich yet so simple, so intricate yet so regulated, so various yet so majestic, should be a mere sound, which is gone and perishes? Can it be that those mysterious stirrings of heart, and keen emotions, and strange yearnings after we know not what, and awful impressions from we know not whence, should be wrought in us by what is unsubstantial, and comes and goes, and begins and ends in itself? It is not so; it cannot be. No; they have escaped from some high sphere; they are the outpourings of eternal harmony in the medium of created sound; they are echoes from our Home; they are the voice of Angels, or the Magnificat of Saints, or the living laws of Divine Governance, or the Divine Attributes; something are they besides themselves, which we cannot compass, which we cannot utter,—though mortal man, and he perhaps not otherwise distinguished above his fellows, has the gift of eliciting them.

Through all these exercises of mind and of heart Newman realised God "training us heavenward", through "all the information it has pleased [Him] to vouchsafe to us whether in nature or in grace." He prayed for himself and his hearers to "the Gracious and Merciful God, the Father of Lights, that in all our exercises of Reason, His Gift, we may thus use it, as He would have us, in the obedience of Faith, with a view to His Glory, with an aim at His Truth, in dutiful submission to His Will, for the comfort of His elect, for the edification of Holy Jerusalem His Church."

To receive into mind and heart the great objects offered to us by Revelation.

To realise, to contemplate that revealed Truth.

To edify or build up the Church's majestic temple of theology.

These were the objects, as now of Newman's preaching, so always of his whole life.

Beginning with the thought of Our Lady meditating God's Revelation, contemplating that Divine Word which she above all creatures held substantially in human mind and body, he seems already on the verge of crying with the Church: Our Lady, Seat of Wisdom pray for us.

CHAPTER XXVII

Peace and Conflict 1840–1841

THE GREAT bundle of Newman's letters to Jemima chronicles every happening and almost every hope and fear of these years. Even if there were more letters to Harriett also that have been destroyed, the messages to her show Jemima as his chief correspondent, sensitively aware of and responsive to his changing feelings. I imagine both she and her husband must have been a little dismayed when, very happy to be godfather to their first child, Newman wrote to John Mozley, "As Jemima has a memory for days, let her know the 2nd of May is the feast of St. Athanasius. I therefore propose he should be called Athanasius Mozley." May 2nd was also, it appeared, Newman's first full day at school and the day he collapsed at Leonforte. Despite these coincidences the parents called their son Herbert, adding Newman as a second name. His uncle's letters often allude to him, telling how a Littlemore parishioner dreamed of him, sending love, glad "that an alliance has been struck up between him and my Aunt. I shall be truly glad to see them."

"Aunt," his father's sister Elizabeth Newman, figures largely in the correspondence: her financial affairs: her comfort, and, above all, her spiritual vagaries. "She has often complained to me," he writes, "about her want of clear perception of religious truths and disordered state of mind . . . I decidedly think that going to those Meeting Houses at Bristol must in every way tend to unsettle her. Nay, the seeing of so many wild people of course—but one can hardly advise her not to go to Frank."

Frank himself was, doubtless, one of the "wild people", for Newman writes (November 1840), "It is a great joy to me, and fitted for this season that I have made it up with Frank," and a few days later, "his tone is, I rejoice to say, as different as possible from what it was years ago." But "I think he has that great defect of imagination or mysticism (so to put it) which will act always in keeping him from the Catholic system." A few months later, it is no question of imagination, but, "most painful

359

indeed," doubts: "Whether the beginning of St. John is written by the Apostle, whether it is inspired, and whether the doctrine is not taken from Philo. And he said in the course of his letter, God forbid he should ever doubt Our Lord's Resurrection. Indeed I do not see where he is to stop. It is like [Blanco] White. It is like the Genevans, the Germans, like Protestantism generally. Whether or not Anglicanism leads to Rome, so far is *clear as day* that Protestantism leads to infidelity."

Nor was Charles any comfort. "He is going on in his old way," writing abusive letters to Frank. "He seems to have written a whole *book* about him, which may dribble through the penny post." In letters to Newman himself Charles "more than hints that he has given up religion. He is very intimate with the Socialists and now does not shrink from the name."

It is little wonder that this visible disintegration within his own family brought moods of depression. In February 1840, he wrote to Jemima, "Everything is miserable." He expected "a great attack on the Bible—indeed I have long done so." Carlyle, "a man of first rate ability . . . quite fascinating as a writer" holds only the view "that Christianity has good *in* it. . . . Then again you have Arnold's school . . . giving up the inspiration of the Old Testament or of all Scripture (I do not say that Arnold himself does). . . . Then you have all your political economists who *cannot* accept (—it is impossible) the Scripture rules about almsgiving, renunciation of wealth, self-denial, etc. . . . All these and many more spirits seem uniting and forming into something shocking."

And then comes the moment of fear of which Jemima all through these years felt the occasional shock, then relief and then renewed fear.

I begin to have serious apprehensions lest any religious body is strong enough to withstand the league of evil but the Roman Church. At the end of the first millenary it withstood the fury of Satan, and now the end of a second is drawing on. It has *tried* strength; what it *has* endured during these last centuries! and it is stronger than ever. We on the other hand have never been tried and come out of trial without practical concessions. I cannot see that we *can* receive the assault of the foe. We are divided among ourselves, like the Jews in their siege. So that it seems to me as if there were coming on a great encounter between infidelity and Rome, and that we should be smashed between them. Certainly the way that good principles have shot up is wonderful! but I am not clear that they are not tending to Rome—not from any necessity in the principles themselves, but from the much greater proximity between Rome and us than between infidelity and us, and that in a time of trouble we naturally look about for allies. I cannot say enough of the wonderful way in which the waters are rising here, and one should be very thankful. The Heads of Houses promise soon to be fairly carried off their legs, and to be obliged to fast and scourge themselves for good company's sake. All this is a miserable prose, a regular talk worth nothing at all, and sure to be falsified by the event.

I am going up to Littlemore till Easter.

To Wood he was writing near the same time, "Anglicanism has never yet been put to the test whether it will bear *life*: it may break to pieces in the rush and transport of existence, and die of joy."

The Littlemore curate, Bloxam, being called home by his father's illness, Newman decided to reside there for Lent 1840, and gives a glimpse at the work left behind in a letter to Jemima: "My Oxford duty is divided between seven persons, and two presses are stopped and one postponed."

Oxford followed him to Littlemore, "Newman's catechizing being," James Mozley writes, "a great attraction this Lent. Men have gone out of Oxford every Sunday to hear it." One feels a little sorry for the children, but James Mozley after listening reports it "very striking, done with much spirit, and the children so up to it, answering with much alacrity," in spite of the gallery of spectators.

Littlemore was a happy spot in those days and, I think, on the whole the year 1840 was a happy year.

In the autumn of 1839, as we have seen, Wiseman's article on the Donatists had given him a bad shock.

The Monophysite controversy had opened his eyes to the fact "that antagonists to Rome and Churches in isolation were always wrong in primitive times", and this he "had felt as a presumption against ourselves"; Wiseman maintained that this fact was "a recognised principle and rule in those ages". The article had, he said, "fidgetted me a good deal. It is the only formidable thing I have seen on the Roman side". But he had rallied quickly. Five years later he writes of this moment:

On my return to Oxford, my immediate business was to set about answering this argument. It is my sincere belief that it is right to resist doubts and to put aside objections to the form of doctrine and the religious system in which we find ourselves. I think such resistance pleasing to God. If it is His will to lead us from them, if the doubt comes from Him, He will repeat the suggestion, He will call us again as He called Samuel, He will make our way clear to us. Fancies, excitements, feelings go and never return—truth comes again and is importunate.[1]

If his fears were right, his Church had not the note of Catholicity, but it might well have other notes. Even upon Catholicity, there was much to be said for the Church of England: and he said it in an Article in the *British Critic* in January 1843.

He lays special stress on the note of sanctity. The English Church has it. The Roman Church has not:

We see it attempting to gain converts among us by unreal representation of its doctrines, plausible statements, bold assertions, appeals to the weaknesses of human nature, to our fancies, our eccentricities, our fears, our frivolities, our false philosophies. We see its agents smiling and nodding and ducking to attract attention, as gipsies make up to truant boys, holding out tales for the nursery and pretty pictures, and gilt gingerbread, and physic concealed in jam, and sugarplums for good children.

He convinced himself. By the end of February, his "personal distress on the point" seems to have left him. But there remained the question: was the Church of England, as he had asserted in the *British Critic* article, *doctrinally* one with the Church of Antiquity? In other words, what of the Thirty-Nine Articles? He was sure they contained "the doctrine of the Old Church. It was a matter of life and death to us to show it." For the rest of 1840 he was writing a Tract (the famous Tract 90) on the subject. But he had no apprehensions as to the results of his enquiry, and the writing of the Tract did not prevent his entering heartily into the life of the parish. The letters to Jemima are full of its details: March 12, 1840: "I have been reforming, or at least lecturing against uncombed hair, and dirty faces and hands; but I find I am not deep in the philosophy of school-girl tidiness." Two days earlier he had written to Wood of another sort of deficiency in his pupils: "I despair almost. The top girls hardly know Adam from Noah." March 13: to Jemima:

[1] Letter to Mrs. William Froude, April 9, 1844.

Can you suggest any method of bringing children punctual, besides going to their parents and making a talk? . . . How far is it good to apply [a] system of bribing? . . . Can you give me any hints in this matter?

[April 1]. The children are improving in their singing. I have had the audacity to lead them and teach them some new tunes. Also I have rummaged out a violin and strung it . . . begun to *lead* them with it, a party of between twenty and thirty, great and little. . . . I have just begun chanting . . . Gregorian chant which the children seem to take to. . . .

. . . I have effected a great reform (for the time) in the girls' hands and faces—lectured with unblushing effrontery on the necessity of their keeping *their work clean* and set them to knit stockings with all their might. Also I am going to give them some neat white pinafores for Church use. . . .

I have drawn up a sort of Liturgy of School Prayers, varying with the season. . . .

I think I shall be here a good deal in future, for it does not do to begin and not go on. If I could get ground I think I should build on it. . . . I live in hopes of your or H's coming through this place in the summer and giving my girls a polishing up.

To Henry Wilberforce he confesses about the same time, "For several days I have been saying to myself, O that Henry would bring his wife here to put my school to rights! I see indeed the girls' hair wanting combing, but I cannot get further in my analysis of the general air of slatternliness which prevails."

In May 1840 nine acres were bought: Newman writes to Tom Mozley for advice on plans for a possible monastery. This idea was never carried out, the only buildings at Littlemore being an old granary turned into cottages and leased by Newman a little later. For the moment the nine acres were being planted with trees—which would, he said, look well by the time he had become an old man. Later in the same year he wrote a jesting letter to his friend Woodgate who had invited him for a visit:

You forget that I am an incipient monk, in my noviciate at least. I am preparing a Monastery at Littlemore and shall shortly retire from the world—so that if the great prospects are destined for me you speak of, I shall be the first Bishop from the Cloister for the last three hundred years—and while I am about it, I think that I will not come out of it except for the Papacy.

Meanwhile Jemima had been busy for more than a year aided by the Mozley sisters in working an elaborate altar cloth for the Church. Several letters are full of nothing else. There were too to be hangings and a pulpit cover: Newman sends measurements and discusses materials. The altar cloth was evidently singularly beautiful but he was anxious whether the background was the best possible—dark was needed to bring out the bright colours of the embroidery. He suggests this in one letter, confirms it in another from Rogers's experience of his sister's bird paintings —which refused to look bright until some dark relief had been introduced.

The altar cloth arrived just before Easter. "The border is exceedingly rich and effective, and the letters of the text are far better than I thought they could have been made. Altogether I am very much rejoiced. . . . Mrs. Barnes [a parishioner] broke out into exclamations about the favoured condition of Littlemore. . . . The colour is very rich. I have some idea of laying down a dark cloth on the pavement to set it off—but shall take advice on so important a point."

On Easter Eve he writes again about the famous work, which later letters show became a model for many other Churches, people writing for the pattern as they had written for the Church plans. Numbers came out from Oxford to see it, he reports triumphantly to Jemima, and later, "The Ogles' cloth is very beautiful but not to compare in effect with ours at Littlemore."

Easter Eve, 8 p.m.: I have just ended the Lenten Fast, and Bloxam has come up and taken tea with me. Then we went to church, and with much care arranged the altar cloth, covering it all over afterwards. It looks beautiful and B. is quite in ecstasies about it. As to Mrs. Barnes, she dreamed of it of a night at first, from astonishment at its elaborateness, and Eliza B. and several others who are workwomen, look at it with amazement. Rogers, taking another view of it, is equally full of admiration. Indeed, we are all so happy that we are afraid of being too happy. We have got some roses, wall-flowers and sweet-briar, and the Chapel smells as if to remind one of the Holy Sepulchre.

I like to think that in a life of much suffering inflicted by persons and circumstances on a nature of singular sensitiveness this same exquisite perception brought also great joys. The beauty of his church adorned for the feast, the scent of the sweet-briar, the singing of his well-trained children, all were far more deeply appreciated by Newman than by the blunted senses we most of us possess. His sisters too and their families were to him a source of joy. He was "foolishly anxious," he admits to Jemima about Harriett—probably when her first and only baby was on the way. And he always worried about her overwork affecting tightly strung nerves. But he rejoiced in her success when she began the series of stories that sold so well and brought her considerable if temporary fame.

The stories were anonymous and the family got a lot of fun out of the guessing that went on. Harriett herself writes to Tom that everyone is conjecturing about the authorship. Rivington "said it was by a relative of Mr. Newman. Louisa (a cousin) insinuated a modest doubt—he persisted—a friend certainly, he said, and a near connection—he believed a sister. Everybody said so." Other friends "said it embodied all Mr. N's principles and must be from a friend." Maria Giberne "wrote and said she could not guess. Except it was 'Noggs' in petticoats. I hope you are sufficiently read in N. Nickleby to understand this. They call J. H. N. Noggs as a pet name and others a Noggs—Noggites or Noggsites—I think it pretty."

Newman on his side wrote: "*The Fairy Bower* is making a sensation here—I have given away my editorial copy—but no matter." Henry Wilberforce had it for review—and compared the writer with Jane Austen! No wonder she went ahead. *The Lost Brooch* and *Louisa* (which Newman thought "admirable" —by far the best she had done) followed *The Fairy Bower*. Also *Family Adventures* of which something has been said earlier but which Newman does not mention.

The "editorial copy" and Wilberforce's review were for the *British Critic* which appears constantly in these letters and which, although hardish labour, was certainly a pleasure. It was the organ of a still undivided movement, nearly every number is reported as a good one, it was a chance to start his young disciples writing, especially as no article was signed. Newman himself and Tom Mozley had to fill last-minute gaps. To James he had given advice for his first article, "do not be too essayish: i.e. do not begin, 'Of all the virtues which adorn the human breast!'— be somewhat conversational and take a jump into your subject. But on the other hand avoid abruptness and pertness. Be *easy* and take the mean—and now you have full directions how to write."

Early in 1841 the peace was broken by the crisis that followed Tract 90—for which Newman himself was utterly unprepared. He has told the story in the *Apologia*, but a glance at the background is needed to make it fully intelligible to those who come to it fresh today.

The Thirty-Nine Articles of Religion are a set of formulae drawn up in the sixteenth century to which not clergymen only but undergraduates had then to subscribe. This excluded from the University all who were not members of the Church of England. In the early eighteenth century Nicholas Amhurst as *Terrae Filius* speaks in bitter sarcasm of this rule. The newly admitted undergraduate, he says, "subscribes the *thirty-nine* articles of religion, though often without knowing what he is doing, being ordered to write his name in a book, without mentioning upon what account; for which he pays *ten shillings and sixpence*." If over sixteen, the undergraduate was obliged also to take the oaths of allegiance and supremacy, "but if the person is not sixteen years of age, and above *twelve*, then he is only to subscribe the thirty-nine articles."[1]

Too young to take an oath of allegiance, yet old enough to subscribe to a complicated doctrinal formula—it is hardly surprising that Amhurst thus advises "gentlemen school boys" designed for Oxford: "You have subscribed the *thirty-nine articles*; but never venture to explain the *sense*, in which you subscribe them; because there are various senses; so many, indeed, that scarce two men understand them in the *same*, and no *true churchman* in that which the *words bear*, and in which they were written."[2]

Aside from the question of a boy's understanding—or lack of understanding—difficulty in signing the articles at their face value often arises in the eighteenth century, generally among Latitudinarians. It is sometimes assumed that the Tractarians were the first to sign the Articles with reservations or in other than an absolute literal sense. This was far from being so. Abbey tells us that Hoadly in his *Answer to Convocation* "fairly maintained his position that 'the articles were never so much as confined to any one particular determinate sense; but on the contrary were by public authority, as long ago as the time of King Charles I declared to admit of several senses, which was then found

---

[1] *Terrae Filius*, pp. 13, 15.   [2] Ibid, p. 17.

expedient even for the honours and use of the highest and strictest Churchmen themselves."[1]

John Jones too, Vicar of Alconbury, in a book published 1749 and much discussed (*Free and Candid Disquisitions*), maintained that "The Thirty-nine articles may be liable to just and reasonable exceptions when compared with the genuine sense of the Word of God, as that sense appears at this day to learned and inquisitive men."[2]

Dr. Clayton, Bishop of Clogher, whose opinions were almost avowedly Arian, "signed light-heartedly," while Archdeacon Blackburne had a scruple in signing on receiving preferment, since he objected "to all theories of subscriptions which allowed a wide latitude of interpretation and made articles mere symbols of general unity and agreement."

"To the end of his life," says Dr. Whitridge in his life of Arnold, "he never believed the damnatory clauses of the Athanasian creed, although he read the Athanasian creed in church and subscribed to the Article about it. In explanation of this seemingly equivocal position it can only be said that it is at once the strength or the weakness of the Protestant Church, depending on one's point of view, that such inconsistency is tolerated and even respected . . . it was not he who gave way but the bishops who ordained him."[3]

In Stanley's Life we read that Archdeacon Clerke said, "Perhaps I should say that it is rather a *forced* interpretation." To which Stanley answered, "Yes it is; but as it was necessary to put some interpretation I thought it met the difficulty better than any other."

While the eighteenth and nineteenth centuries produced chiefly Latitudinarian interpretations there had earlier been attempts to reconcile the Articles with Catholic teaching. Francis a Santa Clara, chaplain of Henrietta Maria, was the only Catholic theologian who made the attempt and he remarks of several articles "This seems difficult" and even "extremely difficult". He concludes "I have laboured (insudavi) to reconcile the articles of the Anglican profession of faith with the definitions of the Catholic Church" (*Paraphrastica Expositio Articulorum Confessiones Anglicanae*, 1646, republished 1865). In the same century Bishop Bancroft's chaplain Rogers, rector of Horningheath

---

[1] Charles J. Abbey: *The English Church and its Bishops*, 1700-1800, p. 222.
[2] Ibid, p. 223.　　　　　　　　[3] *Dr. Arnold of Rugby.*, p. 53.

wrote *The Catholic Doctrine of the Church of England. An Exposition of the 39 Articles* (reprinted by the Parker Society 1854). Although the Catholic interpretation was not, even in the seventeenth century, the most common one it had warrant from some of the very authors of the Articles. Thus in 1571 Cheney, Bishop of Gloucester, objected to the word "only" in the phrase that "the Body of Christ is given taken and received in the Supper only after a heavenly and spiritual manner." Bishop Guest wrote to Cecil "I told him plainly that this word 'only' in the aforesaid Article did not exclude the presence of Christ's body from the sacrament, but only the grossness and sensibleness in the receiving thereof; for I said unto him, that though he take Christ's Body in his hand, receive it in his mouth and that corporally, naturally, really, substantially and carnally, as the Doctors do write, yet did he not for all that see it, feel it, smell it, or taste it. And therefore I told him that I would speak against him therein" . . . Here we have a Tractarian interpretation admitted—nay apparently held—by one of the framers of the Articles.

When then his friends began to ask Newman: What will you do about the Articles? they were simply posing an old problem from a fresh point of view. And it is interesting to note that to him *personally* it was not even a problem. Arnold, Stanley and the rest had felt a difficulty in signing themselves and sympathy with others who might feel the same difficulty. Hampden, as we have seen, had advocated abolition of this test for undergraduates; Arnold, Hawkins and most of the Liberals had stood with him on this issue and they would all have been ready enough to abolish all religious tests. They felt that it was inconsistent in a Church that upheld private judgment to force any formulary upon its children's consciences. Not so Newman. A teaching Church, a branch of the Church Catholic, was bound to impose formularies; he had always maintained the Articles, he had found no difficulty himself in signing them. And probably of all those who signed not thoughtlessly but with consideration, he alone had a considered view of their interpretation. When he decided to write a Tract on the subject, he was only putting into shape and systematising a view he had long held and often partly expressed.

In the Lectures on the Prophetical Office he had described them as "adopted by our Church in a sense equally remote from the peremptory dogmatism of Rome, and from the cold and narrow spirit which breathes in a test." They were "instruments of teaching . . . heads, as it were, of important chapters in revealed truth . . . the basis on and out of which the superstructure of theology may be most conveniently raised."[1]

But the Articles were not the only expression of the faith of the Church of England and the Articles themselves made reference to these others. There were the Creeds; there were the Homilies; there was the Prayer Book . . . The Articles must then be signed with all these other formularies in mind, and if at any point they appeared to contradict Prayer Book or Homilies, some method of reconciliation must be found.

The Articles were, anyhow, ambiguous, in places self-contradictory, and had historically been intended to be ambiguous. They had been drawn up so as to win both Lutherans and Calvinists, to condemn Popery, perhaps, but certainly to win Papists. If they had one palmary principle, it was that of royal as against papal supremacy. "Now was I saying one word in favour of the supremacy of the Holy See, in favour of the foreign jurisdiction? No, I did not believe in it myself." The Tract was not intended as a full and formal explanation but rather as "an enquiry how far in critical fairness the text *could* be opened": not what signatories must, but what they might hold.

Generally, and he believed superficially, the Articles were assumed to be purely Protestant. In fact they were "tolerant" of a Catholic interpretation. Both Rome and England were Catholic, but the former had, surrounding its Catholic Creed, a "dominant circumambient Popery", the latter a "dominant circumambient Protestantism." The Popery was not of the essence of Rome, still less was the Protestantism of the essence of Anglicanism, and he aimed in this Tract at clearing both away.

"The main thesis then of my Essay was this—the Articles do not oppose Catholic teaching; they but partially oppose Roman dogma; they for the most part oppose the dominant errors of Rome ['dominant errors' is his other expression for 'circumambient Popery.'] And the problem was, as I have said, to draw the line as to what they allowed and what they condemned."[2]

Although in 1883 Newman "expressed himself dissatisfied with the reasoning"[3] on one point in the Tract, he maintained to the end of his life that as a whole it was a legitimate interpretation

---

[1] *Via Media*, Vol. I, p. 137.   [2] *Apologia*, p. 54.
[3] *Correspondence with Keble*, etc., p. 76.

of the Articles. The other Tractarians were all in general agreement with it. Keble had approved it before publication, Pusey
heartily endorsed it. Men with a knowledge of history realised
its value. Palmer of Worcester, the chief of the moderate school,
was both historian and theologian. "I feel it my duty," he wrote,
"to express to you, under present circumstances, the gratification
which I have derived from No. 90." While he would hesitate
to commit himself to every line of it he finds it "the *most valuable*
of the series," as tending "to shake people out of their implicit
reception of *traditionary interpretations* which impose human
opinions as little less than articles of faith." Dr. Moberly, later
Bishop of Salisbury, also thought the Tract "*most valuable*. We
want to be taught that we have a higher and holier origin than
the Reformation and the Articles." Perceval thought it "one
of the most important papers that have been put out, and calculated, under God's Blessing to do much good."

I am trying here to tell as vividly as may be a story of which
much is unknown or forgotten, not to go again over the trampled
ground of old arguments. The detailed method of Newman's
interpretation may be read in the *Apologia* or more fully in the
Tract itself. To him it appeared to be just another Tract, which
would be read by the same readers as all the rest, attacked by
the Protestants, useful to his followers, ignored by the wider
public. The whole argument fitted into, was indeed part of, the
via media which he had been preaching for the last eight years.
"You say," wrote John F. Christie a few weeks later, "you could
not have imagined after all you have written on the subject that
you could have been so misunderstood—but then all people do
not carry all you have written under their girdles." Ward
indeed prophesied that the Tract would raise a storm and Newman
had just told him he was a false prophet, when the storm broke
. in Oxford, to spread presently through the whole of England.

On March 9th (1841) Newman writes to Harriett, "I have got
into what may prove a serious mess here. I have just published
a Tract (90) which I did not feel likely to attract attention. . . .
But people are taking it up very warmly—thanks I believe entirely to Golightly."

And a week later, "I fear I am clean dished. The Heads of
Houses are at this very moment concocting a manifesto against
me. Do not think I fear for my cause. We have had too great
a run of luck."

Palmer's phrase, "under present circumstances," referred to the attacks on the Tract—and had his letter been written a few days earlier and circulated in Oxford the outcome might have been entirely different. For his repute stood high with all parties and his churchmanship was unquestioned. The chronology of the affair is an interesting example of the effect of apparent chance.

On March 14th Church writes in great detail to Rogers, who was in Rome. There had been a violent speech by Lord Morpeth against Oxford (as a part of his yearly defence of the Maynooth grant) and an assertion by O'Connell that the Puseyites were breaking their oaths. Rather surprisingly *The Times* defended them, but just at this moment Tract 90 had appeared.

"It came out at an unlucky time," Oxford being galled by Lord Morpeth and O'Connell, and puzzled and alarmed by the tone of the newspapers generally. "Tait of Balliol first began to talk fiercely . . . but he was after all a mere skirmisher set on to rouse people by Golightly, whose genius and activity have contributed in the greatest degree to raise and direct the storm. He saw his advantage from the first, and has used it well."

Certainly this part of the story is a strange one. Golightly had become the fierce crusading enemy: his zeal grew as the days passed. "He first puffed the Tract all over Oxford as the greatest 'curiosity' that had been seen for some time," next nearly bought out the publishers and sent copies to all the Bishops. "In the course of a week he had got the agitation into a satisfactory state and his efforts were redoubled". Some rebuffs were administered —from the Bishop of Exeter and various tutors he had approached. But four senior tutors agreed to act: Churton of Brasenose, Wilson of St. John's, Griffiths of Wadham and Tait of Balliol, "gentlemen who had scarcely the happiness of each other's acquaintance till Golly's skill harnessed them together"; they wrote to the Editor of the Tracts attacking Number 90 for "removing all fences against Rome" and demanding the author's name.

". . . it soon became known [Church is still speaking] that the Heads were furious and meant to move; driven frantic by Golightly and *The Standard*. They met full of mischief."

Newman told them through Pusey and the Provost that he was preparing a pamphlet in clarification and justification of the Tract; but refusing to wait even a few days for this, they issued a condemnation which stated that the Tract "suggested a mode of interpreting the Articles which *evaded* rather than explained them . . . defeated the object and was inconsistent with the observance of the Statutes."

Dr. Routh, like Palmer and Moberly, knew the past history of the Articles too well to join in this condemnation. With Dr. Richards of Exeter he opposed himself to it—but what were they among so many?

Newman received the condemnation "with a calm and lofty meekness, that must have let a new light into these excellent old gentlemen." This "calm and lofty meekness" was clearly a characteristic attitude that half amused his followers and somewhat disconcerted his opponents.

The fighting spirit that instantly collapsed into meekness at the voice of authority was a puzzle to many. Jemima wrote of the comments she had heard, "you must be aware that to persons who have not been brought up with you or long accustomed to your manner of thought, yours is a difficult character. There is something which seems almost paradoxical which they cannot understand."

"The row," Church continues, "which has been prodigious, they say, has made Golly a great man: he now ventures to patronise the Provost, who even condescended to lose his breakfast t'other day to hear Golly prose. He has received letters of thanks for his great and indefatigable exertions from four bishops."

Correspondence in the Liberal camp was also passing between Oxford and the Eternal City. Stanley with a friend was in Rome and he writes to Tait.

O, my dear Belvedere, what have you been doing? Rome is only in a less state of excitement than Oxford. The Pope has just issued a Bull defending the Decrees of Trent, on the ground that they are not contradictory to the Thirty-Nine Articles; and the Cardinals have just sate in conclave on him, and determined that he is against the usages of the Vatican. But to speak seriously: What has happened? First comes a letter from London to Pearson, intimating that a Tract on such a subject has appeared, and that you are in a state of frenzy. Next, an intelligence from papers that a Protest of five Tutors [it was four, not five], Belvedere being one, has appeared in *The Times*. Next, the great manifesto from the Heads themselves, accompanied by a private letter from Twiss to me, announcing that a "convulsive movement" will "not improbably take place, only equal to a moral Niagara ceasing to flow." Pearson and I are in a state of ferment beyond bounds.

Stanley's brief adhesion to Newman had passed but he was one of the few genuine Liberals in his own party. Most of the others were ready enough to persecute views they did not hold. But Stanley, dropping his note of foolery, ends in a tone of deadly seriousness, "Do not draw those Articles too tight, or they will strangle more parties than one. I assure you when I read the monition of the Heads I felt the halter at my own throat."[1] There was little danger for him.

Newman's friends were inclined to stress the personal side of the "row" and the share taken by Golightly, alias Golly, alias Golias. It is true enough that a fanatical individual who runs to and fro—*Goliare* they called it—bringing people together and carrying stories from one to another can produce surprising results. Golightly's own friends declared that there seemed to be a strain of madness in his conduct and he confided to one of them later that he was in fear of his life from the Tractarians!

But surely the matter went far deeper: it was a call to the undying Protestant spirit that still possessed England. Evasions that modified or explained away the fundamental dogmas— eternal punishment in the case of Arnold and Stanley, the Trinitarian definitions in the case of Hampden—all these left the public cold. But let the face of Rome be glimpsed and even Newmanites grew nervous while Protestants raged.

"*I trust to you*," wrote Jemima to her brother, "as a thousand others will. I look to your late answer to the Roman Catholic letters as a pledge for your being carried through this matter without harm. We shall get the tract and though I shall take a long breath before I read it, I will contrive to believe that it does not go too far."

Underlying Protestant feeling complicated a matter that was not of its nature simple—the question of the sincerity of Newman's interpretation. The newspaper storm and the bewilderment even of his friends conveys something of the difficulty one would have in giving a shortened account of the Tract—which, as I have said, I shall not attempt to do. Every step in the argument represents weeks or months of slow rumination and as Newman describes it in the *Apologia* we see the sincerity, even the simplicity, with which he had drawn distinctions that apart from his own mental story sometimes appear too fine. The newspapers had to summarise something that cannot of its nature be summarised. Their

[1] *Life of Stanley*, Vol. I, p. 293.

accounts, however unintentionally, falsified the Tract and gave a tremendous shock to the reader who had not read it, especially if he had not read or had forgotten Newman's previous books. Newman's *Letter to Jelf*—the form taken by his defence and explanation of the Tract—gave to the immediate world of Oxford the sort of reassurance that was only given to the country as a whole twenty years later by the *Apologia*. Dean Hook was representative of the moderately Tractarian country clergy. He wrote to Ward:

My opinion of Tract 90 is diametrically opposed to yours. I think that in spirit it is bad, that in assertion it is false—and I am quite certain that, if it is only by such special pleading men can be kept in the Church of England, they had better leave her at once—for they are fitter for communion with the *vilest and most corrupt of Churches*[1] than which I do verily believe ultra Protestantism bad as it is far better.

Hook was a hasty man and a few days later was telling Newman that "by your letter to Jelf you have entirely regained your ground." . . . Tract 90 is now only "a little bit of a scrape" that will make us "more cautious."

But the condition for regaining lost ground was a continued repudiation of Rome. "I have no thought whatever of going over to Rome," Newman writes to a follower on April 8th, "or letting others. . . . As to my Tract, *you* only see the disturbances it creates. I know the relief and satisfaction it has given, and I am not at all sure on which side the balance lies."

Everyone was reading Tract 90—2,500 copies were sold within a fortnight. "The papers," says Church, "have been full of the row which has stirred up London itself in no common manner." But at first Newman and the rest were by no means dissatisfied, surprised as they might be at the result. The Heads of Houses had gone beyond their competency, they had done "a violent act", and there was considerable reaction against them in Oxford. But, by the very fact that they had not summoned Convocation, an official condemnation by the University had been avoided.

"You see," wrote Newman to Jemima, "no *doctrine* is censured, and my shoulders shall manage to bear the charge . . . I have asserted a great principle and I ought to suffer for it."

[1] Italics mine.

Bishop Bagot was a quiet, almost a sluggish, man and would probably have given much to be ruling some other diocese just then. He liked Newman personally: "the hubbub", Newman writes to Jemima, "required him to do something." The correspondence between Newman and the Bishop lasted some weeks: the Tract was at first to be suppressed; but on March 30 a letter to Jemima runs:

Our Tract affair is settled—on these terms, which others may think a disappointment, but to me is a very fair bargain. I am now publishing a letter to the Bishop at his wish, stating that he wishes the Tracts discontinued, and he thinks No. 90 objectionable as tending to disturb the Church. I am quite satisfied with the bargain I have got, if this is all—as I suppose it will be.

"We have got the principle", he writes to Keble, "of our interpretation admitted, in that it has not been condemned. . . . It will soon be assumed as a matter of course."

Pusey wrote to James Hope: "the immediate excitement seems subsiding, although I fear (in the minds of many) into a lasting impression of our Jesuitism." But "people will abuse Tract 90 and adopt its main principles."[1]

Newman, everyone was saying, had risen marvellously to the occasion. Keble wrote to Pusey that "Newman's coming out as he does . . . will do the cause more good" than the stir made by the Tract could do harm. Church, too, writes of Newman's stand with admiration—but Newman had not yet been tried where trial could be anguish.

It is surprising to note in so sensitive a man how comparatively little he cared for personal criticism or abuse through all this.

It was clearly not a profoundly depressed man who wrote to Bloxam late in June:

They tell me you are at present performing the character of *mope*, and that the due performance of this character forbids your coming as far as Littlemore. If you have nothing better to do, I would come and mope with you at your rooms. . . .
 I am my dear Bloxam,
  Your sympathetic mope,

Looking back on it, he was sensitive to having been "posted up by the Marshall on the buttery hatch of every college of my

[1] *Memoirs of James Hope-Scott*, Vol. I, p. 261.

University after the manner of discommoned pastry-cooks". But from the letters one feels that the real pain began only with the manifestation of what he has called "a living and energetic heterodoxy" in a Church where he had, he hoped, replanted deeply the principles of Catholicity.

"In the summer of 1841," writes Newman, "I found myself at Littlemore without any harass or anxiety on my mind. I had determined to put aside all controversy, and I set myself down to my translation of St. Athanasius; but between July and November I received three blows which broke me."[1]

The first blow was that, in studying Athanasius and his battles with the Arians, "the ghost had come a second time". The year before he had suddenly seen the Anglicans in the same position as Monophysites and Donatists: now he saw them with the semi-Arians. The other two blows were the Bishops' Charges and the affair of the Jerusalem Bishopric.

It is the custom for Bishops and Archdeacons of the Church of England to deliver periodical Charges to their clergy on any point they regard as important—in the years 1841, '42 and '43 most of the Bishops charged, strongly or mildly, against Tractarianism. I have read most of the Charges and there is in them not a great deal to hurt the feelings of the Newmanites (though the Bishop of Chester[2] did describe them as "instruments of Satan to hinder the true principles of the Gospel") but much to shatter their conception of Anglicanism as a part of the Church Catholic.

Newman writes to Hope that "the charges are very serious matters; as virtually silencing portions of the truth in particular dioceses." It must be remembered that the Tractarians believing in a visible Church had to find somewhere the organ for that Church's expression, the authority to be obeyed as its representative; as they did not believe in the Pope, their Bishops *were* their Pope. Hence the dismay these Charges brought Newman. It may be questioned if there was a man in the whole Anglican Church to whom the episcopal office was more sacred. "Sometimes," he told Pusey, "when I have stood by as he [the Bishop] put on his robes, I felt as if it would be a relief if I could have fallen at his feet and kissed them."

Meanwhile there came what Newman called "this fearful business of the Bishop of Jerusalem . . . we are in the way to

[1] *Apologia*, p. 93.
[2] "Who I hope will be arraigned before the proper tribunal for heresy" wrote Newman to Henry Wilberforce, Nov. 8, 1841.

fraternise with Protestants of all sorts—Monophysites, half-converted Jews and even Druses." They were, he lamented, being "unchurched". The British Government in concert with that of Prussia—the move was primarily political—had agreed that the Archbishop of Canterbury should consecrate a Bishop to preside over the Protestant Congregations of the East, thus admitting them to Communion with the Church of England without renunciation of their heresies. "Why," Newman asks in a letter that the *Times* did not publish, "must the successors of Augustine and Anselm become superintendents of a mixed multitude of Protestants?" Lutheranism, Calvinism, were, Newman points out in a letter of protest to his own Bishop, "heresies repugnant to Scripture, springing up three centuries since, and anathematised by East as well as West." This measure he solemnly disowned and protested against "as removing our Church from her present ground, and tending to her disorganisation." He compares the move to giving Bishops to a Baptist or Wesleyan body without asking their reconciliation or abjuration. A minor point but a very relevant one in his eyes was that in entering Jerusalem as English churchmen they infringed the principle that the various Catholic Churches were autonomous, each in its own territory. He had always held Romanists as true Catholics in Europe, schismatics in England. But now, "If England could be in Palestine, Rome might be in England."[1]

Another man, Palmer of Magdalen (not to be confused with Palmer of Worcester), was protesting against the Bishopric—a man recently returned from Russia where he had been trying to get the Tractarian theory approved by the Orthodox Church. Many years later Newman edited his *Notes of a Visit to the Russian Church*. The tale Palmer had to tell must have added to the general atmosphere of gloom. The trouble began with the authorities of the English Church. Wanting before setting out support from his own College he had called on Dr. Routh, to read him a proposed petition to the Grand Duke Alexander for a Russian to be sent to Oxford, and for his own reception in Russia.

"While the Catholic Church of England——"
Here the President, when I showed it to him, interposed: "Leave out the word 'Catholic', sir; it will not be understood."

[1] *Apologia*, p. 99.

"While the Church of England constantly defends the rights of Christian Sovereigns, invaded equally by the ambition of the Roman Pontiff and by democratical licentiousness, she is herself at present in great danger, isolated in a corner of the West, unsupported by the Civil Government and——"

"I would leave that out, sir."

"In a corner of the West, and threatened by the hatred of all the Protestant sects——"

"Leave out the word 'Protestant'."

"Of all the sects, which have leagued with schismatical Papists to overthrow her.

"If your Imperial Highness will be pleased to favour our studies, and to take an interest in the distress of our Churches, it will be doing a benefit to the cause of social order, of submission and humility in the West; and at the same time, by facilitating the union of the Churches, your Imperial Highness will gladden all those who pray for the peace of Christendom.

"May God bless the throne of the Emperor of Russia, and may all the people committed to him obey him as a father. May he never see the anarchical principles of heretical Protestantism coming to disturb his Empire and its Churches; and may it be given to him, on the occurrence of some just opportunity, to deliver the East from the yoke of the Infidels."

"I would leave out this last sentence, sir," said Dr. Routh; "the first clause will not be understood, and the second will seem un-English."[1]

Routh consented to give Palmer a letter to the Russian authorities, but on his suggesting that this letter should come from the college, one of the Fellows exclaimed, "I protest, Mr. President, I protest against this Society giving any encouragement to the idea of inter-communion with the *idolatrous* Greek Church." The Vice-President and others concurring in the opposition, the letter was given by Routh alone. The Archbishop of Canterbury, asked to countersign it, refused to do so "as a matter of caution beneficial to both sides."

In Russia Palmer received much courtesy, but was asked repeatedly whether the English Bishops held Tractarian views and why, if this was the teaching of the Church of England, English chaplains in Russia (who were definitely Protestant) did not teach it to their people. Count Pratasoff, he notes, "seemed staggered at the idea of one visible Church being made

[1] *Notes of a Visit to the Russian Church*, pp. 2-3.

of three Communions differing in doctrine and rites, and two of them at least condemning and anathematizing the others."

The Russians used the word Catholic of the Latins alone: themselves they called Orthodox—all others Protestant. His request for Communion was steadfastly refused. "The Archbishop said, 'You have your own chaplain here, you need not come to us.' 'How,' I asked, 'can the Church of England be in your diocese . . . I am no member of the Church of England in Russia.'"

But this theory of schism attaching to a Church in one place which yet in another was the true Church was a hard theory to convey to a mind unprepared for it.

Archbishop Howley, before deciding against signing Palmer's document, had objected that in asking to be admitted to Communion, he would be offering himself for doctrinal examination to the Orthodox clergy. Palmer in all sincerity had answered that it would be no more than the giving in of his name as ordered also by the Church of England Rubric. But the Archbishop was right. Palmer was told he would have to prove his belief in every article of Orthodox teaching. Moreover he found his Eucharistic faith doubted because of his insistence on distinguishing between the Real Presence (which he believed) and the Romish doctrine of transubstantiation which only affected the *mode* of the Presence. On this matter the Russians told him they agreed with the Catholics, and they obviously suspected him of not really believing more than a spiritual Presence. He was harassed too by the "Liberal" Orthodox who thought to please him by insisting on the Church as a universal invisible society of true believers. Palmer asserted almost passionately the need for absolute truth and the fact of a visible Church of Christ's foundation.

"The Russians," Newman reported to Rogers, "will not believe him against the evidence of all the English they ever saw before." And now he was home with his sad little tale at a time when cheerful news would have been especially acceptable. There was none such.

Somewhat against Newman's judgment, his former curate, Isaac Williams, stood at the turn of the year 41–42 for the Professorship of Poetry. He was the one Tractarian to whom J. A. Froude allows the name of poet. Christopher Dawson remarked to me that he had put Newman's ideas on Antichrist into verse—indeed one finds passage after passage of Newman

turned into verse by Williams, sometimes almost verbatim. His
opponent Garbett was a mere nullity of a man. But Pusey's
support, rather tactlessly given, made Williams's defeat certain.
The Bishop of Oxford asked him to retire—but now Newman
was for his holding out and demanding at least that the Bishop's
letter be made public. Finally, hopeless of success, Williams did
retire before the election took place. It was widely asserted that
his defeat was to be followed by measures that should have the
effect of "driving us clean out of the University." Did this mean,
Newman queried, a new test of the *sense* in which the Articles
were subscribed?

Men were already being asked when they applied for Orders
how they interpreted the Articles. "A dead set", Keble reported,
was made at his curate, who was only a deacon and wanted
priest's orders; and he added, "I am much afraid that this is
the beginning of a system." It was. A man who was not at
Chapel on November 5th was sent for by the Provost of Oriel
and refused testimonials for Orders "because he did not like
the State Service." Keble's curate was refused a second time on
account of his answers on the Eucharist. The Bishop of London
rejected a man for holding *any* sacrifice in the Eucharist, the Real
Presence, that there is a grace in Ordination. "Are you sure",
writes Newman to Church, "that the Bishops will not be drawing
up some stringent declarations of faith?"

All these things were driving people to Rome—and Newman
was working to keep them back while fearing that he would not
long be successful. "It is not love of Rome that unsettles people
but fear of heresy at home." And to Bowden he writes, "I shall
have taught people that there is a Church *somewhere* and the
Archbishop will teach them it is not to be found at home."

For himself the conviction still remained that Rome as well
as England had much to reform. He was able to say in a letter
to Dr. Russell of Maynooth that while both Churches suffered
from the divisions between them "we cannot *remove the obstacles*;
it is with you to do so." Some of these obstacles are mentioned
in the correspondence of 1841–2 with Dr. Russell and other
Catholic friends: they were both political and doctrinal. The
Catholic Church was allied with Liberalism of which the spirit
was "the characteristic of the destined Antichrist". The "services and devotions to St. Mary in matter of fact do most deeply
pain me." He had never said that all the decrees of Trent could

be reconciled with the Articles—Transubstantiation was verbally condemned, and "the doctrine of Transubstantiation is a great difficulty with me as being, as I think, not primitive."

It was no simple alternative for Newman between England and Rome. In a long letter to James Hope he admits that "a great and anxious *experiment* is going on whether our Church be or be not Catholic", and even "that the only way to keep in the English Church is steadily to contemplate and act upon the possibility of leaving it. Surely the Bishops ought to be brought to realise what they are doing.

"But, still on the whole I hope better things."

"A miserable effect is produced", he writes to Keble a little later, "on the minds of young and sensitive persons, when they are accused and remonstrated with as suspected Romanists . . . When great people take up the Oxford Calendar and go through the colleges . . . The familiarity it creates with the idea of Romanism is miserable; and the dreadful unsympathetic atmosphere created . . . is a distinct evil".

Not only young men suffered from this attitude. He writes to Dean Church, on Christmas Day 1841, that letters from his followers to himself "have done great harm. I speak most sincerely when I say that there are things which I neither contemplate nor wish to contemplate, but when I am asked about them ten times at length I begin to contemplate them."

It becomes at this point a little difficult to chronicle the progress of Newman's mind with exactness. Later letters seem to indicate that a greater advance towards Rome had taken place by this date than is shown by the contemporary evidence. Of course his moods varied, but I think that much was sub-conscious as early as 1841 which only three years later he realised to have been in his mind. The vividness with which he saw it later became retrospective: he knew in 1844 that it had been there all the time. But there is, I think, only one letter in which he appears to have thought the sub-conscious advance had been conscious. Writing in July 1845 to tell his old school fellow, the sculptor Richard Westmacott, "that it is morally certain I shall join the Roman Catholic Church", Newman adds the comment: "It has been the conviction of six years from which I have never seceded." Westmacott very naturally retorted that Newman might well have owned it sooner. In fact the letter was written in haste and, as we shall see, the phrase is too strong as it stands. The reality of these years is better told in a letter to Henry Wilberforce (May 16, 1843): "The impression has faded and revived again and again, and strengthened." The reader may be helped to follow the very complex movement of his mind in these six years by the statement Newman made in 1849 of the main phases (in a letter to Rev. Francis Faber, whose uncle had said that in the last ten years of his Anglican career, Newman was a "concealed Romanist"): "*For the first four years* of the ten (up to Michaelmas 1839), I honestly wished to benefit the Church of England at the expense of the Church of Rome.

"For the second four years [1839-1843] I wished to benefit the Church of England without prejudice to the Church of Rome. [In the Apologia (p. 99) he makes a further division: 'From the end of 1841, I was on my death-bed, as regards my membership with the Anglican Church, though at the time I became aware of it only by degrees'.]

"At the beginning of the ninth year [Michaelmas 1843], I began to despair of the Church of England and gave up all clerical duty: and then, what I wrote and did was influenced by a mere wish not to injure it, and not by the wish to benefit it.

"At the beginning of the tenth year [Michaelmas 1844] I distinctly contemplated leaving it, but I also distinctly told my friends that it was in my contemplation.

"Lastly during the last half of the tenth year, I was engaged in writing a book (*Essay on Development*) in favour of the Roman Church and indirectly against the English."

Now, with the Bishop's Charges and the Jerusalem Bishopric, we are at the midway point of the second stage—the end of 1841 when he was on his death-bed, as regards membership of the Anglican Church, though he did not yet realise it. What he did realise was that he must find a lower ground for his defence of the Anglican position. "The Jerusalem Bishopric was the ultimate condemnation of the old theory of the *via media*."[1]

Still "this could be said: still we were not nothing: we could not be as if we never had been a Church: we were 'Samaria'."[2]

[1] *Apologia*, p. 100.　　　[2] *Apologia*, p. 102.

Chapter XXVIII

Subjects of the Day

THIS "lower ground" to which Newman had been forced in defence of the Church of England is developed especially in sermons preached on the four Sundays before Christmas 1841. It was new for him to introduce any allusion to current events in his preaching, but these sermons were designed to allay the doubts and fears both of himself and his followers. He set about writing them in a state of the gravest perturbation. On November 8, 1841, he had written to Henry Wilberforce:

I have no doubt, nor do I think I am likely to have of the salvability of persons dying in the English Church. But I think still it may be that the English Church is not part of the Church Catholic, but only visited with inflowings of grace, and that God may call some persons on to what is higher . . . I have no call at present to go to the Church of Rome, but I am not confident that I may not some day. But it seems to me that there is something most unnatural and revolting in going over suddenly—unless indeed a miracle is granted.

The preparation of the sermons seems to have reassured him. The first three, "The Invisible Presence of Christ," "Inward and Outward Notes of the Church," "Grounds for Steadfastness in our Religious Profession," are all about the internal evidence that "Christ is with us still, in spite of our many sins and great corruptions."

The outward notes of the Church seem in this age to be "partly gone from us and partly going" (and a footnote here refers to the "grievous effect" of the Jerusalem Bishopric). Yet

what are signs and tokens of any kind whatever but the way *to* Christ? What need of *them*, should it so be, through His mercy, that we have found Him? Who asks his way when he has got to his destination? Why seek the shadow if we already have the substance? Why seek Him elsewhere, if we have reason to trust we have found Him here?

St. Paul spoke when about to die not of visible signs but

of an evidence not outward, not visible, not common, but inward, private, incommunicable. "I know," he says, "Him in whom I have believed" . . . and thus, just as we need not read a friend's writing when we hear his voice . . . the blessed Apostle needed not to seek Him abroad, who had graciously condescended to "come under his roof" and manifest Himself unto him.

So, too, even in this dark age,

if you have gained any good thing, not merely in, but through your Church . . . if your soul has been, as it were, transfigured within you, when you came to the Most Holy Sacrament; or if Lent and Passiontide brought to you what you had not before . . . if strange providences and almost supernatural coincidences have hung about the Church's Ordinances; if mercies and judgments have descended through them upon yourselves, or upon those about you; if you have experience of death-beds, and know how full of hope the children of our Church can die;—O! pause ere you doubt that we have a Divine Presence among us still, and have not to seek it.

Admitting the possibility that Christ should leave "a home where He once was," he points in each one of these sermons to the divine signs that

have generally been attendant on the call of God. What prophecies, what miracles, what portents, what judgments were displayed to convince the Jews that Judaism was at an end . . . what plain tokens of God's wrath rested on those ancient heresies . . . so that they left the world almost before men had time to leave them.

Those who had thought of leaving the Church under the stress of recent happenings had commonly done so "in a moment of weakness," or sickness, or "with manifest eccentricity of conduct," often in disobedience to a powerful feeling that held them back:

. . . Let us beware of turning a deaf ear to what may prove to be a Divine token; let us not do despite to a Divine privilege. Angels are our guardians; Angels surely stand in our way, in mercy, not in wrath; Angels warn us back. Let us obey the warning. When St. Peter was fleeing from Rome, shortly before his martyrdom, Jesus Christ met him at the gate, as if entering the city; and the Apostle understood that he was to return. When the Christians were to flee from Jerusalem, Angels went first, crying one to another, "Let us depart hence". Let us fear to go before, or to fall behind, the pillar of the cloud in the wilderness, the Presence of "God and the Lord Jesus Christ, and the elect Angels".

Turning to the Old Testament, which few men have known as he did in its every line, Newman found in the fourth of these sermons a curiously interesting illustration: "Elijah the Prophet of the Latter Days" takes the story of the Kingdoms of Judah and Israel as prophetic of the dark and dreary modern age. Elijah (Elias) lived amid "dimness and confusion, the threatenings of evil, the scattering of the faithful, and the defection of the powerful." He was raised up by God as a prophet to the tribes of Israel who had broken away into schism and fallen into idolatry. Yet neither he nor his successor Elisha (Eliseus) made any attempt to heal the schism or lead the ten tribes back to worship in Jerusalem:

. . . We are accustomed to say that nothing is done, unless all is done; but God's thoughts are not our thoughts, neither our ways His ways. He raises up prophets and gifts them with miraculous power, to do a half work; not to heal the division of the Kingdoms, but to destroy idolatry; not to restore outward unity, but to repress inward unbelief; not to retrace the steps of the wanderers, but to keep them from wandering still farther. . . . Now why this was so ordered we do not know; whether it be, that when once a people goes wrong, it cannot retrace its steps; or whether there was so much evil at that time in Judah also, that to have attempted a reunion would have been putting a piece of new cloth into an old garment, and had it been effected, would have been an hollow, unreal triumph; or whether such good works have a sort of natural march, and the nearer work must first be done, and then that which is farther removed, and men must undo their sins in the order in which they committed them, and thus, as neglect of the Temple was the sin of Jereboam, and Baal-worship the sin of Ahab, so they must ascend back again from Ahab to Jeroboam; but, whatever was the reason, so it was, that Elijah and Elisha kept the people shut up under that system, if it might be so called, in which they found them, and sought rather to teach them their duty, than to restore to them their privileges.

We are back again at the thought of Rome and England—but with this difference: Rome is now seen as Judah, which had remained faithful, England as Israel which had fallen away.

Yet he still believes that there is evil in both, that both need reform. He stills holds men back from Rome, and he has quieted his own doubts about remaining where he is. On December 27, he writes to Maria Giberne:

Do not you mistake quiet for despondency? Our strength is to sit still. People will find it most difficult to oust us if we sit down, fold our arms, hunch up our shoulders and turn sulky. They will think us dangerous —and if they attempt to lift us will find us so dismally heavy as to make the work hopeless—we the while looking at them with grave faces.

Have patience is ever the burden of his song. And even after the comparison with Israel, he will not apply to the English Church the term apostasy—he still thinks Rome is darkened with political and doctrinal error. A curious letter to Dodsworth is dated January 2nd, 1842:

It is not right to anticipate such a calamity as the English Church apostatising. . . . But if it did, other events, equally portentous, might happen with it, which shows how impossible it is to speculate. The same monstrous events (so to speak) which sank us might (in God's inscrutable counsels) rectify other bodies. . . . It is to me quite as impossible that Rome should purify herself as that England should fall away. . . .

At this time, when we see nothing, the notion of an Anglican Church unestablished is beset with difficulties—e.g., the Non-Jurors had Bishops—we have none . . . certainly one feels a most extreme repugnance to creating an additional communion in the present divided state of Christendom. . . . The question of course arises whether or not the Scotch or American Church would be induced to propagate itself in England; or whether it could do so without schism except with the plain avowal that the English Church was heretical.

Newman had been trying for some time to get St. Mary's separated from Littlemore and hold only the latter. He wrote to Jemima in February 1842: "I have several things which puzzle me about St. Mary's pulpit. One special thing is this, which I have felt for years: is it right to be preaching to those who are not in any sense my charge, and whose legitimate guardians, the Heads of Houses, wish them not preached to?"

The Provost of Oriel would not agree to separating the two offices. In that same month of February, 1842, Newman went down to Littlemore for good. "My books are all in motion. . . .

It makes me very downcast." He appointed a resident curate for St. Mary's and gave himself wholly to Littlemore.

The adaptation of the cottages leased in the summer of 1841 made it possible for Newman to receive "inmates" at Littlemore. Soon rumours spread, for the world was intensely curious about him.

Writing twenty years after in the *Apologia* he complains bitterly how he could not be left to his prayers and the anguish of his unresolved doubt: "Wounded brutes creep into some hole to die, and no one grudges it them. . . . One day, when I entered my house, I found a flight of undergraduates inside, Heads of Houses, as mounted patrols, walked their horses round those poor cottages. Doctors of Divinity dived into the hidden recesses of that private tenement uninvited, and drew domestic conclusions from what they saw there." Gossip reached such a point of intensity that his Bishop asked him to contradict the rumour that he had established a monastery of the Roman Catholic pattern. Newman contradicted it in the famous letter of April, 1842, set out in full in the *Apologia*. Abbott and his sort have termed the contradiction dishonest. But it was not. It is true that Newman had often used the words "abbey" and "monastery" in letters to his friends, but always jestingly. As far back as September, 1840, he writes to Maria Giberne of his amusement at her taking seriously his talk of building a magnificent abbey: "Some day or other we may erect there a hovel such as St. Martin lived in or St. Basil." Nearly a year before the Bishop's enquiry he had written to Pusey: "I have given up the notion of a monastic body at present, lest a talk should be made. I have got a room where I can put my books, and myself. Also I have a number of spare cottages. If anyone chooses to come here from London, Oxford, or elsewhere, for any time, he may have a retreat, but without anything of a coenobitium. It is only, in fact, furnishing him with lodgings."

"A very cheap but not nasty place," is how Dalgairns describes the ensemble, "very like almshouses, very anti-Puginian . . . Newman declares his object is not to teach people austerities, but only living in a plain frugal way, so as to get out of the gentleman-parson line". This they certainly succeeded in doing. There were no servants in the house. A woman from the village came to cook the dinner, her son cleaned the boots and knives. During dinner there was reading aloud. The "inmates" took it in turn to answer the bell, Newman included. Mark Pattison has a story of Doctor Simons of Wadham who asked to see "the Monastery", to which Newman retorted, "We have no monasteries here", and slammed the door in his face. But in his pleasant book *Newman and Bloxam* (to which I am indebted for some of these details), R. D. Middleton expresses a well-founded doubt whether Newman's habitual courtesy was likely so to have failed him. Determined not to act the religious superior, Newman begged his younger friends to drop the "Mr." and call him simply "Newman". But unable to bring themselves to this, they usually called him nothing.

"As for our employments," says Dalgairns, "Newman works for the press and I am his cad; when he has no work in hand he reads theology and so do I. . . . This is really the whole mystery of our pseudo-monastery." And in another letter he says, "Bloxam' has also called it the Union Workhouse; and it certainly does look vastly like its name."

Whatever Newman had hoped for in the past, Littlemore never became a monastery. Monks take vows and no vows were taken by the little group in Newman's cottages. Monks wear some sort of habit or uniform, and nothing external distinguished these men from their fellows. But above all there must be in a monastery some element of permanence—and the only permanent person at Littlemore was Newman himself. "At present," he wrote to Maria Giberne in August, 1842, "our rooms here are full, six sets—but men come and go. I have hardly one constant inmate—and in winter perhaps I may be left alone."

Even the three or four who were more or less constant went away for long periods. Many were only there for a few days. Mark Pattison is an amusing instance of a youthful enthusiast whose stomach could not endure a fortnight of the régime which Newman imposed on himself for four years. Perhaps this is not surprising. Those were the days of great meals in colleges and in the houses of the rich or even the well-to-do. Fasting was often compulsory for the poor but nothing annoyed the Heads of Houses and other anti-Tractarians more than the revival of this discipline once so integral a part of Christian life.

The daily rule was severe at Littlemore: the Lent seems to have been terrific. Even outside Lent an early timetable shows only two meals a day—breakfast at 6.30 a.m. and supper at 6 p.m. The hour of rising was five, there was no talking save between 2 and 6.30 p.m. (This must have been a great safeguard against the garrulous, and a necessary protection for the studious.) In addition to the daily Anglican service at the Church, Divine Office was said in the house from the Roman Breviary—omitting the Antiphons of Our Lady as direct invocation of her was not allowed by the English Church. The division of the day is thus summarised in the Oratorian collection of Newman's letters: devotions four and a half hours, study nine, meals one (no wonder Pattison got such bad indigestion with the one full meal bolted in half an hour), recreation two and three-quarters, sleep six and three-quarters.

The Lent of 1844 Newman describes as "lighter this year." What must it have been when heavier?

1. We have eaten no flesh meat (including suet) on Sundays or weekdays.
2. We have not broken fast till 12.
3. At 12 we have taken a slice of bread. The full meal at 5—but we had the choice (which perhaps we never used) of taking the full meal at 12, and the bread at 5.
4. There was no restriction on tea at any hour early or late.
5. Nor [at the full meal] on butter, sugar, salt, fish, etc. Wine on Sundays.

"I have not," he added, "felt any rule so light since I have attempted anything. This I attribute to drinking very freely of tea, as early as 8 or 9 a.m. with sugar in it. I am told I do not look ill."[1]

Although Newman himself practised fasting in this severe fashion and observed celibacy, these remained the two matters in which his own central sanity is noticeable and on which he had throughout the Movement to keep in leash the extravagant views of his more ardent disciples. Morris of Exeter, "a most simple minded conscientious fellow but . . . little possessed of tact and commonsense," having been left in charge of St. Mary's one Michaelmas day preached a sermon on "his monomania of fasting," saying that "it was a good thing whereas angels feasted on festivals, to make the brute creation fast on fast days." Newman telling this to Bowden comments, "May he (*salvis ossibus suis*) have a fasting horse the next time he goes steeple-chasing."

This happened at the end of 1839: a year later F. W. Faber sent on to Newman a letter from the same Morris who had heard a

[1] *Correspondence of Newman with Keble and others*, p. 296.

rumour that Faber was engaged to be married, hoping that it is false and that he will be "saved from Matrimony and all its specious holiness. . . . What has penance to do with the softness of the marriage bed; or how can Divine Wrath be warded off, if we set ourselves in the midst of continual allurements to be easy and comfortable? I much doubt if there is a woman in England who would not think me stark mad for taking up the miserable pittance of penance which I do." In this same letter we are back again at fasting, for "two days without food," says Morris, "would often bring us to our senses. . . . Do be bold in time."

Faber took the letter rather seriously: he had no immediate intentions but supposed he should marry some time "although convinced that celibacy is a higher state, yet I never ventured to think that I could fulfil it." He had received much good from Morris, but "in the present instance . . . I suspect his advice." So he applied to Newman "who have been *ductor dubitantis* to me in so many things before."

Newman's answer pays a perfunctory compliment to the "overpowering moral force" in Morris's letter which "makes one feel little." He agrees with the thought that celibacy itself is both a penance for past sin and a more holy state. As a holy state he would not urge it on any individual; as a penance: "I could urge it strongly did I know on whom to urge it." But to Faber he suggests: "Why hasten a decision which the natural growth of your mind and greater ripeness in knowledge may lay at your door? You may perhaps have an answer in the way of grace. . . . I suppose no general answer can be given except indeed this, that grace can do all things for us; and that . . . he who has the will has the power."

The question occasionally arose for women also. And the contrast between the real gravity with which Newman viewed the whole matter and the attitude of those on the fringe of the movement can be seen in a letter close to Morris's in the files—from Dean Hook, "I am in hopes of establishing a Sisterhood here to assist the Clergy. Can you obtain a Prioress for me?"

The last letters I have found on this topic are of 1843 from a distracted father whose daughter, engaged for three years, suddenly decides to lead a single life for Christ. It is, says the father, Newman's fault, and he wails, "She has broken her solemnly plighted troth to Theophilus."

The external severity at Littlemore was the framework for

intense prayer and meditation and above all "surrender of myself
in all things to God to do with me what He would at any cost.
Various great trials struck me." One of these great trials was the
possibility of "having to join the Church of Rome."

Meanwhile he was projecting a series of lives of the Saxon
saints: "the only saints," he wrote to Jemima, "I dare take."
The continent in the Middle Ages had more romantic, in the post-
reformation period more interesting and practical stories; ours
"I fear have some sameness with them from the scantiness of the
material—they end or almost so with the thirteenth century—but
we must do what we can." A few months later the publishers were
trying to shelve the series: Pusey had told Hope that the first
book—St. Stephen Harding's Life—would cause a fresh row; it
was shown to Gladstone and he too was frightened.

Yet St. Stephen had been chosen as one of the *less* startling of
the saints—if the Church of England could not bear his story, what
was there in her past that she could today endure to look upon?
Newman wrote to Hope:

Church History is made up of three elements—miracles, monkery,
Popery. . . . Take Missions, take Bishops, the Pope comes in everywhere. Go to Aldhelm and his schools; you have most strange miracles.
Try to retire into the country, you do but meet with hermits. No;
miracles, monkery, Popery, are too much for you if you have any
stomach. If the plan is abandoned the significant question will be,
nay is already asked—what then, cannot the Anglican Church bear
the Lives of her Saints!

Finally he wrote to Jemima: "I resolved to give up the plan."
The lives ceased to be a series, but those "done or doing" were
still to be published—"of course whatever one does leads to other
things—if one were *silent* quite, it might lead to despair and
abandonment of Anglo-Catholicism on the part of some."

To Jemima he wrote in September '42: "If I come to you, I
think you will think me vastly aged in this year and a half. I
begin to think myself an old man." And six months later: "My
dear Jemima, my life is done before it seems well begun."

No wonder that the sermons of these years speak of "this
disordered, dreary time, when the heaven above us is so dark
and its stars so hidden": "this late and dark age when Christians
have divided into parties and fight against each other."

Sermons on Subjects of the Day, preached while the Jerusalem affair
was giving proof of a "living and energetic heterodoxy", when the

Bishops were charging against Catholic truth, is the saddest of Newman's books.

We see the Kingdom of God to all appearances broken into fragments . . . heresy of the most deadly character around us and within us . . . invading high places. . . . When men discern duly the forlorn state in which the spouse of Christ at present lies, how can they have the heart to rejoice. . . . What is to be done with this dull, dispirited, wearied, forlorn, foreboding heart of ours?

This sermon—"Feasting in Captivity"—was preached on the sixth anniversary of the consecration of Littlemore. The occasion was marked by a ridiculous minor episode of which Newman writes to Maria Giberne (Sept. 25, 1842): "There was a vulgar stranger there, making a noise, crying Popish, etc. If I had heard him I should have had him thrown out for brawling— he was a little man and we had some stout fellows among us." The little man must have calmed down, for the sermon was preached without disturbance. It is shot through with pain, yet it dwells on the Christian duty of joy. Christ Himself "even in that awful time when His spirit fainted within Him . . . kept the feast—nay, anticipated it." With desire He desired to eat the Pasch with His disciples, Himself the Paschal Lamb "sharing in the typical rite."

And a few days before it, He took part in a public and (as it were) triumphant pageant, as though the bitterness of death had been already passed. He came to Bethany, where He had raised Lazarus; and there they made Him a supper; and Mary took the precious ointment and poured it on His head, and anointed His feet, and the house was filled with the fragrance. And next the people took branches of palm-trees, and went forth to meet Him, and strewed their garments in the way, and cried, "Hosanna, blessed is the King of Israel, that cometh in the Name of the Lord!"
To rejoice, then, and to keep festival, is a Christian duty, under all circumstances. . . . The Holy Eucharist is a Feast: we cannot help feasting, we cannot elude our destiny of joy and thanksgiving, if we would be Christians.

One gleam early in 1843 relieved the general darkness: Dr. Routh asked Newman for the fifth time to be an examiner in the Johnson Theological examination. "It created a newspaper row two years ago even," wrote Newman to Jemina, "and what it will do now I cannot guess. The President is not likely to change—

I shall not (so be it) for any clamour. To complete it, he has made James my colleague—as if my own name were not sufficiently obnoxious without adding his. It will be a trouble to me, since I wished to be quietly here—but it is so good a joke that I can scarcely wish it otherwise." The President, who to the end of his life spoke of the younger man as "the great Newman," stood firm as was expected.

This was the more remarkable since it was only a few weeks since Newman had done something calculated to alienate much sympathy. "My conscience goaded me," he wrote to Jemima, "to eat a few dirty words of mine." This meant a retractation of his past violent attacks on Rome—he listed some of the most violent, and very startling they are thus accumulated: but he makes it clear that he is apologising for the violence, not for the arguments. Naturally enough, it made, as Jemima puts it, "a great hubbub in the world." The letter appeared in the *Conservative Journal*—without signature, because he did not want to make a sensation!—and Golightly is described as "boiling over" in the *Oxford Herald*. The writing of the Retractation was probably what he had in mind when writing to Henry Wilberforce: "I am out of heart, merely because I wish to be out of hot water, and something or other is always sousing me in it again."

He must have been considerably moved towards some sort of apology to Rome by a correspondence a couple of months earlier with Dr. Russell of Maynooth. "He had," says Newman, "more to do with my conversion than anyone else. . . . He let me alone. He also gave me one or two books." One of these was a volume of sermons by St. Alphonsus Liguori: learning from Dr. Russell that some of the saint's more exuberant passages about Our Lady had been omitted, Newman realised that "such passages as are found in the works of Italian Authors were not acceptable to every part of the Catholic world," were therefore not of obligation but a matter of national taste or fancy. He gained much from the volume, much also from the Exercises of St. Ignatius. He still felt that devotion to saints was overdone, but he could not deny that the Catholic could have, and was meant to have, the most immediate access to God. In this mood he wrote the Retractation.

A priest—Fr. Pagani, a Rosminian—took it as meaning more than it did. He wrote warmly to Newman in Latin.

Newman wrote: "*Jam vero in hoc quoque de me minus accurate judicas, quasi ex retractatione mea colligendum sit motum esse quemdam in mente mea erga Ecclesiam tuam,"*—"In this also you appear to judge of me inaccurately as though my Retractation implied that there was some movement towards your Church in my mind."

It was not Catholics alone who gained this impression, although the Retractation is in fact no more than a withdrawal of extreme anti-papal language—language that Hurrell Froude had at the time protested against as uncharitable cursing and swearing. "I have said nothing, of course, on *doctrinal* points," wrote Newman to Pusey, "but only as to *abuse.*"

Some of the sermons in *Subjects of the Day* preached in 1842 and 1843 are even more interesting and touching than the four of 1841 already quoted. Among them is the sermon on Wisdom and Innocence which Kingsley took twenty years after for the text of his attack on Newman's truthfulness. He was not the first. The letters of the time, the newspapers, the stories that ran back and forth, all abound in suggestions that Newman could not be honest in remaining in the Church of England; that he had already been secretly admitted into the Church of Rome, that he was in the pay of the Pope, etc., etc. Tractarianism was the "spurious offspring of Popery," there was madness in the Newman family, "or at least great oddity and liability to twists—and this ought to be an intimation to me not to leave the Church of England." "May Heaven," writes "A Briton", "turn your heart from your evil doings."

A letter signed "Monitor" reminds Newman how the Bishops have condemned his views:

> The Bishop of Oxford as you know in your heart has censured your 90th Tract, and your Roman Breviary devotional extracts, the Bishop of Exeter your 90th Tract in the strongest terms . . . the Bishop of Peterborough your reserve on the Atonement, the Bishops of London, Chester, Calcutta, the general principle of Tridentinising the articles. . . .
>
> Far be it from me to urge you *forward*; but this I tell you, and you know it, that if your heart is reconciled to Rome and her idolatries, you have no business, according to the judgment of all your Bishops, to be ministering where you are.

The Reverend S. T. Warrington tells Newman that a respectable family "understand that Mr. Newman has received money from the Pope to dispose of as he thinks most advantageously to the cause of Romanism."

Under this trial of doubt and suspicion Newman preached
(Feb. 19, 1843) from the text: "Be ye wise as serpents and simple
as doves," a sermon which with its profound realisation of the
paradox contained in Christ's words was of necessity incomprehensible to the "muscular Christian" of the Kingsley school,
to whom subtlety of thought was but the appearance of duplicity.
Still, that he did not understand Newman's thought hardly
excuses his putting words into Newman's mouth. "Truth for its
own sake," he declared twenty years after, "has never been a
virtue with the Roman clergy. Father Newman informs us that
it need not be." When Newman asked where he was supposed
to have made such a statement, Kingsley referred to this sermon,
but never of course was he able to quote the words since Newman
had never used them. The crushing summary made of the
correspondence by Newman is worth quoting, for Kingsley was
the resurrection of the correspondents of these years:

. . . Oh . . . *not* it seems, as a priest speaking of priests; but I
make answer: "Let us have the passage." Mr. Kingsley relaxes:
"Do you know, I like your *tone*. From your *tone* I rejoice—greatly
rejoice—to be able to believe that you did not mean what you said."
I rejoin: "Mean it! I maintain I never *said* it, whether as a Protestant
or as a Catholic!" Mr. Kingsley replies: "I waive that point." I
object: "Is it possible? What? Waive the main question? I either
said it or I didn't. You have made a monstrous charge against me—
direct, distinct, public; you are bound to prove it as directly, as
distinctly, as publicly, or to own you can't!" "Well," says Mr.
Kingsley, "if you are quite sure you did not say it, I'll take your word
for it—I really will." "My *word*!" I am dumb. Somehow I thought
that it was my *word* that happened to be on trial. The *word* of a professor of lying that he does not lie! But Mr. Kingsley reassures me.
"We are both gentlemen," he says, "I have done as much as one
English gentleman can expect from another." I begin to see: he
thought me a gentleman at the very time that he said I taught lying
on system. After all it is not I, but it is Mr. Kingsley who did not mean
what he said. . . .[1]

The very simplicity of the Christian, Newman had claimed in
his sermon, is "a reason why the dove seems but a serpent":
". . . Christians give up worldly advantages; they sacrifice rank
or wealth; they prefer obscurity to station; they do penance rather

[1] Ward: *Newman*, Vol. II, pp. 3-4.

than live delicately; and the world says, 'Here are effects without
causes sufficient for them; here is craft'."

Then again it may often be the duty of Christians to obey as
far as conscience will allow, cheerfully and contentedly to leave
their cause in God's hands, even to be "well pleased that the
world should seem to triumph over them." But in the eyes of that
world "silence itself is suspicious—even silence is mystery. Why
do they not speak out. . . . The submitting to calumny is a proof
that it is too true."

And then again if the silence and simplicity of God's servants
issues in the triumph of their cause "the event seems to show that a
calculation of results has been the actuating principle at bottom!
It is God Who designs, but His servants seem designing; and that
the more, should it so happen that they really do themselves catch
glimpses of their own position in His providential course."

It is curious that at this time when so many assumed that he
was on the point of joining the Church, he was still trying to hold
others back. He went on doing so till near the end of 1843. As
an example there is a correspondence in the file of 1842 with a
man who writes that he is going to cast his lot among the Priesthood of the Church of Rome:

To this result your writings more than aught else have led . . .
you were the first to create those longings within my soul which I now
feel cannot be satisfied but by communion with Rome; and I am fain
to think that you must at times feel yourself sadly straitened within
those narrow bounds to which the Church of England confines you,
even as you regard her. To me she seems composed of shadows, and
to feed her children on wind. Yet permit me to add, that should you
deem it expedient to make any observations in disapproval they shall
receive my most respectful and serious consideration. . . .

Newman wrote on the back of this letter:

Sir, I am not at all surprised that you should have made up your
mind to join the Church of Rome, considering you call an attention
to the question of less than two years "long and deep consideration,
much research, and patient counting of the cost." Allow me to say,
that those who take more pains than you profess to have done, are
accustomed to come to a very different view of their duty.

Young men tending Romewards were sent to Littlemore by
friends who looked to Newman to "quiet them." He says in the

Apologia: "I kept some of them back for several years from being received into the Catholic Church." Most interesting is the story of his own brother-in-law, Tom Mozley, which has never been told.

A visit to France filled Harriett with dislike for the French people and their religion—"Their ways and habits are so unnecessarily uncomfortable. They go out of their way to be miserable and take a great deal of pains to be odious". It had the opposite effect on Tom. He came back in September (1843) determined to be received. Newman rushed over to Cholderton arriving at seven one morning and discussed the matter with Tom for eight hours—as usual urging patience and delay. "I think him excited," he wrote to Jemima, "and no fit judge of what he is doing. The sudden access of truth or apparent truth *does* excite."

Harriett was furious both with her husband and, less reasonably, with her brother. For Newman in all fairness had confessed to Tom his own unsettled state of mind. "I find to my surprise," he wrote to Jemima, "that she considers me *particeps criminis*." His general view of the situation is also given to Jemima:

As to T. you must make greater allowances than perhaps you can make. I spoke so much to him, when I saw him, against his surprising people, that I hoped he would not have been so incautious—but he does not feel the harm and misery of doing so. He is abrupt in all he does, and he is particularly likely to be awkward in a matter of this kind. He thinks it less pain too on the whole to get it over, than to inflict a slow and chronic anxiety ever increasing till the disclosure comes. And then as to his light manner, it is intended (however injudiciously) to soften the pain in the person to whom he writes. Then you cannot estimate what so many (alas!) feel at present, the strange effect produced on the mind when the conviction flashes, or rather pours upon it that Rome is the true Church. Of course it is a most revolutionary, and therefore a most exciting, tumultuous conviction. For this reason persons should not act under it, for it is impossible in such a state of emotion that they can tell whether their conviction is well founded or not. They cannot judge calmly.

In these letters Newman admits to a belief that it will be impossible to hold Tom back permanently, and he said many years later that he had expected Tom to come into the Church when he himself did. Tom, however, settled down (assisted no doubt by Harriett), but others preceded Newman, and his resignation of St. Mary's in the September of 1843, was the result of the conversion of one of the men, Lockhart, who had been living at Littlemore.

Just before Tom Mozley broke the news of his own attraction to Rome, Lockhart had been received by Father Gentili—who wrote Newman an almost apologetic letter of explanation. The trouble was that Lockhart had been an "inmate" at Littlemore and had previously promised Newman that he would wait for three years, of which only just over a year had expired. This promise he did not mention to the priest. "Dr. G. did not," Newman wrote to Keble, "make any overtures to him . . . he writes me word he had a call so very strong that he felt he dare not disobey it."

Newman was much upset. Writing to Lockhart's mother about "the painful news," he says: "The step he has taken has surprised us and grieved us." To Jemima he wrote: "This occurrence will very likely fix the time of my resigning St. Mary's, for Lockhart had been teaching in the school till he went away and at this moment they are expecting him back and inquiring after him. It is a great scandal." In answer to her letters of entreaty that he would at least delay his resignation, Newman wrote:

August 31, 1843.

MY DEAREST JEMIMA,

I am very sorry to put you to such pain. Your letter would have brought me to many tears unless I had so hard a heart. . . . I wonder my late letters have not prepared you. . . . No time is "the" time. You may have thought as you read on "three years ago would not have mattered". Will three years hence be easier? The question is, *ought* it to be done? . . .

My dearest Jemima, my circumstances are not of my making. One's duty is to act *under* circumstances. Is it a light thing to give up Littlemore? Am I not providing dreariness for myself? If others, whom I am pierced to think about, because I cannot help them, suffer, shall I not suffer in my own way?

Everything that one does honestly, sincerely, with prayer, with advice, must turn to good. In what am I not likely to be as good a judge as another? In the consequences? True, but is not this what I have been ever protesting against? Going by expedience, not by principle? . . . If this be a case of duty, and if I be able to judge whether or no it is, I must leave the consequences to Him Who makes it a duty. My sweetest Jemima, of whom I am quite unworthy, rather

MOTHER CHURCH AND HER PUSSEY-ITES, 1842

Punch's Pencillings. No. XXXII

pray that something may occur to hinder me if I am wrong, than take the matter into your own hands.

What his unknown correspondent had said about the Bishops' attitude gave expression to one of the things that weighed most heavily on Newman—especially in relation to his holding St. Mary's. He had written to Keble early in the year:

What increases my difficulty most heavily is the gradual advance, which is making to a unanimous condemnation of No. 90 on the part of the Bishops . . . no one but myself can be answerable for every word of it. The Bishops condemn it without specifying *what* they condemn in it. This gives an opening to every reader who agrees with it on the whole, to escape the force of their censure. I alone cannot escape it. . . . By October next the probability is, that hardly a single Bishop but will have given his voice against it; that is, given his voice against that comment on the Articles on which alone I can hold my living. How can I with any comfort, with any sense of propriety, retain it?

It was all very well for James Mozley to write (August 31, 1843):

You certainly have been singled out for attack by Bishops and Archdeacons. . . . But it seemed almost necessary that you should be. These people know from their connexions with the place who is really at the head of the Movement and single him out. They know perfectly well that you and not Pusey are at the head. . . . You will not be much obliged to me for wishing to keep you as a public butt.

Newman saw just what this singling out as a public butt implied. To Manning's enquiry following his resignation he replied: "The nearest approach I can give to a general account . . . is to say that it has been caused by the general repudiation of the view contained in No. 90 on the part of the Church . . . lay and clerical. . . . It is felt, I am far from denying justly felt, that I am a foreign material—and cannot assimilate with the Church of England."

Yet how deeply his heart was involved in it, how passionately he still clung to it! The publication of the *Sermons on Subjects of the Day* was (he told Keble) "a sort of guarantee to people" that his resignation "did not involve an ulterior step—for no one could suppose that I should be publishing today, and leaving the Church tomorrow."

Two passages in the sermons touch on a thought on which he often dwelt—as have so many when the fear first beset them that they were not within the true Church. How can that Church be other than Christ's in which so many die happily, in which so many live holily: "men so saintly in their lives, so heavenly in their hearts and minds, so self-denying, so obedient. . . . Is it not safe to trust our souls in their company? Is it not dangerous to part company with them in our journey across the trackless wilderness?"

It was the seventh anniversary of the dedication of the Church of St. Mary's at Littlemore—a feast kept year by year with deep rejoicing. This year again the flock were gathered, the Church adorned, friends come from Oxford.

"I am just returned," wrote Pusey to his brother, "half broken-hearted from the commemoration at Littlemore. The sermon was like one of Newman's in which self was altogether repressed, yet it showed the more how deeply he felt the misconception of himself. It implied rather than said farewell. People sobbed audibly, and I, who officiated at the altar, could hardly help mingling sorrow with even that Feast. However, 'the peace of God which surpasseth all understanding' closed all."[1]

"The Parting of Friends" was preached from the text: "Man goeth forth to his work and to his labour until the evening." It begins "When the Son of Man, the First-born of the creation of God, came to the evening of His mortal life, He parted with His disciples at a feast." He had toiled through the long day, had borne its burdens and its heats and now was about to enter on His passion.

. . . But there is nothing gloomy, churlish, violent or selfish in His grief; it is tender, affectionate, social. He calls His friends around Him . . . He desires their sympathy, He takes refuge in their love. He first feasted them, and sang a hymn with them and washed their feet; and when His long trial began, He beheld them and kept them in His presence, till they in terror shrank from it. . . . O, wonderful pattern, the type of all trial and of all duty under it, while the Church endures.

Although then "we indeed today have no need of so high a lesson and so august a comfort" we may think of the changes

[1] Liddon, *Pusey*, Vol. II, p. 374.

of life, the rhythm of the earth's seasons, the good and the evil that God sends us.

. May not His sun set as it has risen? And must it not set if it is to rise again? And must not darkness come first if there is ever to be morning? . . . And cannot He Who can do all things, cause a light to rise even in the darkness?

David building the Temple had brought all that he could of beauty for God's house, "all manner of precious stones, and marble stones in abundance" and the people had rejoiced and their King with them "for that they offered willingly." (Had not Newman, too, and his people rejoiced and offered willingly, if it were only a simple stone building, a beautiful altar cloth and bunches of wild flowers?)

. . . We, too, at this season, year by year, have been allowed in our measure, according to our work and our faith, to rejoice in God's Presence, for this sacred building which He has given us to worship Him in. It was a glad time when we first met here,—many of us now present recollect it; nor did our rejoicing cease, but was renewed every autumn, as the day came round. . . . We have kept the feast heretofore with merry hearts; we have kept it seven full years unto "a perfect end"; now let us keep it, even though in haste, and with bitter herbs, and with loins girded, and with a staff in our hand, as they who have "no continuing city, but seek one to come".

And then he turns to the stories in Scripture of the partings of friends—of Jacob who "kept feast before he set out upon his dreary way . . . received a father's blessing and then was sent afar"; of Naomi when Ruth clave unto her, but Orpah kissed and left her bringing her "the pain we feel when friends disappoint us, and fall in our esteem";[1] the parting of David with Jonathan, "O, hard destiny, except that the All-merciful so willed it that such companions might not walk in the House of God as friends."

David's affection was given to a single heart, but turning to the New Testament Newman recalls the great Apostle who "had a thousand friends, and loved each as his own soul, and seemed to live a thousand lives in them, and died a thousand deaths when he

[1] It is interesting to find by a letter from Manning—and a denial from Newman— that he thought the allusion to Orpah was intended for himself.

must quit them . . . yet we read of his bidding farewell to whole
Churches, never to see them again."

All the sons of men, however great, give us but shadows of Him
Who in Himself gathered all human experience: kept feast like
Jacob, was persecuted like David, like Naomi deserted by His
friends, "cried out 'I thirst' in a barren and dry land . . . like St.
Paul, 'witnessed a good confession,' and beyond St. Paul . . .
'He came unto His own and His own received Him not.' Heavily
did He leave, tenderly did He mourn over the country and city
which rejected Him."

Like the singing of the Reproaches, or the Lamentations in
Holy Week, the little Church was filled with the clear voice making
audible every word of Christ's lament over the once holy city that
had rejected Him:

"O Jerusalem, Jerusalem, which killest the prophets, and stonest
them that are sent unto thee, how often would I have gathered thy
children together, as a hen doth gather her brood under her wings,
and ye would not! Behold your house is left unto you desolate."

From the depths of this grief, in the texture of this love, are
woven the words of the heartbroken appeal to the Church of
England, still seen by him not as a different Church, but as the
Church of the Saxon saints, the Church of St. Ambrose and St.
Augustine. At moments other thoughts had flashed upon him,
but today it is a Catholic Church, a part of the Church Universal,
unfaithful but reclaimable, to which he speaks, to which he
appeals not without many tears:

. . . O, mother of saints! O, school of the wise! O, nurse of the
heroic! of whom went forth, in whom have dwelt, memorable names
of old, to spread the truth abroad, or to cherish and illustrate it at
home! O thou, from whom surrounding nations lit their lamps! O,
virgin of Israel! Wherefore dost thou now sit on the ground and keep
silence, like one of the foolish women who were without oil on the
coming of the Bridegroom? Where is now the ruler in Sion, and the
doctor in the Temple, and the ascetic on Carmel, and the herald in
the wilderness, and the preacher in the market-place? Where are thy
"effectual fervent prayers," offered in secret, and thy alms and good
works coming up as a memorial before God? . . . O my mother,
whence is this unto thee, that thou hast good things poured upon thee
and canst not keep them, and bearest children, yet darest not own

them? Why hast thou not the skill to use their services, nor the heart to rejoice in their love? How is it that whatever is generous in purpose, and tender or deep in devotion, thy flower and thy promise, falls from thy bosom and finds no home within thine arms? Who hath put this note upon thee, to have "a miscarrying womb, and dry breasts", to be strange to thine own flesh, and thine eye cruel towards thy little ones? Thine own offspring, the fruit of thy womb, who love thee and would toil for thee, thou dost gaze upon with fear, as though a portent, or thou dost loathe as an offence; at best thou dost but endure, as if they had no claim but on thy patience, self-possession, and vigilance, to be rid of them as easily as thou mayest. Thou makest them "stand all the day idle", as the very condition of thy bearing with them; or thou biddest them be gone, where they will be more welcome; or thou sellest them for naught to the stranger that passes by. And what wilt thou do in the end thereof? . . .

The sermon had been woven out of the substance of Scripture and the substance of Newman's heart. ".Scripture," he says, "is a refuge in any trouble . . . its language veils our feelings while it gives expression to them. It is sacred and heavenly; and it restrains and purifies, while it sanctions them."

In the last paragraph the veils are torn and the heart speaks openly:

And, O my brethren, O kind and affectionate hearts, O loving friends, should you know any one whose lot it has been, by writing or by word of mouth, in some degree to help you . . .! If he has ever told you what you knew about yourselves, or what you did not know; has read to you your wants or feelings, and comforted you by the very reading; has made you feel that there was a higher life than this daily one, and a brighter world than that you see; or encouraged you, or sobered you, or opened a way to the inquiring, or soothed the perplexed; if what he has said or done has ever made you take interest in him, and feel well inclined towards him; remember such a one in time to come, though you hear him not, and pray for him, that in all things he may know God's Will, and at all times he may be ready to fulfil it.

CHAPTER XXIX

William George Ward

ALTHOUGH I am writing the story of Newman and not a history of the Oxford Movement, I must at this point behave like an old-style novelist, and, leaving Newman in his retreat at Littlemore, return to Oxford and to the sequel of Tract 90—not in his mind, but in the University.

Newman had accepted the application to himself of his line on St. Athanasius: "Thou couldst a people raise but couldst not rule." Yet he had been ruling for years men of greater divergence and strength of opinion who had acted under him as one party. Now he had abdicated and the natural results followed.

From the beginning there had been in the movement two strongly marked divisions—the Establishment men of whom Palmer of Worcester was typical, and the Apostolicals. Very unfairly as regards the preacher, but with considerable justification as regards the Establishment group, Stanley sees in the excitement over Keble's Assize Sermon clear proof that the movement was at its start purely political. For Palmer and his friends, indeed, the danger to the Church, "by law established," bulked large; but for Keble the issues were always spiritual.

Both these groups had looked to Newman for leadership; both had accepted Tract 90, although some (as Dean Hook) had doubted; but almost inspired leadership was called for to make them keep step. And now a third party was arising; far more impracticable, equally devoted to Newman, but differing more widely with both Establishment and Anglo-Catholic than these did with one another. These were the Romanisers, and by common consent the historians of the movement name as their leader William George Ward—usually described as Ward of Balliol—who (according to Tait) "worried Newman into writing Tract 90." In the *Recollections of A. P. Stanley* it is stated that Ward "succeeded Dr. Newman as the acknowledged leader", of the movement as a whole. And since in Newman's words a movement must by definition continue to move and all other parties were chiefly concerned to avoid moving (Pusey really believed and was glad to believe that for several years they had remained stationary), this seems no exaggeration.

Unlike Newman's, Ward's leadership was wholly intellectual and impersonal, and in his own eyes he remained a follower deputising for the true leader. It was he who had first used the phrase *Credo in Newmannum*, and to a priest friend he said: "You Roman Catholics know what it is to have a Pope. Well, Newman is my Pope."

But Newman was not the head of Ward's Church, and the fundamental difference between this new party and the two older groups lay in their attitude towards the Church of England. Newman, Pusey, Froude and Keble had a passionate love for their own Church and drew their Catholic ideas from her formularies and her history. Through those formularies, through that history, Newman was gradually discovering (with intense pain at every step) that his true home was elsewhere. Ward, on the other hand, had started as a Liberal, with no love for the Church of England, no reverence for her history or her formularies. One day a friend, discussing with him the relation of the Anglican service to the older rituals, the Salisbury use, the Hereford use, etc., remarked that the Reformers thought they had done a good work in simplifying and arranging the ritual so that the whole kingdom should have one use, Ward replied: "Yes, and a precious dull use they took care it should be."

Perfectly typical of the half cheerful, half savage irreverence of this new group towards their Church was a squib which appeared in the *Westminster Review*.[1] The occasion was an effort—unsuccessful, as it happened—made in the summer of 1842 to rescind the decree of six years earlier forbidding Dr. Hampden a say in the naming of University preachers. A nameless humorist published a Latin letter (providing his own translation, given here in footnotes), which the Vice-Chancellor was supposed to have written to the country parsons. It begins by explaining the 1836 condemnation of Hampden:

Causa assignata hujus voti singularis erat certa doctrina de Trinitate, quam nasus acutus carissimi nostri Pusey in oblito quodam doctoris istius opere opportunissime detruserat, et in lucem traxerat. Vos

[1] Here quoted from *The Clerk of Oxford*, pp. 345-9.

autem habetis nimium sensum supponere talem absurditatem impulisse nos votum illud proponere, aut nos singulum damnum de doctrina illa aut ulla alia curavisse . . . in hoc voto dando, ut in aliis rebus, panibus et piscibus oculum omnino habuimus. Detestabilis ista administratio, vulgo Melbourne vocata, res summas gerebat.[1]

They had to attack the Melbourne Government, because under it "all the fat of the Church was devoured by Liberals". But now, continues the letter, Peel is in power, and Peel also is favouring the Liberal party in the Church: therefore it would be well to please Peel by reversing the vote on Hampden: the Trinity might well be left as an open question. After all:

Magna res est ponere homines reçtae sortis in vacantibus Episcopatibus; Peelus autem dat Episcopatus; ergo si Episcopatus obtinere volumus, necesse est placere Peelo. Vos autem, rustici mei fratres clerici! probabiliter dicetis, "Quid nobis cum Episcopatu? Sumus homines quieti, sine patronis, sine magnis talentis: non expectamus esse Episcopi; non omnes possumus."[2]

Perhaps not: but *est nulla sciens*—there is no knowing—and in any event you might get benefits from those who are made Bishops. Further, there is one immediate argument for their coming to vote: they must know that:

. . . damnatum bonum prandium paratum sit. Non necesse est loqui: hoc tantum postponit horam prandii: nec prandium decet esse frigidum. Sola res quam habetis facere est vota dare. Si autem Puseyitae isti spurcissimi, iniquissimi, impransi, impransurique, habent impudentiam vobis resistere . . . vos, O rustici clerici! potestis vos utiles facere . . . infernalem strepitum edendo et clamando "Quaestio! Quaestio! Dividite! Dividite!" omnigenarumque bestiarum, aviumque

---

[1] The assigned cause of this somewhat irregular proceeding was a certain doctrine concerning the Trinity, which the sharp nose of our dearest Pusey most opportunely ferreted out in some forgotten work of the doctor, and dragged to light. You however have too much sense to suppose that we had no better reason than the one assigned for the vote, or that we really cared for the doctrine in question more than any other. . . . We, as in other things, had solely an eye for the loaves and fishes. That detestable administration, commonly called "The Melbourne", then carried on the government.

[2] The great thing is to put men of the right sort into the vacant bishoprics; but Peel has the giving of the bishoprics: therefore if we wish to obtain bishoprics, we must please Peel. But you, my reverend country brethren, to whom I chiefly address my observations, will probably say, "What are bishoprics to us? We are quiet men without patrons, without great talents; we do not expect to be bishops; we cannot all be so."

obscenarum voces imitando. Tanto citius prandium obtinebitis,
cutesque vestras vino implebitis.[1]

I suppose his son would have known if this had been written
by W. G. Ward, but—*est nulla sciens*—and I myself cannot get
over the feeling that something so characteristic of my grandfather
was indeed his work.

In doctrine as in worship the great attraction for Ward,
Oakeley, and the rest lay not in the Anglican but in the Roman
Church. From the moment when Ward—who became later the
respected antagonist of Mill and Bentham—discovered that in
Liberalism there was no sufficiently deep philosophy of faith, his
whole bent was towards Rome. He had begun, with his usual
vehemence, by hating the Tractarians, but falling under Newman's spell he was halted in his progress and became as ardent
a Newmanite as he had been a Liberal. For several years this
position contented him; he did not dream of leaving the Church
of England. But neither he nor "good cultivated little Mr.
Oakeley," as Dean Goulburn calls him, would consent to join in
that abuse of Rome hitherto deemed essential to the Tractarian
position. Ward especially preferred to abuse England. Oakeley,
too, had been a tutor of Balliol. At this date he was incumbent of
Margaret Street chapel, the great London centre of the Tractarians
where Ward often preached, while Oakeley was frequently to be
found in the Balliol Common Room.

I find it a little easier to picture my grandfather from having
known Chesterton—although there were important differences
between the two men, especially in that exquisite subtlety of
mind that G.K. had and Ward so lamentably lacked. But in
swiftness, acuteness, keen logical faculty and overpowering sense
of humour they were much alike—and strikingly in the fact that
a certain absurdity of aspect was a bar to their being taken
seriously when they were most serious. "A strange motley discursive man," says Abbott of W. G. Ward. To Tait and Stanley he

---

[1] . . . a dinner will be prepared for those who give their votes to us. There is no
necessity for talking: it only postpones the dinner hour; and the dinner ought not to
get cold. The only thing you have to do is to give us your votes. But if those dirty,
iniquitous, undined and undinable Puseyites should have the impudence to resist
us . . . you, O country clergymen! may usefully employ yourselves . . . in making an
infernal noise, and shouting " Question! Question! Divide! Divide! " and imitating
the voices of all manner of unclean beasts and birds. So much the sooner will you
get your dinner, and fill your skins with wine.

was "the Prince of Controversialists." To Dean Church "the most amusing, the most tolerant man in Oxford." "I never," says Dean Goulburn, "knew any personality equally intense." The picture of him as a mere buffoon has occasionally appeared in modern accounts of Newman and the Movement, but was never suggested by any of his Oxford contemporaries—although some called him the *enfant terrible* of the Party.

Ward's appearance was against him—and to some extent his habits. Below the middle height, immensely fat, "a huge moon-faced man," says Stanley, given, like Whately, to breaking chairs in the Common Room, not merely by sitting but by leaning on them while intent in an argument, singing whole operas with appropriate action while a friend played the piano, immensely untidy, Ward stood out even in an age of "characters" at the University. He was young in a superficially conventional period to win the position, usually accorded to much older men, in which he might go his own way. Lecturer in Logic and Mathematics at Balliol, he was popular with Dr. Jenkyns the famous Master who, says Dean Church, was proud of him; for although not clever himself, he was a judge of a clever man as a jockey might be of a horse. He probably never discovered that one of the joys of the Common Room was an imitation by Ward of his own mannerisms wedded to the pirouettes and pantomimic expressions of a ballerina. Both Ward's figure and the contrast with his deeper moods of philosophical discussion made all this especially piquant, and the younger dons delighted in it "as though," said one of them, "Thomas Aquinas were to dance a ballet." But an older tutor, unable to continue his reading, once sent a scout to enquire into the unseemly noises above his head, "It's only Mr. Ward," the scout reported, "he's a-hacting of a Cherubim."

And then would follow perhaps the curious contrast of the same "magnificent ear and voice" in the college chapel in a "reading of the prayers such as one only hears," says Dean Goulburn, "once in a lifetime . . . simple and natural . . . leaving the impression that the reader was deeply conscious he was addressing Almighty God."

At Balliol Ward's close friends were chiefly Liberals, some of them briefly attracted by Newman—Stanley, Tait, Clough. Tait had been, as we saw, one of the four tutors who attacked Tract 90, and Ward believed that he was doing a service to Newman by issuing two pamphlets: *A Few Words in Defence of Tract 90* and

A Few More Words in Defence of Tract 90, in which he tried to make clearer whatever had been left obscure, his main aim being to defend Newman against the accusation of casuistry. But in doing this he was curiously blind to the peculiar difficulties of Newman's position. In a letter to Pusey he avowed his fears that Pusey's own defence of Tract 90 (which appeared almost at the same time as Ward's second pamphlet) "would tend the more to blind people to Newman's anti-reformation feelings, from their tendency to consider you almost his authorised interpreter . . . ." In fact, as late as April 1841, Newman could write to Ryder, "Pusey has just discovered that I dislike the Reformers."

Poor worried Dr. Pusey! He had sincerely thought that Newman and he stood almost exactly together. He had been willing to subscribe or not subscribe to the Martyrs' Memorial to identify himself with his friend, but he was preparing a defence of Tract 90 which advocated a favourable view of the Reformation. "This question," says Wilfrid Ward, "was the rock on which the Tractarians split and divided into two parties, the Romanisers and the more moderate school. Newman had passed the question over as of small account, and the difference of opinion might have been scarcely noticed had it not been brought into the boldest relief by Mr. Ward."

Newman had maintained that by God's blessing the proceedings of the Reformers had been so overruled that the sin of schism had been avoided and the Church of England had remained Catholic. To this Ward agreed, but thus underlined what he considered Newman's view of the difficulties the Holy Ghost had somehow surmounted: "He intimates, not very obscurely (Tract, p. 79), that in releasing the English Church from the Roman Supremacy her then governors were guilty of rebellion, and considering that they had also sworn obedience to the Pope, for my own part I see not how we can avoid adding— of perjury."

Newman had maintained that there was no difficulty in subscribing the Articles in a Catholic sense: "our Prayer book is acknowledged on all hands to be of Catholic origin, our Articles, also the offspring of an uncatholic age, are through God's good providence, to say the least, not uncatholic."

In Ward's eyes, however, they *were* uncatholic: his own defence for signing them was that no single person in the Church of England could accept them all since they were self-contradictory.

He had first signed them as a Liberal, later as a Catholic—and he invented the phrase that he had signed "in a non-natural sense". It is not surprising that Dean Church should feel that this phrase— caught up and emphasised by the Protestant opposition—did immense harm to the plain man's view of Tractarian good faith. This plain man never reads anything himself, is quite impervious to the attack on his own attitude, for he has never attached any particular sense to any particular article. He feels only that Jesuitry is abroad when he hears such a word as "non-natural."

With the best intentions, too, Ward was not fair to Newman; for to Newman a close historical analysis and an exquisite accuracy—comparable to that required to get the hair-splitting difference between a distant station on the radio and mere static—had made the signing of the Articles no difficulty at all. "I distinctly repudiate," Newman wrote many years later, "that I maintained either in Tract 90 or elsewhere, the right of a man's subscribing to the Thirty-Nine Articles in a non-natural sense . . . I maintained in Tract 90 that the Thirty-Nine Articles ought to be subscribed in their 'literal and grammatical sense'."

Yet neither was Newman wholly with Pusey, and an interesting letter shows how strange he felt it that after such years of intimacy Pusey only realised after a long talk with Ward that he and Newman were after all not in full agreement. And Newman did not repudiate Ward's defence: even if he disliked the word "non-natural", much of what Ward said he too held even if it went beyond what he had yet expressed. Many years later he voiced in the *Apologia* the annoyance he had felt at being pushed to go at Ward's pace and not at his own, but at the time Ward was unconscious of this: he went constantly to Littlemore, he dragged from Newman confirmations of conclusions drawn by him from what Newman had already said, he flourished them triumphantly at Pusey.

Yet, too, Newman was holding Ward back. "Newman has been preaching some most striking sermons," he wrote to a friend, "on the notes of the Church and the duty of staying where we are . . . within the last month he has been favoured with singular intimations of Christ's presence in the sacraments of our Church." And when Lockhart first began to waver Newman announced to Pusey (with obvious satisfaction) that it was Ward who had persuaded him to promise a three years' delay.

In 1841 Newman had handed over the editorship of the

British Critic to Tom Mozley who has graphically described his own difficulties with Ward's numerous involved articles, "uncouth in form," says Wilfrid Ward, "heavy in style, onesided in treatment"; "the handwriting," says Mozley, "was minute and detestable, it defied correction." An article was made up of "bundles of irregular scraps of paper." It was hard to abbreviate, being "without beginning or end." If Pusey is to be pitied, so too is Mozley. Of an occasional attempt he made at alteration he writes:

I did but touch a filament or two in one of his monstrous cobwebs, and off ran he instantly to Newman to complain of my gratuitous impertinence. Newman was then in this difficulty. He did not disagree with what Ward had written; but, on the other hand, he had given neither me nor Ward to understand that he was likely to step in between us. In fact he wished to be entirely clear of the editorship. This, however, was a thing that Ward could not or would not understand.[1]

Ward's articles on the foundations of faith have no place in this narrative, but those in which he stressed the practical corruptions of the English Church, the sinfulness of the perpetual attacks on Rome, and the enchanting hope of reunion, had considerable effect on the Movement. "The Church was going on very well," one Tractarian bitterly complained, "when Mr. Ward unhappily became connected with the *British Critic*, since which time all has gone wrong." But in October 1843, a remarkably fierce attack by Palmer of Worcester brought about the sudden death of the *British Critic*. A moderate Review, the *Christian Remembrancer*, took its place, and Ward now turned to the writing of a pamphlet which became "a fat book which will, I hope," he wrote to Father Whitty, "bring matters to an issue."

This book was *The Ideal of a Christian Church*.

The atmosphere of Oxford during these years is conveyed by various writers of the right and left—by J. A. Froude and Mark Pattison, who from Newmanites later became free-thinkers; by Dean Church in his valuable narrative; by Tait and Stanley's biographers; by Principal Shairp and Oakeley and Wilfrid Ward; by Canon Liddon in his *Life of Pusey*; by the letters of James Mozley and Rogers (Lord Blachford), and James Hope and

[1] Mozley: *Reminiscences*, Vol. II, pp. 225-226.

Gladstone and hundreds of other letters published and unpublished. By Palmer's narrative also—the title of which was as we have seen: *A Narrative of Events connected with the Publication of the Tracts for the Times with Reflections on existing Tendencies to Romanism.* (How lovely to be able to publish under such explanatory titles!)

All these in different fashions tell the same story. The authorities drew little distinction between moderates and extremists. Suspicion grew. Ward resigned his lectureships in Logic and Mathematics on hearing that Dr. Jenkyns was trying in vain to screw up the courage to ask him to do so. "What heresy," he had said, "may he not insinuate under the form of a syllogism." To his immense relief, Ward came in one day and said, "I have come to resign my two lectureships . . . I must, if your views on the question are the true ones, be a most dangerous man." "Really, Ward," said the Master, "this is just like your generosity."

Stanley notes with great pleasure the goodwill prevailing on all sides during these difficult days at Balliol:

Tait was the great mover against Ward and they are still on perfectly good terms with each other. The Master shed tears in the final interview, and is very much disturbed about it; it is said that he is overheard grumbling to himself, "I wish Mrs. Jenkyns would take care of the flowers instead of the cabbages . . ." and then in the next breath, "I wish Mr. Ward would not write such pamphlets." He and everyone else says that no one could have behaved better than Ward about it.[1]

But elsewhere than at Balliol matters went less smoothly. The defeat of Isaac Williams for the Professorship of Poetry, at the beginning of 1842, has already been mentioned, and it was followed by an attack on Dr. Pusey in 1843. Pusey had preached on "The Holy Eucharist a Comfort to the Penitent." The sermon was later printed and no one could find in it statements more extreme than those of the leading Anglican divines. But the men chosen to pronounce on its orthodoxy were mostly bigoted opponents of Tractarianism. It was one of the strangest trials on record.[2] The original accuser was one of the judges; the accused was not allowed to be heard or even to be present, and was bound to secrecy on such information about the trial as was vouchsafed to him. The decision of the court was never promulgated officially. But Pusey was condemned for having taught

---

[1] *Life of Stanley*, Vol. I, p. 297.
[2] See Church, *The Oxford Movement*, p. 285, ff.

doctrine contrary to that of the Church of England and suspended from preaching within the University for two years.

Earlier I have touched on the special difficulty experienced by the Tractarians in setting out their Eucharistic belief, even when their own minds were entirely clear, which was not always the case. The example of the change in Keble's hymn is well-known. They were not sure if they should say, "As in the hands so in the heart," or "Not in the hands but in the heart." Which of the expressions used by the Fathers, used by their own divines, could they safely employ?

A story of Dean Hook, one of the moderates, is more startling than the Pusey incident although of course far less well-known. It took place a few years earlier (1838). Vicar of Leeds at the time, he was accused by his churchwardens of wasting "parish property by pouring away some of the consecrated wine, *which ought to have been kept by them to be consecrated again.*" The Vicar replied that it was impossible for him to give back to the church-wardens "that which had once been consecrated as the blood of Christ." [1] He had poured the wine down the piscina as there was no fire in which it might have been consumed. This, his biographer tells us, "was construed to imply a belief in a corporeal presence of Christ in the elements." Dean Hook, in a letter to the *British Magazine*, strenuously denied believing in transubstantiation; he quoted Cranmer's words, "The Cup of the most Holy Blood," adding that Cranmer was "not very high," and said that he himself had called the consecrated elements "*relatively holy*" (his own italics). He stated, too, that he "thought it not improbable" that the churchwardens who often drank in the vestry some of the *unconsecrated* wine would have no scruple in doing the same with that which had been consecrated, "for which they evidently entertained no respect." Dean Hook was later to cause Pusey a great many heartaches, but at this time he thought Pusey's spirit "beautiful," contrasting it with the bitterness of the Protestant opposition.

Hampden took advantage of his position as Regius Professor to avenge himself on the followers of the men who had most tenaciously attacked him, and young men coming up for Ordination, or even for degrees, were increasingly subjected to what J. A. Froude has called, "an informal inquisition."

[1] W. R. W. Stephens: *Life and Letters of Walter Farquhar Hook*, Vol. II, p. 3 (Italics mine).

The Macmullen case became famous—because Macmullen was a fighter and a successful one. Into an examination for a B.D. degree on which the retention of his Fellowship depended, but which had hitherto been almost a formality, Hampden introduced, says Dean Church: "two propositions which the candidate was to support, framed so as to commit him to assertions which Mr. Macmullen, whose High Anglican opinions were well-known, could not consistently make." The Vice-Chancellor refused the degree, Macmullen fought the decision, first in the Vice-Chancellor's Court and then in the University Court of Delegates. Finally he got his degree; but not many men could or would spend two or three years and employ distinguished lawyers to achieve a B.D. degree.

It is an over-simplification to say, as J. A. Froude does, that it was Tract 90 alone which produced this, and that before its appearance "the Tracts had represented pretty exactly Anglican Oxford." There had always been an opposing current which Tract 90 strengthened and widened.

And I think that in talking of the effect of the Tract, Froude and others do not allow enough for the effect of Newman's absence from Oxford. Had he remained to lead them, the Tractarians would have got over the effect of the Tract as they had got over the effect of Froude's *Remains*. The loss of Newman's leadership, the activities of their own extremists were the really operative factors in their growing unpopularity.

Newman had vainly advised abstention in the contest for the Poetry Professorship. He refused to give advice as being too remote from Oxford affairs when the Evangelical Warden of Wadham— Mr. B. P. Symons—was put forward for the Vice-Chancellorship. But he indicated that his own feelings were for keeping quiet. Often before had the Tractarians gathered their forces, always representing a large proportion, usually a majority of the University voters. But now they were defeated by the overwhelming majority of 882 to 183. All they had achieved was to make themselves doubly unpopular with the new Vice-Chancellor.

The moderates grew more and more bitter—and not un-naturally against the extremists. Palmer begged Newman to denounce Ward. Newman refused, although in a letter he told Hope that he did not go the whole way with Ward and Oakeley, who were moving towards the claim to hold all Roman doctrine while remaining members of the Anglican Church.

As the moderates grew more timid or more exasperated the extremists grew more extreme.

Into this ocean of eddying currents Ward, in June 1844, threw the *Ideal of a Christian Church*, with a mighty splash.

Ward was even more diffuse than Palmer in giving a title to his book. It was called *The Ideal of a Christian Church considered in Comparison with existing Practice; containing a Defence of certain Articles in the British Critic in Reply to Remarks on them in Mr. Palmer's Narrative.*

The leading ideas of this ill-constructed volume of more than 600 pages have been skilfully drawn out by the author's son in *William George Ward and the Oxford Movement*, and the summary there given throws into bold relief the wide agreement and the vast contrast between Ward and Newman.

The main contention of the book was that the aim of a Christian Church is the sanctification of the individual, and that a Church is to be judged by her success in producing saints and in saving souls. "We are, if I may use a homely expression, at a perfect standstill for want of saints and holy men." No Church can hope to achieve this without a complete system of dogmatic, moral and mystical theology. A Church lacking especially "a deep dogmatic theology, exuberant with life, indomitable in energy, that Church is languid in her spiritual functions, wavering and unauthoritative in ruling her own subjects, feeble and prostrate in her external relations. And what the wonder? Saints are the very hidden life of a Church, and saints cannot be nurtured on less than the full Catholic doctrine."

Newman had, in "The Parting of Friends", appealed to the Church of England as Mother of saints and nurse of the heroic, who had of late languished, but might be brought again to her former greatness. He touched her wounds with the tender finger of love. Ward advanced with a heavy stick to beat her about the head. In theory he disapproved of what is commonly called patriotism as "at bottom but base pride and vulgar nationality", and his view of the Church of England was unsoftened by any tender feelings. " . . . Ever since the schism of the sixteenth century," he writes, "the English Church has been swayed by a spirit of arrogance, self-contentment, and self-complacency, resembling rather an absolute infatuation than the imbecility of ordinary pride, which has stifled her energies, crippled her resources, frustrated all the efforts of her most devoted children to raise her from her existing degradation."

P

The headlines of a chapter on, "Our Existing Practical Corruptions" are: "Absence of all system of moral discipline for the poor," "Absence of all system of moral discipline for the rich," "Our Church's total neglect of her duties as guardian of and witness to morality," "Our Church's total neglect of her duties as witness and teacher of orthodoxy," "Powerlessness of our Church to perform her other duties, especially that of protecting and helping the poor, while these are neglected," etc. etc.

On the neglect of the poor his tone is that of Arnold:

Let me ask while all the frightful and accumulated mass of misery which now oppresses our land was gradually during the last sixty years growing to a head, where was the voice of the National Church heard in drawing attention to its growth . . . where was the "poor man's Church?" How is it conceivable that she can at that time have really thought or cared for the poor without becoming cognisant of the fatal disease in progress, and loudly proclaiming its existence to the country and to the world? What other appellation than that of "grossly and miserably corrupt" can we give to a system under which such monstrous neglect was so much as possible?

Yet the Church's rulers, after so horrible a failure had become manifest,

with unruffled brow and complacent voice have still repeated their insane watchwords, "pure and Apostolical", "holy and venerable" Church, and have dared to speak of the corruptions of other Christian bodies, when they should rather have been in lowly and penitential abasement, mourning those of their own.

All this would be exasperating enough to the average Churchman, but Ward went on to avow that Rome was "that quarter where my own eyes are always first directed when in search of spiritual wisdom." He exalted the confessional as a practical means of abasing the proud, he claimed to be allowed "to honour St. Mary as the highest and purest of creatures, to regard the Roman Church with affection and reverence, and to hold a Pope's dogmatic decree as at least exempt from our criticism and comment."

He asked to be allowed to carry High Church principles to their logical limit, to hold all Roman doctrine within the Church of England, avowing his belief that that Church should and finally would "be taught from above to discern and appreciate the plain marks of Divine wisdom and authority in the Roman Church, to repent in sorrow and bitterness of heart our great sin in deserting her communion, and to sue humbly at her feet for pardon and restoration."

It would seem almost as though the University authorities were stunned on the first appearance of the *Ideal*. From June to December they took no action. The *Edinburgh Review* attacked Ward, and Mr. Gladstone condemned him in the *Quarterly* in magisterial phrases. He seized especially on one of Ward's openly avowed weaknesses—his ignorance of history. Ward declared that he took his historical facts from Newman or from Oakeley: that he was "deplorably ignorant" of history. Philosophy and pure reasoning were his strong points. ("I have," he once said, "the mind of an archangel in the body of a rhinoceros.") Letters were passing at the time between Mill and Comte, who both found the philosophy of the book of profound interest. The fact that Ward had started almost in their camp and that his writings appealed to such men was a great argument against him in Gladstone's eyes—"Mr. Ward, strangely bitten with the spirit of the age and owing more of his mental culture to Mr. Mill than to the whole range of Christian Divines with the exception of Mr. Newman." But the supreme offence was the attack on the English Church made with an avowed absence of historical research: "the principle should be maintained, that those who judge without examining . . . should be called to account; and that children—the demand seems not immoderate—should not strike a parent until they have heard her."

Gladstone appears to have been the Grand Old Man in Oxford long before his years warranted the title in public life. His article did Ward much harm. But even Newman was disappointed with the book. He had said to Dalgairns: "The great thing we have to look for now is Ward's *magnum opus*." Anxious to see if it had fulfilled his expectations, Dalgairns went out to Littlemore to find Newman reading it. "It won't do," he said— and sent a message to Ward disapproving the implication "that members of the English Church were at liberty to look upon the existing Roman Church as their authorised teacher."[1] To James Mozley he added: "I cannot see the ground of his main position— that a Church may be utterly without the gift of teaching, yet

[1] *W. G. Ward and the Oxford Movement*, p. 295.

possessed of the gift of the Sacraments." And to James Hope he wrote: "You are quite right in saying I do not take Ward and Oakeley's grounds that all Roman doctrine may be held in our Church and that *as* Roman. I have always and everywhere resisted it." To Keble he wrote that Ward's view "shocks common sense".

But Newman was "much hurt with Gladstone", thinking the article both "unfair as an *ex parte* account of the book" and "cruel just now when [Ward] has everyone upon him." (It is amusing to note Newman's earlier comment to Miss Giberne after Macaulay's brilliant attack on Gladstone's book on Church and State: "When the Isis flows back and St. Mary's spire turns into a railroad train he will begin to waver and repent of his book".)

Dr. Jenkyns no longer felt that Ward was behaving well. He was found pacing his room, the *Ideal* in his hands quoting in tones of astonishment and horror: "We are a corrupted Church," "We are in a degraded condition," "We are to sue for pardon at the feet of Rome humbly,"—and then in accents of yet deeper horror he repeated, "humbly."

An eye-witness has described a scene that followed in the college chapel. It was Ward's turn to read the epistle on the Feast of SS. Simon and Jude, while Dr. Jenkyns on the other side was to read the Gospel. But just as Ward was about to begin, the Master, rushing forward, announced the epistle from the gospel side and began to read *at* him. "The words of the epistle," says Wilfrid Ward, "were singularly appropriate to the situation, and the Master, with ominous pauses and looks at the irreverent Puseyite, who had sown sedition in the Church and blasphemed the Heads of Houses, read as follows slowly and emphatically: 'For there are certain men crept in unawares,' (pause, and look at Mr. Ward), 'who were before of old ordained into this condemnation' (pause and look) 'ungodly men' (pause and look);—and a little later still more slowly and bitterly he read: 'they speak evil of dignities'."[1]

The official wheels were beginning to turn and before the year was out a proposal was put forward by the Hebdomadal Board for three measures to be brought before Convocation: (*a*) to condemn *The Ideal of a Christian Church*; (*b*) to deprive Ward of his degrees; (*c*) to propose a new test whereby the Articles must be

[1] *W. G. Ward and the Oxford Movement*, p. 325.

signed in the sense in which they had been originally uttered and in which the University imposed them. The proposed test proved too much for everyone. An outburst of pamphlets and letters to *The Times* pointed out the width of interpretation hitherto allowed and the great dangers of a new test and especially one "likely to encourage a system of secret and underhand information and to destroy mutual confidence and freedom of intercourse in the University." This was one of seven considerations urged in a protest to *The Times* on January 1st, 1845. A week later a correspondent pointed out that the University was curtailing the liberty given by the Church. Others said that the University had no power to introduce a fresh test, that the whole thing was "a piece of imbecility, such as one is accustomed to see emanate occasionally from the counsels of the Hebdomadal Board." The difficulty was pointed out of knowing at any given moment what exactly was the meaning attached by the University to the Articles. Protestant today it already verged towards Liberalism, might it not tomorrow be Catholic?

The Times itself in a review of one Anglo-Catholic and one Liberal pamphlet (both of which defended Ward's good faith and attacked the Board) remarked that "the Board have done what they always do when they trust to their own unaided wisdom —they have made a sad blunder." And in a leader they called even the move for Ward's degradation "impolitic and ill-considered." A few days later another leader referred to the "well known eccentricity of the Board". In the same issue (just above a notice that soles are now selling at Billingsgate for 1*d.* to 3*d.* a pair) is printed a paragraph stating that opposition to the test does not imply approval of Ward.

The Board in fact had by its folly lost the support of all parties. They withdrew the test, showing thereby that there was no coherent principle on which Ward could be condemned. Some of the fairest minds saw this consequence. The Prebendary of Chichester wrote: "Certainly I shall refuse to make a victim of Mr. Ward on a principle which Convocation rejects." For Ward had challenged all the members of Convocation to prove that their signing was more true to the *natural* sense of the Articles than his own. In effect Oxford said in dropping the test what some even said in letters to *The Times*: "Others may sign as they will. We are going to punish you."

Newman of course saw this clearly. On January 5, 1845, he wrote to James Mozley:

Now that the test seems pretty sure of rejection, do you think nothing at all can be done in Ward's behalf? Really it does hurt one's sense of justice that, considering the atrocious heresies which have been published without censure on the other side, he must be visited so severely for being over-Catholic. Not that I see what can be done. *The Times evasit, erupit.* The *Remembrancer* is quarterly. Combination there can be none, yet I think we shall be sorry when all is over if Ward is thus inequitably condemned.

Is it impossible to persuade men who come up against the Test also to vote for Ward?

I throw this out to relieve my mind. Before the Test was sure of rejection Ward had no claims on anyone.

Earlier he had written to Keble: "I cannot think [the Archbishop] will refuse to Wardism what has before now been granted in our Church to Wesleyans, Sabellians, Socinians and Swedenborgians."

Far from its being possible to do something for Ward it was made clear by the Hebdomadal Board that the dropping of the test meant no relaxation in the attack on Tractarianism. Within a fortnight of the forthcoming election they added a proposal for the condemnation of Tract 90. On the eve of the election the two proctors signified their intention of vetoing this last measure. *The Times* leader (Feb. 12, 1845) is interesting and probably fairly widely representative. It approves the proctors' veto "of the transparently disingenuous manoeuvre of the Hebdomadal Board"; but it hopes

that those who intended to record their votes in Convocation will not refrain from doing so, because one of the questions is withdrawn from their cognizance. Of Mr. Ward and his book we have already given our opinion and, therefore, we shall not be thought to speak from any peculiar love of him when we say that the proceedings of his present enemies require a decisive check. The pliant pertinacity by which these gentlemen appear determined to gain a *"locus standi"* for persecution must be stopped somewhere; and the proposed degradation of Mr. Ward is the point of resistance which is the best, because the most practicable. A beating on that point may possibly convince them that the University, even though excited, will not be unjust—that, though she has no sympathy with the absurd and offensive speculations of a young review-writer, she is prepared to crush in its bud a vindictive and unscrupulous intolerance. In affirming the first of the two questions now at issue she will have effected the first of these purposes; in negativing the second she will declare that the maintenance of pure Protestant doctrine, not personal infliction, is her object—and that she will not allow the powers of Convocation to be put in motion to serve the purposes of a party, bent, it would appear, on destroying by the most unusual measures those who differ from them.

On the same day a column from *The Times* correspondent in Oxford describes the "groups of cap and gown'd in grave and anxious converse on the absorbing theme. The shops of the publishers are visited with a craving regularity of appetite for any new pamphlets to which the occasion may have given birth."

Oxford was aware of crisis. "Heads of Houses, fellows and University authorities of all sorts and degrees of importance emerge from their various book-strewn dwellings in the colleges and mingle with an unwonted condescension in the miniature convocations formed . . . Whispering and bustling agitation pervades the place. Dignity however self-important confesses itself for the nonce the slave of curiosity. . . . The decision of the Proctors appears to be almost universally approved"—but the possibility was widely canvassed that they might not venture to go through with it.

The correspondent believes that Ward's book will be condemned but his degradation rejected. But it is hard to tell since the event may well depend on the country clergy and the new railway, which now ran to Steventon whence access to Oxford was easy enough. "A collision, a defective axle, an asthmatic engine, or a train thrown off the rails might materially affect the numbers in Convocation and so alter the conditions of Mr. Ward's martyrdom."

But it was not really Ward who was in men's minds at this crisis, it was not Ward about whom they talked in college quad-rangles or about whom they fell silent as the press hovered about in search of copy. "It is very remarkable," says Stanley, "how peculiar a feeling is excited the moment that the slightest attempt is made to eject Newman, as if men had an instinctive fear of touching even a hair of his head. Men who had been prepared to sacrifice Ward without a struggle recoiled in horror when they found they were called upon to sacrifice Newman too."[1]

The peculiar meanness of the measure dismayed many. It was four years since Tract 90 had appeared. Newman had left Oxford and his retirement was a profound one. He had given up every fair prospect in the Church, he had not sought to influence the counsels of the University. Thus to drag him forth for punishment seemed shameful. And underneath it, in all the accounts, lies the strange certainty that he could still have been, as he was called, the King of Oxford would he have stooped ever so little to take up his crown.

Men did not really fear what a stupid Hebdomadal Board might do to Newman. ¡They were terrified of what Newman might do. The thought obscurely striving for expression among those anxious groups is uttered by Stanley with his instinctive gift of perception. Ever since "The Parting of Friends" the thought of Littlemore had brought with it a fear "impossible to exaggerate" among "the thinking and feeling part of Oxford"— the fear that Newman might indeed be lost to the Church of England.

There has always [Stanley writes], and especially for the last year, been something so mysterious about Newman's movements, that now that it seemed that he was about to take the final step, one felt the long range of causes before, and the still longer train of consequences behind, throwing every previous secession and every previous move into the remotest distance in comparison. It really reminded me of that one grand scene that I saw in the *Medea*, when the murder takes place within the palace, and the terrified slaves fly backwards and forwards between the chorus and the closed gates, and the chorus mounts the steps of the altar and invokes the sun to hide its rays, and darkness rapidly falls over the stage. No one asked about it in public, but everyone rushed to and fro to ask in private, and recalled the last time that Newman had been seen walking in the streets, how he looked, and what he had said . . . To anyone who has been accustomed to look upon Arnold and Newman as *the* two great men of the Church of England, the death of one and the secession of the other could not but look ominous, like the rattle of departing chariots that was heard on the eve of the downfall of the Temple of Jerusalem.[2]

---

[1] *Life of Stanley*, Vol. I, p. 336.
[2] *Life of Stanley*, Vol. I, pp. 332-3.

CHAPTER XXX

Last Days at Littlemore

THAT VALENTINE'S EVE of 1845 dwelt in men's memory.
Thirty years later Dean Stanley vividly described the
crowded theatre, snow falling heavily, and the undergraduates,
annoyed by the "obnoxious proceedings" (but, one imagines,
chiefly infuriated by their own exclusion from the Sheldonian)
pelting the Vice-Chancellor with snowballs while they loudly
cheered Mr. Ward.[1] The theatre was packed to capacity, the
Latin used in the proceedings curiously broken into by sentences
from the *Ideal*—gravely proclaimed by the Registrar from his
high seat—and by Ward's own speech, made by a special con-
cession in English. Clear, effective, but utterly unconciliating,
he dwelt only briefly on the strong point—namely the difficulty
felt by all parties in subscribing the Articles—while he repeated
several times with the greatest emphasis that he himself believed
"the whole cycle of Roman doctrine" and so believing was
perfectly prepared to sign the Articles once more. Oakeley
insisted on identifying himself with his friend and stood beside him
on the rostrum.

The condemnation of the *Ideal* was a foregone conclusion:
it was carried by 777 to 391, the degradation only by 569 to
511. Then came the proposal for the condemnation of Tract 90.
Amid roars of "Placet" and "Non placet" the senior Proctor's
voice "was heard like a trumpet and cheered enormously" as he
proclaimed, *Nobis procuratoribus non placet.*

The Dean of Chichester threw himself out of his doctor's seat and
shook both Proctors violently by the hand [and] without any formal
dissolution, indeed, without a word more being spoken, as if such an
interposition as the Proctors' *veto* stopped all business, the Vice-
Chancellor tucked up his gown, and hurried down the steps that led

[1] Bloxam wrote long afterwards: "It was a cold east wind that day, and ten or
more members of Convocation, who came up against him, died of the journey."
(Quoted in Middleton, *Newman and Bloxam*.)

from his throne into the area, and hurried out of the theatre; and in five minutes the whole scene of action was cleared.[1]

Curiously enough. Gladstone's vote was cast for Ward on both divisions.

Ward took his condemnation lightly enough and calling on Dr. Pusey began to discuss his own anomalous position—he was still Fellow of Balliol but now only an undergraduate. "They can't expect me," he said, "to wear an Undergraduate's cap and gown, I suppose I must wear my beaver,"—and he began some comic anticipations of disputes in the matter with Dr. Jenkyns when a solemn voice broke in, "The situation seems to me, Mr. Ward, to be one of the utmost gravity. It is indeed a serious crisis. Let us not at such a time give way to a spirit of levity or hilarity."

The speaker was Archdeacon Manning. But the rebuke was wasted—Ward's levity being incurable; he delighted later in repeating Pusey's comment that all the converts to Rome had deteriorated—except Newman who was too perfect and Ward who was too hopeless for any change to be effected. He became a Catholic a little ahead of Newman, who visited him one fast day himself *impransus* and *impransurus*—and found Ward in front of a large beef steak, having entirely forgotten the fast!

This, however, was later; we must now return to Littlemore and to Newman's own story during and before the explosions in the University.

At Littlemore the shouting and the tumult went unheard and unheeded. Newman's letters show him almost indifferent to the outcome. "I believe", he writes to Henry Wilberforce (Feb. 5, 1845), "the Hebdomadal Board decided yesterday whether or not to introduce a censure of No. 90 into Convocation. I have not heard the result; and, be it strange or not, I feel little or no interest about it. I have no curiosity, not I think to go across the way to know, could I by that means get the information." Greater matters had been stirring in his mind since his relinquishment of St. Mary's. Even more may be learnt of these matters by contemplating his life at Littlemore and studying his letters in its light than from the *Apologia* itself.

Very hard was the giving up of the parish. I suppose there was something irritating about Eden, the new vicar, for it was

---

[1] *William George Ward and the Oxford Movement*, p. 342.

evidently felt by Newman's friends as well as by Newman that yielding it up to him was an especially severe trial. "How revolting," wrote James Mozley, "that St. Mary's and Littlemore must come into Eden's hands". Earlier Eden had told Newman that were he vicar of St. Mary's "he would not engage even to let me read prayers at Littlemore, though he did not provide anyone else". But when the time came he seems to have behaved extremely well in very trying circumstances. To begin with, he categorically refused Hawkins' demand that he should repudiate the interpretation of the Articles given in Tract 90. And he kept Copeland, Newman's curate, as Newman had wished. To have the former vicar—and an immensely popular vicar—resident within the parish must have been a trial to him also. To Newman it seemed intolerable that he should write of "*my* people" (he underlines the word in one of Eden's letters). But the letters, if clumsy, are generous. Eden stressed all that had been done by Newman: "I find 'wells which I digged not', means of grace provided for the parish which I should never have had either the energy or the power to have originated".

He begged Newman to second his efforts by daily prayer for the parish, to assist at the anniversary celebrations in 1844. He asked him to continue his priestly visits to an old parishioner, Elizabeth Lenthall, saying, "I know—not I suspect, but I know with certainty—that she receives more comfort from your visits than from those of any more recent acquaintance; in fact than she does from mine".

All this seems unusually large-hearted, but even in old age, Newman still commented acidly on these old letters, while at the time he wrote on one of them, "Eden was all along eager to impress upon me that he, not I, was now vicar of St. Mary's. He calls dear Elizabeth Lenthall 'The poor thing'! One can't make a silk purse out of a sow's ear. He was essentially rude and vulgar". Perhaps he was, but I think he was kind.

Elizabeth Lenthall's own letters to Newman are touching. One of them runs:

If it should please my Heavenly Father, I intend going to Church on Sunday. I return my grateful thanks for your great kindness to me, and may His Holy Spirit support you through all your trials is the sincere prayer of your unworthy servant.

Newman was careful to say no word in the village of his conflict of mind. Jemima noted afterwards that to the end the people seemed wholly unaware of the drama being played at their door. Probably "the poor thing" knew or guessed it. Her death in 1845 Newman felt deeply, writing to Pusey, "It has affected me very much—she was my last link with St. Mary's." There was in him a real clinging to Littlemore village as well as to the parish. It was part of the same tenderness with which he loved his family, with which he clung in memory to the home of his childhood, with which he loved Oriel. He writes to Jemima at different dates, longing to see "Herbert once at Littlemore", begging her to come and to let the group "swell into a caravan" by adding Anne Mozley to the family party. "How glad I should be if you could see this place and our house this year. One knows so little what is before us." He will get them lodgings in Littlemore, or they can stay in Oxford and James Mozley will help him to "fête" them at Oriel. "Our shrubs are growing and at present are greenness itself of all possible shades, and the brooms have been very fine. I wish you could have seen them."

He had resigned the parish on September 18, 1843. On September 29, he wrote to Maria Giberne:

I do so despair of the Church of England, I am so evidently cast off by her, and on the other hand I am so drawn to the Church of Rome that I think it *safer* as a matter of honesty not to keep my living. This is a very different thing from having the *intention* of joining the Church of Rome.

In October came the series of letters to Manning from the first of which quotation has already been made. In the second he writes:

I must tell you then frankly (but I combat arguments which to me, also, are shadows), that it is not from disappointment, irritation or impatience, that I have, whether rightly or wrongly, resigned St. Mary's; but because I think the Church of Rome the Catholic Church, and ours not part of the Catholic Church, because not in communion with Rome; and because I feel that I could not honestly be a teacher in it any longer.

Manning told Pusey, and Newman urged Pusey to tell others privately. The circle was widening of those who had been warned. Yet he did not make his submission to the Church for a full two years—"nor could I have made it at an earlier day without doubt and apprehension, that is with any true conviction of mind or certitude." Meanwhile he kept away from Catholics, and indeed from Catholic practices in so far as he could not hold them also to be Anglican; and continued in lay communion with the Church of England. Yet even upon this matter, his line became definite only gradually; in December, 1843, he could write to Maria Giberne: "I am still a priest of the Church of England and ready when necessary to perform offices in it." A letter to the same correspondent two years later —only a few months before he himself moved—shows that he took the validity of Anglican Orders for granted, but said that this had no bearing on the question whether the Church of England was part of the true Church:

> As to attending the Holy Communion . . . I do not feel any diff^y in your attending. I suppose the state of things is as follows: there is no cause of doubt, as far as I see, that our Church has the Apostolical Succession and the right form of consecration in the Eucharist. If so the Real Presence of Christ is in our Sacrament. At the same time, if we are in Schism, it is (as it were) locked up in the Sacrament and cannot be imparted to the communicant, except by an extraordinary grace.

A consideration that still held him from taking the decisive step was the certainty of the holiness of many souls nourished in the Church of England. Foremost among these was Pusey, and, in the early part of the next year, he met again with that dear friend's child the experience of a happy and holy death that he had already known with Pusey's wife. We last saw Lucy as one of the "Pusey progeny" who climbed on Newman's knee and played with his spectacles: now aged fifteen she shines through the pages of her father's biography as sister to the virgin martyrs of the early Church or to little St. Teresa in our own day. "She is a child of your writings" her father wrote to Newman, "in looking over her books, I find the date of a volume of your sermons, on her birthday, nearly eight years ago (when she was seven) and I asked you for them, as her dear mother had been some time forming her mind in them . . . I asked her whether she had any message for you. She said, 'Give him my respectful love and thank him for all his kindness to me'."

Now she lay dying, without regret for this pleasant world, ready and longing for Heaven. Newman wrote:

Dear Lucy has been made His in Baptism, she has been made His in suffering; and now she asks to be made His by love. Well may you find her sweet countenance pleasant to look upon, when here at a distance I have such pleasure in thinking of her . . . tell her that she is constantly in my thoughts . . . as she who has gone first, is in my mind day by day, morning and evening, continually . . .

After Lucy's death Pusey wrote:

. . . The struggle was so long and so severe that I could not but think it a realizing, in a degree, of a wish that she had named to me (about two years ago, I think), that she might die a martyr. . . . All at once her eyes opened wide, and I never saw such a gaze as at what was invisible to us; after this had continued for some little while, she looked at me full in the face, and there came such an unearthly smile, so full of love also; all expression of pain disappeared and was swallowed up in joy; I never saw anything like that smile: there was no sound, else it seemed almost a laugh for joy, and I could hardly help laughing for joy in answer . . . and now I would not exchange that smile for worlds . . . I cannot sorrow for one whom I have seen with the light of Heaven . . .

The friends, the disciples, the tender family feelings, the tokens of God's love in a life dedicated to Him—all these had come to him in the Church to which he could less and less feel that he belonged. The sermons are full, not only the famous final one but many others, of tender allusions to the parting of friends. He recalls how Christ leaving home for His public ministry "took leave of His Mother at a feast, as He afterwards took leave of His disciples at a feast." He dwells on the fact that at our judgment we shall stand alone before God: "The sympathy of others . . . the smiling countenance, the thrilling heart, which at present are our very life, all will be away from us."

In two retreats each year the method of St. Ignatius was followed and here as with all his spiritual exercises, Newman had deeply at heart that clearing of the mental vision which he believed was to be achieved far more by moral than by intellectual efforts. "I am not so moody," he writes to Jemima, "as when you, dearest, knew me better". And to Keble, "I think I may say, that in some respects my heart and conduct have improved in the course of these five years, and that in respects in which I have prayed for improvement. Then the question comes upon me, why should Providence have granted my prayers in these respects, and not when I have prayed for light and guidance?"

Links with Oxford were being broken. Letters in the files show invitations refused, and in the August Newman writes to Jemima, "I go into Oxford and find myself out of place. Everything seems to say to me, 'This is not your home'. The college seems strange to me, and even the college servants seem to look as if I were getting strange to them."

This was during the last illness of his old friend Bowden—the external event that holds the largest place in Newman's correspondence during the final years at Littlemore. Newman dwells much on memories of their early college years, feeling that Bowden's loss is breaking his last strong link with the past. "In losing him," he writes to Keble, "I seem to lose Oxford." And "One forgets past feelings, else I would say that I never had pain like the present." Although he had on giving up St. Mary's spoken of going into lay communion, he still ministered to Bowden. It was a case of advanced consumption: "He may easily break a vessel in coughing which would be fatal," wrote Newman to Keble. "It is more than I can describe, to see Mrs. Bowden sitting by him in these fits of coughing, she knowing this. His calmness is most wonderful—and hers too . . .

"I am to administer the Holy Communion to him tomorrow morning—and really I do hope I may be able to come here to do the same, again and again."

After all was over, he wrote to Ambrose St. John,

. . . When one sees so blessed an end, and that at the termination of so blameless a life, of one who really fed on our ordinances and got strength from them—and see the same continued in a whole family—the little children finding quite a solace of their pain in the Daily Prayer, it is impossible not to feel more at ease in our Church, as at least a sort of Zoar, a place of refuge and temporary rest because of the steepness of the way.

As an old man, he wrote:

John William Bowden died September 15th, 1844. I sobbed bitterly over his coffin to think that he had left me still dark as to what the way of truth was, and what I ought to do in order to please God and fulfil His will.

There is a slight change in the proportion of the letters—most of them "taking the liberty" or "hoping he will pardon the presumption"—received by Newman after he had resigned St. Mary's. Protestant urgings that he should leave a Church where he did not belong continue, but there are many more in which he is entreated to remain. The rumours that seemed to Stanley so portentous echoed yet more ominously in Newmanite ears and roused many into action. "Cords of silk," wrote Gladstone to Manning at the end of 1843, "should one by one be thrown over him to bind him to the Church. Every manifestation of sympathy and confidence in him, as a man, must have some small effect."

Others had the same thought. Mr. Justice Coleridge wrote to Keble, quoting a friend who wanted Newman to "know how warmly he was loved, honoured and sympathised with by large numbers of Churchmen, so that he might not feel solitary, or, as it were, cast out. What think you of a private address . . . assuring him of gratitude, veneration and love?"

To a friend, the sculptor Westmacott, Newman had written, "I am amused at your calling me 'cloistered'! It is true, but I am a sharper fellow than you think." Keble sent on Coleridge's suggestion, but Newman expressed the fear "that some persons at least, who took part in such an expression of kindness, would think that my present tendencies arose from the want of such expressions, and would hope to stop them by means of it."

Extremely kind letters from Manning, Gladstone and others "have not operated ever so little in shaking" him. Yet his friends did affect him deeply in quite a different way. Had his confidence in himself been equal to his intellectual conviction the struggle would not have lasted so long. "If my confidence in myself," he wrote to Hope in May, 1844, "bore any proportion to the strength of my persuasion, I should not be where I am." And to Keble, in November, "I am kept first from deference to my friends—next by the fear of some dreadful delusion being over me." In another letter he compares the long waiting and the testing of himself to pinching oneself to make certain one is not dreaming.

An unusual element in the situation was that Newman had

himself furnished his friends with the weapons which they now refurbished for use against him. Sometimes they realised this. "I believe," writes Keble, "I really mean what I have learnt from yourself." Ought not Newman, he had urged, to wait for some plain token of God's will. Or again, if the medieval system is the true development of the primitive, "is it not the most natural way for the English Church to recover it *through* primitive Catholicity, instead of being urged directly to it?" And again, "Do you not think it possible (I dare say I borrowed the view from yourself) that the *whole* Church may be so lowered by sin, as to hinder one's finding on earth anything which *seems* really to answer to the Church of the Scriptures?"

"Your published Parochial Sermons," writes an (apparently unknown) admirer, "have been, under God, the means of rousing me from spiritual sleep, and I have from them . . . been led to regard your opinions with a reverence greater than I can express. From your lectures on Romanism also I have been taught the errors which that system, if I may so express myself, contains."

An old schoolfellow writes of the "reality and consistency" which Newman had imparted to his religion, rescuing him from "low views and such as now seem scarcely believing views . . . O Newman, do, do stop with us. What shall we do without you?"

One correspondent writes concerning Newman's rumoured secession:

What confusion to our friends, what triumph to our enemies! And to Rome what an argument to confirm her in her errors and abuses. What hope, humanly speaking, can remain to our poor humbled Church after such a blow . . . to find herself all at once despaired of and deserted by her best champion; one who, under Providence, has been the chief instrument in raising her from her degraded state and, as it were, breathing into her afresh the breath of life! Surely the bare thought of this is enough to make the whole head sick, the whole heart faint . . . I take heart from your own words . . . which seem absolutely to forbid it . . . where you say that till Rome moves towards us, it is *quite impossible* that we should move towards Rome . . .
I am tempted to cry out

> " *Tu Patronus es, tu Parens*
> *Si deseris tu, periimus* ".

"Of course you must leave England," runs another letter, "and go where they [i.e. Roman Catholics] are not schismatics."

And another, "Why should you contradict the truths you have written . . . torturing and puzzling the mind that would be led to reality."

The wish of a dying mother leads yet another correspondent to apologise for presumption in pointing out that "it seems so fearfully responsible a step to be the first (I believe) of either talent or learning during now nearly three centuries since the Bishop of Rome set up rival altars in this land."

A letter from a younger Oxford friend in unsteady writing, much scratched and interlined, must have afforded on a first reading some light relief. The writer had been impelled to its composition by listening to his sisters singing "Lead Kindly Light". The scene is not hard to imagine, soft candlelight, drawn curtains, the pretty dresses of the girls, flowers on the piano and the sentimental feelings that so often follow a few glasses of wine:

> Surely you might take your rest in the Church of your baptism especially regenerated as it is in a great degree through your means . . . you have yourself created feelings of no common kind, which feelings you are *bound* even at a personal sacrifice *tenderly to consider* now you have created them. Call it the penalty of your past beautiful exercise of many excellent gifts.

This "fact" he feels obliged to bring to Newman's attention— and so on for four pages.

Newman was too overwrought to take anything very lightly just then and there is a dramatic element in the change effected by his brief rather stern reply. This unpublished correspondence casts a vivid light on Newman's position with his younger followers and on his qualities as a leader of men.

My Dear Jeffreys,

I am sure your letter is most kindly meant. Its coming from you is a warrant for this. If it had been my good fortune to have been thrown much with you, you would have been better able to judge how far it was necessary for you to send me what you name your "fact".

Perhaps hereafter you will be a better judge how far any man whatever whose state of mind and feelings you did not know ought to be approached with the want of reverence displayed in your letter.

Yours very truly,
John H. Newman.

The answer—in steady handwriting—was a most humble apology. Newman wrote back:

. . . In truth, if there has been one feeling more keen and continual with me than another, it has been the pain to which I am putting friends and well-wishers known and unknown. I have felt it a great deal more than the prospect of what they would think of me;—though that of course has oppressed me too. In all its different shapes has this suffering been upon me, so as almost to affect me morbidly. Would that my suffering of these would relieve theirs. But that is impossible.

My feelings are not so excited just now—perhaps they have had their crisis—and I shall be calmer—but I am not at all certain but my trouble may return. But I have said enough on the point.

It is not a light conviction that can rouse a man of my age with the associations of many years fixed one way, with the resistance to change and exertion which by that time creeps on the mind with an odd aversion to noise or agitation, with a deep contempt of what looks disorderly and extravagant, and with at least a natural love of seeming consistency, to give up his place in the University and go out into the wide world. You must not, however, think such reflections as this are familiar to me, lest, by those who are determined to find some solution of my conduct short of conviction, the paradox itself should be supposed to be a motive.

The same sort of argument had been earlier put forward by James Mozley: his own development as an Anglican had been Newman's work: "May not persons view their own work as in turn some sort of sign or deduction to themselves—reflecting the religious character of their own minds?"

If I have [comments Newman in a pencil note, which he "reconstructed" in March 1878, from a much-rubbed original], as you say, formed you, still have I not first formed *myself*? . . . Knowledge of facts changes the application of principles; and if one man has greater knowledge than another, as having had more opportunities than another of acquiring it, he cannot take that other as his own reflex, as you wish, though he may have imparted to him originally his own principles. Would you not, for instance, move to Rome if you came to think that the English Church had not the Apostolical Succession, and that not against, but because of the principles which you had gained from me. If facts present themselves otherwise to you and to me, you may represent my ethos without being a measure or index of the *conduct* incumbent on me . . . If I formed you at one time I formed others also . . . Who else of my immediate friends are

firm in Anglicanism? Is even Keble? Think of your brother Tom, of
Robert Williams, Samuel F. Wood, William Froude, Henry Wilberforce, George Ryder, Copeland.

Yes, his own arguments had ceased to affect him, for he had
seen them clearly, examined them, seen through them in the
light of deeper study. With his sister Harriett he refused argument
on this very ground, writing to Jemima, "She has not changed.
I have read what she has not read and I have changed. I read
first (as I was bound to do) with other people's eyes, and since
I have read with my own . . . she is resolved to get into argument
with me—and I am resolved (so be it) not to do so."

If the arguments left him unmoved, fear of self-deception and
reverence for his friends still deeply affected him. A report set
on foot by Golightly of Newman's actual reception into the
Roman Church called forth a long letter to Jemima (Nov. 24th,
1844):

As to late reports, I did not properly hear them till they were over
—that is, I heard that there was a paragraph, but did not realise its
preciseness and plausibility . . . It is astonishing what little feeling
certain people have. Golightly and the newspapers would think it
wrong to put out a statement on doubtful authority that I had broken
my leg, yet they have no remorse in circulating what is adapted to
shock friends indefinitely more. But the said G. is a man literally
without bowels. I doubt whether he has any inside, or is more than
a walking and talking piece of mechanism.

I have gone through a great deal of pain, and have been very much
cut up. The one predominant distress upon me has been the unsettlement of mind I am causing. This is a thing that has haunted me day
by day. And for some days I had a literal pain in and about my
heart . . .

Besides the pain of unsettling people, of course I feel the loss I am
undergoing in the good opinion of my friends and well-wishers, though
I can't tell how much I feel this. It is the shock, surprise, terror,
forlornness, disgust, scepticism to which I am giving rise; the difference
of opinion, division of families—all this makes my heart ache.

I cannot make out that I have any motive but indefinite risk to my
own soul in remaining where I am. A clear conviction of the substantial identity of Christianity and the Roman system has now been
on my mind for a full three years. It is more than five years since the
conviction first came on me, though I struggled against it and overcame it. I believe all my feelings and wishes are against change. I

have nothing to draw me elsewhere. I hardly ever was at a Roman service, even abroad—I know no Roman Catholics. I have no sympathy with them as a party. I am giving up everything. I am not conscious of any resentment, disgust, or the like, to repel me from my present position; and I have no dreams whatsoever, far from it, of what I could do in another position. Far from it—I seem to be throwing myself away.

Unless any thing occurs which I cannot anticipate, I have no intention of an early step even now. But I cannot but think—though I can no more realise it than being made Dean of Ch. Ch., or Bishop of Durham—that some day it will be, and at a definite distance of time. As far as I can make out I am in a state of mind which divines call *indifferentia*, inculcating it as a duty to be set on nothing, but to be willing to take whatever Providence wills. How *can* I at my age and with my past trials be set upon any thing? I really don't think I am. What keeps me here is the desire of giving every chance for finding out if I am under the power of a delusion. Various persons have sent me very kind letters, and I really do trust that many are bearing me in mind in their prayers.

It was not only his own arguments they were all using—it was his own method. As he had begged people to wait, so now they all begged him to wait.

But the time for waiting was at last drawing to a close. Seven was a mystic number and he had hoped to have waited seven years from the time of that first blow in 1839. But, "I doubt," he tells Keble in November 1844 "whether I *can* have a clearer conviction than I have without a miracle, if then."

In the same month he wrote to Maria Giberne: "It seems to me I have no call at present to take so awful a step, as you justly call it—but if I may judge by the past and present, I have very little reason to doubt about the issue of things . . . I have little doubt where I shall be this time two years, though my imagination cannot embrace the idea."

So the torment must go on within him and the harassment from without. All the arguments come up over and over again, and the suspicions of him—"the wretchedness of gossiping, talebearing, prying, delating—in short Golightlyism".[1] "Really no one but [Daniel] O'Connell", he says in the letter to Maria Giberne just quoted, "is called so distinctly and so ordinarily a liar, as I am. I think nothing tends to hurt my spirits but this." Suspicion of his motives, suspicion of Rome, appeals to his

[1] Newman to Pusey, Dec. 16, 1844.

tenderness for his friends, all may be read in the dusty but living letters addressed to him and in his answers. It is hard to choose the most vivid passages, where all are so keenly alive. For Keble, Newman had written down his every thought for a period that this revered friend might judge whether there was some hidden sin affecting him. But besides the Keble letters there is important correspondence with Jemima, with Maria Giberne and Henry Wilberforce, Hope, letters to Badeley, to Coleridge and others. To Badeley he compares the Church of England with a patient dying of consumption whose friends explain away every bad symptom. (Doubtless Bowden's dying state suggested the simile.)

We are naturally friends, for we are children of this dying or dead system in which we have lived all our days. We cannot, we will not, believe what the real state of the case is. We cannot be persuaded to open our eyes. Every ominous fact admits of an explanation, and in it we take refuge. Consider the shock with which child, parent or wife hears of the inevitable blow. It is like a dream. Nothing would convince but the actual sight of the calamity which cannot be explained away. No such positive, visible, tangible evidence is attainable in a moral matter. There is no bier and funeral of a church. The fact then escapes unwilling minds: yet it may be as certain to others as the prospective termination of a fatal malady is to the physician. . . .
This is an abrupt, odious letter—but it is an odious subject.

To Jemima, he writes on St. Andrew's Day 1844,

I am not unwilling to be in trouble now, and for others to be— for it is what must be, and the more of it the sooner over. It is like drinking a cup out. I am far from being unmindful of what you say about unsettlement of others being a providential intimation; but there must be a limit to its force, else Jews could never have become Christian in early times, or Nestorian or Monophysite, Catholic in more recent. How St. Paul must have unsettled quiet Jews who were serving God, and heard nothing but ill of Our Lord as a "Samaritan", "deceiver" and "blasphemer"! And this suggests what has ever been felt and said against the Church at all times—namely, that it was corrupt, anti-Christian, etc. This has ever been a note of the Church. And I do believe the Church of Rome has the imputation only in this sense (allowing for Our Lord's parable of the net). It is no new thing that the Church is under odium and in disgrace,

But in his next letter he shows a full realisation that, to those who do not move, the action of those who do may, perhaps must, appear wrong:

I do not wonder at anyone's first impression being, when he hears of the change of religion of another, that he is influenced by some wrong motive. It is the necessary consequence of his thinking himself right; and I fully allow that the *onus probandi* that he is not so influenced lies with the person influenced. . . . A person's feeling naturally is, that there must be something wrong at bottom; that I must be disappointed or restless, or set on a theory, or carried on by a party, or coaxed into it by admirers, or influenced by any of the ten thousand persuasions which are as foreign from my mind as from my heart, but which it is easy for others to assign as an hypothesis. I do not quarrel with persons so thinking.

But still I think that as time goes on, and persons have the opportunity of knowing me better, they will see that all these suppositions do not hold; and they will be led to see that my true motive simply is that I believe the Roman Church to be true, and that I have come to this belief without any assignable fault on my part. Far indeed am I from saying "without fault" absolutely. Were I sure that it was without fault absolutely, I should not hesitate to move tomorrow. It is the fear that there is some secret undetected fault which is the cause of my belief which keeps me where I am, waiting.

He then refers to his written confession to Keble who could detect nothing "bearing on this particular belief". He continues:

In saying this, I am not saying that another is wrong who does not do the same. I am only looking at myself, if God gives me certain light, supposing it to be such, this is a reason for *me* to act; yet in so doing I am not condemning those who do not so act. . . . Our Church may be a place of grace and security to another, yet not to me. . . .

Now, my dear Jemima, I am sure you will feel that I am not arguing, but I wish you to understand where I stand and what I feel—for my own comfort. I have never wished there should be any reserve between us—it is most repugnant to my nature to conceal things . . . it will be a great comfort if you let me be open with you, and to tell you what the state of my mind is. Indeed, there can be no exercise of love between persons without this openness.

The lies told about himself, had, he confessed to his sister, made him realise how false might be such things as the common imputations against the Jesuits and against Catholics in general. Yet all his letters show that he did not like Roman Catholics, and thought very poorly of them. To Coleridge he wrote (November 16, 1844):

What possible reason of mere "preference" can I have for the Roman Church above our own? I hardly ever, even abroad, was at any of their services. I was scarcely ever for an hour in the same room with a Roman Catholic in my life. . . . I know absolutely nothing of them except that external aspect that is so uninviting. In the *Tablet* and *Dublin Review*, in radical combinations and liberal meetings, this is how I know them. My habits, tastes, feelings are as different as can well be conceived from theirs, as they show outwardly.

Again in a letter to Maria Giberne of January 8, 1845, speaking of his doubt as to whether more than one or two Oxford residents are likely to move, he adds:

And I don't know whether I can wish it. The state of the Roman Catholics is at present so unsatisfactory. This I am sure of, that nothing but a simple, direct call of duty is a warrant for anyone leaving our Church. . . . The simple question is, can *I* (it is personal, not whether another, but can *I*) be saved in the English Church? Am *I* in safety, were I to die tonight? Is it a mortal sin in *me*, not joining another communion?

The reference to dying is a reminder of his miserable bodily state through most of this time. In the October, his hand was troubling him: he writes to Jemima that the doctor "has pronounced my difficulty to be a deficiency of nervous power, and to have nothing to do with my hand—I might as well rub my nose for it as my hand or wrist". On November 24 he tells of a swelling at his elbow and "symptoms of the like" at his knee, and there is a postscript: "This is a most abrupt letter, but I have no time, and am tired and out of spirits." Later in November there is toothache; towards Christmas a heavy cold which "kept me from Church yesterday", and in January, an attack of influenza so heavy that he remarks that he had not been in such poor health since the winter of 1828–9.

There is an extraordinary closeness of mind and heart between brother and sister, yet no swerving of principle in either because of it. Jemima still—and throughout her life—clung to the Church of England: she feared lest he might influence her unduly. He wrote (January 23, 1845):

Far am I indeed from being unwilling that you should fear my influence. I have quite responsibility enough about myself without having in a measure to answer for others. It is my principal trouble, as you know, what effect I may have on others. And I have looked forward to it as one especial test of the strength of my convictions, whether I could *bear* that others should be influenced by me. . . . Really I think it is hardly a relief going about—for I see people pained. It quite made me sick to hear H. Wilberforce's wife sigh. . . .

I could not bear to come to you yet—I could not bear the family party—you don't know how poor a creature I am just now, though I should not and do not show it to others.

The mental attitude of a given date must always be borne in mind when writing about it. Even today many of us can remember how responsible our great-aunts and uncles and still more our great-grandmothers (if they lived to know us), felt about our conduct. Go back a hundred years and this is much intensified. Keble fancied it was *his* fault that Newman was lost to the Church of England. Pusey lamented his own failure in the same matter. Jemima Mozley had a truly deep affection and sympathy for her brother, yet at moments she felt she must rebuke him or be false to her own faith. One important letter (written March 15, 1845) answers her criticisms, and must be given at length, even though it contains some slight repetition of earlier letters. It is probably the fullest statement at once of Newman's acute suffering and of the movement of his mind:

I have just received your very painful letter, and wish I saw any way of making things easier to you or to myself.

If I went by what I wished, I should complete my seven years of waiting. Surely more than this, or as much, cannot be expected of me—cannot be right in me to give at my age. How life is going! I see men dying who were boys, almost children, when I was born. Pass a very few years, and I am an old man. What means of judging can I have more than I have? What maturity of mind am I to expect? If I am right to move at all, surely it is high time not to delay about it longer. Let me give my strength to the work, not my weakness—years in which I can profit His cause who calls me, not the dregs of life. Is it not like a death-bed repentance to put off what one feels one ought to do?

As to my convictions, I cannot but say what I have told you already, that I cannot at all make out *why* I should determine on moving, except as thinking I should offend God by not doing so. I cannot make out what I am *at* except on this supposition. At my time of life men love ease. I love ease myself. I am giving up a maintenance involving no duties, and adequate to all my wants. What in the world am I doing this for (I ask *myself* this), except that I think I am called to do so? I am making a large income by my sermons. I am, to say the very least, risking this; the chance is that my sermons will have no further sale at all. I have a good name with many; I am deliberately sacrificing it. I have a bad name with more; I am fulfilling all their worst wishes, and giving them their most coveted triumph. I am distressing all I love, unsettling all I have instructed or aided. I am going to those whom I do not know, and of whom I expect very little. I am making myself an outcast, and that at my age. Oh, what can it be but a stern necessity which causes this?

Pity me, my dear Jemima. What have I done thus to be deserted, thus to be left to take a wrong course, if it is wrong. I began by defending my own Church with all my might when others would not defend her. I went through obloquy in defending her. I in a fair measure succeeded. At the very time of this success, before any reverse, in the course of my reading it breaks upon me that I am in a schismatical Church. From the time my doubts come upon me I begin to live more strictly; and really from that time to this I have done more towards my inward improvement, as far as I can judge, than in any time of my life. Of course I have all through had many imperfections, and might have done every single thing I have done much better than I have done it. Make all deductions on this score, still, after all, may I not humbly trust that I have not so acted as to forfeit God's gracious guidance? And how is it that I have improved in other points if in respect of this momentous matter I am so fearfully blinded? Suppose I were suddenly dying—one may deceive oneself as to what one should do—but I think I should directly send for a priest. Is not this a test of one's state of mind? Ought I to live where I could not bear to die? Again, I assure you it makes me quite uncomfortable travelling, lest some accident should cut me off in my present state. Is this a right frame of mind to be in? Have I lived so many years, have I made such a high profession, have I preached to others so peremptorily, to be myself now in fear of death? What is the difference between me and a poor profligate? We both feel we have a work to do which is undone.

Why should I distress your kind heart with my miseries? Yet you must know them, to avoid the greater misery of looking at me externally and wondering and grieving over what seems incomprehensible. . . .

Palm Sunday. And then on the other hand it comes on me. Have not there after all been persons in my case before now, and were they not right? Were persons never yet in a schismatical or heretical Church, and would not their trial, when they came to see their state, be exactly what mine is? Have Jews never had to turn Christians, and been cursed by their friends for doing so? Can I shock people so much as they did? Is the Church of Rome, can it be, regarded more fearfully than Jews regard Christianity, than Jews regarded St. Paul? —Was he not the prince of apostates? . . .

So, my dear Jemima, if you can suggest any warning to me which I am not considering, well, and thank you; else do take comfort, and think that perhaps you have a right to have faith in me, perhaps you have a right to believe that He who has led me hitherto will not suffer me to go wrong. I am somehow in better spirits this morning, and I say what it occurs to me to say at the time. Have I not a right to ask you not to say, as you have said in your letter, that I shall do *wrong*? What right have you to judge me? Have the multitude who will judge me any right to judge me? Who of my equals, who of the many who will talk flippantly about me, has a right? Who has a right to judge me but my Judge?

CHAPTER XXXI

Development of Doctrine

WITH ALL the suffering he felt at the suffering he would cause, there is a note of certitude about the central issue all through the letters of the end of 1844. In November he had told Keble that he doubted if he could have a clearer conviction. What still held him back? The fear that as he had changed before, he might change again. So he tells us in the *Apologia*. That fear was exorcised but a subtler one remained: in the following March he wrote to Maria Giberne that his convictions were as strong as he supposed they could become "only it is so difficult to know whether it is a call of *reason* or of conscience"— in other words was he moved by his own thinking or by divine grace? He found the answer to both and the issue of his whole struggle in the writing of the *Essay on the Development of Christian Doctrine*.[1]

It is relief indescribable to turn from the agonies of self-examination that marked the Tractarians—and almost all the men of their time—to turn from this to the objective view of reality opened on the mental vision by this great book.

Newman had meant on completing the translation of St. Athanasius—on which he had been working for three years—to take six months' rest,

for really I required it. And then I found all of a sudden this new work come upon me. . . . It will be a sort of obscure philosophical work, if I manage to do it, with little to interest and much to disappoint. But I hate making a splash and, of course, I hate unsettling people, if I could do so I would rather write something which would sink into their minds. . . . I am not, except at times, in the state of distress I was last autumn. My mind is a great deal more made up. . . .

[1] See Appendix C for a most interesting letter on the *Development* used by Jean Guitton but never before published in England.

442

This letter was written June 1, 1845, to Mrs. William Froude, the wife of another brother of Hurrell's, who later followed Newman into the Church. The *Development* had been under way about four months and Newman says "mind and body are getting wearied together, and the book is not yet written through the first time". And a few days later, to the same correspondent: "never has anything cost me (I think) so much hard work and anxiety . . . our time is so divided here, that I have not above six or seven hours at it, and it is so exhausting I doubt whether I could give more".

The really astonishing thing is the speed at which he wrote it. I had always fancied it to have been the main occupation of the four years between Tract 90 and his reception. In fact its writing took only about nine months although the material had been in the gathering for many years.

The main argument of the book is well known. The question asked by history is first answered by a general view of doctrinal developments. Then come seven tests of true developments whereby they may be distinguished from corruptions: preservation of type, continuity of principle, power of assimilation, logical sequence, anticipation of the future, conservative action on the past and chronic vigour. Then follows the application of these principles, made with the largest possible admissions of all the errors, sins and failures that have attended the Church's history.

So much has been written of this book that I will only by an occasional sentence try to suggest a little of how through the writing of it Newman's mind became at peace and only the anguish of the heart remained as he bade farewell to his friends, his family, his University.

We feel in this book more than in anything Newman ever wrote the sweep of genius, surveying history from an eminence won by the toil and sweat of many years, handling a multitude of details yet never for one moment losing the main outlines. He had wanted to give his followers something that should be no mere personal enchantment but might lead them to turn to the profound philosophy so greatly needed by the Christian world.

"The assailants of dogmatic truth," he wrote, "have got the start of its adherents of whatever Creed; philosophy is completing what criticism has begun; and apprehensions are not unreasonably excited lest we should have a new world to conquer before we have weapons for the warfare."

This was his haunting fear, and from what he has said of his own sceptical intellect some have deduced that he fled to Rome to escape infidelity. It was not the least like that. Of a report to the effect that he had actually fallen into scepticism sent to him by J. F. Christie he wrote: "It is totally, utterly false—I thank God so dreadful a calamity as you speak of is quite foreign to me. . . . I suppose indeed there are few people of education to whom sceptical thoughts do not occur, that is from without, e.g., words of sceptical import present themselves to their *eyes bodily* in a printed book. But beyond that I have no confession whatever to make. I never have felt the temptation for an instant from within. . . . To fear a temptation is not to feel it."

He did fear it very greatly, especially for others, and above all for the young. The Church had always been for him the great safeguard, "the concrete representative of things invisible." For very long he had feared his own unsettlement would unsettle others: he was coming to realise that their unsettlement was already a fact: the historical view of the Church its best answer— for by that path he had himself reached an objective reality that he could no more deny than he could deny the existence of the spires and colleges of his own city.

This thing he was looking at—Christianity—was not simply an atmosphere or even a spiritual presence;

It has from the first had an objective existence and has thrown itself upon the great concourse of men. Its home is in the world; and to know what it is we must seek it in the world, and hear the world's witness of it. . . .

Bold outlines and broad masses of colour rise out of the records of the past. They may be dim, they may be incomplete; but they are definite . . . whatever history teaches, whatever it omits, whatever it exaggerates or extenuates, whatever it says or unsays, at least the Christianity of history is not Protestantism. . . .

And Protestantism has ever felt it so. . . . This is shown in the determination . . . of dispensing with historical Christianity altogether, and of forming a Christianity from the Bible alone: men would never have put it aside unless they had despaired of it. It is shown by the long neglect of ecclesiastical history in England, which prevails even in the English Church . . . the only English writer who has any claim to be considered an ecclesiastical historian, is the unbeliever Gibbon. To be deep in history is to cease to be a Protestant.

The fact lies upon the surface of history that the creeds of the Church bear upon them the appearance of change: by what test are we to determine whether change is corruption?

That the hypothesis here to be adopted, a divinely guided Development of Doctrine, accounts not only for the Athanasian Creed but for the creed of Pope Pius, is no fault of those who adopt it. "No one has power over the issue of his principles; we cannot manage our argument and have as much of it as we please and no more."

This was the essential difference between Newman's mind and the minds of many who had gone along with him for some time. They could and did stop at a certain point in Church history, even if the location of that point varied, but Newman must go on to the final issue of the principles he had adopted. Like the other Tractarians he had for long tried to make a test from St. Vincent's *quod semper, quod ubique, quod ab omnibus,* but even this could not be made at once to cover the belief in the Real Presence and disbelief in Papal Authority for which the early centuries offer as much evidence.

Not without humour he speaks of the Anglican view of history as an attempt to "fit the Thirty-nine Articles on the fervid Tertullian," while on the other hand extreme Protestants held that "Christianity slept for centuries upon centuries, except among those whom historians call heretics", while Milman's Church History attempted to whittle away as accretions anything in Christianity that bore kinship to any other religion.

"The question is," he asks, "which of all these theories is the simplest, the most natural, the most persuasive. Certainly the notion of development under infallible authority is not a less grave, a less winning hypothesis than the chance and coincidence of events, or the Oriental Philosophy, or the working of Antichrist, to account for the rise of Christianity and the formation of its theology."

If we compare this book with the *Arians* we see again how very much Newman had learnt from the controversy with Hampden and all that had followed. He had begun by feeling that creeds and definitions were perhaps a necessity but certainly a regrettable one. By now he realised that the laws of the human mind made the development of an idea the only alternative to its corruption or its disappearance, and also the only way in which its full force could be felt and all its aspects apprehended.

While he was advancing in this apprehension he saw Blanco White, he saw the followers of Hampden and of Arnold, receding into a view of Christianity but little removed from complete scepticism.

From the nature of the human mind, time is necessary for the full comprehension and perfection of great ideas. . . .

. . . Whatever may be the risk of corruption from intercourse with the world around, such a risk must be encountered if a great idea is duly to be understood, and much more if it is to be fully exhibited. It is elicited and expanded by trial and battles into perfection and supremacy. . . .

There is no one aspect deep enough to exhaust the contents of a real idea, no one term or proposition which will serve to define it. . . .

The idea which represents an object or supposed object is commensurate with the sum total of its possible aspects, however they may vary in the separate consciousness of individuals. . . .

We cannot teach except by aspects or views, which are not identical with the thing itself which we are teaching . . . ideas are in the writer and reader of the revelation, not the inspired text itself . . . nor could it be maintained that the letter of the New Testament . . . comprises a delineation of all possible forms which a divine message will assume when submitted to a multitude of minds. . .

The refutation and remedy of errors cannot precede their rise; and thus the fact of false developments or corruptions involves the correspondent manifestation of true ones. . .

When it is declared that "The Word became flesh", three wide questions open upon us on the very announcement. What is meant by "the Word", what by "flesh", what by "became". The answers to these involve a process of investigation and are developments.

In the Old Testament story we have a progress of events that looks vague and uncertain but is "directed by Him who works out gradually what He has determined absolutely."

We must distinguish between a revelation and a reception of it, not between its earlier and later stages. . . . We have no reason to suppose that there is so great a distinction of dispensation between ourselves and the first generation of Christians, as that they had a living infallible guidance, and we have not. . . . As creation argues continual governance, so are Apostles harbingers of Popes.

A revelation is not given, if there be no authority to decide what it is that is given.

The Tridentine Creed is met by no rival developments; there is no antagonist system. We have to choose between this theology and none at all.

The onus probandi is with those who assail a teaching which is and has long been in possession . . . found just there, where true developments ought to be found,—namely in the historic seats of Apostolical teaching and in the authoritative homes of immemorial tradition.

To be just able to doubt is no warrant for disbelieving.

All that was to be said later about his own conversion Newman seems by anticipation to answer in this book. Dean Church, not unreasonably, pointed out as an old man that Catholic countries were as deeply marked as Protestant with the scars and seams of infidelity—that the Catholic Church had not here shown the power that Newman held her to have and Anglicanism to lack. But Newman had seen plainly enough the temporary weakness of the Church while he saw, too, the eternal strength ever coming to her rescue. Like Chesterton, who was to write later of the Five Deaths of the Faith, Newman wrote of her sleep and her rising up:

If corruption be an incipient disorganisation, surely an abrupt and absolute recurrence of the former state of vigour, after an interval, is even less conceivable than a corruption that is permanent. . . . After violent exertion men are exhausted and fall asleep; they awake the same as before, refreshed by the temporary cessation of their activity, and such has been the slumber and such the restoration of the Church. She pauses in her course, and almost suspends her functions; she rises again, and she is herself once more . . . change she cannot if we listen to St. Athanasius or St. Leo; change she never will, if we believe the controversialist or alarmist of the present.

This was indeed a period of slumber and Newman had known it well enough when he wrote to Keble (December 29, 1844):

No one can have a more unfavourable view than I of the present state of Roman Catholics—so much so, that any who join them would be like the Cistercians of Fountains, living under trees till their house was built. If I must account for it, I should say that the want of unity has injured both them and us.

Nothing is more touching in Wilfrid Ward's *Cardinal Wiseman* than the pictures of his hopes and fears during these years. And it might well have surprised Newman had he known how near Wiseman's estimate was to his own of the "*low* state in many things" to which the Catholic Church in England had been reduced by the "terrible grinding oppression of three hundred years". "I am ready to acknowledge," he says of the Tractarians

that, in all things, except the happiness of possessing the truth, and being in communion with God's true Church, and enjoying the advantages and blessings that flow thence, we are their inferiors . . . if the Oxford Divines entered the Church, we must be ready to fall into the shade, and take up our position in the background. I will gladly say to any of them "Me opportet minui".

Returning to England from Rome whence he had been longingly gazing at Oxford, Wiseman was more ready than most of the hereditary Catholics to hold out welcoming arms, and more alive to the results of the "state of siege" in England. "We are," he writes,

like the Jews returned to Jerusalem, or like the first family after the flood: we have to reconstruct everything: we must first work with bricks from the slime of the water that had overwhelmed us. . . . The remedy lies deeper than the surface of things . . . it is a work of time and of much patience; and it is hard to judge us by what belongs to our past . . . and with God's blessing to our future state . . .
. . . Let us have an influx of new blood; let us have but even a small number of such men as write in the Tracts, so imbued with the spirit of the early Church, so desirous to revive the image of the ancient Fathers—men who have learnt to teach from St. Augustine, to preach from St. Chrysostom, and to feel from St. Bernard; let even a few such men, with the high clerical feeling which I believe them to possess, enter fully into the spirit of the Catholic religion, and we shall be speedily reformed, and England quickly converted.

It was with no anticipations of human happiness that Newman approached his journey's end: and he knew well enough that as with Christ, so with his followers, the Cross must come before the Resurrection. It was not likely that one who could view unperturbed the Robber Council of Ephesus would find his faith shaken by the bad manners of Cardinal Cullen or the lack of perfect straightness in Cardinal Manning. Nothing in history is as likely to shake our faith in the Church as the sight of a man in the agonies of cancer to shake our faith in God. And that is part of what Newman meant when he said that for him there was no half-way house between Catholicism and infidelity.

CHAPTER XXXII

Loss and Gain

"THERE came in Oxford," says Mark Pattison, "a sudden end of all things and without a new beginning." With Newman's departure "common conversation seemed to have collapsed, to have died out for want of a topic."

He went very quietly, telling only his intimate friends, but telling each of them in a personal letter. So many friends were there that these letters are numerous: all are much alike. Two may be quoted which have not been published: To Maria Giberne he writes:

October 8th, 1845.

Father Dominic the Passionist comes here tonight. He does not know of my intention—he comes to see my friend Dalgairns whom he received into the Church about a week since—I shall ask him to do the same charitable work to me. This will not go till it is over.

The day following he writes to T. W. Allies:

I am to be received into what I believe to be the one true Church and the one Communion of Saints this evening, if it is so ordered. Father Dominic the Passionist is here, and I have begun my confession to him. I suppose two friends will be received with me.

May I have only one tenth part as much faith as I have intellectual conviction where the truth lies! I do not suppose any one can have had such combined reasons poured upon him that he is doing right. So far I am most blessed, but, alas, my heart is so hard and I am taking things so much as a matter of course, that I have been quite frightened lest I should not have faith and contrition enough to gain the benefit of the Sacraments. Perhaps faith and reason are incompatible in one person, or nearly so.

After his general Confession Newman was in fact quite prostrate and had to be helped out of the library. Father Dominic, who received two of the others at the same time, found in them all "such fervour and piety that I was almost out of myself for joy."

For this part of the story *Loss and Gain* is of capital importance. In the talk between Charles Reding and a priest met in the train, we see reflected this fear of Newman lest habitual intellectual conviction was an insufficient basis. From the description of Charles leaving Oxford we can guess at Newman's own bitter pain:

There lay old Oxford before him, with its hills as gentle and its meadows as green as ever. At the first view of that beloved place he stood still with folded arms, unable to proceed. Each college, each church—he counted them by their pinnacles and turrets. The silver Isis, the grey willows, the far-stretching plains, the dark groves, the distant range of Shotover, the pleasant village where he had lived . . . wood, water, stone, all so calm, so bright, they might have been his, but his they were not. Whatever he was to gain by becoming a Catholic, this he had lost. . . . He could not have another Oxford, he could not have the friends of his boyhood and youth in the choice of his manhood.

He knew well that his friends, that his family would not understand, and this, too, is reflected in the story. He is thought to condemn those he is leaving—the reason, that he must leave to save his soul, naturally enough angers them. His old tutor, his friends, his family, feel only that he goes to please himself. "He would be thought to be inflicting merely, not undergoing, suffering. He might say that he had suffered; but he would be rudely told that every one follows his own will, and that if he had given up Oxford, it was for a whim which he liked better than it."

"We all looked up to you," says the convert's mother, "perhaps we made too much of you; well, God be with you; you have taken your line."
Poor Charles said that no one could conceive what it cost him to give up what was so very dear to him, what was part of himself; there was nothing on earth which he prized like his home.
"Then why do you leave us?" she said, quickly; "you must have your way; you do it, I suppose, because you like it."
"Oh really, my dear mother," cried he, "if you saw my heart! You know in Scripture how people were obliged in the Apostles' times to give up all for Christ."
"We are heathens, then!" she replied; "thank you, Charles, I am obliged to you for this"; and she dashed away a tear from her eye.
Charles was almost beside himself. . . .

One wonders what Harriett and Jemima felt when they read all this—Harriett who would never speak to him again, Jemima who lamented but still loved and clung to him. Very brilliantly does the story indicate the impossibility for a convert so to handle the matter as to avoid misconstruction, hurt feelings, condemnation. He goes suddenly—he has not thought enough; he goes slowly, he has confused his mind with too much thinking. He knows no Romanists, how rash and wrong to venture on a *terra incognita*; he knows many Romanists—they have got hold of him. In fact none can like, none can approve the reasons for an act of which they deeply disapprove. And so, while blaming a man for pleasing himself they are fully convinced that in the event he cannot be pleased. Two chapters in *Loss and Gain* portray scenes such as might have occurred with the men who wrote letters to Newman—to snatch the convert from the jaws of Rome, to make of him an Irvingite, or some other strange religionist, or simply to steady him in the *via media*.

And as they talk it over in the Common Room, one man asks another whether there is not a strain of madness in the young man's family.

Christianity, it has been said, does not take from men the burden of life, but it gives them a spirit to bear that burden. The sacrifice of Christ renewed day by day does not lessen the spirit of sacrifice in those who join with Him in its making. Oxford grew none the less fair for Newman, the loss of friends and family, none the less a loss. But it was the choice of his manhood. Perhaps, as Callista in his own later story, moving forward in a solemn measure of adoration and preparation for the sacrifice of her martyrdom, saw Paradise as the hills and skies of Greece, so for Newman the spires of Oxford and the Isis and the clouds and tints of Shotover were transfigured into that abiding City which is to come.

The choice was a far harder one then than it would be today, and in loss of friends far more absolute. When I read that Mr. Rickards would not allow Maria Giberne (full of deepest sympathy over the death of their child) even to see his wife because she had become a Romanist, I at first felt simply that Rickards was a bigoted man. But as I read on I saw that the thing went deeper—that the feeling that it was wiser to separate at least for a time was to be found on both sides. It is expressed by Oakeley among the converts, even by Newman, when he realised he had unintentionally hurt Pusey's feelings. Different views of truth mattered so vitally, so much of the past had been a shared past, so great a field of thought and feeling was involved that men felt though they might still love they had better not see one another. Deeply affectionate correspondence continued, especially between Newman and Pusey, but the old fellowship must end. For the most part Newman's friends contrived in their attitude wonderfully to harmonise loyalty to their Church and to their old leader. Rogers soon, Church and Tom Mozley later, wrote of him beautifully. Keble expressed to him the thoughts of many: "I cannot bear to part with you, most unworthy as I know myself to be; and yet I cannot go along with you. I must cling to the belief that we are not really parted—you have taught me so, and I scarce think you can unteach me. . . . And so, with somewhat of a feeling as if the Spring had been taken out of my year, I am always your affectionate and grateful, J. Keble".

The Protestant papers felt that Newman was only going where he had belonged for years. The *Christian Observer* described "Puseyism" as "that specific modification of Popery and Tractarianism, to which Mr. Hook and some of his colleagues never fully attained; and which Mr. Newman and Mr. Ward have outrun"; while one of their correspondents, calling himself "An outraged Spectator" wrote of a "clique of Tractites, too many of whom have still the dishonesty to eat [the Church's] bread instead of following their companions to the congenial regions of benighted Popery".

Stanley felt, and a good deal later expressed the feeling, that Newman had been unjust when he said that the Liberals had driven him from Oxford—it was, Stanley affirms, Protestants, not Liberals. If in this Stanley represented the younger school he most certainly did not represent Hampden or Hawkins— only sharing with them a lack of realisation that in the defeat of Newman the principle of dogma had also been overthrown in Oxford, that Matthew Arnold and Jowett, Mark Pattison and Froude would be the later expressions of her thought. But Liberal and Protestant were sometimes curiously close, so that Hawkins could actually write to Newman on receiving the resignation of his Fellowship at Oriel:

I cannot forbear expressing the most earnest hope . . . that whatever course you have resolved upon, you may still at least be saved from some of the worst errors of the Church of Rome, such as praying to human mediators, or falling down before images—because in you, with all the great advantages with which God has blessed and tried you, I must believe such errors to be most deeply sinful. But may He protect you!

Among Newman's intimates only one man struck a really harsh note—and he surprisingly was Newman's well-loved, almost brother-in-law, James Mozley. James Mozley's was probably the best mind in the Movement, next to Newman's. He wrote a most able answer to the Development (although oddly he seems to have fancied that Newman's *securus judicat* was a mere argument from size). But even in this otherwise measured statement of the case against Newman's thesis, a strange touch of spite is apparent. "Exerting," he writes, "the privilege of genius, Mr. Newman does not enter the Roman Church as a simple pupil and follower. He enters magisterially. He surveys her with the eye of a teacher. He tells her new truth."

In an article in the *Christian Remembrancer* the discordant note is hit more strongly and held down longer. It was natural enough that Mozley, representing the older (the middle) school of Newmanites, should strike at Ward and Oakeley as "an openly extraneous and openly uncongenial set of adopters and organs" of the Movement, who "partly professed to follow and partly to lead" Newman, as men "whose minds were visibly outside of their Church." Nor can one really resent from one who had been tried by that exuberant person the remark, "Mr. Ward for example, has appealed to the intellectual province, as one which he considers in a special way his own, and he has stated publicly his conviction that he is formed for excellence in it".

All this is highly excusable, but from a man who had so lately exalted Newman as undoubted head of the Movement, who had written to him: "I owe whatever I am to yourself", who had only six months earlier written an article that caused Newman to exclaim, "I did not know how much you loved me", I find it hard to forgive either the general line on Newman's attitude or the concluding paragraph. Newman, Mozley says, had only taken up a movement already begun by others, he had lent it his support. "But the use which this Movement thus had of Mr. Newman's mind, was a loan, alas! and not a gift: the support was had and not the supporter; and this deficiency soon made itself apparent. Mr. Newman's *inward reserve was soon represented and expressed in plain language*[1] by an earnest, active . . . school" (Ward and Co.)

Curiously enough Jemima and Harriett both appear to have been more pleased by their brother-in-law's ardent championship of the Church of England than displeased by his attack on their brother. Both praised the article. Harriett, however, noted that James was in one respect mistaken, for Newman had in earlier days "had a thorough attachment for the Church of England"—"a time before you knew him" (!!)

It is a comfort to learn from the collected letters and Newman's later correspondence with Anne Mozley both that James greatly disliked writing the article and that Newman did not greatly resent it. But the puzzle remains—why did he consent to write it, or having done so why choose phrases that would seem to deny the sincerity that at every step had been shown to so intimate a friend? Mozley had been one of the witnesses of Newman's agony.

The final description of those remaining in the Church of England is no less unfortunately expressed than the direct comment on him who had gone. "The consciousness of being genuine, and not having mean ends in view, and of being in their proper place, and not having any wish to go out of it, begets a cheerful zeal and an active will . . . that temper of holy magnanimity, high purity and heavenly love, which, we thank God, still resides in and witnesses for our Church."

Magnanimity and heavenly love if not absolutely radiating from this article did so from others of Newman's friends. I have already said how deeply the beauty of Pusey's character must impress any one who comes in contact with him, and at this point his courage, generosity and charity are beyond all praise. Courage, for he too had a heavy burden to carry of misunderstanding and reproach, and he was adding to that burden; generosity and charity, for the temptation to blame where you cannot agree, to understand others only by your own lights, is hard to withstand.

Pusey had been for some time preparing himself and others for the blow and he had formed a theory of Newman having had a divine call, individual and not general, "a mysterious

---

[1] Italics mine.

dispensation", as he wrote to Keble. To Woodgate he had written in March 1845:

His convictions are too strong for him, and so now my only hope is that he may be an instrument to restore the Roman Church, since our own knows not how to employ him. His energy and gifts are wasted among us. But for us it is a very dreary prospect.

This was all very well to private friends, but surely a man was a very giant of unconscious simplicity and heroism, who, silenced already by his University, suspect by, yet still loving, his own Church, should have written as he did to the *English Churchman* within a few days of Newman's secession:

. . . There is a jar somewhere. One cannot trust oneself to think, whether his keen sensitiveness to ill was not fitted for these troubled times. What, to such dulled minds as my own, seemed a matter of course, as something of necessity to be gone through and endured, was to his, as you know, "like the piercings of a sword". You know how it seemed to pierce through his whole self. But this is with God. Our business is with ourselves. The first pang came to me years ago, when I had no other fear, but heard that he was prayed for by name in so many churches and religious houses on the continent. The fear was suggested to me, "If they pray so earnestly for this object, that he may be won to be an instrument of God's glory among them, while among us there is so much indifference, and in part dislike, may it not be that their prayers may be heard, that God will give them whom they pray for,—we forfeit whom we desire not to retain?"
And now must they not think that their prayers, which they have offered so long,—at times I think night and day, or at the Holy Eucharist,—have been heard? And may not we have forfeited him because there was, comparatively, so little love and prayer? And so now, then, in this critical state of our Church, the most perilous crisis through which it has ever passed, must not our first lesson be an increase of prayer? . . .
Yet, since God is with us still, He can bring us even through this loss. We ought not indeed to disguise the greatness of it. It is the intensest loss we could have had. They who have won him know his value. It may be a comfort to us that they do. . . . Our Church has not known how to employ him.˙ . . . Here was one marked out as a great instrument of God. . . . He is gone unconscious (as all great instruments of God are) what he himself is. He has gone as a simple act of duty with no view for himself, placing himself entirely in God's hands. And such are they whom God employs. He seems then to

me not so much gone from us, as transplanted into another part of the vineyard, where the full energies of his powerful mind can be employed, which here they were not. . . . It is perhaps the greatest event which has happened since the Communion of the Churches has been interrupted, that such an one, so formed in our Church, and the work of God's Spirit as dwelling within her, should be transplanted to theirs. If anything could open their eyes to what is good in us, or soften in us any wrong prejudice against them, it would be the presence of such an one, matured and grown to such ripeness in our Church, and now removed to theirs. If we have by our misdeeds (personal or other) "sold our brother", God, we may trust, willeth thereby to "preserve life". . . .

It would be very easy indeed to be cynical over this prophecy of Pusey's. One could glance from page to page of Newman's later life and note a procession of difficulties, failures, frustrations —the Achilli Trial, the Irish University, the *Rambler* and *Home and Foreign Reviews*, the abortive translation of the Scriptures, the quarrel between the Oratories, and the piercing pain of his final exclusion from residence in Oxford. The smile might easily become as our one over the lateness of the honour that proclaimed him a Prince of the Church. "The Cloud is lifted at last" are hardly the words in which a chosen instrument receives tokens of esteem from his rulers.

And yet, was Pusey wrong? It is not the matter of a few years— not the space of a movement, however important—but the centuries through which God's Church acts and in which becomes manifest God's choice of His own instruments. "It is the law of God's Providence," Newman wrote, "that we should succeed through failure." And it was through these repeated failures that Newman continued to build up that majestic structure of thought whereby today he has been raised almost to the position of a Father of the Church—more quickly, I think, than ever man before him.

He came to a Church, divine indeed but depressed by the long siege of Protestantism, almost outlawed from England, a Church whose children had forgotten much of their heritage, who lived by the Church's life but knew little of her thought. "We must lay again," he said, "the foundations of Catholic thought. And no foundation is above ground."

Yet so right was Pusey, so wrong James Mozley, that it was in fact the very desire to be used and taught that (together of course with those human elements of character which have emerged in this story) led Newman so often to attempt the works his superiors wanted, and to leave his own special gifts to merely chance exercise. That Newman was a chosen instrument of God none can doubt. That he or others understood that choice, I think few would maintain.

What meanwhile was the personal Gain which in his book and in his life Newman lets us see as outweighing the Loss which was the deliberate and lasting "choice of his manhood"?

"*Secretum meum mihi*," said St. Philip, and no man perhaps has ever told fully the story of his gain when he becomes a freeman of the City of God. Newman begins to tell it in this book, as

the possession of a deep peace and serenity of mind, which he had not thought possible on earth. It was more like the stillness which almost sensibly affects the ears when a bell that has long been tolling stops, or when a vessel, after much tossing at sea, finds itself in harbour. It was such as to throw him back in memory on his earliest years, as if he were really beginning life again. But there was more than the happiness of childhood in his heart; he seemed to feel a rock under his feet; it was the *soliditas Cathedrae Petri*. He went on kneeling, as if he were already in heaven, with the throne of God before him, and angels around; and as if to move were to lose his privilege.

To Maria Giberne, received a couple of months later, he writes:

December 21st, 1845.

And now, my dear Miss Giberne, that you have the power, pray begin your intercessions very earnestly (though I need not say it) for those dear friends of mine, or ours, who are still held back, or rather imprisoned in their old error, and that by their own good feelings and amiable affections. You have all the saints of heaven to aid you now, and especially that first and most glorious of Saints whose name you bear.

To be able to love Our Lady freely, to invoke her and the saints, is a joy often apparent in his letters. And it is said that no one ever forgot the experience of hearing him say Mass; the depth of adoration, the absorption, the concentration on that great action that gives meaning to the Catholic's day—to his life—because it is the breaking through into this world of Heaven's worship.

In *Loss and Gain*, Newman makes the Catholic say to the Anglican:

The idea of worship is different in the Catholic Church from the idea of it in your Church; for, in truth the *religions* are different . . . I declare, to me, he said, and he clasped his hands on his knees, and looked forward as if soliloquising, to me nothing is so consoling, so piercing, so thrilling, so overcoming as the Mass. . . . It is not a mere form of words—it is a great action, the greatest action that can be on earth. It is not the invocation merely, but, if I dare use the word, the Evocation of the Eternal. He becomes present on the altar in flesh and blood, before whom angels bow and devils tremble. This is that awful event which is the scope, and is the interpretation, of every part of the solemnity. Words are necessary, but as means, not as ends; they are not mere addresses to the throne of grace, they are instruments of what is far higher, of consecration, of sacrifice. They hurry on as if impatient to fulfil their mission. Quickly they go, the whole is quick; for they are all parts of one integral action. . . . Quickly they pass; because as the lightning which shineth from one part of the heaven unto the other, so is the coming of the Son of Man. . . . So we, all around, each in his place, look out for the great Advent, "waiting for the moving of the water." Each in his place, with his own heart, with his own wants, with his own thoughts, with his own intention, with his own prayers, separate but concordant, uniting in consummation . . . like a concert of musical instruments, each different, but concurring in a sweet harmony, we take our part with God's priest, supporting him, yet guided by him. There are little children there, and old men, and simple labourers, and students in seminaries, priests preparing for Mass, priests making their thanksgiving; there are innocent maidens, and there are penitent sinners; but out of these many minds rises one eucharistic hymn, and the great Action is the measure and the scope of it.[1]

But what of the intellect? The Church by her worship filled his emotions, but was that also satisfied? Surely the answer is given abundantly in the *Apologia*. Many of those among whom Newman came lacked intellectual distinction (and so had many of those whom he left and those who came with him). But now after many years of struggle his mind could feed fully on reality. In the Appendix to the *Apologia* he analysed, after almost twenty years, what in 1845 he had just begun to discover.

[1] *Loss and Gain*, pp. 327-329.

This Note E on The Anglican Church well shows how Conversion meant no casting aside of positive truth but its completion. In a brief space we can glimpse the unity that underlay the turbulent struggle of his development. I have transposed the order a little as the only way of materially shortening the passage without altering the sense:

The Church of England has been the instrument of Providence in conferring great benefits on me;—had I been born in Dissent, perhaps I should never have been baptised; had I been born an English Presbyterian, perhaps I should never have known Our Lord's divinity; had I not come to Oxford, perhaps I should never have heard of the visible Church, or of Tradition, or other Catholic doctrines. . . . It may be a great creation, though it be not divine, and this is how I judge of it . . . a time-honoured institution, of noble historical memories, a monument of ancient wisdom, a momentous arm of political strength, a great national organ, a source of vast popular advantage, and, to a certain point, a witness and teacher of religious truth. . . . I cannot tell how soon there came upon me,—but very soon,—an extreme astonishment that I had ever imagined it to be a portion of the Catholic Church. For the first time I looked at it from without, and [at] the contrast which was presented to me by the Catholic Church. Then I recognised at once a reality which was quite a new thing with me. Then I was sensible that I was not making for myself a Church by an effort of thought; I needed not to make an act of faith in her; I had not painfully to force myself into a position, but my mind fell back upon itself in relaxation and in peace, and I gazed at her almost passively as a great objective fact. I looked at her;—at her rites, her ceremonial, and her precepts; and I said, "This *is* a religion."

Appendix A

Letter to Mrs. Wilberforce:

November 17, 1834.

My dear Mrs. Wilberforce,

I delayed writing, yet 'twas from the great satisfaction, as well as the pleasure your most acceptable letter gave me—I found my anxiety, as it were, rested—and as being thus at rest, I kept silent, when perhaps I ought to have acknowledged to you how pleased I was. Really, you must not suppose that I do not feel the force and influence of those parts of the Roman Catholic system, which have struck you. To express vividly what I mean, I would say, "I would be a Romanist, if I could. I wish I could be a Romanist." But I cannot—there is that mixture of error in it, which (though unseen of course by many, many pious Christians who have been brought up in it,) effectually cuts off the chance of my acquiescing in it. I admire the lofty character, the beauty, the sweetness and tenderness of its services and discipline. I acknowledge them divine in a certain sense, i.e., remnants of that old system which the Apostles founded. On the other hand I grieve to think of our own neglect in realising the Church system among us, which our Reformers intended to be ours, though we have degenerated from their notions; but after all there is that in Romanism which makes it a duty to keep aloof from it, there is a mixture of corruption, which, when seen, it is a duty to protest against, and *we* have been so circumstanced as to see it: and instead of shutting our eyes to it, we must feel that we are called upon to protest against it. On the other hand, instead of deserting our own Church, because its members are rebellious, rather let us rally in its defence and try to strengthen its hand. Consider the fallen state of the Jews when our Saviour came, how mixed they were with the world, how political, Herod their King a man of Edom, and the Romans their great friends, yet after all did not such as Zachariah, Anna and the rest gain a blessing by quietly going on with their *own* worship as the saints of old, in spite of the degeneracy around them? and at last they gained, by their perseverance the blessing of seeing the Lord Christ. And so we, though we are thought unfashionable and born centuries too late, may go on in our own Church, as our forefathers, secure through the mercy of a blessing from Him, and sure, even though He does not come in our day to make the glory of the Second House greater than that of the first, yet that at least we shall be preparing the way for

460

Him, and may be the means of bringing the blessing on our children's children, though it be delayed.

The more I examine into the R.C. system, the less sound it appears to me to be, and the less safely could I in conscience profess to receive it. I hardly know whether to say anything on the subject, not knowing whether I shall speak to the point; yet perhaps I ought not to be silent on the nature of my objections to it. E.g. it seems so very irreverent and profane a thing to say that our Saviour's own body is carnally present on the Altar. That He is in some mysterious incomprehensible way present I fully believe; but I do not know what way— and since the way is not told us in Scripture or the ancient Fathers I dare pronounce nothing. Much less dare I be so irreverent as to determine that His flesh and blood are there as they were on Calvary. Surely He who came into the apartment the doors being shut, has ways of being there innumerable, such as we know not. We believe that now He has a "spiritual body"—and a spiritual body may be present, the bread and wine still remaining. Therefore it seems safe and according to Scripture to say He is present *in* the bread and wine —but unnecessary and irreverent to insist on saying that the bread and wine are *changed* into that same flesh and blood which were on the Cross.

Again the honour paid to the saints surely is practically a dishonour to the One God. Is it not practically a polytheism? Are not the Saints the gods of the multitude in R.C. countries? is there not a natural *tendency* in the human mind to idolatry, and shall the Church, the pillar of the Truth, cherish it instead of refusing it?

Again, after all excuses, is there not something against one's sense of right in praying to images? is there not a still small voice telling us not to do so?

Again consider what a frightful doctrine purgatory is—not the holiest man who lived but must expect to find himself there on dying, since Christ does not remit all punishment of sin. Now, if Christ has promised to wipe away all guilt and all suffering upon death, what a great affront it must be to Him, thus to obscure His mercy, to deprive the people of the full comfort of His work for them!

I feel very much the weakness and poorness of these remarks, but hope you will take them as they are meant in kindness. It requires many words to do justice to them, and conversation rather than writing. I feel the Roman Catholic system to be irreverent towards Christ, degrading Him, robbing Him *practically* of His sole honour, hiding *His* bounty;—i.e., so far forth as it *is* Roman Catholic—*so far as* it differs from ours. Its high points are our points too, if it would but keep them, and not give up our jewels. But, while what is good in it is reverent, solemn, and impressive, its corruptions *practically* undo all this excellence. Surely we shall be judged according to our conscience, and if we have a clear sight of what is wrong in Rome, we must not follow our inclinations, because Rome has what is attractive in some part of her devotions.

Pray excuse what I feel to be most imperfect. I wish I spoke by mouth, not by letter. Best love to the two Williams. The Revolutionary Ministry is just out and the Duke of Wellington sent for to the King.

APPENDIX B

Littlemore,
Good Friday Evening,
April 5, 1844.

MY DEAR MRS. FROUDE,

I write with some apprehension lest I should be making a great fuss about nothing and to no good—and yet I think too that what I have said and shall say may tend to make you less uncomfortable.

My confidence against the Church of Rome lay in two things, first my feeling that we had the Apostolical Succession—next my conviction that her peculiar doctrines were not held by the Fathers.

As to the first of these, I acknowledged great irregularity in the transmission, and vast and various disorders in our Church. But I got over all by the parallel of the Jewish Church, which was a Church when Christ came, in spite of anomalies as great as ours. My view is drawn out in my last lecture on the Prophetical Office.

As to the second it was to me as clear as day (as it is now) that the honours paid in the Church of Rome to St. Mary were not primitive. On this I rested our case mainly for those honours are at once the furthest removed from primitive usage and especially characteristic of the Roman Church. I have drawn out the general argument in Lecture II on "Romanism as neglectful of Antiquity".

My defence of the English Church against Rome was conducted under the shelter of these two convictions, with the expression of which my lectures begin and end. They were written in 1834–1837; and during 1836 and 7 the Tracts against Rome.

In the Summer of 1839 I was led in the course of my *regular reading* (which is a point on which some stress might be laid) to the Monophysite controversy, and to the Council of Chalcedon and St. Leo's works inclusively. I found what surprised me very much. It struck me at once, but when it began to assume an unsettling character I do not recollect—but I found more matter for serious thought in that history than in anything I had read. The Council of Ch. is the fourth

A.D. 452 Ecumenical Council, which it is generally considered the English Church receives. Our Divines consider its opponents heretics as denying that "Jesus Christ has come in the flesh". Eutyches was condemned then, he said there was but one nature in Our Lord. Now I cannot bring together all the strange things I found in its history. I found the Eastern Church under the superintendence (as I may call it) of Pope Leo. I found that *he* had made the Fathers of the Council unsay their decree and pass another, so that (humanly speaking) we owe it to Pope Leo at this day that the Catholic Church holds the true doctrine. I found that Pope Leo based his authority on St. Peter. I found the Fathers of the Council crying out "Peter hath spoken by the mouth of Leo", when they altered their decree. I found a portentously large body of Christians thrown into schism by this Council, at this day the Church of Egypt, Syria (in part), and Armenia; and that the schismatics [were] not like the Arians of a rationalist [tendency], but with a theology of a warm and elevating character. I found that they appealed, and with much plausibility, to certain of the Fathers, as St. Athanasius and St. Cyril of Alex.—that they professed to be maintainers of antiquity—that they called their opponents (the Catholics) *Chalcedonians*, as we call the R.C.'s Tridentines, that their cause was taken up by the civil power, and created a contention between Emperors and the Church. Further I found there was a large middle party as well as an extreme. There was a distinct Via Media, which indeed the Emperor took up, and there was a large body who went on for some centuries without Bishops. I am writing from memory, but I am sure I am right in all points of consequence—and in a word I found a complete and wonderful parallel, as if a prophecy, of the state of the Reformation controversy, and that we were on the anti-Catholic side.

I will go on with this part of the subject at the expense of the order of time. I add then that from that time to this, the view thus brought before me has grown upon me. I had hitherto read ecclesiastical history with the eyes of our Divines, and taken what they said on faith, but now I had got *a key*, which interpreted large passages of history which had been locked up from me. I found everywhere one and the same picture, prophetic of our present state, the Church in communion with Rome decreeing, and heretics resisting. Especially as regards the Arian controversy, how could I be so blind before! except that I looked at things bit by bit, instead of putting them together. There was Pope Julius resisting the whole East in defence of St. Athanasius, the Eusebians at the great Council of Antioch resisting him, and he appealing to his own authority (in which the historians support him) and declaring that he filled the See of Peter. The lapse of Pope Liberius, carefully as it needs considering, does not interfere with the general view. There were two parties, a Via Media, and an extreme, both heretical, but the Via Media containing pious men, whom St. Athanasius and others sympathise in—there were the kings of the earth taking up the heresy against the Church—there was precisely the same appeal in Scripture, which now attains, and that grounded on a literal interpretation of its text, to which St. Athanasius always opposes the "ecclesiastical sense"—there was the same complaint of introducing novel and unscriptural terms into the Creed of the Church, "Consubstantial" and "Transubstantiation" being both of philosophical origin, and if Trent has opposed some previous councils (which I do not recollect) at least the Nicene Council adopted the very term "Consubstantial" which a celebrated Council of Antioch 60 or 70 years before condemned or discountenanced.

When shall I come to an end?

Ever yrs affectionately,

John H. Newman.

Appendix C

Oratory, Edgbaston, Birmingham,

June, 1st, 1853.

My dear Mr. Ffoulkes,

I am glad I now know whom I am to thank for sending me so kindly the little work entitled "A Counter Theory", and I assure you of the satisfaction I felt at hearing some time since that the unknown author wished to have my opinion on it. What I said in answer was not that it was "sceptical"; I should not have thought of using so unmeaning and disrespectful a word. I merely observed that it seemed to me an expansion of a tract of my own, No. 31 of Tracts for the Times, entitled "The Reformed Church".

I did not know what else to say: for, to tell the truth, I was not able, with such attention as I could give the book, which I am aware was insufficient, to discover how it bore upon the matter in dispute.

In my own book to which it refers, 1st: I laid down what I conceived to be a *fact*. 2nd: I said that fact was a *difficulty*. 3rd: I said it required a *solution*. 4th: I offered a solution in a *theory* of *doctrinal development*.

1. The fact which I thought I saw was this, that, from the very time of the Apostles, in every successive age, there had been in the teaching of the Church, a prima facie appearance (though, for my part, I did not believe it to be more than an appearance) of a change or accession of doctrine.

2. I said that this appearance was a *difficulty* to Anglicans as well as to Roman Catholics: because it attached to the doctrine of the Blessed Trinity, as contained in the Anglican formularies, as well as to the doctrine of the Pope's Supremacy or of the prerogatives of the Blessed Virgin. I compared the language of the Athanasian Creed which speaks of the Son as Immensus, with Bull's admission "Veteres Catholici *paene omnes*, qui Arium praecessere, Filii Dei invisibilem atque *immensam* naturam ignorasse videntur etc., ad mira ista Patrum dicta quis non plane obstupescat, etc. . . . ." D.F.N. iv. 3.

3. I said therefore that Anglicans, as well as Catholics were interested in finding a *solution* of this difficulty. "An argument is needed, unless Christianity is to abandon the province of argument; and those who find fault with the explanation here offered of its historical phenomena, will find it their duty to find one of their own," p. 29.

4. I proposed a theory which covered the whole difficulty, on the part of Anglicans indeed, but also on the part of Catholics. And, I added that, as seeing no other way out of the difficulty except that which this theory opened, I found myself in this position, that I could not protect myself as an Anglican against it [this difficulty] without protecting Catholics against it also.

Here I left the matter in my book: but the practical inference was obvious. This very, this one difficulty had been my great obstacle and argument, my Achilles heel, against acknowledging the claims of the Catholic Church. I had made it the basis of my work on the Prophetical Office of the Church in 1837. I had shown my intimate heartfelt sense of its extreme importance as early as 1834, and implied it at an earlier period still in the Lyra Apostolica. In 1834 I said, "Considering the high gifts, and the strong claims of the Church of Rome and its dependencies on our admiration, reverence, love, and gratitude, how could we withstand it, as we do; how could we refrain from being melted into tenderness, and *rushing into communion* with it, *but for* the words of *Truth* itself, etc. . . . how could we learn to be severe, etc. . . . but for the warning of Moses against even a divinely gifted teacher," etc., etc.?

I quoted this passage in the advertisement to my Essay on Doctrinal Development, and I added, "He little thought, when he so wrote, that the time would ever come, when he should feel the *obstacle*, which he spoke of as lying in the way of communion with the Church of Rome, to be *destitute of solid foundation.*"

I found then, that I had no argument against the Church of Rome but one which was now solved, and which, if considered not solved, *proved too much*, for it tended to throw me back out of the Church of England towards infidelity *quite as logically* as it deterred me from Rome. Nothing then was left to me as a matter of conscience and duty, but to follow those suggestions of reason, of affection, and of faith, which called me to leave "my country and my father's house" for the patrimony of Peter.

Now the very title of your book shows a fairness and earnestness, which is quite in keeping with the interesting letter you now send me, and which I never yet have found in any answer to my argument. For it acknowledges the *need* of a Counter-Theory, by its very title, whereas the replies to me which I have hitherto met with do but suggest objections to me (sound or otherwise), as infidels suggest them to Christianity, without drawing out any whole view of the subject to be set against and to supplant mine.

So far I could not but be pleased with you: but I confess, possibly from my own fault, I did not find any distinct avowal on your part, 1 : whether you admitted or disputed my *broad fact*, viz. in its application to the *Anglican Church* as well as to the Catholic, 2 : and if you did not admit it, how you answered the arguments producible for it, 3 : if you did admit it, *what* is the Theory, *categorically stated*, by which you solved it.

For instance, to the objection, that St. Athanasius's teaching concerning the Blessed Trinity seems different from St. Justin's, I replied that St. Athanasius considered the doctrine in all its aspects, St. Justin in one only: and that partial truth sounds like error. Both fathers saw before them, by the eye of faith, one and the same object: but St. Justin insisting on one portion of it, seemed to deny the others, though, had his meaning been asked, he would have explained himself in St. Athanasius's sense, nay would have confessed that he had spoken unguardedly.

This then was my Theory, I laid it down as a broad principle, that from the nature of the case, the deeper, the richer, the more pregnant a doctrine is, the more difficult is it to state it all, the more difficult is it to say all we think and inwardly hold about it. To bring out one's meaning fully, to state one's view exactly, is a gift. Do we not find occasion to say almost daily, "I only wish so and so were alive now, he would not let his words be thus wrested. I knew him well, I am confident he meant no such thing, etc." If we feel this even about human beings, how much more justly may we feel it about divine!

In like manner, if Firmilian said things about the Roman See, which at first sight are difficult to reconcile with the existing Catholic teaching on the subject, I said that, considering that St. Justin could be obscure on a point of faith, which required no outward position of secular affairs for its exhibition, much more might there be confusion of mind and inconsistency in Catholic controversialists, who wrote about a *practical* doctrine, which the times had not suffered as yet to be fully carried out in act, or made *oculis subjecta fidelibus,* and to which they were addressing themselves in a state of excitement and irritation.

I am sorry I have had to use so many words in bringing out my meaning, but I thought I should be writing to no purpose, unless I

made myself clear at once beyond the need of future "developments".
As to my book, I could have written its subject on its title page, viz.,
"The differences and additions in doctrinal teaching observable in the
history of the Church are but apparent, being the necessary phenomena
incident to deep intellectual ideas." Will you kindly take the trouble
on your part to write down your "Counter Theory", thus categorically
as if in your title page?

I am, my dear Mr. Ffoulkes,
very truly yours,

JOHN H. NEWMAN.

BIBLIOGRAPHY

Newman's own works *passim*, especially *Apologia pro Vita Sua, Arians of the Fourth Century, Development of Christian Doctrine, Difficulties of Anglicans, Essays on Miracles, Lectures on Justification, Oxford University Sermons, Parochial and Plain Sermons* (8 volumes), *Sermons on Subjects of the Day, Verses, Via Media* (2 volumes).

NEWMAN AND HIS CIRCLE

Abbott, Edwin A.	*Anglican Career of Cardinal Newman* (2 vols.)
Ashwell, A. R., M.A.	*Life of the Right Reverend Samuel Wilberforce, D.D.*
Bellasis, Edward	*Coram Cardinale*
Bishops' Charges, 1841	
Blachford, Frederick Lord	*Letters*
Bremond, Henri (tr. H. C. Corrance)	*The Mystery of Cardinal Newman*
Brillioth, Yngve	*The Anglican Revival: Studies in the Oxford Movement*
Burgon, Dean	*Twelve Good Men*
Church, Dean	*The Oxford Movement* (1833–45)
,, ,,	*Occasional Papers*
Church, Mary	*Life and Letters of Dean Church*
Clarke, C. P. S.	*The Oxford Movement*
Clough, Arthur Hugh	*Writings and Memoirs*, edited by his wife.
Coleridge, Rt. Hon. Sir John Taylor	*Memoir of John Keble*
Dawson, Christopher	*The Spirit of the Oxford Movement*
Faber, Geoffrey	*Oxford Apostles*
Froude, James Anthony	*The Nemesis of Faith*
,, ,, ,,	*The Oxford Counter Reformation: Short Studies on Great Subjects*: 4th Series
Froude, Richard Hurrell	*Remains* (ed. Newman and Keble: 4 vols.)
Guitton, Jean	*La Philosophie de Newman*
Hampden, Dr.	*The Scholastic Philosophy considered in its Relation to Christian Theology* (Bampton Lectures)

Harper, Gordon Huntingdon	*Cardinal Newman and William Froude, F.R.S.: a Correspondence*
Hutton, R. H.	*Cardinal Newman*
Liddon, Henry Parry, D.D.	*Life of Edward Bouverie Pusey* (4 vols.)
Lyra Apostolica	
Middleton, R. D.	*Dr. Routh*
,, ,,	*Newman and Bloxam*
Mozley, Harriet	*The Fairy Bower*
,, ,,	*The Lost Brooch*
,, ,,	*Louisa*
,, ,,	*Family Adventures*
Mozley, James	*Collected Letters* (edited by Anne Mozley)
,, ,,	*Literary and Philosophical Essays*
Mozley, Thomas	*Reminiscences, Chiefly of Oriel and the Oxford Movement* (2 vols).
Nédoncelle, M.	*Oeuvres Philosophiques de Newman*
Newman, Cardinal	*Letters and Correspondence of Newman in the English Church, with a brief Auto-biography* (edited by Anne Mozley)
,, ,,	*Correspondence with John Keble and Others* (edited at the Birmingham Oratory)
Newman, Francis	*Contributions, Chiefly to the Early History of Cardinal Newman*
Oakeley, Frederick	*Historical Notes on the Tractarian Movement* (1833–45)
Ornsby, Robert	*Memoirs of James Robert Hope-Scott* (2 vols.)
Palmer, William (of Worcester)	*Narrative of Events Connected with the Publication of "Tracts for the Times"*
Palmer William (of Magdalen)	*Notes of a Visit to the Russian Church*
Pattison, Mark	*Memoirs*
Sieveking, I. Giberne	*Memoir and Letters of Francis Newman*
Stanley, Dean	*Life of Thomas Arnold* (2 vols.)
Stephens, W. R. W.	*Life and Letters of Dean Hook* (2 vols.) Tracts for the Times (6 vols.)
Tristram, Henry	*Newman and his Friends*
Various Authors	*A Tribute to Newman: published Browne and Nolan*
,, ,,	*John Henry Newman: Centenary Essays*

Ward, Wilfrid	*Life and Times of Cardinal Wisemau* (2 vols)
,, ,,	*Life of Cardinal Newman* (2 vols.)
,, ,,	*William George Ward and the Oxford Movement*
,, ,,	*Last Lectures*
Whately, Jane	*Life and Correspondence of Richard Whately, D.D., late Archbishop of Dublin* (2 vols.)
White, Blanco	*Life, by Himself* (ed. Thom, 2 vols.)
,, ,,	*Letters from Spain* (2 vols.)
Williams, Isaac	*Autobiography*
Yonge, Charlotte	*John Keble's Parishes: A History of Hursley and Otterbourne*

BACKGROUND OF THE TIMES

Anonymous	*A Reply to the Calumnies of the Edinburgh Review against Oxford*
Beveridge, William	*Private Thoughts on Religion*
Blakiston, H. E. D.	*Trinity College*
Cox, G. V.	*Recollections of Oxford*
Disraeli, Benjamin	*Sybil*
,, ,,	*Coningsby, or The New Generation*
Gaskell, Mrs.	*Mary Barton*
Halévy, Elie	*History of the English People* (3 vols.)
Hammond, J. L. and Mary	*The Town Labourer* (1716–1832)
,, ,, ,,	*The Skilled Labourer* (1760–1832)
,, ,, ,,	*The Village Labourer* (1760–1832)
Hughes, T. H.	*Tom Brown at Oxford*
Lang, Andrew	*Oxford*
Legg, J. Wickham	*English Church Life from the Restoration to the Oxford Movement*
Leslie, Shane	*George the Fourth*
Mallet, C. E.	*A History of the University of Oxford* (3 vols.)
Melville, Lewis	*Life and Letters of William Cobbett* (2 vols.)
More, Hannah	*Works*
Newton, Thomas, Bishop of Bristol	*Dissertation on the Prophecies*

Overton, Canon	*The Non-Jurors, their Lives, Principles and Writings*
„ „	*The English Church in the 19th Century*
Pearson, Hesketh	*The Smith of Smiths*
Piette, Maximin	*John Wesley in the Evolution of Protestantism*
Rannie, David Watson	*Oriel College*
Roberts, William	*Memoirs of the Life and Correspondence of Mrs. Hannah More*
Seccombe and Scott	*In Praise of Oxford* (2 vols.)
Tawney, Richard Henry	*The Acquisitive Society*
Thackeray, W.	*The Four Georges*
Trevelyan, Sir George Otto	*Life and Letters of Lord Macaulay*
Trevelyan, G.	*English Social History*
Tuckwell, Rev. W.	*Reminiscences of Oxford*

Index

Abbott, E. A., 182, 330, 386, 407
Arnold of Rugby, Dr., 6, 74, 75, 76, 104, 114, 141–2, 145, 153, 176, 199–200, 212, 225, 226, 229–30, 231, 235, 252, 260, 288, 289, 295, 296–7, 312, 325, 331, 350, 360, 367, 368, 416, 422, 446
Arnold, Matthew, 350, 452
Austen, Jane, 61, 250, 270, 299

Bagot, Dr., Bishop of Oxford, 331–2, 375
Beveridge, Bishop, 31–3
Bloxam, Mr., 271, 361, 364, 375, 388, 423
Bowden, John William, 37, 38, 41, 46, 62, 111, 121, 125, 154, 245, 429–30, 436; letters from Newman, 71, 75, 196, 228, 233, 241, 255–6, 289, 298, 312, 332, 335, 380, 389
Bremond, Henri, 136–7, 139
Brillioth, Dr., 84, 237, 291
British Critic, 298, 310, 334, 362, 365, 410–11
British Magazine, 185–6, 205, 241, 252, 413
Bulteel, Mr., 177–8
Burgon, Dean, 93, 185
Butler, Bishop, 101, 160, 262, 302

Caroline, Queen, 55–6
Catholic Church: Catholic Emancipation Bill, 154–7, 158, 164
Newman's early views on, 27–30, 193, 197, 202–11, 221, 256, 262–7, 342–4, 360–1, 362, 374, 380–2, 385–6, 391, 427 and appendices
Newman's Retractation of past attacks on (1843), 393–4
Newman's conversion to (1845), 433–59
Chesterton, G. K., 127, 132, 225, 227, 329, 340, 407, 447
Christian Observer, 61, 242, 310, 452
Christian Remembrancer, 411, 453
Christie, J. F., 203, 326, 370, 444
Church, Richard, later Dean of St. Paul's, 70–1, 224, 248–9, 259, 290, 313, 314, 315, 318, 325, 330, 337, 339, 371, 372, 374, 381, 408, 410, 411, 414, 447, 452
Church of England: Evangelicalism in, 23, 25–33, 78–92, 101–5, 177

Church of England:—contd.
Thirty-Nine Articles, 265, 287–97, 366–74, 380, 409–10, 418–9, 445
Publication of Froude's Remains, 322–33
Bishops' Charges against Tractarians, 331–2, 376, 394
Bishopric of Jerusalem controversy, 376–9, 382, 383
Newman's views on, 257, 260–2, 265, 335–6, 360, 361, 362, 382, 383–6, 399–403, 426, 427, 436, 444–5, 458, 459
See also Oxford Movement
Church Missionary Society, 176–8
Churton, Edward, 74, 96, 329
Clark, Rev. J., 318
Clough of Balliol, 315, 408
Cobbett, William, 55, 166–7, 227–8, 230, 231, 251
Coleridge, Mr. Justice, 430, 436, 438
Conservative Journal, 393
Copeland, W. J., 425, 434
Copleston, Provost of Oriel, 69, 70, 76, 83, 95, 154, 180, 290
Cox, Bedel, 38, 56, 107, 110

Dalgairns, J. B., 387, 388, 417, 449
Darby, John Nelson, 164
Dawson, Christopher, 40, 205, 212, 379
Dodsworth, Mr., letter from Newman, 386
Dominic, Father, 161, 449

Eden, Mr., Vicar of St. Mary's, Oxford, 424–5
Edinburgh Review, 68–9, 130, 296, 325, 331, 417
Evangelicalism, 23, 25–33, 78–92, 101–5, 177

Faber, F. W., 315, 382, 389–90
Faber, Rev. Francis, 382
Family Adventures (Harriett Newman), 11–3, 365
Fairy Bower, The (Harriett Newman), 11–15, 51, 365
Faussett, Mr., 325–6, 332, 333
Ffoulkes, Mr., 163; letter from Newman, 464–7
Fourdrinier, Jemima, see Newman, Jemima, mother

Froude, James Anthony, 84, 146, 315–7, 319, 324, 349–51, 379, 411, 413, 414, 452

Froude, Richard Hurrell: Ancestry and character, 146–8
Elected Fellow of Oriel, 115, 141
Friendship with Newman, 115, 125, 132, 135, 136, 137, 148, 158, 176, 184, 243, 298, 309, 314
Travels with Newman, 189–99, 203, 204–6
Religious thought, 204–13, 405
Life of austerity, 84, 272, 330–1, 339
Views on Catholic Church, 204, 205–8
Otherwise mentioned, 163, 178, 180, 181, 186, 237, 239, 240, 248, 255, 394
Publication of *Remains*, 322–33
Quoted, 213, 224
Letters from Newman, 182, 183, 242–3, 275

Froude, William, 434, 443
Froude, Mrs. William, letters from Newman, 361–2, 443, 462–4
Fry, Mrs., 227, 325

Gentili, Father, 398
George IV, King, 55–6
Giberne, Maria, 121–3, 124, 126–7, 129, 149–50, 171, 271, 308, 309, 436, 451, 457
Letters from Newman, 304, 309, 311, 334, 336, 386, 387, 388, 418, 427, 435, 438, 449, 457
Gladstone, W. E., 240, 315, 326, 412, 417, 418, 424, 430
Golightly, Mr., 128, 314, 328–9, 370, 371, 372, 373, 434
Goulburn, Dean, 260, 407, 408
Grey, Lord, 230–3
Guitton, Jean, 343, 345, 350, 442
Gutch, Dr., John, 100

Hale, W. H., 323
Halévy, Elie, 225, 226
Hampden, Dr. (afterwards Bishop), 141–2, 145, 180, 255, 287–97, 307, 312, 339, 353, 368, 405–6, 413–4, 445–6, 452
Hawkins, Dr., 74, 75, 76, 97, 101, 102–3, 137, 141, 144, 146, 152–3, 155, 178–81, 183, 188, 219, 288, 368, 425, 452–3
Henrietta Maria, Queen, 367
Hook, Dean, 312, 374, 390, 404, 413, 452
Hooker, Bishop, 160, 211
Hope, James (afterwards Hope-Scott), 62, 315, 323, 375, 414, 436; letters from Newman, 376, 381, 391, 411, 418, 430
Hume, David, 24, 26, 347–8
Hutton, R. H., 97, 251, 265, 307

Irish Bishoprics Bill, 183–4, 199, 233–4

Jager, Abbé, 252, 257
Jeffreys, Mr., 432–3
Jelf, Mr., 112, 374
Jenkyns, Dr. (Balliol), 38–9, 181, 188, 231, 408, 412, 418
Johnson, Dr. Samuel, 27, 85, 88, 212, 257, 338
Jowett of Balliol, 153, 452

Keble, John: Fellow of Oriel College, 75
Influence on Newman, 75, 76, 132, 135, 146, 158, 333, 334, 436, 437, 439
Friendship with Froude, 147, 148, 243, 324
and the Oxford Movement, 176, 233, 237, 238, 243, 255, 375, 404, 405, 413, 431
Sermon on National Apostasy, 233, 237–8
Otherwise mentioned, 130, 152, 218, 226, 233, 235, 272, 283, 314, 335, 380, 430, 434
Letter to Newman on his conversion, 452
Letters from Newman, 25, 239, 241, 298, 332, 375, 381, 398, 399, 418, 420, 429, 430, 435, 447
Keble, Tom, 332, 333
Kingsley, Charles, 317, 349, 356, 394, 395
Kinsey, Dean of Trinity, 43, 66, 73

Lake, Dean, 313, 315
Laud, Archbishop, 133, 208, 209, 211, 252, 258, 262, 325
Laurie, Mr., 5
Lee, Dr., President of Trinity College, 34
Lenthall, Elizabeth, 425–6
Library of the Fathers, 255, 298, 307, 310
Liddon, Henry Parry, D.D., 100, 101, 141, 142, 253, 254, 411
Littlemore, parish life, 153, 163, 164–5, 174–5, 269–71, 301, 303–5, 328, 338, 361, 362–5, 392, 400, 424–5; Community life at, 363–5, 376, 386–91, 398, 449
Lloyd, C., Bishop of Oxford, 94, 95, 98, 111–12, 125, 177, 252
Lockhart, William, 246, 398, 410
Lost Brooch, The (Harriett Newman), 59–60, 130, 365
Lyra Apostolica, 186, 190, 223, 252, 465

Macaulay, Lord, 87, 212, 232, 234
Macaulay, Zachary, 87
Macmullen, Mr., 414
Manning, Henry Edward, 256, 273, 315, 399, 424, 426, 430
Marsh, Mr., Vicar at Hampstead, 127–8
Martyrs' Memorial, Oxford, 327–8, 409

Mayers, Walter, 25, 31, 32, 60, 99, 102, 121, 124, 136, 165; letters from Newman, 42, 52, 54

Maynooth, 234, 326, 371, 380, 393

Melbourne, Lord, 289, 290, 406

Methodism, *see* Evangelicalism

More, Hannah, 27, 30, 78, 80, 86, 87, 88–91, 191, 243

Morris of Exeter, 389–90

Mozley, Anne, 24, 26, 119, 154, 164, 171, 218, 270, 308, 364, 426, 454; *quoted*, 184, 191, 285, 316

Mozley, James, 245, 247–8, 312, 315, 318, 319, 338, 365, 411, 425, 426, 453–4; *quoted*, 238, 255, 278–9, 285, 290, 291, 293–4, 304–5, 308, 361, 399, 433; letters from Newman, 417, 420, 433–4

Mozley, John, 285, 359

Mozley, Tom, 14, 94, 112, 178, 186–8, 199, 231, 243, 245, 258, 274, 299–301, 304, 315, 363, 365, 397–8, 411, 434, 452; *quoted*, 11, 62, 76, 78–9, 93, 111–12, 147, 174, 175, 227, 246

Mullins, John. 34, 169, 359

Newman, Charles Robert, brother, 1, 2, 8, 9, 12, 40, 61, 128, 167–71, 172, 281–2, 283, 285, 360

Newman, Elizabeth, aunt, 16–21, 168, 281, 359; letters from Newman, 21, 54, 63, 91

Newman, Francis (Frank), brother, 1, 6, 8–9, 52, 55, 59, 60, 61, 62, 63–4, 66, 87, 98, 99, 117, 118, 121, 131, 164–7, 168, 170, 171, 172, 255, 268, 281, 359–60

Newman, Harriet, sister, 1, 9–10, 11–15, 21, 22, 55, 98–9, 119, 120, 121, 122, 123, 124, 127, 129, 130, 131, 134–5, 161–2, 168, 172, 173–4, 274, 280–1, 282, 299–301, 308, 359, 365, 397–8, 434, 451, 454; letters from Newman, 9–10, 124, 161, 200–1, 370

Newman, Jemima, mother, 1, 2, 3, 6, 16–22, 54, 110, 117–31, 134, 161–3, 172–5, 268–71, 277, 278, 279–86, 300; letters, 11, 17, 18–19, 20, 45, 49, 65, 110, 117, 118, 172–5, 270, 280, 282, 283; letters from Newman, 3, 6, 40, 46, 48–9, 63–4, 65, 66, 98, 99, 110, 111, 117, 118, 124, 125, 141, 156, 158–60, 181–2, 189, 190–9, 216, 222–3, 280

Newman, Jemima, sister, 1, 3, 21, 111, 123, 124–5, 126, 128, 130, 131, 270, 285, 359, 360, 364, 372–3, 426, 438–9, 451, 454; letters from Newman, 2, 10, 50, 51–2, 57, 99, 120, 162, 169, 171–2, 177, 200, 203, 215, 232, 260, 285, 286, 299, 300, 301, 305, 306–7, 360–1, 362–3, 364, 374, 375, 386, 391, 393, 397, 398, 428, 429, 434–5, 436, 437, 439–41

Newman, John, grandfather, 1

Newman, John, father, 1, 11, 16–20, 21, 40, 44, 45, 49, 53, 54, 60–2, 63, 105–6, 168; letter to Newman, 2

Newman, John Henry: Ancestry, birth and childhood, 1–23

Family life, 48, 49, 57, 60–7, 98–9, 105–6, 117–31, 134–5, 148–51, 161–75, 268–71, 278–86, 298–301, 308–9, 359–60, 365, 450–1

Early religious influences, 13, 23–33, 58–61, 62, 64–7, 76, 84, 87, 96–7, 101–5, 132, 135, 137–40

Residence at Trinity College, Oxford (1817), 34–55, 62

Fellow of Oriel College (1822), 68–77, 93–4, 302

Tutor at Oriel (1826), 112–16, 178–82, 186–8

Ordained deacon (1824), 100; priest (1825), 103, 104, 113

Curate at St. Clement's, Oxford (1824), 100–5, 107, 111, 113

Vice-Principal, Alban Hall (1825), 110–11, 113

Vicar at St. Mary's, Oxford (1828), 153, 161, 163, 175, 386–7; resigned (1843), 426

and Catholic Emancipation Bill, 154–8

Preaches University Sermons, 132–40, 176, 317–21, 339–42, 345–58, 383–5

Travels to Rome via Mediterranean, 189–203

Illness in Sicily, 215–23

Edits Froude's *Remains*, 322–33

Editor of *The British Critic*, 310, 410–11

Tract 90 published (1841), *see* Tracts for the Times

Views on Catholic Church, 27–30, 193, 197, 202–11, 215, 221, 256, 262–7, 305–6, 341–4, 360–1, 362, 374, 380–2, 385–6, 391, 393–9, 426–7, 438 and appendices

Retractation of past attacks on Catholic Church (1843), 393–4

Admitted into the Catholic Church (1845), 433–59

Friendships, *see* Bowden, Froude, Keble, Pusey, Whately and H. Wilberforce

Views on celibate clergy, 31, 271–8, 339, 389–90

Views on dogmatic principle, 287–97

Love of music, 11, 32, 45–6, 55, 57, 72, 144, 163

As a leader, 314–21, 404, 405

See also Littlemore *and* Oxford Movement

BOOKS and WRITINGS mentioned and quoted:

Newman, John Henry:—*contd.*
Apologia, 24, 25–6, 29, 31, 78, 97, 104, 137, 149, 157, 158, 170, 200, 204–5, 221, 223, 245, 253, 256, 277, 287, 303, 343, 344, 346, 369, 370, 373, 374, 376, 377, 382, 387, 397, 410, 424, 442, 458
Callista, 139, 218, 321, 451
Development of Christian Doctrine, Essay on the, 161, 345, 354, 382, 442–8, 464–7
Diary, 40–1, 57–9, 60, 62, 65, 70, 71, 72, 95–6, 97, 98, 103, 104, 106, 113, 118, 134, 149, 184
Difficulties of Anglicans, 305–6
Discussions and Arguments, 206–12
Dream of Gerontius, 218
Elucidations, 290–3, 295
Essays Critical and Historical, 334
Grammar of Assent, 24, 345, 348
History of the Arians, 137, 144, 182–3, 184, 185, 255, 345, 351, 445
Idea of a University, The, 70
Lead, Kindly Light, 23, 222, 432
Lectures on Justification, 306–7
Letter to Jelf, 374
Letters and Correspondence including *Autobiographical Memoir*, 50, 102, 103, 104, 113, 244, 275, 344
Loss and Gain, 31, 35, 39, 78, 105–6, 139, 279, 312, 313, 337, 450–1, 457, 458
Occasional Sermons, 139
Oxford University Sermons, 132–3, 134, 136, 137, 138, 345, 346–7, 350, 351–4
Parochial Sermons, 32, 132, 176, 255, 356, 431
Sermons on Subjects of the Day, 391–2, 394, 399
Tract 90, see Tracts for the Times
Via Media, 257, 259, 306, 369
Newman, Mary, sister, 1, 3, 10, 11, 15, 111, 119, 120, 121, 122, 123, 124, 126, 127, 128, 129, 130, 149–51, 154
Newton, John, 86, 89
Newton, Thomas, Bishop of Bristol, 21, 26–30, 46
Nicholas, George, 4, 18, 19, 34
Non-Jurors, 147, 204, 208, 212–14, 252, 297, 324–5, 386

Oakeley, Frederick, 126, 313, 320, 321, 337, 338, 407, 411, 414, 417, 423, 451, 453
O'Connell, Daniel, 154, 256, 371, 435
Oriel College, Oxford, 58, 63, 68–77, 78, 93, 94, 95, 96, 97, 102, 110–16, 143–6, 152–6, 158, 178–82, 215–16, 220, 227, 242, 259, 290, 294, 295, 298, 302, 380, 386
Overton, Canon, 79, 213–14
Oxford Herald, 327, 393

Oxford Movement: Social conditions leading to, 224–36
Development towards, 76, 84, 91–2, 101, 132, 141–8, 153–4, 176–8, 204–14
Opening stages of, 237–56
Attack on Popery, 256–67, 306, 342–3
Tracts for the Times, *see* Tracts
Publication of Froude's *Remains*, 322–33
Oxford reaction to, 252, 311–21, 361, 404, 408–22
W. G. Ward and *The Ideal of a Christian Church*, 404–22

Pagani, Father, 393–4
Paine, Thomas, 24, 26, 27, 80
Paley's *Evidences of Christianity*, 347–50, 353
Palmer, William, 232, 239, 242–3, 249, 370, 404, 411–12, 414, 415
Palmer of Magdalen, 377–9
Pattison, Mark, 45, 72, 180, 181, 315, 350, 388, 389, 411, 449, 452
Peel, Robert, 154–7, 179, 183, 406
Perceval, Arthur, 239, 243, 370
Pope, J., letters from Newman, 96, 247, 277, 289, 294–5
Przywara, Father, 306, 307
Pusey, Edward Bouverie: Friendship with Newman, 100, 110, 146, 171–2, 254, 272, 336, 400, 427, 428, 439, 452, 454–6
Character, 96–7, 254, 296, 454
Religious opinions, 146
Marriage, 171–2, 254, 336
and the Oxford Movement, 253–4, 304, 307–8, 311, 327, 329, 375, 380, 399, 405, 409, 410, 412–13, 454–6
Death of his daughter, 427–8
Otherwise mentioned, 74, 152, 155, 218, 228, 233, 237, 271, 295, 313, 314, 335, 424, 426
Pusey, Lucy, 427–8

Record, 242, 310
Rickards, Samuel, 120, 128–9, 177–9, 185, 202, 245, 272, 278, 301, 304, 451
Rogers, Frederick (Lord Blachford), 146–7, 186, 187–8, 216, 220, 246, 247, 248, 272, 307, 311, 315, 322–3, 326, 333, 337, 338, 364, 371, 411, 452; *quoted*, 288; letters from Newman, 187–8, 201–2, 225, 240, 311, 312, 334, 343, 379
Rose, Hugh, 183, 185, 186, 188, 238–9, 272–3, 290
Routh, Martin (Magdalen), 255, 257–9, 307, 338, 372, 377–8, 392
Russell, Dr. (Maynooth), 380, 393
Ryder, George Dudley, 273–4, 335, 409, 434

St. Mary's, Oxford, 73–4, 102, 114, 133–4, 135, 153–4, 259, 304–5, 312, 314, 317–21, 334, 345, 386, 398, 424–5, 430
Sandford, D. K., 68
Santa Clara, Francis a, 367
Shairp, J. C., 313, 315, 317, 411
Short, Mr., tutor, 37, 43, 44, 45, 62, 68, 72
Smith, Sydney, 69, 83, 233, 234
Stanley, Arthur P., 259–60, 290, 311–12, 315, 316, 350, 367, 368, 372–3, 404, 407, 408, 411, 412, 421–2, 423, 452
Stephen, James, 331
Stephen, Leslie, 214, 355, 356
Symons, B. P., 414

Tait, Dr. (later Archbishop of Canterbury), 304–5, 371, 372, 407, 408, 411, 412
Temple, Frederick (later Archbishop of Canterbury), 83; *quoted*, 312
Times, 419–21
Tracts for the Times, 237–46, 249–51, 252, 253, 254, 256, 298, 311, 331–5, 338, 354–5
Tract 90, 304, 362, 366–76, 394, 399, 404, 408–10, 414, 420–4, 443
Trinity College, Oxford, 34–5, 36–7, 42–3
Tristram, Father Henry, *quoted*, 44
Trollope, Anthony, 250–1
Tuckwell, Rev. W., 39, 94, 95, 113, 144, 153, 177
Tyler, Dean of Oriel, 72, 97, 113–14

Undergraduate, The, 46

Vere, Aubrey de, *quoted* on Newman, 315

Walpole, Horace, 88, 90
Ward, Wilfrid, 350, 411, 447
Ward, W. G., 259–60, 271, 312, 315, 318, 329, 351, 370, 374, 404–24, 452, 453,

454; *Ideal of a Christian Church*, 411 415–22
Wellington, Duke of, 154, 156, 157, 255, 327, 462
Wesley, John, 27, 84, 85, 86, 87, 88, 160
Westmacott, Richard, 381, 430
Whately, Dr. (later Archbishop of Dublin): At Oriel College, 74, 75, 76, 93–4, 145, 155
Principal of Alban Hall (1825), 110–11
Friendship with Newman, 93–5, 97, 99, 108, 115–16, 125, 132, 133, 136, 137, 183, 247, 278, 335
Religious views, 101, 134, 142
Otherwise mentioned, 141, 158, 180, 199, 227–8, 245, 294, 318
Quoted, 241, 264–5, 288, 297
White, Blanco, 91, 125, 141, 142–6, 163, 226, 294–6, 360, 446
Wilberforce, Henry: Friendship with Newman, 128, 129, 163, 184, 187, 217, 272, 273, 275, 276, 315, 344, 363, 436
Letters from Newman, 187, 273, 276, 303, 322, 334, 363, 376, 382, 383, 424
Otherwise mentioned, 130, 185, 365, 434
Wilberforce, Robert, 129, 141, 176, 178, 181, 185, 275, 315
Wilberforce, Samuel, 77, 104, 247, 273; *quoted* on Newman, 316
Wilberforce, William, 27, 78, 86, 87–8, 89, 129
Wilberforce, Mrs., letter from Newman, 460–2
Williams, Isaac, 96, 148, 149, 163, 253, 271, 285, 286, 322, 329, 333, 354–5, 379–80, 412
Wilson, R. F., *quoted*, 323
Wiseman, Monsignor (later Cardinal), 203, 204, 205, 256, 343, 344, 361, 447–8
Wood, S. F., 333, 361, 434
Woodgate, H. A., 149, 177, 178, 363, 455

Yonge, Charlotte, 235–6, 271